A Question of Commitment

Studies in Childhood and Family in Canada

Studies in Childhood and Family in Canada is a multidisciplinary series devoted to new perspectives on these subjects as they evolve. The series features studies that focus on the intersections of age, class, race, gender, and region as they contribute to a Canadian understanding of childhood and family, both historically and currently.

Series Editor
Cynthia Comacchio
Department of History
Wilfrid Laurier University

Manuscripts to be sent to
Brian Henderson, Director
Wilfrid Laurier University Press
75 University Avenue West
Waterloo, Ontario, Canada, N2L 3C5

A Question of Commitment
Children's Rights in Canada

R. Brian Howe and
Katherine Covell, editors

Wilfrid Laurier University Press
[WLU]

We acknowledge the financial support of the Government of Canada through the Book Publishing Industry Development Program for our publishing activities.

Library and Archives Canada Cataloguing in Publication

A question of commitment : children's rights in Canada / R. Brian Howe and Katherine Covell, editors.

(Studies in childhood and family in Canada series)
Includes bibliographical references and index.
ISBN 978-1-55458-003-3

1. Children's rights—Canada. 2. Children—Government policy—Canada. 3. Child welfare—Canada. 4. Convention on the Rights of the Child (1989). I. Howe, Robert Brian II. Covell, Katherine III. Series.

HQ789.Q48 2007   323.3'520971   C2007-901788-6

Cover design by P.J. Woodland. Text design by C. Bonas-Taylor.

∞

This book is printed on Ancient Forest Friendly paper (100% post-consumer recycled).

Printed in Canada

Published by Wilfrid Laurier University Press
Waterloo, Ontario, Canada
www.wlupress.wlu.ca

This book is dedicated to Senator Landon Pearson for her tireless efforts on behalf of children and their rights.

Contents

Foreword

On December 11, 1991, a group of children from every province and territory surrounded Prime Minister Brian Mulroney in the Rotunda of Parliament to sign along with him a document celebrating Canada's ratification of the United Nations Convention on the Rights of the Child (CRC). Poinsettias rose in tiers around the great central pillar and coloured lights twinkled among the gargoyles. Two local school choirs sang "O Canada!" in French and English and everyone clapped. As the chair of the Canadian Coalition for the Rights of the Child I spoke to the children about their rights and, on behalf of the people of Canada, Mr. Mulroney promised to respect them.

So, fifteen years later, how have we done? How well have we fulfilled the promises we made that day? Our successes and failures are what this book is all about.

We were full of hope on that snowy December afternoon, but, as with all the other major UN-sponsored human rights instruments Canada has ratified, the domestic implementation of the CRC has been neither as quick nor as comprehensive as we would have liked. In fact, in many ways, we have been more successful on the international scene than at home. As a country we have been seen as a leader in the field of children's rights; we have negotiated, signed, ratified, or adopted numerous international conventions, statutes, protocols, and declarations over the past decade that directly reference children. Child rights–based programming has been a priority for our official development assistance, and we remain strong supporters of the eight millennium goals to reduce poverty and improve lives by 2015, most of which involve children. Furthermore, we have formally recognized at international conferences that the rights of the child, like all human rights, are universal, indivisible, interdependent, and interrelated. But here at home we often compartimentalize those rights due to jurisdictional issues as well as to a tendency toward specialization. As you read each chapter of this important book, please keep in mind the UNICEF slogan "All Rights for All Children." To underline the holistic nature of children's rights, the child's right to the highest attainable standard of health (Article 24), for example, must include a recognition of the family's role in health care. To take another example, while a child's civil and political rights (Articles 12, 13, 14, and 15) are dependent on a full understanding of the concept of "evolving capacities," they should be respected even if they run counter to the administrative requirements of the school or other institution in which the child is present.

Anyone who reads the CRC carefully will recognize what a remarkable document it is. It is almost a miracle that during the dying years of the Cold War, representatives of both East and West could have come together and crafted an instrument so respectful of the humanity of the child. It has changed fundamentally the ways in which those of us who care about children think about them and interact with them. The standards set by the Convention should not be seen as entitlements that set the child against the adult world. On the contrary, they represent the highest norms of civilized behaviour. Because they are vulnerable, children have the right to our protection. But at the same time, they also have the right to be treated with respect. And it is only within a culture of respect that constructive social responsibility is able to emerge.

At the UN Special Session on Children, the children reminded us that "they are not the sources of problems," but "the resources that are needed to solve them." The twenty-first century will belong to them and to their children. It is their dreams and aspirations—shaped by the families into which they are born and the circumstances that surround them as they grow up—that will give the century its final definition. Our challenge is to offer them the protection and respect they deserve so that the horrors of the twentieth century will never be repeated and humanity will thrive.

The children who were with us in 1991 are adults now, living and working among us. Some of them probably have children of their own. For their sake and for the sake of all the children in the world, we need to continue working together, learning from our mistakes, and pushing for necessary changes in programs and policies, listening all the time to the voices of the young. This book is an excellent contribution to the dialogue we must continue to hold, a base to move forward from, and I congratulate the editors for assembling such a rich array of knowledgeable and concerned authors.

The Honourable Landon Pearson
Canadian Senator 1994–2005
Advisor on Children's Rights to the Minister of Foreign Affairs
Landon Pearson Resource Centre for the Study of Childhood and
Children's Rights, Carleton University

Acknowledgments

The editors express their appreciation to the following child rights special-
ists who willingly shared their thoughts as this book was being conceived:

The Honourable Landon Pearson
Tara Collins
Sandra Griffin
Judy Finlay

We also wish to thank the anonymous reviewers for their very helpful
and positive comments.

Introduction
A Question of Commitment

R. Brian Howe

The overarching question for this book is this: How committed are the governments of Canada to the rights of the child? There is no question about their *official* commitment. In 1991, with the approval of all the provinces except Alberta, the federal government ratified the United Nations Convention on the Rights of the Child, thereby committing all governments in Canada to a policy of ensuring that Canadian laws, policies, and practices are in conformity with the rights of the child as described in the Convention. Alberta hesitated at first, but in 1999 it too gave its support to the Convention.[1]

But official commitment is not the same thing as actual commitment. Official commitment is when a government makes a pledge to pursue a particular course of action or policy. In ratifying the UN Convention, Canada's federal and provincial governments of Canada were pledging to implement it. Actual commitment is when a government demonstrates its official commitment by taking concrete measures, be they in the form of laws, policies, or programs. It does so whatever obstacles and challenges stand in its way. The obstacles are a test of a government's commitment. The effort that a government takes to overcome the obstacles and to achieve results is a measure of its commitment. This book assesses the level of the commitment by Canadian governments to the rights of the child, by examining and assessing developments in Canada in the 1990s and 2000s.

R. Brian Howe, Department of Political Science and Children's Rights Centre, Cape Breton University

A government's commitment is not an all-or-nothing affair. It varies in degree and can be described as follows, in ascending order of strength. First is symbolic commitment, where government support for a particular course of action is at a low level. This sort of commitment may be real but it is also shallow, as reflected in a highly limited range of government action, weak efforts, and heavy reliance on symbolism, with words substituting for deeds.[2] Second is wavering commitment, where government authorities are ambivalent about a course of action—positive and enthusiastic at certain times but doubtful or hesitant or forgetful at others. This is reflected in government action that occurs in spurts, as well as in efforts that are modest or that weaken when authorities are confronted with obstacles. The result is forward and backward developments without clear signs of progress. Third is expanding commitment. Here, a government's initial commitment is shallow or wavering but then increases over time, as reflected in strengthening efforts and in an increasing range of government activities to overcome obstacles and achieve results. Efforts may ebb and flow, but there are clear signs of progress on most or all fronts. Finally, fourth is deep commitment, where government authorities maintain a high level of commitment to a course of action and demonstrate that commitment in strong and sustained action to achieve results on all fronts and in determined efforts to overcome challenges. Efforts ultimately lead to positive outcomes that are widely recognized and appreciated among all those in the children's rights policy community.

This book attempts to identify and explain the level of Canada's commitment to the rights of the child, as reflected in its record. This chapter will provide a brief background of the significance of the UN Convention on the Rights of the Child (hereafter, the CRC or the Convention) and examine Canada's commitment to it. Throughout this book, we assume that the Convention and a rights-based approach have great value as a means to improve the lives of children. It is beyond the scope of this book to provide a philosophical defence of children's rights or the Convention. We leave this to others.[3] But briefly put, we follow Joel Feinberg in the belief that claims based on rights—rather than actions based on benevolence or pity or a sense of duty—have value in conveying the understanding that the holders of rights are persons worthy of respect.[4] It is not out of pity or benevolence or paternalism that children have a legitimate claim to the things they need for their healthy development. Rather, it is because they—as persons worthy of respect—have rights. It is their due.

The Significance of the Convention

An event of major significance occurred in 1989. The UN Convention on the Rights of the Child was unanimously approved by the UN General Assembly. It then was signed and ratified by virtually all the world's countries during the 1990s, making it the most widely and most quickly signed and ratified convention in world history. Only the United States and Somalia have yet to ratify the Convention.[5]

At first glance, from an international perspective, one might wonder whether the CRC has had any significance at all. In looking at the continuing or worsening situation of children globally—children with HIV/AIDS, child soldiers, children labouring in sweatshops, children working in the sex trade—it is understandable that one might question the value of the Convention.[6] Yet despite the problems, there are good reasons to believe that the Convention has been a significant step forward. Children are in a better position with it than without it. That there is an ongoing gap between a principle and a practice does not rule out the importance of a principle.

To begin with, the Convention serves as a new global standard on the treatment of children.[7] By providing a systematic and comprehensive statement on children's rights that did not exist before, the CRC represents a new global conception of children that is far different from the older conceptions of children as parental property or as vulnerable "not yets" in need of the state's protection.[8] From the perspective of the Convention, children—defined as all young persons under eighteen—deserve respect and support not out of pity or a sense of duty but because they have inherent rights. The claim that children have basic human rights, and that these deserve priority in public policy and law, has forcefulness beyond a claim based on pity or duty.[9] A claim based on rights, together with a global consensus about the validity of the claim, is a significant moral prod for action. It is much better to have this moral prod than not to have it.

It is impressive that 192 countries have agreed to recognize and affirm this new conception of children. It also is impressive that they have agreed to the general meaning of children's rights as rights to the so-called three Ps in the CRC: (1) rights of provision (provision of health care, education, economic welfare), (2) rights of protection (protection from abuse, neglect, violence, exploitation), and (3) rights of participation (a voice in decisions affecting the child).[10] And it is impressive that they have agreed to the Convention's three guiding principles: (1) non-discrimination, where children are to be protected from all forms of discrimination, (2) the best interests of the child, where a primary consideration in all actions concerning children is their best interests, and (3) participation, where children have the right to be heard and their views given weight in accord with their age and maturity.[11] With such widespread international agreement, it is virtually impossible for countries to defend themselves against failure to act on the basis that they do not support the concept of children's rights. They might try to defend themselves by saying that they have done more than what has been suggested by critics or that their shortcomings and failures are due to unforeseen circumstances. But they cannot deny their official support of the Convention. This is an advance.

Furthermore, the Convention is significant because it is legally binding international law. In 1959 the Universal Declaration of the Rights of the Child was adopted by the UN General Assembly and was agreed to by virtually all the world's countries. But this was a declaration of moral ideals, not a legally binding international treaty. In contrast, the CRC is a legally binding treaty.[12] By ratifying the Convention, a state party has agreed to implement the articles of the CRC (if not already implemented) and to ensure that its laws, policies, and practices are in compliance with the Convention. A country may choose not to act immediately, but it is obligated to do so over time. This may not be a system of "hard law" in the sense that the rights found in the CRC are capable of immediate enforcement through a court of law. Except for those few countries that have chosen to incorporate the CRC directly into domestic law, this is not a situation in which, when a right has been violated, a legal case can be taken to a court or official agency and a remedy ordered by that court or agency. Rather, it is a system of "soft law" in which the law is enforced indirectly and over time through a reporting system and on the basis of public opinion and national and international peer pressure.[13]

Under the Convention, a state party makes a report to an expert committee—the UN Committee on the Rights of the Child—every five years. The country documents how well it has been complying with the Convention and what measures it has taken to implement the articles of the CRC. The UN Committee then reviews the country's report, along with shadow reports from child advocacy organizations and UN agencies (e.g., UNICEF), and then issues a report back to the country—called concluding observations—in which it notes progress and shortcomings. The shadow reports are an important element in the process because they are a source of alternative information and act as a check and balance. On the basis of information in the country and shadow reports, the committee makes recommendations for improvements where needed. Based on these recommendations, countries are expected to improve their performance, though they are not legally obligated to act on the recommendations.

The Convention ultimately is enforced through the court of public opinion and on the basis of moral and political pressure. A state party typically does not want to be embarrassed by criticism or chastised as a country that does not honour its international commitments. Although it may not be hard law, the Convention is significant because it is legally binding. A country cannot respond to criticism simply by saying that it is not bound by the CRC. Inadequate though it might be, there is pressure to demonstrate progress. Some pressure is better than no pressure.

Finally, the Convention is significant because it provides an opportunity that did not exist before for the global improvement of the situation of children. At a symbolic level, the CRC sends out the important message that children are bearers of rights and that those rights deserve priority in public policy and law. At an advocacy level, the CRC provides child advocacy organizations with a tool and a standard by which to monitor and criticize the shortcomings and failures of governments and to pressure for improvement. And at a legal level, although far from ideal, it provides a formal process through which governments in Canada and elsewhere are required to account for their effort or lack of effort at implementation. That government officials are obligated to explain themselves is a mechanism that did not exist before. Although this does not mean that governments actually will improve their performance, it does give them an incentive to do so that otherwise would not have existed.

It would be naive to think that the simple recognition of children's rights and the simple endorsement of the Convention would suddenly and majestically improve the lives of children. Much depends on how rights are interpreted and applied. We know from Canada's historical experience with rights in other contexts—for example, with the rights of women and Aboriginal rights—that despite the recognition and use of rights by courts and governments, rights can be interpreted narrowly and conservatively and in ways that do little to alleviate hardship or oppression. If children's rights are recognized but interpreted and applied in a similarly restrictive way—for example, as rights that belong only to autonomous persons and that thus apply only to older children for particular purposes—little will be done substantially to improve the lives of children. So it is important to realize that rights alone do not spell progress. However, as pointed out by Martha Minow and John Eekelaar, when children's rights are given a broad interpretation that considers children as independent persons with voices of their own, and not simply as persons dependent on their parents or on paternalist state officials to represent their best interests, the possibilities for progress are enhanced.[14] When the Convention can be understood and applied as intended by its framers—that is, as including participation rights as well as protection and provision rights, as requiring action in the area of social and economic rights as well as of other rights, and as requiring the voices of children as part of the determination of the best interests of the child—the prospects are much greater that children's rights can be an effective means for improving the lives of children. This highlights the importance of effective implementation.

The Test of Canada's Commitment

Before 1991, like many other countries, Canada recognized and provided for the rights of children in particular areas of law and public policy. Under the Young Offenders Act (1984), for example, the federal government provided for the due process rights of youth in conflict with the law. At the same time, provincial governments provided children with certain rights in education; they also enacted child protection legislation. But with the ratification of the CRC in 1991, in all areas of law and policy dealing with children, Canada became officially committed to ensuring the implementation of the rights of the child.[15] As required by the Convention's article 4, Canada was obligated to "undertake all appropriate legislative, administrative, and other measures for the implementation of the rights recognized in the present Convention." It was to do so through a reporting and monitoring system in which Canada would send reports to the UN Committee on the Rights of the Child for review (it sent reports in 1994 and 2001) and make the reports widely available to the public.

This was the easy part. Making a pledge is not difficult; the hard part is demonstrating that the commitment is real. The real test of Canada's commitment—following ratification—was whether it would succeed in overcoming obstacles and translating the provision, protection, and participation rights of the child into practice. The grade that Canada would receive on this test would be based on its record. If the record showed that successive federal, provincial, and territorial governments in Canada had done little or had vacillated in implementing the rights of the child, this would signify symbolic or wavering commitment. If the record showed that these governments had increased their efforts over time or had undertaken strong and sustained measures after 1991, this would indicate a deep or expanding level of commitment. The proof would be in the reading of the record.

The test of Canada's commitment would consider whether this country had overcome three obstacles in particular. The first of these related to a complicated and sometimes contentious system of federalism.[16] Under Canada's constitution, the federal government has the authority to make international treaties or conventions, but it does not have the sole authority to implement them.[17] When a subject matter falls under provincial jurisdiction, it is the provinces (and territories) that bear the responsibility for implementation. It sometimes happens that for ideological or other reasons, a particular province or territory, or group of provinces and territories, is hesitant or resistant about implementing change in a particular area. It also sometimes happens that in areas where jurisdiction is unclear, a provincial or federal government may claim that a matter is not in their jurisdiction, thus blocking change.

Furthermore, the federal government is responsible for certain child-related matters—criminal law, divorce, Aboriginal affairs—but it is the provinces (and territories) that bear the lion's share of responsibility, including in the areas of health care, child care, education, child protection, social assistance, and early childhood education. This system poses problems, because although the provinces have major child-related and family-related responsibilities, they often do not have the financial resources to fulfill them. Most depend heavily on the federal government for fiscal transfers—through cost-sharing arrangements and equalization payments—to fund programs and fulfill their obligations. Moreover, many of the transfers are in the form of conditional grants, which gives the federal government leverage in areas of provincial jurisdiction. Given these complications, a major stumbling block to implementing the rights of the child is the requirement for cooperation between the federal and provincial governments (and the territorial and Aboriginal governments as well) and the difficulties of coordinating efforts.

A second obstacle to be overcome is the availability of adequate financial funding.[18] Implementing the rights of children, especially social and economic rights, takes a lot of money. Apart from the problem of fiscal imbalance between the federal government and the provinces, a more general potential problem is that Canadian governments—like governments everywhere—are able to claim that economic difficulties do not allow for a greater spending on children. Indeed, the decade following Canada's ratification was an era of fiscal restraint—sometimes severe fiscal restraint—by both federal and provincial governments. This problem was foreseen in the early 1990s as Canada and other countries were preparing to ratify the Convention. In 1990, Prime Minister Brian Mulroney co-chaired the World Summit for Children, where attention was given to the issue of children's basic needs and to situations where governments assign children low priority in their budgets despite their official commitment to children. It was agreed, therefore, that there be a global plan of action for the survival, protection, and development of children. Within this global plan, it was further agreed that individual countries were to design their own plans, to make financial resources available for children, and to abide by the principle of "first call for children."[19] This principle essentially said that the needs of children should be given first priority in a nation's budget—in hard economic times as well as in good economic times. A challenge for the implementation of the rights of the child is to ensure that governments take this principle seriously.

A third obstacle is the lack of public and political pressure for implementation. In Canada as elsewhere, government action—as a general rule—is strongly influenced by political pressure.[20] Yet in the area of children's rights, little pressure comes from the chief stakeholders—Canada's children. They do not vote, they have little money and resources, and they seldom are involved in organizational and lobbying activities. To make up for this, strong pressure could come from child advocacy organizations.[21] However, important though their role is in raising children's rights issues, there are limits to what these organizations can do. They are relatively few in number, and they lack the resources and membership for sustained lobbying and influence. Pressure also could come from public opinion in support of children, but—thanks to a lack of public education— most Canadians have little knowledge of children's rights and little understanding of the importance of implementation.[22] Among those who do have opinions about children's rights, many have negative or ambivalent views based on what they see as too many rights for children, especially for young offenders. In the absence of education on the rights of the child, there is little public awareness about the importance of the CRC and thus little public pressure for implementation. To some degree, public pressure does emanate from the notion that children are not to be blamed for misfortunes such as poverty and abuse. This provides child advocates with a platform for mobilizing public support to address particular problems such as child poverty and child abuse. For the most part, though, the pressure is based on sympathy rather than on the rights of children and is not directed at a fuller implementation of the Convention.

This leaves implementation dependent largely on the political will of politicians and senior government officials. This is a challenge for implementation, because amidst the multiple demands on government, in the absence of strong and sustained pressure, it is easy for children's rights issues to become ignored or squeezed out by other issues. Even when politicians would like to take the initiative, they often want or need public pressure to justify a course of action. Because the Convention is soft law rather than hard law, without public awareness and sustained pressure, it may be attractive to take the path of least resistance and delay or forgo implementation.

Signs of Canada's Commitment

If Canadian governments were to meet the test, how could we tell? It is reasonable to assume that four basic things would have to happen as signs of their commitment. The first three—all recommended to Canada by the UN Committee on the Rights of the Child—are related to process, the fourth to substantive outcomes.

First, the Convention would have to become incorporated into Canadian law and the objectives of public policy. If Canada were fully committed to the rights of the child, it would incorporate the Convention into its domestic law (if not already incorporated) so that it could be applied in Canadian courts and injected into child-related policy goals. There are several ways in which a country can proceed after ratifying the CRC. One option, a path chosen by Belgium, is to directly incorporate the Convention into domestic law. In Belgium the Convention is "self-executing"— in other words, having been ratified, it has the force of law and can be invoked in a Belgian court of law.[23] Another option, one chosen by countries such as South Africa and Norway, is to incorporate the Convention either into the constitution or into key legislation and policies.[24] South Africa has incorporated the rights of the child into its 1996 constitution (article 28). Norway has amended a number of pieces of legislation—its human rights act, children's act, adoption act, and child welfare act—for the purpose of incorporating the Convention and giving it direct application. Finally, another option is to assume that to a large degree the CRC already has been incorporated into domestic law and public policy goals. From this perspective, all that is required is occasional change in the law when new needs arise. If Canada were to choose the first or second option and make explicit reference to the Convention in new laws and policy goals, this would be an indicator of commitment.

It is important to note, however, that the simple incorporation of the Convention into domestic law is not enough in itself. Even when the rights of the child are recognized in the law, governments still must to put the law into effect, and courts must interpret the law in such a way that governments have a positive obligation to implement rights. Governments have been known, of course, to stall on their obligations, and the courts have been known to interpret rights in a restrictive manner. For example, in interpreting the Canadian Charter of Rights and Freedoms, the Supreme Court of Canada ruled in the *Gosselin* case (2002) that the state does not have a positive obligation to ensure minimum economic standards for citizens.[25] This ruling was by a slim majority of the Court; even so, it illustrates the potential for narrow interpretations of rights. Simple incorporation and the recognition of children's rights in the law do not in themselves ensure progress. Nonetheless, it is an important and necessary step in the right direction.

Second, special institutions in support of children's rights—a children's commissioner or a children's ombudsman—would have to be established.[26] The Convention assumes that children and youth are partners in implementing the rights of the child. It assumes that children are subjects with rights of participation—not passive objects—and that the state has the responsibility to give institutional support to children. As recommended by the UN Committee, an important means by which a country can give support to children is by establishing an independent office for children—a children's ombudsman or commissioner—working with and on behalf of children. These offices would have the task of listening to children and advocating for children, addressing problems or grievances, spreading public awareness about the Convention, and making reports to the UN Committee on the Rights of the Child about a country's progress or lack of progress. Countries such as Norway, Sweden, Costa Rica, and Iceland have taken steps in this direction.[27] Norway provides a model, having established an independent children's ombudsman as early as 1981 (well before the adoption of the Convention). This office hears from children directly, consults with child and youth organizations, monitors Norway's implementation of the Convention, and advises the Norwegian government on developing child-friendly legislation and policies. If Canada were to establish a similar national office, this also would provide evidence of Canada's actual commitment.

Third, an effective coordinating and monitoring mechanism for children's rights would have to be put into place.[28] A major problem for implementation is the very size and complexity of modern government. Matters concerning children and their families spill across many government departments and agencies and down through different levels of government. This complexity is especially pronounced in federal states such as Canada, where provincial (and territorial) governments have major responsibility for social and family policies. Given this complexity, and given the need to give children a distinct focus amid all the complexities and the multiple demands on government, there is a need for a permanent government mechanism or structure, one that can monitor the overall implementation of the Convention as well as coordinate governmental efforts for this purpose. Where this coordination is lacking, and where children are not given a distinct and ongoing focus in government efforts and priorities, there is a greater likelihood that issues of children's rights will be ignored or marginalized. There also is a greater likelihood that reports to the UN Committee will be done at the last minute, with little consultation and long-term planning among government officials between reports. So it is important for Canada to establish an effective and permanent coordinating and monitoring mechanism. If Canada were to do this, this would be further evidence of its commitment.

Fourth and most important, Canadian governments would have to achieve substantive results in implementing the specific articles of the Convention. They might not do any of the first three items, but if they were to carefully study their obligations under the CRC; invite and listen to feedback from child advocacy organizations, children, and the UN Committee; review laws and policies and make adjustments where needed; and actualize the articles of the Convention in a serious and progressive way, they would be showing themselves committed to the rights of children. This would involve demonstrating genuine progress· in each of the three Ps—provision, protection, and participation rights. It also would involve working to improve the situation of vulnerable populations of children identified as having experienced historical disadvantages or marginalization. In particular, it would involve improving the situation of Aboriginal children, children in alternative care, homeless children and street youth, immigrant and refugee children, and children with disabilities.

At first glance, there is good reason to be suspicious about Canada's commitment. Canada has failed, first of all, to incorporate the Convention into its domestic law.[29] It perhaps is understandable that, on ratification, the CRC was not automatically incorporated into Canadian law. Some countries, such as Belgium, subscribe to the doctrine of monism; that is, international treaties have automatic legal application on ratification. In contrast, Canada operates on the basis of dualism: it is legally bound by an international treaty, but a treaty is not automatically part of domestic law and has no internal effect until it has been incorporated through the enactment of legislation. In dualist systems, the Convention has to become incorporated statute by statute. However, unlike other dualist countries such as Norway, Canada has chosen not to incorporate the CRC into domestic law. The federal government has operated under the assumption that the CRC already has been incorporated into domestic law through the Charter of Rights and Freedoms, federal and provincial human rights legislation, and other federal and provincial legislation.[30] The position of the federal government has been that before it ratified the CRC, it consulted with the provinces and made the determination that Canadian laws already were in conformity with the Convention. It was necessary to take this approach because issues of children's rights cut across all jurisdictions and because the federal system is so complex. Thus, from the federal government's point of view, there has been no need to incorporate the Convention since 1991.

This, however, is highly dubious. How can it be said, for example, that the rights of Aboriginal children or the participation rights of the CRC have already been implemented into all Canadian law? Aboriginal children continue to suffer from deep poverty, and children in general do not have the right to be heard in all areas of law. Canadian law may be consistent with the standards of the Convention in regard to some or many children's rights, but incorporation has yet to be realized. No doubt there are difficulties inherent in incorporating the CRC into Canadian law. There are also difficulties with court decisions that adopt the values of an international convention that has yet to be incorporated. In his minority opinion in *Baker v. Canada*, Justice Iacobucci stressed the point that a convention has no force or effect until its provisions have been put into legislation and that judges should avoid adopting the values of a convention for fear of compromising the principles of democracy and Parliamentary government.[31] Thus in the interests of democracy and the Parliamentary tradition, it is important that steps be taken to incorporate the CRC through implementing legislation. If the federal and provincial governments are confident about their commitment to the rights of children, why have they not made their commitment explicit through incorporation since 1991, as dualist countries such as Norway have done?

Canadian governments have chosen not even to refer to the Convention in most child-related legislation enacted since ratification. A review of federal, provincial, and territorial legislation since 1991 shows that there has been no mention of the CRC except in the federal Youth Criminal Justice Act (in which the CRC is referred to only in the preamble, where it has no legal effect); in provincial adoption acts dealing with international adoptions; and in the Northwest Territories Child Protection Act.[32] Thus the Convention has little direct legal application in Canada. Moreover, because the Convention has little or no effect, Canadian judges have seldom referred to it in decisions.[33] In *Baker v. Canada* (1999) the majority of the Supreme Court did hold that "the values reflected in international human rights law may help inform the contextual approach to statutory interpretation and judicial review."[34] In other words, the Court was saying, it was appropriate for judges to use the CRC as an aid in interpreting the law. This would not be at odds with democracy, as it would be presumed that the Canadian Parliament and provincial legislatures would want to respect and uphold the values enshrined in the CRC. This approach was confirmed in *Canadian Foundation for Children, Youth and the Law* (2004), where the Supreme Court stated that Canadian law "should be construed to comply with Canada's international obligations."[35] However, as pointed out by Jutta Brunnée and Stephen Toope, in the absence of incorporation, the Court has given the Convention a "hesitant embrace": at best, the CRC has been deemed to have "persuasive force" but not "obligatory force."[36]

Canada also has failed to establish a special institution for the rights of the child at the national level.[37] In the late 1990s, child advocates made a strong effort to create a new national office for children, to be called the Children's Commissioner.[38] But this effort ultimately fell on deaf ears. Possible reasons included the lack of sufficient pressure by child advocates, a belief among federal officials that such an office was not required as the needs of Canada's children were already well taken care of, and a fear that an independent office might cause the federal government political embarrassment, just as other independent offices have done in the past.[39] The failure of this effort does not mean that there are no official offices for children in Canada. At the provincial level, most provinces have established child advocacy or child ombudsman offices. However, these do not exist in all provinces—there still is not one on Prince Edward Island—and none have been founded in the three territories.[40] Where they do exist, they perform important tasks, but their mandates are limited to particular areas of children's rights—usually in the fields of child protection and care or youth justice. Their mandates do not include monitoring the implementation of the Convention or promoting the Convention rights of children.

Finally, Canada has failed to establish an effective coordinating and monitoring mechanism in support of implementing the Convention. The federal government does have a structure in place for coordinating international treaties, including the CRC. The Continuing Committee of Officials on Human Rights, an administrative body within the Department of Canadian Heritage with representation from all jurisdictions, is responsible for ensuring coordination among the different levels of government and for facilitating the preparation of Canada's reports to the UN Committee on the Rights of the Child.[41] However, it has become clear that both the Continuing Committee and the process are highly inefficient and ineffective. The committee meetings are secretive and without the benefit of public or parliamentary input and without the sort of ministerial involvement that would elevate their importance. The compilation of the reports is very slow; the reports are long and overly complicated (different jurisdictions prepare them differently); there is little systematic monitoring of issues and developments; and little effort is made to disseminate the UN Committee's Concluding Observations for the purpose of discussion and follow-up. There is little effort even to make the Concluding Observations and the Convention known to the public, to MPs, or to government officials. Indeed, in its 2003 Concluding Observations, the UN Committee questioned whether provincial governments were even aware of the Convention. That the committee had to urge federal officials "to ensure that the provinces and territories are aware of their obligations under the Convention" speaks volumes about the lack of an effective coordinating, monitoring, and educating mechanism.[42]

In Search of Substance

All of this does not mean that Canada has not made substantive progress in the actual implementation of the rights of the child. Failure to provide for a coordinating mechanism, to establish a national children's commissioner, or to incorporate the Convention into Canadian law does not necessarily mean that Canada has failed to translate the words of the Convention into practice. It still may be the case that Canada has done much to provide for the rights of provision, protection, and participation. It still may also be the case that Canada has done much to advance the rights of vulnerable and disadvantaged populations of children. The chapters that follow will explore the question of substantive progress. The areas chosen are based on issues and concerns highlighted by the UN Committee as well as by Canada's child advocacy community.

The first part of the book deals with leading issues in the areas respectively of provision, protection, and participation rights. In the area of provision rights, in chapter 2, Ken Battle examines the problem of child poverty, with particular attention to Canada's evolving system of child benefits as a means of dealing with the problem. In chapter 3, Martha Friendly looks at the issue of early learning and child care and the measures taken by Canadian governments to address shortages and to ensure quality care. In chapter 4, Cheryl van Daalen-Smith reviews developments in the area of child health care and assesses initiatives taken by policy-makers. In the area of protection rights, in chapter 5, Joan Durrant deals with the issue of corporal punishment and with Canada's efforts to protect children from violence and assault. In chapter 6, Anne McGillivray examines the problem of child sexual abuse and exploitation and assesses developments in Canadian law. In chapter 7, Myriam Denov deals with Canada's response to youth in conflict with the law and examines the new Youth Criminal Justice Act. In chapter 8, Shannon Moore gives special attention to an important new feature of the youth justice system: programs of restorative justice. In the area of participation rights, in chapter 9, Kelly Campbell and Linda Rose-Krasnor examine the child's right to be heard in family and school settings and the extent to which this right has been provided for. In chapter 10, Katherine Covell deals with participation on the basis of the child's right to know his or her rights through programs of children's rights education in Canadian schools.

The remainder of the book is devoted to vulnerable and disadvantaged populations of children. Marlyn Bennett examines the situation of Aboriginal children in chapter 11 and issues of poverty, health, and child welfare. In chapter 12, Tom Waldock analyzes children's rights in alternative care and issues in the child protection and child care system. In chapter 13, Sonja Grover looks at the situation of homeless children and street youth and at government measures to protect them from economic and sexual exploitation. In chapter 14, the same Sonja Grover examines problems facing refugee children and asylum seekers and developments related to their rights. Finally, in chapter 15, Richard Sobsey analyzes and assesses the degree to which the rights of children with disabilities are provided for in Canada. In the conclusion, an attempt will be made to bring together the different analyses and answer the question of Canada's commitment to the rights of the child.

Notes

1 Support was in the form of a letter from Premier Klein to Prime Minister Chrétien in 1999.
2 The classic work on the role of symbolism in politics is M. Edelman, *The Symbolic Uses of Politics* (Urbana: University of Illinois Press, 1964).
3 M. Freeman, "Taking Children's Rights More Seriously," in P. Alston, S. Parker, and J. Seymour, eds., *Children, Rights, and the Law* (Oxford: Oxford University Press, 1992), pp. 52–71; J. Eekelaar, "The Importance of Thinking That Children Have Rights," also in Alston, Parker, and Seymour, pp. 221–35; M. Minow, "Rights for the Next Generation: A Feminist Approach to Children's Rights," *Harvard Women's Law Journal* 9 (1986): 1–24.
4 J. Feinberg, "The Nature and Value of Rights," *Journal of Value Inquiry* 4, no. 4 (1970): 55–97. For an application of Feinberg's claims theory to children, see Eekelaar, "The Importance."
5 Among the Americans' objections were that the rights of children could undermine parental rights and that the death penalty for juvenile offenders could no longer be used.
6 A global picture of violence and threats against children is presented in the 2006 UN study on violence against children. See UN General Assembly, *Report of the Independent Expert for the United Nations Study on Violence against Children,* A/61/299 (August 2006).
7 E. Verhellen, *Convention on the Rights of the Child* (Kessel-Lo: Belgium: Garant, 1994).
8 S.N. Hart, "From Property to Person Status: Historical Perspective on Children's Rights," *American Psychologist* 46, no. 1 (1991): 53–59; Verhellen, "Facilitating Children's Rights in Education," *Prospects* 29, no. 2 (1999): 224–31; K. Covell and R.B. Howe, *The Challenge of Children's Rights for Canada* (Waterloo: Wilfrid Laurier University Press, 2001), pp. 16–22.
9 M. Freeman, *The Moral Status of Children: Essays on the Rights of the Child* (The Hague: Kluwer Law International, 1997), pp. 19–41.

10 T. Hammarberg, "The UN Convention on the Rights of the Child—and How to Make It Work," *Human Rights Quarterly* 12 (1990): 97–105.

11 M. Hill and K. Tisdall, *Children and Society* (London: Addison Wesley Longman, 1997), pp. 28–30.

12 J. Doek, "The Current Status of the United Nations Convention on the Rights of the Child," in S. Detrick, ed., *The United Nations Convention on the Rights of the Child* (Dordrecht: Martinus Nijhoff, 1992), pp. 632–40.

13 D. Stasiulis, "The Active Child Citizen: Lessons from Canadian Policy and the Children's Movement," *Citizenship Studies* 6, no. 4 (2002): 508; "The UN Convention on the Rights of the Child as a Touchstone for Research on Childhoods" (Editorial), *Childhood* 6, no. 4 (1999): 403.

14 Minow, "Rights for the Next Generation"; Eekelaar, "The Importance."

15 K. Covell and R.B. Howe, *The Challenge of Children's Rights for Canada* (Waterloo: Wilfrid Laurier University Press, 2001), pp. 22–32; S. Toope, "The Convention on the Rights of the Child: Implications for Canada," in M. Freeman, ed., *Children's Rights: A Comparative Perspective* (Aldershot: Dartmouth Publishing, 1996), pp. 33–64.

16 R. Andreychuk and L. Pearson, *Who's in Charge Here? Effective Implementation of Canada's International Obligations with Respect to the Rights of Children* (Ottawa: Senate Standing Committee on Human Rights, 2005), pp. 59–68.

17 P. Hogg, *Constitutional Law of Canada* (Toronto: Carswell, 1992), pp. 281–99.

18 Toope, "The Convention on the Rights of the Child," pp. 51–52.

19 Covell and Howe, *The Challenge of Children's Rights for Canada,* p. 38.

20 Most theories of the formation of public policy are society-centred; that is, they posit that pressures or interests in society are a key influence. However, in both state-centred theory and institutionalism, it is assumed that the structure of the state and autonomous state actors play central roles. See S. Brooks, *Public Policy in Canada: An Introduction* (Toronto: Oxford University Press, 2003), pp. 22–45.

21 Leading national organizations advocating for the rights of the child in Canada include the Canadian Coalition for the Rights of Children (formed in 1989), the Defence for Children International—Canada (1989), the Organization for the Protection of Children's Rights (1983), the Canadian Children's Rights Council (1992), the International Bureau for Children's Rights (1994), the National Children's Alliance (1996), UNICEF Canada (1955), World Vision Canada (1957), and Save the Children Canada (1921). There are also a number of provincial bodies as well as organizations that focus on particular issues of children's rights such as corporal punishment, child care, and child poverty.

22 R.B. Howe and K. Covell, *Empowering Children: Children's Rights Education as a Pathway to Citizenship* (Toronto: University of Toronto Press, 2005), pp. 35–42.

23 Covell and Howe, *The Challenge of Children's Rights for Canada,* p. 31.

24 UNICEF, *Summary Report of the Study of the Impact of the Implementation of the Convention on the Rights of the Child* (Florence: UNICEF Innocenti Research Centre, 2004), pp. 3–8.

25 *Gosselin v. Quebec (Attorney General),* 2002 SCC 84, [2002] 4 S.C.R. 429. Louise Gosselin claimed that her rights to security of person and equality under the

Canadian Charter of Rights and Freedoms had been infringed by the Quebec government's decision to sharply reduce social assistance for single individuals, forcing her into deep poverty. Although there was strong dissent, the majority on the Court held that the right to security of person does not mean that the state has to guarantee adequate living conditions.

26 UNICEF, *Summary Report*, pp. 9–14.

27 See Howe and Covell, *Empowering Children*, pp. 38–39; R. Hodgkin and P. Newell, *Implementation Handbook for the Convention on the Rights of the Child* (New York: UNICEF, 1998), pp. 70–71.

28 Emphasized by the UN Committee on the Rights of the Child both in 1995 and 2003. See CRC/C/15/Add.37 (June 1995) and CRC/C/15/Add.215 (October 2003). See also UNICEF, *Summary Report*, pp. 15–18.

29 R. Joyal, J.-F. Noel, and C.C. Feliciati, eds., *Making Children's Rights Work: National and International Perspectives* (Montreal: Editions Yvon Blais, 2005), pp. 30–31; Andreychuk and Pearson, *Who's in Charge Here?* pp. 74–87.

30 Andreychuk and Pearson, *Who's in Charge Here?* pp. 46–48.

31 *Baker v. Canada (Minister of Citizenship and Immigration)*, [1999] 2 S.C.R. 817.

32 Based on a search of the database of the Canadian Legal Information Institute (http://www.canlii.org), September 2005.

33 From 1991 to December 2005, the UN Convention was referred to in only fifty-four cases (based on a search of http://www.canlii.org).

34 *Baker v. Canada,* at para. 70.

35 *Canadian Foundation for Children, Youth and the Law v. Canada (Attorney General)*, 2004 SCC 4, [2004] 1 S.C.R. 76, at para. 31.

36 J. Brunnée and S. Toope, "A Hesitant Embrace: Baker and the Application of International Law by Canadian Courts," *Canadian Yearbook of International Law* 40 (Vancouver: UBC Press, 2002), pp. 3–60.

37 Joyal, Noel, and Feliciati, *Making Children's Rights Work*, pp. 23–27, 31; Andreychuk and Pearson, *Who's in Charge Here?* pp. 62–63.

38 A leading figure in this effort was Senator Landon Pearson.

39 Examples include the Privacy Commissioner, the Commissioner of Official Languages, and, of course, the Auditor General of Canada.

40 Some municipalities have established child advocacy offices. Toronto, for example, designates a councillor as a "children's advocate"; that person is responsible for issuing periodic reports.

41 Andreychuk and Pearson, *Who's in Charge Here?* pp. 53–59.

42 CRC/C/15/Add.215 (October 2003), p. 3.

Bibliography

Andreychuk, R., and L. Pearson. 2005. *Who's in Charge Here? Effective Implementation of Canada's International Obligations with Respect to the Rights of Children*. Ottawa: Senate Standing Committee on Human Rights, pp. 59–68.

Brooks, S. 2003. *Public Policy in Canada: An Introduction*. Toronto: Oxford University Press.

Brunnée, J., and S. Toope. 2002. "A Hesitant Embrace: Baker and the Application of International Law by Canadian Courts." *Canadian Yearbook of International Law* 40. Vancouver: UBC Press.

Covell, K., and R.B. Howe. 2001. *The Challenge of Children's Rights for Canada*. Waterloo: Wilfrid Laurier University Press.

Doek, J. 1992. "The Current Status of the United Nations Convention on the Rights of the Child." In S. Detrick, ed., *The United Nations Convention on the Rights of the Child*. Dordrecht: Martinus Nijhoff, pp. 632–40.

Edelman, M. 1964. *The Symbolic Uses of Politics*. Urbana: University of Illinois Press.

Eekelaar, J. 1992. "The Importance of Thinking That Children Have Rights." In P. Alston, S. Parker, and J. Seymour, eds., *Children, Rights, and the Law*. Oxford: Oxford University Press, pp. 221–35.

Feinberg, J. 1970. "The Nature and Value of Rights," *Journal of Value Inquiry* 4, no. 4: 55–97.

Freeman, M. 1992. "Taking Children's Rights More Seriously." In P. Alston, S. Parker, and J. Seymour, eds., *Children, Rights, and the Law*. Oxford: Oxford University Press.

———. 1997. *The Moral Status of Children: Essays on the Rights of the Child*. The Hague: Kluwer Law International.

Hammarberg, T. 1990. "The UN Convention on the Rights of the Child—and How to Make It Work." *Human Rights Quarterly* 12: 97–105.

Hart, S.N. 1991. "From Property to Person Status: Historical Perspective on Children's Rights." *American Psychologist* 46, no. 1: 53–59.

Hill, M., and K. Tisdall. 1997. *Children and Society*. London: Addison Wesley Longman.

Hodgkin, R., and P. Newell. 1998. *Implementation Handbook for the Convention on the Rights of the Child*. New York: UNICEF.

Hogg, P. 1992. *Constitutional Law of Canada*. Toronto: Carswell.

Howe, R.B., and K. Covell. 2005. *Empowering Children: Children's Rights Education as a Pathway to Citizenship*. Toronto: University of Toronto Press.

Joyal, R., J. Noel, and C.C. Feliciati, eds. 2005. *Making Children's Rights Work: National and International Perspectives*. Montreal: Editions Yvon Blais.

Minow, M. 1986. "Rights for the Next Generation: A Feminist Approach to Children's Rights." *Harvard Women's Law Journal* 9: 1–24.

Stasiulis, D. 2002. "The Active Child Citizen: Lessons from Canadian Policy and the Children's Movement." *Citizenship Studies* 6, no. 4: 508.

Toope, S. 1996. "The Convention on the Rights of the Child: Implications for Canada." In M. Freeman, ed., *Children's Rights: A Comparative Perspective*. Aldershot: Dartmouth Publishing, pp. 33–64.

UNICEF. 2004. *Summary Report of the Study of the Impact of the Implementation of the Convention on the Rights of the Child*. Florence: UNICEF Innocenti Research Centre.

"UN Convention on the Rights of the Child as a Touchstone for Research on Childhoods" (editorial). 1999. *Childhood* 6, no. 4: 403.

UN General Assembly. 2006. *Report of the Independent Expert for the United Nations Study on Violence against Children.* A/61/299.

Verhellen, E. 1994. *Convention on the Rights of the Child.* Kessel-Lo, Belgium: Garant.

———. 1999. "Facilitating Children's Rights in Education." *Prospects* 29, no. 2: 224–31.

Child Poverty
The Evolution and Impact of Child Benefits

Ken Battle

Introduction: Family Policy at a Crossroads?

Canada is officially committed to the goal of eliminating child poverty. In 1989, as the Convention on the Rights of the Child (CRC) was being adopted by the United Nations, Canada's House of Commons unanimously passed a resolution—endorsed by all parties—to seek an end to child poverty in Canada by the year 2000. In 1990, at the World Summit for Children, Canada agreed to the principle of "first call for children"; in other words, the basic needs of children were to receive priority in the allocation of a state's resources, in hard times as well as in good times. In 1991, in ratifying the CRC, Canada agreed to implement measures on behalf of children to the "maximum extent" of its resources (article 4) and to implement "the right of every child to a standard of living adequate for the child's physical, mental, spiritual, moral, and social development" (article 27).

No government questions the importance of the objective of eliminating or reducing child poverty or of the proposition that poverty is contradictory to one of the key principles of the CRC—the best interests of the child. Unfortunately, the track record of governments in fighting child poverty has been decidedly mixed. On the negative side are cuts to social assistance benefits, the radical shrinkage of Employment Insurance coverage, and low minimum wages. On the positive side is a range of efforts— ranging from modest to substantial—that have been made in recent years to combat child poverty and better meet the basic needs of children

Ken Battle, Caledon Institute of Social Policy

through improvements in the three main pillars of Canadian family policy—child benefits, child care, and parental leave. However, the years 2005 and 2006 bracket what could well turn out to be a turning point in family policy. At risk are decades of hard work on the part of experts, advocates, and policy-makers—not to mention the well-being of millions of Canada's children and parents and the international competitiveness of Canadian employers who benefit from strong social infrastructure.

In the late 1990s and early 2000s, some progress was made with all three pillars. In 2000 there was a doubling of the maximum duration of combined maternity and parental leave benefits under Employment Insurance (EI), to fifty weeks, to allow parents more time at home with newborns and newly adopted children. In 2005 the Liberal government negotiated bilateral agreements on child care with all ten provinces, and hoped to bring the territories onside soon after. These initiatives built on previous agreements in 2000 and 2003 by which Ottawa has been transferring billions of dollars to the provinces, territories, and First Nations to help them build a national system of early learning and child care services. In its 2003 budget the federal government announced a series of additional enrichments to the Canada Child Tax Benefit through to 2007 as part of its ongoing commitment to the federal–provincial/territorial National Child Benefit reform launched in 1998. This major reform to the structure of child benefits built on a lengthy process of "relentlessly incremental"[1] changes beginning in the late 1970s and evolving through the 1980s and 1990s.

However, the January 2006 election brought to power a new government intent on making a 180-degree turn in federal policy on child care and child benefits. The Conservatives abandoned the previous Liberal administration's recently negotiated bilateral agreements on child care with the provinces, which will be honoured for only one year; this about-turn will have a drastic chilling effect on the provinces' plans to improve and expand their early learning and child care services.[2] Most of the money saved by axing the bilateral agreements will be used instead to launch a "Universal Child Care Benefit" (known during the election campaign as the "Choice in Child Care Allowance") that, despite its name, is not a child care program but rather a child benefit—and a seriously flawed one at that.

This chapter explores the role and evolution of child benefits, a key—but much underestimated and misunderstood—instrument for poverty reduction and strengthening families as well as an indispensable element of any modern social security system.[3]

No Magic Bullets

Child poverty, like poverty in general, tends to rise and fall with economic recessions and recoveries. Overall, there has been no long-term reduction in the incidence of child poverty, which stood at 12.8 percent in 2004.[4] However, child poverty rates would have been even higher were it not for child benefits, as will be explained later. Figure 2.1 illustrates the trend in the percentage of low-income children between 1980 and 2004, using estimates calculated by Statistics Canada based on its after-tax low-income cut-offs. Children raised by single-parent mothers run a much higher risk of poverty (40.0 percent at last count, 2003) than children in two-parent families (8.1 percent).

Canada fares poorly in international comparisons of child poverty. Among the twenty-three nations shown in Figure 2.2, Canada's child poverty rate—15.7 percent, or one child in six—placed us sixth highest.[5]

Child poverty is a complex and enduring problem. Children are poor because their parents are poor, and their parents are poor for any number of reasons. Low wages, non-standard employment, unemployment,

Figure 2.1: Low-income rate, Canadian children, 1980–2004

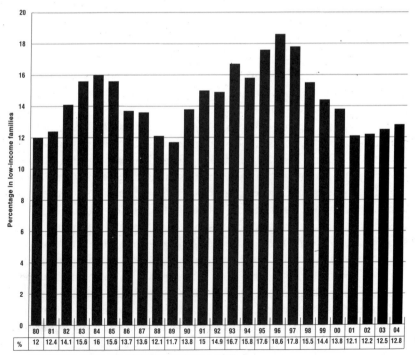

	80	81	82	83	84	85	86	87	88	89	90	91	92	93	94	95	96	97	98	99	00	01	02	03	04
%	12	12.4	14.1	15.6	16	15.6	13.7	13.6	12.1	11.7	13.8	15	14.9	16.7	15.8	17.6	18.6	17.8	15.5	14.4	13.8	12.1	12.2	12.5	12.8

Data: Statistics Canada 2006, using after-tax low-income cutoffs.

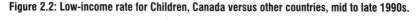

Figure 2.2: Low-income rate for Children, Canada versus other countries, mid to late 1990s.

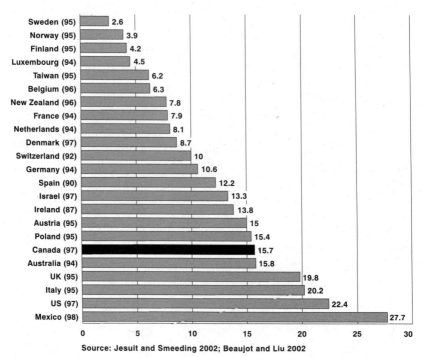

Source: Jesuit and Smeeding 2002; Beaujot and Liu 2002

marriage breakup, inadequate education, and outmoded work skills are among the many factors fuelling the troubling statistic that one child in eight lives in a low-income family.

There are no magic bullets to vanquish child poverty. The problem is too varied, too complex, and too entrenched to be solved by a single social program or policy. Child poverty demands action on a number of fronts by a variety of actors besides government, including employers, unions, the education system, advocacy groups, and communities. A broad range of instruments and institutions affect poverty directly or indirectly. They include fiscal and monetary policies, lifelong learning, minimum wages, social assistance, early learning and child care services, efforts to build community capacity and foster community-based social and economic development, employment development services, health care, child support, social housing, parental leave and leave for family responsibilities, respite care, supports for persons with disabilities, family-friendly workplace practices and—the subject of this chapter—child benefits. Communications to raise public awareness and improve understanding also play an important role. Examples are the famous 1989 Commons resolution to work toward the elimination of child poverty by the year 2000, and the annual report cards on child poverty from Campaign 2000. Some of these measures and policies seek to prevent poverty, others to ease the severity and lessen the harmful impact of poverty, still others to place and keep child poverty on the political agenda.

Child Benefits in Canada

In 1998 the federal and provincial/territorial governments embarked on one of the most significant changes in the history of Canadian social policy—the National Child Benefit (NCB). Because it involves a substantive if not radical restructuring of federal and provincial/territorial child benefits, the initiative—which is still in process, due to its multiyear implementation—has sparked criticism from both left and right. Despite empirical evidence as to its positive impact, the NCB remains one of the least understood of recent public policy reforms, having failed to register on the radar of most journalists and politicians.

To properly understand why Canada's child benefits required so fundamental a reform, we must briefly explain their basic purposes and trace their evolution.[6]

Core Objectives

In Canada, child benefits—meaning cash payments on behalf of children, delivered in the form of either cheques or income tax reductions—historically have pursued two fundamental and related objectives, characterized as the "antipoverty" and "horizontal equity" objectives. Under the antipoverty objective, child benefits seek to help fill the gap between the earnings of low- and modest-wage parents and their families' income needs, based on the long-recognized and still highly relevant reality that a market economy does not vary wages and salaries to take into account the number of family members dependent on that income. The horizontal equity objective views child benefits as one way for society to provide some financial recompense for the fact that families at all income levels with children to support bear expenses that childless households at the same income level do not.

These twin objectives are interrelated. Both assume that society has an interest and obligation to help parents with their childrearing costs because children are viewed at least partially as a "public good" or "investment": children grow up to become workers, taxpayers, and citizens, so it is in the interest of everyone—including those without children—that parents do not face undue financial strain in the childrearing "work" that they perform, in effect, in part on behalf of everyone. The antipoverty objective acknowledges that lower-income families have the least financial capacity and also seeks to mitigate the higher personal and societal risks of child poverty in terms of children's immediate and long-term health, learning capacity, and educational performance. For low-income families the antipoverty and horizontal-equity objectives of child benefits effectively are the same. Concern about the horizontal-equity objective typically has focused on non-poor families, which have suffered a substantial decline (and, for some high-income families, disappearance) in their child benefits since the mid-1980s.

The long-term trend has been toward greater "targeting" of child benefits—that is, with gearing amount to need as measured by family income and with raising the maximum payments. Since the late 1970s the antipoverty objective has been accorded greater weight at the expense of the horizontal-equity objective. However, even though it calculates the amount of payments on the basis of family income, Canada's child benefits system is not—contrary to what some people think—targeted narrowly at the poor in terms of eligibility; rather, it is a broad-based system that covers the large majority of families—about nine in ten.

Evolution of Child Benefits

The history of Canadian child benefits can be divided into five main periods. The first phase, between the two world wars, can be characterized as "regressive targeting." The personal-income-tax system provided a children's tax exemption that delivered its benefits in the form of income-tax savings; these savings increased with taxable income and excluded families that did not owe income tax—the majority, in those times of widespread poverty and modest average incomes.

The arrival of universal, monthly Family Allowances in 1945 heralded the second phase, "untargeted universality." Child benefits were extended to include low- and modest-income families; even so, the better off still got more (because they received both the children's tax exemption and Family Allowances). The 1970s ushered in the third phase, "progressive universality." Family Allowances were tripled, indexed to the cost of living, and made taxable. A new, "income tested" program administered through the personal-income-tax system—the refundable child tax credit—delivered its maximum payments to low-income families, smaller amounts to middle-income families (amounts that decreased as incomes increased), and nothing to the well off.

The fourth phase, "progressive targeting," began in the 1980s and continued through the 1990s. The children's tax exemption was reduced in 1987 and then converted to a non-refundable child tax credit in 1988. Whereas the children's tax exemption was a regressive program providing benefits in the form of income-tax savings that increased with income, the non-refundable child credit gave virtually all taxpaying families equal income-tax savings (though it still excluded families below the taxpaying threshold and was worth less than the maximum in the case of families whose income tax liability was less than the value of the non-refundable credit). The equivalent-to-married exemption—a child benefit paid on behalf of the first child in single-parent families—also was converted to a non-refundable credit. The refundable child tax credit enjoyed a substantial boost in the latter half of the decade, including a new supplement for children under seven.

The federal government announced the imminent demise of universal child benefits in 1989 by requiring upper-income families to repay more or (if their incomes were high enough) all of their Family Allowances through a clawback. The measure was phased in over three years, so that as of 1991 well-off families received what amounted to temporary Family Allowances in that they had to pay back, through the clawback at income-tax time, the benefits they had received the previous year. The federal child benefits system, which had been fully indexed to the inflation rate since 1973, was partially de-indexed as of 1985—a significant albeit stealthy and regressive change that was not rescinded until 2000.

The 1990s brought a formal break with universality and a shift to a wholly income-tested federal child benefits system. In 1993 the three major federal child benefits—Family Allowances, the refundable child tax credit, and the non-refundable child tax credit—were replaced by a single, income-tested Child Tax Benefit that increased benefits for working-poor families with children, maintained benefits for other low-income families, reduced benefits for middle-income families, and removed benefits from high-income families.

In 1997, Canada entered a fifth phase of child benefits, an "integrated child benefit," that broadened the scope of reform to include provincial and territorial programs. This large-scale reconstruction of Canadian child benefits, the NCB, is discussed next.

Building an Integrated Child Benefit: The National Child Benefit

Rationale for Reform

To understand the rationale underlying Canada's unfolding NCB reform, it is necessary to recount the major weaknesses of the child benefits system that it is now replacing. To begin with, the old "system" was not really a system in any rigorous sense of the word; rather, it was an unco-ordinated group of programs provided by two levels of government.

The federal child benefits system, which for much of its history suf-fered from an irrational distribution of benefits, was rationalized in 1993 into a single, income-tested Child Tax Benefit (renamed Canada Child Tax Benefit in 1998, though the new program is much the same). While the benefits are geared to net family income, the program is not targeted narrowly at the poor. This "broad-based" characteristic—while no longer universal, the system still reaches nine in ten families with children—advances the social policy objective of social cohesion, in that the large majority of families are served by the same program and no vulnerable group is excluded.

Another of the Canada Child Tax Benefit's virtues is its anonymous, non-stigmatizing, and efficient administration, through the same income-tax system that covers Canadians in all income groups throughout the country. Recipients qualify and requalify for benefits based on a simple test of their income; there is almost never any direct contact between recipi-ents and administrators. Benefits are delivered on a frequent (monthly) basis. Until the advent of the NCB, all the provinces and territories deliv-ered what amounted to cash child benefits through their social assistance systems, which provided benefits on behalf of children as well as adults. There was little if any explicit coordination with federal child benefits, and the two differed in terms of purpose, design, and delivery.

Child benefits delivered through provincial and territorial social assis-tance (popularly known as welfare) have pursued only an antipoverty objective, and (along with adult benefits) have been intended to provide sufficient funds for a family to buy basic necessities. They are meant to replace income from earnings and other sources, whereas federal child benefits are intended only to supplement other sources of income.

Income-tested child benefits have performed well in terms of foster-ing social cohesion and inclusion; in contrast, needs-tested social assis-tance in Canada has always been an exclusionary, socially marginalizing, and divisive social program. The welfare system is often highly discre-tionary and involves a relatively high degree of client–worker interaction. Welfare imposes a significant social stigma on its recipients. It is a highly complex system that is top-heavy with rules and regulations and in which recipients typically are treated in a manner that tends to reinforces their economic powerlessness. As a result, their employment skills and self-confidence may "rust" and atrophy.[7]

Federal and provincial child benefits also differ significantly in scope: Federal child benefits throughout their history have served all or (since 1991) almost all families with children; welfare-embedded child benefits are restricted mainly to non-working poor families and typically exclude other low-income families such as the working poor and those on Employment Insurance. The record shows that welfare benefits are politically vulnerable to cuts, be they overt (as a result of rate reductions) or covert (as a result of non-indexation and complicated rule changes).

One inherent problem in the uncoordinated non-system of federal income-tested child benefits and provincial needs-tested child benefits is that it has never been able to deal effectively with the problem of persistent and extensive child poverty in Canada, because social assistance is so narrowly targeted and so unpopular. The blunt reality is that the benefits offered by social assistance will always be extremely low, perhaps *because* the program itself is so stigmatized—as well as stigmatizing.

Another significant problem with the two-tiered non-system of child benefits is the "welfare wall," a term coined by the Caledon Institute of Social Policy.[8] Welfare families have long received child benefits from two sources: provincial social assistance benefits paid on behalf of children, and federal child benefits. Other low-income families—notably the working poor and the Employment Insurance poor—have typically received federal child benefits only. Families on welfare have enjoyed considerably more generous child benefits than those paid to other low-income families (indeed, about double the benefits), and this cash advantage does not count the value of the social assistance system's income-in-kind benefits, such as supplementary health and dental; nor does it count shelter allowances and special benefits such as winter clothing allowances.

Just before the NCB was introduced in July 1998, combined federal–provincial child benefits ranged annually from around $2,220 to $2,820 per child for social assistance families in most provinces (add another $213 per year for each child under seven, for whom the child care expense deduction was not claimed), whereas federal child benefits for children in working-poor families were a maximum $1,520 annually for one child. For two children, the gap between welfare families and other low-income families was even wider. For example, for families with one child under seven and one child over seven, total child benefits for a social-assistance family from the federal and provincial governments amounted to $5,253 per year—close to double the $2,753 in federal child benefits for other low-income families with children (using a rough average of $1,500 per child per year for welfare assistance–provided child benefits, excluding the special adult equivalent benefit for the first child in single-parent families).

The term "welfare wall" has been used as the central metaphor in NCB reform to dramatize the features of the tax/transfer system—in this case, child benefits—that can erect barriers to moving from social assistance into the workforce. Parents on social assistance who managed to find paid work risked forfeiting thousands of dollars in welfare-provided cash child benefits and in-kind benefits, on top of seeing their (typically low) wages reduced by federal and sometimes provincial income taxes as well as federal payroll taxes, and stressed by employment-related costs such as child care, clothing, and transportation.

Formula for Reform

The federal–provincial/territorial NCB seeks to lower the welfare wall by creating an integrated, non-stigmatizing child benefit that treats all low-income families equally, whether they are working or not, while enabling the provinces to take additional actions to assist low-income families.

The main engine of reform is the federal child benefit. As Ottawa increases payments under the Canada Child Tax Benefit (CCTB), the provinces and territories can reduce their social assistance–provided child benefits by the amount of the federal increase, as long as the provinces/territories "reinvest" the resulting savings in other programs and services for low-income families with children—such as child care and other early childhood development services, supplementary health care, income-tested child benefits, and earnings supplements.

Governments' goal is to raise the CCTB to the point where, alone or in combination with provincial/territorial income-tested child benefits, it will displace basic welfare-embedded child benefits—estimated at about $2,500 per child in 1998, or about $3,000 in today's dollars. That level of maximum benefit would achieve the objective of an "integrated child benefit": all low-income families, regardless of their major source(s) of income, would receive the same amount of child benefit, and the distinction between child benefits for the working poor and those for the non-working poor would in this way be eliminated.

Objectives of Reform

The federal and provincial governments have set three formal objectives for the NCB: "to help prevent and reduce the depth of child poverty; to promote attachment to the workforce—resulting in fewer families having to rely on social assistance—by ensuring that families will always be better off as a result of finding work; and to reduce overlap and duplication through closer harmonization of program objectives and benefits and through simplified administration."[9]

In a 1997 report written for the federal and British Columbia governments,[10] the Caledon Institute of Social Policy proposed several additional objectives: adequacy, fairness, dignity and independence, and economic stabilization.

Once the "displace welfare" child benefits target of a maximum $2,500 (in 1998 dollars) per child per year is reached, the CCTB should be raised further, within the first decade of the twenty-first century, to reach about $5,000 (in current 2006 dollars) maximum per child annually, which is our rough estimate of the basic cost of raising a child in a low-income family (Caledon has recommended that a study be conducted to arrive at more accurate and detailed estimates). A number of social-advocacy groups, such as the broad-coalition Campaign 2000, have endorsed Caledon's $5,000 target. Caledon has also urged the federal government to improve child benefits for modest- and middle-income families—which have seen losses since the 1980s—to strengthen its performance regarding the horizontal equity goal. Adequacy also requires full indexation; the federal government achieved this as of 2000, but the provinces have not yet followed suit.

The objectives of dignity and independence are being advanced through the broad-based, income-tested CCTB. Finally, resurrecting a traditional but long-lost objective of Canadian child benefits, Caledon has recommended that the system also be seen as an important part of economic stabilization—as an efficient vehicle to put cash into the hands of parents and thereby maintain consumer demand during downturns and cushion the effects of recessions.

Progress

A series of annual government reports, as well as the first formal evaluation, show progress toward all three of the NCB's objectives. Indeed, the target of $2,500 (about $3,000 in today's money) for an integrated child benefit has been surpassed, effectively launching the program on the road to adequate child benefits dreamed of by social advocates and think tanks.

The federal government has followed through on its commitment to the NCB through substantial annual increases to the maximum payment from the CCTB. The 2003 federal budget announced a further multi-year series of significant enrichments to the CCTB through 2007. These commitments are sufficient to complete the first stage of the NCB reform— creating an *integrated child benefit*—and to launch a second stage of reform (to build an *adequate child benefit*).

The maximum CCTB payment for a first child has risen from $1,650 in its first year (July 1998 to June 1989) to $2,632 for July 2003 to June 2004 and will reach a projected $3,243 for July 2007 to June 2008. The maximum benefit for a second child has risen from $1,425 for July 1988 to June 1989, to $2,423 for July 2003 to June 2004, to a projected $3,016 for July 2007 to June 2008; and for the third and each additional child from $1,425 to $2,427 to a projected $3,020 over the same period.

These are among the largest benefit increases in the history of Canadian social policy. Expressed in inflation-adjusted 2007 dollars, the maximum benefit for the first child was $1,974 in 1997, the year before the NCB reform began. By July 2007 it is projected to reach $3,243—a substantial $1,269 or 64 percent real increase over 1997.

The NCB reached its $2,500 target in July 2005, when the maximum payment for the first child was $2,521 in constant 1988 dollars ($2,950 in current 2005 dollars). This level marked the completion of a new architecture for child benefits—an *integrated child benefit* providing equal and portable benefits to all low-income families and delivered through an inclusive system that also serves the large majority of non-poor families. Total expenditures on federal child benefits increased in real terms (constant 2007 dollars) from $6.5 billion in 1997 to a projected $10.1 billion in 2007—a boost of $3.7 billion, or 56.9 percent. The new investments in the CCTB much more than make up for the reductions in expenditures on federal child benefits that occured in the 1980s: by 2007, Ottawa will be spending $10.1 billion, which is $2.6 billion (35.2 percent) more than its 1984 expenditure of $7.5 billion (constant) on child benefit programs.

Provincial and territorial governments and First Nations communities have been reinvesting federally driven welfare savings and have also invested their own money in a range of other programs and services for low-income families.[11] Total provincial, territorial, and First Nations reinvestments and investments went from $270 million in 1998–99 to $486 million in 1999–2000, $593 million in 2000–1, $726 million in 2001–2, $769 million in 2002–3, $879 million in 2003–4, and $919 million in 2004–5. Child care took first place (29 percent in 2003–4), followed by income-tested child benefits and earnings supplements (26 percent), early childhood development and children-at-risk initiatives (16 percent), other (14 percent), First Nations (6 percent), supplementary health care (5 percent), and youth initiatives (4 percent).

As expected, increases to federal payments through the National Child Benefit Supplement—the part of the CCTB that is targeted to low-income families—have yielded modest reductions in the number of low-income children and families, as well as in the incidence and depth of poverty.[12] In 2000 the increase in child benefits reduced the number of low-income children by 53,300 (16,100 in one-parent families and 37,200 in two-parent families) and the number of low-income families with children by 22,900 (8,600 one-parent families and 14,300 two-parent families), which represents a 5.1 percent decline in the number of low-income families.

The higher child benefits slightly lowered the incidence of poverty among families with children, which fell by 0.6 percent (from 11.6 to 11.0 percent) in 2000. The impact was greater among one-parent families, whose poverty rate fell by 1.2 percent (from 29.4 to 28.2 percent). The incidence of poverty among two-parent families declined by 0.5 percent as a result of the NCB (from 7.6 to 7.1 percent).

Families that were lifted above the poverty line by the NCB saw an average $1,800 or 7.5 percent increase in their disposable income ($1,250 or 6.0 percent for one-parent families, $2,100 or 8.3 percent for two-parent families), which rose from $23,800 to $25,600 in 2000. Families that remained below the poverty line experienced an average $700 or 4.1 percent increase in their disposable income thanks to the NCB ($500 or 3.1 percent among single-parent families, $900 or 4.8 percent among two-parent families). Overall, their average disposable income increased from $16,900 to $17,600. The reform increased the average disposable income of working-poor families with children by $1,200 or 7.0 percent, from $16,700 to $17,900.

Among families that remained below the poverty line, the NCB reduced the total poverty gap—that is, the total dollar amount below Statistics Canada's low-income cutoffs—by $320 million or 9.6 percent ($100 million or 7.6 percent for one-parent families, $220 million or 11.0 percent among two-parent families). For working-poor families, the total low-income gap declined by $269 million or 14.0 percent. These are substantial improvements.

There also is evidence of a positive impact on the "welfare wall" (i.e., the set of barriers that families face that can make them worse off working than if they stayed on welfare. In 1997, before NCB reform, a single parent with one child age four gained only 3.8 percent in disposable income if he or she moved from welfare to full-time work at the minimum wage; in 2001, that parent's disposable income rose by 12.7 percent thanks to increases in child benefits for working poor families (to bring their child benefits closer to the level of families on welfare). For a two-parent family with two children aged ten and thirteen, the move from welfare to full-time work at minimum wage gained them 30.8 percent in 1997 but 37.9 percent in 2001 as a result of the NCB.

Two case studies suggest that the NCB is helping reduce welfare dependency.[13] One case study of single-parent families estimated that, controlling for the effects of various factors, a $1,200 annual real increase in minimum-wage income over welfare income resulted in a 20 percent increase in the rate at which these families leave welfare and a corresponding 17 percent decline in both the average and median duration of spells on assistance. The second case study determined that the NCB's replacement of welfare child benefits with an integrated income-tested child benefit (providing equal benefits to all low-income families, whether working poor or welfare poor) contributed to a 14.5 percent cumulative reduction in welfare caseloads of families with children, compared to those without children.

The NCB has also helped reduce overlap and duplication of federal and provincial/territorial programs—the third formal objective of the reform. In a number of jurisdictions the federal CCTB is also being used to deliver provincial/territorial child benefits, resulting in administrative savings and efficient delivery to families.

Canada's NCB reform has attracted international attention. Revenue and Treasury officials from the United Kingdom visited Canada to look at the design and delivery experience of the CCTB system when developing their own integrated system to address child poverty in Britain.

While increases to child benefits under the NCB have had generally modest effects, the CCTB as a whole has packed a much bigger antipoverty punch. A Finance Canada study found that the low-income rate for families with children in 1999 would have been 16.8 percent had the federal government not provided the CCTB.[14] With the CCTB at its 1999 rate, the incidence of family poverty was 13.1 percent in 1999. With the CCTB at its 2004 rate, 12.4 percent of families with children would have been below Statistics Canada's low-income cutoffs in 1999—4.4 percentage points lower, which represents a sizable reduction of 26 percent in the poverty rate.

Child benefits are contributing a growing share of the incomes of working-poor families. For a family with one child and earnings of $15,000, the CCTB increased from 10.1 percent of earnings in 1977 to 18.0 percent in 2004 and will reach 21.6 percent by 2007. For a two-child family earning $25,000, the CCTB went from 12.2 percent of earnings in 1997 to 20.7 percent in 2004 and will rise to 25.0 percent by 2007.

The increase in federal child benefits for low-income families is striking over both the short and the long term. In 2007 the CCTB will pay almost quadruple what Family Allowances delivered in 1946 for a low-income family with two children: $6,511 versus $1,697 (in inflation-adjusted 2007 dollars). Figure 2.3 illustrates the trend for a family with two children.

The CCTB is also being used as a platform to help deliver other child-related benefits. A number of provinces and territories have elected to have their own child benefits delivered through the federal income-testing and delivery machinery. In 2003 the federal government added a Child Disability Benefit to the CCTB. Payable on behalf of children with severe disabilities who are in low- and modest-income families with children,

Figure 2.3: Federal cash child benefits for low-income families with two children, 1946–2007

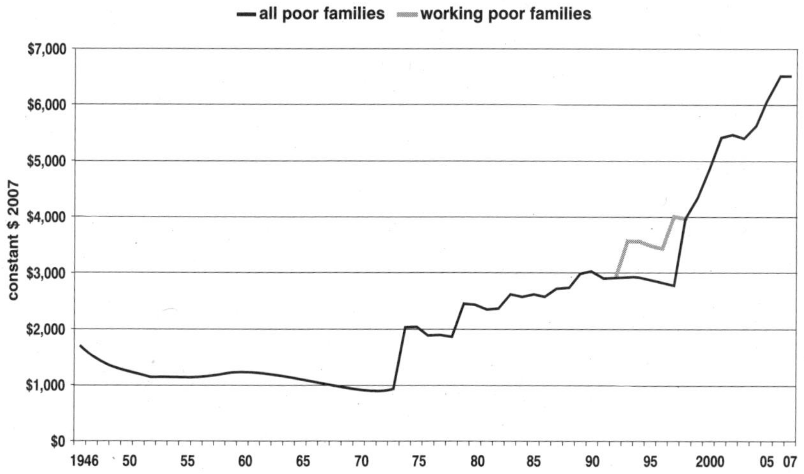

— all poor families   — working poor families

the Child Disability Benefit is currently worth a maximum of $2,000. The year 2004 brought another CCTB-delivered new program, the Canada Learning Bond. Intended to help low-income families save toward their children's post-secondary education, the Canada Learning Bond will pay $500 at birth and $100 each year thereafter (to a cumulative total of $2,000) for each child in families that receive the CCTB's National Child Benefit Supplement (i.e., that portion of the CCTB targeted to families with net incomes under $35,595).

Another tiny but still noteworthy advance—one ignored by all—is that Ottawa recently began modestly restoring child benefits for non-poor (mainly modest- and middle-income) families through changes to the CCTB's parameters. In so doing, the federal government has broadened the scope of reform beyond the child benefit system's antipoverty objective to at least tacitly acknowledge the need to improve its horizontal equity performance. Thus the two fundamental objectives of child benefits are being simultaneously strengthened, even if the weight is still heavily on the antipoverty goal.

Criticisms of the National Child Benefit

The complexities of Canada's child benefits system, and the broad scope and rather complex nature of the federal–provincial/territorial NCB—extending as it does beyond income support to social and health services—have placed that system beyond the understanding of the Canadian public, most journalists and, indeed, all but a handful of politicians. So the

NCB debate has been confined largely to social-advocacy and social-policy NGOs as well as to a few economic think tanks. Several criticisms have been made of the system, the two most common of which are considered here.[15]

The most damning allegation against the NCB is that it "discriminates against social assistance families, the poorest of the poor." Welfare families have not received an increase in their child benefits; rather, they have seen only an increase in the proportion coming from the federal CCTB and, in some provinces and territories, new income-tested child benefits, and a concomitant decline in the share from social assistance. Critics have vilified this as a "clawback" of the National Child Benefit Supplement (i.e., that part of the CCTB that has been increased). In contrast, the working poor and other low-income families not on welfare have enjoyed a substantial rise in their child benefits. To make matters worse, the NCB—touted by its supporters as a key advance in antipoverty strategy—arrived after several years of overt or covert cuts to social-assistance benefits, cuts that have shrunk families' incomes, and amidst increasing efforts on the part of most provinces to require recipients to enter the workforce (e.g., through workfare programs and the tightening of eligibility rules in many provinces).

This criticism, parroted by a generally uninformed media, misses or rejects the essential purpose of the NCB, which is to restructure income-security policy for families by equalizing child benefits for all low-income families—that is, by raising payments for poor families not on welfare assistance to the levels paid to welfare families.

This core feature of the NCB has resulted in a great deal of confusion, a field day for government critics, and not a little honest anxiety on the part of highly vulnerable social assistance recipients. A key issue here is strategy: had Ottawa gone with a big-bang approach (as proposed in a 1995 Caledon report) rather than an incremental, multi-year, phased-in approach, and had it placed enough money on the table, it could not only have displaced welfare-embedded child benefits immediately, but also raised the level of the new CCTB high enough to exceed the previous amount of combined federal and provincial/territorial child benefits payable to social-assistance families. Welfare families still would have seen a smaller net increase in child benefits than the working poor, but at least the former would have been better off than before. As well, the idea that one type of benefit was simply replacing another would have been apparent and easily explained. The incremental strategy that was adopted instead has fuelled criticisms of the NCB.

However, even without a real increase in child benefits for social-assistance families, it can be argued those families are better off under the

NCB. Welfare is a highly stigmatizing program prone to overt cuts or stealthy erosion on the part of the provinces. For example, a get-tough-on-welfare plank was a prominent part of Ontario's Harris government election platform, and it followed through with a 21.6 percent cut in social assistance for most recipients in October 1995. The cuts did not harm their political fortunes and indeed may well have helped. The Ontario Conservatives were subsequently handily re-elected, unlike the previous two provincial administrations, which had raised welfare rates.

Income-tested social programs, in contrast to needs-tested welfare, have seen real and substantial increases in benefit rates for lower-income recipients, with broad public support. The CCTB, which was fully indexed as of 2000, is in a far better position than social assistance to enjoy further increases in the coming years. Thus if one is worried about the adequacy of welfare recipients' incomes, the best option is to provide a larger proportion of their incomes out of a politically popular and expanding program such as the CCTB.

Moreover, it is vital to remember that the population on social assistance is a dynamic and ever-changing group. Around half of welfare recipients rejoin the workforce every year. Under the old system, those recipients lost all of their welfare-delivered child benefits. But, to borrow a term from pension terminology, the CCTB is a "portable" benefit that accompanies families no matter what their primary income source: welfare families no longer lose child benefits when they move into the workforce, and working-poor families continue to receive their child benefits from the federal government even when they move to social assistance or Employment Insurance. Families that improve their earnings continue to receive the CCTB—albeit in smaller amounts as their income increases—and they do so far up the income scale.

As well, families on welfare receive the CCTB, without stigma, just like the large majority of Canadian families. Payment is automatic and painless and involves little or no contact with government officials. Moreover, some social-assistance families will benefit from some of the provincial reinvestments (not all of which are focused on the working poor), though more so if they move into the workforce.

The NCB holds out the promise of more than just a restructuring and enhancement of child benefits. By removing a large group (children) from social assistance caseloads, it marks a major step forward in the essential task of dismantling the archaic and harmful welfare system and replacing it with more effective programs for working-age adults. (The Caledon Institute is currently developing a new architecture of adult benefits.)

The second main criticism of the NCB comes from the right. Some economists content that the NCB reform could be shooting itself in the foot, as it were, by imposing high effective marginal tax rates that supposedly sap the work ethic of the very families it is supposed to help. (By "effective marginal tax rate," we mean the percentage of additional income paid in income and payroll taxes and forgone due to income-tested programs' reduction rates.)

The CCTB has resulted in higher marginal tax rates for some working-poor families (those currently in the $22,000 to $36,000 net family income range) because of the wish to target limited new spending on low-income families. For example, an Ontario family with net income of $25,000 in 2001 saw its effective marginal tax rate rise from 39.5 percent to 54.2 percent as a result of the high reduction rate imposed on the National Child Benefit Supplement. At the same time, although more difficult to measure due to the complicated rules for social assistance, welfare recipients who move into the labour market enjoy a large decrease in their marginal tax rates.

The impact of this mix of higher and lower effective marginal tax rates on labour market behaviour remains an open question. The factors that can influence families' decisions regarding paid work (e.g., choice of full-time or part-time work, social assistance over work, overtime) are highly complex and cannot simply be assumed as given according to the usual (and rather simplistic) interpretation of orthodox economic theory. Many variables are in play, including social expectations, opportunities and the perception of future opportunities, transportation and child care availability, and employer's provision of family-friendly policies—and it is not clear, nor does economic theory suggest, that the marginal tax rate is the most important of all these variables.

The NCB has objectives beyond the labour market. Child benefit reform's impact on the incidence and depth of poverty and disposable income is just as important—if not more so—than the effect of that reform on labour-market behaviour.

Toward an Adequate Child Benefit

The next challenge is to build the integrated child benefit into an *adequate child benefit* that will pay substantially larger amounts to low-income families (both welfare families and the working poor) and to modest- and middle-income families. The initial stage of the federal–provincial NCB reform focused on low-income families, which made both fiscal and policy sense. Payments to the poor, however, must continue to increase in order to reach the $5,000 level of an adequate child benefit system. The 2003 federal budget put Canada well along the road to an adequate child benefit by committing Ottawa to a series of increases that will reach

$3,243 for the first child by 2007. The federal government should commit to a final series of investments to achieve the target of $5,000.

But building the CCTB into a stronger system of income security for Canadian families with children will not be accomplished if the federal government continues to limit increases to the poor alone: such a strategy would further widen the child-benefits gap between poor and non-poor families (the latter suffered losses during the reforms prior to the creation of the CCTB). Rather, benefit enhancements toward the goal of a $5,000 maximum payment for low-income families should gradually be extended up the income ladder to improve payments to modest-income and middle-income families as well. Increases to the CCTB should, like the program itself, be geared to family income—that is, the largest increases should go to low-income families, followed by modest-income and then middle-income families. As Ottawa expands the CCTB, the provinces and territories can, if they choose, phase out their own child benefits and redirect the money to services for families—services such as child care, early childhood development, and supplementary health and dental care.

Universal Child Care Benefit: Obstacle or Opportunity for Reform?

As mentioned at the beginning of this chapter, the centrepiece of the new Conservative government's child care plan is a $1,200 "Universal Child Care Benefit." (A second initiative—still in the planning and consultation stage—is a one-time-only tax credit incentive for employers and community groups to create a planned 250,000 child care spaces over five years starting in 2007.) The Universal Child Care Benefit (UCCB) is a stealth scheme that will result in severe inequities and that could turn the clock back on decades of child benefit progress.[16]

The key to deciphering the UCCB is to distinguish between its *face value* and its *true value*. All families receive $100 per month for a total of $1,200 a year—the *face value*—for each child age five and under. But the new scheme comes with a hidden price—higher income taxes and the loss of a benefit for young children—that will substantially diminish its *true* (net) *value*.

Take the example of a two-earner couple in Ontario raising two children (one under six) and earning $40,000. That level of earnings is modest for that size family: it is not that far above Statistics Canada's estimated after-tax low-income cut-off of $33,152 for cities of 500,000 or more, where most Ontarians live. It is only 44 percent of the $90,500 estimated average income for two-earner families with children.

Table 2.1: True (net) value of Universal Child Care Benefit, families in Ontario, 2006

Earnings	One-earner couples	Two-earner couples	One-parent families
0	951	951	951
10,000	951	951	951
20,000	768	923	768
30,000	768	641	623
50,000	738	935	577
100,000	805	826	679
200,000	971	679	643

The $1,200 Universal Child Care Benefit increases the family's taxable income, so it pays $265 more in federal and Ontario taxes. The family also loses $249 from the CCTB's young child supplement, payable on behalf of each child six and younger for whom the child care expense deduction is not being claimed. The family ends up with a net Universal Child Care Benefit worth $686—just 57 percent of the $1,200 face value.

Table 2.1 gives the results for three different families in Ontario with the same income. While the precise numbers will differ, the same irrational and inequitable pattern of benefits will hold for the other provinces and territories as well.

Net benefits show no rational relationship to need. One-earner couples earning $100,000 will end up with more net Universal Child Care benefits than families with only $10,000 or one-tenth their earnings ($971 and $951, respectively). Working-poor families will get less than welfare families ($768 at $20,000 versus $951 on welfare), thus raising the welfare wall that the NCB reform has sought to lower. The figures differ, but the same unfair distribution applies to two-earner families as well as to single parents.

The Universal Child Care Benefit will distribute different net amounts to different families according to income level, as shown in Figure 2.4. Only at low income levels will the three family types get the same benefit. Net benefits will drop for all family types between around $20,000 and $40,000, though single parents will fare worst. Two-earner couples will do best of the three family types between $50,000 and $100,000. One-earner couples will have the largest net benefit between $25,000 and $49,000 and from $101,000 and upwards.

Single parents will generally fare worst under the new scheme. Above $25,000, single parents will get the smallest net benefit at all income levels (except between $51,000 and $74,000, where one-earner couples get least), while one-earner couples will for the most part do best.

Figure 2.4: Net Universal Child Care Benefit, families with one child, by family type and income, Ontario, 2006

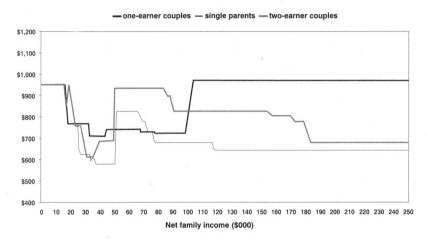

Things could have been even worse. Ottawa will not be counting the Universal Child Care Benefit as net income for the purposes of calculating eligibility for and benefits from income-tested programs such as the CCTB and the GST credit; otherwise, net benefits would have been even lower for low- and modest-income families, since the additional $1,200 would have increased their income and thus reduced their geared-to-income benefits. And the provinces and territories have said they will allow welfare families to keep the Universal Child Care Benefit and not deduct it from their social assistance.

The Universal Child Care Benefit will do little if anything to address the core problem facing Canadian families—the lack of affordable, quality child care. Nor can $1,200 a year do much to help families pay for child care, since it will offset only a fraction of the cost of child care for most. Canada's lack of attention to meeting the rights of children to early learning and child care is detailed by Martha Friendly in the next chapter.

The Universal Child Care Benefit is really a child benefit, not a child care program. It will go to all families with children, regardless of their child care needs. Families can choose to spend the new benefit (and existing federal and provincial/territorial child benefits) on child care, but it is not tied to that use. It's their choice.

To fix its design flaws, the federal government should deliver the Universal Child Care Benefit through the proven and cost-effective CCTB—a program that all parties and governments support. The maximum CCTB for a young child reached $3,426 in July 2006. Adding the

$1,200 Universal Child Care Benefit to the CCTB would boost this amount to $4,626—close to the $5,000 target for an adequate maximum child benefit. As well, the young child supplement to the CCTB should be restored.

If the $1,200 were added to the CCTB's base benefit, almost all families would get—and keep—the full $1,200 increase, since the CCTB is non-taxable and serves all but high-income families. The CCTB-plus-$1,200 option is a win–win design that would both combat poverty and improve child benefits for the large majority of non-poor families. An ill-conceived and inequitable scheme could have been instead a major advance in Canadian social policy.

Conclusion

The question asked in the introduction to this book was this: What does Canada's record show about the country's commitment to the rights of the child? In the area of combatting child poverty through child benefits, although Canada's efforts are not framed in the language of children's rights, Canada's record does reflect a growing level of commitment. Through the expansion and reconstruction of child benefits, there has been a modest but promising reduction in the incidence and depth of child poverty in Canada and a significant lowering of the welfare wall.

However, the level of commitment cannot yet be described as deep. Canada is well on the road to reaching an *adequate child benefit* that can make a more significant dent in child poverty, though substantial further investments in the CCTB are still required. Unfortunately, the Conservative government's flawed Universal Child Care Benefit will turn the clock back on many years of progress in child benefits, and also will siphon away badly needed federal investments to help the provinces and territories build a quality early learning and child care system. The future of both child benefits and child care at this point remains a question mark.

Notes

1 K. Battle, *Relentless Incrementalism: Deconstructing and Reconstructing Canadian Income Security Policy* (Ottawa: Caledon Institute of Social Policy, 2001).

2 Child Care Advocacy Association of Canada, *The Financial Reality behind the Federal Child Care Spaces Initiative: A Mismatch of Mythic Proportions* (Ottawa: CCAAC, 2006).

3 This chapter draws heavily from Caledon Institute writings on child benefits and child care, most of which can be downloaded from http://www.caledonist .org.

4 Statistics Canada, *Income Trends in Canada 1980–2004* (Ottawa: Queen's Printer, 2006).

5 Data are from R. Beaujot and J. Liu, *Children, Social Assistance, and Outcomes: Cross-National Comparisons,* Luxembourg Income Study Working Paper no. 304 (Syracuse: Maxwell School of Citizenship and Public Affairs, Syracuse University, June 2002). Also, from D. Jesuit and T. Smeeding, *Poverty Levels in the Developed World,* Luxembourg Income Study Working Paper no. 321 (Syracuse: Maxwell School of Citizenship and Public Affairs, Syracuse University, 2000). Figure 2.2 gives the most recent estimates of national poverty rates, based on income data collected mainly in the mid-1990s; the Canadian figures are for 1997. Note that these international data are calculated using a definition that sets the poverty line at half of adjusted median disposable income; by contrast, Canadian data use the low-income cutoffs, which produce higher estimates. The international results should not be compared to the LICO-based low-income data used in this chapter.

6 K. Battle and M. Mendelson, *Child Benefit Reform in Canada: An Evaluative Framework and Future Directions* (Ottawa: Caledon Institute of Social Policy, 1997).

7 National Council of Welfare, *Welfare in Canada: The Tangled Safety Net* (Ottawa: NCW, 1987).

8 K. Battle and S. Torjman, *The Welfare Wall: The Interaction of the Welfare and Tax Systems* (Ottawa: Caledon Institute of Social Policy, 1993).

9 Department of Finance Canada, *Working Together Towards a National Child Benefit System* (Ottawa: Queen's Printer, 1997).

10 Battle and Mendelson, *Child Benefit Reform in Canada.*

11 Federal/Provincial/Territorial Governments, "National Child Benefit Progress Report, 2000, 2004," http://socialunion.gc.ca.

12 Ibid., "2002." All figures in this section are from this source.

13 Ibid., "2002."

14 Department of Finance, *Tax Expenditures and Evaluations 2002* (Ottawa: Queen's Printer, 2002).

15 D. Durst, ed., *Canada's National Child Benefit: Phoenix or Fizzle?* (Halifax: Fernwood Publishing, 1999). See also Battle, *The National Child Benefit: Best Thing since Medicare or New Poor Law?* (Ottawa: Caledon Institute of Social Policy, 1997).

16 The Caledon Institute of Social Policy published three papers as the Conservatives' scheme moved from election proposal to budget design. See Battle, *The Choice in Child Care Allowance: What You See Is Not What You Get* (Ottawa: Caledon Institute, 2006); idem, *The Incredible Shrinking $1,200 Child Care Allowance: How to Fix It* (Ottawa: Caledon Institute, 2006); and K. Battle, S. Torjman, and M. Mendelson, *More Than a Name Change: The Universal Child Care Benefit* (Ottawa: Caledon Institute, 2006).

Bibliography

Battle, K. 1997. *The National Child Benefit: Best Thing since Medicare or New Poor Law?* Ottawa: Caledon Institute.

———. 2001. *Relentless Incrementalism: Deconstructing and Reconstructing Canadian Income Security Policy.* Ottawa: Caledon Institute.

————. 2006. *The Choice in Child Care Allowance: What You See Is Not What You Get*. Ottawa: Caledon Institute.

————. 2006. *The Incredible Shrinking $1,200 Child Care Allowance: How to Fix It*. Ottawa: Caledon Institute.

Battle, K., and M. Mendelson. 1997. *Child Benefit Reform in Canada: An Evaluative Framework and Future Directions*. Ottawa: Caledon Institute.

Battle, K., and S. Torjman. 1993. *The Welfare Wall: The Interaction of the Welfare and Tax Systems*. Ottawa: Caledon Institute.

Battle, K., S. Torjman, and M. Mendelson. 2006. *More Than a Name Change: The Universal Child Care Benefit*. Ottawa: Caledon Institute.

Beaujot, R., and J. Liu. 2002. *Children, Social Assistance, and Outcomes: Cross-National Comparisons,* Luxembourg Income Study Working Paper no. 304. Syracuse: Maxwell School of Citizenship and Public Affairs, Syracuse University.

Child Care Advocacy Association of Canada. 2006. *The Financial Reality behind the Federal Child Care Spaces Initiative: A Mismatch of Mythic Proportions*. Ottawa: CCAAC, 2006.

Department of Finance Canada. 1997. *Working Together Towards a National Child Benefit System*. Ottawa: Queen's Printer.

Durst, D., ed. 1999. *Canada's National Child Benefit: Phoenix or Fizzle?* Halifax: Fernwood Publishing.

Federal/Provincial/Territorial Governments. Various years. "National Child Benefit Progress Report." http://socialunion.gc.ca.

Jesuit, D., and T. Smeeding. 2000. *Poverty Levels in the Developed World*. Luxembourg Income Study Working Paper no. 321. Syracuse: Maxwell School of Citizenship and Public Affairs, Syracuse University.

National Council of Welfare. 1987. *Welfare in Canada: The Tangled Safety Net*. Ottawa: NCW, 1987.

Statistics Canada. 2006. *Income Trends in Canada 1980–2004*. Ottawa: Queen's Printer.

Early Learning and Child Care
Is Canada on Track?

3

Martha Friendly

Introduction

Shortly after the Convention on the Rights of the Child (CRC) was adopted by the UN General Assembly in 1989, the Canadian Council on Children and Youth (CCCY) held a consultation to discuss the Convention's implications for Canada. In the consultation's Proceedings (1990), Landon Pearson, chair of the CCCY, made several significant observations. Noting that the consultation had been organized to clarify the implications of the Convention for Canadian domestic policy, she said that "we [Canada] fall short of the standards set by the Convention with respect to child care, juvenile justice, sexual exploitation, child abuse and economic support." Furthermore, she declared that "we can be proud of our Government's international commitment to the concept of children as persons with human rights that must be respected. Although our status as a federated state means that the process of ratification will be slower here than in most other countries, we have been assured that the will exists at the federal, provincial, and territorial levels of government to proceed. From now on, the Convention will have to frame all policy discussions with respect to children, both at home and abroad."[1]

Child care was one of the key policy issues addressed by the council's pre-ratification consultation. Among the participants' conclusions were the following:

- Adequate child care should conform to standards set by the federal government, be based on a sound knowledge of child development and

Martha Friendly, Childcare Resource and Research Unit, University of Toronto

at the same time, acknowledge the practices of minority groups and indigenous people;
- The government must recognize that child care policy is not simply day care. It involves such things as family responsibility leave, pregnancy and parental leaves, more flexible working arrangements and prenatal support and care;
- The emphasis in any child care policy should be on facilities and parental leave provisions, not tax measures;
- There was strong support among the participants for the long-term objective of a high quality, universal state-supported child care system in Canada.[2]

In an article on child care in the Proceedings, Friendly noted that there was—at that time—no national child care policy but that a majority of preschool-age children were in non-parental child care arrangements as their mothers participated in the paid labour force. She concluded: "It is clear that there will need to be some new directions in child care policy.... If child care policy is to be in the best interests of children, Canadian governments need to take another look at what we know about the best ways to design and implement a high quality child care system that will truly meet the needs of all Canadian families and children."[3]

Governments in Canada have "taken another look" at child care not once but several times since 1990. Yet in 2007, Canada still has no national child care policy. Rather, as noted by Ken Battle in chapter 2, the Harper government has elected to provide a choice in child care allowance: an allowance that fails to overcome the problem of a national lack of affordable, quality child care. Today a higher proportion of preschool-age children are in non-parental child care than in 1990 as a considerably higher proportion of their mothers participate in the paid labour force. The number of regulated child care spaces has grown somewhat over the years, but access has remained substantially the same as it was when the Convention on the Rights of the Child was introduced, and research on quality shows that even regulated child care programs are more likely to be mediocre than excellent.[4] Thus, the concern expressed about child care in 1990—that access to high-quality regulated early learning and child care is still for the few, not the majority—still pertains in 2007.

This chapter's starting place is with the Convention's assumption, stated in article 18(3), that child care is a right and that governments have a responsibility to ensure that this right is addressed. The definition of "child care" or early learning and child care used here includes child care centres as well as other "care" services such as regulated family day care and nursery/preschools whose primary purpose is "early childhood education." While kindergartens are separate from child care programs in Canada, they are part of the same "early learning and child care concept." And some parts of family resource programs, which are more focused on supporting parents than on providing "care" or "early childhood education," are part of the concept as well. These are all intended to enhance child development and well-being and to support parents in a variety of ways, whether they are in or out of the paid workforce.

This chapter reviews the Canadian political and social context for child care; reviews the current child care situation; discusses the articles of the Convention that pertain to early learning and child care; and concludes that Canada has not taken seriously the issue of children's right to early learning and child care.

The Canadian Context for Early Learning and Child Care

In the 1980s and 1990s, child care became a mainstream policy and program area in most industrialized nations and part of the social fabric in many countries. Not so in Canada. In most industrialized countries—even the United States—considerably more preschool-age children attend early childhood programs than is the case here. In most of the countries of Western Europe, many children aged six or under—and most three-to-six-year-olds—attend decent-quality, publicly funded early learning and child care programs.[5]

Since the CRC was introduced in 1990, there has been considerable debate and learning in Canada about child care, or early learning and child care, as it has come to be called. However, while federal and provincial governments have introduced several reforms[6] to the family policy package in recent years, Canada has failed to make progress toward a system of universal high-quality early learning and child care or even toward establishing widespread access to high-quality programs.

Canadian Demographic Trends Affecting Early Learning and Child Care

A number of demographic trends—most of which are not unique to Canada—contribute to the need for early learning and child care or have implications for how it is delivered. These include the following: a substantial increase in the labour participation rate of mothers of young children; a shrinking child population; intensified presence of visible minorities, including Aboriginal people, especially in cities; a stubbornly high child poverty rate; and improved provisions for maternity and parental leave. A parallel trend—while not a demographic one—has been

Table 3.1 Labour force participation rate of mothers with children 0 to 15 years (rounded)

	1995 (%)	1998 (%)	2001 (%)	2003 (%)
With youngest child 0–3	61	65	66	68
With youngest child 3–5	69	71	73	75
With youngest child 6–15	76	78	81	82

the growing expert and public appreciation of the importance of the early years and the role that early childhood education can play in enhancing child development and children's lives.

For child care, perhaps the most important social and economic change in families has been the shift from a single-breadwinner family model to one in which the expectation is that both fathers and mothers will be employed while their children are young. Canadian employment patterns among mothers with young children have changed dramatically over the past quarter century. In 1976 the labour force participation rate for women with children under sixteen was 39 percent. The rates have risen steadily since then: in 1992, mothers' labour-force participation rates were 61, 69, and 76 percent, depending on the age of the child (see Table 3.1).[7] By 2003, 66 percent of mothers of children younger than three were employed (as were 75 percent of women whose youngest child was between three and five and 82 percent whose youngest child was between six and fifteen).

Having two earners in the family has been an important component of economic security over the past decade, during which unemployment, increased casualization of the labour force, and stagnating incomes have had a significant impact on young families. Indeed, where family incomes have improved over the last decade, it has largely been due to having two earners working longer hours.[8] At the same time, the increased prevalence of single-parent families with young children means that these factors have an even bigger impact on single mothers, who are more likely to be poor and who, if employed, are more likely to have low-waged jobs that are more insecure and that offer fewer benefits. It is also worth noting that more children are experiencing life in single-parent families and that they are doing so at increasingly younger ages.[9] This underscores why it is so important that child care be of high quality during the very years that are so critical to child development.

The demographic environment also includes a shrinking child population. In the 1990s, child populations in Canada—particularly the cohort under age six—declined, especially in regions experiencing out-migration.[10] Since 1992 the number of children five and under years has decreased in all provinces.[11] In Canada as a whole, the five-and-under cohort decreased from 2.257 million in 1992 to 2.046 million in 2003. Most provinces lost population in the six-to-twelve year age group as well.[12]

Canada has long been a diverse nation. That Canada relies heavily on immigration for population replacement has implications for child care policy and programs. Immigrants and refugees now form a substantial portion of the population in some cities; in 2001 they accounted for 18.3 percent of Canada's total population, up from 17.4 percent in 1996.[13] Most new immigrants settle in Canada's largest urban areas, and as a result, more than 50 percent of the kindergarteners in some classes in Toronto, Vancouver, and Montreal were born outside Canada or are from recently immigrated families.[14]

At the same time, First Nations and other Aboriginal people form a majority in some regions. As a result of migration into cities, today half of all Aboriginal people live in large urban areas.[15] That their birth rates tend to be considerably higher than the national average has significant implications for the form and content of early learning and child care programs.

Another demographic trend that shapes child care is that over the past fifteen years—throughout the 1990s and 2000s—child and family poverty has increased. In 2003 more than one million children—almost one Canadian child in six—lived in poverty. Poor children come disproportionately from lone-parent, mother-led families or are from recently immigrated or Aboriginal families.[16] Poverty is more common among families with younger children (both two- and single-parent families) and in these families it is more likely to be severe and of long duration.[17]

The introduction of the supplement to the Canada Child Tax Credit (sometimes called the National Child Benefit or NCB), introduced in 1998 to provide financial support to low-income families with employed parents, is also part of the poverty/child care context. Both the NCB and provincial welfare reforms have encouraged or pressed more parents (mothers) with young children to join the paid labour force, and these people often take low-waged insecure jobs. This policy design, which requires or encourages parental employment for mothers of young children, has significant implications for how child care services are designed and distributed.

Finally, maternity and parental leaves are part of the context for child care programs as these determine when parents are likely to begin to need alternative care for very young children. Typically, in contrast to the 1970s or 1980s, women now have an ongoing attachment to the labour force throughout the childbearing years. Almost 90 percent of Canadian women who were employed when pregnant returned to work within a year after birth, with 60 percent having returned within six months of childbirth.[18] Canadian maternity/parental leave provisions are shared between the federal and provincial governments. Provinces set the length and conditions of leave under employment legislation, and the federal government provides benefits under Employment Insurance (EI).

In 2001 the federal government increased the parental-leave portion of the benefit to thirty-five weeks, making a total benefit covering fifty weeks combined maternity/parental available to eligible new parents. All provinces and territories have amended their employment legislation to allow for an extended parental leave that matches or exceeds the federal benefit period. The EI benefit pays 55 percent of wages (up to a ceiling of $413 in 2005) for eligible workers. However, for a variety of reasons (including self-employment and the number of hours worked), many new parents are not eligible.

The Early Childhood Learning Context

In addition to these demographic, social, and economic elements, over the past fifteen years profuse child development research has reinforced ideas that were—until recently—new to many Canadians: that learning begins at birth, that young children learn through play, that development in the early years forms a platform for future success, and that early childhood education programs have an important role to play in how children develop.[19] The strength of this research has convinced observers from diverse areas of interest such as economics, politics, and health to embrace the idea that high-quality early learning and child care is the foundation for lifelong learning as well as fundamental for a prosperous twenty-first-century society.[20] The change in terminology to "early childhood education and care"—used internationally—and "early learning and child care"—a Canadian term—signals the growing acceptance of these ideas. It also signals the breadth of the related idea that early childhood education and child care are—as stated by Carol Bellamy, General Director of UNICEF in the 1990s—"inseparable."[21]

At an individual level, most parents seem convinced that early learning and child care programs are valuable for their children. Experience in all regions of Canada shows that if kindergarten, nursery school, preschool, and child care centres are available and affordable, families will enrol their children in them.[22] Indeed, some parents line up for hours on kindergarten registration day or put their names on child care and preschool waiting lists before the child is born. This signals that Canadian parents everywhere, across social/economic/cultural groups, seek opportunities for their children to "get the best start in life."

Over the past two decades or so, the Canadian purposes for providing early learning and child care have swung back and forth, between those associated with the child (life-long learning, school readiness, alleviating at-risk status) and those associated with parents (supporting employment, women's equality, balancing work and family, reducing poverty, social integration).[23] Most recently, the purposes associated with the child have gravitated toward an emphasis on human development as it is interpreted in conceptions about prosperity in modern societies. Economists, including American Nobel Prize winner James Heckman, are now frequently cited in Canada as part of arguments that universal early learning and child care must be part of any strategy for building human capital—something considered vital to modern competitive countries.[24] This conception of development views childhood as a preparatory stage and children as adults-in-training whose value lies in their future contributions to society, both social and economic. In this conception, early learning and child care programs ought to be judged by the extent to which they can help produce children who are "school ready."

The human capital approach has most recently been one of the main Canadian drivers in the early learning and child care debate. A contrasting idea about children—more consistent with that of the CRC—is that children are citizens with rights and with voices that should be listened to. This idea, which emphasizes the importance of early childhood as a stage in its own right—has been much less clearly articulated in Canada.[25] These two poles of ideas about early childhood programs and the nature of children will obviously not be played out in black and white; the point to be made is that whether early learning and child care is primarily a program to support parental employment, or a program for alleviating poverty and its effects, or a program primarily for children is not at all clear in Canada. This conceptual gap in ideas distinguishes Canada from countries with better developed early learning and child care systems.[26]

The State of Early Learning and Child Care in Canada

Canadian Political Realities

Senator Landon Pearson's observation, quoted earlier in this chapter, that "our status as a federated state means that the process of ratification will be slower here than in most other countries"[27] was prophetic. Senator Pearson had at that time "been assured that the will exists at the federal, provincial, and territorial levels of government to proceed"; but while Canada and all provinces did ratify the Convention, in the fifteen years since ratification we have made little or no progress toward complying with it in the area of early learning and child care.

The case of early learning and child care illustrates the substantial shifts in political understandings about Canadian federalism that have occurred over the past decade. These shifts have had a powerful impact on social programs, particularly child care. Except for programs intended for specific populations for whom the federal government has responsibility,[28] under Canadian constitutional conventions, health, social, and educational programs such as early learning and child care have been assumed to be the responsibility of provincial/territorial governments ever since Confederation.[29] However, while there have always been tensions between federal and provincial governments regarding programs within provincial jurisdiction, it has long been accepted that Ottawa has a role to play in maintaining overarching policy frameworks of national principles and in providing financing. For example, in health, this took the form of a series of pieces of national health legislation that culminated in the Canada Health Act of 1986.

In the 1990s a further shift to provincial domination occurred, involving a move to executive decision making as intergovernmental agreements became the norm. From the mid-1990s on, the Social Union Framework Agreement (SUFA) laid out how these intergovernmental agreements would work; it provided the framework for subsequent agreements by defining how national social programs would be developed or modified.

Within these historical understandings and shifts over time, an examination of how early learning and child care has developed in Canada will provide some explanation for its current state and future prospects.

A Short History of Early Learning and Child Care

As early as the 1900s, a number of provinces had child care facilities, often operated by religious groups or charities. There was virtually no government involvement until the Second World War, when an order-in-council established the Dominion-Provincial-War-time Agreement, the first federal intervention in organized child care (1942). This agreement offered 50 percent cost sharing to assist provinces in providing child care for children whose mothers were working in essential war industries.[30] Only Ontario and Quebec participated in this agreement. After the war, the federal government withdrew its support and all six of the Quebec child care centres closed, as did many of Ontario's. After the war, the federal government played no further role in child care until 1966.

The federal government's second foray into child care, in 1966, was an indirect one, but it had an important impact on the way child care has developed ever since. The Canada Assistance Plan (CAP), the national welfare program, was introduced in 1966 to prevent or ameliorate poverty. Through the child care provisions of the federal Canada Assistance Plan Act, the Government of Canada provided cost-sharing agreements to the provinces for welfare services, including child care. For the purpose of 50–50 cost sharing, CAP treated child care like other welfare services— that is, it established federal conditions for cost sharing. The federal government's conditions stipulated that its funds could pay only for services for needy (or potentially needy) families; also, to be eligible for funding as a welfare service, child care had to be regulated and either public or not-for-profit. The way CAP was designed, federal funds were to be used almost exclusively for fee subsidies for families who had been income- or means-tested and found to be eligibile. This illustrates how, at the time, the federal government shaped social programs by tying financing to conditions.

Social services are a provincial responsibility in Canada, so the provinces were not compelled to participate. However, though it took a decade, eventually all the provinces cost-shared their eligible child care costs with the federal government. In this way, CAP began to spur the development of child care services throughout Canada and to shape their evolution throughout the 1970s and 1980s.

The residual approach to funding meant that regulated child care emerged as a welfare service rather than a universal or educational one. But as mothers with young children entered the paid labour force in growing numbers—reaching a majority in the 1980s—middle-class families also began to use child care centres, most of which served both subsidized and fee-paying families. Although funding was always limited, the supply of regulated child care services grew throughout Canada, with most of the provinces developing and refining service delivery, regulation, and funding in the 1970s and 1980s. Beginning in 1971, parental out-of-pocket child care expenses were allowed as a tax deduction under the Income Tax Act and maternity benefits for eligible new mothers were included under the Unemployment Insurance Act.

In 1970 the Royal Commission on the Status of Women called for a National Day-Care Act. This was the first national recognition of child care as part of the growing recognition of women's equality. The provinces— beginning with Quebec in 1979—began to provide some global funding (in addition to fee subsidies for low-income families) to child care centres to reduce fees for parents across the economic spectrum and to improve staff wages. Public demands for a national child care program—led by the growing feminist movement—grew throughout the 1980s. At the same time—separated conceptually, administratively, and programmatically from "care"—public kindergarten was established in almost every province and territory, becoming an entitlement in most jurisdictions. Thus, by the mid-1980s most Canadian five-year-olds (and, in Ontario, four-year-olds) had been enrolled in public, mostly part-day kindergarten programs.

Early Learning and Child Care in the 1980s and 1990s

Between 1984 and 1995, three significant attempts were made to develop a national approach to child care, with successive federal governments announcing that a national strategy for child care would be developed. Each of these—the Task Force on Child Care set up by the Trudeau government (1984), the Special Committee on Child Care of the Mulroney government (1986), and the aborted national child care program based on the Chrétien Liberals' 1993 Red Book election commitment—was initiated by a federal government. Each recognized the primacy of the provinces in social and educational services such as child care. However, none of them succeeded in producing a pan-Canadian strategy or approach to early childhood education and care, each for its own reasons.[31]

Early Learning and Child Care in the 1990s to 2006: From the CHST to a National Learning and Child Care Program

In the mid-1990s, Canada's political arrangements underwent a shift that had significant implications for early learning and child care and, indeed, for social programs overall. In 1996 all federal dollars for provincial health, education, and welfare, including those under the CAP, were subsumed in a block fund, the Canada Health and Social Transfer (CHST).[32] Social-policy experts expressed fears that without federal leadership through setting conditions and pinpointing funding, provincial spending would become less accountable both to the federal government and to the public, especially as federal funds had been substantially reduced and there was considerable pressure to make budget cuts. The new, more provincialized arrangements were formalized in February 1999, when the federal government and the nine provinces comprising "the rest of Canada" outside Quebec signed the Social Union Framework Agreement (SUFA). These features of Canadian federalism continued to play a key role in the development of a national early learning and child care program through 2005. Throughout these years, child care was off national policy agendas and, indeed, lost ground in some provinces such as Ontario.[33]

A 1997 intergovernmental agreement on a National Children's Agenda was intended to provide a policy framework for initiatives to support young children and their families. It set out four broad goals: (1) all children should be as physically, emotionally, and spiritually healthy as they can be, with strong self-esteem, coping skills, and enthusiasm; (2) all children would have their basic needs for food, shelter, clothing, and transportation met and would be protected from abuse, neglect, discrimination, exploitation, and danger; (3) all children should have opportunities to reach their potential for good physical and social development, language skills, numeracy, and general knowledge; and (4) all children should be helped to engage with others, to respect themselves and others, and to develop an understanding of the rights and responsibilities of belonging to a wider society.[34] There was little or no follow-up to determine whether and how these goals were being met.

"The Beginning" and the Next Step toward a National Child Care Program

While "child development" and child poverty—not child care—garnered political attention in the last part of the 1990s, child care remained off policy agendas until 2003, when another intergovernmental agreement— the Multilateral Framework on Early Learning and Child Care—was put in place by the federal Human Resources Minister, Jane Stewart, and provincial/territorial social services ministers. The ministers' communiqué declared that "this early learning and child care framework represents another important step in the development of early childhood development programs and services,"[35] while Stewart called the agreement "the beginning of a very solid national day-care program for Canadians."[36]

But it was the next step toward a national early learning and child care program that would be historic, for it would mark the first time that a national child care program had been promised since Brian Mulroney's Progressive Conservative government in 1986. This commitment came in the 2004 election campaign, when the federal Liberals promised to develop a national early learning and child care system based on four principles: quality, universality, accessibility, and developmental programming (QUAD). The campaign platform promised $5 billion over five years (new dollars) to begin to build the system. Most of this money was to be transferred to the provinces/territories through the CST, but $100 million was to be used for "accountability and data" and a further $100 million for early learning and child care for First Nations communities (on reserve).

After the Liberals won the 2004 election, they began negotiations with the provinces using the SUFA model—that is, proceeding by securing assent from the provinces. The federal government insisted on one condition—that the federal funds be used for regulated early learning and child care programs—and as a result it proved impossible to come to enough of an agreement to execute a multilateral accord. Instead, in 2005, nine provinces signed agreements-in-principle with Ottawa on early learning and child care.[37]

These agreements marked the first time that a Canadian government had followed through with an election commitment to improve child care at the national level. There was considerable variation in the provinces' directions as described in the agreements-in-principle; even so, in signing them, the provinces were committing themselves to developing detailed action plans based on the four QUAD principles, as modified in intergovernmental meetings. Each agreement included a provincial commitment to collaborative infrastructural work in such areas as data systems and a national quality framework. In signing the agreements-in-principle, the federal government was promising five-year funding agreements with each province upon production of a provincial action plan specifing how the federal transfer funds would be spent. In Novmber 2005, two provinces, Manitoba and Ontario, released their action plans and concluded five-year funding agreements with the Government of Canada.

The End of the National Early Learning and Child Care Program

After the January 2006 election, the new minority Conservative government announced that the processes set in motion by these agreements would end. It also announced that all jurisdictions—the three provinces with five-year funding agreements (Quebec, Ontario, and Manitoba),[38] the seven provinces that had not yet released the action plans they had devised, and the three territories—would get federal funding for one year; federal funding would then terminate on March 31, 2007.

In its place the Conservative government promised individual cash payments to parents—the "Choice in Child Care Allowance," as detailed in the previous chapter. This was to consist of a payment to all families with children under six of $1,200, taxed in the hands of the lower-income spouse. In addition, the Conservatives said they would initiate a Community Childcare Investment Program (capital funding) amounting to $10,000 per space to "help employers and communities create child care spaces in the workplace or through cooperative or community associations by establishing a tax credit."

The cancellation of the previous government's early learning and child care commitment through agreements with the provinces was the first announcement the new government made after the swearing-in ceremony.

The following section describes the current state of early learning and child care in each province/territory.

The Current State of Early Learning and Child Care

Currently, each of Canada's fourteen jurisdictions—ten provinces, three territories, and the federal government—has its own approach to early learning and child care. Each has a number of programs for "care" and "education" as well as programs for meeting other objectives such as ameliorating the effects of poverty and supporting parents.

Each province and territory has a provincial program of regulated child care. This usually includes nursery schools or preschools, centre-based full-day child care, and regulated family child care. Provincial child care legislation sets standards for these services and establishes funding arrangements, usually under a social or community services ministry. Provincial/territorial governments are also responsible for public kindergartens, which in most jurisdictions are part-time for five-year-olds under ministries of education. Generally, kindergarten programs for five-year-olds (four-year-olds in Ontario) are a public responsibility, while "care" and early childhood education programs for children younger than five, such as nursery schools, are assumed to be a private, family responsibility. Besides these provincial/territorial programs, there are a variety of care and education programs—for example, Aboriginal Head Start—that are under the aegis of the federal government. These programs are supplemented by family resource programs (primarily intended to support parents) and by an assortment of cash payments and are complemented by paid maternity and parental leave.

According to Statistics Canada (2005) data,[39] between the mid-1990s and 2001 the proportion of children aged six months to five years who were in child care outside the nuclear family increased significantly, with more child care–using families shifting to child care centres and relatives.[40] These unregulated arrangements are sometimes provided by a relative or by an unregulated family child care provider or in-home caregiver. In 2005, there were regulated child care spaces for only a minority of children with both parents (or a single parent) in the paid labour force. Overall, the proportion of all children twelve or under for whom there was a regulated child care space was 15.5 percent in 2004, up from 7.5 percent in 1992.

As of this day, no region of Canada provides a system of well-designed and well-funded early childhood education and care services to meet the needs of a majority—or even a large minority—of families with children. The quality of early learning and child care programs and access to them vary enormously by region and circumstances. Overall, regulated early learning and child care programs across Canada are in short supply or—like public kindergarten—are insufficiently sensitive to working parents' needs.

Early learning and child care programs vary considerably across Canada. Quebec's system—while only partly developed—is better than most in most ways. Beginning in 1997, the Quebec government undertook a massive reorganization of its child care system and transformed it into the early childhood care and education component of a new family policy that included improved maternity/parental leave. Quebec's 1997 Act Respecting Childcare Centres and Childcare Services, which came into effect in 1997, stipulates that *every child is entitled to receive good, continuous, personal childcare until the end of primary school*[41]—a conception that is closer to that of the Scandinavian countries than to the rest of Canada. Quebec's educational services for children now have three major components: early childhood agencies (*centres de la petite enfance* [CPEs]), school-age child care programs, and full-day kindergarten for all five-year-olds. CPEs include non-profit child care centres—*installations*—and regulated family day care. In addition, for-profit child care centres—*garderies*—have been increasing in Quebec over the last two or three years.

The differences between Quebec and the rest of Canada can be seen in access figures, including the cost to parents—Quebec charges a flat rate of $7 a day ($150 a month) rather than a user fee that can be as high $1,200 a month. (See Figures 3.1 and 3.2.) Quebec has taken some steps toward improving quality; for example, it has doubled the required complement of ECE-trained staff.[42] Even so, like the rest of Canada, Quebec has problems with the quality of its child care programs.[43]

There is enormous variation not only among provinces but also among regions. Children in rural and remote communities, infants and school-age children with special needs, and Aboriginal children are especially underserved.[44] Outside Quebec, regulated child care is not funded—or funded in only a limited way—and is often too costly for ordinary families.[45] Research shows that too often it is not high-quality enough to be "developmental"[46] or, as the CRC would put it, in the best interests of children.

And child care for children older than six is also outside the experience of many families. Young school-aged children may be alone after school or attend recreation or other community programs that are not intended to provide "care"—that is, they may not "conform with the standards established by competent authorities, particularly in the areas of safety, health, in the number and suitability of their staff, as well as competent supervision," as described in article 3 of the CRC.

Figure 3.1 Percent of children 0–12 for whom a regulated full- or half-day child care space is available, by province/territory, 2004

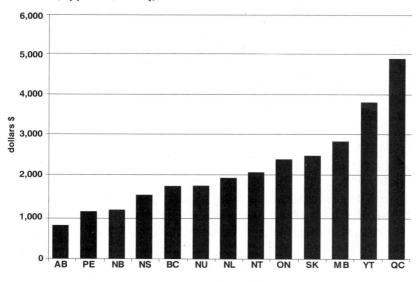

Figure 3.2 Public spending per regulated child care space, by province/territory, 2004

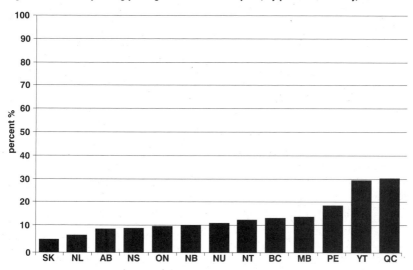

Early Learning and Child Care and the Convention

The articles that relate to early learning and child care in the CRC emanate from the ideas in the Convention's Preamble that children are entitled to special care and assistance, that families should be afforded the necessary protection and assistance to allow them to assume their parental responsibilities, and that every child should be fully prepared to live an individual life in society as an individual separate from the family. The CRC states three broad kinds of rights intended to protect children's interests—protection rights, participation rights, and provision rights. The articles pertaining to early learning and child care relate mainly to provision rights.

The following section identifies and discusses those CRC articles (see the appendix for full Convention articles) that make a contribution to conceptualizing early learning and child care as an issue of children's rights.

Article 18 (clauses 2 and 3 in particular) is the article of the Convention that is most directly concerned with early learning and child care. It identifies child care—"institutions, facilities and services for the care of children" and "child care services"—specifically. This article's focus on "children of working parents" in clause 3 is, by today's standards, somewhat out of date in that much broader conceptions of blended early learning and child care have superseded earlier ideas about "care" for children of working parents. More current conceptions of early learning and child care have shifted some emphasis to the child's needs and rights from the needs and rights of parents (or mothers) as drivers of public policy. However, both emphases remain important.

Two points in article 18 are particularly important for early learning and child care policy. First, the article clearly assigns responsibility for "rendering appropriate assistance to parents" and for "ensuring that children of working parents have the right to benefit from child care services and facilities" to State Parties—national governments—rather than parents, provinces, or local communities. And second, it is significant that this article identifies the benefit to children from child care as a right. These two points are important ones to consider when reviewing State Parties' approaches to public support for early learning and child care.

Article 4 is one of the most important articles in the CRC, not only for child care but overall. It declares that the national government (the State Party) should fulfill its responsibility for ensuring that the commitment to children's rights is met. Article 4 is about the concept of First Call. As Griffin points out, the concept of First Call was coined by UNICEF to signify that the best interests of the child must be a priority. This should not depend on whether a particular party is in power, or the economy has been well managed, or interest rates are rising or falling, or a country is at war. It means that in ratifying the Convention, signatory nations have pledged not only that they will harmonize their national laws with the Convention's principles but also that they will take responsibility for institutionalizing appropriate "legislative and administrative" mechanisms to ensure compliance.

Note well that the article's caveat with regard to economic, social, and cultural rights—acknowledgment that a State Party's available resources may be limited and that the "international cooperation framework" may need to be oriented toward helping countries comply with the Convention—does not apply to Canada as an affluent country with considerable wealth and as a provider, not a recipient, of international aid. Note also that the article does not include a caveat regarding specific political arrangements such as federalism within a State Party. This absence of a limitation recognizing compliance difficulties arising from assignment of issues such as child care to a lower-level jurisdiction is consistent with the UN's comments regarding Canada's lack of progress toward compliance with the CRC in the 1990s.[47]

Article 3 (especially clause 3) is also an overarching article. It is highly relevant to early learning and child care as it relates to quality. When "facilities responsible for the care ... of children" do not "conform with the standards established by competent authorities, particularly in the areas of safety, health, in the number and suitability of their staff, as well as competent supervision," it is hard to make the argument that the provision of child care is good for children. This concept is entirely consistent with the research that focuses on the best interests of the child. Participation in good-quality child care is a benefit to children developmentally and an asset to their quality of life in the short term, whereas poor-quality child care may be a negative experience in both the short term and long term.[48]

It is again important to note that from the perspective of the Convention, the responsibility for ensuring that the facilities are good places for children falls on the State Party, not the parents. Clause 2 has it that the State Party's assurance of care and protection must recognize the rights and duties of parents and guardians. This is consistent with the role of parents set out in article 18 as "hav[ing] the primary responsibility for the upbringing and development of the child." However, both articles set out the responsibility of State Parties to provide parents with the assistance they require to perform their parenting role.

Article 23 is concerned with the right of "a mentally or physically disabled child to "enjoy a full and decent life, in conditions which ensure dignity, promote self-reliance and facilitate the child's active participation in the community." However, the Convention's concept in 1990 as set out in this article—"recognizing the right of the disabled to special care"—is not fully consistent with contemporary ideas about including children with special needs in regular early learning and child care as a human right.[49] Over time, the concept of equity for children with special needs has progressed from neglect and institutionalization, to the development of separate facilities, to (more recently) the idea that all individuals have the right to participate fully in their community and in society, which includes being welcomed into inclusive programs and being given the opportunity to participate alongside typically developing peers. This idea—if not the full practice—of inclusion has become mainstream in Canada. From this perspective, today the language of clause 1 of article 23 could be interpreted to mean that in Canada, "enjoy[ing] a full and decent life, in conditions which ensure dignity, promote self-reliance and facilitate the child's active participation in the community" means full inclusion.

Article 24 is much more about access to health care and to prevention in a traditional sense rather than about the more contemporary notion of "social determinants of health," which was relatively unexplored when the CRC was signed in 1990. Today, it is widely recognized that early childhood experiences have a long-term effect on physical and mental health. The 1996 Report on the Health of Canadians noted: "There is strong evidence that early childhood experiences influence coping skills, resistance to health problems and overall health and well being for the rest of one's life."[50] Early childhood development provides a platform for adult employment, education, income, status, and lifestyle, and these in turn are linked to adult health.

Early learning and child care is only one of a number of factors that are known to have an impact on children in the early years. Sufficient family income, adequate food and good nutrition, a healthy environment, proper housing, and early childhood education programs all have an effect on childhood health in the preschool years, then on the young school-aged child, and on into adulthood. Some of these factors (a healthy environment, good nutrition, early childhood education) affect children directly, and some (adequate income, access to reliable child care) have their main impact more indirectly, through their effects on the child's first and primary environment, the family. Although these factors are all important, there is strong research support for the idea that early learning and child care programs are an important—even a determining—factor that affects children both directly and more indirectly through their impact on their parents.[51]

Article 27 is highly pertinent to early learning and child care in the sense that reliable child care is a family support program needed to enable parental employment, and thus is directly linked to the child's standard of living. While clause 2 is clear (as are other parts of the Convention) that the primary responsibility for securing the "conditions of living necessary for the child's development" is the parents', clause 3 once again assigns responsibility for assisting parents as they implement this right to the State Party.

This is pertinent to child care in the most traditional sense of child care as an employment support program. Without affordable and reliable child care, parents—usually mothers—may be forced to stay out of the paid labour force, to work at poorly paid part-time employment, or not to take advancement. Some women—especially single mothers—are driven into dependence on social assistance and into poverty. Because child poverty can have negative consequences for children's well-being and development, children's lives and their future possibilities are enhanced if their families are supported economically. Paid work may not necessarily provide an adequate living standard; that said, unless parents have employment income, children will lack even the possibility of escaping poverty.

Article 28 recognizes the child's right to education, "with a view to achieving this right progressively," but the CRC as it was written does not specifically recognize the right to education in early childhood, nor does it recognize the inseparability of early childhood education and child care. However, today the idea that high-quality child care should be viewed as educational in that it can play an important developmental role in early childhood is well supported by research.[52] Observations of models for blended early learning and child care services in countries such as Sweden, Denmark, Spain, and Italy have contributed to this contemporary understanding even in countries like Canada and the United States, which have maintained care and education for young children as two separate silos. Carol Bellamy, UNICEF's former executive director, sums this up when she says: "There is a growing consensus that child care and early childhood education are inseparable."[53] An early learning and child care program that is of high quality will provide intellectual and social simulation that promotes cognitive development and social competence, with effects that can persist into elementary school to establish a foundation for later success.[54] This pertains regardless of social class (although poor children may derive more benefit) and regardless of whether the mother is in the paid workforce.

The idea of blended early child education and child care should not, however, be seen to suggest that early childhood programs should be didactic or teacher driven or that "school readiness" is necessarily the sole legitimate goal for children. As Peter Moss[55] represents the ideas underlying this concept, it concerns "the development of the child through active involvement with the environment and others by exploring, questioning, experimenting and debating."

The concept of the purposes of education addressed in article 29 is a broad and fundamental one that bridges age groups and varying national ideas about education.

In relation to early childhood education, article 29 addresses the idea of "quality" in its broadest sense, transcending the basic health, safety, and facility requirements discussed in articles 3 and 18. Different societies—and even different communities and individuals in a society—have different ideas about the specific purposes of education. This article bridges those diverse perspectives to reinforce the idea that although there is no single universal definition of quality early learning and child care, certain values are so critical to the well-being of children that they need to be viewed as the foundations of any definition of quality in education.

Article 30 does not specifically address the right of minorities or people of indigenous origin to early learning and child care in their own culture or language. Even so, an analysis of the role that such programs can play tells us why article 30 is relevant to early learning and child care. In Canada, this is especially so for communities that have historical claims to special status—Aboriginal communities and French-language communities outside Quebec—with regard to maintenance of language and culture.

In Conclusion

This chapter has reviewed the political and social context for early learning and child care, discussed the child care situation in 2007, and analyzed the articles of the Convention that pertain. Nine of the Convention's articles—in particular, the ones relating to disabilities, health, education, standard of living, and minority and indigenous populations—apply to early learning and child care. Through these articles, the Convention addresses early learning and child care from various perspectives, including care for working parents, education, health, family support, and equity.

Child care as an issue of children's rights under the Convention has not moved forward appreciably since 1990 in Canada. It is noteworthy, perhaps, that in the first report of the UN Committee on the Rights of the Child in 1995,[56] in a very short list of "positive factors" observed about Canada, one referred to Canada's leading role in adopting the Convention initially; three referred to mechanisms that no longer exist (the National Centre for Crime Prevention, the Family Support Enforcement Fund, and the Children's Bureau); one referred to local and community—not national—actions; and the last referred to Canada's participation in international cooperation projects through international organizations such as UNICEF—surely not a very strong list of positive factors.

The rest of the report is a much longer list of Principal Subjects of Concern and Suggestions and Recommendations. The first of the Principal Subjects of Concern is a strongly worded observation that—while Canada's official report made the argument that "the federal nature of Canada is a complicating factor in the implementation of the Convention"[57]—Canada is "bound to observe fully the obligations assumed by ratifying the Convention." It then the suggests that a permanent mechanism to do this be established. The 1995 committee report makes a number of strong recommendations—for example, that Canada ensure "full implementation of article 4" and allocate of adequate resources to ensuring children's economic, social, and cultural rights. It should be remembered that this report was received at a time when Canada was devolving power to the provinces, eliminating CAP, making massive cuts to social programs, and declaring that national improvements to child care were off the political agenda.[58]

Canada's second periodic report to the UN Committee was made in 2001. The committee's second response (2003) expressed concerns about the high cost of child care and the absence of national standards and made twenty-nine recommendations. Of these, the most directly pertinent to early learning and child care was a request that Canada "undertake a comparative analysis at the provincial and territorial levels with a view to identifying the variations in child care provisions and their impact on children; devise a coordinated approach to ensure that quality child care is available to all children, regardless of their economic or geographic status." In addition, there were recommendations that Canada "ensure that the principle of "best interests of the children" is integrated in, among other things, all revisions of legislation concerning children," that Canada "ensure that the provinces and territories are aware of their obligations under the Convention and that the rights in the Convention must be implemented within all the provinces and territories through legislation and policy and other appropriate measures," and that Canada "ensure a coherent and comprehensive rights-based National Plan of Action, targeting all children; and ensure systematic monitoring of the implementation of the National Plan of Action."[59]

While the UN has called on world government leaders to "make children—the youngest most especially—the priority at all policy tables ... and to ensure that this has the necessary financial and political support,"[60] there has never been a sustained, consistent approach to public policy of the sort that is required in order to establish an early learning and child care system that would comply with the CRC. At the level of government that is responsibile for early learning and child care—the provinces and territories—child care has often moved backwards, then forwards, then backwards again in almost all jurisdictions instead of moving steadily forward to meet long-term goals. Indeed, in some jurisdictions it has virtually stagnated for a decade.

This chapter has traced how early learning and child care in Canada became public-policy issues and how both have been on and off public-policy agendas since the 1970s. As the data describing accessibility and quality show, little progress has been made. Most recently, the first serious attempt at the level of the State Party to forge a cross-Canada program with agreed-upon principles of quality, universality, accessibility and developmental programming was cancelled by the subsequent government.[61]

The introduction to this book provides an insightful analysis of four ascending levels of governmental commitment to the Convention—symbolic, wavering, expanding, and deep. What do developments in Canada—since ratification of the CRC—reveal about governmental commitment to early learning and child care? They reveal that the level of commitment falls somewhere between symbolic and wavering. This assessment is notwithstanding the relatively steady—albeit sometimes slow and not always sustained, especially when governments change—progress made in Quebec and to some extent in Manitoba. And if the spurts of progress that have occurred have been motivated at all by consideration of the Convention's articles and processes, this is not apparent. Indeed, it would be fair to say that the issue of early learning and child care as a children's right has not been addressed by governments at any level[62] and that the Convention has played little if any role in governments' considerations of early learning and child care. As the introduction points out in a general sense: "There is good reason to be suspicious about Canada's strength of commitment."

As this chapter has discussed, the years of the CRC paralleled an era in Canada during which the role of the federal government vis-à-vis the provinces diminished and the role of government as a leader, facilitator, and provider of services and programs was challenged in favour of the marketplace, "the community," and individual families. These developments have created an environment in which "firm and demonstrable" commitment with ongoing forward movement does not occur and is, in some quarters, hard to justify.

As Sheila Kamerman, an international expert in early learning and child care policy, has documented, there are some clear international trends regarding early learning and child care in such areas as financing, governance, balance with family policies (such as maternity/parental leave), focus on quality, and attention to infants and toddlers. Most countries have achieved close to universal coverage for older preschool-age children.[63] Over the past fifteen years, nations with a variety of histories, cultures, fiscal capacities, and political arrangements have set in motion public policies for high-quality early learning and child care programs. This tells us that vision, commitment, and political will can go a long way to turning symbolic commitments to children's rights into a reality that makes a difference on a day-by-day basis for children.

Notes

1 Canadian Council on Children and Youth, *On the Right Side: Policies for Children in the '90s: Canada and the Convention on the Rights of the Child* (Ottawa: CCCY, 1990), p. iv.

2 Ibid., p. 6.

3 Ibid., p. 37.

4 H. Goelman, G. Doherty, D. Lero, A. LaGrange, and J. Tougas, *You Bet I Care! Caring and Learning Environments—Quality in Child Care Centres across Canada* (Guelph: Centre for Families, Work and Well-Being, University of Guelph, 2001).

5 OECD, Directorate for Education, *Starting Strong II: Early Childhood Education and Care,* Final report: Thematic Review of Early Childhood Education and Care. Paris: OECD, 2006.

6 Canada introduced the Canada Child Tax Credit with the low-income supplement and improved the duration of benefits for maternity/parental leave in the 1990s. But in the 1990s, Canada also abolished its national welfare program (the Canada Assistance Plan) and the federal presence in housing, both of which play a role in the social safety net for families.

7 Statistics Canada, *Labour Force Historical Review,* StatsCan #71F0004XCB (Ottawa: StatsCan, 2004).

8 K. Johnson, D.S. Lero, and J. Rooney, *Work–Life Compendium 2001: 150 Canadian Statistics on Work, Family, and Well-Being* (Guelph: Centre for Families, Work and Well-Being, University of Guelph; and Ottawa: HRDC, Women's Bureau, 2001).

9 N. Marcil-Gratton and C. Le Bourdais, *Custody, Access, and Child Support: Findings from the National Longitudinal Survey of Children and Youth* (Montreal: Département de démographie, Université de Montréal, 1999).

10 Childcare Resource and Research Unit, *Trends and Analysis: Early Childhood Education and Care in Canada 2004* (Toronto: CRRU, University of Toronto, 2005).

11 Comparable data are not available for the territories.

12 However, because this age group increased somewhat in the three largest provinces, the 6–12 age group grew somewhat in Canada as a whole, from 2.68 million in 1992 to 2.764 million in 2003.

13 G. Doherty, M. Friendly, and J. Beach, *OECD Thematic Review of Early Childhood Education and Care: Background Report for Canada* (Paris: OECD, 2003).

14 F. Larose, B. Terrisse, J. Bedard, and T. Karsenti, *Preschool Education Training: Skills for Adapting to a Changing Society* (Toronto: Council of Ministers of Education of Canada, 2001).

15 Statistics Canada, "Aboriginal Peoples of Canada: A Demographic Profile, 2001 Census" (2003a), http://www.statcan.ca/IPS/Data/96FOO30XIE2001007.htm.

16 Campaign 2000, *Child Poverty in Canada: Report Card 2000* (Toronto: Campaign 2000, 2000).

17 National Council of Welfare, *Preschool Children: Promises to Keep* (Ottawa: NCW, 1999).

18 Statistics Canada, "Benefiting from Extended Parental Leave," *The Daily*, March 21, 2003, http://www.statcan.ca/Daily/English/030321/d030321b.htm.

19 T. David, ed., *Teaching Young Children* (London: Paul Chapman Publishing, 1999); J.R. Moyles, ed., *The Excellence of Play* (Philadelphia: Open University Press, 1995); J. Shonkoff and D. Phillips, eds., *From Neurons to Neighborhoods: The Science of Early Childhood Development* (Washington, DC: National Academy Press).

20 S. Kamerman, M. Neuman, J. Waldfogel, and J. Brooks-Gunn, *Social Policies, Family Types, and Child Outcomes in Selected OECD Countries* (Paris: OECD Directorate for Employment, Labour, and Social Affairs, 2003).

21 UN Children's Fund, *The State of the World's Children 2001: Early Childhood* (New York: UNCF, 2001), p. 71.

22 M. Friendly and J. Beach, *Early Childhood Education and Care in Canada 2004* (Toronto: CCRU, University of Toronto, 2005). For example, when Quebec (see Quebec section) opened the publicly funded early learning and child care system for 0–4 year olds to children whose parents were not in the paid labour force, their participation swelled waiting lists for scarce spaces.

23 M. Friendly and M. Oloman, "Early Childhood Education on the Canadian Policy Landscape," in J. Hayden, ed., *Landscapes in Early Childhood Education* (New York: Peter Lang, 2000), pp. 69–82.

24 J. Heckman, *Invest in the Very Young*, Address at the University of Montreal (Montreal: Centre of Excellence for Early Childhood Development, 2004).

25 OECD Directorate for Education, *Thematic Review of Early Childhood Education and Care*, Canada Country Note (Paris: Author, 2004).

26 M. Friendly, G. Doherty, and J. Beach, *What Do We Know about Quality in Early Learning and Child Care, and What Do We Think? A Literature Review* (Toronto: CCRU, University of Toronto, 2006).

27 Canadian Council on Children and Youth, *On the Right Side*, p. iv.

28 Under the Constitution Act of 1867, for example, the federal government's jurisdiction over "Indians and lands reserved for Indians" was connected to contemporary funding of early learning and child care services on reserve.

29 Of course, early learning and child care didn't exist at the time of Confederation, nor did Medicare, the Canada Pension Plan, or other social programs.

30 This did not include farming and other rural occupations that women carried out while men left for the war; consequently, some provinces did not qualify for child care assistance from the federal government.

31 M. Friendly, "Child Care and Canadian Federalism in the 1990s: Canary in a Coal Mine," in G. Cleveland and M. Krashinsky, eds., *Our Children's Future: Child Care Policy in Canada* (Toronto: University of Toronto Press, 2001).

32 The CHST was replaced by the CHT (health) and the CST (everything else) in 2005.

33 Childcare Resource and Research Unit, *Ontario's Spending for Regulated Child Care, 1942–2001,* Briefing Note (Toronto: CRRU, University of Toronto, 2002).

34 Federal/Provincial/Territorial Council of Ministers on Social Policy Renewal, *National Children's Agenda: Developing a Vision* (Ottawa, 1999).

35 Government of Canada, "Federal/Provincial/Territorial Agreement on Early Learning and Child Care" (2003), http://www.socialunion.gc.ca/elcc_e.htm.

36 V. Lawton, "Ottawa, Provinces Sign Day-Care Deal," *Toronto Star,* March 1.

37 Neither the territories nor Quebec signed agreements-in-principle because their negotiations with the federal government followed a different pattern from those between Ottawa and the rest of Canada.

38 Each of the three five-year agreements (Manitoba, Quebec, and Ontario) contains a pro forma "escape clause" which specifies that either partner to the agreement may cancel it with one year's notice.

39 These data are from the National Longitudinal Study of Children and Youth.

40 Note that the number of children 0–12 dropped over the decade while the number of child care spaces rose from 372,000 to 745,000.

41 Government of Quebec, An Act Respecting Childcare Centres and Childcare Services (Quebec City: Government of Quebec, 1997), para. 2.

42 This was increased in CPE or not-for-profit centres but not in for-profit centres, which are still bound by the old requirement that one-third of the staff in a centre qualify as ECEs.

43 C. Fournier and D. Drouin, *Grandir en Qualité 2003: Educational Quality in Childcare Centre Daycares (installations de CPE)—Highlights* (Quebec: Institute de la Statistique du Québec, 2004). For a more detailed analysis of Quebec's initiatives, see J. Tougas, *Quebec's Early Childhood Care and Education: The First Five Years,* Occasional Paper #17 (Toronto: CRRU, University of Toronto, 2002).

44 OECD, Canada Country Note.

45 For more detail, province by province, and comparative data over time, see Friendly and Beach, *Early Childhood Education and Care.*

46 Goelman et al., *You Bet I Care!*

47 UN Committee on the Rights of the Child, *Consideration of Reports Submitted by State Parties under Article 44 of the Convention: Concluding Observations on the Rights of the Child—Canada* (New York: UNCRC, 1995).

48 J. Shonkoff and D. Phillips, eds., National Research Council and Institute of Medicine, *From Neurons to Neighborhoods: The Science of Early Childhood Development* (Washington, DC: National Academies Press, 2000).

49 M. Bach, "Social Inclusion as Solidarity: Rethinking the Child Rights Agenda," in T. Richmond and A. Saloojee, eds., *Social Inclusion: Canadian Perspectives* (Halifax: Fernwood Publishing, 2005).

50 Federal/Provincial/Territorial Advisory Committee on Population Health, 1996. *Report on the Health of Canadians*, prepared by the committee on population health for a meeting of the Ministers of Health, Toronto, September 10–11, 1996 (Ottawa: Public Health Agency).

51 NRC and Institute of Medicine, *From Neurons to Neighborhoods.*

52 OECD, *Starting Strong: Early Childhood Education and Care,* Summary R: Thematic Review of Early Childhood Education and Care (Paris: OECD, 2001).

53 UNCF, *The State of the World's Children 2001*, p. 71.
54 NRC and Institute of Medicine, *From Neurons to Neighborhoods.*
55 P. Moss, "Setting the Scene: A Vision of Universal Children's Spaces," in Daycare Trust, ed., *A New Era for Universal Childcare?* (London: Daycare Trust, 2004), pp. 19–28.
56 UNCRC, *Consideration of Reports.*
57 Ibid., p. 3.
58 Friendly and Oloman, 2000, "Early Childhood Education."
59 http://www.hri.ca/fortherecordCanada/documentation/tbodies/crc-c-15-add215.htm.
60 UNICEF, *The State of the World's Children 2001.*
61 Childcare Resource and Research Unit, *The State of the National Early Learning and Child Care Program and Provincial Contexts*, Briefing Note (Toronto: CRRU, University of Toronto, 2006).
62 Except for the City of Toronto, which included a right to child care as one plank in its Children's Charter. However, the City of Toronto has neither the jurisdictional responsibility nor the funding for child care.
63 Kamerman et al., *Social Policies.*

Bibliography

Bach, Michael. 2005. "Social Inclusion as Solidarity: Rethinking the Child Rights Agenda." In T. Richmond and A. Saloojee, eds., *Social Inclusion: Canadian Perspectives*. Halifax: Fernwood Publishing.

Campaign 2000. 2000. *Child Poverty in Canada: Report Card 2000*. Toronto: Campaign 2000.

Canadian Council on Children and Youth. 1990. On the Right Side: Policies for Children in the '90s: Canada and the Convention on the Rights of the Child. Ottawa: CCCY.

Childcare Resource and Research Unit. 2002. *Ontario's Spending for Regulated Child Care, 1942–2001*. Briefing Note. Toronto: CRRU, University of Toronto.

———. 2005. *Trends and Analysis: Early Childhood Education and Care in Canada 2004*. Toronto: CRRU, University of Toronto.

———. 2006. *The State of the National Early Learning and Child Care Program and Provincial Contexts*. Briefing Note. Toronto: CRRU, University of Toronto.

David, T., ed. 1999. *Teaching Young Children*. London: Paul Chapman Publishing.

Doherty, G., M. Friendly, and J. Beach. 2003. *OECD Thematic Review of Early Childhood Education and Care: Background Report for Canada*. Paris: OECD.

Federal/Provincial/Territorial Advisory Committee on Population Health. 1996. *Report on the Health of Canadians*. Prepared for a meeting of the Ministers of Health, Toronto, September 10–11, 1996. Ottawa: Public Health Agency.

Federal/Provincial/Territorial Council of Ministers on Social Policy Renewal. 1999. *National Children's Agenda: Developing a Vision*. Ottawa.

Fournier, C., and D. Drouin. 2004. *Grandir en Qualité 2003: Educational Quality in Childcare Centre Daycares (installations de CPE)—Highlights*. Quebec: Institute de la Statistique du Quebec.

Friendly, M. 2001. "Child Care and Canadian Federalism in the 1990s: Canary in a Coal Mine." In G. Cleveland and M. Krashinsky, eds., *Our Children's Future: Child Care Policy in Canada*. Toronto: University of Toronto Press.

Friendly, M., and J. Beach. 2005. *Early Childhood Education and Care in Canada 2004*. Toronto: CCRU, University of Toronto.

Friendly, M., G. Doherty, and J. Beach. 2006. *What Do We Know about Quality in Early Learning and Child Care, and What Do We Think? A Literature Review*. Working documents from the Quality by Design Project. Toronto: CRRU, University of Toronto.

Friendly, M., and M. Oloman. 2000. "Early Childhood Education on the Canadian Policy Landscape." In J. Hayden, ed., *Landscapes in Early Childhood Education*, New York: Peter Lang, pp. 69–82.

Goelman, H., G. Doherty, D. Lero, A. LaGrange, and J. Tougas. 2001. *You Bet I Care! Caring and Learning Environments—Quality in Child Care Centres across Canada*. Guelph: Centre for Families, Work and Well-Being, University of Guelph.

Government of Canada. 2003. "Federal/Provincial/Territorial Agreement on Early Learning and Child Care." http://www.socialunion.gc.ca/elcc_e.htm.

Government of Quebec. 1997. *An Act Respecting Childcare Centres and Childcare Services*. Quebec City.

Heckman, J. 2004. *Invest in the Very Young*. Address at the University of Montreal, Centre of Excellence for Early Childhood Development.

Johnson, K., D.S. Lero, and J. Rooney. 2001. *Work-Life Compendium 2001: 150 Canadian Statistics on Work, Family, and Well-Being*. Guelph: Centre for Families, Work and Well-Being, University of Guelph; and Ottawa: HRDC, Women's Bureau.

Kamerman, S., M. Neuman, J. Waldfogel, and J. Brooks-Gunn. 2003. *Social Policies, Family Types, and Child Outcomes in Selected OECD Countries*. Paris: OECD Directorate for Employment, Labour, and Social Affairs.

Larose, F., B. Terrisse, J. Bedard, and T. Karsenti. 2001. *Preschool Education Training: Skills for Adapting to a Changing Society*. Toronto: Council of Ministers of Education of Canada.

Lawton, V. 2003. "Ottawa, Provinces Sign Day-Care Deal: 50,000 New Spots over Five Years, $900M Program 'Essential First Step.'" *Toronto Star*, March 14.

Marcil-Gratton, N., and C. Le Bourdais. 1999. *Custody, Access, and Child Support: Findings from the National Longitudinal Survey of Children and Youth*. Montreal: Département de démographie, Université de Montréal.

Moss, P. 2004. "Setting the Scene: A Vision of Universal Children's Spaces." In Daycare Trust, ed., *A New Era for Universal Childcare?* London: Daycare Trust, pp. 19–28.

Moyles, J.R., ed. 1995. *The Excellence of Play.* Philadelphia: Open University Press.

National Council of Welfare. 1999. *Preschool Children: Promises to Keep.* Ottawa: NCW.

OECD, Directorate for Education. 2001. *Starting Strong: Early Childhood Education and Care.* Summary Report: Thematic Review of Early Childhood Education and Care. Paris: OECD.

———. 2004. *Thematic Review of Early Childhood Education and Care.* Canada Country Note. Paris: OECD.

———. 2006. *Starting Strong II: Early Childhood Education and Care.* Final Report: Thematic Review of Early Childhood Education and Care. Paris: OECD.

Shonkoff, J., and D. Phillips, eds. 2000. *From Neurons to Neighborhoods: The Science of Early Childhood Development.* Washington, DC: National Academy Press.

Statistics Canada. 2003a. "Aboriginal Peoples of Canada: A Demographic Profile, 2001 Census." http:// www.statcan.ca/IPS/Data/96FOO30XIE2001007 .htm.

———. 2003b. "Benefiting from Extended Parental Leave." *The Daily,* March 21, 2003. http://www.statcan.ca/Daily/English/030321/d030321b.htm.

———. 2004. *Labour Force Historical Review.* StatsCan #71F0004XCB. Ottawa: StatsCan.

Tougas, J. 2002. *Quebec's Early Childhood Care and Education: The First Five Years.* Occasional Paper #17. Toronto: CRRU, University of Toronto.

UN Children's Fund. 2001. *The State of the World's Children 2001: Early Childhood.* New York: UNCF.

UN Committee on the Rights of the Child. 1995. Consideration of Reports Submitted by State Parties Under Article 44 of the Convention: Concluding Observations on the Rights of the Child—Canada. New York: UNCRC.

A Right to Health
Children's Health and Health Care through a Child Rights Lens

Cheryl van Daalen-Smith

Holding another person's life in one's hand, endows this metaphor
with a certain emotional power that we have the power to determine
the direction of something in another person's life. We're to a large
extent inescapably dependent upon one another. We are mutually
and in a most immediate sense in one another's power.

—Knud Logstrup, 1997[1]

Introduction: Holding Another in Our Hands

The Danish philosopher Knud Logstrup reminds us that we "hold another
in our hands," and in this way we find our ethical responsibilities. He
states that our existence demands that we protect the lives of those who
lay themselves open to us and who place themselves in our hands.[2] The
health of Canadian children lies in our hands, and while it may seem a tall
order, the UN Convention on the Rights of the Child (CRC) is a beacon
that can surely guide us in our policies and practices regarding children's
health and health care.

This chapter on children's rights to health and health care is firmly
rooted in hope. For hope is central to health and quality of life. Canada's
health care system for children and youth is ripe for dialogue concerning
the provision, protection, and participation rights of children.[3] Canadian
pediatric nurses, pediatricians, child psychologists, and others have a
rich history as highly motivated advocates for children, youth, and their
families.

Cheryl van Daalen-Smith, School of Nursing, York University

The analysis provided here invites a broad adoption of the CRC on all issues concerning children's health and health care. It separates children's rights to health from their right to health care; it is the latter that tends to dominate most health discourses. While article 24 of the CRC and the 2003 Concluding Observations of the UN Committee on the Rights of the Child serve as important pivots for this chapter, a broader application of the CRC will be urged. This chapter has three sections: (1) children's rights to health, (2) children's rights to health care, and (3) children's rights *in* health care. The aims of this chapter are two: to urge the broadest application in Canada of the CRC for child health initiatives, and to urge health care practitioners and policy-makers to think beyond article 24 and view the entire Convention as a health convention.

Children and youth have a right to health, to health care, and most assuredly—while engaged *with* health care services and programs—to other basic rights. Rights should not be dependent on age, geography, level of well-being, or status. Every child has an intrinsic right to health and well-being.

Children's Rights to Health

Health is the increased becoming of who we are most deeply.
—Anonymous

In signing the CRC, Canada was agreeing that children have a right to health and health care. An entire text could be written about the state's responsibility to protect and promote children's health. Understood in the broadest terms, from autonomy, dignity, and justice to education and freedom from harm, "health" underpins the CRC. The key article in the Convention that describes children's health rights is article 24. This article describes the right of the child to the enjoyment of the highest attainable standard of health and to facilities for the treatment of illness and rehabilitation of health. In addition, under article 2, the principle of non-discrimination requires that these health rights be accessible to every child regardless of his or her situation or status, and, under article 3, all decisions affecting the health or health care of the child require that the best interests of the child be a primary consideration. However, a broader definition of health would encompass all the substantive rights in the CRC.

Defining Health

In order to understand how health is ensured through the implementation of the CRC, a broad conceptualization is necessary. The word "health" is derived from the Old English word "hael," meaning whole. According to the World Health Organization (WHO), health is much more than the mere absence of disease. Health is most often experienced as harmony of body, mind, spirit, and environment.[4] Health is a state of physical, mental, and social well-being.[5] According to the Ottawa Charter for Health Promotion, the prerequisites for health include food, water, shelter, a stable ecosystem, equity, peace, and social justice.[6] Raphael goes further and adds that in order to achieve health, one must also have social inclusion, security, health care services, and adequate income, and that particular attention must be paid to an individual's well-being during childhood.[7] Labonte says that health is most often experienced as a sense of control over one's life and living conditions, as having hope, as being able to do things one enjoys, and as having a sense of purpose, belonging, and connectedness to others. In addition, he argues that health includes a sense of being energized, being loved, loving, fitting in, doing, giving, receiving, sharing, and having meaning in life; it encompasses happiness, creativity, spiritual contentment, wholeness, and playfulness.[8]

Health and quality of life are related, and this relationship is central to a discussion of children's health. For example, various health scholars understand health as wholly related to the notion of "human becoming" and have argued that the role of health professionals is to advocate for the quality of life of people for whom we care.[9] Quality of life is often defined as the degree to which a person can take advantage of important possibilities in his or her life. According to Raeburn and Rootman, the capacity to make the most of opportunities depends to a great extent on how much control a person feels she or he has. Control has to do with autonomy and the ability to do things. It also involves how much choice a person has, which in part is an environmental or social issue.[10] To have one's rights respected by default enables health, quality of life, and well-being.

Given that health is the continued enjoyment of dignity, respect, choice, agency, autonomy, belonging, and purpose, the CRC *is* a document that advocates health. The congruence between broad definitions of health, health determinants, and quality of life and the rights outlined in the Convention has been established[11] and still remains powerful. This congruence and the way the CRC can ensure child health is encapsulated in Table 4.1.

This is a text about children's health. In arguing for the enactment of policies and practices that breathe life into the CRC,[12] all of the recommendations put forth here promote the health of Canadian children and youth. When health is understood in its broadest sense, the CRC emerges as a health treaty. Viewing children's health and health care through a child rights lens ensures that children will become "who they are most deeply."

Table 4.1: Children's health and the CRC

Determinants of health/QOL	Relevant articles from the CRC
Food, water, shelter	24 (c) – The right to adequate nutrition, clean drinking water; 24(d) – The right to give all segments of society basic knowledge of nutrition
Stable ecosystem	24(4) The right to protection from environmental toxins
Autonomy Choice	12 – The views of children and youth must be heard and given due weight; 13 – Freedom of expression; 8 – The right to preserve one's identity 17 – The right to access information
Safety/Peace Dignity Equity	2 – The right to be free from any form of discrimination (all protection rights) 20 – The right to be protected by the state 19 – The right to protection from abuse, neglect, punishment, and mental violence 7 – The right to a name, and nationality; 16 – The right to privacy 4 – The right to implementation of the CRC
Freedom Belonging Purpose Being Connectedness Being loved Receiving Becoming	31 – The right to freedom from work; freedom of thought, conscience, religion 1 – The right to be a child 15 – Freedom of association 28/29 – The right to education 24 – The right to health 26/27 – The right to social security and an adequate standard of living for the child's physical, mental, moral, and social development 7 – The right to be cared for by their parents (if safe); 18 – State Parties must render appropriate assistance to parents in the performance of their childrearing responsibilities; 30 – The right to enjoy one's culture, religion, language
Social justice	3 – The best interests of the child are always to be factored into decisions/policies 6 – The right to survival and development 24 – The right to accessible health care; 28/29—(All provision rights) 6 – The right to survival and development; 24 – The right to enjoy the highest attainable standard of health possible; 31 – The right to rest, leisure, play; The entire CRC

Based on R. Labonte, Ottawa Charter for Health Promotion, and Population Health Model

How Is Canada Doing?

I want all of our children to have dreams—not bad dreams, but
good dreams. Dreams about what they want to become, [and]
how they can strengthen each other.   —Ovide Mercredi[13]

In 2003 the UN Committee on the Rights of the Child, in its Concluding
Observations, expressed concern with Canada's record on providing for
children's health and health care. Particular concern was focused on Aboriginal children and children in remote and rural areas and on prov-
incial/territorial differences in accessibility:[14]

> The Committee is encouraged by the commitment of the (Canadian)
> Government to strengthen health care for Canadians by increasing
> the budget and focusing on Aboriginal Health Programs. However,
> the Committee is concerned at the fact acknowledged by the State
> Party that the relatively high standard of health is not shared equally
> by all Canadians and notes that provincial and territorial equal com-
> pliance is a matter of concern, in particular as regards universality
> and accessibility in rural and northern communities and for children
> in Aboriginal Communities. The Committee is particularly concerned
> at the disproportionately high prevalence of the sudden infant death
> syndrome (SIDS) and fetal alcohol syndrome disorder (FASD) among
> Aboriginal children. The Committee recommends that the State Party
> undertake measures to ensure equal enjoyment of all children with
> the same quality of health services, with special attention to indigenous
> children and children in rural and remote areas. The Committee is
> encouraged by the average declining trend of infant mortality rates in
> the State Party, but is deeply concerned at the high mortality rate
> among the Aboriginal population and the high rate of suicides and
> substance abuse among youth belonging to this group. The Commit-
> tee suggests that the State Party continue to give priority to studying
> possible causes of youth suicide and the characteristics of those who
> appear to be most at risk and take steps as soon as practicable to put
> in place additional support and prevention and intervention programs,
> be it in the field of mental health, education, employment or another
> field, which could reduce this tragic phenomenon.

The Committee's comments were quite correct in highlighting the
higher risk for emotional, social, and physical health problems among
Canada's indigenous children and youth. Marlyn Bennett of the First
Nations Child and Family Caring Society of Canada (FNCFCS) reflects on
the special problems of Aboriginal child poverty and child welfare in chapter 11. Martha Friendly in chapter 3 describes the lack of early learning
and child care for Aboriginal children. Canada's Aboriginal children are

at disproportionate risk of poor health outcomes. In Canada as a whole, sudden infant death syndrome (SIDS)—although declining—remains the leading cause of death for infants between twenty-eight days and one year of age. Among Canada's Aboriginal children, the rate of SIDS (1.5 per 1,000 live births) is three times the national average.[15] There are no national data describing the rates of fetal alcohol spectrum disorder (FASD); however, research suggests a 10.9 to 1 ratio of Aboriginals to Caucasians.[16] An additional alarming fact concerns the recent emergence of type 2 diabetes among Aboriginal children in Canada. Type 2 diabetes's onset typically occurs during adulthood, yet the rates of pediatric diabetes in this group have been found to be among the highest in the world.[17] Angela Campbell argues that the most striking disparity between Aboriginal and non-Aboriginal pediatric health is in fact found in the increased rates of Aboriginal children with type 2 diabetes. She adds that the correlation between diabetes and the social and economic history of Canada's Aboriginal people calls out for us to consider how culture, race, and poverty affect the state of children's health.[18] The rates of suicide among Aboriginal youth between ten and nineteen are six times higher than those of their non-Aboriginal peers. The average youth suicide rate across Canada is 18 deaths per 100,000. Among Aboriginal youth it is 108 per 100,000.[19]

In response to the problem of suicide, Canada launched its National Aboriginal Youth Suicide Prevention Strategy in 2004.[20] This was designed to reduce risk factors and promote preventive measures in Aboriginal communities. In this program, Health Canada provided resources to support communities and improve mental health; these resources included intervention and counselling services, suicide prevention programs, and education and employment strategies. However, organizations such as the FNCFCS believe that more must be done.[21]

The Canadian Paediatric Society (CPS), in response to a challenge put before it in 1999 by First Nations Chief Ovide Mercredi to find answers to the health needs of Aboriginal children, partnered with the FNCFCS and other Aboriginal health and social service organizations to arrange a national summit aimed at improving the health of Aboriginal children and youth. After nearly seven years of planning, the CPS held the summit in 2005. Aboriginal and non-Aboriginal health professionals, social workers, educators, parents, researchers, advocates, and others collaborated to articulate a new vision of health. The CPS wanted participants to think differently about Aboriginal children's health issues with the goal of creating sustained, positive change.[22] The outcome was a report that emphasized the need for Aboriginal people to lead any efforts relating to the health and well-being of their children. That report stated that new relationships based on reciprocity and mutual respect must characterize any further initiatives on health care and that non-Aboriginal health care providers have an obligation to listen.[23] This summit was a historic event and one that many hope will bring meaningful change.

The disparities faced by Canada's Aboriginal children regarding access to the prerequisites of health—food, water, shelter, education, justice, equity, and a stable ecosystem—are disturbing.[24] One dramatic illustration of the problem arose in October 2005 when Assembly of First Nations National Chief Phil Fontaine called for immediate action to address the water crisis facing residents of Kashechewan in Northern Ontario.[25] Despite federal and provincial awareness that this reserve had been under a boil-water advisory since 2003, nothing had been done. Some have argued that the preventable tragedy of 2005 that confronted children and adults living on the Kashechewan First Nations Reserve amounted to a pulse check of Canada's attention to the health and well-being of indigenous communities. I would argue that this abomination went far beyond a pulse check; in fact, it was a stroke that originated in Canada's carotid artery: one that gave many warning signs.

As noted by the UN Committee on the Rights of the Child, health problems do not exist only for Aboriginal children. There are problems of uneven access to health care as a function of the province or territory of residence of the child—a situation that is at odds with the CRC's principle of non-discrimination. In its recent report the CPS described the patchwork of health legislation that exists across Canada regarding disease prevention, health promotion, and injury prevention. For example, programs for immunizations, contraception, smoking reduction and cessation, obesity prevention, and promotion of physical activity vary widely across jurisdictions. So do laws relating to recreational safety, car seat use, and graduated driver licensing.[26]

While the Committee's Concluding Observations highlighted disparities in health care accessibility and the increasing health problems facing Aboriginal children, Canada's report and subsequent observations missed an important opportunity to discuss children's environmental health and the specific health care rights of children with disabilities. For example, according to the Canadian Association of Physicians for the Environment (CAPE), children face a much higher risk of environmental toxin exposure and a greater risk for various forms of cancer.[27] Also, the Canadian Institute of Child Health (CICH) has emphasized the importance of adopting environmental protections in order to address the heightened vulnerability of children to toxins. The CICH has noted the links between exposure to such toxins as smog, mould, lead, pesticides, and environmental tobacco smoke, and impaired intellectual development, behavioural problems, and neurodevelopmental disorders such as autism and cancer.[28] Childhood cancers, in particular, have been increasing since the ratification of the CRC. As of 2004, childhood leukemia rates had risen by 62 percent, childhood brain cancers by 50 percent, and childhood bone cancers by 40 percent.[29] Furthermore, as reported in 2006 by the Commission for Environmental Cooperation (CEC), childhood asthma rates have been increasing steadily, quadrupling since 1986.[30] The CEC noted that asthma affected 1 in 10 Canadian children in 2006, with the highest rates among boys between eight and eleven. Asthma was found to be linked to poor air quality, second-hand tobacco smoke, pesticides, and ground-level ozone.

The Canadian Association for Community Living (CACL) continues to alert provincial and federal governments regarding the financial burden endured by families of children with disabilities. This hardship continues despite the CACL's appearance before the UN Subcommittee on the Status of Persons with Disabilities of the Standing Committee on Human Resources Development. To date, the strong pressure on provincial and federal policy-makers to enact a disability tax credit in order to ensure adequate, affordable, and dignified support has gone unheeded.[31] The issue of health care for children with disabilities is considered in detail by Richard Sobsey in chapter 15.

Shifting "Upstream" to Protect Children's Health

Butterfield[32] has argued that nurses and other health care professionals need to think "upstream." The metaphor is that of a fast-flowing stream. "Downstream," nurses, doctors, counsellors, and others are hard at work pulling drowning people from the rapids. Shifting to an "upstream" approach in children's health involves walking "upstream" in order to discover what is pushing children and youth into the stream in the first place. This shift must involve understanding the causes of health problems in children and young people and doing everything possible to address them.

In *A Canada Fit for Children*,[33] a policy document developed in response to the May 2002 UN special session on children, the Government of Canada identified population health as the best approach for health program and policy development. Population health programs focus on the maintenance and improvement of the health of the entire population and the reduction of inequities in health status among groups within the population.[34] What makes populations healthy? According to Canada's Population Health Model,[35] the primary factors are income and social status, social supports and networks, the social environment (i.e., how cohesive it is), personal health practices, quality of education and child development, health care access, and the existence of gender, class, culture, literacy, and age discrepancies. Our stratified culture continues to exclude many children and youth based on religion, ability, race, size, sexual orientation, gender, and so on, and this also has an impact on a population's health.

The CRC requires that State Parties attend to these factors and has framed them as separate articles in the Convention. By reiterating them under article 24, it has ensured that these are seen not as utopian luxuries (as some critics of the Convention have charged) but rather as critical components of health and quality of life.

Upstream factors like these *are* the answer to FASD, to the staggeringly high rates of Aboriginal youth suicide, to SIDS rates, and so forth. For those children identified as most at risk, programs and policies to address the core determinants of health are urgently needed. A new MRI machine always garners much attention and subsequent funding; meanwhile, small community-based programs for Canada's poor, indigenous, and otherwise disadvantaged people fail to attract serious interest or sufficient health care funding.

This is a bias, and furthermore, it reflects an attitude toward health care that is prejudicial to children. Article 24 clearly states that we must root out and put an end to this mindset. The path to the top of the stream will be found only after we fully comprehend how the provision, protection, and participation rights articulated in the CRC ensure child health. Having broadened article 24 to encompass more far-reaching definitions of health and health determinants, health professionals and policy-makers will be able to succeed in protecting children's rights to health.

Children's Rights to Health Care

Article 24.1 of the CRC requires Canada to ensure children that have equitable access to health care services for the treatment of illness and the rehabilitation of health. Further, article 24.2 calls on Canada to ensure the provision of necessary medical assistance and health care to *all* children, with an emphasis on the development of primary health care, and to develop preventative health care programming. As noted earlier, the UN Committee on the Rights of the Child has pointed out Canada's shortfalls in meeting these requirements and has stated that Canada's relatively high standard of health care is *not* shared equally by all Canadians. Equitable provincial and territorial compliance is a matter of concern, especially regarding universal access to health care in rural, Aboriginal, and northern communities. The Committee has recommended that Canada take measures to ensure equal quality of health care services for all Canadian children.

But access is a problem not only for children in rural, northern, and Aboriginal communities. It also is a problem for children and youth with disabilities and of sexual minority status. According to the CACL, children with disabilities face greater barriers to adequate health care. The CACL estimates that nearly 7 percent of Canada's children and youth have disabilities and that these children continue to face social exclusion. According to article 23 of the Convention, children with disabilities have the right to a full and decent life. Yet Canadian society still does not provide adequate support for them, and as a result of their social exclusion they are often institutionalized, overmedicated, and improperly reviewed by medical teams. Too often they live in families with low incomes and are excluded from regular education.[36]

Furthermore, according to a report funded by Health Canada and initiated by the Coalition for Lesbian and Gay Rights of Ontario (CLGRO), gay, lesbian, bisexual, two-spirited, transgendered, or queer (GLBTQ) children and youth face prejudicial, hostile, or insufficient health care treatment.[37] In the "Systems Failure" report on the experiences of sexual minorities in Ontario's health care and social service systems, the experiences of youth participants with health care services were described and found problematic. The report found that misinformation and the practice of defining these people by their sexual orientation, rather than for the reason they sought health care, was adversely affecting the quality of the health care they received.[38] Many Canadian pediatric health centres take pride in their dedication to culturally sensitive health care provision; even so, there is room for improvement in how children who are disabled, mentally ill, or GLBTQ receive health care. Sensitivity training in order to provide dignified care for *all* children remains an area of growth in Canadian pediatric health care.

What has been done to address these concerns? There have been a number of positive developments, including a landmark legal case concerning the rights of children to health care. *Auton et al. v. the Supreme Court of British Columbia* (2002) considered this fundamental question: "Has there been a breach of the petitioners' Charter rights?"[39] This case focused on the right of children to receive state-funded health services. The court ruled that Connor Auton's right to early intensive intervention for his autism had not been met, and cited the CRC in its decision. That children with autism are forced to endure needless years of legal wrangling is evidence that governments continue to resist having to ensure that the right of *all* children to health and health care are met. Notwithstanding ongoing resistance and false claims of fiscal restraint, this case has set a legal precedent and may in fact help Canada's children have their right to health care deemed inarguable.

A second development has been a recent acknowledgement of the problem of access to health and health care. In September 2005, Prime Minister Paul Martin announced at a first ministers' meeting that access to health care in northern and rural communities would be a government priority.[40] Since then, a number of new federal and provincial initiatives have been undertaken for children as well as for adults. Telehealth is one such initiative.

Telehealth was developed in Canada with the aim of addressing geographic isolation and unequal access to cutting-edge health care. Telehealth programs use videoconferencing technology to provide patient consultation as well as education for health professionals. Telehealth aims to provide health care services from a distance; it views itself as an extension of the commitment to provide "the right health care, at the right place, at the right time."[41] Although the development of Telehealth[42] has been a helpful response to the shortage of health professionals in rural regions, many argue, however, that the program is inadequate and that it actually provides a false sense of security while permitting a continuing gap in health care services.

Among other initiatives are various provincial and territorial incentive programs designed to attract physicians to work in rural and northern areas. In Ontario, for example, legislation has been approved that will locate more nurse practitioners in rural and impoverished settings.[43] The recent founding of the Northern Ontario School of Medicine[44] reflects the assumption that physicians are more likely to work where they grew up. More schools of medicine and other health professions must be established in northern and rural communities. This must become a priority. No child should suffer discrimination in health services based on geography. While incentive programs aimed at attracting primary health practitioners to rural and northern communities continue, these programs have yet to achieve sustainability.

Community health centres (CHCs), in contrast, have proven to be effective, efficient, and relevant.[45] CHCs provide primary health care services and programs that are accessible and seamless and that meet the changing health needs of communities and people. CHCs address the broad determinants of health and provide accessible, community-driven health care to residents in the neighbourhoods they serve. The Central Toronto Community Health Centre is an example. Its mission is to serve as a resource for improving health and quality of life. The centre achieves its goals through health promotion, harm reduction, education, community development, and advocacy and by providing medical, nursing, dental, and counselling services.[46]

There is much evidence to support the development of similar centres in rural, Aboriginal,[47] and northern communities. For the next ten years, perhaps every new hospital or rehabilitation centre should be located in a rural or northern communy in Canada. Such a decision by the federal government would demonstrate a clear commitment to ameliorating geographical disparities. A final point: cultural competence in health care delivery[48] must become a core component of ethical practice.

It is not enough to parachute doctors and nurses, most of whom have been trained in Western biomedical curricula, into Aboriginal communities. Recruitment posters by Health Canada for nurses to go to Aboriginal communities use the slogan: "Are you the new Nurse?"[49] This seems to acknowledge the inadequacy of health care services for Canada's indigenous peoples. Health Canada and health professionals need to partner with Aboriginal communities and provide culturally relevant care. The Department of Indian Affairs, in collaboration with several Aboriginal groups, has designed a culturally relevant community health model that focuses on wellness.[50] This type of model involves partnering with a community's healers and leaders in order to best meet the needs of that community. One size does not fit all, and Canada needs to reflect its self-declared cultural diversity in the health care services it provides.

In summary, although there has been acknowledgement of the problem of uneven accessibility and although a number of new measures have been taken to address this, inequities continue to face Aboriginal and rural children as well as children with disabilities and of sexual minority status. The challenges presented have particular relevance to children. Children who lack state-sanctioned citizenship have little if any agency to improve their health status or their access to quality health services. In addition, because children are generally not considered to have moral agency—or the ability to contribute meaningfully to policy decisions concerning their health as a Canadian aggregate—their needs are further obscured by adult-centred free-market policies. Rarely are children's voices heard about their own struggles with addiction, their lack of access to clean drinking water, or their lack of access to physical and/or recreational activities. The common denominator is that their voices are missing. And this is a breach of their rights.

Children's Rights *in* Health Care

Absent from article 24 and from the 2003 Concluding Observations of the UN Committee is any reference to children's rights *in* health care. Virtually all of the rights described in the CRC apply to the health care system. These rights include the right to be heard in health decision making, the right to privacy and confidentiality with regard to medical information, the right to respect for culture and religion, the right to rest, leisure, play, and association, and the right to be educated about one's rights. There are a number of problems with how Canada is implementing these articles in the Convention dealing with these rights. I will focus on two areas of concern: awareness of the CRC among health professionals (article 42), and the child's right to a voice in health decisions (article 12).

The Problem of Awareness

Article 42 requires that adults and children be made aware of the rights of the child as described in the CRC. As urged by the UN Committee on the Rights of the Child, it is particularly important that professionals working with children—including health care professionals—be made aware of those rights. This is because with knowledge, professionals will be keener to respect the Convention rights of the child and to inform children themselves of their basic rights. However, few pediatric health care professionals are familiar with children's rights despite the UN Committee's repeated recommendation that State Parties integrate the Convention into training curricula for professional groups who work with children.[51] On one hand, posters such as the one developed by the CICH and booklets such as the one developed by the Canadian Coalition for the Rights of Children (CCRC) have been made available. Also, the mission statements of organizations such as the CICH and the Canadian Association of Paediatric Health Centres (CAPHS) reflect increasing awareness of the CRC. On the other hand, the Convention has not been integrated into the mission statements or philosophies of the Canadian Paediatric Centre and many other relevant organizations. Overall, the Convention has not been implemented in any systematic, sustainable, or policy-based way, and this inattention has left the Convention's policy and practice implications largely misunderstood or unrecognized by most health care professionals.[52]

Canada's future pediatric practitioners must be taught the CRC while in university or college. Pediatrics must be reaffirmed as a specialty worthy of compulsory study for all health professionals. All health professionals will engage with children or youth over the course of a career, and whether those children are patients, significant persons to their patients, or the community aggregate, understanding of children's rights will be critical. In addition, for those who go on to work in privileged positions as pediatric health professionals after graduation, every health care institution, service, or agency must not only be well versed in the Convention itself, but also make training in the Convention a compulsory component of each employee's orientation. An expectation must be developed across the country that practice rooted in children's rights is a component of competence for pediatric health care practitioners. Annual articulation of such practice should be made a part of every performance review template.

It is clear that Canada's eleven tertiary pediatric health centres,[53] Canadian schools of nursing,[54] and medical schools[55] urgently require explicit attention to the Convention in order to fulfill Canada's responsibility to implement it.

Broadly speaking, the CRC constitutes a promise to ensure the health and well-being of Canadian children; as such, it should *ground* and *frame* the work of pediatric health care professionals. There is no reason that this cannot be. The provision, protection, and participation rights afforded to Canadian children by the CRC *fit* with the various codes of ethics of most of the health professionals who work with children in Canada's health care system (see Table 4.2).

Table 4.2. The Congruence of the Canadian Nurses Association Code of Ethics (2002), the Canadian Medical Association Code of Ethics (2004), the Canadian Psychological Association Code of Ethics (2000), and the UN Convention on the Rights of the Child (1989)

Values within the CNA, CPA, and CMA Codes of Ethics	Related child rights embraced through ethical practice
Health and well-being Beneficence Non-malfeasance Responsible caring	The right to: education; the highest standard of health care; enjoyment of the highest attainable health; a safe standard of living; if disabled, the right to special care and education that will help one's achievement of self-reliance and the enjoyment of a full life in society
Choice Refusal to participate or support practices that violate basic human rights	The right to: have one's opinion's heard; freedom of association; leisure and recreation; have a say regarding decisions that affect one
Dignity, respect, autonomy	The right to: freedom of expression; personal identity; privacy; and respect
Justice Consideration of the well-being of society in matters affecting health Responsibility to society	The right to : know one's rights; protection from abuse, discrimination, and neglect; a society that considers one's best interests; freedom from harm

The Problem of Participation

Participation rights are specified in articles 12 and 13 of the CRC. In chapter 9, Campbell and Rose-Krasnor discuss children's participation rights in the family and more generally in the community. Children also have the right to a voice in matters that affect them, including health matters; and they have a right to seek, receive, and impart information, including health information. Given that some adults believe that children are incompetent or incapable of making informed decisions about their own health or life, children's rights to have their views considered are often denied. Children and youth must be free to share their opinions regarding all matters that affect them, and under article 12 these views must be given "due weight in accordance with the age and maturity of the child." Yet many health professionals and institutions view this right as problematic.

Lowden notes that there has been much debate concerning children's rights, ethics, and health care.[56] She explains that children's rights are influenced by various conceptualizations of children and childhood. She highlights the ambiguity and inconsistency in how consent laws are interpreted and enacted.[57] Debates more often than not centre on a child's right to refuse treatment. She argues that a child's right to consent is not balanced by the right to withhold consent,[58] and that this privileges adults' beliefs about what is in the "best interest" of a given child or youth over the views of the child.

In some circles, decisions regarding a child's right to consent to or refuse treatment are rooted in "age of majority" legislation—legislation that further marginalizes children and youth by suggesting that they are not a part of a so-called majority and so are not to be afforded the same rights and freedoms as adults. According to Barb Wilson, Communications Advisor to the Canadian Medical Protective Association (CMPA), it is now more widely recognized that many young patients reach what is called the "age of discernment" before they reach the legal age of majority for consent—in this context, to medical treatment. She goes on to explain that legislation exists in each province and territory with respect to setting an age of majority. "In British Columbia, New Brunswick, Nova Scotia, Newfoundland and the Territories, that age is 19. In the remaining provinces, it's 18. Legislation in a number of provinces and territories has codified the law on consent, including the reliance on maturity in assessing a young person's right to consent to, or refuse, medical treatment. Only Quebec has established a fixed age of fourteen years, below which the consent of a parent or guardian or court is necessary for the purposes of proposed treatment" (personal communication, November 23, 2006).

The debate across the country regarding a child's right to consent to health care is palpable. According to Ontario's Chief Child Advocate, Judy Finlay, the many discrepancies that exist among provinces and territories concerning children's right to consent to or refuse health care treatment have given rise to a further denial of article 12.[59] In Ontario, for example, consent is determined through a child's ability to pass tests of understanding and appreciating the consequences of a medical treatment. But in provinces such as Alberta, it is based on a specific age—eighteen. In Nova Scotia, it is based on a different age—nineteen. *Consent and Confidentiality in Health Services* is a new report that examines critical issues relating to consent and confidentiality for children and youth engaged with the health care system.[60] This report concludes with a helpful list of critical principles associated with the ethical understanding of consent and confidentiality. Firmly rooted in the CRC, these recommendations are helpful for health care professionals hoping to navigate article 12. They start with the notion of "presumed capacity." The argument is that children should be presumed capable of consenting to treatment and to decisions regarding the release of personal information. Children should not be presumed incapable simply because of age, disability, status, or medical condition.[61] Second, the notion of "developing capacity" is introduced. Children should be given the opportunities and assistance they need to develop their competence to make health decisions. The intent of this principle is for all adults involved in a young child's life to take responsibility for developing the capacity in the child.[62] Finally, consent should be conceived of as an ongoing process rather than an isolated event. A good consent process, the report's authors argue, involves an ongoing and active dialogue between the child and the medical practitioner, and in some cases the guardian or other adult. The ideal process allows all involved parties to consult one another, share fears, concerns, and information, and invite and respond to one another's ideas. Consent must be informed.[63]

Canadian pediatric health professionals strive to inform children and youth regarding their health status, the available treatments, and the potential results. At times, however, this information is tempered based on what the individual practitioner decides is *appropriate* for a child based on age, supposed cognitive ability, and mental health status. The information that a child or youth receives is often decided by the adults who are providing the service. Pediatric health professionals *must* ensure that children or youths be provided with all available information regarding their health and the options in front of them, even if this information leads to a refusal of treatment.

In addition, the current process of reading one's medical chart is one of disincentive, financial implications, and judgment. The Personal Health Information Act (PHIA) of Ontario, for example, has a mechanism whereby individuals can access their medical records. However, the experience of the Ontario Office of Child and Family Services Advocacy has been that the PHIA does not necessarily help children and youths gain access to these charts. For example, if the health professional who is holding the chart believes that release of the information might result in a risk to the treatment or recovery of the individual, the request can be denied.[64] Again, the view of an adult takes precedence over the view of children or youths.

Further problems of inadequate provision for child participation have been noted by Youth Net, a mental health promotion and intervention program run by youths for youths.[65] According to Youth Net, children and youths with mental health problems often encounter judgment, lack of interest, or disregard on the part of health care professionals. Youth Net was launched following the 1993 report *Youth Mental Health and Illness*.[66] This report found that young people were seriously concerned about their own mental health, were dissatisfied with the mental health services they were receiving, and felt most comfortable talking to peers regarding their mental health and well-being. Youth Net is one of Canada's strongest youth-derived and youth-led health care initiatives. It now provides training to health care professionals regarding child and youth mental health and how to reach youth. Similarly, in Ontario, the Validity project explores the lived experience of depression for girls and young women. Many participants in this project have described problematic experiences with what were supposed to be youth-centred mental health services. They have often found their depression discounted, merely medicated, or inordinately pathologized. One participant summed up her recommendation to health care professionals in this way: "I don't want to be treated; I want to be heard!"[67]

Unfinished Business

Canada's ratification of the UN Convention on the Rights of the Child was a significant event. It elevated the importance of the health rights of children, and it committed Canada to a policy of ensuring that these rights would be put into effect. However, despite the new programs and the progress that has occurred since 1991, major problems remain. Canadian children in general are facing increasing rates of childhood cancers, respiratory illnesses, and childhood obesity. For Canadian Aboriginal children in particular, the rates of SIDS, FASD, and youth suicide have been high—much higher than among non-Aboriginal children. For Aboriginal children, children in northern and rural communities, children with disabilities, and children of sexual minority status, there has been uneven accessibility to health care services. All children in Canada have encountered a lack of provision for their participation in health care decisions as well as a lack of awareness of children's rights among health professionals.

All of these problems suggest a lack of governmental commitment to the CRC. That the CRC has not been incorporated into health legislation or into standards of practice governing health professionals and pediatric practitioners speaks volumes. Standards of practice set by national licensing boards should include the CRC as a core component of competent and ethical pediatric practice. The CRC should be made explicit in acts that govern health professional practice. Ontario's Regulated Health Professions Act (RHPA)[68] is a provincial law that applies equally to twenty-three health professions in Ontario. It provides a set of guidelines that govern ethical and professional health care practice. It could, and should, be broadened to include a subsection pertaining to working with children and youth. Within this section there should be an explicit inclusion of the health care professional's responsibility to understand and embrace the Convention in her/his own practice with children. Furthermore, future accreditation procedures enacted by the Canadian Council on Health Services Accreditation should incorporate an assessment of every pediatric institution's implementation of the CRC in policies, practices, and programming.[69] Pediatric health care accreditation should assess the presence of sustainable measures to ensure that children's rights are protected when they receive care.

The training of health professionals should be adjusted to make room for education on the rights of the child. Curriculum relating to the CRC should be made compulsory in all health professional programs in Canada. There should be provision not only for initial education but also for continuing education on the rights of the child and the related responsibilities for health professionals. Sensitivity training should be a core component of ongoing clinical competence for Canadian pediatric health professionals. Health professionals should be aware of a duty to inform children of their basic rights, and on their arrival[70] in any Canadian health care institution or service, children should be given information concerning their rights.

The participation rights of children need to be much more closely integrated with the health care system. Article 12 of the CRC *requires* provision for the input of the child into health decisions, not simply a right to consent or withhold consent at some arbitrary age. Canadian provincial laws on consent need to be reviewed to ensure a system for providing for the child's rights to be heard. Moreover, health professionals should be made more aware of their role with regard to child participation. Pediatric health care professionals must be like sunflowers. Sunflowers adjust. Sunflowers turn to face the sun and, as the sun moves, so does the sunflower. The only model that will adequately meet Canada's responsibility to respect the rights of children is one that situates the child "with" the health care practitioner in *all* aspects of care. To practise in such a manner, to take one's cues from the children and youths with whom we partner, will require steadfast attention to article 12. Health practitioners have the power to create space for any child or youth to be heard literally, be it on a Bliss Board or through careful attention to the signals they impart. Article 12 calls on practitioners to view children and young people as competent citizens now, not at some later, age-based date; it also requires practitioners to give up paternalistic, ego-driven practice.

Health care provision should be co-constructed with children and youth and mirror their expressed needs. Provision must be a relational exchange, not a series of tasks done *to* children that renders them passive recipients of decisions made by adults. Balancing the principle of the best interests of the child and principle of child participation is no easy task. However, not to balance these two key CRC principles when considering children's rights in health care is no longer an option. Canada has ratified the CRC, and health professionals have the obligation to do everything possible to commence and maintain the discussion regarding the Convention, children's rights, and how it all comes together differently for every child and youth. To accept that someone else, especially the patient, knows better than anyone else what he or she wants or needs, is the journey that must be travelled. How practitioners view patients determines what they do.

Conclusion: Unfolding Our Hands

I conclude with a special word to fellow health care professionals. This chapter discussed children's rights to health, children's rights to health care, and children's rights *in* health care. In this discussion, an expanded view of what the CRC holds for children's health was presented. With this expanded view in mind, it behooves us as current and future health professionals to embrace a child rights lens in order to view children's rights to health and health care and our role in both. The CRC is a valuable tool, one to be placed in practitioners' back pockets for daily reference. It is our collective responsibility to ensure children's equitable access to health care *and* to health.

Those privileged with a professional role that encompasses child health *must* focus in on the determinants of child/youth health, children's interface with Canada's health care system, and the ways in which we can ensure voice and choice. Health must be protected. Access to health care must be equitable and sustainable. Health care provision should be co-constructed with children and youth and mirror their needs as expressed. Provision must be a relational exchange rather than a series of tasks done *to* children that renders them as passive recipients of decisions made by adults. We must strive to ensure that the view of health is one that extends beyond the bedrails to include children's lives in their social and cultural milieu.

The Convention anchors children's rights to health, rights to health care, and rights *in* health care. There must be a willingness to embrace it, not simply read it. As this discourse comes to a close, I invite health care professionals to unfold your hands and welcome two things. First, welcome the enlightenment that will come from understanding the application of the CRC to children's health and health care. The fact that children have rights does not mean that adults do not. Second, welcome children and young people as citizens now rather than as "not-yets" who are incapable of having a say in decisions that affect their lives.

For many, working with children and safeguarding their health is a calling. It truly is a sacred privilege to hold children and youth in your hands, even for a fleeting moment. When they put themselves in our care, and we really see them through a child rights lens, we can help ensure that children and youth are healthier, happier, and have a better quality of life. Unfold your hands to children and their rights and go forward.

Notes

1 K. Logstrup, *The Ethical Demand* (Notre Dame: University of Notre Dame Press, 1997).
2 Ibid., p. 18.
3 K. Covell and R.B. Howe, *The Challenge of Children's Rights for Canada* (Waterloo: Wilfrid Laurier University Press, 2001), pp. 8–9.
4 J. Watson, *Nursing: The Philosophy and Science of Caring* (Boulder: Colorado Associated University Press, 1985).
5 World Health Organization, *Constitution* (Geneva: WHO, 1946).
6 WHO, Health and Welfare Canada (HWC), and Canadian Public Health Association (CPHA), *Ottawa Charter for Health Promotion* (Ottawa: CPHA, 1986).
7 D. Raphael, "Introduction to the Social Determinants of Health," in Raphael, ed., *Social Determinants of Health: Canadian Perspectives* (Toronto: Canadian Scholars' Press, 2004), p. 85.
8 R. Labonte, "Exploring Health: In *ParticipACTION*" (Toronto: Centre for Health Promotion, University of Toronto, 1998), pp. 15–20.

9 R. Rizzo Parse, "Human Becoming: Parse's Theory of Nursing," *Nursing Science Quarterly* 5 (1992): 35–42.

10 Ibid., p. 55.

11 R.C. Mitchell, "Implementing Children's Rights in British Columbia Using the Population Health Framework," *International Journal of Children's Rights* 8, no. 4 (2001): 333–49.

12 Ibid., p. 345.

13 Canadian Pediatric Society, "Hold Summit for Aboriginal Kids, Mercredi Says," *CPS News*, September–October 1999.

14 CRC/C/15/Add.215 (October 2003).

15 Public Health Agency of Canada, "Canadian Perinatal Surveillance System: Sudden Infant Death Syndrome," http://www.phac-aspc.gc.ca/rhs-ssg/factshts/sids_e.html.

16 A.E. Chudley, J. Conry, J.L. Cook, C. Loock, T. Rosales, and N. LeBlanc, "Fetal Alcohol Spectrum Disorder: Canadian Guidelines for Diagnosis," *Canadian Medical Association Journal* 172, no. 5 (2005): S1–S21; F. Boland, M. Duwyn, and R. Serin, "Understanding FAS," *Correctional Service of Canada Forum* 12, no. 1 (2000).

17 Health Canada, First Nations and Inuit Health Branch, "Aboriginal Diabetes Initiative: Introduction," http://www.hc-sc.gc.ca/fnihb/cp/adi/introduction.htm.

18 A. Campbell, "Type 2 Diabetes and Children in Aboriginal Communities: The Array of Factors That Shape Health and Access to Health Care," *Health Law Journal* 10 (2002): 147–68.

19 C. Goar, "Tackling the Issue of Teen Suicide," *Toronto Star,* February 11, 2004; CPS, "Issue Backgrounders: Aboriginal Child Health," http://www.cps.ca.

20 See http://www.hc-sc.gc.ca/fnih-spni/promotion/suicide/index_e.htm.

21 See http://www.fncfcs.com.

22 See http://www.cps.ca.

23 CPS, "Many Hands, One Dream: New Perspectives on the Health of First Nations, Inuit, and Metis Children and Youth," Conference Proceedings, http://www.cps.ca.

24 The list is provided in the Ottawa Charter.

25 Assembly of First Nations, "A Community in Crisis: National Chief Calls for Urgent Action on Unsafe Drinking Water in Kashechewan First Nation," http://www.afn.ca/article.asp?id=1768.

26 CPS, "Are We Doing Enough? A Status Report on Canadian Public Policy and Child and Youth Health," http://www.cps.ca.

27 See http://www.cape.ca.

28 Canadian Institute of Child Health, "The Environment and Health," http://www.cich.ca.

29 "Cancer and the Environment," *Briarpatch* 32 (January 2004).

30 Commission for Environmental Cooperation, *Children's Health and the Environment in North America* (Montreal: CEC, 2006), http://www.cec.org.

31 See http://www.disabilitytax.ca/subs/cacl-e.html.

32 P. Butterfield, "Thinking Upstream: Conceptualizing Health from a Population Perspective," in Butterfield, *Community Health Nursing: Promoting the Health of Aggregates* (Boston: W.B. Sauders, 1993), pp. 68–80.

33 Government of Canada, *A Canada Fit for Children: Canada's Plan of Action in Response to the May 2002 United Nations Special Session on Children* (Ottawa, 2004).

34 Ibid., p. 22.

35 Health Canada, *Strategies for Population Health: Investing in the Health of Canadians* (Ottawa: Advisory Committee on Population Health, Health Canada, 1996).

36 See http://www.cacl.ca/english/priorityresouces/childyouth.

37 Coalition for Lesbian and Gay Rights of Ontario, "Systems Failure: A Report on the Experiences of Sexual Minorities in Ontario's Health-Care and Social-Service Systems" (Toronto: Project Affirmation [CLGRO], 1997), p. 69.

38 Ibid.

39 See http://www.featbc.org/decision.htm.

40 Prime Minister's Office, "A Ten Year Strategy to Strengthen Health Care," September 16, 2005, http://pm.gc.ca/eng/news.

41 See http://www.sickkids.ca/telehealth.

42 See http://www.telehealth.ca.

43 See http://www.cnpi.ca.

44 See http://www.normed.ca.

45 A. Dievler and T. Giovannini, "Community Health Centers: Promise and Performance," *Medical Care Research* 55, no. 4 (1998): 405–31.

46 See http://www.ctchc.com.

47 See http://www.ainc-inac.gc.ca/ch/rcap/sg/si25_e.html.

48 J. Campinha-Bacote, "The Process of Cultural Competence in the Delivery of Health Care Services: A Model of Care," *Journal of Transcultural Nursing* 13, no. 3 (2002): 181–84.

49 See http://www.healthcanada.gc.ca/nursingjobs.

50 Department of Indian Affairs, "Healing Centres," http://www.ainc-inac.gc.ca/ch/rcap/sg/si25_e.html.

51 See, for example, CRC/C/15 Add.37 (June 1995). For a broader discussion, see R.B. Howe and K. Covell, *Empowering Children* (Toronto: University of Toronto Press, 2005), pp. 29–35.

52 R.C. Mitchell, "Ideological Reflections on the DSM-IV (Or Pay No Attention to That Man behind the Curtain, Dorothy!)," *Child and Youth Care Forum* 32, no. 5 (2003): 281–98.

53 See http://www.caphc.ca.

54 See http://www.casn.ca.

55 See http://www.afmc.ca.

56 J. Lowden, "Children's Rights: A Decade of Dispute," *Journal of Advanced Nursing* 37, no. 1 (2002): 100–107.

57 Ibid., p. 100.

58 Ibid., p. 105.

59 J. Finlay, personal communication, November 3, 2005.

60 J. Finlay, J. Magazine, and A. Hotrum, *Consent and Confidentiality in Health Services: Respecting the Right to Be Heard* (Toronto: Office of Child and Family Service Advocacy, 2005).

61 Ibid., p. 29.

62 Ibid., p. 30.
63 Ibid., p. 31.
64 Government of Ontario, Personal Health Information Protection Act (Toronto: Queen's Park, 2004), S. 52(1)e.
65 See http://www.youthnet.on.ca.
66 I. Manion and S. Davidson, "Canadian Youth Mental Health and Illness Survey," http://www.acsa-caah.ca/ang/journal/pt0812/pt0812_a11.html.
67 Centre for Addiction and Mental Health, *Hear Me, Understand Me, Support Me: What Young Women Want Service Providers to Know about Depression* (Toronto: CAMH, 2005).
68 See http://192.75.156.68/DBLaws/Statutes/English/91r18_e.htm.
69 See http://www.cchsa.ca.
70 Mitchell, "Children's Rights and Secure Care Providers," in M. Smith, ed., *Secure in the Knowledge: Perspectives on Practice in Secure Accommodation* (Glasgow: Scottish Institute for Residential Child Care, Glasgow School of Social Work, and Universities of Strathclyde and Glasgow, 2005).

Bibliography

Assembly of First Nations. 2005. "A Community in Crisis: National Chief Calls for Urgent Action on Unsafe Drinking Water in Kashechewan First Nation." http://www.afn.ca/Article.asp?id=1768.

Boland, F., M. Duwyn, and R. Serin. 2000. "Understanding FAS." *Correctional Service of Canada Forum* 12, no. 1.

Butterfield, P. 1993. "Thinking Upstream: Conceptualizing Health from a Population Perspective." In P. Butterfield, *Community Health Nursing: Promoting the Health of Aggregates*. Boston: W.B. Saunders.

Campbell, A. 2002. "Type 2 Diabetes and Children in Aboriginal Communities: The Array of Factors That Shape Health and Access to Health Care" *Health Law Journal* 10 (2002): 147–68.

Campinha-Bacote, J. 2002. "The Process of Cultural Competence in the Delivery of Health Care Services: A Model of Care." *Journal of Transcultural Nursing* 13, no. 3: 181–84.

Canadian Institute of Child Health. "The Environment and Health." http://www.cich.ca.

Canadian Pediatric Society. 1999. "Hold Summit for Aboriginal Kids, Mercredi Says." *CPS News*, September–October.

Canadian Paediatric Society. 2005. "Are We Doing Enough? A Status Report on Canadian Public Policy and Child and Youth Health." http://www.cps.ca.

———. 2005. "Many Hands, One Dream: New Perspectives on the Health of First Nations, Inuit, and Metis Children and Youth." Conference Proceedings. http://www.cps.ca.

———. 2006. "Issue Backgrounders: Aboriginal Child Health." http://www.cps.ca.

"Cancer and the Environment." 2004. *Briarpatch* 32 (January).

Centre for Addiction and Mental Health. 2005. *Hear Me, Understand Me, Support Me: What Young Women Want Service Providers to Know about Depression.* Toronto: CAMH, 2005.

Chudley, A.E., J. Conry, J.L. Cook, C. Loock, T. Rosales, and N. LeBlanc. 2005. "Fetal Alcohol Spectrum Disorder: Canadian Guidelines for Diagnosis." *Canadian Medical Association Journal* 172, no. 5: S1–S21.

Coalition for Lesbian and Gay Rights of Ontario. 1997. *Systems Failure: A Report on the Experiences of Sexual Minorities in Ontario's Health-Care and Social-Service Systems.* Toronto: Project Affirmation, CLGRO.

Commission for Environmental Cooperation. 2006. *Children's Health and the Environment in North America.* Montreal: CEC. http://cec.org.

Covell, K., and R.B. Howe. 2001. *The Challenge of Children's Rights for Canada.* Waterloo: Wilfrid Laurier University Press, 2001.

Department of Indian Affairs. 2005. "Healing Centres." http://www.ainc-inac .gc.ca/ch/rcap/sg/si25_e.html.

Dievler, A., and T. Giovannini. 1998. "Community Health Centers: Promise and Performance." *Medical Care Research* 55, no. 4: 405–31.

Finlay, J., J. Magazine, and A. Hotrum. 2005. *Consent and Confidentiality in Health Services: Respecting the Right to Be Heard.* Toronto: Office of the Child and Family Service Advocacy.

Goar, C. 2004. "Tackling the Issue of Teen Suicide." *Toronto Star,* February 11.

Government of Canada. 2004. *A Canada Fit for Children: Canada's Plan of Action in Response to the May 2002 United Nations Special Session on Children.* Ottawa.

Government of Ontario. 2004. Personal Health Information Protection Act. Toronto: Queen's Park.

Health Canada. 1996. *Strategies for Population Health: Investing in the Health of Canadians.* Ottawa: Advisory Committee on Population Health, Health Canada.

Health Canada, First Nations and Inuit Health Branch. 2002. "Aboriginal Diabetes Initiative: Introduction." http://www.hc-sc.gc.ca/fnihb/cp/adi/ introduction.htm.

Howe, R.B., and K. Covell. 2005. *Empowering Children: Children's Rights Education as a Pathway to Citizenship.* Toronto: University of Toronto Press.

Labonte, R. 1998. "Exploring Health." In *ParticipACTION.* Toronto: Centre for Health Promotion, University of Toronto.

Logstrup, K. 1997. *The Ethical Demand.* Notre Dame: University of Notre Dame Press.

Lowden, J. 2002. "Children's Rights: A Decade of Dispute." *Journal of Advanced Nursing* 37, no. 1: 100–107.

Manion, I., and S. Davidson. 1993. "Canadian Youth Mental Health and Illness Survey." http://www.acsa-caah.ca/ang/journal/pt0812/pt0812_all.html.

Mitchell, R.C. 2000. "Implementing Children's Rights in British Columbia Using the Population Health Framework." *International Journal of Children's Rights* 8, no. 4: 333–49.

————. 2003. "Ideological Reflections on the DSM-IV-R (or Pay No Attention to That Man behind the Curtain, Dorothy!)." *Child and Youth Care Forum* 32, no. 5: 281–98.

————2005. "Children's Rights and Secure Care Providers." In M. Smith, ed., *Secure in the Knowledge: Perspectives on Practice in Secure Accommodation*. Glasgow: Scottish Institute for Residential Child Care, Glasgow School of Social Work, and Universities of Strathclyde and Glasgow.

Prime Minister's Office. 2005. "A Ten Year Strategy to Strengthen Health Care." September 16. http://pm.gc.ca/eng/news.

Public Health Agency of Canada. 1999. "Canadian Perinatal Surveillance System: Sudden Infant Death Syndrome." http://www.phac-aspc.gc.ca/rhs-ssg/factshts/sids_e.html.

Raphael, D. 2004. "Introduction to the Social Determinants of Health." In D. Raphael, ed., *Social Determinants of Health: Canadian Perspectives*. Toronto: Canadian Scholars' Press.

Rizzo Parse, R. 1992. "Human Becoming: Parse's Theory of Nursing." *Nursing Science Quarterly* 5: 35–42.

Watson, J. 1985. *Nursing: The Philosophy and Science of Caring*. Boulder: Colorado Associated University Press.

World Health Organization. 1946. *Constitution*. Geneva: WHO.

World Health Organization, Health and Welfare Canada (HWC), and Canadian Public Health Association (CPHA). 1986. *Ottawa Charter for Health Promotion*. Ottawa: CPHA.

Corporal Punishment
A Violation of the Rights of the Child

Joan E. Durrant

To carve out legal exemptions to this basic principle of human rights risks opening the door to abuse as a matter of course, rather than a standard violated truly "in extremis." It is far better to embrace a standard that might be violated in extraordinary circumstances than to lower our standard to accommodate a remote contingency, confusing personnel in the field and sending precisely the wrong message.[1]

Introduction

In the previous chapter, Cheryl van Daalen-Smith described many of the health problems that challenge Canada's children when their rights are infringed upon. This chapter focuses on another very real threat to children's health and well-being: the use of corporal punishment. Section 43 of Canada's Criminal Code states that "Every schoolteacher, parent or person standing in the place of a parent is justified in using force by way of correction toward a pupil or child, as the case may be, who is under his care, if the force does not exceed what is reasonable under the circumstances."[2]

This law, ancient in its origins, remains in force today. It provides a legal justification for acts that, if committed against an adult, would constitute criminal assault. The Criminal Code defines assault as the intentional use of force against another person without that person's consent,

Joan E. Durrant, Department of Family Studies, University of Manitoba yet Section 43 removes the protection of assault laws for one group of citizens on the basis of their age. Vigorously defended by the Government of Canada and upheld by the highest court in the land,[3] Section 43 stands as a powerful symbol of the status of children's rights in this country.

Corporal Punishment and the UN Convention

The UN Convention on the Rights of the Child (CRC) is the first international human rights instrument to explicitly call for the prevention of all forms of violence against children. Article 19 requires ratifying states to "take all appropriate legislative, administrative, social and educational measures to protect the child from all forms of physical or mental violence, injury or abuse" while in the care of parents or other caregivers. Why, then, does Section 43 still exist? Perhaps the answer lies in the definition of "violence." If striking a child for the sake of correction, training, or deterrence is not an act of violence, then article 19 does not apply to corporal punishment.

The UN Committee on the Rights of the Child (the treaty body that monitors states' implementation of the CRC) has explicitly declared this "discipline versus violence" dichotomy to be a false one that inherently degrades children's dignity. As long ago as 1994, the Committee explicitly stated that corporal punishment of children violates the principles of the Convention. The Committee has criticized legal concepts that provide defences to punishment, such as "reasonable chastisement" and "lawful correction," as well as the arbitrary nature of defining whether a particular punishment is "reasonable." It rejects the view that some level of corporal punishment may be in the interests of children. Since 1994, the Committee has recommended to more than 140 states—including Canada—that physical punishment of children in families be prohibited.[4]

So, the question remains: Why, in the face of its clear obligation to prohibit physical punishment, has Canada actively and strenuously upheld the law that justifies it? The answer to this question can only be found through an understanding of the law's history and evolution, and through an examination of the cultural beliefs reflected in this history.

Ancient History and Contemporary Judgments

Section 43 dates from a time when correction by force was seen as essential to a child's socialization, when it was considered necessary to break a child's will, and when the father had the power of life and death over his wife and children. Its origins are found in the laws of Imperial Rome, where corporal punishment was considered educational and virtuous and where children's legal status was equivalent to that of slaves. When the first reform that protected children from being killed by their fathers was enacted in AD 365, the concept of "reasonable chastisement" entered into law.[5]

Through the ensuing centuries, a reform that was originally intended to provide protection to children became transformed into a protection for adults. This protection entered into English common law, which also allowed the use of corporal punishment by husbands against wives, by masters against apprentices, by ships' officers against their crew, and by judicial authorities against prisoners. When the common law was codified in 1892, protection from assault laws was extended to all of these "persons in authority" except for husbands.

Since its original codification, the criminal law has undergone several notable reforms: protection for masters who physically punished their apprentices was removed in 1955; judicial whipping of prisoners was abolished in 1972; and protection for ships' officers was removed in 2003. But the ancient law allowing fathers to punish their children with impunity lives on in contemporary Canadian law. Today, children—the smallest and most vulnerable among us—are the only Canadians who are deprived of full legal protection from physical assault.

Defining "Reasonable" Force

Perhaps the most symbolic phrase in Canadian law is the one which states that physical force against a child is justified "if the force does not exceed what is reasonable under the circumstances." This phrase establishes a zone of non-violent violence. The notion of "reasonable" force against a child is based on an assumption that physical punishment of a child is not, by definition, an act of violence. The definition of violence against children is based not on principle, but on an arbitrary assessment of the merits of the punishment.

The factors that have been considered by the courts—even in recent years—as legitimating physical punishment are numerous.[6] They have included the acceptability of "instilling respect even through fear,"[7] the "corrective potential" of "injured dignity,"[8] the "salutary effect" of slapping,[9] and the necessity of obtaining a "submissive response."[10] Legitimating circumstances have even been found to include the judge's own childhood experiences: in acquitting a father of assault, a Manitoba judge ruled that kicking and hitting are "mild indeed compared to what I received in my home."[11]

The zone of non-abusive punishment has been found to include the use of objects and the infliction of injury: "Case law recognizes and Parliament apparently sees using a belt as acceptable punishment";[12] "striking with a belt is perhaps a little distasteful but is authorized by law";[13] "punishment causing bruises is not necessarily excessive";[14] "raising welts does not amount to bodily harm."[15] In fact, since 1990 at least thirteen judicial rulings have not found physical injury (e.g., bruises, welts, swollen lip, swollen eye, bleeding nose) to constitute evidence of unreasonable force.[16] In 2001 an Ontario court revealed just how broad the zone of "reasonable" force is when it ruled that Section 43 does not restrict punishment to what is appropriate or proportional or that it must be a last resort.[17]

Challenges to Section 43

Committee Reports and Private Members' Bills: 1976 to 2001

In light of the fundamental violation of children's rights to protection and dignity that Section 43 presents, its repeal has been recommended numerous times over the past thirty years. For example, in 1980 the Senate Standing Committee on Health, Welfare and Science recommended that Section 43 "be reconsidered in view of the sanction which this type of provision gives to the use of violence against children." In 1981 the House of Commons Standing Committee on Health, Welfare and Social Affairs recommended that Section 43 be "repealed immediately." More recently, direct attempts have been made in Parliament and the Senate to remove Section 43. Between 1994 and 2001, seven private members' bills were introduced.[18] However, none was referred to a committee for study.

The Constitutional Challenge to Section 43: 1999 to 2004

Owing to the government's inaction on Section 43, an alternative remedy has recently been sought—action through the courts. In 1999 a legal challenge to Section 43 was filed in the Ontario Superior Court on the grounds that the section violates the Charter of Rights and Freedoms.

Background

Canada's Charter of Rights and Freedoms[19] sets out the essential rights and freedoms of all Canadians. All Canadian laws must be consistent with the terms of the Charter. Until recently, if a law was seen to violate the Charter, that law could be challenged in the courts. Until 2006, the Court Challenges Program of Canada[20] provided financial support to such challenges if they were seen as important and if they advanced equality rights guaranteed under the Charter.[21] An individual or an organization could apply to this program for funding to challenge an existing law on the grounds that it violated one or more terms of the Charter.

In 1995, Dr. Ailsa Watkinson[22] of the University of Regina initiated the legal process of challenging the constitutionality of Section 43 of the Criminal Code. She received funding from the Court Challenges Program to argue that Section 43 constitutes age discrimination and is thus a violation of children's rights under the Charter. She invited the Canadian Foundation for Children, Youth, and the Law[23] to argue the case before the courts. In December 1999 the foundation filed the challenge in the Ontario Superior Court.

The Foundation's Argument

The foundation argued that Section 43 violates three sections of the Charter:

> Section 7: "Everyone has the right to life, liberty, and security of the person, and the right not to be deprived thereof except in accordance with the principles of fundamental justice."

> Section 12: "Everyone has the right not to be subjected to any cruel and unusual treatment or punishment."

> Section 15(1): "Every individual is equal before and under the law and has the right to the equal protection and equal benefit of the law without discrimination and, in particular, without discrimination based on race, national or ethnic origin, colour, religion, sex, age or mental or physical disability."

Section 1 of the Charter allows governments to put some limits on essential rights, as long as those limits are reasonable and justified in a free and democratic society. Therefore, a law that limits a right guaranteed under the Charter may still be valid if it conforms to Section 1. The foundation argued that Section 43 of the Criminal Code is not justified under Section 1 of the Charter.[24]

The foundation further argued that Section 43 is a violation of four articles of the UN Convention on the Rights of the Child:

> Article 3: "In all actions concerning children ... the best interests of the child shall be a primary consideration."

> Article 18: [With regard to parental responsibilities,] "the best interests of the child will be their basic concern."

> Article 19: "States Parties shall take all appropriate legislative, administrative, social and educational measures to protect the child from

all forms of physical or mental violence, injury or abuse, neglect or negligent treatment, maltreatment or exploitation, including sexual abuse, while in the care of parent(s), legal guardian(s) or any other person who has the care of the child."

Article 28: "States Parties shall take all appropriate measures to ensure that school discipline is administered in a manner consistent with the child's human dignity and in conformity with the present Convention."

The Court Decisions

In its ruling of July 2000, the Ontario Superior Court recognized the "growing body of evidence that even mild forms of corporal punishment do no good and may cause harm." It was noted in the decision that not a single expert witness on either side of the case advocated or recommended physical punishment as a form of discipline. Despite these findings, the Court ruled that section 43 is constitutional—that it does not violate the Charter of Rights and Freedoms.

This decision was appealed to the Ontario Court of Appeal. The lower court's decision was upheld in January 2002. The Supreme Court of Canada granted leave to appeal this decision. The appeal was heard in June 2003. On January 30, 2004, a split 7–2 decision was announced. The majority of judges had ruled that Section 43 does not violate the constitutional rights of children but, rather, recognizes their developmental needs.[25] In the decision, Chief Justice McLachlin wrote that "Section 43 is not arbitrarily demeaning. It does not discriminate. Rather, it is firmly grounded in the actual needs and circumstances of children."

Three judges on the Supreme Court panel viewed Section 43 as a violation of children's Charter rights. Justice Arbour held that it violated Section 7 of the Charter (security of the person) and stated that "children remain the only group of citizens who are deprived of the protection of the criminal law in relation to the use of force." Justice Deschamps found a breach of Section 15 of the Charter (equality rights): "Far from corresponding to the actual needs and circumstances of children, s. 43 compounds the pre-existing disadvantage of children as a vulnerable and often-powerless group whose access to legal redress is already restricted." Justice Binnie also found that Section 43 violates Section 15 of the Charter, but determined that this violation was justified for parents (but not for teachers) under Section 1 of the Charter: "There can be few things that more effectively designate children as second-class citizens than stripping them of the ordinary assault provisions of the Criminal Code."

The Supreme Court's Definition of Reasonable Force

The Supreme Court not only found Section 43 constitutional as it stands, but also explicitly defined a zone of acceptable violence. According to the decision, the use of force against a child is justified if:

1. it is administered by a parent (teachers may not use corporal punishment[26]),
2. the child is between the ages of two and twelve years, inclusive,
3. the child is capable of learning from it,
4. it constitutes "minor corrective force of a transitory and trifling nature,"
5. it does not involve the use of objects or blows or slaps to the head,
6. it is not degrading, inhuman or harmful, and
7. it is corrective—that is, not the result of the caregiver's "frustration, loss of temper or abusive personality."

While stating that "the gravity of the precipitating event is not relevant," the Court also determined that the question of what is "reasonable under the circumstances ... must be considered in context and in light of all the circumstances of the case."

Therefore, in its 2004 decision, in direct contradiction of article 19 of the CRC, the Supreme Court upheld the justification of reasonable corrective force against children, spelling out the circumstances in which Canada's assault laws do not apply. The Court justified its position by stating that the CRC does not explicitly require State Parties to ban all corporal punishment of children. In doing so, the Court ignored repeated criticisms of Canada's law by the CRC:

In the framework of its mandate, the Committee has paid particular attention to the child's right to physical integrity. In the same spirit, it has stressed that corporal punishment of children is incompatible with the Convention and has often proposed the revision of existing legislation, as well as the development of awareness and educational campaigns, to prevent child abuse and the physical punishment of children.[27]

Certain States have tried to distinguish between the correction of children and excessive violence. In reality the dividing line between the two is artificial. It is very easy to pass from one stage to the other. It is also a question of principle. If it is not permissible to beat an adult, why should it be permissible to do so to a child? One of the contributions of the Convention is to call attention to the contradictions in our attitudes and cultures.[28]

The Committee recommends that the physical punishment of children in families be prohibited [in Canada].[29]

The Committee recommends that States parties review all relevant legislation to ensure that all forms of violence against children, however light, are prohibited.[30]

[States should] enact or repeal, as a matter of urgency, their legislation in order to prohibit all forms of violence, however light, within the family and in schools, including as a form of discipline, as required by the provisions of the Convention.[31]

The Committee is deeply concerned that [Canada] has not enacted legislation explicitly prohibiting all forms of corporal punishment and has taken no action to remove section 43 of the Criminal Code, which allows corporal punishment ... The Committee recommends that the State party adopt legislation to remove the existing authorization of the use of "reasonable force" in disciplining children and explicitly prohibit all forms of violence against children, however light, within the family, in schools and in other institutions where children may be placed.[32]

The guidelines for States in preparing their periodic reports to the Committee on their implementation of the CRC, which were adopted in October 1996, ask whether legislation (criminal and/or family law) prohibits all forms of physical and mental violence, including corporal punishment.[33]

The Supreme Court's Application of the Principle of the Best Interests of the Child

Article 3 of the CRC states that "in all actions concerning children, whether undertaken by public or private social welfare institutions, courts of law, administrative authorities or legislative bodies, the best interests of the child shall be a primary consideration."

The foundation had argued that laws affecting children must be in their best interests and that a legal justification of physical punishment violates this principle. The Court's response was that the "best interests of the child" is indeed a legal principle that has been established in domestic law and in international conventions to which Canada is a party. It noted that this principle is recognized in the Immigration and Refugee Protection Act, the Youth Criminal Justice Act, the Divorce Act, the Family Relations Act, the Child and Family Services Act, and the Children's Law Reform Act, among other statutes.[34] However, the Court stated that there is an absence of "consensus that the principle is vital or fundamental to our societal notion of justice." While it is "widely supported in legislation and social policy, and is an important factor for consideration in many contexts ... it is not, however, a foundational requirement for the dispensation of justice."[35] The Court also found that this principle cannot be applied with precision or with full agreement about its application.[36] Therefore, the Court concluded, the "best interests of the child" is not a principle of fundamental justice.

This conceptualization of the "best interests of the child" principle contrasts sharply with that seen in other nations where it has become a cornerstone of legal and policy decision making. In Norway, for example, the CRC has been fully implemented in law through a 2003 amendment to the Human Rights Act, meaning that the Convention *is* the law in that country.[37] When conflicts arise between the Convention and other Norwegian legislation, the Convention now takes precedence.

Another example is Sweden, where Parliament unanimously approved the implementation of Child Impact Assessments in 1999 as part of its national strategy for implementing the CRC.[38] These assessments must be conducted in the case of any government decision affecting children; this places the burden of proof on those who propose policies contrary to the child's best interests. A five-step procedure has been developed for the implementation of these assessments and for the application of their findings.[39]

Senate Private Member's Bills S-21: 2004 and S-207: 2006

Following the Supreme Court decision, ongoing efforts have been made to provide children with full legal protection. In December 2004, Senator Céline Hervieux-Payette introduced a private member's bill to the Senate that would have repealed Section 43 (Bill S-21, An Act to Amend the Criminal Code: Protection of Children).[40] This bill passed second reading in the Senate in March 2005 and was subsequently referred to the Senate Committee on Legal and Constitutional Affairs for study. Witnesses were called before the committee in June 2005. Those hearings were adjourned toward the end of that month. When a new federal government was elected in January 2006, the bill died on the Order Paper. In April 2006, Senator Hervieux-Payette introduced a new bill (Bill S-207, An Act to Amend the Criminal Code: Protection of Children).[41] Debate on this bill was adjourned in June 2006 for summer recess. Its fate was unknown at the time of writing.[42]

Why Does Canadian Law Still Justify Physical Punishment?

Why have the Canadian government and the Canadian courts continued to justify the physical punishment of children, leaving Section 43 unchanged for more than one hundred years? The key arguments that the government and the courts have put forward to retain this law are presented in this section, and their validity is examined.

Argument 1: Physical Punishment Is an Effective Socialization Tool

According to the Ontario Court of Appeal, Section 43 "de-criminalizes only non-abusive physical punishment by parents or teachers where the intention is to correct, and correction is possible ... The legislative purpose of s.43 is to permit parents and teachers to apply strictly limited corrective force to children without criminal sanctions so that they can carry out their important responsibilities to train and nurture children without harm that such sanctions would bring to them, to their tasks and to the families concerned."[43] In other words, Section 43 carves out a zone of non-abusive violence—a zone that the Court saw as necessary in bringing up children.

But is physical punishment a useful tool for correcting, training, and nurturing children? This question can be answered by the findings of several decades of social-science research. In 2002 the results of a meta-analysis of this research were published, providing a comprehensive picture of the developmental outcomes associated with common forms of physical punishment.[44] The findings demonstrated that physical punishment is consistently linked to negative behavioural indicators such as increased child aggression, higher risk of delinquency, and weaker internalization of moral standards. Physical punishment also was consistently associated with negative emotional indicators, namely poorer mental health and impaired parent–child relationships. In sum, physical punishment has not been shown to be an effective method for training or nurturing children.

The relationships between physical punishment and negative developmental outcomes have been confirmed elsewhere. For example, the Canadian Psychological Association has concluded that "physical punishment has been consistently demonstrated to be an ineffective and potentially harmful method of managing children's behaviour."[45] Similarly, the Canadian Paediatric Society has concluded that "the research that is available supports the position that spanking and other forms of physical punishment are associated with negative child outcomes."[46] The argument that physical punishment is an effective socialization tool and should, therefore, be protected by law is not supported by the evidence.

Argument 2: Law Reform Would Infringe on Parents' Rights

It might be argued that regardless of the research evidence, parents have the right to determine their methods of discipline. The difficulty with this argument is that, in fact, no person has the "right" to hit or otherwise assault another person. Section 43 does not bestow on parents a right to assault their children. Rather, it provides them with a *privilege* or an *excuse* should they commit such an assault for the purpose of correction.[47]

In the words of Howe and Covell,[48] "it is children who have fundamental rights and it is parents, adults, and state officials who have responsibilities to provide for those rights." The UN Convention affirms that "parents or, as the case may be, legal guardians, have the primary responsibility for the upbringing and development of the child," but it also specifies that in the discharge of those responsibilities, "the best interests of the child will be their basic concern" (article 18). The Convention recognizes parents' "responsibilities, rights and duties ... to provide, in a manner consistent with the evolving capacities of the child, appropriate direction and guidance in the exercise by the child of the rights recognized in the present Convention" (article 5).

Therefore, under the terms of the Convention, parents do not have the right to violate children's rights to protection. Rather, they have the right and the duty to guide children's exercise of their protection rights and to promote their best interests. And children have the right to parents who will guard those interests.[49]

Argument 3: No Other Country Has Criminalized Physical Punishment

In its 2002 Memorandum of Argument requesting that the Supreme Court refuse to hear an appeal of the lower court's decision, the Attorney General of Canada stated that "no other country has criminalized all forms of corrective physical force."[50] This claim was repeated in 2005 in the statement of the Department of Justice to the Senate Committee on Legal and Constitutional Affairs regarding Bill S-21. In fact, at the time when the initial challenge was filed in the Ontario Superior Court, ten countries had explicitly abolished all corporal punishment. By the time the Ontario Court of Appeal had released its decision, this number had increased to thirteen. By the time the Attorney General's factum was submitted to the Supreme Court, this number had increased to fourteen. Today, fifteen countries have prohibited all corporal punishment.[51]

In its 2002 Memorandum of Argument, the Attorney General noted correctly that most of these prohibitions are found in the civil laws of these countries and do not, therefore, create a new crime of corporal punishment.[52] However, these civil prohibitions were enacted *in addition to* the repeal of the criminal defence to corrective assault. Parents in these countries are subject to the criminal laws on assault whether they strike a child or an adult. The purposes of the civil code prohibitions—which are implemented *in addition to* repeal of the criminal defence—are to remove any ambiguity about whether corporal punishment is allowed and to affirm children's rights to full protection in law. As the Swedish Minister of Justice stated in 1979:

> With the new clause in the Children and Parents' Code there can be no doubt that a disciplinary measure against a child is a criminal offence if a corresponding act against another person is punishable as maltreatment under the Penal Code.[53]

Similarly, the German government has stated that

> pursuant to the new prohibition, the corporal effect must exceed a certain degree of intensity before it may have criminal law consequences, but this level of intensity is now reached when a child is slapped. As a consequence, a parent may now be punished for causing bodily injury pursuant to §223 of the Criminal Code (Strafgesetzbuch), if he or she exceeds this threshold of violence in the course of his or her childrearing. For parents, this means that they are subject to the same limits in their relationship to their children as they are in society in general.[54]

Not only is Canada far from the first country to consider recognizing children's rights to full protection, it is becoming more of a laggard every day. Three countries (the Netherlands, Slovenia, and the Slovak Republic) have announced that they are committed to prohibiting all corporal punishment in the near future. Four others (Belgium, the Czech Republic, Greece, and Ireland) have been found by the European Committee of Social Rights to be in breach of their human rights obligations under article 17 of the European Social Charter[55] and are expected to act on that decision.[56]

The issue of eliminating of corporal punishment is steadily climbing the global human rights agenda. In 2004, for example, the Parliamentary Assembly of the Council of Europe adopted a resolution calling for a Europe-wide ban on corporal punishment of children.[57] Paulo Sérgio Pinheiro, appointed by UN Secretary-General Kofi Annan to lead the first comprehensive global study on violence against children in 2003, stated in his Final Report to the UN General Assembly that full law reform is a fundamental necessity in the worldwide effort to eliminate violence against children: "The central message of the study is that *no violence against children is justifiable, and all violence against children is preventable.* The Study reveals that in every region, in stark contradiction to human rights obligations and children's developmental needs, much violence against children remains legal, State-authorized and socially approved. The Study aims to mark a definitive global turning point: an end to the justification of violence against children, whether accepted as 'tradition' or disguised as 'discipline'"[58] (original emphasis). The report recommends that world-wide prohibition of all violence against children be completed by 2009.[59]

In 2005 the Andean Commission of Jurists requested the Inter-American Commission on Human Rights to seek an advisory opinion from the Inter-American Human Rights Court regarding whether corporal punishment of children is a breach of their human rights. If the court accepts the petition and issues an advisory opinion which confirms that states have legal obligations to prohibit all forms of corporal punishment, law reform will proceed across the Americas. Thus, rather than assuming a leadership role, Canada increasingly lags behind in protecting the fundamental rights of children.

Argument 4: Parents Will Be Prosecuted for Minor Offences

In its 2004 decision, a majority of the Supreme Court stated that Section 43 "ensures the criminal law will not be used where the force is part of a genuine effort to educate the child, poses no reasonable risk of harm that is more than transitory and trifling, and is reasonable under the circumstances. Introducing the criminal law into children's families and educational environments in such circumstances would harm children more than help them."[60]

This statement reflects a concern that, in the absence of Section 43, parents will be charged and prosecuted for occasional "minor" offences carried out with good intent (e.g., slapping a toddler's hand for touching a dangerous object). Indeed, the Canadian government views this position on the law as being in the best interests of children and as a form of child protection. In documentation submitted to the UN Study on Violence Against Children, the Government of Canada stated that "the Government does not support the 'spanking' of children but neither does it condone the criminalization of Canadian parents for disciplinary conduct that is undertaken in a reasonable way that takes into account the needs and best interests of children ... it is not in the best interests of the child or Canadian society to bring the full force of the criminal law to bear on parents who give a mild, non-injurious spank to a child."[61]

While this position may, on the face of it, appear to be a rational compromise, it betrays an assumption that children's rights to protection must be trumped by parents' fears of prosecution. In no other area of law do we accept such compromise. The Criminal Code does not carve out a zone of non-criminal assault for husbands who correct their wives, guards who correct their prisoners, or nurses who correct their elderly patients.

In each of these cases, the standard is clear and absolute in order to protect the rights of the vulnerable party. In each case, assault cannot be excused on the basis of corrective intent, as such assault is seen to violate the victim's right to dignity and physical integrity. The law reflects our principles of fundamental rights.

But, that said, would repeal of Section 43 result in prosecution of parents for minor violations of the law? Federal and provincial Crown counsel guidelines recognize two principles in this respect: (1) sufficiency of proof, and (2) public interest.[62] According to Carter,[63] "in the absence of section 43 or a judge-made replacement, any distinction that might be drawn between corrective force administered by parents and teachers, and other kinds of force would have to be made in the context of Crown Counsel's application of the principle of public interest. The existence of the public interest principle respects the common law position that sufficiency of evidence will not, alone, compel the prosecution of a charge."[64]

Carter concludes that "the repeal of the corporal punishment defence could be understood to provide authoritative content to the concept of "public interest."[65] Factors that could be considered in assessing whether prosecution of a parent is in the public interest include "the possible counter-productivity of a prosecution; undue harshness or oppressiveness of a conviction under the circumstances; [and] the opinion of the victim."[66]

To illustrate: the criminal law does not delineate a zone of non-criminal theft and provide an excuse in law. This is to ensure that those who taste grapes in the supermarket will not be criminally charged. What the law does do is make the principle clear, and then prosecutorial discretion permits the application of the law in a manner that serves the public interest. Just as it would not be in the public interest to charge the occasional grape taster, it would not be in the public interest—or in the child's interest—to charge a parent who spanks a child in a moment of panic for running into traffic.

In her dissenting opinion to the Supreme Court decision, Justice Arbour noted that the common-law defence of *de minimus non curat lex* (the law does not take account of trifles) prevents the prosecution of minor violations of the law.

> Generally, the justifications for a de minimis excuse are that: (1) it reserves the application of the criminal law to serious misconduct; (2) it protects an accused from the stigma of a criminal conviction and from the imposition of severe penalties for relatively trivial conduct; and (3) it saves courts from being swamped by an enormous number of trivial cases ... In part, the theory is based on a notion that the evil to be prevented by the offence section has not actually occurred. This

is consistent with the dual fundamental principle of criminal justice that there is no culpability for harmless and blameless conduct.[67]

I am of the view that an appropriate expansion in the use of the de minimis defence—not unlike the development of the doctrine of abuse of process—would assist in ensuring that mere technical violations of the assault provisions of the Code that ought not to attract criminal sanctions are stayed. In this way, judicial resources are not wasted, and unwanted intrusions of the criminal law in the family context, which may be harmful to children, are avoided. Therefore, if s. 43 were to be struck down, and absent Parliament's re-enactment of a provision compatible with the constitutional rights of children, parents would be no more at risk of being dragged into court for a "pat on the bum" than they currently are for "tasting" a single grape in the supermarket.[68]

Whether the Criminal Code retains a defence to corrective assault for parents, then, reflects the priority placed by the government on children's rights to protection versus parents' access to a legal justification for violating those rights. "A Criminal Code provision that insulates violent conduct towards children from criminal liability does not enhance children's security in any way[69] ... Children deserve to see the end of the way in which the law formally compromises their dignity and security interests."[70]

Other countries have dealt with this issue simply and decisively, by prioritizing the principle of children's rights to protection and acknowledging the reality of prosecutorial decision making. For example, in addressing this issue with regard to the explicit prohibition on corporal punishment enacted in Sweden in 1979, the Swedish Minister of Justice stated that "it would be certainly unfortunate if the state could prosecute and punish any infringement, however slight, of a prohibition against corporal punishment. The rules governing warrant for prosecution also ensure the right of refusal to prosecute trifling acts which in themselves fall within the domain of what is punishable."[71]

In 2000 the Israeli Supreme Court struck down the criminal defence to corrective assault, stating that "we cannot reach a compromise on account of the risk to the welfare and well-being of the minors ... We cannot endanger the physical and mental well-being of a minor by any kind of physical punishment; truth has to be clear and unequivocal, and the message is that physical punishment is not allowed ... We will give the prosecution discretion not to charge in the absence of public interest."[72]

The German government has stated that "The public prosecutor's office will still only press criminal charges in serious cases and can, in particular, waive these when the family accepts social education, family-oriented therapy or other supporting measures."[73]

The Supreme Court of Canada, in contrast, has prioritized the protection of adults over the rights of children. Its decision insulates adults from legal liability, yet in doing so it compromises the dignity and security of children.[74]

Argument 5: Canadians Do Not Support Law Reform

In its 2002 Memorandum of Argument, the Attorney General stated that the majority of Canadians do not support the repeal of Section 43.[75] No evidence, however, was provided for this statement. Following the Attorney General's submission, and five months before the release of the Supreme Court's decision, Decima Research[76] conducted a national poll on Canadians' attitudes. The results indicated that most Canadians do in fact support the repeal of Section 43.

With regard to teachers, 69 percent of respondents agreed that Section 43 protection should be ended. Agreement was highest among younger Canadians (76 percent of 18- to 34-year-olds) and women (75 percent). With regard to parents, 51 percent of respondents agreed with ending Section 43 protection. Again, agreement was highest among younger Canadians (58 percent) and women (59 percent). However, ending Section 43 protection for parents would be supported by 72 percent of respondents if guidelines were in place to prevent prosecutions for minor offences, by 72 percent if research showed that physical punishment is ineffective and potentially harmful, and by 80 percent if research showed that repeal would contribute to decreasing child abuse. It follows that the majority of Canadians would in fact support full law reform if they were provided with information on prosecutorial discretion and social-science research findings.

Argument 6: Public Education Is a More Powerful Agent of Change Than Law Reform

In its 2002 Memorandum of Argument, the Attorney General claimed that there was no evidence to demonstrate that striking down Section 43 would lead to changes in public attitudes, while there was evidence that this goal could be accomplished through public education.[77] It also was claimed that "Canadian attitudes towards the use of physical punishment and the level of force which is appropriate have changed over time without any change to s.43."[78] In its 2004 decision, the Supreme Court of Canada confirmed this position, stating that Parliament has decided not to reform the criminal law, "preferring the approach of educating parents against physical discipline."[79]

The relationship between law reform and attitudinal change is a complex one. Certainly, attitudinal shifts can generate legislative change, but law reform can also shift norms. An evaluation of the merits of the Supreme Court's position can be undertaken by examining approaches taken in other countries.

In Sweden, the criminal defence to corrective assault was struck down in 1957, when a majority of Swedes still believed that corporal punishment was necessary in childrearing and virtually all children were struck by their parents.[80] By 1968, only 42 percent believed that corporal punishment was necessary. In 1979 the Civil Code prohibition was enacted; two years later, the proportion of Swedes who believed that physical punishment is necessary had declined to 26 percent. By 1994 only 11 percent of Swedes were positively inclined to even mild physical punishment, and the vast majority of children had never experienced it.[81]

At the time of the Swedish prohibition, massive public education initiatives were undertaken. But these initiatives focused on the law reform. In other words, law reform became the lever for public education.[82] The prohibition and its accompanying public education campaign resulted in almost universal knowledge of the law within two years of its enactment.[83] Today, every new parent is told about the corporal punishment prohibition during their first visit to a well-baby clinic. This information provides a framework for discussing of the issue and an opportunity for bolstering the transformation of the norm. The law sets a clear standard so that all professionals can convey the same message to parents and all parents hear the same unambiguous message.[84]

Attitudinal and behavioural shifts are already evident in Germany, where a prohibition on corporal punishment was enacted in 2000.[85] As was the case in Sweden, the prohibition provided the opportunity to launch a two-year nationwide multimedia campaign with the theme "More Respect for Children." Among parents who tend to use corporal punishment, the proportion who believe that this is their natural right fell from 46 to 35 percent between 1996 and 2001. Between 1992 and 2002, the proportion of German youth who felt that their parents had a right to slap them fell from 80 to 50 percent.

Between 1992 and 2002, the proportion of adolescents who reported having been slapped lightly on the face decreased by 15 percent; the proportion who had been slapped severely on the face decreased by 69 percent; the proportion who had been beaten with a rod had decreased by 88 percent; and the proportion who had been beaten to the point of bruising had decreased by 90 percent.[86]

Are these changes specifically attributable to the prohibition itself? This may be partially the case, but it is also true that the process of law reform in Germany took several years. A proposal to prohibit corporal punishment was first debated in the German parliament in the early 1990s. While the proposal failed at the time, the public discourse that ensued likely contributed to the attitudinal and behavioural change that has been observed.[87]

Interestingly, although *attitudes* might have begun to shift during the 1990s, the public's *knowledge* of the law was utterly lacking at that time: "Nobody, not even lawyers or the courts, [knew] how hard blows may be ... The orientational function of this norm is almost completely zero ... Only a meager fraction of adults (3.7%) are familiar with the German norm."[88] Thus, prior to the explicit prohibition, almost no Germans knew what their law permitted.[89] But by 2001, 90 percent or more of parents knew that severe slaps to the face, beatings with rods, and thrashings were not permissible, and more than 80 percent knew that beating a child's bottom with the hand is not permissible (although parents were less certain about the milder forms of corporal punishment—over 60 percent still thought that smacks on the bottom and light slaps on the face were still permitted).[90]

Moreover, knowledge of law reform appears to contribute to a redefinition of violence in the public mind. German parents who knew about the law reform were more likely than those who did not know about it to define the following acts as violence: a slap across the face for disobedience (39 vs. 28 percent), a forceful smack on the bottom (25 vs. 16 percent), and a thrashing (57 vs. 45 percent).[91]

As a result of the educational campaign that accompanied the prohibition, more than 90 percent of professionals employed in child- and family-serving institutions knew about the law within a year of its passage. This group is seen by the German government as a "multiplier" that can spread the information more broadly to the general public.[92]

The Interdependence of Law and Education

Both law reform and public education will be more effective if they are consistent and are implemented simultaneously. Law reform will be ineffective if parents are unaware of the change and its rationale. But public education aimed at altering attitudes and behaviour will be undercut by a law that justifies and enshrines the very same attitudes and behaviours that those educational campaigns aim to eliminate.

Section 43 educates. It states that corrective force against children is "justified." In law, a justification asserts the *rightfulness* of an act.[93] This means that Section 43 does not merely provide a defence or excuse for an act that would not otherwise be condoned; it provides a justification for an act that is thereby considered to be *the right thing to do*, making it unique among legal defences to assault.

For example, when one person assaults another for the purpose of self-defence, all parties in the case agree that an assault has taken place and that assault is a crime and a rights violation. The defendant does not attempt to prove that an assault did not take place. Rather, the defendant argues that the assault was excusable owing to exceptional circumstances. Even if the defendant is successful, the principle remains intact: every individual has the right to freedom from assault.[94] Section 43, in contrast, provides more than an excuse; it provides a justification that renders the physical punishment of children not merely excusable, but a non-criminal act. The act only becomes an assault in the eyes of the law if the Crown can establish that the act was "unreasonable." Section 43 explicitly tells Canadians that hitting children has educational value, is sometimes necessary, and is sometimes deserved.[95]

The primary purpose of law reform in the nations that have undertaken it has been to convey a principle, which is that children, like adults, have the fundamental right to protection from all forms of violence. The law itself is a mechanism for public education about that principle. As stated by the European Committee of Social Rights,[96] "to prohibit any form of corporal punishment of children is an important measure for the education of the population in this respect in that it gives a clear message about what society considers to be acceptable. It is a measure that avoids discussions and concerns as to where the borderline would be between what might be acceptable corporal punishment and what is not."

While some would argue that the purpose of criminal law is not to educate, it also could be argued that this is actually its fundamental purpose. Law sets a standard for behaviour in a society; it demarcates rightful from wrongful behaviour; it codifies the values of a nation; and it serves as a deterrent to rights violations. While it is not always effective in accomplishing these purposes, it is the standard against which behaviour is judged. It tells us where the line is drawn. Section 43 tells us that the use of corrective force with children meets the standard of our nation. No amount of public education can change that standard. In the words of Justice Deschamps, in a dissenting opinion to the 2004 Supreme Court decision, "the Charter infringement in this case is discriminatory at a very direct and basic level. It clearly impairs the equal rights of children to bodily integrity and security in a much more intrusive way than necessary to achieve a valid legislative objective. The provincial and policy mechanisms available do not change this effect."[97]

Conclusion

In 1972 the Criminal Code was amended so as to forbid corporal punishment of prison inmates. This amendment reflected a belief that such punishment is not an acceptable means of improving behaviour and that even those who have committed criminal acts retain their fundamental human rights.[98] This amendment did not affect prison authorities' ability to use force to restrain inmates, to defend themselves or others, or to maintain order. But it did remove the legal sanction for punishing inmates physically, and in so doing it asserted those individuals' rights to dignity and physical security.

At this time in history, we must ask ourselves why two-year-old children merit any less protection. As long as our law declares corporal punishment of children to be justifiable, we cannot claim to be a nation that respects children or their rights. Section 43 is more than a powerful symbol of children's status in Canada; it also is a practical obstacle to effective child protection. It undermines the efforts of parent educators, social workers, pediatricians, and other professionals to encourage parents to stop hitting; it backs up those parents who believe that hitting children is the right thing to do; it advises uncertain parents that hitting is sometimes necessary; and it contributes to the risk of escalation that is inherent in situations of conflict.[99] But perhaps the most important message of Section 43 is the one it sends to children. Instead of affirming their full personhood and their right to a non-violent upbringing, it affirms their lesser status and the belief that they deserve to be hit. In this new millennium, perhaps we can take our inspiration from Sweden, the first country to tell children explicitly that they have the right to not be hit. More than a quarter of a century ago, the Swedish government told children in law that they are "entitled to care, security and a good upbringing. Children are to be treated with respect for their person and individuality and may not be subjected to corporal punishment or any other humiliating treatment."[100]

Do the children of Canada deserve any less?

Notes

1 J. McCain, "Torture's Terrible Toll," *Newsweek*, November 21, 2005, 34–36 at 36.

2 Criminal Code, S. 43.

3 *Canadian Foundation for Children, Youth and the Law v. Canada (Attorney General)*, 2004 SCC 4.

4 Committee on the Rights of the Child, UN Doc. CRC/C/15/Add 37. 1995.

5 For more on the history of this law, see A.E. McGillivray and J.E. Durrant, "Child Corporal Punishment: Violence, Law, and Rights," in R. Alaggia and

C. Vine, eds., *Cruel but Not Unusual: Violence in Canadian Families* (Waterloo: Wilfrid Laurier University Press, 2006).

6 McGillivray, "He'll Learn It on His Body: Disciplining Childhood in Canadian Law," *International Journal of Children's Rights* 5 (1998): 193–242.

7 *R. v. Wetmore*, New Brunswick, 1996, 172 N.B.R. (2nd) 224.

8 *R. v. Spenard*, unreported, Ontario 1996.

9 *R. v. Park*, Newfoundland 1999, 178 NFLD & PEI Reports 194, Nfld.

10 *R. v. Pickard*, unreported BC, 1995, de Villiers, J No. 2861.

11 *R. v. K. (M)*, Manitoba, 1993, 16 CR (4th), 121 Manitoba Ct. of Appeal.

12 *R. v. C. (G)*, Newfoundland, 2001, 51 WCB (2nd) 417, NFLD 2001.

13 *R. v. L.A.K.*, Newfoundland, 1992, 04 Nfld. and P.E.I. R. 118 NFLD.

14 *R. v. Wheeler*, unreported, Yukon, 1990, Faulkner J. No. 191.

15 *R. v. N.S.*, unreported, Ontario, 1999, Karam, J. OJ 320.

16 See http://www.repeal43.org/acquittals.html.

17 *R. v. Bell*. Ontario, 2001, 49 WCB (2d) 507.

18 1994 Bill C-296 House of Commons, MP Svend Robinson; 1996 Bill C-305 House of Commons, MP Svend Robinson; 1996 Bill S-14 Senate, Senator Sharon Carstairs; 1997 Bill C-276 House of Commons, MP Libby Davies; 1998 Bill C-368 House of Commons, MP Tony Ianno; 1999 Bill C-273, House of Commons, MP Libby Davies; 2001 Bill C-329, House of Commons, MP Libby Davies.

19 The Charter came into effect on April 17, 1982, as part of a package of reforms contained in the Constitution Act, 1982. Section 15, which guarantees equality rights, came into effect three years later; the delay was to give governments time to bring their laws into line with that section. Further information on the Charter can be found at http://www.canadianheritage.gc.ca/progs/pdp-hrp/canada/guide/index_e.cfm.

20 See http://www.ccppcj.ca.

21 This program was eliminated by the federal government in September 2006.

22 Ailsa Watkinson's background includes twelve years working for the Saskatchewan Human Rights Commission. She holds a Ph.D. in educational administration. Her doctoral research was on the Courts' interpretations of the Canadian Charter of Rights and Freedoms and their possible consequences for the decision-making role of administrators. She is the author of *Education, Student Rights, and the Charter* and a co-editor of *Contesting Fundamentalisms*. She is the president of the Canadian Association of Elizabeth Fry Societies and was instrumental in instigating a systemic human rights investigation filed with the Canadian Human Rights Commission into the treatment of women prisoners. The final report, *Protecting Their Rights: A Systematic Review of Human Rights in Correctional Services for Federally Sentenced Women,* was issued on January 28, 2004, and can be accessed at http://www.chrc-ccdp.ca.

23 The Canadian Foundation for Children, Youth, and the Law administers a non-profit legal aid clinic (Justice for Children and Youth) that provides legal representation to low-income children and youth in the Toronto area and assists them in obtaining fair and equal access to legal, educational, medical, and social resources. It also advocates for law and policy reform and monitors and responds to legal developments affecting children. Its work is

based on the principle that children and youth must be recognized as individuals under the law. Further information can be found at http://www.jfcy.org.
24 For detailed Charter analyses, see M. Carter, "The Constitutional Validity of the Corporal Punishment Defence in Canada: A Critical Analysis of Canadian Foundation for Children, Youth, and the Law versus Canada (Attorney General)," *International Review of Victimology* 12: 189–211; S.G. Grover, "Negating the Child's Inclusive Right to Security of the Person: A Charter Analysis of the s. 43 Canadian Criminal Code Defense to Corporal Punishment of a Minor," *Murdoch University Electronic Journal of Law* 10; S. Turner, *Something to Cry About: An Argument against Corporal Punishment of Children in Canada* (Waterloo: Wilfrid Laurier University Press, 2002); A. Watkinson, "Corporal Punishment and Education: Oh Canada! Spare Us!" in M.M. Casimir, ed., *The Courts, the Charter and the Schools: The Impact of the Charter of Rights and Freedoms on Educational Policy and Practice* (Toronto: University of Toronto Press, 2006).
25 The Supreme Court's decision may be viewed at http://www.lexum.umontreal.ca/csc-scc/en/rec/index.html.
26 The Court ruled that teachers may use reasonable force only to "remove a child from a classroom or to secure compliance with instructions, but not merely as corporal punishment." To date, however, teachers remain identified in Section 43 as among those authorities who are "justified in using force by way of correction of a pupil or child."
27 November 8, 1994, CRC/C/24.
28 October 10, 1994, CRC/C/SR 176.
29 June 20, 1995, CRC/C/15/Add.37.
30 September 22, 2000, CRC/C/97.
31 September 28, 2001, CRC/C/111.
32 October 27, 2003, CRC/C/15/Add.215.
33 CRC/C/58.
34 *Canadian Foundation for Children, Youth and the Law v. Canada (Attorney General),* 2004 SCC 4 (see para. 9).
35 Ibid. (see para. 10).
36 Ibid. (see para. 11).
37 Ministry of Children and Family Affairs, UN Special Session on Children, *Norway's National Plan of Action* (Oslo: MCFA, n.d.), http://www.odin.no/bld/english/doc/reports/004021–220008/hov003-bu.html.
38 See http://www.sweden.gov.se/content/1/c6/02/38/18/068d0933.pdf.
39 For more information on child impact assessments in Sweden, see Durrant, "From Mopping Up the Damage to Preventing the Flood: The Role of Social Policy in the Prevention of Violence against Children," *Social Policy Journal of New Zealand* 27: 1–17; Ministry of Health and Social Affairs, *Strategy to Implement the UN Convention on the Rights of the Child* (Stockholm: MHSA, 2004), http://www.sweden.gov.se/content/1/c6/02/38/18/068d0933.pdf; L. Sylvander, *Child Impact Assessments: Swedish Experience of Child Impact Analyses as a Tool for Implementing the UN Convention on the Rights of the Child* (Stockholm: MHSA, MFA, 2001).
40 See http://www.parl.gc.ca/38/1/parlbus/chambus/senate/bills/public/pdf/s-21_1.pdf.

41 See http://www2.parl.gc.ca/content/Senate/Bills/391/public/S-207/S-207_1/ S-207_text-e.htm.

42 For details of these bills and their progress through the Senate, see http://www .repeal43.org/bill_s21.html.

43 Ontario Court of Appeal of Section 43, paras. 29–30.

44 E.T. Gershoff, "Corporal Punishment by Parents and Associated Child Behaviors and Experiences: A Meta-analytic and Theoretical Review," *Psychological Bulletin* 128 (2002): 539–79.

45 See http://www.cpa.ca/documents/policy3.pdf.

46 See http://www.cps.ca/english/statements/PP/pp04–01.htm.

47 For a full discussion of this distinction, see Turner, *Something to Cry About.*

48 R.B. Howe and K. Covell, "Child Poverty in Canada and the Rights of the Child, *Human Rights Quarterly 25*, no. 44 (2003): 1069.

49 Grover, "Negating the Child's Inclusive Right to Security of the Person."

50 *Canadian Foundation for Children, Youth and the Law v. Canada (Attorney General)* [2002] S.C.C.A. No. 113, *Respondent's Memorandum of Argument in response to the Application for Leave to Appeal,* para. 3.

51 These countries are Sweden (1979), Finland (1983), Norway (987), Austria (1989), Cyprus (1994), Denmark (1997), Croatia (1998), Latvia (1998), Germany (2000), Israel (2000), Bulgaria (2000), Iceland (2003), Ukraine (2004), Hungary (2004), and Romania (2005). Italy and Portugal have not enacted explicit prohibitions; however, their Supreme Courts have struck down the criminal defence (Council of Europe 2005). These Court decisions have been interpreted by the European Committee of Social Rights as prohibitions on all corporal punishment (July 2005, Conclusions XVII-2).

52 Attorney General of Canada, *2002 Memorandum of Argument* (see para. 20).

53 Swedish Minister of Justice, stated in 1979 (p. 3).

54 Federal Ministry for Family Affairs, Senior Citizens, Women, and Youth, and Federal Ministry of Justice, *Violence in Upbringing: An Assessment after the Introduction of the Right to a Non-Violent Upbringing* (Berlin: Ministries, 2003), p. 5.

55 European Committee of Social Rights, July 2005, "Conclusions XVII-2," http://www.coe.int/t/e/human_rights/esc/3_reporting_procedure/2_recent _conclusions/2_by_year/Conclusions_XVII-2_Vol1.pdf.

56 For a state-by-state analysis of the legality of corporal punishment around the world, see http://www.endcorporalpunishment.org.

57 Recommendation 1666 (2004).

58 "World Report on Violence against Children, Introduction," http://www .violencestudy.org/a405.

59 Ibid., para. 116.

60 Supreme Court, *2004 Decision* (see para. 59).

61 "Canada's Response to the World Report on Violence against Children," September 1005, response to question 5, p. 6, http://www.pch.gc.ca/progs/pdp-hrp/ docs/vac-vce/tdm_e.cfm.

62 B.P. Archibald, 1998, in M. Carter, "Corporal Punishment and Prosecutorial Discretion in Canada," *International Journal of Children's Rights* 12 (2004): 41–70.

63 Carter, "Corporal Punishment."

64 Ibid., p. 54.

65 Ibid., p. 60.

66 Ibid., p. 57.

67 Justice Arbour's opinion of the s. 43 Supreme Court decision (see para. 204).

68 Ibid. (see para. 207).

69 Carter, "Corporal Punishment," p. 57.

70 Ibid., p. 62.

71 Swedish Minister of Justice, stated in 1979 (p. 3).

72 Criminal Appeal 4596/98 *Plonit v. A.G.* 54(1)P.D., p. 145.

73 Federal Ministry for Family Affairs, *Violence in Upbringing*, p. 5.

74 Carter, "Corporal Punishment."

75 Attorney General of Canada, *2002 Memorandum of Argument* (see para. 3).

76 Decima Research Inc., *Toronto Public Health—Family Abuse Prevention* (Toronto: Decima Research, 2003).

77 Attorney General of Canada, *2002 Memorandum of Argument* (see para. 28).

78 Ibid. (see para. 28).

79 Supreme Court, *2004 Decision* (see para. 59).

80 J. Stattin, H. Janson, I. Klackenberg-Larsson, and D. Magnusson, "Corporal Punishment in Everyday Life: An Intergenerational Perspective," in J. McCord, ed., *Coercion and Punishment in Long-Term Perspectives* (Cambridge: Cambridge University Press, 1995).

81 Durrant, "Legal Reform and Attitudes toward Physical Punishment in Sweden," *International Journal of Children's Rights* 11 (2003): 147–74.

82 S. Bremberg, Swedish National Board of Public Health, Chair, Commission on Parental Support, personal communication, May 21, 2003.

83 K.A. Ziegert, "The Swedish Prohibition of Corporal Punishment: A Preliminary Report," *Journal of Marriage and the Family* 45 (1983): 917–26.

84 For more information on parent support and education in Sweden, see C.A. Ateah, J.E. Durrant, and J. Mirwaldt, "Physical Punishment and Physical Abuse of Children: Strategies for Prevention," in Ateah and Mirwaldt, eds., *Within Our Reach: Preventing Abuse across the Lifespan* (Halifax: Fernwood Publishing and RESOLVE [Research and Education for Solutions to Violence and Abuse], 2004).

85 Federal Ministry for Family Affairs, *Violence in Upbringing*.

86 Ibid.

87 K.D. Bussman, *Evaluation of the German Prohibition of Family Violence against Children* (Toledo, Spain: European Society of Criminology, 2002).

88 D. Frehsee, "Violence toward Children in the Family and the Role of Law," in W.H.D. Frehsee, W. Horn, and K.D. Bussman, eds., *Family Violence against Children* (Berlin: de Gruyter, 1996), p. 6.

89 Ibid.

90 Federal Ministry for Family Affairs, *Violence in Upbringing*.

91 Ibid.

92 Ibid.

93 Grover, "Negating the Child's Inclusive Right"; Turner, *Something to Cry About*.

94 Grover, "Negating the Child's Inclusive Right."

95 An analysis of Web postings in the days immediately following the release of the Supreme Court's decision revealed that 60 percent of writers interpreted the decision as permission to spank children. J.E. Durrant, N. Sigvaldason, and L. Bednar (2006, under review). What did the Canadian public learn from the Supreme Court decision on physical punishment?

96 European Committee of Social Rights, *Conclusions XV–2.*

97 Justice Deschamps, in response to the Supreme Court, *2004 Decision* (see para. 240).

98 Turner, *Something to Cry About.*

99 M.M. Bernstein, "The Decision of the Supreme Court of Canada Upholding the Constitutionality of Section 43 of the *Criminal Code of Canada*: What This Decision Means to the Child Welfare Sector," *OACAS Journal* 48 (2004): 2–14; Durrant, "Corporal Punishment"; Vatcher, "Corporal Punishment of Children ... The Current Law, the Constitutional Challenge, and Implications for Future Social Work Practice," *OACAS Journal* 44 (2000).

100 Parenthood and Guardianship Code, 1989/1981.

Bibliography

Archibald, B.P. 1998. "The Politics of Prosecutorial Discretion: Institutional Structures and the Tensions between Punitive and Restorative Paradigms of Justice." *Canadian Criminal Law Review* 3: 68.

Ateah, C.A., J.E. Durrant, and J. Mirwaldt. 2004. "Physical Punishment and Physical Abuse of Children: Strategies for Prevention." In Ateah and Mirwaldt, eds., *Within Our Reach: Preventing Abuse across the Lifespan*. Halifax: Fernwood Publishing and RESOLVE (Research and Education for Solutions to Violence and Abuse).

Bernstein, M.M. 2004. "The Decision of the Supreme Court of Canada Upholding the Constitutionality of Section 43 of the *Criminal Code of Canada*: What This Decision Means to the Child Welfare Sector." *OACAS Journal* 48: 2–14.

Bussman, K.D. 2002. *Evaluation of the German Prohibition of Family Violence against Children*. Toledo, Spain: European Society of Criminology.

Carter, M. 2004. "Corporal Punishment and Prosecutorial Discretion in Canada." *International Journal of Children's Rights* 12: 41–70.

———. 2005. "The Constitutional Validity of the Corporal Punishment Defence in Canada: A Critical Analysis of Canadian Foundation for Children, Youth, and the Law versus Canada (Attorney General)." *International Review of Victimology* 12: 189–211.

Council of Europe. 2005. *Eliminating Corporal Punishment: A Human Rights Imperative for Europe's Children*. Strasbourg: Council of Europe Publishing.

Decima Research Inc. 2003. *Toronto Public Health—Family Abuse Prevention*. Toronto: Decima Research.

Durrant, J.E. 2003. "Legal Reform and Attitudes toward Physical Punishment in Sweden." *International Journal of Children's Rights* 11: 147–74.

————. 2005. "Corporal Punishment: Prevalence, Predictors, and Implications for Child Behaviour and Development." In S.N. Hart, ed., *Eliminating Corporal Punishment: The Way Forward to Constructive Child Discipline*. Paris: UNESCO.

————. 2006. "From Mopping Up the Damage to Preventing the Flood: The Role of Social Policy in the Prevention of Violence against Children." *Social Policy Journal of New Zealand* 27: 1–17.

European Committee of Social Rights. 2001. "Conclusions XV–2, Volume 1." http://www.humanrights.coe.int/cseweb/GB/index.htm.

Federal Ministry for Family Affairs, Senior Citizens, Women, and Youth, and Federal Ministry of Justice. 2003. *Violence in Upbringing: An Assessment after the Introduction of the Right to a Non-Violent Upbringing*. Berlin: Federal Ministries.

Frehsee, D. 1996. "Violence toward Children in the Family and the Role of Law." In Frehsee, W. Horn, and K.D. Bussman, eds., *Family Violence against Children*. Berlin: de Gruyter.

Gershoff, E.T. 2002. "Corporal Punishment by Parents and Associated Child Behaviors and Experiences: A Meta-analytic and Theoretical Review." *Psychological Bulletin* 128: 539–79.

Grover, S.G. 2003. "Negating the Child's Inclusive Right to Security of the Person: A Charter Analysis of the s. 43 Canadian Criminal Code Defense to Corporal Punishment of a Minor." *Murdoch University Electronic Journal of Law* 10.

McCain, J. 2005. "Torture's Terrible Toll." *Newsweek,* November 21, 34–36.

McGillivray, A. 1998. "He'll Learn It on His Body: Disciplining Childhood in Canadian Law." *International Journal of Children's Rights* 5: 193–242.

McGillivray, A.E., and J.E. Durrant. 2006. "Child Corporal Punishment: Violence, Law, and Rights." In R. Alaggia and C. Vine, eds., *Cruel but Not Unusual: Violence in Canadian Families*. Waterloo: Wilfrid Laurier University Press.

Ministry of Children and Family Affairs. n.d. *UN Special Session on Children: Norway's National Plan of Action*. Oslo: MCFA. http://www.odin.no/bld/english/doc/reports/004021–220008/hov003-bu.html.

Ministry of Health and Social Affairs. 2004. *Strategy to Implement the UN Convention on the Rights of the Child*. Stockholm: MHSA. http://www.sweden.gov.se/content/1/c6/02/38/18/068d0933.pdf.

Stattin, J., H. Janson, I. Klackenberg-Larsson, and D. Magnusson. 1995. "Corporal Punishment in Everyday Life: An Intergenerational Perspective." In J. McCord, ed., *Coercion and Punishment in Long-Term Perspectives*. Cambridge: Cambridge University Press.

Sylvander, L. 2001. *Child Impact Assessments: Swedish Experience of Child Impact Analyses as a Tool for Implementing the UN Convention on the Rights of the Child*. Stockholm: MHSA, Ministry for Foreign Affairs.

Turner, S. 2002. *Something to Cry About: An Argument against Corporal Punishment of Children in Canada*. Waterloo: Wilfrid Laurier University Press.

Vatcher, C.A. 2000. "Corporal Punishment of Children ... The Current Law, the Constitutional Challenge, and Implications for Future Social Work Practice." *OACAS Journal* 44.

Watkinson, A. 2006. "Corporal Punishment and Education: Oh Canada! Spare Us!" In M.M. Casimir, ed., *The Courts, the Charter and the Schools: The Impact of the Charter of Rights and Freedoms on Educational Policy and Practice*. Toronto: University of Toronto Press.

Ziegert, K.A. 1983. "The Swedish Prohibition of Corporal Punishment: A Preliminary Report." *Journal of Marriage and the Family* 45: 917–26.

Child Sexual Abuse and Exploitation
What Progress Has Canada Made?

Anne McGillivray

Introduction: Sex and Rights

Sexual expression in consensual and non-exploitive relationships is a healthy or at least inescapable part of growing up, a matter for the private realm of family and community. When is it a matter for the law? All societies set limits based on age and relationship, but limits vary from culture to culture and across history. The purpose of this chapter is to examine Canada's progress in the legal protection of children from sexual exploitation and abuse, in light of Canada's obligations under the UN Convention on the Rights of the Child (CRC).[1] The CRC combines basic human rights of expression, autonomy, and security of the person with child-specific rights, including security from abuse and exploitation. The product of ten years of deliberation by an international committee, it bears the marks of compromise. The overlap between CRC articles 19 and 34 reflects how difficult it is to define sexual abuse and exploitation, and, in the compromise reference to "unlawful" sexual activity, to set the age of consent.

As Joan Durrant described in the previous chapter, children have the right to be protected from all forms of violence. Article 19 requires that the state "take all appropriate legislative, administrative, social and educational measures to protect the child from all forms of physical or mental violence, injury, or abuse, neglect or negligent treatment, maltreatment or exploitation, including sexual abuse." Measures include "identification, reporting, referral, investigation, treatment and follow-up," and

Anne McGillivray, Faculty of Law, University of Manitoba

judicial involvement "as appropriate." Article 34 requires that the child be protected "from all forms of sexual exploitation and sexual abuse." It calls for "national, bilateral, and multilateral measures to prevent: (a) the inducement or coercion of a child to engage in any unlawful sexual activity; (b) the exploitative use of children in prostitution or other unlawful sexual activity; (c) the exploitative use of children in pornographic performances and materials."

To abuse is to "misuse, wrongly take advantage of or maltreat, injure, esp. repeatedly." This usage dates from the sixteenth century, according to the Shorter Oxford. Child abuse is the "severe maltreatment of a child, esp. by beating or neglect or sexual assault." Abuse implies both a familial or institutional context and a continuing pattern of conduct. To exploit is to "utilize for one's own ends, take advantage of." UNICEF defines sexual exploitation as "sexual abuse by the adult and remuneration in cash or kind to the child or a third person"; in this way the child is treated both "as a sexual object and as a commercial object."[2] The Manitoba Strategy on Sexual Exploitation calls it "coercing, luring or engaging a child, under the age of 18, into a sexual act, and involvement in the sex trade or pornography, with or without the child's consent, in exchange for money, drugs, shelter, food, protection or other necessities."[3] Exploitation adds a commercial dimension to abuse.

Protection rights limit basic human rights of expression and association and must be justified. Where the lines of sexual protection are set is highly controversial. Canadian law reform over the past twenty years has been more active in this area than in any other area of child protection. We agree that young children should be protected from all forms of sexual activity (but what about the masturbation panics of earlier centuries?). We agree that children should be protected from sexual exploitation (but what about a child of the age of consent engaging in legal prostitution?) and from inappropriate sexual conduct (but why is the heterosexual child privileged over the homosexual child?). At what age is a child capable of real, informed consent? What circumstances peculiar to the child vitiate consent? Is child pornography harmful because real children are harmed in its making, or because it normalizes illicit sex with children even if no real children are depicted? Canada has had the moral obligation and legal power to prosecute child sexual offences committed by Canadians on foreign soil for well over a decade, yet only one prosecution has succeeded. Why? Child sexual abuse and exploitation are the province of federal criminal law and provincial child protection agencies, both of which have had the power since the late nineteenth century to place children at risk in state custody. Cases may come before both and be dealt with by either. New technologies have opened new ways to exploit children, and meanwhile, child prostitution, sex tourism, and pornography are increasingly appearing on rights agendas.

In its first report to the CRC Committee (1994), Canada set out its Criminal Code provisions for child sexual abuse and assault.[4] In its second report (2003), Canada noted that "the Convention has been specifically considered in legislative developments in the areas of child prostitution, child sex tourism, criminal harassment and female genital mutilation."[5] The preamble to the Protection of Children and Other Vulnerable Persons Act of 2005 (hereafter "Bill C-2"), proclaimed in force on November 1, 2005, and January 2, 2005, cites the CRC and the Optional Protocol: "Whereas the Parliament of Canada has grave concerns regarding the vulnerability of children to all forms of exploitation, including child pornography, sexual exploitation, abuse and neglect; whereas Canada, by ratifying the United Nations Convention on the Rights of the Child, as undertaken to protect children from all forms of sexual exploitation and sexual abuse, and has obligations as a signatory to the Optional Protocol to the Convention on the Rights of the Child on the sale of children, child prostitution and child pornography ... "

The act created the offences of exploiting a child between ages fourteen and eighteen, and voyeurism; it also redefined child pornography, increased sentences, and broadened the availability of testimonial aids for victims. The new exploitation offence was the Liberal government's answer to the question of whether the age of consent should be raised from fourteen to sixteen. The present Conservative government tabled Bill C-22 on July 2005, raising the age of consent to sixteen. However, the effectiveness of this latter bill has yet to be tested in the courts.

Before examining these latest measures in what may be the most active area of reform in criminal law, I consider the number of child victims and the law predating the CRC (including a brief history of marriage, incest, rape, and sodomy), as well as the Badgley Report and Bill C-15 (1988). I then turn to post-CRC reforms in the areas of prostitution, sex tourism, pornography, Internet luring and voyeurism, and witnesses and offenders. I conclude with some thoughts about Bill C-22 and the status of children. Criminal Code provisions are referenced in parentheses.

How Many Children?

The incident-based Uniform Crime Reporting Survey collects data from 122 police services in nine provinces, accounting for 61 percent of reported crimes.[6] In 2003, children were victims of two in ten violent crimes and six in ten sexual assaults (9,352 of 15,319). Sexual assault reports taper off after age thirteen. Eight in ten sexual assault victims are girls. Almost half the female victims of sexual assault are under ten, two in ten are eleven to thirteen, and three in ten are fourteen to seventeen. Sexual assaults are the most likely crimes against girls and the least likely against boys. The assailant was a stranger in only 5 percent of cases. In the rest, all but 2 percent were male relatives and seven in ten were fathers or brothers.

Some cases go directly to child protection agencies without police involvement. Police may direct cases to agencies without charging, or lay charges without agency involvement.[7] The 2003 Canadian Incidence Study of Reported Child Abuse and Neglect found that only three out of one hundred (2,935) substantiated child protection cases involved sexual abuse, down from (an already low) nine out of one hundred in 1998.[8] Girls were victims in more than six in ten cases. In seven in ten cases, victims were between eight and fifteen years old.

Reported cases are the tip of the iceberg. The 1999 General Social Survey found that almost nine in ten sexual assaults against children between fifteen and seventeen were not reported, compared to seven out of ten physical assaults.[9] Children are screened from view by family privacy, political powerlessness, and lack of knowledge; the situation is worse for younger children, whose parents are their gatekeepers and who may not know that what is being done to them is a crime. Underreporting is the norm. The 1997 Ontario Supplement, a general population survey, found that one in eight girls and one in twenty-three boys is sexually abused, compared to one in three boys and one in five girls.[10] Girls are three times more likely than boys to be sexually abused (12.8 percent of girls to 4.3 percent of boys). More girls are severely sexually abused (11.1 percent) than boys (3.9 percent). Rates of reported abuse were steady between 1998 and 2003, which suggests that either abuse or reporting is down. Research on child prostitution is sorely lacking.

The cost of violence against children in 1998 was $15.7 billion, of which 13 percent was paid by the state for police, courts, legal aid, and special education services and 15 percent by victims for counselling and medical care. The remaining costs, in lost employment opportunities, fell on both victims and the state.

Marriage, Incest, Rape, and Sodomy

Consent vitiates crime except where consent is unlawful or unlawfully obtained. The age at which a girl can consent to sexual activity and a boy and a girl to marriage varies widely with history, social status, and culture. In England around the twelfth century, for example, an upper-class girl could be betrothed at three and married at twelve. Generally, the age of marriage coincided with menarche.[11] On reaching the age of consent (seven), the child with paternal consent could reject the marriage. By 1315, church courts were supreme in matters of fornication, marriage, adultery, and bastardry, while the law courts were concerned with temporal effects such as damages for a lost marriage.[12] At present in Canada, the age of marriage with parental consent is sixteen, except in Nunavut and the Northwest Territories, where it is fifteen.[13]

Incest, historically, was not about intercourse but about marriage within a forbidden range of relationships. Sexual intercourse within incestuous degrees of relationship but outside marriage was not incest but adultery or fornication. A 1215 act, for example, prohibited the marriage of those closer than fourth cousins, and a 1533 act forbade marriage to a deceased wife's sister.[14] After 1669, first cousins could marry but marriage to any in-law was prohibited. Punishment was left to the church courts until 1650, when—with other offences against morality—it became subject to the law courts and the death penalty. With the restoration of the monarchy, control returned to the church. England's 1908 Punishment of Incest Act made incest a crime and removed the ban on marriage with a sister-in-law. Incest was included in Canada's 1892 Criminal Code (s. 155), which criminalized sexual intercourse with a parent, grandparent, sibling, child, or grandchild. The code exempts those under "restraint, duress or fear," implicitly including children. The Canadian Law Reform Commission recommended repeal on grounds of desuetude, but withdrew the recommendation when the 1984 Badgley Report[15] showed that police relied on the offence in prosecuting child sex crimes.[16]

At one time, the age of consent outside of marriage was nine or ten. Despite a 1576 act raising the age to twelve,[17] the courts continued to recognize younger ages. The harm being addressed was not to the child but to the proprietary rights of the father in a daughter's chastity. Focus on (moral) harm to the child began to come to the fore in nineteenth-century movements against cruelty to children and the "white slave trade" of child prostitution. This crusade was led by feminist Josephine Butler and investigative journalist W.T. Stead.[18] Prosecution remained a problem, however.[19] The age of consent was raised to thirteen in the 1875 English Offences Against the Person Act and to 16 in the 1885 Criminal Law Amendment Act, confirmed in the 2003 act. The 1885 act introduced the offence of gross indecency between males, thus criminalizing private homosexual acts. It was under this law that Oscar Wilde was sentenced to two years' hard labour for his use of underage and under-class "rent-boys." Gross indecency (now "indecent acts") was included in the 1892 Canadian Criminal Code (s. 173) to prosecute offences not caught by rape, sexual intercourse with girls, sodomy, or incest.

The crime of rape was defined as non-consensual sexual intercourse consisting of penile penetration of the vagina of a woman not married to the accused. Marriage gave a husband absolute access to the body of the wife under the doctrine of coverture, which made man and wife legally one, that one being the man. Distrust of women and girls was reflected in judge-made requirements that the complaint be recent, that it be corroborated, and that the victim's sexual reputation be examined; all these acted as deterrents to complaint. The evidence of young children was freely taken in the criminal courts until the arrival of lawyers in the late eighteenth century. Sworn evidence could be taken if the child knew the Christian catechism. Children required adults to prosecute on their behalf, but the office of the public prosecutor was not fully established until the nineteenth century. For much of history, relief for a child abused or exploited by an adult with legal custody was unavailable. Civil courts were reluctant to interfere with the father's ownership rights—later called "custody" or "family privacy"—until the late nineteenth century, when child protection legislation permitted apprehension of abused children and courts began to assert their parens patriae jurisdiction in abuse cases.[20] A major deterrent to prosecution was the ruin of reputation of both accuser and accused. Penalties ranging from whipping to life imprisonment further raised the stakes. Sons of the English rich were often banished to British colonies as remittance men, receiving an allowance and prosecutorial immunity on condition that they not return.

The Canadian Criminal Code set out the offences of sexual intercourse with a stepdaughter, foster daughter, or female ward, with a female under fourteen, with a female under age sixteen "of previously chaste character," and with a female employee under twenty-one. These were meant to protect girls outside paternal control as wards, domestic servants, and workers. Collectively called "statutory rape," the laws protected only girls, prosecuted only males, and permitted no defence of consent or mistake of fact. Girls were popularly known as "jail bait" seducers of innocent men. The laws were struck with the enactment of Bill C-15 (below).

Sodomy was illegal in Canada and Britain until the 1960s. Queen Victoria refused to include female same-sex relations in the 1885 Criminal Law Amendment Act (above). Homosexuality was decriminalized in England in 1967 in England. Canada followed suit in 1969, when Trudeau famously declared that "the state has no place in the bedrooms of the nation." Even so, the Criminal Code (s. 159) prohibits anal intercourse except between spouses and consenting adults over eighteen. Boys are reluctant to report sexual violation by males for fear of being labelled gay, and by females, as this supposedly is a desirable induction into manhood.

The penalty for sexually using girls was borne by the child herself. Loss of chastity and pregnancy out of wedlock meant loss of employment, marriage, and social status, and the resulting child was legally branded a bastard. Justification for laws controlling sexuality shifted over time from protecting paternal interests in a daughter's chastity (seen in tort suits for conversion of interest by fathers against lovers or unapproved husbands), to morality under protestant reform movements, to curtailing male vice, to preventing disease and teen pregnancy. In 1985, for example, the Ontario Provincial Court ruled that the offence of intercourse with a girl under fourteen did not offend the equality provisions of the Charter because the "medical hazard" of intercourse is borne by girls.[21] That sexually abusing or exploiting a child is a profound breach of social trust, and that bodily integrity is a right of the child, are very new ideas.

Badgley, Bill C-15, and Beyond

Nineteenth-century child-saving movements raised the profile of sexual abuse and exploitation. Freudian theory inspired a focus on family healing as well as a rejection of the claims of abused girls in the professional social work of the twentieth century, reducing sexual abuse to an obscure category of neglect.[22] The "new" social work rejected the criminal focus of late-nineteenth-century reformers. The sex offender became the mythical stranger, not the father he so often turned out to be, property of psychiatry and not the law. Sexual abuse was pushed back into secrecy. Child prostitution became a matter of choice, not exploitation. Rights movements of the 1960s challenged the dominance of professional discourse over knowledge and law. Feminist consciousness-raising sessions in the 1970s uncovered the prevalence and damage of sexual abuse in the closed institutions of childhood and family. As the sexual use of children is "always" wrong (and therefore politically right), it has now usurped all other areas of child protection in criminal law reform.

Just as women came to dominate the nascent sociology of the later nineteenth century and the social work profession born from it, so have women now begun to numerically equal men in the legal profession; this has brought a feminist consciousness to law and legal practice. Social work has shifted from family therapy to victim protection. Beginning in the early 1980s, police involvement increased and police response to child victims improved to the point that Badgley (below) credited police as most likely to believe the child. At the same time, reporting rates tripled and criminal charges were laid in up to half of cases, many of them pushed into court by female prosecutors.

Statutory rape was doomed by the 1982 Charter of Rights and Freedoms and the equality provisions proclaimed in 1985, and by new information about sexual abuse and exploitation that showed the criminal law's lack of fit. Rape and its marital exemption were dropped in 1983, replaced by a three-tiered sexual assault provision patterned on newly reformed physical assault provisions. Rape, it was argued, "is primarily an act of violence, not passion; an assault with sex as the weapon,"[23] although some judges expressed regret for the loss of the emotionally charged word "rape." Recent complaint and corroboration requirements were abolished, and "rape shield" laws were enacted to protect victims' reputations (ss. 274–276). This was to be accompanied by reform to archaic child sex laws, as announced by Canada during the 1979 Year of the Child.

The Committee on Sexual Offences Against Children and Youth, headed by Robin Badgley, began its work three years later.[24] The committee heard from police, social workers, child protection groups, and medical practitioners across Canada. The hearings fanned public awareness and system response.[25] Bill C-15 (1988) can be seen as an effect of criminalizing abuse, rather than the cause. Bill C-15 created child-specific, gender-neutral offences that did not require penile penetration—sexual interference, invitation to sexual touching, sexual exploitation (ss. 150–153). If reasonable efforts had been made to find out the age of the victim, then mistake of fact would acquit—statutory rape was gone. Statutory limitation periods were abolished, leading to a flood of "historical" cases coming before the courts. The reforms were controversial. They encouraged lying girls to lie. They were a paternalistic intervention into girls' lives. They submitted abused children to the further abuse of the criminal process by making the child relive the abuse and by exploiting the child's testimonial frailty. Key proposals of the Badgley Committee were not implemented.

Responsibility for child abuse shifted from Justice Canada to Health Canada. Special advisor Rix Rogers's 1990 checklist of the "long-range direction of federal initiatives regarding child sexual abuse"[26] included recommendations of the Badgley Report[27] and the Fraser Report[28] on child prostitution and pornography, as well as Bill C-15. Rogers concluded, perhaps predictably, that "long-term prevention of child sexual abuse will require the continued commitment and involvement of all members of society."

Conditions of consent were clarified in 1992 Criminal Code reforms (s. 273). Consent must be voluntary; it cannot be given by the words or acts of a third party; and the victim must be capable of consent legally, physically, and mentally. Consent cannot be given to a person in a position of trust (dependency), power, or authority. Consent can be refused by words or by conduct and can be withdrawn at any time. As children (and adults) with a physical or mental disability are frequent targets of sexual exploitation and as consent is compromised by disability, the Criminal Code (s. 153.1) was amended in 1998 to prohibit sexual exploitation of the disabled regardless of age. Yet myths about "jail bait" abound in the courts. In 1997, three incidents of sexual intercourse between a twenty-nine-year-old man and a twelve-year-old girl resulted in a conditional sentence of nine months.[29] Justice Twaddle for the Manitoba Court of Appeal stated that "the girl, of course, could not consent in the legal sense, but nonetheless was a willing participant."[30] "She was apparently more sophisticated than many of her age and was performing many household tasks including baby-sitting the defendant's children. The defendant and his wife were at the time somewhat estranged. The relationship which developed was entirely inappropriate and criminal, but the circumstances do distinguish the case from those in which a child has been interfered with by force or deception." After national headlines decrying "the mature babysitter case" and complaints to the Canadian Judicial Council, Justice Twaddle wrote a public letter of apology.

The consent provisions were challenged in 1999 by Steve Ewanchuk, a carpenter who assaulted a seventeen-year-old girl during a job interview despite her repeated requests that he stop.[31] His acts were "more hormonal than criminal," she did not enter his office trailer "in a bonnet and crinoline," she had a boyfriend and a baby, and a slap to the face or knee to the groin ought to have been her response, wrote Justice McClung for the Alberta Court of Appeal. The Supreme Court of Canada ruled that consent to sexual activity can never be implied, that no means no, and that rape myths still dogging the law of consent must be banished.

Badgley recommended that anal sex be reserved for those over eighteen on the murky ground that sexual orientation is not established until adulthood. Anal intercourse (formerly, sodomy) provisions were left standing. The law was struck down on Charter equality grounds by the Ontario[32] and Quebec[33] Courts of Appeal. Also, provincial courts in almost every province legalized consent at fourteen, and subject to other consent provisions. Yet Parliament has not struck down the criminal provision, nor did Bill C-2 (2006) and Bill C-22 (2006) address it.

Canada's regime is unique in recognizing graduated age provisions based on physical and social development and cognitive ability. This reflects earlier law but is tailored to the harms recognized by the Badgley and others. Children of twelve can consent to sexual acts with those not more than two years older (s. 153). Children of fourteen can consent to sex with any person, except where the person is in a position of trust or authority or the relationship is one of dependency. What constitutes such a relationship is a question of fact and of the accused person's understanding, and this has led to a bewildering array of cases. Bill C-2 left the age of consent standing, and instead expanded the age range and definition of child sexual exploitation, at the same time increasing the possible sentence. The Criminal Code (s. 150.1, s. 153) now states that children under eighteen cannot consent to a sexually exploitive relationship. Exploitation can be inferred from the nature and circumstances of the relationship, including the age of the child, the difference in age between victim and offender, the evolution of the relationship, and the degree of control or influence exerted over the victim.

Prostitution

Prostitution is legal. Criminal law is aimed at the mischief attending prostitution—communication for the purpose of prostitution, living off the avails, keeping bawdy houses, corrupting minors, and so on. Child prostitution is controversial. If a child can consent to sex at fourteen, then why should the child not consent to commercial sex? Is it a choice or a crime, and whose crime is it? Badgley thought it might be necessary to criminalize child prostitutes, locking them up to seal them from life of prostitution.[34] Bill C-15 (1988) linked criminal procurement to sexual exploitation, negating consent. Bill C-27 (1997) created two prostitution-related offences (Criminal Code s. 212.1). Aggravated procurement—forcing a child under eighteen into prostitution for personal profit by threats, violence, intimidation, or coercion—is punishable by a sentence of five to fourteen years. Obtaining or attempting to obtain sex from a person whom the accused believes to be under eighteen or who is represented as under eighteen is punishable by a sentence of up to five years. Bill C-27 also provided for testimonial supports and publication bans. To forestall Charter problems, the phrase "attempts to obtain" was replaced by "communicates ... for the purpose of obtaining" by Bill C-51 (1999).

A series of conferences highlighted commercial sexual exploitation. The 1996 World Congress Against the Sexual Exploitation of Children, in Stockholm, at which Canada affirmed its commitment and signed the CRC Protocol, was followed by a second congress in Yokohama in 2001. The 1998 conference Out from the Shadows: International Summit of Sexually Exploited Youth, held in Victoria, B.C., inspired by Stockholm, included fifty-four "experiential" youth delegates from Canada, the United States, and Latin America. At the 2001 United Nations Special Session on Children, rescheduled for 2002 because of the New York terrorist attacks, Canada successfully argued for the inclusion of rights language in the outcome document "A World Fit for Children." That document calls for countries to protect children from abuse, exploitation, and violence. Canadian premiers at the 1999 Quebec First Ministers Conference agreed to harmonize the provinces' child-protection responses to child prostitution.

Some provinces have since enacted special legislation. Alberta's 1999 Protection of Children Involved in Prostitution Act (discussed further by Sonja Grover in chapter 13), for example, mandates protective apprehension of children for up to three days, with judicial extension for longer periods and fines for pimps and johns of up to $25,000.[35] Manitoba, for its part, has developed a multifaceted response that includes amended child protection legislation, increased fines for johns and pimps (up to $50,000), and voluntary treatment and safe house programs.[36]

The problem is severe. A 1996 Alberta Task Force found that at least one in ten street prostitutes is a child, who entered the trade at an average age of fifteen. Eight of ten were sexually abused in a family context. According to Jane Runner of Manitoba ChildFind, ten to fifteen children between eight and fourteen are on Winnipeg streets every night, yet more than nine in ten police arrests are of women and children, not their clients.[37] Car stalkers approach young children playing in their yards, offering them $5 to pull up their shirts, more for sexual touching. Poor Aboriginal children are targeted. Enforcement problems include finding the children and getting their evidence before the courts. Only two charges for "picking up" minors have been laid in Winnipeg in the past ten years. Professor Susan Strega suggests that police are reluctant to charge the middle-class married men who are the majority of johns.[38] In 2005 a joint force of social workers and police uncovered a child prostitution ring run by two women, involving more than thirty girls and boys between twelve and sixteen, who were being compelled to perform sexual acts with clients.[39] Charges of living off the avails of prostitution, corrupting children, and procuring children for the purposes of prostitution were laid. Runner suggests that more than one hundred children may have been involved.

Child Sex Tourism

The South Asian sex playground established by the U.S. military for troops on leave during the Vietnam War led to a lucrative international child sex trade after the troops went home. Organized sex tours were shut down in their countries of origin, but foreign exploitation continues. If criminal consequences for exploiting children elsewhere are unlikely, can Canada prosecute its own citizens? Jurisdiction is based on territory, but the Criminal Code allows exceptions (s. 6.2). The Criminal Code (s. 273.3) was amended in 1993 to criminalize taking a child out of Canada in order to commit a sexual act illegal in Canada if the country in which the act occurred so requested. Also, commercial child prostitution could be prosecuted without a request. Bill C-27 (1997) amended the Criminal Code (s. 7) to deem acts of sexual abuse and exploitation by Canadians overseas to be acts committed in Canada. The Bill also reinforced prohibitions against female genital mutilation, criminal harassment, and child prostitution. The CRC is cited in the preamble. In 2001, Canada signed the CRC Optional Protocol on child prostitution and pornography.[40] Bill C-15A (2002) eliminated the requirement that the foreign country request prosecution. This eliminated the distinction between commercial and "non-commercial" exploitation. Bill C-49 (2005) established a framework for prosecuting all forms of trafficking in people.

The sole Canadian conviction to date—that of Don Bakker in May 2005—was by way of a guilty plea.[41] Following his arrest for sexually assaulting three Vancouver sex-trade workers, police found self-made videotapes showing Bakker engaged in sex acts with seven Cambodian girls aged seven to twelve. In sentencing him to five years concurrent for each of seven counts of invitation to sexual touching (fellatio), the court stated: "The constitutionality of the tourist sex laws is not a foregone conclusion, and it has not been examined by any court. In those circumstances, the fact of the guilty plea is meaningful, because just the legal issues might have kept this case going before the courts for some considerable period of time."

Pornography, Internet Luring, and Voyeurism

Unless it is obscene, pornography is legal. Defining obscenity has occupied the courts for centuries. The tension is between freedom of expression and the cultural value of art and literature (famously including the now unobjectionable *Ulysses* and *Lady Chatterley's Lover*) and the protection of public morality. The Fraser Report (1983)[42] and the Badgley Report (1984)[43] justified prohibiting child pornography on the basis of the harm done to real children used in its making. The Supreme Court ruled in 1992 that depictions of explicit sex that are not violent, dehumanizing, or degrading are obscene only if children are employed in its production.[44] The Criminal Code was amended in 1993 (s. 163.1) to prohibit visual or written materials, however produced, that show "a person who is or is depicted as being under the age of eighteen years and is engaged or is depicted as engaged in explicit sexual activity," or that depicts for a sexual purpose the sexual organ or anus of a child, or that advocates or counsels sexual activity with a person under eighteen, unless the material has an educational, scientific, or medical purpose or "artistic merit." The CRC prohibits "the exploitative use of children in pornographic performances and materials." The CRC Optional Protocol prohibits "any representation, by whatever means, of a child engaged in real or simulated explicit sexual activities or any representation of the sexual parts of a child for primarily sexual purposes."

The meaning of "artistic merit" was challenged in 2001 by Robin Sharpe. The Supreme Court ruled that artistic merit, however slight, should be interpreted liberally to protect freedom of expression.[45] The possession of artistic materials (poems, drawings, stories) by their maker for his or her exclusive use, and of visual records made for private use by consenting couples that do not show illegal sexual activity, is not criminal. Sharpe's acquittal on retrial with respect to his possession of homemade stories[46] left a bitter taste for many. That the artistic merit applied not only to imaginary drawings but also to materials depicting real children under s. 163.1 was "a blinding stupidity."[47] Real children are hurt, however artful the representation.

The controversy following *Sharpe* led to two Bill C-2 (2006) reforms. First, "artistic merit" was replaced with "legitimate purpose" (which replaced "public good" in an earlier version, although "public good" is a defence to the new voyeurism offence [below] and to corrupting morals [s. 163]). The Criminal Code now states: "No person shall be convicted of an offence under this section if the act that is alleged to constitute the offence (a) has a *legitimate purpose* related to the administration of justice or to science, medicine, education or art; and (b) *does not pose an undue risk of harm* to persons under the age of eighteen years" (emphasis added). Second, it is now illegal to possess materials "whose dominant characteristic is the depiction, for a sexual purpose, of [unlawful] sexual activity against a person under the age of eighteen years" even though no child was used in the making. Advocating or counselling unlawful sex is still an offence, but it is no longer an element of the offence of possession. What is a legitimate purpose when it comes to artistic expression will fuel future Charter challenges. Condemnation, as Professor Bruce Ryder notes, should focus on materials that harm real children in their making or that constitute hate propaganda by advocating or counselling sexual violations of children.[48]

Prosecution rates for possessing and distributing child pornography increased from 20 cases in 1998 to 159 in 2003; most of them resulted in a conditional sentence.[49] When Antonio Marinelli took his computer to a Winnipeg repair shop in 1997, technicians found one pornographic image featuring a child. Police investigation turned up 3,600 obscene digital images, some depicting sex with children as young as five. Many had been distributed to other users. In 2005, after eight years and sixty adjournments, Marinelli pleaded guilty to possession of child pornography and received a conditional sentence of two years.[50] He must remain under curfew, permit searches of his house, not contact children under eighteen, and perform one hundred hours of community service. Bill C-2 introduced a mandatory minimum prison sentence of fourteen days for viewing and ninety days for publishing or distributing; this sentence was applied by Winnipeg courts within days of its proclamation. "Investigators say it is unlikely hardcore users will be deterred but say those on the 'fringe' might think twice about downloading images if it means time behind bars."[51] In a 2005 Winnipeg case, videotapes of sexual acts involving at least eight young victims were found.[52] The accused was charged with sexual assault, sexual interference, possessing child pornography, and supplying a controlled substance to a minor.

There is a virtual arms race between law enforcement and digital technologies relating to Internet distribution, Web, spy, and digital cameras, chat rooms for child luring, distribution sites, and self-made and self-distributed child pornography.[53] Bill C-15A (2002) amended the Criminal Code to prohibit use of the Internet to lure or exploit children for sexual purposes (s. 172) or to send, make available, export, or access child pornography (s. 163). Downloading images is not required: knowingly viewing such images is sufficient. The court can order deletion of pornographic materials, seize computers and disks, prohibit Internet access, and issue peace bonds. Enforcement also has taken new forms. Cybertip.ca, pioneered in Manitoba in 2002, tracks child pornography, prostitution, luring, and sex tourism in order to enhance police investigations and shut down offending websites. As of 2004, 1,200 tips had been sent in, with pornography accounting for almost nine of ten, luring one of ten, and the remainder prostitution and sex tourism. Since 2002, twenty-three arrests have been made and 1,700 websites removed.[54] The Manitoba Integrated Child Exploitation Unit, also set up in 2002, is staffed by ten full-time investigators and relies on special prosecutors to deal with the "booming caseloads" of child pornography—up to thirty cases at a time.[55] The typical offender is white, middle aged, and employed. Rating systems ("naked posing," "genital close-up," etc.) assist prosecution.[56] Showing actual images to the court increased the Manitoba conviction rate to 90 percent. Other provinces are following suit. In 2005, cybertip.ca became a national website. The 2004 National Strategy to Protect Children from Sexual Exploitation relies on cybertip.ca and SchoolNet.ca. Investigations are handled through the RCMP National Child Exploitation Coordination Centre.

"Peeping Tom-ism," named for the mythical peasant who spied on Lady Godiva's nude ride for peasant rights in eleventh-century Coventry, may have been an offence at English common law. If so, it was not included in the Criminal Code. The equivalent offence was prowling by night, now trespassing by night (s. 177). Bill C-2 created the offence of voyeurism (s. 162). Voyeurism is observing or visually recording for a sexual purpose, in circumstances where there is a reasonable expectation of privacy, a person who is (or is reasonably expected to be) nude, or whose genitals, anus, or breasts (if female) are exposed, or who is engaged in explicit sexual activity. "No person shall be convicted of an offence under this section if the acts that are alleged to constitute the offence serve the public good and do not extend beyond what serves the public good."

The Child Witness

The criminal justice system—laws, rules of evidence, policing, prosecution, the courtroom, the judge—was not set up with children in mind. Judicial developments in the eighteenth and early nineteenth centuries effectively barred children's testimony through presumptions of incapacity and requirements for corroboration. Reforms beginning with Bill C-15 (1988) have been aimed at ensuring the availability and reliability of children's evidence by supporting children who are testifying. Bill C-15 permitted the use of screening devices to shield the child witness from the accused and the admission of the child's videotaped statement, in lieu of examination in chief (s. 715). As the child must still attend court, accept the statement, and be cross-examined, this fell short of the Badgley Report recommendations that would have made the child's courtroom testimony unnecessary.[57] Bill C-15 abolished the requirement that the child's evidence be corroborated in a material way; it also amended the Canada Evidence Act (s.16) to eliminate judicial examination of the child's understanding of Christianity as a prerequisite for taking the oath. Children under fourteen could make a solemn declaration or testify on promise to tell the truth if they could show that they understood the nature of a promise and could communicate the evidence. In 1990 the Supreme Court clarified common-law rules of evidence to recognize the unique character of children's evidence;[58] in 1993 it affirmed the constitutionality of videotaped evidence.[59]

Problems remained. Videotapes raised more problems than they solved, child-friendly courtrooms were more rare and less friendly than hoped, the self-represented accused could question the victim, there were violations of privacy owing to the narrowness of publication bans, the Canada

Evidence Act retained the presumption of incapacity in children under fourteen, and judges imposed adult standards in examinations for capacity, with sometimes ludicrous results. Also, the provisions were available only to child victims of sex crimes. Other children testifying in the case, and child victims of other crimes, were excluded from Bill C-15's provisions.

Bill C-2 amended the Canada Evidence Act and the Criminal Code (s. 486) to permit the child to testify on promising to tell the truth. The capacity of children under fourteen is presumed. No inquiry can be made into capacity. The sole requirement is the ability to understand and answer questions. Evidence thus taken has the same weight as if under oath. This applies to any child witness in any criminal proceeding. Other reforms include bans on electronic and Internet transmission where a publication ban is in place. The public can be excluded from any proceeding. The accused may not cross-examine the victim. A support person can accompany a witness on the stand.

Witnesses can refuse these protections, as did a twenty-three-year-old woman in a Winnipeg case heard in 2006.[60] Sexually abused from the age of eleven, she rejected the judge's offer of protection and chose to undergo cross-examination by her self-represented father in a jury trial. The cross-examination reads as follows: "*Q*: You paint this picture here of this cowering little girl waiting for her big bad daddy to come home and abuse her. Well, I remember coming home and you opening the door and hearing 'Daddy's home, daddy's home' as you cuddled me and welcomed me home. Am I lying when I say that? *A*: I was happy to see you. You were my dad. *Q*: I'm not here to call you a liar. I'm saying you're out of your mind. *A*: All I know is you said you loved me. That's why you were doing it." The accused was convicted.

The Offender

Reforms may benefit children even where children are not the target. Post-CRC reforms to sentencing, the laws of intoxication, DNA warrants and registries, sex offender registries and file flagging, and orders to produce personal records of a complainant have affected those charged with child sexual abuse and exploitation.

The old adage "He who kills drunk shall be hanged sober" was rejected in later criminal law. Extreme intoxication, even if self-induced, was considered to negate the mental element (knowledge, awareness) needed to convict, including for sexual assault. The intoxication defence was narrowed by Bill C-72 (1995). The Criminal Code (s. 33) now states that self-induced intoxication is a marked departure from the ordinary standard of reasonable care and cannot be used as a defence to assault or any other interference with the bodily integrity of another person.

Bill C-104 (1995) enabled judges to issue warrants for collecting DNA samples from suspects in sexual offence and serious violent offence cases. Bill C-3 (2000) set up a national DNA data bank, and Bill C-13 designated Internet luring and child pornography as offences that must be included in the bank. Sex offender registries and criminal record flagging were problematic. Early registries that included names of suspected as well as convicted offenders were shut down on Charter grounds, while records sealed because of passage of time or pardons frustrated police background checks. Bill C-7 (2000) amended the Criminal Records Act to allow sealed and pardoned sex offender files to be flagged for RCMP access. Bill C-16 (2004), the Sex Offender Information Registration Act, was passed, requiring identifying information on sex offenders to be registered in an RCMP national data bank (s. 490).

Bill C-41 (1996) codified sentencing principles and added abuse of the offender's child to the list of justifications for imposing more severe sentences (s. 718). Bill C-2 broadened this to include the abuse of any child. Bill C-2 also imposed mandatory minimum sentences of fourteen days for summary conviction and forty-five days for conviction on indictment (ss. 151 and 152) for sexual interference, invitation to sexual touching, and sexual exploitation. Bill C-45 (1995) permitted holding high-risk offenders who caused death or serious bodily harm for the full duration of sentence, as was done in the case of Karla Homolka. Bill C-55 (1997) amended the Criminal Code (s. 753) to establish the category of long-term offender where a finding of dangerous offender (the designation of Paul Bernardo) is unavailable. If the crime is sexual assault, sexual touching, sexual exploitation, indecent exposure, child pornography, or a related offence, and if there is a pattern of such offending, or if the conduct shows a future risk of "injury, pain or other evil to other persons," a longer sentence and post-sentence supervision of up to ten years are justified. "Fear of sexual offence" was added to the peace bond sections of the code (s. 180), and was used to place post-sentence restrictions on Homolka in June 2005.

The Charter right to a fair trial requires full access to all evidence that may assist the defence. A 1991 Supreme Court decision to admit evidence of prior sexual conduct[61] led to the 1992 amendment of the Criminal Code's rape shield provisions (s. 276). The new rules were challenged on Charter grounds by Bishop Hubert O'Connor in 1995. Charged with the rape of two girls in the 1960s in the B.C. Indian residential school over which he presided as priest and principal, O'Connor demanded that the prosecution give him the school, medical, welfare, and counselling records of his alleged victims, if necessary by legal compulsion of the victims.[62] Bill C-46 (1997) amended the Criminal Code (s. 278) to require that in sexual assault and sexual exploitation cases, requests for disclosure of records in which there is a reasonable expectation of privacy must go through a judicial process to protect victim privacy and prevent fishing expeditions.

Concluding Thoughts

How do we make sense of the remarkable spate of reforms to criminal laws governing the sexual abuse and exploitation of children? Certainly, it shows the passion engendered by the sexual use of children. It shows the difficulty of distinguishing consent from exploitation, rights from protection, love from manipulation, art from obscenity, and law from morality. It shows that reform here is politically easy. No politician is going to vote against a law that purports to protect a child from abusive or exploitive sex. The focus on sex lets us say that we are protecting children's rights even while we avoid the tough rights questions such as poverty, neglect, physical abuse, and correction of children by force. It serves a distractive function. At least we are rid of child-blaming language (jail bait or sophisticated) and stereotypes of sex offenders that belie the reality. Old barriers to prosecution, punishment, and tracking are reduced or altogether gone.

Men have long dominated law, religion, and the production of images of women and children; they have also defined sexual transgression and the conditions of consent in moral terms of purity and corruption since the inception of the common law in the eleventh century and the Roman law that influenced it. Modern reforms reflect a shift from morality-based definitions of harm toward a more child-centred approach, a growing appreciation of children's rights, and a recognition of the role of the CRC. In raising the age of consent from fourteen to sixteen, Bill C-22, introduced in 2006, may signal a return to (legally imposed) morality and a retreat from rights.

Private members' bills raising the age to sixteen with a close-in-age exception of two years did not pass reading, nor was the age raised in the flurry of amendments beginning with Bill C-15 in 1988 and ending, one might have thought, with Bill C-2 and its creation of the new offence of sexually exploiting a child over fourteen. This was Parliament's answer to the question of age. Bill C-22, An Act to amend the Criminal Code (age of protection), introduced in June 2006 by Justice Minister Vic Toewes, re-opened it.[63] The minister told Parliament that raising the age of consent from fourteen to sixteen would "better protect youth against sexual exploitation by adult predators."[64] The "age of consent" would be renamed the "age of protection" as the aim was not to criminalize consensual sexual activity but to protect youth from predators. A child of fourteen or fifteen could consent to sexual activity with a person less than five years older. Other consent provisions would still apply. There would be a time of transition for children already married or in a common-law relationship outside the set limits. Provinces might have to raise the age of marriage. The minister alluded to Internet luring and to the support of Beyond Borders, the Canadian affiliate of ECPAT, to support the bill.[65]

The shift from consent, a question of rights, to the limiting language of protection requires justification.[66] There are no data on whether the present age of consent makes Canada a target destination for Internet luring or sex tourism (as claimed by the minister), nor are there data on whether children of sixteen are more or less capable of consent than children of fourteen. The real question for rights and law is the manipulation of consent, whether it is by superior age or status, or authority, or power over the child, however gained. Despite the minister's claim that Bill C-22 places the onus on adults, the focus is the child and her chastity. The omission of gay youth from the bill, even though courts across Canada have overturned the age restriction, lends support to this reading of Bill C-22.

Moral corruption is no longer a compelling basis for criminal sanctions.[67] The focus of prohibition and reform should be the eradication of conditions that lead to hatred and violence against children. Raising the status of women in domestic and international law led to better social, legal, and political conditions for women than prevailed even twenty-five years ago. Reforming the law of rape and placing domestic assault on a legal par with stranger assault in the early 1980s were key to raising women's status. Until the nineteenth century, both women and children were legally subject to corrective assault by husbands and fathers. Canada retains the anachronistic defence of correction to the physical assault of children, despite the CRC's censure and despite a challenge to the law based on the Charter of Rights and Freedoms and the CRC.[68] In an odd twist, the courts have allowed the defence of correction in sexual assault cases.[69] In 1995, for example, the Alberta Court of Appeal ruled that the bare-bottomed spanking of a twelve-year-old stepdaughter was not sexual assault but physical correction, while other sexual acts such as "suggestive nuzzling and hugging in the chest area" were dismissed as "horseplay."[70] Unless the status of children is similarly raised, sexual exploitation and abuse will continue. Ensuring the right of the child to live free of physical violence will reinforce the right of the child to live free of sexual violence. Parliament is flying on one wing.

Notes

1 United Nations, *Convention on the Rights of the Child* (New York: UN, 1989).
2 UNICEF, World Congress Against Commercial Exploitation of Children, "Declaration and Agenda for Action" (1997), http://www.hartford-hwp.com/archives/28/024.html.
3 Manitoba, "Manitoba Strategy Responding to Children and Youth at Risk of, or Survivors of, Sexual Exploitation" (2004), http://www.gov.mb.ca/fs/childfam/strategy_on_sexual_exploitation.
4 Canada, "Report to the Committee on the Rights of the Child (CRC/C/11/Add.3) to December 31, 1992" (1994), http://www.pch.gc.ca/progs/pdp-hrp/docs/crc/index_e.cfm.
5 Canada, "Report to the Committee on the Rights of the Child (CRC/C/83.Add.6) to December 31 1999" (2003), http:// www.pch.gc.ca/progs/pdp-hrp/docs/crc-2001/index_e.cfm.
6 Statistics Canada, "Children and Youth as Victims of Violent Crime," *Juristat* 25, no. 1 (2003).
7 T. Landau, "Policing the Punishment: Charging Policies under Canada's Corporal Punishment Laws," *International Review of Victimology* 12 (2005): 121–38.
8 N. Trocmé et al., *Canadian Incidence Study of Reported Child Abuse and Neglect—2003*. Major findings. 2005, http://www.phac-aspc.gc.ca/cm-vee/csca-ecve/index.html.
9 Statistics Canada, "Children and Youth."
10 H.L. MacMillan et al., "Prevalence of Child Physical and Sexual Abuse in the Community: Results from the Ontario Health Supplement" *Journal of the American Medical Association* 278 (1997): 131–35.
11 "World Sex Atlas: Growing Up Sexually," pp. 763 et seq. (and see generally), http://www.ipce.info/booksreborn/janssen/atlas/GrowingUpSexually1.pdf.
12 J.H. Baker, *An Introduction to English Legal History,* 4th ed. (Toronto: Butterworths, 2002), pp. 129, 440.
13 This will change if Bill C-22 is enacted; see below.
14 J. Shaffer, "Familial Love, Incest, and Female Desire in Late Eighteenth- and Early Nineteenth-Century British Women's Novels—Critical Essay," *Criticism* (1999), http://www.findarticles.com/p/articles/mi_m2220/is_1_41/ai_56905045.
15 Canada, Badgley Report.
16 A. McGillivray, "Abused Children in the Courts: Adjusting the Scales after Bill C-15" (1990) *Manitoba Law Review:* 549–79.
17 18 Eliz.1 c.7.
18 A. McGillivray, "Child Physical Assault: Law, Equality, and Intervention." (2004) *Manitoba Law Journal* 30: 133–66.
19 K. Stevenson, "Observations on the Law Relating to Sexual Offences: The Historical Scandal of Women's Silence [1994]," *Web Journal of Current Legal Issues* 4 (1999), http://webjcli.ncl.au.uk/1999/issue4/stevenson4.html.
20 McGillivray, "Child Physical Assault: Law, Equality, and Intervention" (2004) 30 *Manitoba Law Journal:* 133–66.

21 *R. v. M.E.D.* 47 C.R. (3d) 382.

22 McGillivray, "Reconstructing Child Abuse: Western Definition and Non-Western Experience," in M.D.A. Freeman and P. Veerman, eds., *The Ideologies of Children's Rights: International Studies in Human Rights* 23 (Dordrecht, Boston, and London: Martinus Nijhoff, 1992), pp. 213–36.

23 M. Carter, "The Corrective Force Defence (Section 43) and Sexual Assault," (2000) 6 *Criminal Law Review:* 35 (citing the Hon. Flora MacDonald).

24 Canada, Badgley Report.

25 McGillivray, "Abused Children in the Courts."

26 R. Rogers, *Reaching for Solutions,* Summary Report of the Special Advisor to the Minister of National Health and Welfare on Child Sexual Abuse in Canada (Ottawa: Health and Welfare Canada, 1990); idem, Status Report on the Federal Response to *Reaching for Solutions* (Ottawa: Health and Welfare Canada, 1993).

27 Canada, Badgley Report.

28 Canada, Special Committee on Pornography and Prostitution, *Pornography and Prostitution in Canada* [Fraser Report] (Ottawa: Minister of Supply and Services, 1985).

29 McGillivray, "*R. v.* Bauder: Seductive Children, Safe Rapists, and Other Justice Tales" (1999) 25 *Manitoba Law Journal:* 359–83.

30 *R. v. Bauder* (unreported) 23 May 1997.

31 *R. v. Ewanchuk,* [1999] 1 S.C.R. 330.

32 *R. v. M.* (1995), 98 C.C.C. 3rd 481.

33 *R. v. Roy* (1998) 125 C.C.C. 3rd 442.

34 Canada, Badgley Report.

35 See J. Koshan, "Alberta (Dis)Advantage: The Protection of Children Involved in Prostitution Act and the Equality Rights of Young Women" (2003) 2 *Journal of Law & Equality*": 210 for a discussion of problems with the Alberta legislation.

36 Telephone interview, Jane Runner, Manitoba Childfind, 1 December 2005.

37 Telephone interview, Professor Susan Strega, University of Manitoba, 30 November 2005.

38 Ibid.

39 B. Owen, "Child-sex Operation Affected 30 Kids, Police Say," *Winnipeg Free Press,* November 2, 2005.

40 United Nations, Optional Protocol to the Convention on the Rights of the Child on the Sale of Children, Child Prostitution, and Child Pornography. New York: UN.

41 *R. v. Bakker* [2005] B.C.J. No. 1577.

42 Canada, Fraser Report.

43 Canada, Badgley Report.

44 *R. v. Butler* [1992] 1 S.C.R. 452.

45 *R. v. Sharpe* [2001] 1 S.C.R. 45.

46 *R. v. Sharpe* [2002] B.C.J. No. 610 (B.C.S.C.). Sharpe's remaining convictions were left standing.

47 B. Ryder, "The Harms of Child Pornography Law" (2003) 36 *University of British Columbia Law Review:* 101–135.

48 Ryder, "The Harms." "Public incitement and willful promotion of hatred against an identifiable group" is prohibited by s. 319 of the Criminal Code.

49 Statistics Canada, "Children and Youth as Victims of Violent Crime."

50 M. McIntyre, "Conditional Sentence Ends Child Porn Case," *Winnipeg Free Press,* November 11, 2005.

51 D. Kuxhaus, "Child Porn Fills Dockets," *Winnipeg Free Press,* December 12, 2005.

52 B. Owen and M. McIntyre, "Police Find Rape Videotapes," *Winnipeg Free Press,* December 16, 2005.

53 For one such story, see K. Eichenwald, "Through His Webcam, Boy Joins Sordid, Online World," *New York Times,* December 20, 2005.

54 http://www.cybertip.ca/en/cybertip.

55 D. Kuxhaus, *Winnipeg Free Press,* "Child Porn Fills Dockets."

56 L. Reynolds, "Just Ordinary Guys, Up on Child Porn Charges," *Winnipeg Free Press,* December 30, 2005.

57 McGillivray, "*R.* v. *Laramee:* Forgetting Children, Forgetting Truth" (1991) 6 *Criminal Reports:* 325–42.

58 *R. v. Khan* [1990] 2 SCR 530; *R.* v. *B.G.* [1990] 2 S.C.R. 3.

59 *R. v. D.O.L.* [1993] 4 S.C.R. 419.

60 M. McIntyre, "Man Convicted of Sexually Abusing Young Daughter," *Winnipeg Free Press,* January 10 and 12, 2006.

61 *R. v. Seaboyer* [1991] 2 S.C.R. 577.

62 *R. v. O'Connor* [1995] 4 S.C.R. 411. O'Connor was convicted on retrial and sentenced to two and one-half years' imprisonment.

63 The bill was before the Justice Committee at the time of writing (November 2006). The text at first reading can be accessed at http://www2.parl.gc.ca/HousePublications/Publication.aspx?Language=E&Parl=39&Ses=1&Mode=1&Pub=Bill&Doc=C-22_1&File=24#1.

64 House of Commons Debates, *Hansard* 141, no. 72, 1st Session, 39th Parliament, October 30, 2006. The minister proposed lowering the age of criminal responsibility from twelve to ten at the August 16, 2006, Canadian Bar Association meeting (and debated this with the author on national television when the minister was justice critic for the Official Opposition). In a speech to the Faculty of Law, University of Manitoba, on November 24, 2006, the minister retreated from this position, stating that lowering the age was the responsibility of provincial justice ministers. Yet under the Constitution, the age of onset of criminal responsibility is solely within the power of the federal Parliament. Attributing incapacity to consent to sex in those under sixteen and, at the same time, capacity to engage in intentional crime in ten-year-olds is contradictory.

65 ECPAT (End Child Prostitution, Child Pornography, and the Trafficking of Children for Sexual Purposes). See D. Butt, "Canada's Age of Consent Still 14! Why the 'Exploitive' Relationship Offence Fails Children," *Beyond Borders Newsletter* no. 7 (2005); D. Matas, "Guarding Our Children," *Beyond Borders Newsletter* no. 9 (2006). Winnipeg lawyer David Matas makes the legally curious point that the kidnapper of two boys aged eleven and fourteen could not be charged with the abuse of the fourteen-year-old "unless it can be established either that Whitmore sexually exploited the child or that the child did

not consent to sex." Kidnapping would bar consent, and there is no consent to anal sex (which, presumably, would be an interest of the chronic pedophilic kidnapper) for another four years.

66 McGillivray, "Why Children Do Have Equal Rights: In Reply to Laura Purdy" (1994) 2 *International Journal of Children's Rights:* 243–58.

67 Ryder, "The Harms."

68 McGillivray, "He'll Learn It on His Body: Disciplining Childhood in Canadian Law" (1998) 5 *International Journal of Children's Rights:* 193–242; "Child Physical Assault"; idem, "Child Corporal Punishment: Violence, Law, and Rights" (with J. Durrant), in R. Alaggia and C. Vine, eds., *Cruel but Not Unusual: Violence in Canadian Families—A Sourcebook of History, Theory, and Practice* (Waterloo: Wilfrid Laurier University Press, 2006), pp. 177–200.

69 Carter, "The Corrective Force Defence."

70 *R. v. M. (W.F.)* (1995) 41 *Criminal Reports* (4th).

Bibliography

Baker, J.H. 2002. *An Introduction to English Legal History,* 4th ed. Toronto: Butterworths, 2002.

Butt, D. 2005. "Canada's Age of Consent Still 14! Why the 'Exploitive' Relationship Offence Fails Children." *Beyond Borders Newsletter,* no. 7.

Canada. 1984. Report of the Committee on Sexual Offences Against Children and Youths [Badgley Report]. Ottawa: Minister of Supply and Services.

———. 1985. Special Committee on Pornography and Prostitution, *Pornography and Prostitution in Canada* [Fraser Report]. Ottawa: Minister of Supply and Services.

———. 1994. Report to the Committee on the Rights of the Child (CRC/C/11/Add.3) to December 31, 1992. http://www.pch.gc.ca/progs/pdp-hrp/docs/crc/index_e.cfm.

———. 2003. Report to the Committee on the Rights of the Child (CRC/C/83.Add.6) to December 31, 1999. http://www.pch.gc.ca/progs/pdp-hrp/docs/crc/index_e.cfm.

Canada, House of Commons Debates. 2006. *Hansard* 141, no. 72, 1st Session, 39th Parliament, October 30.

Carter, M. 2000. "The Corrective Force Defence (Section 43) and Sexual Assault." 6 *Criminal Law Review:* 35.

Eichenwald, K. "Through His Webcam, Boy Joins Sordid, Online World" *New York Times,* December 20, 2005.

Koshan, J. 2003. "Alberta (Dis)Advantage: The Protection of Children Involved in Prostitution Act and the Equality Rights of Young Women." 2 *Journal of Law and Equality:* 210.

Kuxhaus, D. 2005. "Child Porn Fills Dockets." *Winnipeg Free Press*, December 12.

Landau, T. 2005. "Policing the Punishment: Charging Policies under Canada's Corporal Punishment Laws." *International Review of Victimology* 12: 121–38.

MacMillan, H.L., et al. 1997. "Prevalence of Child Physical and Sexual Abuse in the Community: Results from the Ontario Health Supplement." *Journal of the American Medical Association* 278: 131–35.

Manitoba. 2004. "Manitoba Strategy Responding to Children and Youth at Risk of, or Survivors of, Sexual Exploitation." http://www.gov.mb.ca/fs/childfam/strategy_on_sexual_exploitation.

Matas, D. 2006. "Guarding Our Children." *Beyond Borders Newsletter,* no. 9.

McGillivray, A. 1990. "Abused Children in the Courts: Adjusting the Scales after Bill C-15." 19 *Manitoba Law Journal Annual Survey of Manitoba Law*: 549–79.

———. 1991. "*R. v. Laramee:* Forgetting Children, Forgetting Truth." 6 *Criminal Reports:* 325–42.

———. 1992. "Reconstructing Child Abuse: Western Definition and Non-Western Experience." In M.D.A. Freeman and P. Veerman, eds., *The Ideologies of Children's Rights: International Studies in Human Rights* 23: 213–36. Dordrecht, Boston, and London: Martinus Nijhoff.

———. 1994. "Why Children Do Have Equal Rights: In Reply to Laura Purdy." 2 *International Journal of Children's Rights:* 243–58.

———. 1998. "He'll Learn It on His Body: Disciplining Childhood in Canadian Law." 5 *International Journal of Children's Rights:* 193–242.

———. 1999. "*R. v. Bauder:* Seductive Children, Safe Rapists, and Other Justice Tales." 25 *Manitoba Law Journal:* 359–83.

———. 2004. "Child Physical Assault: Law, Equality, and Intervention." 30 *Manitoba Law Journal:* 133–66.

———. 2006. "Child Corporal Punishment: Violence, Law, and Rights" (with Joan Durrant). In R. Alaggia and C. Vine, eds., *Cruel but Not Unusual: Violence in Canadian Families—A Sourcebook of History, Theory, and Practice.* Waterloo: Wilfrid Laurier University Press.

McIntyre, M. 2005. "Conditional Sentence Ends Child Porn Case." *Winnipeg Free Press,* November 11.

———. 2005. "Man Convicted of Sexually Abusing Young Daughter." *Winnipeg Free Press,* January 10 and 12.

Owen, B. 2005. "Child-Sex Operation Affected 30 Kids, Police Say." *Winnipeg Free Press,* November 2.

Owen, B., and M. McIntyre. 2005. "Police Find Rape Videotapes," *Winnipeg Free Press,* December 16.

Reynolds, L. 2005. "Just Ordinary Guys, Up on Child Porn Charges." *Winnipeg Free Press*, December 30.

Rogers, R. 1990. *Reaching for Solutions.* Summary Report of the Special Advisor to the Minister of National Health and Welfare on Child Sexual Abuse in Canada. Ottawa: Health and Welfare Canada.

———. 1993. Status Report on the Federal Response to *Reaching for Solutions Canada,* 1993. Ottawa: Health and Welfare Canada.

Ryder, B. 2003. "The Harms of Child Pornography Law." 36 *University of British Columbia Law Review:* 101–35.

Shaffer, J. 1999. "Familial Love, Incest, and Female Desire in Late Eighteenth-
and Early Nineteenth-Century British Women's Novels." *Criticism.* http://
www.findarticles.com/p/articles/mi_m2220/is_1_41/ai_56905045.

Statistics Canada. 2003. "Children and Youth as Victims of Violent Crime."
Juristat 25, no. 1. Ottawa: StatsCan.

Stevenson, K. 1999. "Observations on the Law Relating to Sexual Offences:
The Historical Scandal of Women's Silence [1994]." *Web Journal of Current Legal Issues* 4. http://webjcli.ncl.au.uk/1999/issue4/stevenson4.html.

Trocmé, N., et al. 2005. *Canadian Incidence Study of Reported Child Abuse
and Neglect—2003.* Major findings. http://www.phac-aspc.gc.ca/cm-vee/
csca-ecve/index.html.

United Nations. 1989. Convention on the Rights of the Child. New York: UN.

UNICEF. 1997. "World Congress against Commercial Exploitation of Children: Declaration and Agenda for Action." http://www.hartford-wp.com/
archives/28/024.html.

"World Sex Atlas: Growing Up Sexually." http://www.ipce.info/booksreborn/
janssen/atlas/GrowingUpSexually1.pdf.

Cases Cited

R. v. Bakker [2005] B.C.J. No. 1577 (BC Provincial Court)

R. v.. Bauder [1997] M.J. No. 270 (Manitoba Court of Appeal)

R. v. Butler [1992] 1 S.C.R. 452 (Supreme Court of Canada)

R. v. M.E.D. (1985) 47 *Criminal Reports* (3rd) 382 (Ontario Provincial Court)

R. v. D.O.L. [1993] 4 S.C.R. 419 (Supreme Court of Canada)

R. v. Ewanchuk [1999] 1 S.C.R. 330 (Supreme Court of Canada)

R. v. Khan [1990] 2 SCR 530 (Supreme Court of Canada)

R. v. M. (1995), 98 C.C.C. 3rd 481 (Ontario Court of Appeal)

R. v. M. (W.F.), (1995) 41 *Criminal Reports* (4th) 330 (Alberta Court of Appeal)

R. v. O'Connor [1995] 4 S.C.R. 411 (Supreme Court of Canada)

R. v. Roy (1998) 125 C.C.C. 3rd 442 (Quebec Court of Appeal)

R. v. Seaboyer [1991] 2 S.C.R. 577 (Supreme Court of Canada)

R. v. Sharpe [2001] 1 S.C.R. 45 (Supreme Court of Canada)

R. v. Sharpe [2002] B.C.J. No. 610 (BC Supreme Court)

Youth Justice and Children's Rights
Transformations in Canada's Youth Justice System

Myriam Denov

Introduction: Trends in Youth Justice and Children's Rights

The weight is still balanced in favour of the young offender in this country. The protection of society, the protection of our children, is still outweighed by the so-called rights of violent and delinquent young Canadians. All we are asking is that the scales be evened out, that the rights of victims, the rights of our children be given priority. We ask that the protection of society outweigh the protection of violent young offenders who have no respect for the lives and rights of others.[1]

Few issues in Canada have stirred public debate as much as youth crime and the way our criminal justice system responds to young offenders. Many Canadians appear to support the notion of children's rights in theory; yet as the above quotation clearly illustrates, implementing children's rights in everyday practice—especially for children in conflict with the law—remains an ongoing challenge. In a socio-political context that has long advocated punitive responses to youth crime, the idea of ensuring rights for young offenders may invoke varying degrees of discomfort and opposition, as it may be perceived as a direct or indirect threat to the rights of victims of crime or to the overall protection of society. Moreover, guaranteeing the rights of young offenders enables young people to exercise choices, ask questions, challenge procedures, and

Myriam Denov, Faculty of Social Work, McGill University

have the opportunity to be heard in proceedings; all of this may defy traditional assumptions about young people and the criminal justice process.

Having ratified the UN Convention on the Rights of the Child (CRC) in 1991, the Canadian government pledged its commitment to meeting the needs and respecting the rights of Canadian children,[2] including children in conflict with the law. Through articles 37 and 40, the CRC sets out the fundamental principles that should guide the treatment of children who come into conflict with the law and that recognize their rights of general due process. Article 37 provides guarantees for children deprived of their liberty. It states that every child who is deprived of his or her liberty should be treated in a manner that takes into account the needs of persons his or her age—for example, the need to maintain contact with family members (articles 37 and 9) and friends (article 15); to engage in play, leisure and recreational activities, cultural life, and the arts (article 31); to enjoy their own culture, practice their own religion, and use their own language (article 14 and 30); and to continue their education (article 28). Also, children who are incarcerated should be separated from adult offenders (article 37). When ratifying the CRC, Canada made a reservation with respect to article 37(c). This article requires that children who are deprived of their liberty "be separated from adults unless it is considered in the child's best interest not to do so ... save in exceptional circumstances." Canada has chosen not to be bound by this provision, and as a result, young offenders can be housed in adult facilities.

Article 40 addresses the right of every child who has infringed the penal law (or who is accused of having done so) to be treated in a manner that takes into account the child's age and the desirability of promoting his or her reintegration into society. Article 40 discourages a focus on punishment; it also embodies the right to due process of law as well as the principle that recourse to formal proceedings and deprivation of liberty should be avoided whenever possible and appropriate.

The CRC serves as an umbrella treaty for three international juvenile justice instruments: the 1985 UN Standard Minimum Rules for the Administration of Juvenile Justice (the Beijing Rules); the 1990 UN Guidelines for the Prevention of Juvenile Delinquency (the Riyadh Guidelines); and the 1990 UN Rules for the Protection of Juveniles Deprived of their Liberty (the Havana Rules).

Yet despite the presence of these protective international conventions and their near global ratification, abuses and violations of the rights of children in conflict with the law continue to occur worldwide. In fact, evidence gathered and presented in many state party reports indicates that policies toward imprisoned children violate as many as twenty of the Convention's forty-one substantive rights provisions.[3] Examples of these state violations are numerous and occur internationally; six years after the genocide in Rwanda, 4,545 children were in prison awaiting resolution of their cases. More than 450 of these children had been formally cleared of any involvement in the genocide, yet only 196 of them had been released as of June 2003.[4]

U.S. officials have admitted that an undisclosed number of children under sixteen and as young as thirteen have been interrogated and incarcerated at its military prison camp at Guantánamo Bay, Cuba. Officials refuse to disclose the nationality of the children but have reported that they were brought from Afghanistan in 2003 on suspicion of terrorism.[5] The children have been declared "enemy combatants" by the U.S. military. As such, they are being held indefinitely without having been charged with any offence; nor have they been given access to legal counsel. One of the young prisoners is said to be Omar Khadr, a Canadian national who was captured on July 27, 2002, at the age of fifteen by U.S. Special Forces in eastern Afghanistan and who is being held at Guantánamo for allegedly throwing a grenade that killed a U.S. sergeant. Canadian officials have been unable to gain access to Khadr.[6]

In a similar vein, U.S. government documents obtained by the American Civil Liberties Union have revealed that children as young as eleven have been held at Abu Graib, the Iraqi prison at the centre of the U.S. prisoner-abuse scandal. There have been reports and allegations of abuse and deprivation among the children.[7] The United States is one of two nations that has not ratified the CRC;[8] however, it is a signatory to the treaty and thus has an obligation not to defeat its object and purpose.

The execution of young offenders is also an international concern. Though it clearly contravenes the CRC, five of the world's countries have, since 2000, executed juvenile offenders: China, Democratic Republic of Congo, Iran, Pakistan, and the United States. In the past five years the United States has executed thirteen juvenile offenders whereas the rest of the world combined has carried out five such executions. As of January 2004, more than seventy juvenile offenders were sitting on death row in the United States.[9]

These examples illustrate not only the ongoing direct violations of the CRC in relation to youth justice, but also the difficulty in monitoring and implementing the CRC in practice. The examples also capture the growing international trend toward punitive responses to crime and criminality, especially toward children and youth, in contravention of the spirit of the CRC. Numerous authors have commented on the growing "homogenization" of criminal justice, particularly in Western societies, driven by the spread of punitive penal policies from the United States.[10] Increasingly, these punitive policies are leaching into the realm of juvenile justice, where we are witnessing the diminution of a welfare-based mode of governance in favour of various "justice"-based responsibilization and managerial strategies.[11] While there are of course exceptions to this rule, discourses of "getting tough" on youth crime continue to pervade Western state policies and practices concerning youth justice, with inevitable implications for the implementation of children's rights and the principles of the CRC.

What are the implications of such trends for Canada? What has been Canada's response to youth justice both historically and presently? And how does Canada measure up with regard to its compliance to the CRC in the area of youth justice? This chapter traces the evolution of children's rights and youth justice in Canada and the various discourses that have accompanied this evolution. It also evaluates the extent to which the new Canadian law on youth justice, the Youth Criminal Justice Act, supports and affirms the rights-based principles of the CRC.

History, Transformation, and Rights in Canadian Youth Justice

With the introduction and implementation of the CRC, children are now viewed as subjects—that is, as individuals with distinct human rights and as active participants in their own development. But these perceptions of children have not always prevailed. Movements advocating for the rights of all children, including children in conflict with the law, have existed for centuries, but the actual implementation of these rights in everyday policies and legal practices is relatively new across the globe. An examination of Canada's historical perceptions, policies, and practices with regard to the rights of children reveals a particular trajectory. Covell and Howe[12] identify three distinct stages in this history. In the first stage, Canadian children were perceived largely as objects under the direct control of parental authority. In the second stage, children were considered a highly vulnerable population in need of state protection. In the final stage, children were regarded as subjects with inherent rights of their own. Perhaps not surprisingly, Canada's treatment and management of children and youth in conflict with the law has often paralleled these changing notions and perceptions of children and their rights. This section traces the changing perceptions of children over time and how these varying discourses have been reflected in Canada's treatment of youth in conflict with the law.

Children as Objects: The Absence of Legal Rights and Protections

According to Covell and Howe,[13] from colonial times into the nineteenth century, perceptions of Canadian children reflected a social laissez-faire philosophy whereby children were viewed predominantly as possessions and objects of parental authority. Parents were legally required to provide their children with the necessities of life; beyond that, childrearing practices and discipline were left to the complete discretion of the parents, who had the right to inflict "reasonable chastisement." Moreover, no laws or legislation existed to protect children from potentially harmful abuse, exploitation, or neglect. Reflecting the absence of legal rights and protections for children, as well as the overarching view of children as objects, during this era there was no protective or separate system of juvenile justice in Canada. Children and adults were thought to be acting with the same level of intent while engaging in criminal behaviour and were thus held equally accountable for their crimes. Thus, children over thirteen who came into conflict with the law were governed in much the same way as adults: they came before the same judges, they were sentenced to the same prisons, and they received the same punishments as adults.[14] Without question, these laws and practices left children in conflict with the law vulnerable to many forms of abuse, exploitation, and maltreatment.

The Vulnerable Child and Parens Patriae: The Introduction of the Juvenile Delinquents Act

In the context of a newfound sentimentality toward children and an increased humanitarianism, from the time of Confederation to the mid-twentieth century, children were no longer perceived as objects of parental authority or as possessions, but instead as a special class of persons who were inherently vulnerable and in need of protection. Reflecting a welfare-oriented approach and premised on the concept of parens patriae (literally, "parent of the country"), the role of the state was to protect children from cruelty and abuse. As such, if parents failed to adequately protect and provide for their children, the state had a duty to intervene on those children's behalf. While the view of children as possessions had altered, there was, as yet, no prevailing discourse on the importance of upholding or promoting children's inherent rights. Instead, children continued to be viewed as objects in need of care, whether by their parents or the paternalistic state.

This changing philosophy and welfare-oriented approach had a powerful impact on the creation of new protective laws and legal principles for children and paved the way for a separate juvenile justice system. During this era, children in conflict with the law were no longer viewed as having the same level of intent as adults; instead, delinquent children were perceived as "misdirected and misguided" and thus in need of aid and assistance. With the passing of the Juvenile Delinquents Act (JDA) in

1908, children were no longer governed and judged according to adult legal principles. Now, legislation and carceral institutions not only recognized childhood as a unique stage of life but also located the causes of child delinquency in the child's immediate environment, including difficult life circumstances and corrupting role models. Moreover, there was an overarching assumption that children were infinitely malleable and highly amenable to rehabilitation.[15] Given all this, the social protection of youth was thought to be best achieved by focusing resources on their rehabilitation and by protecting them from the full glare of public accountability.[16] Under the JDA, little emphasis was placed on due process, such as the right to legal representation. Moreover, rules of evidence were relaxed and youth courts enjoyed enormous discretion in terms of the processes to be followed and the resulting sentences.[17] The philosophy of this era also supported the use of indeterminate sentences for young offenders, this based on the perceived utility of providing involuntary treatment for as long as it was in the best interests of the young offender. The welfare-oriented JDA remained in force with little dissent until the 1960s.

Children as Subjects? The Creation of the Young Offenders Act, and the Youth Criminal Justice Act: The Clash between "Rights" and "Accountability"

After the Second World War, state paternalism and a welfare-oriented regime gradually gave rise to a new perception of children as individuals not in need of state protection. Instead, they were viewed as endowed with inherent civil, political, and social rights; consequently, it was the duty of the state and of parents to provide for these rights. A variety of declarations came into play that solidified the growing perception of children as subjects who are entitled to full human rights. One such instrument was the non-binding UN Declaration of the Rights of the Child in 1959; another was the declaration of 1979 as the year of the child; then, in 1989, came the creation and implementation of the CRC.

In the Canadian context of heightened awareness of human rights, growing social and civil rights movements, and the constitutional entrenchment of the Canadian Charter of Rights and Freedoms in 1982, it became increasingly difficult to justify the lack of legal rights for youth in conflict with the law, the use of indeterminate sentences, and the abuse of due process rights, all inherent to Canada's JDA. Canadians also began to interrogate the paternalistic principles of the JDA and to question more closely the notion of the "reformable young offender."[18] This changing political and social context led to the demise of the JDA and its replacement by the Young Offenders Act (YOA) in 1984.

The YOA was a turning point in Canadian juvenile justice. Unlike the JDA, which focused heavily on rehabilitation, the YOA placed a stronger emphasis on the philosophy of punishment. It also marked a shift to a law-and-order approach; as a consequence, young people and other marginalized groups would now be singled out as risky populations in need of control.[19] Moving away from the child-welfare philosophy of the JDA, the YOA emphasized due process and advocated that young offenders be held accountable for their actions—albeit not as accountable as adults.[20] The YOA held seemingly contradictory principles in that it referred to young people as being in a "state of dependency" and as having "special needs and requir[ing] guidance and assistance" as well as "supervision, discipline, and control."[21] On one hand, the YOA provided for the special needs of children in conflict with the law, advocated alternatives to youth imprisonment, and promoted children's legal rights and freedoms. On the other hand, it called for increased youth accountability and responsibility and emphasized the need to protect victims and society.[22] Many suggest that the latter principles were given greater authority and credence: "The [YOA] favours a strategy that pays lip service to the possibilities inherent in alternative measures, overemphasizes individual responsibilities and traits and, in the end, witnesses a steady entrenchment of punishment and incarceration."[23]

Interestingly, with the establishment of the CRC in 1989, the broader international discourse on children's rights gained momentum and prominence, all the while emphasizing the importance of rehabilitative and reintegrative strategies for children in conflict with the law. This was in stark contrast to the principles reflected in the YOA and to the voices of those many Canadians who clamoured for harsher punishments for young offenders. Articles 37 and 40 of the CRC advocated that young offenders be arrested, detained, and imprisoned *only* as a last resort and emphasized "promoting the child's reintegration and ... a constructive role in society"; yet the YOA had introduced a new set of principles that called for "supervision, discipline, and control."[24] Moreover, after being introduced in 1984, the YOA underwent three sets of revisions, all of which placed a stronger emphasis on punishment, crime control, and deterrence.[25] Clearly, there was a growing disjuncture between the rehabilitative and rights-based principles in the CRC and the seemingly punitive philosophy of the YOA.

When Canada ratified the CRC in 1991 it pledged to amend its laws over time so as to harmonize them with the CRC. However, the disjuncture between the CRC and the YOA continued to grow in the years following ratification. The YOA became subject to much public concern and criticism as Canadians continued to express high anxiety over the youth crime problem and the youth justice response. Concern was fuelled in part by the widespread public perception that juvenile crime was escalating out of control and that the YOA was contributing to (or at least associated with) a substantial increase in youth crime.[26] Demands for politicians to get tough on youth crime grew especially loud in the late 1990s: almost three-quarters of respondents in a national opinion poll stated that they had little or no confidence in the YOA.[27] Similarly, a nationwide petition circulated in 2000 generated almost one million signatures of individuals demanding harsher sentencing for juveniles.[28] Nearly two-thirds of Canadians supported lowering the age of criminal responsibility from twelve to ten years.[29] Approximately two-thirds of the public opposed the existence of a separate youth justice system, and 93 percent thought that youth court sentences were too lenient.[30] Clearly, public discourses of deterrence and crime control were being prioritized over discourses of rights for young offenders.

Yet concern about rising youth crime has not always coincided with actual trends. Sixty percent of the public polled in 2000 believed that youth crime was rising, when in fact these rates had been declining for almost a decade.[31] The Canadian public's views on youth crime have been shaped in part by high-profile cases of homicide involving juvenile offenders both in Canada and abroad. Perhaps the best known of these cases are the murders of Jamie Bulger in England and Reena Virk in Canada and the massacre at Columbine High School in Colorado. In this context of growing fear and "moral panics" regarding youth crime,[32] many Canadians have advocated that the "government create a legal framework that reflected current social values—one that commands respect, fosters values such as *accountability* and *responsibility* ... makes it clear that criminal behaviour will lead to *meaningful consequences* [and that reflects the needs for a] broader, more comprehensive approach to youth justice that looks beyond the justice system for solutions to youth crime."[33]

The punitive reaction to youth crime had a predictable effect on politicians. In the 2000 federal election, all opposition parties except the Bloc Québécois promised to introduce reforms that would toughen the juvenile justice system. In response to public and political pressure to get tough on youth crime, the government tabled youth justice reforms that were intended to address the "disturbing decline in public confidence in the youth justice system."[34] In April 2003 the YOA was replaced by the Youth Criminal Justice Act (YCJA).

In introducing the YCJA, the Canadian government was seeking to appease two diverse groups. First were the vocal law-and-order critics of the youth justice system, who emphasized the need for greater accountability, especially for serious violent offenders. Second were the child-advocacy groups, who were clamouring for a more supportive and pre-ventive approach to youth justice, one that would place less emphasis on custody and more on effective community-based responses to young offend-ing.[35] These groups represented the major players in youth justice reform; however, there were other realities that Canada needed to consider when creating a new youth justice law. One was the reality that Canada was already known internationally for having one of the harshest regimes for young offenders in the Western world.[36] Since 1987 the incarceration rates for young offenders had increased by 26 percent,[37] making Canada's rate of juvenile incarceration one of the highest in the world—higher than the rates in both the United States and Britain.[38] Canada jails nearly four times as many youth as adults, despite abundant evidence that punish-ment is generally not effective and may actually increase crime rates.[39] The federal government recognized that Canada was relying too heavily on expensive and often ineffective court-based responses and custody for the majority of young offenders who had not committed serious offences.[40]

The government also needed to consider its commitment to children's rights as expressed in the CRC. Through ratification, Canada had agreed to amend its laws over time so as to harmonize them with the CRC. The creation of the YCJA offered not only an important opportunity for har-monization, but also an obligation to incorporate the CRC's distinct guide-lines into the proposed new law. Canada also needed to take into account the recommendations of the Committee on the Rights of the Child, the monitoring mechanism to which state parties were accountable. Canada had submitted two reports to the Committee, in 1994 and 1999, that out-lined this country's progress in meeting the CRC's obligations. The Com-mittee responded by urging Canada to revoke its reservations to article 37 of the CRC; to create more legislation and programs that would include the voices and participation of young people in the justice system, policy-making, and community life; to renew its commitment to Aboriginal chil-dren; and to coordinate and disseminate information and programs to address economic disparity, child poverty, and discrimination, to name but a few calls to action.[41] These were important issues to consider in amending the youth justice law.

Examining the Youth Criminal Justice Act: Rights or Rhetoric?

The Canadian government has declared that the YCJA is "more consis-tent with national and international human rights in protecting the inter-ests of children."[42] However, preliminary research has revealed elements of both compliance and failure to comply with key aspects of the CRC.[43] This section explores the strengths of the YCJA in relation to the CRC and

Canada's progress in the areas of juvenile justice and children's rights. It then addresses some of the limitations of the new law and points out where Canada can improve its promotion of the rights of children in conflict with the law.

Areas of Compliance with the CRC

Limiting the Use of Custody

Given Canada's notably high rates of youth incarceration, the YCJA contains a number of measures designed to reduce the use of incarceration in youth courts. As noted earlier, article 37(b) of the CRC declares that "the arrest, detention or imprisonment of a child shall be in conformity with the law and shall be used only as a measure of last resort and for the shortest appropriate period of time." In greater compliance with the CRC, youth courts are prohibited from imposing a custodial sentence in many cases in which custody would have been imposed under the YOA. Whereas custody might have been imposed for a violent offence, section 39(1) of the YCJA "places restrictions on the use of custody for non-violent offences, requiring a history of failing to comply with non-custodial sentences, a pattern on non-violent offending or exceptional circumstances."[44] In cases where custody is possible under the YCJA, the court is required at a number of points to consider all possible alternatives to custody before imposing a term of imprisonment (s. 39[2]).

Increased Emphasis on the Principles of Rehabilitation and Reintegration

Article 40(4) of the CRC requires that a variety of dispositions be available to children in conflict with the law "such as care, guidance, supervision orders, counseling, probation, foster care, education and vocational training programs and other alternatives to institutional care." There are a number of references to rehabilitation in the YCJA—in the preamble to the Act, in the Declaration of Principle, and in the sentencing purpose and principles. To ensure that rehabilitation plays a more important role in sentencing at the youth court level, the YCJA has increased the scope of alternatives to judicial proceedings and has increased the variety of dispositions and alternatives to custody. The stronger emphasis on rehabilitation in youth court should direct judges toward the use of alternative sanctions and away from the imposition of terms of imprisonment. Moreover, the federal government has promised to increase funding to the provinces and territories to ensure the implementation and availability of community-based dispositions.[45]

Regarding reintegration, article 40(1) of the CRC highlights the need for children in conflict with the law to be "treated in a manner consistent with the promotion of the child's dignity and self worth ... promoting the child's reintegration and the child's assuming a constructive role in society." The YCJA places greater emphasis than the YOA on the concepts of rehabilitation and reintegration, and this is consistent with article 40(1). The following extract of the YCJA illustrates this emphasis: "The youth criminal justice system is intended to rehabilitate ... and reintegrate (s. 3 (1) (a)); The criminal justice system for young persons must ... emphasize the following: rehabilitation and reintegration ... enhanced procedural protection ... and timely intervention" (s. 3 (1) (b)).

While the YOA contained similar principles, the YCJA has other, more practical, provisions that promote rehabilitation and reintegration. For example, in the past, children tended to serve the entirety of their custodial sentence in a residential facility. In keeping with the promotion of rehabilitation, there is a presumption within the YCJA that the last third of the sentence will be served on conditional supervision in the community.

Increased Attention to Survival and Development

Article 6 of the CRC guarantees the right to life and to survival and development to the maximum extent possible. The YCJA has the capacity to contribute to the survival and development of young people in conflict with the law, given its repeated references to rehabilitation and reintegration and the increased focus on non-judicial options and alternatives to custody. However, the degree to which these goals will be met will depend on the extent to which these aspects of the law will be implemented. Given this country's social, political, and economic diversity, there is likely to be a great deal of provincial variation in implementation.

The Promotion of Child Participation

Many youth who have passed through the youth justice system have said that they were not effectively heard or involved in proceedings throughout the youth justice process. A young Aboriginal woman who had many dealings with the police and the courts asserted:

> With myself, they don't involve you in the decisions that affect you, and most of the time they tell you what to do. Like you have probation, you have to be home at a certain time, or you have to go to school or you have to talk to this person or its mediation and they make you feel like you're not important and that everything that you do is wrong. Even yourself, your well-being, like who you are is wrong. Like you're not important. You're actually not worth anything. It's how a lot of

them approach you. Cops, the court system and youth workers and jail. You're just treated like an animal.[46]

Article 12 of the CRC requires that "the child shall in particular be provided the opportunity to be heard in any judicial or administrative proceedings affecting the child, either directly, or through a representative or an appropriate body, in a manner consistent with the procedural rules of national law." The provisions in the YOA (s. 3(1)(e)) that offered the potential for the voices of young people to be heard have been reiterated in the YCJA. Section 3(1)(d)(i) of the YCJA recognizes the right of children in conflict with the law to "be heard in the course of and to participate in the processes, other than the decision to prosecute, that lead to decisions that affect them." The YCJA should be commended for requiring that young persons be given an opportunity to be heard in proceedings that affect them;[47] however, there is no concurrent obligation for the young person's views to be taken into account in the decision-making process. Compliance with article 12 of the CRC could be improved if this were addressed through a statutory regulation or obligation to incorporate children's views in a predisposition report or in sentencing considerations. It is important to note, however, that there is a clear distinction between policy as *formulated* and policy as *implemented*. While the YCJA has provided for the voices of young people to be heard, time will tell whether those provisions will inject truly *meaningful* youth participation into everyday practice.

Increased Attention to the Plight of Aboriginal Youth and Overrepresentation

Article 2 of the CRC asserts that "State Parties shall respect and ensure the rights set forth in the present CRC to each child within their jurisdiction without discrimination of any kind, irrespective of the child's ... race, colour, sex, language, religion, political or other opinion, national, ethnic or social origin, property, disability, birth or other status." The plight of Canada's Aboriginal children in health, child poverty, and child welfare is described in chapters 4 and 11. In addition, in Canada, Aboriginal youth and youth from certain immigrant and visible minority groups are overrepresented in the justice system.[48] For example, Aboriginal youth are overrepresented at every stage of the criminal justice process including arrests, convictions, and populations in youth detention facilities.[49] In 1999, Aboriginal youth accounted for nearly one-quarter of youth admissions to custody, yet they represent only 7 percent of youth aged twelve to seventeen.[50] One study found that, statistically, Aboriginal youth had a better chance of going to jail than graduating from high school.[51] This carceral overrepresentation is more pronounced in the Prairies, British Columbia, and Ontario: in Manitoba, 75 percent of sentenced custody admissions were identified as Aboriginal youth even though only 16 percent of Manitoba's youth population is Aboriginal. Green and Healy have illuminated the serious implications of this problem: "If the current high number of Aboriginal youth already in custody were to increase at the same rate as the overall Aboriginal population, the resulting effects would be crippling, both within the youth justice system and Canadian society as a whole."[52]

The causes of this overrepresentation are complex and include factors such as colonization, poverty, and social and cultural upheaval; that said, the role that conscious or unconscious racism may play in charging and detention practices and even in judicial decision making must be considered.[53] While Section 3(1)(c)(iv) of the YCJA states that "measures taken against young persons who commit offences ... should respect gender, ethnic, cultural and linguistic differences and respond to the needs of Aboriginal young persons," this is only a guideline and is not operative as are other legal requirements in the law. However, in 2002, during readings of the YCJA, the Canadian Senate objected to the new law's lack of attention to the special needs of Aboriginal youth. In response, the law was changed to include a sentencing principle, similar to Section 718.2(e)[54] of the Canadian Criminal Code. This section of the code, came into effect in 1996 for adult offenders, requires judges to consider alternatives to incarceration for Aboriginal adult offenders at the time of sentencing.[55] This sentencing principle has been incorporated into the YCJA for consideration when sentencing Aboriginal young offenders (sec. 50.1); furthermore, Section 38(2)(d) directs judges when sentencing young offenders to consider "all available sanctions other than custody that are reasonable in the circumstances ... for all young persons, *with particular attention to the circumstances of aboriginal young persons*" (emphasis added).

Alternatives may include youth justice committees and conferences. These can be convened to recommend appropriate measures at various stages of the process and have the potential to positively affect rehabilitation efforts as well as indirectly address the overrepresentation of Aboriginal youth in custody.[56]

The inclusion of this sentencing principle and reference to Section 718.2(e) of the Criminal Code may also serve to address the recommendation of the Committee on the Rights of the Child that the Canadian government "pursue its efforts to address the gap in life chances between Aboriginal and non-Aboriginal children."[57] However, the extent to which judges will incorporate these principles into their sentencing decisions for Aboriginal youth remains to be seen.

Areas of Non-Compliance with the CRC

The Best Interests of the Child?

"The best interests of the child" is one of the overarching principles of the CRC. Article 3(1) states that "in all actions concerning children, whether undertaken by public or private social welfare institutions, courts of law, administrative authorities or legislative bodies, the best interests of the child shall be a primary consideration." Though the YCJA recognizes the CRC in its preamble, the act neglects to mention "best interests" in its declaration of principles in Section 3. While the government has argued that the YCJA is "more consistent with national and international human rights in protecting the interests of children while, at the same time, protecting public safety,"[58] the emphasis seems to be on the latter. The fact that the YCJA does not have the child's best interests as one of its guiding principles demonstrates inadequate compliance with the CRC. In 1995, Canada was informed by the Committee that "principles relating to the best interests of the child and prohibition of discrimination in relation to children should be incorporated into domestic law and it should be possible to invoke them before the courts."[59] This has yet to be fully realized.

The Reality of Punishment, Custody, and the
Language of Accountability

Notwithstanding the limits placed on the use of custody, punishment—although not expressly stated as such—still appears to be a key objective of the YCJA.[60] The emphasis on proportionate and meaningful consequences (punishment) is a fundamental point of departure between the YCJA and the CRC's emphasis on rehabilitation. In the past, the Committee has questioned Canada's overuse of custodial dispositions for young offenders. According to the CRC, detention and imprisonment are to be used "only as a measure of last resort and for the shortest appropriate period of time" (article 37). The YCJA has attempted to address this trend by limiting custody for less serious offences; in other areas, though, custody remains an option for those convicted of more serious offences. In fact, elements of the new law will result in harsher sentences for young offenders convicted of the most serious offences. Additionally, custody can be imposed in cases where a youth has failed to comply with two previous non-custodial dispositions, such as probation. Although several sections of the YCJA appear to encourage a reduction in the use of custody for youth, the act nevertheless fails to make rehabilitation a priority. True compliance with the CRC would require youth justice policies and laws that shift the focus from incarceration to rehabilitation. Also, greater emphasis would need to be placed on creating long-term measures to prevent youth crime.

A punitive approach is also reflected in other aspects of the YCJA—especially its terminology. For example, the term "disposition," which was used in the YOA, has been replaced in the YCJA by the stronger term "sentence." Furthermore, although the act includes several sections that encourage rehabilitation and reintegration, this step forward is unfortunately countered by the act's focus on "accountability"—a word that is typically intended to project a "get tough" approach to criminal justice and that places the best interests of society over those of the young person. For example, the term "accountability" appears twice in the YCJA's Declaration of Principles and once in the Preamble, whereas the notion of the "best interests" of the child is entirely absent. Moreover, in its overview of the act's core principles, the Justice department notes that the "protection of society is the paramount objective of the youth justice system."[61] This approach to youth justice is in sharp contrast to that of the CRC, which clearly instructs that the emphasis should be placed not on punishment or the protection of society, but rather on rehabilitation and reintegration programs (article 40) and that the best interests of the child should be the primary consideration (article 3). As a member of the Committee stated: "The rehabilitation of offenders should be the primary objective, not the third, following the protection of society and the punishment of the child in the interest of society."[62] Compliance with the CRC would require a more protective rather than punitive youth justice system.

The Failure to Ensure Differential Treatment of Adult and Young Offenders

The CRC emphasizes the importance of ensuring that young offenders be treated differently from adult offenders. However, several examples illustrate Canada's uniform treatment of young and adult offenders. For example, article 37 of the CRC stipulates that "every child deprived of liberty shall be separated from adults unless it is considered in the child's best interest not to do so." However, as noted earlier, when ratifying the CRC, Canada reserved the right not to be bound by this provision, and this has made it possible for children to be held in adult remand or correctional facilities. To comply with the CRC and to ensure that the best interests of the child are of primary importance, Canada would have to remove its reservation on the requirement that young offenders be kept separate from adults. In assessing Canada's record in 1995, the Committee suggested that Canada consider withdrawing this reservation. To date, Canada has refused. Some have argued that this refusal stems from Canada's desire to avoid having to build more youth detention centres.[63]

The contentious issue of applying adult sentences to youth reflects another example of the new law's failure to treat young and adult offenders differently. The YCJA could strengthen this trend, as young offenders can now receive an adult sentence, post adjudication. Moreover, the list of offences for which a youth can receive an adult sentence has been expanded. The YCJA has lowered the age of presumptive transfer (i.e., to an adult facility) from sixteen to fourteen. Thus, under Section 61, young persons who commit certain serious offences (murder, attempted murder, manslaughter, aggravated sexual assault, or repeat violent offences) can, at the option of the province, receive an adult sentence when they are as young as fourteen. This expansion of the use of adult sentences for young offenders has eroded the boundaries between the youth and adult criminal justice systems and is contrary to the spirit of the CRC.

Inadequate Attention to Meeting the Special Needs of Youth

Youth custody facilities are filled primarily with marginalized youth, including Aboriginals, the poor, and the disabled.[64] It is estimated that up to 75 percent of the children in custody have some form of disability.[65] The YCJA lacks provisions that specifically address the importance of accommodating the special health or other needs of young persons in custody or under supervision. The law has introduced a new sentencing provision called "intensive rehabilitative custody," but this is directed toward a very select group of youth who have committed a serious violent offence and/or who are suffering from a mental illness or emotional disturbance (s. 42[7]). Moreover, the imposition of this sentence is contingent on the existence and availability of such programming in the provinces. To date, very few such programs have been established for adolescents. Additionally, it is unclear how the system will deal with the greater number of young offenders serving their sentences in adult correctional facilities. A correctional officer has noted that "overcrowded institutions and continued budget reductions make special treatment of young offenders within adult facilities unlikely."[66] Given the CRC's emphasis on protecting minority and indigenous children, it will be particularly important to monitor the application of adult sentences for Aboriginal, visible-minority, and female offenders.

The governing principles of the YCJA could be further improved if they included consideration of other disadvantages faced by young persons in conflict with the law, particularly in relation to social and economic disadvantages. This would be further support for the principle set out in the Preamble to the CRC, which states that "in all countries in the world, there are children living in exceptionally difficult conditions and that such children need special consideration." By failing to address this principle in the YCJA, certain areas of the act, such as those which consider the importance of family stability when arriving at community alternatives to sentencing or custody, could discriminate against socially disadvantaged youth who have not had access to the same social supports as more advantaged youth. For example, family stability and school attendance are factors considered in pre-sentence reports and in sentencing. However, social disadvantage is not sufficiently addressed by the YCJA.

The YCJA also falls short of a child's right to privacy as indicated in the CRC. According to article 16 of the CRC, "no child shall be subject to arbitrary or unlawful interference with his or her privacy, family, home or correspondence, nor to unlawful attacks on his or her honour or reputation. The child has the right to protection of the law against such interference or attacks." Arguably, the YCJA is in remiss of this article in that it permits the publication of the names of all youth convicted of a crime who receive an adult sentence. In addition, the names of fourteen-to-seventeen-year-olds given a youth sentence for murder, attempted murder, manslaughter, aggravated sexual assault, or repeat violent offences can now also be made public. The YCJA also allows potentially harmful disclosure of information to victims and other individuals deemed acceptable by the court. Moreover, there is no requirement that the court consider the young person's best interests in having such information disclosed. These practices, which allow for the possibility of harmful stigmatization, fail to comply with article 16 of the CRC.

Regional Disparities

Regional disparities may preclude uniform treatment of young offenders in all regions of Canada, as the YCJA contains many provisions that entitle the provinces to apply specific sections as they wish. For example, Section 61 of the YCJA permits each province/territory to set an age for which young persons between fourteen and sixteen can be sentenced as adults for certain offences. Thus, a fourteen-year-old from one province could be subjected to an adult sentence, whereas a fourteen-year-old from another province who committed the same offence could have the benefit of being sentenced as a young offender. In essence, this allows for discrimination based on both age and location, which contravenes article 2 of the CRC.

Sections 7, 18, 19, 86, 87, and 157 of the YCJA all address programs and procedures for dealing with youth involved with the criminal justice system. Each section states that provinces "may" (except for Sections 86 and 87, which state that provinces "shall") establish such programs, thus enabling disparity in application. Furthermore, there is no requirement for consistency between provinces, and as a result, custody and reintegration decisions—as well as the quality of care or protection that young people receive—could vary greatly depending on jurisdiction.

The Committee had admonished Canada for the "disparities between provincial or territorial legislation and practices which affect the implementation of the CRC."[67] Given that both provincial and federal governments were made aware of this contravention of article 2 prior to the development of the YCJA, the continued disparity of Canada's youth justice system is particularly disconcerting.

Conclusion: Mixed Models and Competing Discourses

A historical look at Canada's responses to youth crime reveals a philosophy that has shifted from welfarism to justice to just deserts to restoration and responsibility. Each of these approaches and philosophies has influenced the degree to which the rights of children in conflict with the law have been prioritized.

While the YCJA has taken many commendable and progressive steps toward protecting and promoting the rights of children in conflict with the law, these steps forward have been countered by an apparent disregard for key elements of the Convention. This highlights the contradictory nature of several principles and provisions of the YCJA. With the introduction of the new law in 2003, youth justice in Canada has developed into a particularly complex agglomeration of competing and contradictory policies and discourses, which include retribution, responsibility, rights, and rehabilitation. This mixed model of proportionality, punishment, and rehabilitation is clearly illustrated in Section 38(1) of the YCJA, wherein the purpose of sentencing for young offenders is deemed to include "*just sanctions that have meaningful consequences* for the young person and that promote his or her *rehabilitation and reintegration* into society" (emphasis added). Under this sundry approach, the promotion and assurance of children's rights has become only one element among an array of competing interests and issues, and this raises serious concerns for ensuring compliance to the CRC. To meet the standards of the Convention, regional disparities in the treatment of young offenders need to be addressed, as do issues relating to discrimination, privacy, and the erosion of the boundaries between young and adult offenders. Ways must be found to ensure that the "best interests of the child" are of equal importance to the "protection of society."

The YCJA also appears to create a potentially dangerous bifurcation among young offenders. Minor offending is increasingly being decriminalized, and minor offences—including first-time offences—are less and less subject to formal sanctions under the YCJA. Yet at the same time, the YCJA has reserved increasingly serious sanctions for those who commit more serious offences by lowering the age of eligibility for a presumptive adult sanction from sixteen to fourteen years. It has also extended the reach of a presumptive adult sentence to those who have committed a third or serious violent offence. As Campbell[68] suggests, this bifurcation into two groups of "serious" and "minor" offenders has important implications. It suggests that youth who commit minor offences are deemed worthy of the investment of time and resources on the part of the state, whereas the more violent offenders are excluded from society—they are perceived as beyond help and are essentially warehoused. This clearly contravenes the spirit of the CRC, which advocates for the rights and protections of *all* children in conflict with the law.

For many children's rights advocates, the new law does not go far enough in its protection and promotion of child rights. For example, the Canadian arm of Defence for Children International takes the position that the new juvenile justice legislation does not meet the standards of the CRC: "[The YCJA] will do nothing to address the question of discrimination which results in higher percentages of poor children, of indigenous children and of black children. It pays lip service but provides no protection for the best interests of the child as a 'primary consideration.' It does not establish an effective mechanism to assure the right of the child to be heard."[69]

The Committee on the Rights of the Child has also expressed concern over the YCJA's compliance with the CRC: "The Committee is encouraged by the enactment of the new legislation in April, 2003. The Committee further welcomes crime prevention initiatives and alternatives to judicial processes. However, the Committee is concerned at the expanded use of adult sentences for children as young as 14, that youth custody is among the highest in the industrialized world, that mixing of juvenile and adult offender in detention facilities continues to be legal, and that access to youth records and public identification is permitted."[70]

While the new law continues to have its critics, it is important to acknowledge that Canada has begun to report significant decreases in youth incarceration since the implementation of the YCJA owing to the wider availability of community alternatives, though it has done so from a very high base figure.[71] While there continues to be significant variations across the country, populations in youth custody facilities declined by 20 to 50 percent in the months after the YCJA was enforced.[72] According to Statistics Canada, in 2003–4, caseloads in Canada's youth courts declined 17 percent from the previous year. Judges heard 70,465 cases involving young people during 2003–4, down from 105,538 in 1991–92, a difference of 33 percent.[73] Meanwhile, the rate for those who received a warning, caution, or referral to a community program in lieu of charges rose 30 percent.[74] These changes bode well for the promotion of children's rights and compliance with the CRC. Ultimately, however, YCJA's effectiveness in reducing the use of custody will depend on the way that criminal justice professionals—including and especially judges—interpret and implement the statute.

The CRC represents a political tool that can be used to influence the ways in which Canada's youth justice laws and policies evolve and the degree to which children's rights are respected. However, it is clear that national (and international) politics play a salient role in the implementation of children's rights in youth justice law and policy. As demonstrated in the epigraph to this chapter, in an era in which the protection of society and punitive responses to youth crime are the accepted norm, ensuring the rights and best interests of young offenders may not be high on the political agenda of governments. Greater education for the public on the realities of youth justice would bode well for a more protective and children's rights–based youth justice system. Greater use of restorative justice, as described in the next chapter, would also bode well for increased consistency with children's rights.

Notes

1 Reform Party M.P. Jack Ramsay, House of Commons Debates, 1995.
2 For this paper, the definition of a child will coincide with the definition set out in the UN Convention on the Rights of the Child (CRC). According to the Convention, a child is "every human being below eighteen years" (article 1). "Children" refers equally to boys and girls. Incidentally, under the Canadian Criminal Code (with the enactment of the Young Offenders Act and the more recent Youth Criminal Justice Act), a "young offender" refers to a young person (twelve through seventeen as of the date of the alleged offence) who has been found guilty of an offence.
3 S. Meuwese, *Kids Behind Bars* (Amsterdam: Defence for Children International, 2003).
4 UNICEF, "Juvenile Justice," http://www.unicef.org/protection/index_juveniljustice .html.
5 O. Burkeman, "Children Held at Guantanamo Bay," *The Guardian*, April 24, 2003, http://www.guardian.co.uk/international/story/0,3604,942310,00.html.
6 Ibid.
7 BBC News, *US Held Youngsters at Abu Graib* (2005).
8 Somalia, which has no interim government, has also failed to ratify the CRC.
9 Amnesty International (2005), http://www.amnesty.ca/child/report.php.
10 D. Garland, *The Culture of Control* (Oxford: Oxford University Press, 2001).

11 J. Runcie, "The Globalization of Crime Control—the Case of Youth Justice," *Theoretical Criminology* 9, no. 1 (2005): 35–64.

12 K. Covell and B. Howe, *The Challenge of Children's Rights for Canada* (Waterloo: Wilfrid Laurier University Press, 2001).

13 Ibid.

14 During this period, children under the age of seven were deemed incapable of committing a criminal act and could therefore not be held responsible. However, children between the ages of seven and thirteen were able to employ the defence of *doli incapax*—the inability to form criminal intent required under the law—and could thus avoid criminal liability.

15 B. Hogeveen, "History, Development, and Transformations in Canadian Juvenile Justice, 1800–1984," in K. Campbell, ed., *Understanding Youth Justice in Canada* (Toronto: Pearson Education, 2005).

16 N. Bala, "The Development of Canada's Youth Justice Law," in K. Campbell, ed., *Understanding Youth Justice in Canada* (Toronto: Pearson Education, 2005).

17 G. Green and K. Healy, *Tough on Kids: Rethinking Approaches to Youth Justice* (Saskatoon: Purich Publishing, 2003).

18 Hogeveen, "History, Development, and Transformations."

19 S. Alvi, "A Criminal Justice History of Children and Youth in Canada," in B. Schissel and C. Brooks, eds., *Marginality and Condemnation* (Halifax: Fernwood Publishing, 2002).

20 Bala, "The Development of Canada's Youth Justice Law."

21 Young Offenders Act (YOA), Section 3.

22 S. Bell, *Young Offenders and Juvenile Justice: A Century after the Fact* (Scarborough, ON: Nelson, 2002).

23 Alvi, "A Criminal Justice History."

24 YOA, Section 3.

25 Bell, *Young Offenders and Juvenile Justice.*

26 Bala, "What's Wrong with YOA Bashing? What's Wrong with the YOA? Recognizing the Limits of the Law," *Canadian Journal of Criminology* 36 (1994): 247–70.

27 Angus Reid Group, *Canadian Attitudes toward the Young Offenders Act* (Ottawa: Angus Reid, 1998).

28 J. Tufts and J. Roberts, "Sentencing Juvenile Offenders: Comparing Public Preferences and Judicial Practice," *Criminal Justice Policy Review* 13, no. 1 (2002): 46–64.

29 Angus Reid, *Canadian Attitudes.*

30 J. Sprott, "Understanding Public Opposition to a Separate Youth Justice System," *Crime and Delinquency* 44 (1998): 399–411.

31 J. Roberts, "Sentencing Juvenile Offenders in Canada: An Analysis of Recent Reform Legislation," *Journal of Contemporary Criminal Justice* 19, no. 4 (2003): 413–34.

32 B. Schissel, *Blaming Children: Youth Crime, Moral Panics, and the Politics of Hate* (Halifax: Fernwood Publishing, 1997).

33 Canada, Department of Justice, *Canada's Youth Criminal Justice Act* (2001), http://www.canada.justice.gc.ca/en/dept/pub/ycja/youth.html.

34 A. McLellan, [press release], remarks by [then] federal Justice Minister, Department of Justice (May 12, 1999).

35 Bala, "The Development of Canada's Youth Justice Law."

36 P. Mallea, *Getting Tough on Kids: Young Offenders and the "Law and Order" Agenda* (Winnipeg: Canadian Centre for Policy Alternatives, 1999).

37 Canadian Centre for Justice Statistics (CCJS), "Justice Data Fact Finder," *Juristat* 16 (1997): 9.

38 Alvi, "A Criminal Justice History."

39 Green and Healy, *Tough on Kids.*

40 Bala, "The Development of Canada's Youth Justice Law."

41 International Save the Children Alliance, *Children's Rights: Reality or Rhetoric? The UN Convention on the Rights of the Child: The First Ten Years* (London: ISCA, 1999).

42 Department of Justice Canada. http://canada.justice.gc.ca/en/ps/yj/repository/2overvw/2010001a.html.

43 M. Denov, "Children's Rights or Rhetoric? Assessing Canada's Youth Criminal Justice Act and Its Compliance with the UN Convention on the Rights of the Child," *International Journal of Children's Rights* 12, no. 1 (2004): 1–20.

44 Bala, *Youth Criminal Justice Law* (Toronto: Irwin Law, 2003), p. 411.

45 Ibid.

46 Green and Healy, *Tough on Kids*, pp. 35–36.

47 There are many other examples of the YCJA providing for the participation of young people, including Sections 25, 34, 39(6), 42(1), 48, 56, 59(1), and 63(1).

48 Various groups of immigrant and visible minority youth are discriminated against by the youth criminal justice system; however, there has been more documentation to date about the situation of Aboriginal youth, so that group will be the focus of this section.

49 Royal Commission on Aboriginal Peoples, "Aboriginal Peoples and the Criminal Justice System," *Report of the National Round Table on Justice Issues* (Ottawa: Canada Communications Group, 1993).

50 Statistics Canada, *Aboriginal Peoples in Canada: Canadian Centre for Justice Statistics Profile Series* (Ottawa: StatsCan, 2001).

51 Saskatchewan, *Report of the Indian Justice Review Committee* (Saskatoon: Government of Saskatchewan, 1992).

52 Green and Healy, *Tough on Kids*, p. 91.

53 N. Bala, "Juvenile Justice: International Themes and a Canadian Perspective," in A. Trahan, ed., *A New Vision for a Non-Violent World: Justice for Each Child,* proceedings of the 4th Biennial International Conference of the International Association of Women Judges (Quebec: Editions Yvon Blais, 1999), pp. 305–13.

54 *Criminal Code,* R.S.C. 1985, c. C-46, s. 718.2(e).

55 Section 718(2)(e) is not without its critics. Roach and Rudin (2000) and Stenning and Roberts (2001) have argued that the new provision will not significantly reduce Aboriginal overrepresentation in the Canadian prison system. See K. Roach and J. Rudin, "Gladue: The Judicial and Political Reception of a Promising Decision," *Canadian Journal of Criminology* 42 (2000): 355–88; P. Stenning and J. Roberts, "Empty Promises: Parliament, the Supreme Court, and the Sentencing of Aboriginal Offenders," *Saskatchewan Law Review* 64 (2001): 137–68.

56 L. Chartrand, "Aboriginal Youth and the Criminal Justice System," in K. Campbell, ed., *Understanding Youth Justice in Canada* (Toronto: Pearson Education, 2005).
57 Committee on the Rights of the Child, *Concluding Observations of the Committee on the Rights of the Child: Canada* (2003), CRC/C/15/add.215, p. 13.
58 Department of Justice Canada. http://canada.justice.gc.ca/en/ps/yj/repository/2overvw/2010001a.html.
59 UNICEF, *Implementation Handbook for the Convention on the Rights of the Child* (New York: UNICEF, 1998), p. 43.
60 L. Chartrand, "Aboriginal Youth."
61 Canada, Department of Justice, *Canada's Youth Criminal Justice Act: A New Law, A New Approach* (Ottawa: Minister of Public Works and Government Services Canada, 1999).
62 UNICEF, *Implementation Handbook*, p. 545.
63 Society for Children and Youth of British Columbia, *The UN Convention on the Rights of the Child: Does Domestic Legislation Measure Up?* (Vancouver: SCYBC, 1998).
64 S. Artz, D. Nicholson, and C. Rodrigez, "Understanding Girls' Delinquency: Looking beyond Their Behaviour," in K. Campbell, ed., *Understanding Youth Justice in Canada* (Toronto: Pearson Education, 2005).
65 Green and Healy, *Tough on Kids*.
66 L. Cuddington, "Young Offenders: A Correctional Policy Perspective," *Forum* 7, no. 1 (1995): 2–43, http://www.198.103.98.138/crd/forum/e07/e071m.htm.
67 UNICEF, *Implementation Handbook*, p. 27.
68 K. Campbell, *Understanding Youth Justice in Canada* (Toronto: Pearson Education, 2005).
69 S. Meuwese, *Kids behind Bars*, p. 42.
70 Committee on the Rights of the Child, *Concluding Observations*, p. 12.
71 J. Runcie, "The Globalization of Crime Control—the Case of Youth Justice," *Theoretical Criminology* 9, no. 1 (2005): 35–64.
72 Bala, "The Development of Canada's Youth Justice Law."
73 S. Rook, "Fewer Youths Heading to Court Statscan Says," *Globe and Mail*, June 25, 2005, A8.
74 Ibid.

Bibliography

Alvi, S. 2002. "A Criminal Justice History of Children and Youth in Canada." In B. Schissel and C. Brooks, eds., *Marginality and Condemnation*. Halifax: Fernwood Publishing.

Amnesty International. 2005. http://www.amnesty.ca/child/report.php.

Angus Reid Group. 1998. *Canadian Attitudes toward the Young Offenders Act*. Ottawa: Angus Reid.

Artz, S., D. Nicholson, and C. Rodrigez. 2005. "Understanding Girls' Delinquency: Looking beyond Their Behaviour." In K. Campbell, ed., *Understanding Youth Justice in Canada*. Toronto: Pearson Education.

Bala, N. 1994. "What's Wrong with YOA Bashing? What's Wrong with the YOA? Recognizing the Limits of the Law." *Canadian Journal of Criminology* 36: 247–70.

———. 1999. "Juvenile Justice: International Themes and a Canadian Perspective. In A. Trahan, ed., *A New Vision for a Non-Violent World: Justice for Each Child*. Proceedings of the 4th Biennial International Conference of the International Association of Women Judges. Quebec: Les Editions Yvon Blais, pp. 305–13.

———. 2003. *Youth Criminal Justice Law*. Toronto: Irwin Law.

———. 2005. "The Development of Canada's Youth Justice Law." In K. Campbell, ed., *Understanding Youth Justice in Canada*. Toronto: Pearson Education.

BBC News. 2005. *US Held Youngsters at Abu Graib*.

Bell, S. 2002. *Young Offenders and Juvenile Justice: A Century after the Fact*. Scarborough, ON: Nelson.

Burkeman, O. 2003. "Children Held at Guantanamo Bay." *The Guardian*. April 24. http://www.guardian.co.uk/international/story/0,3604,942310,00.html.

Campbell, K. 2005. *Understanding Youth Justice in Canada*. Toronto: Pearson Education.

Canada, Department of Justice. 1999. *Canada's Youth Criminal Justice Act: A New Law, A New Approach*. Ottawa: Minister of Public Works and Government Services Canada, 1999.

———. 2001. "Canada's Youth Criminal Justice Act." http://www.canada.justice.gc.ca/en/dept/pub/ycja/youth.html.

Canadian Centre for Justice Statistics. 1997. "Justice Data Fact Finder." *Juristat* 16, no. 9.

Chartrand, L. 2005. "Aboriginal Youth and the Criminal Justice System." In K. Campbell, ed., *Understanding Youth Justice in Canada*. Toronto: Pearson Education.

Committee on the Rights of the Child. 2003. *Concluding Observations of the Committee on the Rights of the Child: Canada*. CRC/C/15/Add.215.

Covell, K., and B. Howe. 2001. *The Challenge of Children's Rights for Canada*. Waterloo: Wilfrid Laurier University Press.

Cuddington, L. 1995. "Young Offenders: A Correctional Policy Perspective." *Forum* 7, no. 1: 43. http//www.198.103.98.138/crd/forum/e07/e071m.htm.

Denov, M. 2004. "Children's Rights or Rhetoric? Assessing Canada's Youth Criminal Justice Act and Its Compliance with the UN Convention on the Rights of the Child." *International Journal of Children's Rights* 12, no. 1: 1–20.

Garland, D. 2001. *The Culture of Control*. Oxford: Oxford University Press.

Green, G., and K. Healy. 2003. *Tough on Kids: Rethinking Approaches to Youth Justice*. Saskatoon: Purich Publishing.

Hogeveen, B. 2005. "History, Development, and Transformations in Canadian Juvenile Justice, 1800–1984." In K. Campbell, ed., *Understanding Youth Justice in Canada*. Toronto: Pearson Education.

International Save the Children Alliance. 1999. *Children's Rights: Reality or Rhetoric? The UN Convention on the Rights of the Child: The First Ten Years*. London: ISCA.

Mallea, P. 1999. *Getting Tough on Kids: Young Offenders and the "Law and Order" Agenda*. Winnipeg: Canadian Centre for Policy Alternatives.

McLellan, A. 1999, May 12 [press release]. Remarks by [then] federal Justice Minister, Department of Justice.

Meuwese, S. 2003. *Kids behind Bars*. Amsterdam: Defence for Children International.

Roach, K., and J. Rudin. 2000. "Gladue: The Judicial and Political Reception of a Promising Decision." *Canadian Journal of Criminology* 42: 355–88.

Roberts, J. 2003. "Sentencing Juvenile Offenders in Canada: An Analysis of Recent Reform Legislation." *Journal of Contemporary Criminal Justice* 19, no. 4: 413–34.

Rook, S. 2005. "Fewer Youths Heading to Court, Statscan Says." *Globe and Mail,* June 25, A8.

Royal Commission on Aboriginal Peoples. 1993. "Aboriginal Peoples and the Criminal Justice System." *Report of the National Round Table on Justice Issues*. Ottawa: Canada Communications Group.

Runcie, J. 2005. "The Globalization of Crime Control—the Case of Youth Justice." *Theoretical Criminology* 9, no. 1: 35–64.

Saskatchewan. 1992. *Report of the Indian Justice Review Committee*. Saskatoon: Government of Saskatchewan.

Schissel, B. 1997. *Blaming Children: Youth Crime, Moral Panics, and the Politics of Hate*. Halifax: Fernwood Publishing.

Society for Children and Youth of British Columbia, Canada. 1998. *The UN Convention on the Rights of the Child: Does Domestic Legislation Measure Up?* Vancouver: SCYBC.

Sprott, J. 1998. "Understanding Public Opposition to a Separate Youth Justice System." *Crime and Delinquency* 44: 399–411.

Statistics Canada. 2001. *Aboriginal Peoples in Canada: Canadian Centre for Justice Statistics Profile Series*. Ottawa: StatsCan.

Stenning, P., and J. Roberts. 2001. "Empty Promises: Parliament, the Supreme Court, and the Sentencing of Aboriginal Offenders." *Saskatchewan Law Review* 64: 137–68.

Tufts, J., and J. Roberts. 2002. "Sentencing Juvenile Offenders: Comparing Public Preferences and Judicial Practice." *Criminal Justice Policy Review* 13, no. 1: 46–64.

UNICEF. 1998. *Implementation Handbook for the Convention on the Rights of the Child*. New York: UNICEF.

———. 2005. "Juvenile Justice." http://www.unicef.org/protection/index _juveniljustice.html.

Restorative Justice
Toward a Rights-based Approach

8

Shannon Moore

Introduction

Restorative justice is sourced in ancient and contemporary indigenous epistemologies found the world over and is best viewed in contrast to mainstream, colonialist systems of justice found in countries such as Canada.[1] Today it is a global social movement, about a quarter of a century old, that aims to transform understanding, responses to crime, and various social harms.[2] Restorative practice is built on a communitarian value base, a perspective of interconnectedness, a focus on full participation, a respect for human social and interpersonal relationships, and an emphasis on the voices of victims of harm.[3] In restorative practice the healing of harm done is the central focus. Accordingly, the emphasis is on oral and emotive responses and on interventions that are non-hierarchal and non-linear. The range of restorative justice practices is vast and may include dyads, groups, or entire communities, as well as fact sharing, acceptance of responsibility, mutual resolution, restitution, reduction in fear, and even a challenge to social inequity.

From the perspective of the UN Convention on the Rights of the Child (CRC), restorative justice and children's rights can be understood as theoretically congruent, for they are premised from similar principles. Moreover, through their interconnection in practice, they have the potential to facilitate more ethical and democratic responses to young people in

Shannon Moore, Department of Child and Youth Studies, Brock University conflict with the law. Also, practices based on restorative justice and children's rights correspond in many ways to Canada's domestic and international legal commitments, including those relating to the CRC and the UN Basic Principles of Restorative Justice.[4] Each of these UN metanarratives has been adopted by Canada, having been drafted with significant Canadian input.[5] Yet despite the potential applications of these interconnected principles, only recently have they been linked in Canadian discourse.[6] These principles have yet to become established in integrated practice in partnership with Canada's young people. However, movement toward this, and toward a fully fledged system of rights-based restorative justice, is both desirable and possible for Canada. This journey may be informed by several international developments[7] and by a Canadian model for rights-based restorative justice.[8]

Rights-based restorative justice[9] as a framework for domestic policy and practice can be understood in the context of (a) recent legislative developments in Canada and (b) a practical focus on fair, proportionate, and democratic interventions with young people in conflict with the law. Canada ratified the CRC in 1991, adopted the UN Basic Principles of Restorative Justice in 2002, and enacted the federal Youth Criminal Justice Act (YCJA) in 2003 (see previous chapter). These events suggest that Canada is committed to a system of youth justice that will integrate the principles of restorative practice with those of children's human rights.[10] The YCJA has emerged as a major legislative engine driving rights-based initiatives, notwithstanding the substantial obstacles that have yet to be addressed if restorative practice and children's are to be actualized in practice.

This chapter presents a focused discussion on policy and practice related to restorative justice in the context of the principles and provisions of the CRC. It is hoped that this chapter will encourage a dialogue about rights-based restorative practice by exploring and critically reflecting on recent developments and obstacles affecting Canada. To this end, the chapter begins with an overview of definitions, major themes, and principles in restorative practice. It then explores the Canadian context of restorative justice programs and critically analyzes recent developments. After this, it discusses the practice of restorative justice in terms of relevant articles in the CRC. The chapter concludes with reflections on rights-based restorative practice.

From Canada's Retributive System of Justice Toward Restorative Justice

Canada acquired its retributive justice system from the Europeans during the era of colonization in the seventeenth and eighteenth centuries.

The indigenous justice systems that existed before then continued to prevail informally within First Peoples communities; meanwhile, Canada's official system of justice began to increasingly reflect European legal and political norms. Canada's criminal law and criminal justice policy, with its focus on retribution and punishment, was "invented by Western culture within the process of colonization and the formation of Eurocentrism"[11] and essentially "overlooks millennia of First Peoples history."[12]

In contrast to Canada's retributive system of justice, restorative justice is an approach associated with ancient pre-colonial teachings. Aboriginal communities in Canada were imbued with vibrancy, spirituality, and social order long before colonization.[13] Restorative practice reflects the values of indigenous systems of justice in Canada (and elsewhere) and implies certain processes and outcomes. This approach has a practical goal: to restore balance to the lives of victims of crime as well as peace within the community, while allowing offenders the chance to redeem themselves and develop a sense of responsibility for the harm they have done.[14] Very unlike European justice, restorative practice focuses on accountability, respect, disharmonies in relationships, and capacity building. Its processes aim to reduce antagonisms. Retributive justice, in contrast, focuses on a single act of crime, is both adversarial and punitive, and can increase the isolation and alienation of offenders in relation to the community.[15]

Restorative justice is defined by its focus on healthy human relationships and on healing the effects of wrongdoing through the promotion of dialogue among individuals within communities.[16] In this way it is context-bound and co-constructed within the social worlds of those affected by crime, harm, and conflict.[17] The principles of restorative justice can be summarized as follows. First, the perpetration of crime and the infliction of harm are fundamentally violations of human beings or human relationships as they rupture the well-being of individuals, communities, and societies. Second, the goals of the restorative process are to repair harm done and to restore relationships between individuals and community in ways that bring about greater equilibrium among all those involved. Third, all restorative processes must be voluntary and must respect the rights of individuals to choice. This is achieved through sensitive consideration of power relationships and the social and structural inequities within society. Fourth, victims of crime must always be of central concern and must be given the choice to participate in the process. Fifth, perpetrators of wrongdoing are extended the opportunity to accept responsibility for the harm they have caused and a choice to participate in a restorative process. These five principles all emphasize the importance of human interpersonal and social relationships.[18] Restorative justice takes shape in a fluid way; it reflects the needs of particular individuals and communities and at the same time is connected with a single arena through the values of empowerment, accountability, honesty, respect, engagement, volunteerism, restoration, inclusiveness, collaboration, and problem solving.[19]

Restorative programs that authentically reflect the diversity and unique needs of communities are congruent with the basic principles of restorative justice. However, such programs resist prescribed formulations and bureaucratic regulations and so are difficult to evaluate.[20] As a result, standardization has become a key concern now that restorative processes are becoming increasingly integrated into mainstream systems. Ideally, restorative practice with young people will address these concerns through an "emphasis upon the responsibility of the wider family group for their young relatives, rights of children and young people, affirmation of cultural diversity, and encouragement of community-state partnerships."[21] These process qualities are congruent with rights-based restorative justice as they emphasize concern for ethical and democratic practice.[22]

Many variations in contemporary restorative approaches are possible, such as family group conferencing, youth justice committees, community-based hosting processes, healing circles, reconciliation and conferencing, and victim–offender mediation. All of these programs and processes share the same guiding principles as were listed above and thereby establish a template for balancing the diversity and unity that are both so essential in our increasingly pluralistic society.[23] At the same time, there can be large differences among programs regarding the degree of autonomy that communities retain to design them and the amount of government interference they accept. In Canada's unique political landscape, each province and territory independently decides how restorative justice is to be translated into practice, and this had led to considerable variation across the country.

Canadian Context for Restorative Justice Programs

Currently, restorative justice processes are being integrated into mainstream, correctional, and grassroots programs throughout rural and urban Canada. Restorative approaches have in fact been used informally in a broad range of communities for more than thirty years. The roots of contemporary restorative practice can be traced back to the work of Mark Yantzi in the Kitchener–Waterloo region of Ontario and also to Community Justice Initiatives—an organization that continues to thrive today.[24] Community Justice Initiatives is known worldwide as having started the first restorative justice program.[25] Today, restorative justice informs responses to wrongdoing in every Canadian province and territory through programs based in corrections, communities, and schools.

In 1998 a survey of restorative justice in Canada conducted by Correctional Services Canada found that two hundred programs were operating that year.[26] In 2003 a report commissioned by Justice Canada noted that community and restorative programs featuring youth justice committees numbered 262.[27] These committees have been established to work in partnership with the justice system and are founded on principles of restorative justice, although they are regulated in a manner that leads to prescribed processes. In contrast, community-centred approaches to restorative justice respond to specific local needs. Many restorative justice initiatives are unlike youth justice committees in that they are grassroots and have been developed through community organizations or First Peoples communities.[28] That these initiatives can choose to operate independently reflects a flexible approach to programming that is intended to be responsive to the unique needs of particular communities.

Current and accurate data regarding Canadian programs are difficult to gather, because so many programs are informal. Clearly, though, the numbers are still growing, which perhaps indicates their effectiveness. This expansion probably also reflects the call for community-based programming under the new YCJA. After the YCJA came into effect in 2003, public- and private-sector support for these programs grew, while public education increased awareness.[29]

As Myriam Denov noted in chapter 7, the YCJA allows the provinces and territories a great deal of autonomy in the design and delivery of community and restorative justice programs. Thus there continues to be considerable variation across the country. An overview of some programs is provided next, by province and territory.

In British Columbia it is estimated that as many as ninety restorative justice programs are currently operating, eighteen of which are in First Peoples communities.[30] Most of these programs are community based and provide services to young people, including children under twelve.[31] For instance, in Vancouver, both the John Howard Society of the Lower Mainland and the Vancouver Aboriginal Transformational Justice Service provide services for youth. In Greater Victoria, seven programs offer restorative justice services. These programs utilize a wide variety of models, including community accountability panels, victim–offender programs, family group–community conferencing mediation, and mentorship, assessment, and counselling services.

In Alberta an estimated 102 youth justice committees are responsible for community and restorative justice programming. For example, in Edmonton, the Community Conferencing Association focuses on serving youth through a conferencing model, and Native Counselling Services of Alberta offers a variety of services to youth, including to those under twelve. In Calgary, programs focus on a conferencing model such as used by the Alberta Seventh Step Society and the Calgary Community Conferencing Project. Other programs, such as one in Red Deer, focus on family group conferencing or victim–offender mediation.[32]

In Saskatchewan there are four government-designated community justice committees to provide programming and an additional fifty non-designated initiatives in Aboriginal communities.[33] Most of these programs use the victim–offender mediation model and family group conferencing.

In Manitoba there are about fifty-eight designated youth justice committees, although it is unclear how many are active. In places such as Brandon, services include family and community conferencing, victim–offender mediation, circles of support, and circle sentencing. In Winnipeg, Onashowewin focuses mainly on young people using victim–offender mediation, conferencing, and circle sentencing.[34] Also, Manitoba Keewatinook Okimakanak (MKO) First Nations Justice focuses on developing and implementing a system of Aboriginal justice in Manitoba. It is operating in ten First Nation communities. Its mandate is to empower First Nations to assume direction and control of the criminal justice process, through a model that is restorative and culturally relevant.[35]

In Ontario, it is estimated that fifty-six programs founded on principles of restorative justice are currently operating. Twenty-seven of these are community-based restorative justice projects, and sixteen provide services for youth.[36] There are also twenty-three government-sponsored youth justice committees in the province.[37] It is expected that these committees will expand to more locations across the province, although it is important to note that many of the established committees are currently inactive. An example of an emerging program is the multifaith "Hosting" pilot project, which is found in five regions in southern Ontario. Also, six Aboriginal community-based programs are listed in the province.[38]

In Quebec, eight restorative justice programs are identified, and seven of these serve young people specifically. All of the programs for young people seem to focus on victim–offender mediation and also provide some family group conferencing. In Montreal, two programs seem to be based on restorative justice principles, although the details are unclear.[39]

In New Brunswick, six restorative justice programs are operating, and three of these provide services to young people. For instance, Moncton has three programs: two focus on training and community education, while the John Howard Society offers community justice forums for young people in addition to services for adults. In Fredericton, the Department of Criminology serves young people with a circle-of-support format, and alternative measures are the focus of Victim Services and Restorative Justice of the Department of Public Safety.[40]

In Newfoundland and Labrador, an estimated thirty-two designated youth justice committees have been endorsed by Justice Canada.[41] In addition, it is estimated that three non-designated restorative justice programs are providing youth services. In St. John's, the John Howard Society serves about one thousand young offenders annually. Also in St. John's, Circles of Support is developing a program for young people.[42]

The Nova Scotia Restorative Justice program, under the direction of Dr. Don Clairmont, is a national leader; its goal is to implement restorative justice throughout the criminal justice system in that province. The premise in Nova Scotia is that restorative justice can have applications throughout the justice process, from pre-charge to corrections. Launched in 1999 with federal government support after two years of planning, this program is now fully funded provincially. Programming is carried out by non-profit agencies. Restorative justice in Nova Scotia is considered "institutionalized," in the sense that it is available across the province through the Department of Justice.[43]

On Prince Edward Island, programs are operating in Charlottetown and Stratford. The Island's Restorative Justice Network, for example, has a mandate to serve young people through victim–offender mediation and conferencing.[44]

In the Northwest Territories there are thirty designated community justice committees (similar to youth justice committees), although only about twenty-three seem to be active.[45] Currently, only two restorative justice programs are listed on the NWT justice website. These are in Fort Smith and Inuvik. They are supported by the Community Justice Division of the Department of Justice in NWT, and they focus on developing safer and healthier communities through alternative justice programming.[46] The Inuvik Justice Committee specifically offers youth programming for alternative measures and diversion. In Fort Smith, youth programming includes victim–offender mediation, family group conferencing, circle sentencing, and justice committees.[47]

In Nunavut the Community Justice Program (Department of Justice Nunavut) has a mandate to promote crime prevention, services for victims, and greater community involvement and control in responses to crime.[48] This mission statement reflects principles of restorative justice. There are twenty-five government-designated community justice committees in the territory, though it is unclear how many are currently active. A recent publication exploring the integration of principles of restorative practice, child rights, wisdom from Inuit Elders, and cross-cultural counselling for school-based programming indicates possible future directions for rights-based restorative practice with young people in this northern context.[49]

In Yukon, nine restorative justice programs seem to be operating. Many of them offer services in First Peoples communities. Processes focus on victim–offender mediation, conferencing, and circle sentencing.[50]

Generally, there is considerable variation in program development, implementation, and services. This seems to reflect Canada's vast cultural and regional diversity. Also, the ideological and philosophical differences that distinguish government-regulated youth justice committees from grassroots community-centred or First Peoples agencies seem to have an impact on how these programs are implemented and monitored. For example, several youth justice committees across the country that are regulated and funded by Corrections Canada are inactive; programs that respond flexibly to the unique needs of their communities seem to have greater longevity—perhaps as a result of greater local legitimacy. At the same time, many grassroots programs take an approach that moves away from certification, government regulation, and endorsement in order to retain flexibility and community accountability.[51] Unfortunately, this had led to a dearth of rigorous evaluations for many programs (Nova Scotia being a noteworthy exception) and to a lack of standardization founded on the UN Basic Principles of Restorative Justice.[52] Furthermore, programs are currently being developed, piloted, or revised, and this presents a challenge when reporting the current status of restorative justice.

Critical Analysis: Toward Ethical and Democratic Restorative Practice

The practice of restorative justice is not without controversy.[53] While these programs have proven strengths, it is essential to acknowledge these critiques in order to safeguard the integrity of practice. For example, restorative programming may "widen the net" of youth justice systems if the focus becomes increased intolerance and a heightening of social control. By their very nature, restorative justice processes are community centred and rely on citizen volunteers for support. Thus they depend on a critical mass of investment, interest, and knowledge of alternative approaches in order to sustain themselves. In addition, the YCJA is likely to encourage a bifurcation of youth justice, with restorative justice resorted to for minor offences and traditional justice applied to more serious offences.[54]

Further critiques have emerged from social justice and feminist movements[55] and are consistent with critical social pedagogy and rights-based thinking: "The issue of power in relationships is very important when you consider alternative dispute resolution processes because ADR focuses on people who share a problem and share the resolution of the problem. When there is power imbalance between people who share the problem it may be difficult to engage in an equitable problem solving process and generate an equitable resolution to the problem."[56]

From this, it follows that by recognizing the complexity of justice, we are more likely to take into account the challenges of equality, power relationships, and vulnerability when designing programs. Furthermore, youth justice stakeholders have a responsibility to ensure ethical practice with everyone—perhaps most especially with individuals who have been victimized or who are vulnerable, including young people—by establishing a climate of equality, mutuality, and solidarity. One way to achieve this is to ensure that supports are provided for individuals in order to account for power differentials as well as personal needs—especially in "adultist" institutions.[57] Also, processes need to emphasize informed consent and voluntary participation. Victims' needs must be a central focus; power relations need to be addressed and equalized; and all proceedings must be physically, emotionally, and psychologically "safe" to the maximum possible extent.[58]

Another valid critique of restorative justice is that the real emphasis of "restoration" is on the return of individuals to a state of *dis*equilibrium."[59] We can begin to address this criticism by focusing on the impact of power relations, equality, and vulnerability as highlighted in social justice and feminist discourse.[60] The aim of healing justice must be transformation in a context of mutuality, equality, and solidarity, rather than restoration to imbalance.

Canadian sociologist and justice activist Ruth Morris[61] has outlined several critiques of restorative justice that have led her to emphasize transformative justice. She makes the following three points. First, it is unhealthy to talk about restoring victims as this involves restoring a past without addressing the trauma of victimization. Second, structural-distributive injustices in society and the justice system are not adequately or consistently addressed by restorative processes. Third, the term "restorative justice" suggests that there was justice originally, which was then lost—and this is often not the case. In essence, according to Morris, transformative justice may be truer to the intentions of restorative justice and a focus on lasting change and healing. Moreover, in the author's experience working with young people, a children's rights approach has the potential to provide a framework for a more transformative restorative justice. Integrating the CRC in policy and practice would help safeguard the well-being of vulnerable participants and raise their voices in a context of safety and full participation. Once we understand the links between restorative justice and child rights, a safe, ethical, and transformative experience of justice may be realized.

Contextualizing Restorative Justice and Children's Rights

In light of Canada's international commitments to the CRC and the UN Basic Principles of Restorative Justice, the lens provided by rights-based restorative justice[62] could provide an effective standard of practice in systems of youth justice. Certainly, viewing restorative practice in the context of children's and young people's rights reveals several links between these constructs. Much like human rights, restorative justice is not a new concept: both have roots that can be traced through the millennia, notwithstanding their recent appearance in discourses influencing how we relate to and create space for children and young people in mainstream society.[63] In Canada this is demonstrated through community-based initiatives, provincial restorative-justice programs, and the YCJA, which reflects an openness to seriously engage with restorative justice processes.[64] Similarly, an interest in rights-based policy and practice has slowly evolved across service sectors in Canada over the past decade. In addition, one can find restorative justice principles in Aboriginal, indigenous, and ancient cultures the world over, not only in North America but also in ancient Celtic traditions and in regions of Africa and Asia, for instance. Thus, it should not be surprising that in a contemporary sense, "over 80 countries use some form of restorative justice in addressing crime, [and] the number could be closer to 100."[65]

Canada is acknowledged as one of the pioneers in this alternative community-centred perspective. This country's first community-based justice program was founded in 1974.[66] Also, Canada made a significant contribution to the drafting of the UN Basic Principles of Restorative Justice and affirmed the merit of these guidelines through early adoption.[67] This was a show of global leadership, yet the application of restorative processes has been inconsistent in Canada. The YCJA states that alternatives to the criminal justice system are to be the initial response to young people in conflict with the law for the first time; yet how this policy is translated is up to the individual provinces and territories. Urban and rural communities then get to decide how they will put restorative justice into practice locally. Also, funding is inconsistent or non-existent in many regions, and local citizen volunteers must be mobilized to support the process. These factors have led to inconsistent engagement with and knowledge about restorative justice. Yet at the same time, this fluid interpretation of policy and practice constitutes an opportunity to shape responses to wrongdoing in a manner that reflects the specific needs and values of individuals and communities.

As a social democratic industrial state, Canada has fallen behind other OECD nations in implementing the CRC, even though it was an early supporter, having ratified the convention in 1991.[68] Some of the same obstacles impeding the implementation of the CRC have also plagued the wider adoption of restorative justice. At least to some degree, this is a function of the political structure of Canada. For example, Canada co-hosted the 1990 UN World Summit for Children in New York and promoted the CRC from its inception. Despite this, the CRC has not been integrated into federal legislation, except that CRC principles are mentioned in the recent YCJA.[69] In addition to this, provincial and territorial governments have the constitutional right to decide for themselves whether to embrace the CRC as government policy. One outcome of these political realities has been a lack of awareness of both the CRC and restorative justice among organizations and individual citizens despite national campaigns and federal endorsement.[70] This political reality suggests why there has been so little research and practice in Canada that links restorative justice to children's rights.[71]

Finally, restorative justice and children's rights share congruent principles and assumptions as discussed in the introduction. Rights-based restorative justice[72] has been conceptualized as an approach to youthful offending that focuses on fair, proportionate, ethical, and democratic interventions. Moreover, a rights-based approach for working with young people in conflict with the law is articulated by CRC article 40(1), which asserts that all young people are to be "treated in a manner consistent with the promotion of the child's dignity and work, which reinforces the child's respect for human rights and freedoms of others and which takes into account the child's age and the desirability of promoting the child's reintegration and the child's assuming a constructive role in society." When the focus is on full participation, the voices of victims, offenders, and young people can be heard in matters that affect them. In this way, the principles of CRC articles 2, 3, 6, and 12 can be emphasized in harmony with the UN Basic Principles of Restorative Justice in a rights-based restorative justice framework.[73]

A rights-based framework supports the expansion of responses toward youthful offending beyond the punitive and the retributive. The premise that every young person has an innate citizenship indicative of their equality in relation to human rights is a central link between restorative practice and the CRC.[74] Shared by all young citizens under the principles of both the CRC and restorative justice is the assertion that every young person deserves respect as well as opportunities to be heard, to express their concerns, and to fully participate in matters that concern them.[75] To establish ethical practice, as emphasized earlier, it is also essential to consider power relations. This is especially so in situations of vulnerability or victimization, when calls are being made for compensation.[76] Further open discussion of children's rights within restorative justice policy and practice could strengthen programs for young people in conflict with the law and safeguard their well-being.

The approach outlined above would reinforce non-discrimination (see CRC, article 2) so that all young people have the same human rights regardless of their social and cultural context and whether they are victims or perpetrators of harm. The best interests (see CRC, article 3) of all young participants ought to be central to processes and outcomes. Furthermore, particular attention to the survival and developmental needs of all young participants (see CRC article 6) would prompt appropriate processes and outcomes in the context of the power relations that are typical in circumstances of victimization. Finally, all people affected by crime must have an opportunity to fully and voluntarily participate in restorative justice and have their views heard (CRC, article 12).[77]

In Canada, this author is unaware of any program in which children's rights under the CRC are being established as part of an integrated practice with restorative approaches, although pilot projects are currently being conceptualized.[78] As Katherine Covell points out in chapter 10, most Canadians are unaware that the CRC even exists and that Canada is accountable to the world community to ensure that the rights of young people are protected.[79] Only recently has discourse regarding children's rights and restorative justice entered federal legislation, and the principles linking these frameworks remain essentially unexplored in Canadian practice.[80] Given the general lack of mainstream knowledge about the CRC in Canada, the incorporation of principles of children's rights into the YCJA is especially important. This legislative development arose from a series of consultations with advocates from across Canada, including activists, scholars, and promoters of child rights, who brought the CRC to the clear attention of the House of Commons Standing Committee on Justice and Human Rights.[81] This Senate committee then contributed to the revamping of youth justice in Canada. Still, the natural congruence between the principles of restorative justice and those of children's rights— both centre on respect, accountability, and full participation—has yet to be fully explored, or fully reflected in the law.

Awareness of restorative justice and the CRC continues to evolve in Canada. This has proven to be a long, complex political and practical endeavour shaped by ideological changes in how we understand young people. These shifts in understanding date back to the early 1900s. Over the past century, social constructions of young people, justice, and human rights in Canada have been strongly influenced by ideologies inherited from Britain and France.[82] In addition, policy and mainstream practices serving children have paralleled changes in women's rights over the past century. Early in the last century, young people were perceived as objects of parental authority. After the Second World War, this perspective shifted so that young people came to be viewed as vulnerable and in need of protection. Although past perspectives are difficult to transform, in recent years children have come to be understood the world over as social actors and as citizens and subjects of their lives, rather as than problems to be solved.[83] Note well that world views regarding children and childhood arising from Aboriginal and minority communities are not often visible in the historic literature or in academic discourses, which have tended to embrace mainstream colonial ideologies.

Our conceptualizations of young people continue to evolve and to shape how we respond in the policy and practice arenas. Thus, the meanings attributed to behaviours perpetrated by young people in conflict with the law are socially constructed and will continue to modify as Canadians begin to more fully understand and respect young people from the perspective of human rights. The social construction of youthful offending is often described as deviance, and researchers in Canada and beyond this nation's borders have begun to explore the links between this theoretical stance and retributive responses that focus on social control in the justice system.[84]

Restorative Justice Contextualized by CRC Article 40

A children's rights approach is guided mainly by article 40 of the CRC. Article 40(1) asserts that young people in conflict with the law are to be "treated in a manner consistent with the promotion of the child's dignity and worth, which reinforces the child's respect for human rights and freedoms of others and which takes into account the child's age and the desirability of promoting the child's reintegration and the child's assuming a constructive role in society." Many aspects of article 40 reflect the principles of restorative justice. There is an emphasis on respecting young people as rights-bearing citizens regardless of their behaviours or wrongdoing (see also article 2 on non-discrimination). Opportunities for young people to be held accountable to those affected by their actions reflect the assumption that young people must be encouraged to respect and understand the rights and freedoms of others and how their wrongdoing can affect others (accountability is a central principle of restorative justice).

These restorative principles provide an opportunity to reintegrate young people into their communities as they strive to repair the harms caused by their actions. The impact of wrongdoing is expressed by all parties in restorative processes; this, in turn, challenges young participants to bring their best selves forward, to be socially accountable, and to contribute to society in more constructive ways (see also article 12 on participation and voice).

Similarly, the YCJA uses language that is consistent with article 40 and the principles of restorative justice. This is reflected in the following sections of the YCJA: "Fair and proportionate accountability that is consistent with the greater dependency of young persons and their reduced level of maturity" (s. 3(ii)(b)). This statute is also consistent with article 6, which refers to healthy development. Clearly, there is an emphasis in restorative justice on ensuring the safety of vulnerable participants.

The YCJA continues these points: "enhanced procedural protection to ensure that young persons are treated fairly and that their rights, including their right to privacy, are protected" (s. 3(ii)(b)).

Ontario's chief advocate for children, youth, and families, Judy Finlay, addressed the above statute in relation to her experience consulting with young people about justice during an interview with the author in March 2005: "In some ways the YCJA is more restrictive in terms of rights than the Young Offenders Act—especially in terms of privacy, so there are some issues that don't offer privacy. Other areas are more expansive and more inclusive in terms of young people—seeing them not as criminals but as young people and reflecting on that differently."[85] This statement highlights the challenge of transforming legislation into policy and meaningful practice. In order to facilitate ethical and democratic practice for young people, whole systems will need to be considered, including the interaction of CRC principles and provisions with the values imbedded in restorative processes. Central to a rights-based and restorative justice approach is respect—in relation both to privacy and to other dimensions of selfhood.

Recognition of the challenge of transforming legislation such as the YCJA into meaningful policy and practice is central to understanding the social and political context of restorative justice and child rights. Finlay expands on this point: "During the early phases of the development of the YCJA there was far more rights-based language and then with the whole debate a lot was pulled out. I was more hopeful in the early days. I think if people embrace the YCJA the rights will follow. It depends on how people choose and interpret the act provincially and territorially."[86]

The principles of restorative justice and child rights need to be interpreted by justice stakeholders at all levels of the system. This is a particular challenge, given Canada's political landscape. The provinces and territories are autonomous when it comes to interpreting statutes, and as a consequence, much depends on a given region's social and political climate. So a logical first step would be to educate policy-makers and practitioners regarding the core principles of the CRC and restorative justice (article 42). The YCJA is innovative in the sense that it is the first piece of federal legislation to clearly articulate principles of the CRC and restorative justice. Yet impediments to rights-based practice remain, because these principles are presented only in the introduction to this legislation and are not embedded in the remainder of the act.[87]

A rights-based approach to youth justice calls for measures to respond to the factors that lead to incarceration. For instance, article 40(4) states: "A variety of dispositions, such as care, guidance and supervision orders; counselling; probation; foster care; education and vocational training programs and other alternatives to institutional care shall be available to ensure that children are dealt with in a manner appropriate to their well-being and proportionate both to their circumstances and the office."

Further reinforcing the need for alternative measures, the YCJA stipulates that custody "may be imposed for a violent offence." But then Section 39(1) restricts the use of custody for non-violent offences and requires a history of failing to comply with non-custodial sentences—a pattern of non-violent offending, for example.[88] In this way, alternatives to sentencing such as restorative practice are federally legislated as the initial course of action for first-time offenders. It follows that in the YCJA's declaration of principles, express reference to the CRC and the need for enhanced rights for young people facing the state's criminal law power has been made. This includes the requirement that all levels of the justice system consider extrajudicial measures—such as restorative justice—before proceeding with judicial options. This in effect recognizes article 40 and the merit of restorative justice. Again, the challenge remains to develop an integrated rights-based restorative practice.

Restorative Justice Contextualized by Article 30

The especially vulnerable circumstances of Aboriginal children are well documented throughout this volume. Friendly, van Daalen-Smith, Denov, Bennett, and Waldock discuss the overrepresentation of Aboriginal children in many areas of risk to healthy development. Aboriginal Canadians (Inuit, Metis, and First Nations) also are disproportionately represented in the criminal justice system as victims and offenders of crime and are described as the "most vulnerable group of children and youth in Canada today and in the future."[89] Aboriginal Canadians are more likely to be "born into poverty, suffer health problems, be victims of maltreatment, be placed away from their families and communities in provincial and territorial child welfare systems or be incarcerated in youth correctional facilities."[90] This increased risk of Aboriginal young people becoming involved in the youth justice system is reflected in an incarceration rate eight times higher than among non-Aboriginal youth. Moreover, it is evident that young people in contact with the welfare system often cross over into the justice systems.[91] These facts call attention to the need for social justice in relation to structural and distributive inequities in Canada.

Given the reality of increased risk factors for Aboriginal young people and the indigenous pre-colonial roots of community-based justice, contextualizing restorative justice with article 30 of the CRC could support an important youth justice response: "In those States in which ethnic, religious or linguistic minorities or persons of indigenous origin exist, a child belonging to such a minority or who is indigenous shall not be denied the right, in community with other members of his or her group, to enjoy his or her own culture, to profess and practice his or her own religion, or to use his or her own language." The ancient foundations of restorative practice are congruent with the traditional teachings represented in the diverse cultures of Aboriginal Canadians.[92] Returning to the communitarian values of restorative processes in response to Aboriginal youth in conflict with law is arguably in accord with article 30. Here, it is important to emphasize that there are important distinctions to be made between restorative justice and Aboriginal justice in Canada.[93] If we accept that the cause of Aboriginal overrepresentation in the justice system is colonization, we then understand that the aim of Aboriginal justice is decolonization through community building.[94] Restorative justice in this context has a different focus, in the sense that such processes may strengthen communities, but community building is not the essential standard for measuring success.[95]

The YCJA also references to article 30 and restorative practice in the following sections of the YCJA:

> respect gender, ethnic, cultural and linguistic differences and respond to the needs of aboriginal young persons and of young persons with special requirements. (s. 3(iv)(a))

> timely intervention that reinforces the link between the offending behaviour and its consequences. (s. 3(iv)(b))

> within the limits of fair and proportionate accountability, the measures taken against young persons who commit offences should:

(i) reinforce respect for societal values,

(ii) encourage the repair of harm done to victims and the community

(iii) be meaningful for the individual young person given his or her needs and level of development and, where appropriate, involve the parents, the extended family, the community and social or other agencies in the young person's rehabilitation and reintegration. (s. 3)

Taken together, the above sections further affirm an emphasis on restorative, timely, value-based, and socially and culturally sensitive responses to offending behaviours.

Nevertheless, since the YCJA became law, significant advances have not been made with regard to Aboriginal young people. Finlay confirms this failure: "Because we have so many aboriginal young people in the child welfare system the rate is far higher than non-aboriginal—largely because of poverty and because of some of the conditions on reserve— and history and residential schools and alcoholism ... unless we assist communities in healing and assist communities in looking after and managing their own children then we going to have them gravitate to the justice system we know ... I think higher than 20%, a conservative estimate—come to the youth justice systems from the child welfare system."[96] Hence, the challenges faced by Aboriginal young people in this country may take decades to transform meaningfully through Aboriginal and social justice.

Finlay also described how large numbers of young people in the child welfare system often migrate into the justice system—which means removing them from reserves because rural Northern communities lack resources for youth justice. Indeed, the challenges faced by Aboriginal young people are indicative of "an element of racism—if the same circumstances existed for non-aboriginal people I am wondering if we would be as tolerant."[97] There is a "legislative requirement to pay 'particular attention to the circumstances of Aboriginal young persons.'"[98] A rights-based restorative justice framework has the potential to transcend binary notions of right-doing and wrong-doing and to address the underlying causes of behaviours such as racism, and distributive and structural injustices.

Accurate Knowledge: Article 42

To realize rights-based restorative practice, Canadians will need accurate knowledge about the principles and provisions of children's rights (article 42)[99] and the UN Basic Principles of Restorative Justice. Ideological and political barriers impede this initial and essential step.[100]

Notwithstanding Canada's adoption of the CRC and the UN Basic Principles of Restorative Justice, individuals responsible for extrajudicial responses are generally unaware of, and receive little or no training in, the principles of either UN metanarrative. Youth justice stakeholders could benefit from knowledge of rights-based restorative justice in that it would help them standardize practices.[101] So, the first step to implementation and monitoring of a rights-based restorative practice is widespread education.[102]

Accountability to the International Community: Article 44

When Canada ratified the CRC, it was committing itself to uphold a minimum standard of care for children and young people. It was also committing itself to report its progress in meeting the Convention's standards to the Committee on the Rights of the Child every five years (article 44).[103]

The Committee on the Rights of the Child expressed concern in 1995 and in 2003 regarding the complicated nature of Canada's governance and the division of responsibilities among federal, provincial, and territorial systems in matters affecting young people. First, the Committee emphasized the importance of article 12 and the right of young people to be heard, with an emphasis on judicial proceedings. Related to article 12 are articles 2 (on non-discrimination) and 3 (on best interests), which explicitly call for integration of the CRC into domestic law. Finally, the Committee reinforced the need to protect children who belong to vulnerable and disadvantaged groups, such as Aboriginal children.[104] Rights-based restorative justice was developed in response to these critiques and aims to contribute to fulfilling Canada's responsibility to article 44.[105]

Canada has also endorsed the UN Economic and Social Council resolution on the basic principles and use of restorative justice programs in criminal matters. This resolution recognizes calls for the significant growth of restorative justice worldwide and for such initiatives to draw from traditional and indigenous forms of justice. In addition, the resolution suggests an evolving response to crime that respects the dignity and equality of each person, builds understanding, and promotes social harmony by healing victims, offenders, and communities.[106] The CRC and UN Basic Principles of Restorative Justice point to Canada's responsibilities to international law and for leadership in relation to the human rights of young people.

Closing Reflections

There is an opportunity for Canada to engage in a rights-based restorative practice, given historic and contemporary developments here. Current frameworks have the potential and the legal mandate to support the integration of the CRC and the UN Basic Principles of Restorative Justice in systems affecting young people. In the context of social change, "the concept of globalization has gradually permeated criminology ... and widespread experimentation with restorative justice offers possibilities for rehabilitation ... epitomized by the United Nations Convention on the Rights of the Child."[107] It will remain a challenge to sustain fidelity to the principles of rights-based restorative justice and respond to the diversity of communities in our pluralistic society. This responsiveness to a community-centred approach is the heart of restorative justice and the factor that made Canada a world leader in these processes more than thirty years ago. Leadership is now needed in the arena of social justice and in restorative practices that address racism and structural and distributive inequities. A critical-transformational value base is required that can promote healing through awareness of diversity, difference, and the uneven global experiences of young people.[108]

Notes

1   S.A. Moore and R.C. Mitchell, "Rights-Based Restorative Justice: Towards Critical Praxis with Young People in Conflict with the Law," in *UN Children's Rights Convention: Theory Meets Practice—Proceedings of the International Interdisciplinary Conference on Children's Rights,* 18–19 May 2006, Ghent, Belgium, ed. A. Ang, I. Delens-Ravier, M. Delplace, C. Herman, D. Reynaert, V. Staelens, R. Steel, and M. Verheyde (Mortsel, Belgium: Intersentia, in press).

2   G. Johnstone and D. Van Ness, eds., "Handbook of Restorative Justice," Devon: Willan Publishing, 2007.

3   Moore and Mitchell, "Rights-Based Restorative Justice."

4   United Nations, UN Basic Principles on the Use of Restorative Justice Programs in Criminal Matters (New York and Geneva: Economic and Social Council, 2002).

5   Moore and Mitchell, "Rights-Based Restorative Justice."

6   Ibid. See also S.A. Moore, W. Tulk, and R.C. Mitchell, "Qallunaat Crossing: The Southern–Northern Divide and Promising Practices for Canada's Inuit Young People," *First Peoples Child and Family Review* 2, no. 1 (2005): 117–29.

7   T. Gal, "Child Victims and Restorative Justice: The Appeal, the Risks," paper presented at New Frontiers in Restorative Justice: Advancing Theory and Practice, Centre for Justice and Peace Development, Massey University, Albany, New Zealand, December 2–5, 2004, http://www.restorativejustice.org/

articlesdb/articles/5636 on 14 January 2006; A. Skelton, "Juvenile Justice Reform: Children's Rights and Responsibilities Versus Crime Control," paper presented at the Children's Rights in a Transitional Society Conference, Centre for Child Law, University of Pretoria, RSA, October 30, 1998, http://www .restorativejustice.org/articlesdb/articles/313; A. Wolthuis, "Restorative Aspects in the Dutch Juvenile Justice System," Defence for Children International, October 2000, http://www.defenceforchildren.nl/ariadne/loader .php/en/dci/eng/activities/Justice; Child Rights International, "Draft Recommendations," paper presented at the plenary Violence in the Home and Family, June 16, http://www.crin .org/violence/search/closeup.asp?infoID=5740; U. Kilkelly, R. Kilpatrick, L. Lundy, L. Moore, P. Scaton, C. Davey, C. Dwyer, and S. McAllister, *Children's Rights in Northern Ireland,* research commissioned by the Northern Ireland Commissioner for Children and Young People (Belfast: Queen's University, 2005).

 8 Moore and Mitchell, "Rights-Based Restorative Justice."

 9 Ibid.

10 M. Denov, "Children's Rights or Rhetoric? Assessing Canada's Youth Criminal Justice Act and Its Compliance with the UN Convention on the Rights of the Child," *International Journal of Children's Rights* 12 (2004): 1–20.

11 P. McLaren, *Revolutionary Multiculturalism: Pedagogies of Dissent for the New Millennium* (Boulder: Westview Press, 1997), p. 45.

12 E. Neegan, "Excuse Me Who Are the First Peoples of Canada? A Historical Analysis of Aboriginal Education in Canada Then and Now," *International Journal of Inclusive Education* 9, no. 1 (2005): 3–15.

13 G. Radwanski and J. Luttrell, *Will of a Nation: Awakening the Canadian Spirit* (Toronto: Stoddart, 1992).

14 M. Umbreit and R. Coates, "Multicultural Implications of Restorative Juvenile Justice," *Federal Probation* (December 1999): 44–51; Moore, Tulk, and Mitchell, "Qallunaat Crossing."

15 Moore and Mitchell, "Rights-Based Restorative Justice."

16 S.A. Moore, "Restorative Justice and Education: Emergent Connections and Possibilities," *Connections* (2001): 110–15; idem, "Towards an Integrated Perspective: Restorative Justice, Cross-Cultural Counselling, and School-Based Programming," in M.H. France, M.C. Rodriguez, and G.G. Hett, eds., *Diversity, Culture, and Counselling: A Canadian Perspective* (Calgary: Detselig, 2004); Moore, Tulk, and Mitchell, "Qallunaat Crossing;" H. Zehr, *Changing Lenses: A Focus on Crime and Justice* (Scottsdale: Herald Press, 1995).

17 Moore, Tulk, and Mitchell, "Qallunaat Crossing."

18 Moore, "Towards an Integrated Perspective."

19 Restorative Justice Consortium, *Principles of Restorative Processes* (London: Restorative Justice Consortium, 2004), http://www.restorativejustice.org/ articlesdb/authors/1138.

20 R. Morris, *Stories of Transformative Justice* (Toronto: Canadian Scholars' Press, 2000).

21 J. Pennell and G. Burford, "Feminist Praxis: Making Family Group Conferencing Work," in H. Strang and J. Braithwaite, *Restorative Justice and Family Violence* (Cambridge: Cambridge University Press, 2004), p. 108.

22 Moore and Mitchell, "Rights-Based Restorative Justice."

23 Moore, Tulk, and Mitchell, "Qallunaat Crossing"; Moore, "Transdisciplinary Critical Multicultural Pedagogy in Canadian Higher Education," in D. Zinga, ed., *Navigating Multiculturalism* (Toronto: University of Toronto Press, in press).

24 G. Nyp, *Pioneers of Peace: The History of Community Justice Initiatives in the Waterloo Region 1974–2004* (Kitchener: Community Justice Initiatives, 2004); see also Community Justice Initiatives, http://www.cjiwr.com.

25 "Community Justice Initiatives," http://www.cjiwr.com.

26 Correctional Service of Canada, *Inventory of Canadian Events and Initiatives Related to Restorative Justice* (Ottawa: CSC, September, 1998), http://www.justice.gc.ca/en/ps/voc/rjpap.html#restorative.

27 Han and Associates, *National Survey of Youth Justice Committees, Justice Canada* (Ottawa: Department of Justice, 2003), http://canada.justice.gc.ca/en/ps/rs/rep/2003/rr03yj-7/rr03yj-7_04_00.html on 14 January 2006.

28 Ibid.

29 Ontario Multifaith Council on Spiritual and Religious Care, "Annual Report 2004–2005: Restorative Justice," http://www.omc.ca/pdf/2005annualreport.pdf.

30 Han and Associates, *National Survey*.

31 *Restorative Justice Oak Bay*. http://www.rjob.ca/index.asp.

32 CSC, "Restorative Justice Week 2003, 16–23 November," http://www.csc-scc.gc.ca/text/forum/restore2003/basic/12_e.shtml; Han and Associates, *National Survey*.

33 Han and Associates, *National Survey*; CSC, "Restorative Justice Week 2003: Basic Resource Kit," http://www.csc-scc.gc.ca/text/forum/restore2003/basic/12_e.shtml; Commission on First Nations and Metis People and Justice Reform, "Summary of Restorative Justice Initiatives in Saskatchewan Round Table, March 2003," http://www.justicereformcomm.sk.ca/sumMarB-2003.gov.

34 Commission on First Nations, "Summary."

35 Manitoba Keewatinook Ininew Okimowin, "Justice Portfolio," http://www.mkonorth.com/justice.html.

36 Conflict Resolution Network, "Restorative Justice in Canada," http://www.crnetwork.ca.

37 Youth Justice Committees in Ontario, "Overview of Youth Justice Committees," http://www.yjcontario.ca/overview.html.

38 Department of Justice Canada, *Community-based Justice Programs Ontario* (Ottawa: Aboriginal Justice Strategy, n.d.), http://canada.justice.gc.ca/en/ps/ajs/programs/ontario.html.

39 Conflict Resolution Network, *Restorative Justice in Canada*.

40 Ibid.

41 Han and Associates, *National Survey*.

42 Conflict Resolution Network, *Restorative Justice in Canada*.

43 D. Clairmont, "The Nova Scotia Restorative Justice Initiative Final Evaluation Report," December 2005, File #4500009896; idem, "Restorative Justice in Nova Scotia," *Isuma* 1 (Spring 2000), http://www.isuma.net/v01n01/clairmon/clairmon_e.shtml.

44 Conflict Resolution Network, *Restorative Justice in Canada*; Department of Justice Canada, "An Inventory of Government-Based Services That Support the Making of Enforcement and Custody and Access Decisions, Prince Edward Island," http://canada.justice.gc.ca/en/ps/pad/reports/invent/pe.htm.

45 Han and Associates, *National Survey.*
46 Department of Justice, Northwest Territories, "Community Justice," http://www.justice.gov.nt.ca/CommunityJustice/CommunityJustice.htm.
47 Conflict Resolution Network, *Restorative Justice in Canada.*
48 Department of Justice Nunavut, "Community Justice," http://www.justice.gov
.nu.ca/english/commjust.html.
49 Moore, Tulk, and Mitchell, "Qallunaat Crossing."
50 Department of Justice, Yukon, "Community Justice Committees and Information," http://www.justice.gov.yk.ca/prog/cjps/cj/comjuscom.html.
51 Morris, *Stories of Transformative Justice.*
52 Moore and Mitchell, "Rights-Based Restorative Justice"; J. Braithwaite, "Setting Standards for Restorative Justice," *British Journal of Criminology* 42 (2002): 563–77.
53 T. Rugge, J. Bonta, and S. Wallace-Capretta, "Evaluation of the Collaborative Justice Project: A Restorative Justice Program for Serious Crime" (Ottawa: Department of Public Safety and Emergency Preparedness, 2005); J. Latimer, C. Dowden, and D. Muise, "The Effectiveness of Restorative Justice Programs: A Meta-Analysis" (Ottawa: Research and Statistics Division, Department of Justice, 2001), http://canada.justice.gc.ca/en/ps/rs/rep/2001/meta.html.
54 S. Charbonneau, "The Canadian Youth Criminal Justice Act 2003: A Step Forward for Advocates of Restorative Justice?" in E. Elliott and R. Gordon, eds., *New Directions in Restorative Justice: Issues, Practice, Evaluation* (Devon: Willan, 2005), 75.
55 H. Strang and J. Braithwaite, *Restorative Justice and Family Violence* (Cambridge: Cambridge University Press, 2002).
56 Provincial Association Against Family Violence, *Keeping an Open Mind: A Look at Gender Inclusive Analysis, Restorative Justice, and Alternative Dispute Resolution* (St. John's: Department of Justice, 2000a), p. 21.
57 Moore and Mitchell, "Rights-Based Restorative Justice."
58 Ibid.; Provincial Association Against Family Violence, *Making It Safe: Women, Restorative Justice, and Alternative Dispute Resolution* (St. John's: Department of Justice, 2000b), p. 21; Transition House Association of Nova Scotia, "Abused Women in Family Mediation: A Nova Scotia Snapshot" (unpublished Report, THANS, 2000).
59 Strang and Braithwaite, *Restorative Justice and Family Violence.*
60 Provincial Association Against Family Violence, *Keeping an Open Mind;* idem, *Making It Safe.*
61 Morris, *Stories of Transformative Justice.*
62 Moore and Mitchell, "Rights-Based Restorative Justice."
63 Moore, Tulk, and Mitchell, "Qallunaat Crossing"; P. Moss and P. Petrie, *From Children's Services to Children's Spaces—Public Policy, Children, and Childhood* (London: Routledge/Falmer, 2002).
64 Moore, *Towards an Integral Transformation through the Looking Glass of Restorative Justice* (unpublished Ph.D. dissertation, University of Victoria, 2003); Department of Justice, Canada, "Youth Criminal Justice Act Backgrounder" (Ottawa), http://canada.justice.gc.ca/en/news/nr/2003/doc_30864
.html.

65 D. Van Ness, "An Overview of Restorative Justice around the World," paper presented to the UN 11th Congress on Crime Prevention and Criminal Justice, Bangkok, April 22, 2005, http://64.233.161.104/search?q=cache :HHisu8JbPgsJ:www.pficjr.org/programs/un/11thcongress/danspaper/down load+restorative+justice+global+around+the+world&hl=en.

66 Nyp, *Pioneers of Peace.*

67 ECOSOC, "Resolution to Be Adopted July 1–26, 2002," http://www.unodc.org/ pdf/crime/terrorism/2002/19eb.pdf; Corrections Canada, http://www.csc-scc .gc.ca/text/portals/rj/rjflyer_e.shtml.

68 The OECD is a consortium of twelve nations with similar economic and development structures. Moore, Tulk, and Mitchell, "Qallunaat Crossing"; Mitchell, "Ideological Reflections on the DSM-IV-R (or Pay No Attention to That Man behind the Curtain, Dorothy!)," *Child and Youth Care Forum* 32, no. 5 (2003): 281–98; idem, "Canadian Health Care and Child Rights—What Are the Links?" *Canadian Journal of Public Health/Revue Canadienne de Santé Publique* 94, no. 6 (2003): 414–16.

69 I. Cotler, Testimony to the Senate of Canada Standing Committee on Human Rights Hearings (2005), http://www.parl.gc.ca/common/Committee_SenProceed .asp?Language=E&Parl=38&Ses=1&comm_id=77; R. Andreychuk, Standing Committee Chair on Human Rights Hearings to Examine and Report upon Canada's International Obligations in Regards to the Rights and Freedoms of Children, 2005, http://www.parl.gc.ca/38/1/parlbus/commbus/senate/com-e/ huma-e/rep-e/rep09feb05-e.htm.

70 Mitchell, "Canadian Health Care and Child Rights?"

71 Moore, Tulk, and Mitchell, "Qallunaat Crossing."

72 Moore and Mitchell, "Rights-Based Restorative Justice."

73 Ibid.

74 Ibid; R.B. Howe and K. Covell, *Empowering Children: Children's Rights Education as a Pathway to Citizenship* (Toronto: University of Toronto Press, 2005).

75 Mitchell, "Postmodern Reflections on the UN Convention on the Rights of the Child: Towards Utilizing Article 42 as an International Compliance Indicator," *International Journal of Children's Rights* 13, no. 3 (2005): 315–31.

76 Moore, *Towards and Integral Transformation.*

77 Moore and Mitchell, "Rights-Based Restorative Justice."

78 Mitchell "Postmodern Reflections"; Moore, "Towards an Integrated Perspective." For more information, see Centre for Justice and Reconciliation, "ECOSOC Endorses Basis Principles of Restorative Justice," http://www.pficjr .org/programs/un/ecosoc.

79 Moore and Mitchell, "Rights-Based Restorative Justice."

80 Ibid.

81 Mitchell, "Postmodern Reflections."

82 Moore and Mitchell, "Rights-Based Restorative Justice"; Denov, "Children's Rights or Rhetoric?"; Department of Justice Canada, "Youth Criminal Justice Act Explained," http://www.justice.gc.ca/en/ps/yj/repository.

83 Personal communication with J. Finlay, Ontario's Chief Advocate for children, youth, and families and President of the Canadian Council of Provincial Child and Family Advocates, March 11, 2005.

84   A. James, C. Jenks, and A. Prout, *Theorizing Childhood* (London: Blackwell Publishers, 1998).

85   Mitchell, "Postmodern Reflections"; Howe and Covell, *Empowering Children*; H. Giroux, *The Abandoned Generation—Democracy beyond the Culture of Fear* (New York: Palgrave Macmillan, 2003).

86   J. Tanner, "Teenage Troubles: Youth and Deviance in Canada" (Toronto: Nelson Thomson, 2001); J. Muncie, "The Globalization of Crime Control—the Case of Youth and Juvenile Justice Neoliberalism, Policy Convergence, and International Conventions," *Theoretical Criminology* 9, no. 1: 35–64.

87   Personal Communication with J. Finlay.

88   Ibid.

89   Ibid.

90   Denov, "Children's Rights or Rhetoric?"

91   J. Finlay, Testimony to the Senate of Canada Standing Committee on Human Rights (2005, submission p. 10), http://www.parl.gc.ca/common/Committee _SenProceed.asp?Language=E&Parl=38&Ses=1&comm_id=77.

92   Ibid.

93   Ibid.

94   Moore, Tulk, and Mitchell, "Qallunaat Crossing."

95   J. Rudin, "Aboriginal Justice and Restorative Justice," in E. Elliott and R. Gordon, eds., *New Directions in Restorative Justice: Issues, Practice, Evaluation* (Devon: Willan, 2005), pp. 89–114.

96   Ibid.

97   Moore and Mitchell, "Rights-Based Restorative Justice."

98   Personal communication with J. Finlay.

99   Ibid.

100 D. Cooley and A. Borgida, *It Takes a Community: Report of the Stakeholder Consultation on Alternatives to Custody for Young Persons* (Youth Justice Services: Ministry of Children and Youth Services, 2005); C. Blackstock, Testimony to the Senate of Canada Standing Committee on Human Rights (February 7, 2005), http://www.parl.gc.ca/common/Committee_SenProceed .asp?Language=E&Parl=38&Ses=1&comm_id=77.

101 Mitchell, "Postmodern Reflections."

102 Ibid.

103 Moore and Mitchell, "Rights-Based Restorative Justice."

104 Ibid.

105 Ibid.

106 UN Committee on the Rights of the Child, "Concluding Observations on Canada" (1995), http://www.pch.gc.ca/progs/pdp-hrp/docs/crc/crcconc_e.cfm.

107 Moore and Mitchell, "Rights-Based Restorative Justice."

108 ECOSOC, Resolution to Be Adopted July 1–26, 2002; CSC, Restorative Justice and Dispute Resolution Branch, http://www.csc-scc.gc.ca/text/portals/ rj/rjflyer_e.shtml.

109 Muncie, "The Globalization of Crime Control," p. 35.

110 W. Schafer, "The Uneven Globality of Children," *Journal of Social History* 38, no. 4 (2005): 1027–39.

Bibliography

Andreychuk, R. 2005. Standing Committee Chair on Human Rights Hearings to Examine and Report upon Canada's International Obligations in Regards to the Rights and Freedoms of Children. http://www.parl.gc.ca/38/1/parlbus/commbus/senate/com-e/huma-e/rep-e/rep09feb05-e.htm.

Blackstock, C. 2005. Testimony to the Senate of Canada Standing Committee on Human Rights Hearings. http://www.parl.gc.ca/common/Committee_SenProceed.asp?Language=E&Parl=38&Ses=1&comm_id=77.

Braithwaite, J. 2002. "Setting Standards for Restorative Justice." *British Journal of Criminology* 42 (2002): 563–77.

Charbonneau, S. 2005. "The Canadian Youth Criminal Justice Act 2003: A Step Forward for Advocates of Restorative Justice?" In E. Elliott and R. Gordon, eds., *New Directions in Restorative Justice: Issues, Practice, Evaluation*. Devon: Willan, 2005.

Child Rights International. 2005. "Draft Recommendations." Paper presented at the plenary Violence in the Home and Family, June 16. http://www.crin.org/violence/search/closeup.asp?infoID=5740.

Clairmont, D. 2000. "Restorative Justice in Nova Scotia." *Isuma* 1, no. 1. http://www.isuma.net/v01n01/clairmon/clairmon_e.shtml.

———. 2005. Nova Scotia Restorative Justice Initiative Final Evaluation Report, File #4500009896. Halifax.

Commission on First Nations and Metis People and Justice Reform. 2003. "Summary of Restorative Justice Initiatives in Saskatchewan Round Table." http://www.justicereformcomm.sk.ca/sumMarB-2003.gov.

"Community Justice Initiatives." http://www.cjiwr.com/.

Conflict Resolution Network. "Restorative Justice in Canada." http://www.crnetwork.ca.

Cooley, D., and A. Borgida. 2005. *It Takes a Community: Report of the Stakeholder Consultation on Alternatives to Custody for Young Persons*. Toronto: Ministry of Children and Youth Services, Youth Justice Services.

Correctional Services Canada. 1998. *Inventory of Canadian Events and Initiatives Related to Restorative Justice*. Ottawa: Corrections Canada. http://www.justice.gc.ca/en/ps/voc/rjpap.html#restorative.

———. 2003a. "Restorative Justice Week 2003, 16–23 November." http://www.csc-scc.gc.ca/text/forum/restore2003/basic/12_e.shtml.

———. 2003b. "Restorative Justice Week 2003: Basic Resource Kit," http://www.csc-scc.gc.ca/text/forum/restore2003/basic/12_e.shtml.

Cotler, I. 2005. Testimony to the Senate of Canada Standing Committee on Human Rights Hearings. http://www.parl.gc.ca/common/Committee_SenProceed.asp?Language=E&Parl=38&Ses=1&comm_id=77.

Denov, M. 2004. "Children's Rights or Rhetoric? Assessing Canada's Youth Criminal Justice Act and Its Compliance with the UN Convention on the Rights of the Child." *International Journal of Children's Rights* 12: 1–20.

Department of Justice, Canada. 1993. *Canada's System of Justice*. Ottawa: Department of Justice.

———. n.d. "An Inventory of Government-Based Services That Support the Making of Enforcement and Custody and Access Decisions, Prince Edward Island." http://canada.justice.gc.ca/en/ps/pad/reports/invent/pe.htm.

———. n.d. "Community-based Justice Programs Ontario. The Aboriginal Justice Strategy." Ottawa: Aboriginal Justice Strategy, n.d. http://canada.justice.gc.ca/en/ps/ajs/programs/ontario.html.

———. "Youth Criminal Justice Act Backgrounder." Ottawa. http://canada.justice.gc.ca/en/news/nr/2003/doc_30864.html .

———. n.d. "Youth Criminal Justice Act Explained." http://www.justice.gc.ca/en/ps/yj/repository.

Department of Justice, Northwest Territories. "Community Justice." http://www.justice.gov.nt.ca/CommunityJustice/CommunityJustice.htm.

Department of Justice, Nunavut. "Community Justice." http://www.justice.gov.nu.ca/english/commjust.html.

Department of Justice, Yukon. "Community Justice Committees and Information." http://www.justice.gov.yk.ca/prog/cjps/cj/comjuscom.html.

ECOSOC. 2002. "Resolution to Be Adopted July 1–26." http://www.unodc.org/pdf/crime/terrorism/2002/19eb.pdf.

Finlay, J. 2003. *Cross-over Kids: From Care to Custody*. Toronto: Office of the Child and Family Service Advocacy.

———. 2005. Testimony to the Senate of Canada Standing Committee on Human Rights. http://www.parl.gc.ca/common/Committee_SenProceed.asp?Language=E&Parl=38&Ses=1&comm_id=77.

Gal, T. 2004. "Child Victims and Restorative Justice: The Appeal, the Risks." Paper presented at New Frontiers in Restorative Justice: Advancing Theory and Practice, Centre for Justice and Peace Development, Massey University, Albany, New Zealand, December 2–5. http://www.restorativejustice.org/articlesdb/articles/5636.

Giroux, H.A. 2003. *The Abandoned Generation—Democracy beyond the Culture of Fear*. New York: Palgrave Macmillan.

Han and Associates. 2003. "National Survey of Youth Justice Committees, Justice Canada." Department of Justice Canada. http://canada.justice.gc.ca/en/ps/rs/rep/2003/rr03yj-7/rr03yj-7_04_00.html.

Howe, R.B., and K. Covell. 2005. *Empowering Children: Children's Rights Education as a Pathway to Citizenship*. Toronto: University of Toronto Press.

James, A., C. Jenks, and A. Prout. 1998. *Theorizing Childhood*. London: Blackwell Publishers.

Johnstone, G., and D. Van Ness, D., eds. 2007. *Handbook of Restorative Justice*. Devon: Willan Publishing, 2007.

Kilkelly, U., R. Kilpatrick, L. Lundy, L. Moore, P. Scaton, C. Davey, C. Dwyer, and S. McAllister. 2005. *Children's Rights in Northern Ireland*. Research commissioned by the Northern Ireland Commissioner for Children and Young People. Belfast: Queen's University.

Latimer, J., C. Dowden, and D. Muise. 2001. "The Effectiveness of Restorative Justice Programs a Meta-Analysis." Research and Statistics Division, Department of Justice. http://canada.justice.gc.ca/en/ps/rs/rep/2001/meta.html.

Manitoba Keewatinook Ininew Okimowin. n.d. "Justice Portfolio." http://www.mkonorth.com/justice.html.

McLaren, P. 1997. *Revolutionary Multiculturalism: Pedagogies of Dissent for the New Millennium.* Boulder: Westview Press.

Mitchell, R.C. 2003a. "Ideological Reflections on the DSM-IV-R (or Pay No Attention to That Man behind the Curtain, Dorothy!)." *Child and Youth Care Forum* 32, no. 5: 281–98.

———. 2003b. "Canadian Health Care and Child Rights—What Are the Links?" *Canadian Journal of Public Health/Revue Canadienne de Santé Publique* 94, no. 6: 414–16.

———. 2005. "Postmodern Reflections on the UN Convention on the Rights of the Child: Towards Utilizing Article 42 as an International Compliance Indicator." *International Journal of Children's Rights* 13, no. 3: 315–31.

Moore, S.A. 2001. "Restorative Justice and Education: Emergent Connections and Possibilities." *Connections* (2001): 110–15.

———. 2003. *Towards an Integral Transformation through the Looking Glass of Restorative Justice.* Unpublished Ph.D. dissertation, University of Victoria.

———. 2004. "Towards an Integrated Perspective: Restorative Justice, Cross-Cultural Counselling, and School-based Programming." In M.H. France, M.C. Rodriguez, and G.G. Hett, eds., *Diversity, Culture, and Counselling: A Canadian Perspective.* Calgary: Detselig.

———. (in press). "Transdisciplinary Critical Multicultural Pedagogy in Canadian Higher Education." In Dawn Zinga, ed., *Navigating Multiculturalism.* Toronto: University of Toronto Press.

Moore, S.A., and R.C. Mitchell. (in press). "Rights-Based Restorative Justice: Towards Critical Praxis with Young People in Conflict with the Law." In *UN Children's Rights Convention: Theory Meets Practice—Proceedings of the International Interdisciplinary Conference on Children's Rights,* 18–19 May 2006, Ghent, Belgium, ed. A. Ang, I. Delens-Ravier, M. Delplace, C. Herman, D. Reynaert, V. Staelens, R. Steel, and M. Verheyde. Mortsel, Belgium: Intersentia.

Moore, S.A., W. Tulk, and R.C. Mitchell. 2005. "Qallunaat Crossing: The Southern–Northern Divide and Promising Practices for Canada's Inuit Young People." *First Peoples Child and Family Review* 2, no. 1: 117–29.

Morris, R. 2000. *Stories of Transformative Justice.* Toronto: Canadian Scholars' Press.

Moss, P., and P. Petrie. 2002. *From Children's Services to Children's Spaces—Public Policy, Children, and Childhood.* London: Routledge/Falmer.

Muncie, J. (2005). "The Globalization of Crime Control—The Case of Youth and Juvenile Justice Neoliberalism, Policy Convergence, and International Conventions." *Theoretical Criminology* 9, no. 1: 35–64.

Neegan, E. 2005. "Excuse Me Who Are the First Peoples of Canada? A Historical Analysis of Aboriginal Education in Canada Then and Now." *International Journal of Inclusive Education* 9, no. 1: 3–15.

Nyp, G. 2004. *Pioneers of Peace: The History of Community Justice Initiatives in the Waterloo Region 1974–2004*. Kitchener: Community Justice Initiatives.

Ontario Multifaith Council on Spiritual and Religious Care. 2004–5. "Annual Report: Restorative Justice." http://www.omc.ca/pdf/2005annualreport.pdf.

Pennell, P., and G. Burford. 2004. "Feminist Praxis: Making Family Group Conferencing Work." In Heather Strang and John Braithwaite, eds., *Restorative Justice and Family Violence*. Cambridge: Cambridge University Press.

Provincial Association Against Family Violence. 2000a. *Keeping an Open Mind: A Look at Gender Inclusive Analysis, Restorative Justice, and Alternative Dispute Resolution*. St. John's: Department of Justice.

———. 2000b. *Making It Safe: Women, Restorative Justice, and Alternative Dispute Resolution*. St. John's: Department of Justice.

Radwanski, G., and J. Luttrell. 1992. *Will of a Nation: Awakening the Canadian Spirit*. Toronto: Stoddart.

Restorative Justice Consortium. 2004. *Principles of Restorative Processes*. London: Restorative Justice Consortium. http://www.restorativejustice .org/articlesdb/authors/1138.

"Restorative Justice Oak Bay." http://www.rjob.ca/index.asp.

Rudin, J. 2005. "Aboriginal Justice and Restorative Justice." In E. Elliott and R. Gordon, eds., *New Directions in Restorative Justice: Issues, Practice, Evaluation* Devon: Willan.

Rugge, T., J. Bonta, and S. Wallace-Capretta. 2005. *Evaluation of the Collaborative Justice Project: A Restorative Justice Program for Serious Crime*. Ottawa: Department of Public Safety and Emergency Preparedness. http:// ww2.psepc-sppcc.gc.ca/publications/Corrections/cjp/cjp_toc_e.asp.

Schafer, W. "The Uneven Globality of Children." *Journal of Social History* 38, no. 4 (2005): 1027–39.

Skelton, A. 1998. "Juvenile Justice Reform: Children's Rights and Responsibilities versus Crime Control." Paper presented at the Children's Rights in a Transitional Society Conference, Centre for Child Law, University of Pretoria, RSA, October 30. http://www.restorativejustice.org/articlesdb/ articles/313.

Strang, H., and J. Braithwaite, eds. 2002. *Restorative Justice and Family Violence*. Cambridge: Cambridge University Press.

Tanner, J. 2001. *Teenage Troubles: Youth and Deviance in Canada*. Toronto: Nelson Thomson.

Transition House Association of Nova Scotia. 2000. "Abused Women in Family Mediation: A Nova Scotia Snapshot." Halifax: THANS.

Umbreit, M., and R. Coates. 1999. "Multicultural Implications of Restorative Juvenile Justice." *Federal Probation* (December 1999): 44–51.

United Nations. 2002. *UN Basic Principles on the Use of Restorative Justice Programs in Criminal Matters*. New York and Geneva: Economic and Social Council.

United Nations Committee on the Rights of the Child. 1995. "Concluding Observations on Canada." http://www.pch.gc.ca/progs/pdp-hrp/docs/crc/crcconc_e.cfm.

Van Ness, D. 2005. "An Overview of Restorative Justice around the World." Paper presented to the UN 11th Congress on Crime Prevention and Criminal Justice, Bangkok, April 22. http://64.233.161.104/search?q=cache :HHisu8JbPgsJ:www.pficjr.org/programs/un/11thcongress/danspaper/download+restorative+justice+global+around+the+world&hl=en.

Wolthuis, A. 2000. "Restorative Aspects in the Dutch Juvenile Justice System." Defence for Children International. http://www.defenceforchildren.nl/ariadne/loader.php/en/dci/eng/activities/Justice.

Youth Justice Committees in Ontario. "Overview of Youth Justice Committees." http://www.yjcontario.ca/overview.html.

Zehr, H. 1995. *Changing Lenses: A Focus on Crime and Justice*. Scottsdale: Herald Press.

The Participation Rights of the Child
Canada's Track Record

Kelly Campbell and Linda Rose-Krasnor

Introduction: What Are Participation Rights?

The idea that children should take part in decisions about their lives is not new. For example, when developmental psychologist Diana Baumrind first discussed her classic parenting styles in 1966, she described the (ideal) authoritative parent as one who values children's development as autonomous and independent persons and who provides opportunities for child participation.[1] What is relatively new, however, is the assertion that children have the *right* to have opportunities for participation. In fact, the Convention on the Rights of the Child (CRC) was the first international document on children's rights specifically to articulate participation rights.[2]

The Convention describes children's participation[3] rights in articles 12 through 17. Article 12, the key article about participation rights, states that children have the right to express their views in all matters affecting them. This general right of expression is what is usually meant when people refer to children's right to participate. However, in addition, children also have the specific rights to freedom of expression and information (article 13), freedom of thought, conscience, and religion (article 14), freedom of association and peaceful assembly (article 15), privacy (article 16), and access to media (article 17). Throughout this chapter, we will use the term participation to refer explicitly to the right of children to express their views (as described in article 12), recognizing that the form and extent of this expression will vary as a function of the characteristics

Kelly Campbell and Linda Rose-Krasnor, Department of Psychology, Brock University of the child, particular situation, and cultural context. Although we will not address them directly, we consider the principles presented in articles 13 to 17 to be necessary to support children in expressing their general participation rights.

In addition to describing specific rights, the CRC also has an overall philosophical framework that consists of four principles that "influence the way each right is fulfilled and serve as a constant reference for the implementation and monitoring" of children's rights.[4] The framers of the Convention included participation as one of these guiding principles; thus, it also informs the implementation of *all* rights under the Convention. The framers have made a clear statement that, to be fully committed to the implementation of the CRC, a country must make extensive provisions to allow children to be heard.

There are two important things to note about participation rights under the CRC. First, article 5 specifically states that children's participation rights apply to decisions made in "all matters" that affect them. Therefore, children's participation rights apply within various domains, including the family, schools, local communities, and national politics. Also, the right of children to participate applies at different levels. It may refer to an individual, a specific group (e.g., a classroom or community), or children as a whole.[5]

Second, the Convention describes children's right to express their views; it does not say they have the right to make all decisions themselves. This is made clear in article 12, which states that the view of the child should be "given due weight in accordance with the age and maturity of the child." That is, when decisions that affect children are being made, adults should seek their input. Even very young children should be given opportunities to participate in age-appropriate ways (in fact, there is no lower age limit provided for any of the rights in the CRC). However, the extent to which a child's view plays a role in the final decision depends on the child's age and maturity, with children who are more mature being given more opportunities to make decisions than less mature children. Thus, parents and other adults are to protect and guide children, but they also should provide children with gradual increases in autonomy that allow for age-appropriate opportunities to express their views and make decisions. In fact, article 5 specifically states that adults have a *responsibility* to provide children with guidance in exercising their rights in a manner consistent with their evolving capacities.

This provision of increasingly demanding—but age-appropriate— opportunities for decision making also should contribute to children's abilities to make good decisions in the future. This is related to Vygotsky's concept of the "zone of proximal development," which refers to a range of task difficulty that is just above a child's current capacities.[6] Vygotsky suggested that with adult help, children can master tasks in this zone and thereby advance their skills. In a cyclic process, their new skills then increase the level of their zone of proximal development. Participation in age-appropriate decisions (i.e., within the zone of proximal development), with suitable support, will increase competence; based on this greater maturity, the child should be given even more opportunities for participation and greater weight should be given to the child's input.

So it is important for adults to find a balance between protecting children and providing opportunities for participation and decision making. Achieving this balance may be difficult, however. It requires that adults understand the child's current capabilities and the nature of opportunities needed to facilitate development. Furthermore, this balance must be dynamic, changing over time in response to the child's development. Adults must adjust participation opportunities and guidance as the child's capabilities increase. The difficulties associated with finding this balance may create tension in the implementation of participation rights, an issue that we will discuss later in the chapter.

Why Are Participation Rights Important?

Children's participation in decision making has been associated with many benefits. The Centre of Excellence for Youth Engagement has described the benefits of children's participation at individual, social, and systems levels.[7] Individual benefits are those that occur to the youth personally, such as the development of decision-making skills. Covell and Howe have suggested that children without the opportunity to participate in decision-making opportunities are "less capable of making rational decisions in later childhood and adulthood, times when the penalties for poor decisions are typically more severe."[8] Making decisions and effecting change also may contribute to children's development of a sense of self-efficacy, which has been associated with positive adjustment.[9] Furthermore, the experience of being heard can teach children that their opinions are important, increasing their sense of self-worth. As Melton stated, "Nothing is more fundamental to the experience of being taken seriously than simply having a say, being heard politely, and having one's perspective considered."[10] Finally, participation in democratic decision-making processes may encourage the development of democratic values and promote civic involvement throughout the lifespan.[11]

Social benefits include improvements to youth's relationships and social networks. These benefits may take the form of specific relationships that are advantageous for youth. For example, many coaches or youth group leaders become mentors to youth. In addition, being involved in the community may provide an opportunity to widen social networks, expose the youth to individuals with different backgrounds and perspectives, and increase social capital. Furthermore, participation may allow the youth to develop specific social skills (e.g., negotiation, communication).[12]

Systems benefits are improvements to organizations and structures that occur as a result of youth involvement. Youth often provide a fresh perspective, which can improve the operations of youth programs and services. For example, Lansdown[13] described a 1993 project designed to obtain input from four-to-five-year-old children in a poor district of London. The local council had been trying to provide play areas with grass, but discovered that the children did not want grass in their play areas. Instead, the children preferred concrete, because grass made it impossible for them to see broken glass and discarded needles from drug addicts. Youth involvement also can provide direct benefits to organizations. In one study, three-quarters of the adults interviewed reported that having youth participate in decision making had positive influences on organizational functioning and increased overall efficiency.[14] Furthermore, youth participation in schools and communities can foster a sense of community and cooperation among both youth and adults.[15] This may lead to indirect benefits for youth themselves, as healthier communities produce healthier children.

The Call for Participation Rights

In the sixteen years since Canada ratified the Convention, various groups have expressed their belief in the importance of children's participation and have called on the Canadian government to provide opportunities for children to exercise this right. First, the UN Committee on the Rights of the Child has expressed its concern that the principle of respect for the views of children is not adequately reflected in national legislation and policies.[16] Second, Canadian non-governmental organizations (NGOs) have suggested that Canada should provide more meaningful opportunities for youth participation.[17] Third, youth who participated in a 1998 online survey identified participation rights (i.e., the rights to "express ourselves, say what we think, and be listened to when we do) as one of the top ten rights for young people.[18] Finally, Canada's national plan of action ("A Canada Fit for Children") developed in response to the UN General Assembly Special Session on Children, states that children's participation is one of the "principles based on Canadian values," according to which "we commit to implementing the Plan of Action."[19]

Therefore, there is great pressure on the Canadian government to provide for children's participation rights. The participation of children in matters that affect them is a fundamental right that is beneficial to both children and society. The importance of participation and the government's role in providing participation opportunities have been recognized by various groups. Moreover, when the Canadian government ratified the Convention in 1990, it made a legally binding commitment to provide for this right.

But what have Canadian governments actually done to support children's participation rights? We begin to address this question by discussing indications of the governments' overall philosophy and general progress regarding children's participation. We then discuss specific progress that governments have made in three participation domains: family, education, and government. Finally, we evaluate the progress made and provide suggestions for next steps.

Canada's Progress?

Since the ratification of the Convention, the Canadian government has articulated a general philosophy that is consistent with the principle of children's participation rights. For example, when meeting with the UN Committee for the Rights of the Child in 2003, Senator Landon Pearson stated that there had been "a recent trend in Canada to assume that children had the right to participate."[20] In addition, "A Canada Fit for Children" states that Canada recognizes that "children themselves have important contributions to make to the decisions that affect their own development, as well as that of their communities."[21]

Furthermore, there have been some federal actions that appear to reflect this philosophy. First, the federal government promotes public education about children's rights. The Human Rights Program of the Department of Heritage distributes five thousand free copies of the Convention each year and has also funded the development of "Say It Right!," the youth edition of the Convention.[22] Also, in 1993 the federal government established November 20 as National Child Day, designed to promote awareness of the Convention. Second, the federal government provides funding for research on children's participation. For example, in 2000 Health Canada funded the Centre of Excellence for Youth Engagement; this centre's mandate is to find, describe, and build models of effective strategies for engaging youth in meaningful participation.[23] Another example is the Public Health Agency of Canada's sponsorship of a study designed to survey youth participation in Canadian communities and to identify best practice models of youth participation.[24] Third, the federal government has supported youth participation at a national and international level. For example, it has funded national and international youth conferences and taken a leading role in supporting youth participation at the UN General Assembly Special Session on Children, by organizing workshops to help prepare youth representatives from around the world for their role.[25]

Overall, then, it appears that the Canadian government recognizes the importance of children's participation rights and has acted to support these rights. However, there also have been criticisms of the government's actions. As Howe notes in chapter 1, one criticism is the lack of a federal child advocate or ombudsman, despite calls for the development of such a position from both Canadian NGOs[26] and the UN Committee for the Rights of the Child.[27] However, children's advocates/ombudsmen exist in eight provinces,[28] and in 1996 they joined to form the Canadian Council of Provincial Child and Youth Advocates. Furthermore, the topic of the council's 2005 annual meeting was youth engagement, with the focus on ways to involve youth in decision making both provincially and nationally.[29]

Although the establishment of these provincial advocates and their council is a positive step, there are problems with these offices. First, none of the children's advocates in Canada have a general mandate to apply all of the Convention rights recognized.[30] Although provincial mandates differ, every advocate is concerned with vulnerable children (e.g., youth in care. youth in the justice system) or those accessing other government services (e.g., health, education). Second, the fact that mandates vary from province to province leads to variation across the country in the redress mechanisms available to youth;[31] this is one of the reasons that a federal-level advocate or ombudsman is needed—a need recognized by the Council itself.[32]

Therefore, despite significant progress in the Canadian government's approach to children's participation rights, there have been significant criticisms and suggestions for next steps. We now will analyze progress in the government's role in supporting children's participation rights in the family, educational, and civic domains.

Participation in the Family

Children may be involved in family decisions about day-to-day choices (e.g., meals, clothing), activities (e.g., which movies to see), or more serious issues (e.g., health care, custody). Participation within the family is especially important because, for most children, the family is the first context in which they have the opportunity to participate in decisions affecting them. As a result, the model of participation learned within the family may shape the child's expectations about participation in other contexts. A child who is provided appropriate participation experiences at home will likely expect such opportunities in other contexts. However, a child who is not provided with these opportunities at home likely will not expect them in other contexts, and may not be prepared to participate meaningfully when such opportunities are presented.

Once again, it is important to stress that participation is not equivalent to self-determination. As noted above, article 5 of the Convention describes parents' rights and responsibilities to guide their children in exercising their rights, and article 12 states that the weight given to children's opinions should be proportional to their age and maturity. Rather, it is children's exposure to and input into the decision-making process that is important. Gary Melton, a prominent children's rights scholar, has stated that "the initial and typical focus on the question of who will decide (or the age of the child at which the decision maker will change) not only pits parents against children unnecessarily and indeed erroneously, it diverts attention from the underlying principle."[33] The underlying principle is the idea that children and parents should work together to make decisions. Children should be invited to express their opinions and, when the parents' decision is contrary to the child's wishes, the reasons behind this decision should be explained and discussed. Interestingly, in a study of family decision making, children themselves have expressed this principle.[34] Most children described "having a say" as more important than "getting their own way." One child stated that a fair decision was when "everybody has a say about what they want to do even if we don't get to do it."[35] Similarly, Eccles and her colleagues found that adolescents who thought they had little opportunity to participate in family decision making reported more conflicts with their parents, relied more on their friends for help than their parents, and were more willing to disobey their parents than those who were satisfied with their participation opportunities.[36]

The Convention requires that parents seek children's input, discuss and explain, and gradually increase children's autonomy with age and maturity. This is consistent with Baumrind's definition of authoritative parenting.[37] Authoritative parents set and enforce age-appropriate limits and expect their children to display behaviour at levels consistent with their developmental level. However, they also seek their children's input in appropriate ways to assist them with limit setting and other decision making. Such parents discuss these issues with their children, provide explanations when they are not following the children's wishes, and display high warmth and affection. In addition to being consistent with children's participation rights, authoritative parenting has been associated with positive outcomes, including increased self-esteem, self-control, peer acceptance, and decision-making skills.[38]

Thus, one way the Canadian government can support children's participation rights within the family is to provide parent education programs that will inform parents of the importance of children's participation and the benefits of authoritative parenting. In fact, Canada is actually obligated under article 18 of the Convention to assist parents in their performance of their child-rearing responsibilities—an obligation that parent education programs would help fulfill. The need for parent education is recognized in "A Canada Fit for Children," which states that parents will be provided with the skills and knowledge they need and that positive and effective parenting will be promoted in Canada.[39] To fulfill this need, the Canadian government supports a number of parent education programs. For example, Health Canada (now the Public Health Agency of Canada) has developed "Nobody's Perfect," an education and support program for parents who are young, single, isolated, or of low socio-economic status.[40] In Ontario, the Ontario Early Years Centres provide parent education activities on diverse topics, including general parenting skills and behaviour management.[41] The Public Health Agency of Canada also distributes an educational video for parents called "Welcome to Parenting: The First Six Years."[42]

The funding of parent education programs such as these is a positive step. However, the majority of parent education programs in Canada focus on parenting young children (up to age five or six). This is a concern, considering that parents of teenagers are particularly likely to need help finding a balance between guiding and protecting their children and providing for their adolescents' increasing autonomy needs. Indeed, those programs that do exist for parents of adolescents are designed specifically for families experiencing difficulties. Furthermore, because the target audience of most parenting programs is families with young children, they focus on issues such as nutrition and toilet training rather than on children's participation rights. Therefore, there is a clear need for government-funded programs to educate parents (and especially parents of adolescents) about the importance of participation and children's rights.

Another way that Canadian governments can support children's participation rights within the family is through legal means. For example, Covell and Howe have suggested that Canada could enact legislation that would obligate parents to consult their children on matters affecting them, as has been done in many European countries.[43] Although liability would be rare—the goal would be to educate parents through the law—this would make a strong statement of principle and help create a culture in which listening to children is normative. As yet, however, no Canadian government has included such provisions in their legislation.

Thus, through education, the government can *encourage* parents to provide participation opportunities for their children. However, when families are experiencing difficulties, the government often plays a more direct role in ensuring children's participation rights. In cases of abuse and neglect, decisions need to be made about removal from the home, placement in care, and returning to the home. In divorce cases, decisions about custody and visitation must be made. In these circumstances, there is an opportunity to require courts to seek input from children and take their wishes into account. Space limitations prevent us from describing in detail the provisions for children's participation rights in these areas, given that each province has different legislation and there are separate laws for child protection, adoption, and divorce.

However, we can tell you that there is wide variation in the extent to which children's participation in custody and visitation decisions is required. In some cases there are extensive provisions for children's participation rights. For example, New Brunswick's Family Services Act gives children the right to be heard in any matter under the act, and children between twelve and sixteen have the right to retain council and legal aid.[44] In Alberta, a 1997 amendment to the Child Welfare Act allows children sixteen and younger to apply for access to their grandparents.[45] Children in Quebec are given the right to be heard in every application affecting their interests, if appropriate for their age and competence, but are not granted more active roles such as retaining council.[46] In contrast, the federal Divorce Act contains no requirements for the child's views to be considered in determining best interests in custody and access proceedings.[47] Note also that, in their report to the UN Committee, the Canadian government stated that some authorities believe participation in such proceedings may be too traumatic for children.[48]

However, despite the lack of formal requirements for children's participation in many court proceedings, judges and lawyers often do consider their views. This raises concerns about the training of the individuals who are questioning the children, particularly young children. More formal recognition of the need to seek children's input in such proceedings likely will prompt the development of more measures to support children's participation; this should include training for court officials and formal procedures for obtaining children's input.

Participation in Educational Settings

Educational settings appear to be particularly appropriate contexts for the development, exercise, and promotion of children's participation rights. Schools are relatively protected environments, in which children can learn and practise decision-making skills in domains that affect their lives (e.g., school discipline, extracurricular activities). More than many other adults, educators are likely to have the skills and daily opportunities necessary to support children's participation in an age-appropriate manner. Indeed, these chances to promote development through participation fit naturally within the educational mandate of schools. Student participation also can provide educators with unique and valuable sources of information (e.g., student needs, difficulties) for educational policy and planning. In addition, schools have a long history of youth participation through elected student councils. In fact, the educational sector is one domain in which youth participation has been secured explicitly through legislation. Finally, it has been argued that, as government institutions, schools are obligated to provide for the age-appropriate participation of children as laid out in the Convention.[49]

Children's participation in educational contexts has increased in the past sixteen years, and there are some exciting examples of student involvement in school governance and policy. One example is the school survey done by Nutana Collegiate Secondary School in Saskatoon. The survey, instituted in 1990, assesses the needs of its changing student population.[50] Students, parents, community members, educators, and other professionals were involved in the creation of the surveys and interpretation of their results. Through this survey, the Nutana staff identified challenges that made it difficult for many young people to attend school, such as troubled home situations, pregnancy, and addiction. Based on this student input, several major changes were made to address these barriers, including instituting a quarter-semester system that allowed two additional entry points into the school year. In this way, students who needed to take time away from school would have to wait less time before re-entry. Furthermore, an integrated service model provided community support for students on the school campus, reducing the amount of time students had to miss school to obtain assistance. Similarly, British Columbia's Ministry of Education has conducted an annual student survey since 2002, and these results become part of the schools' planning process.[51]

In addition to providing input into adult decision making through surveys and similar information-gathering techniques, Canadian youth have had more direct advisory roles in educational policy development. For example, provincial and federal governments increasingly have included youth on advisory boards and committees. In New Brunswick, for example, students on the Curriculum Advisory Committee help make policy recommendations to the provincial government.[52]

Furthermore, in the late 1980s and 1990s, local school councils and advisory committees were established in many provinces and territories, and provision was made for student representation on these units at the secondary level[53] (student representation on elementary school councils is either optional or excluded). The primary function of these councils is advisory; however, student representatives also can be found on local boards of education, which have greater decision-making authority. In Ontario, for example, the Education Quality Improvement Act 1997 established the position of non-voting pupil representative on boards of education.[54] Similarly, the Northwest Territories Education Act states that students may select a representative to attend and participate in public meetings of the district educational authorities.[55]

Douglas McCall's report on youth involvement in public decision making provides an example of how youth participation on school boards can work.[56] In the B.C. community of Richmond, the school board has included a full-time student since 1993. The student trustee is elected as part of a slate of candidates and functions as a regular board member in representing the entire community (note that this representation model contrasts with other models, in which student trustees are selected specifically to represent young people and to promote youth-related issues). The duties of the Richmond student trustee are the same as those of other trustees, including sitting and chairing on committees, attending board meetings, and regularly visiting schools. McCall concluded that the student trustee's status is a reflection of that community's acceptance of the value of youth participation in the school system, including an enhanced role for high school student councils.

Many provinces also require that students with exceptionalities be consulted in the development of their individualized program plans. In B.C., for example, such young people are given the opportunity to participate actively in the development of their educational plans.[57] Similarly, in Newfoundland and Labrador, children "at risk" have been involved in the integrated support services planning process since 1995.[58] Unfortunately, perhaps, these rights of participation in individualized planning typically are made explicit only for exceptional children and not for all students.

In spite of considerable progress in including youth in educational policy, planning, and practice, significant limitations to meaningful participation remain. For example, Smith and colleagues[59] presented an in-depth analysis of student engagement in five elementary and five secondary Canadian schools (two from each of five provinces). These researchers identified only one school from their case studies that valued children's input in everyday institutional practices; overall, "students had relatively limited influence on school policy and practices."[60] Furthermore, they found that traditional mechanisms for youth participation in schools (e.g., student councils) were not recognized by the students as "serious forms of representation and voice."[61]

In addition, all is not well for the student trustee initiatives; serious limitations to their effectiveness have been noted by both analysts and the trustees themselves. Marques, for example, concluded that the section of the Ontario legislation establishing student trustees is "badly flawed and has been poorly implemented by many school boards."[62] Indeed, the roles of student representatives vary considerably across the province.[63] Student trustees only attend board meetings in some regions; in others, trustees also chair a student advisory group, provide reports, and sit on committees. In addition, some student trustees are elected and others are appointed. A report from the Ontario Student Trustees' Association also identified these issues as problematic and further described the overall lack of resources available to support student representatives on boards. These difficulties have prompted calls for changes in the legislation regulating student trustees, including targeted funding for their role, the democratic selection of trustees, and a full vote for student trustees.[64] In addition, the creation of representative student advisory committees is recommended, to allow for greater diversity of youth input than is possible with a small number of student trustees.

We have focused on students' general participation in schools—that is, their basic right to input in decision making. Schools are also important contexts for the exercise of children's specific participation rights, such as freedom of expression, information, religion, and peaceful assembly. However, it is important to note that these are complex issues that often involve conflicting rights and responsibilities. For example, in the case of school newspapers, school officials may feel that students' right to freedom of expression conflicts with the school's responsibility to protect students from harmful or explicit content. Also, there have been numerous cases in Canada in recent years in which schools have attempted to ban students from wearing religious articles or clothing, either because the articles may be dangerous (e.g., the kirpan—a ceremonial dagger worn by male orthodox Sikhs) or because they conflict with school policy (e.g., hijabs and turbans).[65] In complex situations with competing rights (e.g., protection vs. expression), it is certainly not the case that students' participation rights should "trump" all others automatically. However, as Leanne Johnny has pointed out, school policies and decisions about such issues are usually made without the input of students.[66] Canadian schools and school boards need continuing dialogue and discussion—with input from students themselves—to develop policies and guidelines that appropriately balance the competing rights in these situations.[67]

Civic Participation

Youth participation in civic affairs may take many forms. The authors of the 2003 Citizen Re: Generation report,[68] for example, identified eight "modes" of civic participation: giving; volunteering; voting; activism; political party involvement; social and recreational participation; faith-based organized activities; and employment. Space limitations do not allow us to discuss each of the ways that youth actively participate in society. Therefore, we will focus on youth involvement in two civic domains (governance and voting), which will serve to illustrate how government initiatives have encouraged youth participation.

Youth Participation in Governance

Municipal and regional governments have shown considerable leadership in promoting youth engagement. Vancouver's 1995 Civic Youth Strategy[69] was based on the principle that youth are an important resource for the city, and it ensures that their voices will be heard by city officials. A youth council meets monthly and develops activities that promote connections between young people and government officials. Similarly, in 1998, Toronto established the Toronto Youth Cabinet (TYC) to be the "official voice for youth at City Hall."[70] TYC membership is open to those fifteen-to-twenty-four-year-olds who apply and complete an orientation procedure, as well as a day-long anti-oppression training. All members can vote at membership meetings; they also elect an executive committee, which meets biweekly and is mentored by city politicians. The TYC promotes youth activism and engagement; it also advocates for youth issues, programs, and services.[71] Following the 2005 Boxing Day shootings in Toronto, for example, TYC members held a widely reported news conference to speak out against youth violence and offer suggestions for prevention.[72] Calgary[73] (Alberta), the northwestern region of Ontario,[74] and Gatineau[75] (Quebec) are other noteworthy examples of local and regional government initiatives to increase youth civic involvement.

Many provincial and territorial governments also have developed continuing structures for youth consultation in policy and program development. The Nova Scotia Youth Advisory Committee, for example, has twelve to fifteen members between fifteen and twenty-four years old.

This committee advises the Minister for Youth on government policies and programs, provides information and advice about youth concerns, and fosters youth-initiated projects.[76] Similarly, Manitoba's MB4Youth Advisory Council consists of twelve to fifteen youth (between fifteen and twenty-four) who are selected on the basis of their community leadership. This council provides feedback to the Minister of Education, Citizenship and Youth on issues such as employment, civic engagement, and health; helps with youth events; assists in improving the "youth friendliness" of programming; and increases young people's awareness of programs and services.[77] Another similar structure is the New Brunswick Advisory Council on Youth, consisting of thirteen members appointed by the premier. Some of the activities of the 2005 council included a campaign to recognize youth community engagement and build youth capacity, facilitate consultations with young people on democratic reform, and establish a youth network to help control tobacco use.[78] Notably, New Brunswick was the only province to give young people their own response section in the 2001 Canadian report to the UN Committee on the Rights of Children.

Each of these provincial examples is of a youth committee that is appointed by government officials. A different model of provincial youth consultation is FINALY (Futures in Newfoundland and Labrador's Youth), which is a youth-driven organization established in 1996 that is open to provincial youth (fifteen-to-thirty-year-olds) on application.[79] FINALY elects thirteen members to the Provincial Youth Council, which coordinates and oversees the program and expresses youth perspectives on relevant issues.

One example of youth consultation at the provincial level is a 2005 Ontario Web-based initiative, consisting of a three-step "democracy challenge," to engage young people in improving democracy.[80] First, youth were invited to submit ideas for activities that would engage young people in the democratic process. Second, the government publicized the projects in an "idea bank" and invited young people to evaluate them. Implementation of selected projects will be the final step. When this process is completed, it will provide a useful model for actively engaging a potentially diverse group of youth in the development and implementation of services affecting them.

At the federal level, Environment Canada established a Youth Round Table in 1997 to advise the government on environmental issues and government programs, as well as to provide assistance in making such programs accessible to a wide diversity of youth.[81] The Round Table comprises up to eighteen youth and prepares an annual report of its activities. In addition, the federal government has involved young people in ad hoc consultations around specific issues. For example, five of the youth delegates to the UN General Assembly Special Session on Children created the Child Engagement Experts Resource Team (CEERT), which assisted in the development of "A Canada Fit for Children," Canada's national plan of action.

Although considerable progress has been made in the inclusion of youth on government advisory committees, the creation of youth-driven processes in governance, and ad hoc consultations with youth, much remains to be done. In a 2000 report surveying thirty Canadian communities,[82] Caputo concluded that youth often found it difficult to have their voices heard by local governments and were often frustrated by inaction on issues relevant to them, in spite of some municipal opportunities for young people to participate.

Youth Participation in Voting

Canadian governments have created a number of promising programs designed to increase youth engagement in the democratic process through voting. Indeed, this issue has received considerable attention, given that young citizens have the lowest voting rate.[83] To address this concern, Canadian federal and provincial governments developed the Student Vote program, designed to promote future voting behaviour, increase political interest, and help students learn to make good decisions and learn critical thinking skills."[84] In this program, grade-five to grade-twelve students vote in mock elections that parallel real ones; they listen to candidates debate, learn about platforms, and vote for real parties. Elections Canada provides the thousands of participating schools with its "official" ballot boxes. On student election day, students vote for candidates in their local ridings and count the ballots; results are then phoned into a central returning office. The outcome is released on the actual election night and widely reported by the media. The first Student Vote was conducted during the Ontario 2003 provincial election campaign, followed by federal Student Votes in 2004 and 2006 and provincial votes in Alberta in 2004 and British Columbia in 2005. This is a highly successful program; more than 450,000 students and 2,400 schools, for example, participated in the mock 2006 federal election.[85]

Another example of Canada's commitment to youth voting is the federal government's sponsorship of the 2003 National Forum on Youth Voting.[86] Supported by Elections Canada, the conference focused on finding ways to encourage youth electoral participation. This event brought together youth and adult delegates in a collaborative effort to increase youth involvement in the democratic process.

Analysis and Recommendations

We have reviewed many exciting initiatives undertaken by Canadian governments to implement children's participation rights. However, we also have noted many concerns and shortcomings. Why haven't Canadian governments done more? To answer this question, we now discuss three general issues that contribute to the difficulties in fully implementing children's participation rights: the need for cultural transformation; difficulty balancing participation and protection; and practical barriers. We also make specific action recommendations for Canadian governments that will increase their compliance with this important aspect of the Convention.

The Need for Cultural Transformation

Governmental support of children's participation rights needs to occur in the context of a societal culture that values children's participation. Governments are unlikely to create legislation and policies that contrast too greatly with public opinion, and government employees are unlikely to work hard to implement such policies if they conflict with their personal values. Furthermore, without a culture that values and supports children's participation, government laws and policies may not have much impact. As Covell and Howe have pointed out, even if children have the legal right to participate, they may not have the capacity or motivation to do so without the encouragement provided by a "culture of listening to children."[87]

A shift toward such a culture has started in Canada, as evident in our review of the progress made in providing opportunities for children's participation. There are increasing efforts to seek youth input, and there is growing recognition of the value of youth participation. However, it is also clear that not all Canadians have fully embraced these values, given the patchwork way in which these rights have been implemented.

In a country as large and multicultural as Canada, there are cultural and regional differences in the extent to which children's participation is valued and supported. This can lead to resistance when governments attempt to implement legislation or policies that create national standards. Obviously, some recognition and allowance for such differences is necessary in order to accommodate variation in cultural norms and local needs. However, it is also important to have some consistency in the basic rights, services, and opportunities provided to children. In fact, the UN Committee on the Rights of the Child has expressed concerns that Canada's federalist system, in which many children's issues are the responsibility of the provinces and territories, will lead to situations in which the minimum standards of the Convention are not applied to all children.[88] Clearly such a situation is undesirable. However, given that almost all countries in the world have ratified the Convention, its basic principles (and the minimum standards suggested by them) should be applicable to almost all communities and cultural groups.[89]

Therefore, there is a need for further cultural transformation in Canada, so that all individuals, communities, and cultural groups will recognize and support children's participation rights. To this end, Canadian governments must increase the saliency and awareness of these issues. That is, they must educate Canadians about children's rights so that the importance and value of listening to children becomes part of the public consciousness. Such education could come in a number of forms.

One form of education would be to directly inform Canadians about children's participation rights, which Canadian governments are obligated to do under article 42 of the Convention. As noted previously, the Department of Heritage distributes free copies of the Convention; there is also information available on numerous government websites. However, it is important that Canadian governments develop more active means of educating the general public about children's participation rights. Additionally, governments should develop and implement education programs targeted to specific groups. As discussed above, education programs are needed for parents (particularly parents of adolescents) and for individuals who work with youth (e.g., judges, lawyers). It is particularly important that these educational programs be targeted to specific groups because the meaning and implementation of child participation rights may vary along dimensions such as culture and context. Governments then could make it a condition of funding that education and training programs include this content in their curricula. It is also important to educate children about their rights—a topic that Katherine Covell discusses in the next chapter.

A second form of education is the indirect education that occurs with the implementation of legislation. Enacting laws and policies that support children's participation rights in various domains will help the public learn that these rights exist and may provide models of how they can be implemented. For example, Sweden's anti-spanking laws have been credited with bringing about attitudinal and behavioural change among the population.[90] In Canada, legislation that would guarantee children's right to be heard in various domains would be useful. For example, legislation that would require parents and other adults to consider children's views in court proceedings is recommended. In particular, the creation of a federal children's advocate or ombudsman would be an important step for the

Canadian government, both practically and symbolically. This would increase Canada's compliance with the Convention and provide children with accessible and meaningful ways to express their views; it also would make a statement that Canada values children's input and opinions.

Finally, one of the best ways to educate Canadians about children's participation rights is to continue to support and create opportunities for children to become involved in their environments in meaningful ways. Often organizations seek youth input as a symbolic gesture, but then gradually become aware that youth participation improves their organization and the services it offers. In a study of youth involvement in organizational governance,[91] many of the adults interviewed admitted entering the process with stereotypes about young people's motivations and abilities, but indicated that after working with the youth they became convinced that young people contribute positively to their organization. The adults also expressed the view that the youth perspective was "vital to bridging the gap between organizational leadership and the services that the organization provided."[92] Thus, seeking youth input and assistance can help adults and organizations improve services that provide for children's other rights. The Canadian government should provide leadership in helping organizations (including their own departments) involve youth; in addition, giving the youth themselves experience in meaningful and well-publicized engagement would set the stage for more widespread youth participation. Youth conferences, such as those funded by Heritage Canada, are an important example of the type of activity, which builds the capacity of both adults and youth to participate in decision making and policy formation.[93]

One of the most exciting ways to create meaningful opportunities for youth participation at the systems level would be to create a Canada-wide youth forum. This forum would meet to discuss issues of relevance to youth, develop media releases to encourage public debate on these issues, make recommendations to the House of Commons and Senate, and provide excellent opportunities for young Canadians to develop personal skills and obtain valuable experience. The youth forum could consist of a diverse and representative group of young people, selected by the provinces. This national youth forum could be modelled on the European Youth Forum,[94] in which participating countries develop their own processes for selecting representatives. These selection processes are part of country-specific systems of youth engagement initiatives and structures that promote youth participation at the local, regional, and national levels. The mission of European Youth Forum is to "empower young people to actively participate in the shaping of Europe and the society in which they live" and "works for the interests of all young people in

Europe." For a Canadian youth parliament to work, however, the federal government would have to commit itself to both the principle of youth participation and the provision of material resources necessary to staff and implement the program.

Balancing Participation with Protection

Even among those who have embraced the values of youth participation, there is disagreement about the proper balance between protecting children and allowing them to play an active role in decision making in domains that affect them. Adults may have conflicting values about their responsibilities to protect children from harm *and* provide them with autonomy. The fact that our society is unclear about these issues is reflected in the inconsistencies in the ages at which we allow young people various privileges and responsibilities. In Canada, for example, youth can consent to sexual relations at fourteen, drive and quit school at sixteen, watch adult movies at eighteen, and drink and vote at nineteen. Gideon Koren and his colleagues[95] have pointed out that we allow young people to babysit at eleven or twelve, expecting them to perform difficult tasks, make complex judgments, and take responsibility for a younger child. However, we do not allow these same children to consent to participation in medical research, and this reveals incongruities in the ways we assess children's maturity in these situations. Children themselves have expressed frustration with this situation; in a report by the Canadian Teacher's Federation, one young person asked, "Why are we told to act like adults and then treated like children?"[96]

Parents and those working with youth have difficulty assessing when children are able to make decisions independently, a situation that is further complicated by extensive variation among youth in these abilities. Lansdown has stated that "although very considerable thought and energy has been invested in developing principles and practice in respect of children's participation in decision-making in recent years, relatively little attention has been given to developing the tools for assessing whether and when children have the competence and maturity to take responsibility for that decision-making on their own behalf."[97] Canadian governments should support the development and use of competency assessment tools, and make them widely available to others working with children. Such tools would be particularly helpful to parents and could be incorporated into parent education programs. These tools also would be helpful for individuals working with youth, such as judges and doctors, in situations where they may have to make competency judgments. For example, British Columbia's Infants Act gives children with the capacity the right to consent to health care without obtaining parent/guardian consent. However, it is left in the hands of the doctors and nurses to assess whether the child has the capacity to consent. Without clear guidelines, medical personnel are unlikely to risk either angering parents or legal action to allow children to make their own decisions. As a result, such laws may rarely be put into practice. Clearly, guidelines and tools to assist in these situations are necessary. (See chapter 4 for further discussion of children's participation rights in health care.)

Above, we discussed the idea that adults need to provide children with age-appropriate decision-making opportunities and guidance. Greater focus on children's increasing autonomy may be useful in overcoming concerns about the perceived risks of allowing young people to make decisions. Melton has suggested that there are risks involved whenever a person is given a new area of responsibility, regardless of age.[98] Instead of trying to decide the particular age at which children are competent to make decisions, we should focus on developing mechanisms that help teach children to make decisions in the context of their increasing autonomy. Melton discussed the fact that North America does a good job of this in the area of driving licences; youth are given learner's permits with many restrictions, then graduated licences with fewer restrictions, and finally a full, unrestricted licence. He suggests that this framework could easily be applied to other areas of decision making (e.g., decisions about school courses) "so that parents and other adults gradually shift from being instructors to 'co-pilots' to supervisors to limited supervisors (i.e. supervisors only under certain especially risky conditions)."[99] Canadian governments should develop legislation and policies that will provide this "learner's permit" structure in other domains of relevance to young people.

Practical Barriers

Even if Canadian governments create legislation and policies that provide for children's participation rights and a supportive cultural shift occurs, there may be practical obstacles to children's participation that remain. In our research, we have identified a number of these barriers to the implementation of participation initiatives.

First, the specific logistics of creating structures for youth participation (e.g., youth boards, student trustees) may not be clear to those involved. For example, there may be questions such as, "Do we seek youth input on all issues, or only those directly related to youth?" and "Should youth be involved in committees and project planning, or only in advisory roles?" Melton notes that "statutes typically are silent about the corollary questions. The result is that service providers and bureaucrats often have little idea of how to implement the standard for decision making."[100] There frequently are calls from people and organizations facing these issues for manuals outlining "best practices" of youth participation. In conducting our research, we have come across numerous examples of such documents.[101] The problem may not be a lack of guidelines but rather finding and accessing them. One solution may be for the government to help maintain and promote a national, Web-based clearinghouse for the identification and distribution of these documents, such as the one being developed by the Centre of Excellence for Youth Engagement, in order to promote the sharing of ideas and experience across organizations.

Second, concerns are often raised about the selection processes used to choose the youth who participate in various endeavours. The young people who sit on community boards or government committees are rarely elected by fellow youth; occasionally they are selected by application, but more often the youth who are already vocal in the community are invited to participate. As a result, these youth may not be representative of the general youth population. There also are concerns about renewal within organizations. When youth representatives and the organizations with which they work have a positive relationship, they may see no need for the youth to move on, which can result in thirty-year-old "youth representatives." Thus, we recommend that organizations put mechanisms in place to assist "aging" youth in the transition from their role as a youth representative to other meaningful roles.

Third, there is a problem with a lack of follow-through from youth input. As noted above, Caputo reported that Canadian youth were often frustrated by government inaction on issues relevant to them, following youth participation.[102] Such inaction may result from issues such as political concerns or a lack of funding. However, it is often interpreted as tokenism—that is, the government had never intended to follow through on youth recommendations and sought their input only as a symbolic gesture. Youth may become cynical and disengaged if youth recommendations are not acted on. Furthermore, there appears to be little evaluation of such initiatives (e.g., "What is the quality of the youths' experience?" "What are the problems and concerns with the process?" "How can processes be improved?"), especially from the perspective of the youth themselves. We suggest that the government support the development of good evaluation tools for these purposes and make them available in the national clearinghouse suggested above.

Finally, concerns have been expressed about the sustainability of youth participation initiatives. In their report to the UN Committee on the

Rights of the Child, Canadian NGOs stated that "children's fundamental freedoms are very dependant on the good intentions of adults."[103] Although some structured initiatives are in place (e.g., provincial youth councils), much of the Canadian youth participation appears to be the product of a small number of committed adults. Once these adults move on, these initiatives may collapse and disappear. Instead of relying on ad hoc committees, governments need to put more effort into developing formal structures for youth participation that will become part of the infrastructure.

Conclusion

The right of children to express their views in matters affecting them is not only a fundamental right under the UN Convention on the Rights of the Child (article 12), but is also one of the Convention's guiding principles. Children's participation rights mean they should have the opportunity to express their views but not that they be allowed to make all decisions themselves. Children's development is optimized when they are provided with age-appropriate decision-making opportunities and guidance that allow for gradual increases in autonomy.

Having ratified the Convention, Canadian governments are obligated to provide for children's participation rights. We have reviewed actions taken by each level of the Canadian government to promote children's participation rights in the family, education, and government domains. We have discussed many promising initiatives, such as parent education programs, school surveys, and youth councils. However, there is much room for improvement, despite considerable progress in the promotion of participation rights.

In our analysis of the current Canadian situation, we discussed three general issues that contribute to difficulties in implementing children's participation rights. First, Canada needs to create a culture in which the voices of children and youth are valued and respected. This cultural shift is in progress, but tensions relating to conflicting beliefs and values have impeded its progress. To promote this cultural shift, Canadian governments need to directly educate Canadians about children's participation rights by developing education programs for parents and individuals working with youth. Canadian governments also should indirectly educate Canadians through additional legislation and policies in support of children's participation, as well as provide effective models of participation.

Second, even among those who have embraced children's participation rights, there is tension in determining the proper balance between protecting children and allowing them to be active decision makers. Establishing an appropriate balance between these protection and participation rights is a complex task that requires sensitivity to the children's changing needs and abilities. To assist parents and those working with youth to make such judgments, governments should support the development of child-competency assessment tools. Furthermore, to allow for age-related increases in children's competence, Canadian governments should focus on developing legislation and policies that would apply the "graduated licensing" framework to other areas of decision making.

Finally, even when legislation and policies support children's participation rights, there are a number of practical obstacles to their implementation. These include difficulties accessing best practices, concerns about the representativeness and renewal of youth representatives, lack of follow-through and evaluation of youth participation, and concerns about the sustainability of initiatives supporting youth participation. To address these concerns, we have suggested that Canadian governments support the development of a national clearinghouse of information regarding best practices, work to develop a National Youth Forum, develop and use good evaluation tools to assess the effectiveness of youth participation initiatives, and focus on developing formal structures for youth participation that will become part of the government infrastructure. Working together, adults and youth can develop opportunities for youth participation that will benefit both young Canadians and our society in general.

Notes

1 D. Baumrind, "Effects of Authoritative Parental Control on Child Behavior," *Child Development* 37, no. 4 (1966): 887–907.
2 K. Covell and R.B. Howe, *The Challenge of Children's Rights for Canada* (Waterloo: Wilfrid Laurier University Press, 2001), p. 25.
3 The term "participation" is not actually used in these articles. However, UN documentation about the Convention uses the term in reference to this group of articles as well as when describing the guiding principle of participation.
4 UNICEF, "Framework for the Protection, Care, and Support of Orphans and Vulnerable Children Living in a World with HIV and AIDS" (July 2004), http://www.unicef.org/uniteforchildren/knowmore/files/Framework_English.pdf.
5 G. Lansdown, *Promoting Children's Participation in Democratic Decision Making* (Florence, Italy: UNICEF Innocenti Research Centre, 2001), p. 9.
6 L. Vygotsky, *Mind in Society: The Development of Higher Psychological Processes* (Cambridge, MA: Harvard University Press, 1978).
7 M. Busseri, K. Campbell, M. Pancer, and L. Rose-Krasnor, "Testing a Model for Youth Engagement and Positive Outcomes," poster presented at the annual meeting of the American Psychological Association, Toronto, August 2003.

8 Covell and Howe, *The Challenge of Children's Rights for Canada*, p. 9.
9 J. Klein-Hessling, A. Lohaus, and J. Ball, "Psychological Predictors of Health-Related Behaviour in Children," *Psychology, Health and Medicine* 10 (2005): 40.
10 G.B. Melton, "Parents *and* Children: Legal Reform to Facilitate Children's Participation," *American Psychologist* 54 (1999): 936.
11 Gary B. Melton, "Parents *and* Children: Legal Reform to Facilitate Children's Participation," *American Psychologist* 54: 938.
12 Lansdown, *Evolving Capacities and Participation* (Gatineau: CIDA Child Protection Unit, 2004), p. 21.
13 Gerison Lansdown, *Promoting Children's Participation in Democratic Decision Making*, p. 5.
14 Shepherd Zeldin, "Youth as Agents of Adult and Community Development: Mapping the Processes and Outcomes of Youth Engaged in Organizational Governance," *Applied Developmental Science* 8, no. 2 (2004): 75–90.
15 Ibid.
16 UN Committee on the Rights of the Child, "Considerations of Reports Submitted by States Parties under Article 44 of the Convention: Concluding Observations: Canada" (1995), CRC/C/15/add.37, p. 4.
17 Covell, *Canada's Non-Governmental Organizations.* Report submitted for the UN General Assembly Special Session (Ottawa: Canadian Coalition for the Rights of Children, February 2001), p. 17.
18 See http://equalitytoday.org/edition3/united.html.
19 Government of Canada, *A Canada Fit for Children: Canada's Follow-Up to the United Nations General Assembly Special Session on Children* (Ottawa: Public Health Agency of Canada, 2004), p. 38.
20 UN Committee on the Rights of the Child, *Summary Record of the 895th Meeting: Consideration of Reports of States Parties: Second Periodic Report of Canada* (September 2003), CRC/C/sr.895, p. 3.
21 Government of Canada, *A Canada Fit for Children*, p. 16.
22 Canadian Heritage, *Convention on the Rights of the Child: Second Report of Canada* (Ottawa: Canadian Heritage, 2001), p. 16.
23 Centre of Excellence for Youth Engagement, "Vision," http://www.tgmag.ca/centres/vision_e.htm.
24 T. Caputo, *Hearing the Voices of Youth: Youth Participation in Selected Canadian Municipalities* (Ottawa: Public Health Agency of Canada, 2000).
25 Canadian Coalition for the Rights of Children, *UN Convention on the Rights of the Child: How Does Canada Measure Up? Update to Canada's Report to the UN Committee for the Rights of Children* (Ottawa: CCRC, 2003), p. 4.
26 Ibid., p. 18.
27 UN Committee on the Rights of the Child, *Considerations of Reports*, p. 4.
28 Currently, Prince Edward Island, New Brunswick, and the territories do not have child advocates, although New Brunswick is in the process of establishing such an office.
29 Nova Scotia Office of the Ombudsman, News release: "Canadian Council of Provincial Child and Youth Advocates Meet in Halifax," September 28, 2005, www.gov.ns.ca/news/details.asp?id=20050928007.

30 C. Giroux, "Child Advocacy Institutions: Providing Effective Protection for Child and Youth Rights," speech presented on behalf of the Commission des droits de la personne et des droits de la jeunesse du Québec and the Canadian Council of Provincial Child and Youth Advocates at the international conference Making Children's Rights Work: National and International Perspectives (Montreal: November 2004).

31 CCRC, *The UN Convention: How Does Canada Measure Up?* p. 18.

32 Giroux, "Child Advocacy Institutions."

33 Melton, "Parents *and* Children," p. 939.

34 I. Butler, M. Robinson, and L. Scanlan, *Children's Involvement in Family Decision-making* (York, UK: Joseph Rowntree Foundation, July 2005), p. 2.

35 Ibid.

36 J.S. Eccles, C. Miller Buchanan, C. Flanagan, A. Fuligni, C. Midgley, and D. Yee, "Control versus Autonomy during Early Adolescence," *Journal of Social Issues* 47, no. 4 (1991): 53–68.

37 Baumrind, "Effects of Authoritative Parental Control on Child Behavior."

38 See Covell and Howe, *The Challenge,* 105–107, for discussion.

39 Government of Canada, *A Canada Fit for Children,* p. 52.

40 Public Health Agency of Canada, "Family and Parenting: Nobody's Perfect," http://www.phac-aspc.gc.ca/dca-dea/family_famille/nobody_e.html.

41 Government of Ontario, "Ontario Early Years Centre," http://www.ontario earlyyears.ca/oeyc/en/home.htm.

42 Public Health Agency of Canada, "Family/Parenting: Welcome to Parenting," http://www.phac-aspc.gc.ca/dca-dea/family_famille/welcometo_e.html.

43 Covell and Howe, *The Challenge,* p. 103.

44 Canadian Heritage, *Convention on the Rights of the Child,* p. 208.

45 Ibid., p. 123.

46 Quebec Civil Code, 1991, Chapter II, c. 64, a. 34.

47 Covell and Howe, *The Challenge,* p. 121.

48 Canadian Heritage, *Convention on the Rights of the Child,* p. 17.

49 Howe and Covell, "Schools and the Participation Rights of the Child," *Education and Law Journal* 10: 107–23; L. Johnny, "UN Convention on the Rights of the Child: A Rationale for Implementing Participatory Rights in Schools," *Canadian Journal of Educational Administration and Policy* 40: 1–20.

50 Del Williams, personal communication, November 2005; Nutana Team, "Linking Research to Policy and Practice for Children and Youth in Saskatchewan Schools," presented at the Centre for Early Childhood Development Conference (2001), www.tgmag.ca/centres/e/resourcesdb/detail_e.php?recordid=40.

51 Government of British Columbia, "Citizenship and Social Responsibility Survey," http://www.bced.gov.bc.ca/citizen_survey.

52 New Brunswick Advisory Council on Youth, http://www.gnb.ca/0049/activities-e.asp.

53 Such provisions have been made in Alberta, British Columbia, Saskatchewan, Manitoba, Ontario, Quebec, New Brunswick, Nova Scotia, and Newfoundland and Labrador. See S. Critchley, "The Nature and Extent of Student Involvement in Educational Policy-Making in Canadian School System," *Educational Management and Administration* 31, no. 1 (2003): 87–106.

54 E. Marques, "Youth Involvement in Policy-Making: Lessons from Ontario School Boards," Policy Brief no. 5 (Ottawa: Institute on Governance, 1999).

55 Education Act, S.N.W.T. 1995, c. 28, Sections 23 and 24, http://www.canlii .org/nt/laws/sta/1995c.28/20051121/whole.html.

56 D.S. McCall, "Selected Case Studies of Youth Involvement in Public Decision-Making," http://www.phac-aspc.gc.ca/dca-dea/7–18yrs-ans/participation _e.html.

57 Government of British Columbia, "Special Education Services: A Manual of Policies, Procedures and Guidelines," http://www.bced.gov.bc.ca/specialed/ ppandg/iep_1.htm.

58 Government of Newfoundland and Labrador, "Guidelines to Be Followed by Education, Health, Human Resources, and Employment Justice Personnel to Facilitate the Implemenation of the Individual Support Services Planning Process" (November 1997), http://www.mcscy.nl.ca/guidelinesissp.html.

59 W.J. Smith, L. Butler-Kisber, L.J. LaRocque, J.P. Portelli, C. Shields, C. Sturge Sparkes, and A.B. Vibert, "Student Engagement in Learning and School Life: The Executive Summary" (Montreal: McGill University, Office of Research on Educational Policy, n.d.).

60 Ibid., p. 6.

61 Ibid., p. 11.

62 Marques, "Youth Involvement in Policy-Making," p. 2.

63 Ontario Student Trustees' Association, "The Student Trustee Today and Tomorrow" (OSTA, 2005); Marques, "Youth Involvement in Policy-Making."

64 OSTA, "The Student Trustee"; Marques, "Youth Involvement in Policy-Making."

65 See S. Shariff, "Balancing Competing Rights: A Stakeholder Model for Democratic Schools," *Canadian Journal of Education* 29, no. 2 (2006): 476–96.

66 Johnny, "UN Convention on the Rights of the Child," 1–20.

67 For a discussion of these issues and the presentation of a model to help school officials balance competing rights, see Shariff, "Balancing Competing Rights."

68 R. Baranard, D.A. Campbell, and S. Smith, with contributions from D. Embuldeniya, *Citizen Re:Generation Understanding Active Citizen Engagement among Canada's Information Age Generation* (Toronto: D-Code, 2003).

69 City of Vancouver Youth Outreach Team, "Civic Youth Strategy," http://www.vancouveryouth.ca/who_we_are/civic_youth_strategy.

70 Toronto Youth Cabinet, "About the TYC," http://www.torontoyouth.com/youth _cabinet/about/index.php.

71 Ibid.

72 CTV.ca, "Youth Group Demands Anti-Violence Action," http://toronto.ctv.ca/ servlet/ArticleNews/local/CTVNews/20051227/youth_cabinet_newser_051227 ?s_name=&no_ads=.

73 City of Calgary, "Guide to Youth Friendly Practices: Youth Engagement," http://www.calgary.ca/docgallery/bu/community_strategies/cys_guide.pdf.

74 Regional Multicultural Youth Council, Multicultural Association of Northwestern Ontario, "Who Are We," http://my.tbaytel.net/manwoyc/who.html.

75 Ville de Gatineau, "Commission Jeunesse," http://www.adogatineau.ca/home .asp.

76 Nova Scotia Youth Secretariat, "Youth Advisory Council," http://youth.ednet
    .ns.ca/council/council.htm.

77 Manitoba Education, Citizenship and Youth, "MB4Youth Advisory Council,"
    http://www.edu.gov.mb.ca/youth/Initiatives/MB4YouthAdvisoryCouncil.html.

78 New Brunswick Advisory Council on Youth, "Current Activities," http://www
    .gnb.ca/0049/activities-e.asp.

79 Futures in Newfoundland and Labrador's Youth, "About Us," http://www
    .finaly.ca/about_us.htm.

80 Democratic Renewal Secretariat, "Democracy Challenge—Welcome,"
    http://www.democraticrenewal.gov.on.ca/english/youth/default.asp.

81 Environment Canada, "What Is the YRTE?" http://www.ec.gc.ca/youth/
    yrte_e.html.

82 Caputo, *Hearing the Voices of Youth*.

83 Statistics Canada, "Study: Political Activity among Young Adults," *The Daily*,
    December 6, 2003, http://www.statcan.ca/Daily/English/051206/d051206b.htm.

84 See http://www.studentvote.ca.

85 Student Vote, "2006 Federal Election Results," http://www.studentvote.ca/
    federal/index.php.

86 See http://www.elections.ca/eca/eim/article_search/article.asp?id=42&lang=
    e&frmPageSize=&textonly=false.

87 Covell and Howe, *The Challenge*, p. 102.

88 UN Committee on the Rights of the Child, *Considerations of Reports*, p. 3.

89 Covell and Howe, *The Challenge*, p. 159.

90 Ibid., p. 133.

91 Zeldin, "Youth as Agents of Adult and Community Development."

92 Ibid., p. 85.

93 M. Pancer, L. Rose-Krasnor, and L. Loisell, "Youth Conferences as a Context
    for Development," *New Directions in Youth Development* 96 (2002): 47–64.

94 S. McCart, "Youth Policy in the European Union: Intriguing Ideas for
    Canada," paper presented at A Place for Youth conference October 2005,
    Toronto; "European Youth Forum Work Plan 2005–2006," adopted by the
    General Assembly (Madrid, November 2004), http://www.youthforum.org/en/
    downloads/0678–04FINAL.pdf.

95 G. Koren, D. Birenbaum Carmeli, Y.S. Carmeli, and R. Haslam, "Maturity of
    Children to Consent to Medical Research: The Babysitter Test," *Journal of
    Medical Ethics* 19 (1993): 142–47.

96 Canadian Teachers' Federation, *A Cappella: A Report on the Realities, Con-
    cerns, Expectations, and Barriers Experienced by Adolescent Women in Canada*
    (Ottawa: CTF, 1999), as cited in Caputo, "Hearing the Voices of Youth: A
    Review of Research and Consultation Documents" (Ottawa: Health Canada,
    1999), p. 9.

97 Lansdown, *Evolving Capacities*, p. 8.

98 Melton, "Parents *and* Children," p. 939.

99 Ibid., p. 940.

100 Ibid., p. 937.

101 Examples include the City of Calgary's *Guide to Youth Friendly Practices*
    (n.d.); J. Lui and A. Moarif on behalf of the Civic Youth Strategy of the City

of Vancouver, *Guidelines and Tools for an Effective Youth Engagement Strategy* (n.d.); and *InvolveYouth: A Guide to Involving Youth in Decision-Making* (City of Toronto: InvolveYouth Campaign, 2004).

102 Caputo, *Hearing the Voices of Youth: Youth Participation in Selected Canadian Municipalities* (Ottawa: Health Canada).

103 CCRC, *UN Convention: How Does Canada Measure Up?* p. 37.

Bibliography

Baranard, R., D.A. Campbell, and S. Smith, with contributions from D. Embuldeniya. 2003. *Citizen Re:Generation Understanding Active Citizen Engagement among Canada's Information Age Generation.* Toronto: D-Code.

Baumrind, D. 1966. "Effects of Authoritative Parental Control on Child Behavior." *Child Development* 37, no. 4: 887–907.

Busseri, M., K. Campbell, M. Pancer, and L. Rose-Krasnor. 2003. "Testing a Model for Youth Engagement and Positive Outcomes." Poster presented at the annual meeting of the American Psychological Association, Toronto.

Butler, I., M. Robinson, and L. Scanlan. 2005. *Children's Involvement in Family Decision-making.* York, UK: Joseph Rowntree Foundation.

Canadian Coalition for the Rights of Children. 1999. *UN Convention on the Rights of the Child: How Does Canada Measure Up?* Ottawa: CCRC.

———. 2003. *UN Convention on the Rights of the Child: How Does Canada Measure Up? Update to Canada's Report to the UN Committee for the Rights of Children.* Ottawa: CCRC.

Canadian Heritage. 2001. *Convention on the Rights of the Child: Second Report of Canada.* Ottawa: Canadian Heritage.

Caputo, T. 1999. *Hearing the Voices of Youth: A Review of Research and Consultation Documents.* Ottawa: Health Canada.

———. 2000. *Hearing the Voices of Youth: Youth Participation in Selected Canadian Municipalities.* Ottawa: Public Health Canada.

Centre of Excellence for Youth Engagement. n.d. *Vision.* http://www.tgmag.ca/centres/vision_e.htm.

City of Calgary. n.d. "Guide to Youth Friendly Practices: Youth Engagement." http://www.calgary.ca/docgallery/bu/community_strategies/cys_guide.pdf.

City of Vancouver Youth Outreach Team. n.d. "Civic Youth Strategy." http://www.vancouveryouth.ca/who_we_are/civic_youth_strategy.

Covell, K. 2001. *Canada's Non-Governmental Organizations.* Report submitted for the UN General Assembly Special Session. Ottawa: Canadian Coalition for the Rights of Children.

Covell, K., and R.B. Howe. 2001. *The Challenge of Children's Rights for Canada.* Waterloo: Wilfrid Laurier University Press.

Critchley, S. 2003. "The Nature and Extent of Student Involvement in Educational Policy-Making in Canadian School System." *Educational Management and Administration* 31, no. 1: 87–106.

CTV.ca. 2005. "Youth Group Demands Anti-Violence Action." http://toronto.ctv
.ca/servlet/ArticleNews/local/CTVNews/20051227/youth_cabinet_newser
_051227?s_name=&no_ads=.

Democratic Renewal Secretariat. n.d. "Democracy Challenge—Welcome."
http://www.democraticrenewal.gov.on.ca/english/youth/default.asp.

Eccles, J.S., C.M. Buchanan, C. Flanagan, A. Fuligni, C. Midgley, and D. Yee.
1991. "Control versus Autonomy during Early Adolescence." *Journal of
Social Issues* 47, no. 4: 53–68.

Education Act, S.N.W.T. 1995, c. 28, Sections 23 and 24. http://www.canlii.org/
nt/laws/sta/1995c.28/20051121/whole.html.

Environment Canada. n.d. "What Is the YRTE?" http://www.ec.gc.ca/youth/
yrte_e.html.

Futures in Newfoundland and Labrador's Youth. n.d. "About U." http://www
.finaly.ca/about_us.htm.

Giroux, C. 2004. "Child Advocacy Institutions: Providing Effective Protection for Child and Youth Rights." Speech presented on behalf of the Commission des droits de la personne et des droits de la jeunesse du Québec
and the Canadian Council of Provincial Child and Youth Advocates at the
international conference Making Children's Rights Work: National and
International Perspectives, Montreal.

Government of British Columbia. n.d. "Citizenship and Social Responsibility
Survey." http://www.bced.gov.bc.ca/citizen_survey.

———. n.d. "Special Education Services: A Manual of Policies, Procedures, and
Guidelines." http://www.bced.gov.bc.ca/specialed/ppandg/iep_1.htm.

Government of Canada. 2004. *A Canada Fit for Children: Canada's Follow-
Up to the United Nations General Assembly Special Session on Children*.
Ottawa.

Government of Newfoundland and Labrador. 1997. "Guidelines to Be Followed by Education, Health, Human Resources, and Employment Justice
Personnel to Facilitate the Implementation of the Individual Support Services Planning Process." http://www.mcscy.nl.ca/guidelinesissp.html.

Government of Ontario. n.d. "Ontario Early Years Centres." http://www.ontario
earlyyears.ca/oeyc/en/home.htm.

Howe, R.B., and K. Covell. 2000. "Schools and the Participation Rights of the
Child." *Education and Law Journal* 10: 107–23.

Johnny, L. 2005. "UN Convention on the Rights of the Child: A Rationale for
Implementing Participatory Rights in Schools." *Canadian Journal of Educational Administration and Policy* 40: 1–20.

Klein-Hessling, J., A. Lohaus, and J. Ball. 2005. "Psychological Predictors of
Health-Related Behaviour in Children." *Psychology, Health and Medicine*
10: 31–43.

Koren, G., D. Birenbaum Carmeli, Y.S. Carmeli, and R. Haslam. 1993. "Maturity of Children to Consent to Medical Research: The Babysitter Test."
Journal of Medical Ethics 19: 142–47.

Lansdown, G. 2001. *Promoting Children's Participation in Democratic Decision Making*. Florence, Italy: UNICEF Innocenti Research Centre.

————. 2004. *Evolving Capacities and Participation*. Gatineau: Canadian International Development Agency (CIDA) Child Protection Unit.

Manitoba Education, Citizenship, and Youth. n.d. "MB4Youth Advisory Council." http://www.edu.gov.mb.ca/youth/Initiatives/MB4YouthAdvisoryCouncil .html.

Marques, E. 1999. "Youth Involvement in Policy-Making: Lessons from Ontario School Boards." Policy Brief no. 5. Ottawa: Institute on Governance.

McCall, D.S. n.d. "Selected Case Studies of Youth Involvement in Public Decision-Making." http://www.phac-aspc.gc.ca/dca-dea/7-18yrs-ans/participation _e.html.

McCart, S. 2005. "Youth Policy in the European Union: Intriguing Ideas for Canada." Paper presented at A Place for Youth Conference, Toronto.

Melton, G.B. 1999. "Parents *and* Children: Legal Reform to Facilitate Children's Participation." *American Psychologist* 54: 935–44.

New Brunswick Advisory Council on Youth. n.d. "Current Activities." http:// www.gnb.ca/0049/activities-e.asp.

Nova Scotia Office of the Ombudsman. 2005. News release: "Canadian Council of Provincial Child and Youth Advocates Meet in Halifax." http://www .gov.ns.ca/news/details.asp?id=20050928007.

Nova Scotia Youth Secretariat. Youth Advisory Council. n.d. http://youth.ednet .ns.ca/council/council.htm.

Nutana Team. 2001. "Linking Research to Policy and Practice for Children and Youth in Saskatchewan Schools." Presented at the Centre for Early Childhood Development Conference. http://www.tgmag.ca/centres/e/ resourcesdb/detail_e.php?recordid=40.

Ontario Student Trustees' Association. 2005. "The Student Trustee: Today and Tomorrow." Report of the Ontario Student Trustees' Association. N.p.: 2005.

Pancer, M., L. Rose-Krasnor, and L. Loisell. 2002. "Youth Conferences as a Context for Development." *New Directions in Youth Development* 96: 47–64.

Public Health Agency of Canada. n.d. "Family and Parenting: Nobody's Perfect." http://www.phac-aspc.gc.ca/dca-dea/family_famille/nobody_e.html.

————. n.d. "Family/Parenting: Welcome to Parenting." http://www.phac-aspc .gc.ca/dca-dea/family_famille/welcometo_e.html.

Quebec Civil Code, 1991, Chapter II, c. 64, a. 34.

Regional Multicultural Youth Council, Multicultural Association of Northwestern Ontario. n.d. "Who Are We." http://my.tbaytel.net/manwoyc/who .html.

Shariff, S. 2006. "Balancing Competing Rights: A Stakeholder Model for Democratic Schools." *Canadian Journal of Education* 29, no. 2: 476–96.

Smith, W.J., L. Butler-Kisber, L.J. LaRocque, J.P. Portelli, C. Shields, C.S. Sparkes, and A.B. Vibert. n.d. "Student Engagement in Learning and School Life: The Executive Summary." Montreal: McGill University, Office of Research on Educational Policy.

Statistics Canada. 2003. "Study: Political Activity among Young Adults." *The Daily*. http://www.statcan.ca/Daily/English/051206/d051206b.htm.

Student Vote. n.d. "2006 Federal Election Results." http://www.studentvote.ca/federal/index.php.

Toronto Youth Cabinet. n.d. "About the TYC." http://www.torontoyouth.com/youth_cabinet/about/index.php.

UNICEF. 2004. "Framework for the Protection, Care and Support of Orphans and Vulnerable Children Living in a World with HIV and AIDS" (July). http://www.unicef.org/uniteforchildren/knowmore/files/Framework_English .pdf.

UN Committee on the Rights of the Child. 1995. "Considerations of Reports Submitted by States Parties under Article 44 of the Convention: Concluding Observations: Canada." CRC/C/15/add.37.

————. 2003. *Considerations of Reports Submitted by States Parties under Article 44 of the Convention: Concluding Observations: Canada*. CRC/C/15/add.215.

————. 2003. *Summary Record of the 895th Meeting: Consideration of Reports of States Parties: Second Periodic Report of Canada*. CRC/C/sr.895.

Ville de Gatineau. n.d. "Commission Jeunesse." www.adogatineau.ca/home.asp.

Vygotsky, L. 1978. *Mind in Society: The Development of Higher Psychological Processes*. Cambridge, MA: Harvard University Press.

Youth Forum. 2004. "European Youth Forum Work Plan 2005–2006." Adopted by the General Assembly, November. http://www.youthforum .org/en/downloads/0678–04FINAL.pdf.

Zeldin, S. 2004. "Youth as Agents of Adult and Community Development: Mapping the Processes and Outcomes of Youth Engaged in Organizational Governance." *Applied Developmental Science* 8, no. 2: 75–90.

Children's Rights Education
Canada's Best-Kept Secret

Katherine Covell

Introduction

Canada is justly proud of its human rights record, its Charter of Rights, and that it ratified the Convention on the Rights of the Child in 1991. As a self-proclaimed world leader in human rights, it is ironic that the Convention on the Rights of the Child (hereinafter the Convention) remains Canada's best-kept rights secret. In ratifying the Convention, Canada agreed to make its provisions widely known. Yet more than a decade after ratification, there remains little knowledge among the public about the Convention.[1] The dearth of knowledge is particularly evident among children—those for whom the Convention is intended. Rather than systematic education about the provisions and principles of the Convention, there have been sporadic initiatives and a seeming reluctance to act in more than a symbolic manner. The UN Committee on the Rights of the Child repeatedly has called for the integration of the Convention into school curricula. That call appears not to have been heard.

In this chapter, it will be shown that there is little evidence in Canada of commitment to children's rights education in schools, and that systematic implementation would require some changes in teacher training and in the orientation of education officials. A model of children's rights education, and its outcomes, will be described. First, however, it is important to clarify what is meant by children's rights education.

Katherine Covell, Department of Psychology and Children's Rights Centre,
Cape Breton University

What Is Children's Rights Education?

The Convention on the Rights of the Child has nine articles that address children's rights *to* and *in* education. The focus of this chapter is on children's rights *in* education. However, first, it is important to note that articles 23 and 28 specify children's rights to education. These rights include the right to free primary education, and to accessible secondary and higher education, and the right of children with disabilities to appropriate education and supports. Canada's record in education generally is consistent with articles 23 and 28. Children with emotional and behavioural difficulties continue to experience some exclusion from the regular classroom, but overall, Canada's record on inclusion of children with exceptionalities is improved.[2]

Children's rights *in* education specify what and how children should be taught. The umbrella term of children's rights education is used for these rights. Children's rights education is the explicit teaching of the rights in the Convention in an environment that itself models and respects those rights. Education does not just occur in the classroom. Children learn both from the formal curriculum and from the informal or "hidden" curriculum. The hidden curriculum—the way students are treated by teachers and administrators, teaching styles, disciplinary strategies, the school's policies and practices—has a profound impact on what students learn.[3] It is, therefore, important not only to teach children in their classrooms what their specific rights are, but also to respect and promote children's rights in all aspects of school life.

The overarching content and goals of children's rights education are specified in articles 29 and 42; the appropriate pedagogy and the basis for school rules and regulations are described in articles 12 to 15. In addition, article 16 protects the child's privacy and has relevance to policies such as locker searches, and under article 28, children have the right to disciplinary procedures that protect the dignity of the child and are in conformity with the other Convention rights. True children's rights education requires that curricula and school policies and practices be consistent with all of these articles. The rights of the Convention are interrelated and were not intended to be in a hierarchy. This is very clear in rights relating to education.

Article 29 specifies the goals and the general content of education. First, teachers are expected to provide education that promotes the optimum physical, social, and cognitive development of each child. Education, then should take into account the development of the whole child, with attention paid to much more than the dissemination of information. The child's physical development should be promoted through physical education as well as health and nutrition teachings, and the child's social development should be promoted through the provision of appropriate opportunities for social interaction, and teaching through such means as role play and cooperative learning. Such pedagogy is consistent with articles 12 to 15. In addition, a vast body of education research demonstrates the value of such teaching strategies to the optimum cognitive and social development of the child.[4] This pedagogy, then, also meets the criteria of best interests described in article 3. Second, teaching should develop in each child a respect for the rights of all others, as well as an appreciation of equality, multiculturalism, world peace, and the natural environment. The development of respect for human rights is unlikely unless children are taught appropriately about the nature of rights and what fundamental human rights have been promised to them as described in article 42. When children are taught appropriately about their Convention rights, there is a significant increase in their respect for the rights of all others.[5]

Article 42 requires that appropriate and active means be used to disseminate information about the principles and provisions of the Convention. It is not enough to have information available. Children are to be taught explicitly about their Convention rights. Signatories to the Convention are required—not simply encouraged—to inform children (as well as adults) of the rights of children under the Convention. It is interesting to note here that this is the only human rights Convention that includes a dissemination duty.[6] Perhaps the architects of the Convention foresaw the reluctance of the general public to accept that children are bearers of fundamental rights. Regardless, it is obvious that the exercise of rights by children, and the protection of and advocacy for children's rights by adults, cannot occur in the absence of knowledge. The logical place to reach and educate children is in schools. In fact, the Committee on the Rights of the Child has repeatedly recommended that schools take responsibility for educating children about their rights.[7]

Articles 12 through 15 obligate teachers to use a democratic pedagogy in the classroom, and obligate school administrators to allow for student input into school decision making. Teachers and administrators should provide opportunities for the age-appropriate exercise of the rights of freedom of expression; access to information; freedom of thought, conscience, and religion; and freedom of association and peaceful assembly. Of course, the freedoms are not absolute. Articles 3 and 5 are also of relevance here. Article 5 obligates educators, because they are legally responsible for the child, to provide direction and guidance to their students in the exercise of their rights. Article 3, as the overarching principle of the Convention, requires that the best interests of the child be a primary consideration in all pedagogical and classroom-management decisions. It is particularly interesting here that since the early writings of Dewey, research in education repeatedly has shown that the type of education that is in the best interests of the child is that which is consistent with the Convention—supportive relationships among students and teachers, collaborative deliberation in democratic classrooms, and discussion of social issues.[8]

Children's rights education, then, is education whose goals, content, and pedagogy are consistent with and focus on the Convention. It is education that fully recognizes the citizenship and rights-bearing status of the child, in the classroom and out of it. Children's Convention rights are taken seriously, and talk is combined with action.[9] The Convention is taught in a democratic classroom environment characterized by mutual respect among students and between teacher and students. The rights of the Convention provide an overarching framework into which topics, policies, and practices are fit. For example, children do not simply learn that they have a right to have their voices heard (article 12); they are also listened to, and they participate meaningfully in school decision making, classroom charters, school councils, and school newspapers. Children are not simply told to "say no to drugs"; they are provided an opportunity for peer deliberation about how experimentation with drugs may interfere with their rights to maintain a high standard of health (article 24) and about their right to be protected from the production, use, and trafficking of illicit substances (article 33). Children are not simply taught about governments, geography, and history; they can also examine such issues as sustainable development, war, labour conditions, world religions, art, music, and literature, from a rights-based perspective.

Are Canadian Schools Committed to Children's Rights Education?

Schools are under provincial/territorial jurisdiction. This, of course, precludes the federal government from mandating the inclusion of the Convention in their teaching. Nonetheless, the federal government has made some effort to disseminate information about the Convention to children, and to encourage schools to do so. Children's rights information brochures and websites have been developed, children's rights conferences have been held, and the development of children's rights curriculum materials has been funded. The federal government's efforts may be most apparent through their annual National Child Day initiatives and through the work of Senator Landon Pearson.

National Child Day, November 20, was designated by the federal government in 1993 to honour children by commemorating the signing of the UN Declaration on the Rights of the Child (November 20, 1959) and the UN Convention on the Rights of the Child (November 20, 1989). Each year, there are suggested activities and some resources are made available to enable those who so wish to celebrate the day. The original intent was to focus on children's rights. More recently, the focus has been narrowed. According to the Public Health Agency of Canada website (July 2005), "Celebrating National Child Day is about celebrating children as actors in their own lives and in communities, as active citizens who can and should meaningfully contribute to decision-making as we create a Canada fit for children." There are also suggestions for activities, including holding a bottle drive to raise money for a local charity, donating used clothing to a local shelter, exchanging decorated school T-shirts with another school, and volunteering time in the community. Laudable perhaps, but one is hard pressed to see how such activities reflect any of the Convention rights, or in fact differ from suggestions made in the 1950s, decades before the Convention was signed. To be fair, it should be acknowledged that there are also suggestions for activities to "show knowledge" of children's rights, such as writing poems or taking pictures, but these presume knowledge of the Convention that may not be present. Regardless, there is little evidence of eager teachers adopting these suggestions and celebrating National Child Day in their classrooms.

Senator Pearson was named Advisor on Children's Rights to the Minister of Foreign Affairs in 1996, and in 1999 Personal Representative of Prime Minister Jean Chrétien to the 2002 Special Session on Children of the UN General Assembly. Senator Pearson contributes to raising awareness of children's rights through many initiatives, including the involvement of children in conferences and consultations, and through her newsletter *Children and the Hill*. Her efforts may have increased the awareness of the importance of children's rights in Canada. But, given the nature of federalism, however successful dissemination efforts are at the national level, there is no requirement that her initiatives be adopted by the provinces and territories.

As noted above, education is under exclusive provincial/territorial jurisdiction. There is a strong tradition of jurisdictional autonomy in education, as well as significant variation among provinces and territories in curricula.[10] The federal government, then, cannot require that schools include children's rights in their curricula, policies, or practices. Note, however, that it is not only the federal government that is obligated by the Convention. Each province and territory has also approved the Convention and is required to act in ways that are consistent with the Convention's principles and provisions. This includes how education is provided. Using the definition of children's rights education given above, there is little evidence that demonstrates consistency with the Convention's education goals, content, or pedagogy.

Broadly speaking, the goals described in article 29 may be accepted, at least rhetorically; but the reality is that the focus of education across the nation is more often on technology and global competitiveness than on the optimum development of the child or the development of respect for others. Especially in the wake of the terrorism of this new millennium, concerns have been expressed over what type of education is most important for children. Should the focus of education be on enabling and maintaining democracies or on enabling and maintaining capitalism? The Canadian Teachers' Federation, among other groups, has been studying whether schools should teach the content and skills necessary for participation in a global democratic society, or for participation in a global competitive marketplace.[11] Suzanne Majhanovich[12] described this dichotomy as education for life versus education to make a living. Whereas the Convention recognizes their interconnectedness and requires the inclusion of both, most schools have opted to emphasize education to make a living. The fact of globalization has resulted in schools being concerned with enabling competitiveness in the global marketplace; primacy is given to technology, with an emphasis on economics. In many schools, the addition of computer technology has been facilitated by the reduction of funding and supports to physical education.[13] Not surprisingly, most Canadian schools do not meet the national standard of 150 minutes a week of physical education.[14] Initiatives to teach or promote tolerance, multiculturalism, and equality issues have been relegated to low-status occasional foci, such as "Black History Month," rather than being integral to curricula. Overall, what appears to have been adopted is a "flavour of the month" approach. As social problems become more or less salient (anti-bullying, anti-racist, anti-gambling, drug prevention), programs to cope with them appear and disappear.

Education consistent with article 42, the most fundamental aspect of children's rights education, is even more rare. There is no lack of resources to teach children about their rights. To promote education and to assist states in fulfilling their Convention obligations, UNICEF has developed a special Education for Development program, which provides resources and educational materials—directly and through the Internet—for the teaching of children's rights. Similarly, Save the Children Canada has programs for children's rights education and a variety of resources available. In addition to these NGO efforts, academics have provided children's rights education curricula. Children's rights curriculum resource materials designed and evaluated in Canadian schools have been made available for teachers to use with students in kindergarten through grade three,[15] and with students in grades six, eight, and twelve.[16] Most recently, a number of children's books about their Convention rights have been developed for children from kindergarten through grade nine.[17] These materials also are used by some schools and some teachers. But for the most part in Canada, children's rights education has been limited to federal government initiatives as described above, to NGO initiatives such as the materials provided by UNICEF, and to rights education programs provided by Save the Children Canada.

Only in one province has there been any systematic inclusion of children's rights in school curriculum. Working in cooperation with the Cape Breton University Children's Rights Centre, the Province of Nova Scotia has incorporated children's rights education activities into the province-wide Health and Social Studies curriculum from kindergarten through grade six, with knowledge of the Convention being a required learning outcome at grade six. The history of this initiative illustrates the glacial pace of curriculum change.

Funded by Canadian Heritage and in cooperation with the Cape Breton–Victoria School Board, the Cape Breton University Children's Rights Centre in 1997 began a program of children's rights education in local schools. A curriculum was developed that fit with existing health and social studies curricula and that conformed to existing learning outcomes and curriculum design. The curriculum was evaluated in seven grade six classrooms (involving 175 children) during the 1997–98 school year. Grade six was chosen as an introductory point for the curriculum, as research indicates that children around age eleven have an increased capacity for understanding abstract concepts such as rights. For additional support, information and resources for teachers, students, and parents were placed on the centre's website. Teachers were given training at a workshop at the beginning of the school year, and a handbook was developed for parents to address issues as well as to provide basic information about the Convention.

Evaluation data from the Centre's researchers and independent evaluations from the school board converged to demonstrate that the rights curriculum was successful. Children whose teachers had used the rights curriculum, compared with a demographically equivalent group, evidenced a more adult-like understanding of rights (that they of necessity include responsibilities), more supportive attitudes toward minority children, and perceived greater levels of peer and teacher support. These children also reported that they enjoyed the curriculum activities. Their teachers reported the positive and enthusiastic responses of students to the curriculum and a deeper understanding of rights and responsibilities.[18] The success of this project led to a request from the school board for a follow-up curriculum at the grade eight level, and to the initiation of discussions to incorporate children's rights activities into the provincial curriculum. The grade eight curriculum was developed with funding from the Canadian Race Relations Foundation. It extended the application of the Convention rights to interpersonal issues salient to the age— equality, alcohol and drug use, the environment and health, youth justice, abuse and exploitation, rights and sexuality, employment and education. Like the grade six curriculum, the effects of the grade eight curriculum were evaluated at the end of the school year; again, the impact was found to be very positive. In essence, the data indicated that learning about their rights using role play, debate, discussion, and cooperative learning increased the students' self-esteem, perceived peer and teacher support, and rights-respecting attitudes and behaviours.[19]

In the meantime, discussion with provincial education officials continued. Their Convention obligations were pointed out to them, as well as the benefits of incorporating children's rights education into classroom teachings. Department officials continually expressed interest but also concern that there might be insufficient emphasis on children's responsibilities. In addition, officials had difficulty appreciating the need to pay attention to the Convention, given that Canada already had its Charter of Rights. Discussions continued, and in 2000 the department agreed to a process of incorporating children's rights education into the Nova Scotia health and social studies curriculum from grades K through six, with concentration in grade six. However, before it could be introduced, for financial reasons, the Government of Nova Scotia put a freeze on new education curricula. The freeze was to be lifted in 2002. During this time, discussions took place with regard to incorporating the grade eight curriculum into the province's Personal Development and Relationships curriculum for junior high school students. In 2001, education officials in the province expressed their intent to incorporate children's rights into the Personal Development and Relationships grade eight curriculum.

Children's rights education finally was introduced in 2003, from K to six. In the meantime, the grade eight curriculum remains in local use, and a new grade twelve curriculum examining Canada's children's rights obligations internationally has been developed (funded by the Canadian International Development Agency) and is being used informally in Global Citizenship classes. Whether these curricula also will be adopted by the province remains unclear.

The Nova Scotia initiative is a good step in the right direction; even so, it falls short. Students in elementary schools may well learn that the Convention exists, and they may learn what the articles are, but the necessary democratic teaching and management styles have not been adopted.

In consequence, it is expected that children will not fully appreciate the nature of their rights, nor feel empowered to promote and protect their own and others' rights. In fact, there is a possibility that children will become cynical about rights if they are told they have them but are not provided opportunities to exercise them. A focus solely on article 42 does not meet the criteria of children's rights education. Nonetheless, with the exception of individual schools and perhaps some school districts, the Nova Scotia initiative appears to be the best that Canada has to offer at this time. Until it also adopts the democratic pedagogy required by the Convention, it remains only a step in the right direction.

The pedagogy required by articles 12 through 15 is rare in Canadian public schools. With the exceptions noted in the previous chapter, most schools deny children's participation rights. The most common classroom situation continues to involve rote learning and hierarchical student–teacher relationships. Participatory learning—role play, debate, discussion, cooperative learning, and so forth—while clearly in the child's best interests, are not often in evidence in Canadian classrooms, except for very young children.[20]

Even when teaching initiatives are outside the classroom and intended to promote citizenship, there is little student participation in their design or implementation. For example, community action projects, increasingly used for civic learning, have very limited student direction. Rather, students typically are limited to helping behaviours such as working in community soup kitchens or hospitals.[21] And these community-involvement initiatives typically are not self-directed. School councils have limited functions and limited membership. There is more student initiation in school councils, but typically school councils are composed of elite students, those with high grades or those selected by school staff as known cooperators.[22] Likewise, school newspapers are contributed to by few students, and in most schools, staff continue to control or limit the content of newspapers. School dress codes, often hotly debated, also are decided upon in the absence of student input. The extent to which students are denied a voice, and their freedom of expression rights, was highlighted in the 1999 decision by an Edmonton school to forbid several students to participate in their grade nine graduation ceremonies. Lisa Cote was denied participation because she had dyed her hair blue, and Gavin Mader was denied participation because he had "jelled his hair and combed it into unsightly spikes."[23]

Contrary to the allowance for participation and for freedom of thought, conscience, and religion, and contrary to access to information of benefit to the child's well-being, there are many examples of violations of these rights. Sitch and McCoubrey[24] describe an appalling litany of rights violations in Canadian schools. These include the denial of rights information as well as drug and other searches that violate children's privacy rights as described in article 16 of the Convention. For example, in December 1998, twenty high-school students in Ontario were required to submit to a strip search after some money was reported missing. The students actually were required to remove their clothing (including their underwear) in front of their peers and teacher. This was a highly intrusive and disturbing violation of these students' right to privacy and right to be treated with dignity. It simply would not have happened with adults. And yes, it turned out that the money was lost, not stolen. In another case, a junior high-school student in Nova Scotia was searched for drugs after another student reported him to the vice-principal. The student was searched without counsel and without the usual privacy considerations afforded adults under the Charter of Rights and Freedoms.[25] Other cases have involved disciplinary action taken against a student who sang a banned song ("Let's Talk about Sex") while off school property during a lunch hour, and a refusal to allow a homosexual teen to take his partner to his high-school graduation party. This latter is a particularly egregious example of rights violations.

In 2002 in Ontario, seventeen-year-old Marc Hall was in court seeking an injunction against the Durham Catholic District School Board.[26] His school had refused to allow Marc to take his boyfriend to his high-school prom. The board, which is not exempt from the Convention, claimed that under religious freedom, they could discriminate against homosexual students. Hall did win the injunction, but what was the message sent to the students and to other Canadians who watched this story unfold through the media? The discrimination practised by the board must be expected to be a very powerful educational tool since it carried the weight of authority. And the discrimination stood in sharp contradiction to Marc Hall's rights under the Convention. The board, it would seem, was educating students that it is legitimate to discriminate and act disrespectfully toward students of sexual-minority status. This stands in contradiction to article 29's requirement for teaching that promotes understanding, respect, tolerance, and equality. The board's behaviour had infringed on Hall's article 13 right to freedom of expression, his article 14 right to freedom of thought and conscience, and his article 15 right of freedom of association. In expressing his homosexuality by taking his boyfriend to the prom, he was not posing a threat to national security or to public health and safety, or to the morals or rights of others. These are the limiting criteria. Moreover, the board's discriminatory treatment toward Hall stands in sharp contrast to the best-interests principle described in article 3. In the social-science literature it is clear that homosexual students are common targets of harassment, bullying, and violence and that these experiences have profound developmental consequences.[27]

The violation of students' rights to access (age-appropriate) information as described in article 13 most often takes the form of withholding information about sexuality. This was seen most recently in Nova Scotia. During the school year 2004–5, many students were not provided access at school to a new Department of Health information booklet about sexuality. In response to rising rates of sexually transmitted diseases, decreasing knowledge about sexuality, and decreasing ages of sexual involvement, the province's Office of Health Promotion developed an excellent resource to educate children from grades seven through twelve. The booklet was meant to be used disseminated and discussed in school classes. The resource was evidence-based; it stressed the importance of healthy choices and it promoted tolerance for youth of sexual-minority status. Its content and style were consistent with a large body of social-science literature demonstrating the links between appropriate sexuality education and delayed sexual activity and more responsible sexual behaviour. Clearly, this resource was in the best interests of children. Of eight school boards in the province, one has not yet decided whether to allow distribution (Conseil Scolaire Acadien), one has decided there will be no distribution (Strait Regional), and the remaining six boards require parental permission, either for junior high-school students or for all students. Interestingly, one board (Cape Breton–Victoria Regional) is allowing only parents to obtain the resource, saying that parents can then allow their child access to it if they choose.[28] Arguments against the distribution of the booklet not only are denying the best interests of children and children's right to access to information, but also are denying the reality of Canadian legislation. Since it is legal in Canada to have sex with a peer at the age of twelve (and with an adult, other than one in authority over the child, at the age of fourteen), it is important that children be provided access to information that will facilitate healthy decision making.

In summary, there is little evidence of children's rights education. Most children do not learn that there is such as thing as a Convention on the Rights of the Child ratified by their government. And even those who do learn about the Convention, do so in a traditional educational environment in which the rights of the Convention are neither modelled nor respected. Schools in Canada continue to function as though the Convention has not been ratified by their governments.

Implementing Children's Rights Education

For Canada to show real commitment to children's rights education, there will first have to be a genuine appreciation among education officials of the importance and usefulness of children's rights as an overarching principle for school functioning. In this area, the federal government could play a key role in disseminating information about the Convention. If provincial education ministers are unaware or unconvinced of the importance of children's rights education, they cannot be expected to undertake implementation efforts.

Canada's education ministers have a forum in which they can discuss issues of common interest and commit to pan-Canadian strategies if they so choose. The Council of Ministers of Education, Canada (CMEC) was established in 1967 to enable cooperation among the provinces and territories, and the federal government. It would seem, then, that this body should be the initial target of federal government strategies to encourage children's rights education. And in accord with their mandate, the CMEC could work in partnership with the federal government toward the implementation of children's rights education in every province and territory. In fact, it should not be a hard sell. The goals and content of education described by the Convention, and the empirical evidence on the outcomes of children's rights education,[29] are congruous with the CMEC's goals and priorities in this new millennium.

In 2000 the CMEC was part of the 14th Commonwealth Education Ministers Conference, held in Halifax, Nova Scotia. During the conference, the ministers raised concerns about globalization, endorsed the importance of citizenship education, and recognized the importance of the moral and spiritual dimensions of education, noting the need to use education to encourage acceptance and respect for diversity.[30] In the outcome statement, the ministers agreed on the values of education. They agreed that education should "promote values of democracy, human rights, citizenship, good governance, tolerance." They noted the pivotal role of teachers in accomplishing the goals of education, and they called for strengthened teacher training.[31] Children's rights education is a demonstrated means of encouraging acceptance of diversity and in fact of promoting the values, skills, and attitudes that are fundamental to democratic citizenship.[32]

Unfortunately, the goals and priorities agreed on in the Halifax Statement seem to have been overshadowed by other concerns. Priority action plans decided on recently have related to (1) Aboriginal education, (2) literacy, and (3) post-secondary education capacity.[33] Moreover, the listing of "other initiatives" fails to include any reference to promoting the values of democracy, human rights, citizenship, good governance, or tolerance. Not surprisingly, there is an emphasis on education outcomes. New technologies and testing and assessment approaches have primacy. Moreover, the current or planned initiatives make no reference to teacher training initiatives.

Children's rights education is unlikely to become a reality in Canada unless there are extensive changes in teacher training. In 2005 an examination of university teacher education course descriptions in Canada revealed no required or elective courses on children's rights. Some included consideration of rights, but not children's rights. For example, a course offered at Acadia University called ED 5273, "Education and the Law," is described as examining various legal principles, including teacher and student rights. The essential focus, however, is on the educational implications of the Canadian Charter of Rights and Freedoms. The Charter does include children, but it is only the Convention that provides a clear, comprehensive, and systematic statement specifically about the rights of children. And it is the Convention that is of the most importance to children. Some universities did include in their descriptions the importance of considering children's needs, but again, not their rights (e.g., University of Lethbridge, ED 5633, "Governance, Collaboration and Community Engagement"). In contrast, many offered a wide variety of courses on technology and computer applications in education. In the one university that offers upper-level courses in children's rights to all its students (Cape Breton), students in education are neither required to take any of these courses, nor are they given credit for children's rights courses as electives.

Besides receiving no training in the Convention, teachers typically receive inadequate training in the pedagogy required by the Convention. The overwhelming evidence throughout the education literature is that teachers are poorly prepared to teach in other than traditional ways.[34] Fundamental to children's rights education is teachers' ability to listen to their students. Rudduck and Flutter noted the importance of teachers specifically being trained to listen to their students, to help students express their learning needs, and to respect the participation rights of children.[35] Building on the concept of reflection,[36] Carol Rodgers stressed the importance of teachers developing their capacity to think critically about what and how their students are learning.[37] Part of this requires that teachers be aware of and respect the participation rights of their students. That teachers have not been taught the importance of children's voices and agency in their own learning is reflected also in the difficulty many teachers have in allowing their students to engage in non-traditional learning activities such as role play and drama.

Teachers tend to be skeptical about the value of role play and drama and social-issues discussion. They are dismissive of these activities, which they tend to see as mere fun, or a waste of time, or an inappropriate opportunity for students to socialize, or a break from real teaching.[38] Teachers need to be taught not only the benefits of such activities, but also the benefits of student engagement in and enjoyment of classroom activities. Effective teaching strategies such as role play should not be dismissed because the students have fun with them.

Teachers also lack training in cooperative learning. Although the effectiveness of cooperative learning has been well established,[39] its techniques are not often part of teacher training. In the absence of adequate training, cooperative learning often fails and, like role play and social-issues discussion, is dismissed as a waste of time. When teachers have not been trained in how to organize and facilitate effective groups, there can be individualistic learning or competition within a group, or there can be some students who do the work for the entire group. Teachers need to be taught how to design and supervise cooperative learning so that these problems do not arise; they also need to be taught the benefits of cooperative learning over whole-class competitive approaches. An excellent short summary of the benefits and best practices in cooperative learning is provided by Mary Hamm and Dennis Adams.[40] This summary could readily be used as the core for teaching training.

The effects of the gaps in teacher training may be exacerbated by their current experiences in the classroom. Many Canadian teachers have expressed concerns about increasing workloads as a consequence of new responsibilities, larger classes, fewer resources, and loss of support personnel.[41] Canadian teachers are left exhausted by cutbacks to funding and by new curricula, new assessment protocols, and endless policy changes.[42] Teachers are constantly faced with new curricula that encourage highly ritualized and hierarchical teacher–student relationships.[43] And while they are adopting these curricula and ensuring that new standards are met, they are expected to attend to the increasingly wide variety of needs and learning styles of the individual children in the class.[44] As in much of the industrialized world, education in Canada has become framed in economic terms, with an increasing emphasis on standards, accountability, and testing.[45] As a result, the focus in the classroom is on speedy task completion and rote learning.[46] Competence continues to be understood as possession of facts. Teachers feel they must teach for testing rather than learning.

A Model for Children's Rights Education

Children's rights education at this time is most advanced in Hampshire County in England. Ironically, the Hampshire Initiative grew from the Nova Scotia children's rights programming. But where Nova Scotia has essentially limited its children's rights education to consistency with article 42, the Hampshire education authorities have made children's rights part of the overall ethos of their schools. In Hampshire, children learn about children's rights in a rights-respecting, participatory environment. Children's rights education permeates the formal and the informal teachings. True commitment to children's rights education is evident.

Impelled by an awareness of how secular schools have been disadvantaged by their lack of universal values or principles, and by reading the research findings from the Cape Breton initiative, Hampshire's education officials have adopted children's rights education as their overarching values framework. Led by Chief Inspector John Clarke and County Inspector for Intercultural Education Ian Massey, three groups of teachers and administrators spent study leave in Cape Breton. They have since developed a comprehensive program of children's rights education, including teacher training in Hampshire, the largest education district in England, with more than 200,000 students.[47]

Hampshire provides a model for children's rights education as a result of its efforts not only to incorporate children's rights education across the formal curriculum but also to make it the core of the school ethos. Schools engage children with the daily practice of children's rights by making those rights a part of school codes of conduct as well as regulations, mission statements, classroom charters, and student council activities. Preliminary evaluations suggest that the objectives of improving the culture of schools, establishing a stronger moral framework for values and behaviours, and promoting rights-respecting attitudes and behaviours are being met.

In April and May 2005 an evaluation of the Hampshire children's rights education initiative, called Rights Respect and Responsibility (RRR), was conducted by researchers from the Cape Breton University Children's Rights Centre. By then, RRR had been introduced to three hundred primary and elementary schools. The evaluation included interviews with eleven participating principals and twelve classroom teachers as well as a survey completed by a further seventy-five teachers. The evaluation was designed to assess their experiences with (1) the RRR training provided, (2) the challenges faced implementing and sustaining RRR, and (3) the impact of RRR on students' behaviours and attitudes and on teachers' own classroom experiences. The data collected pointed to an overall very positive early experience with the RRR initiative.

In both interview and survey responses, the training was described in very positive terms. Teachers reported that they had encountered few difficulties adjusting their teaching styles. Some changes had been necessary to accommodate the greater participation of students. These included the development of new, rights-based class and school charters with student input, the provision of greater autonomy to student councils (with teacher support and guidance), the greater involvement of students in school and community liaisons, and modifications of teacher behaviour to ensure that the rights of each child were respected. The following examples are illustrative.

The first example concerns exemplary changes in student involvement in an elementary school. As part of an effort to gain broad support for the initiative and forestall potential concerns, it was deemed necessary to present information about children's rights and the RRR initiative to a special meeting of the school's governors. Students played a key role in the presentation of the information at the meeting. In addition, a change of policy was made at the school to allow for the presence of students at parent–teacher meetings. This new inclusive policy was highly successful, resulting in a significant increase in attendance at these meetings and improved relationships among teachers, parents, and students. The second example concerns an individual child. The teacher, in this case, described her realization that behaviour consistent with children's rights required that she listen to every child—even a boy whose constant demands for attention she had always found particularly obnoxious. She decided that she would really listen to this boy for five minutes each morning. To her delight, this short period satisfied his need for attention. The child was no longer demanding and no longer seemed obnoxious. The teacher's relationship with this pupil, and her feelings toward him, were vastly improved, as was his behaviour and his ability to concentrate on his work. The positive outcome of the respect for children's rights reflected in this teacher's behaviour is but one indication of an overall improved classroom situation.

Consistent with earlier predictions, children's rights education empowered the students by providing a rights-based framework for understanding and decision making.[48] This was evident in the social *and* cognitive domains.

In the social domain, the difference was most apparent in how student disagreements were handled. One respondent described the impact as follows: "Children developed strategies for ensuring that rights are upheld, and promoted equality in the classroom and playground." There had been a notable change from confrontational and adversarial approaches to conflict resolution to the use of rights-based explanations;

there had also been increased respect for the protection of the rights of all children. Teachers reported that children were using rights discourse to settle problems and that children were more ready to accept responsibility for their errors and to behave appropriately when a rights-based explanation of what is unacceptable was used. Children who in the past had been intimidated by bullies were now empowered to speak up. Teachers reported that such children were responding with reference to their rights—for example, "Stop that, I have the right to play." Interestingly, teachers reported that the bullies tended to pay attention and respond with statements such as, "Oh yeah, I forgot." As such, RRR also has proven very effective as a behaviour-management strategy. In turn, classroom environments have improved. In the words of the children: "The class has changed a lot since last year because they used to be mean and nasty to each other. This year they are starting to respect each other more." "They get along better and cooperate more and there is no upset when they have to work with someone different."* The children's perceptions of improved behaviour are reflected in the detention and exclusion statistics documented at Elson Junior School. Both have dropped significantly (detentions by almost 50 percent and exclusions by more than 70 percent) since the introduction of the RRR initiative.

In the cognitive domain, some children were empowered to take control of their learning through enhanced self-awareness. An example here is that of a ten-year-old boy, a fidgety boy whose work was never completed. The teacher noted a complete change—the boy started to concentrate and complete his work neatly and even before many others in his class. In fact, the teacher reported, the change was so dramatic that the class applauded the boy's work one morning. She asked the boy what had led to his new effort. He replied, "Knowing I have the right to learn—it's up to *me* not to be distracted."

What had not been predicted was that teaching RRR would also empower teachers. The data indicate that teaching RRR has the potential to increase teachers' sense of self-efficacy and enjoyment of teaching and to engender more positive attitudes toward their pupils. It was reported that teaching RRR was a morale-boosting experience. Teachers said it reminded them that their day-to-day interactions with children really do have the potential to improve society and that they can do so much more than get children through their tests. It reminded them, they said, of why they went into teaching. Teachers also reported being empowered and motivated toward increased professionalism in their interactions with students rather than guided by personal feelings. The example

---

* Quotes provided by Basil Kupersamy, Elson Junior School.

above of the teacher who reported the realization that article 12 meant she must listen to every child illustrates this well. Perhaps the best exemplification of teachers' responses to RRR is seen in the following statement by a principal: "If I told my teachers we were not going to do the rights work any more, I'd have a riot on my hands."

The data also revealed a link between the positive impact on teachers and the positive impact on students. As found in earlier research, the more teachers appreciate children's rights and teaching children's rights, the greater the impact of children's rights education on their students.[49] This is not surprising. As discussed elsewhere, teacher attitudes do much to determine classroom functioning and school ethos.[50] Teachers respond to their pupils in ways that are consistent with their perceptions of those pupils.[51] Increasingly. the evidence shows that teachers everywhere are feeling stressed and negative about their pupils and their careers.[52] In particular, global trends in education toward more testing, have left many teachers feeling that their expertise and professionalism have been found wanting.[53] We should expect, then, that when teachers are feeling more positive and empowered there will be a marked improvement in their students' motivation, learning, and behaviour.

The Hampshire County model is important in illustrating what commitment to children's rights education entails and what the outcomes are. It seems clear from the preliminary assessment that when administrators are truly committed to children's rights education, and when teachers have the confidence and motivation to implement it, then children can be educated in ways that are consistent with all their rights in education as described in the Convention on the Rights of the Child. Perhaps the Hampshire experience, begun in Canada, will motivate Canadian educators to rethink their commitment to children's rights education.

Notes

1 R. Joyal, J.F. Noel, and C.C. Feliciati, eds., *Making Children's Rights Work: National and International Perspectives* (Cowansville: Editions Yvonne Blais, 2005).
2 N.L. Heath, H. Petrakos, C.A. Finn, A. Karagiannakis, D. McLean-Heywood, and C. Rousseau, "Inclusion on the Final Frontier: A Model for Including Children with Emotional and Behavior Disorders in Canada," *International Journal of Inclusive Education* 8, no. 3 (2004): 241–60.
3 A. Seaton, "Reforming the Hidden Curriculum: The Key Abilities Model and Four Curricular Forms," *Curriculum Perspectives* 22, no. 1 (2002): 9–15.
4 R.B. Howe and K. Covell, *Empowering Children: Children's Rights Education as a Pathway to Citizenship* (Toronto: University of Toronto Press, 2005).

5 Covell and Howe, "Moral Education through the 3 Rs: Rights, Respect, and Responsibility," *Journal of Moral Education* 30, no. 1 (2001): 31–42; Covell and Howe, "The Impact of Children's Rights Education: A Canadian Study," *International Journal of Children's Rights* 7 (1999): 171–83; J. Decoene and R. De Cock, "The Children's Rights Project in the Primary School 'De Vrijdagmarkt' in Bruges," in E. Verhellen, ed., *Monitoring Children's Rights* (The Hague: Martinus Nijhoff, 1996), pp. 627–36; A. Hughes and H. Filer, *The Rights of the Child: Impact of Teaching in Year 6 Class* (Andover, UK: Knights Enham Junior School, June 2003); E. Murray, *Impact of Children's Rights Education on Primary-Level Children* (unpublished paper, Mount Royal College, Calgary, 2002).

6 J.V. Lanotte and G. Goedertier, "Monitoring Human Rights: Formal and Procedural Aspects," in Verhellen, ed., *Monitoring Children's Rights* (The Hague: Martinus Nijhoff, 1996), pp. 73–111.

7 R. Hodgkin and P. Newell, *Implementation Handbook for the Convention on the Rights of the Child* (New York: UNICEF, 1998).

8 Howe and Covell, *Empowering Children.*

9 P. Alderson, "Human Rights and Democracy in Schools—Do They Mean More Than 'Picking Up Litter and Not Killing Whales?' *International Journal of Children's Rights* 7 (1999): 85–205.

10 Howe and Covell, "Teaching Children's Rights: Considerations and Strategies," *Education and Law Journal* 9, no. 1 (1998): 97–113.

11 D. Wall, M. Moll, and G. Froese-Germaine, *Contemporary Approaches to Citizenship Education* (Ottawa: Canadian Teachers Federation, 2000).

12 S. Majhanovich, "Conflicting Visions, Competing Expectations: Control and Deskilling of Education," *McGill Journal of Education* 7, no. 2 (2002): 159–76.

13 Howe and Covell, *Empowering Children.*

14 Canadian Association for Health and Physical Education, Recreation, and Dance, http://www.cahperd.ca.

15 Murray, *Impact of Children's Rights Education;* idem, *Exploring Children's Emerging Conceptions of their Participation Rights and Responsibilities* (unpublished dissertation, University of Victoria, 1999).

16 Howe and Covell, *Empowering Children.*

17 See *Grover Children's Rights and Peace Education Publishers* (2005), http://www.groverbooks.net.

18 Covell and Howe, "The Impact of Children's Rights Education."

19 Covell and Howe, "Moral Education through the 3 Rs."

20 Howe and Covell, *Empowering Children.*

21 K. Bickmore, "Teaching Conflict and Conflict Resolution in the School: (Extra) Curricular Considerations," in A. Raviv, L. Oppenheimer, and D. Bar-Tal, eds., *How Children Understand War and Peace* (San Francisco: Jossey-Bass Publishers, 1999), pp. 233–59.

22 Ibid.

23 R. Cairney, "Confronted," *See Magazine,* June 24, 1999, http://www.seemagazine.cm/Issues.

24 G. Sitch and S. McCoubrey, "Stay in Your Seat: The Impact of Judicial Subordination of Students' Rights on Effective Rights Education," *Education and Law Journal* 1 (2001): 173–202.

25 *R. v. M. (M.R.),* [1998] 3 S.C.R. 393.

26 *Hall (Litigation guardian of) v. Powers* (2002). O. J. No. 1803. File No. 02-CV-227705CM3.

27 Covell, *Violence against Children in North America,* Report to the UN Global Study on Violence (Toronto: UNICEF Canada, 2005).

28 L. Lowe, "What's the Fucking Problem?" *The Coast* (2004), http://www.thecoast.ca/BAS04/fucking.html.

29 Covell and Howe, "Moral Education through the 3Rs"; Covell and Howe, "The Impact of Children's Rights Education"; Decoene and De Cock, "The Children's Rights Project."

30 Commonwealth Secretariat, Communique: 14th Conference of Commonwealth Education Ministers, Halifax, November 26–30 (London: Commonwealth Secretariat, Information and Public Affairs Division, 2000).

31 Conference of Commonwealth Education Ministers, "Education for Our Common Future: The Halifax Statement on Education in the Commonwealth" (London: Commonwealth Secretariat).

32 Howe and Covell, *Empowering Children.*

33 Council of Ministers of Education of Canada, "CMEC Update June 2005," http://www.cmec.ca.

34 Howe and Covell, *Empowering Children.*

35 J. Rudduck and J. Flutter, "Pupil Participation and Pupil Perspective: Carving a New Order of Experience," *Cambridge Journal of Education* 30, no. 1 (2000): 75–90.

36 J. Dewey, *How We Think* (Buffalo: Prometheus Books, 1933).

37 C.R. Rodgers, "Voices Inside Schools: Seeing Student Learning: Teacher Change and the Role of Reflection," *Harvard Educational Review* 72, no. 2 (2002): 230–53.

38 Howe and Covell, *Empowering Children.*

39 R. Slavin, *Cooperative Learning: Theory, Research, and Practice* (Boston: Allyn & Bacon, 1995).

40 M. Hamm and D. Adams, "Collaborative Inquiry: Working toward Shared Goals," *Kappa Delta Pi Record* (2002): 115–18.

41 Covell and Howe, "The Impact of Children's Rights Education."

42 Majhanovich, "Conflicting Visions, Competing Expectations."

43 R. Hancock and M. Mansfield, "The Literacy Hour: A Case for Listening to Children," *Curriculum Journal* 13, no. 2 (2002): 183–200.

44 S. Katz, L. Earl, and D. Olson, "The Paradox of Classroom Assessment: A Challenge for the 21st Century," *McGill Journal of Education* 36, no. 1 (2001): 13–26.

45 M. Priestly, "Global Discourses and the National Reconstruction: The Impact of Globalization on Curriculum Policy," *Curriculum Journal* 13, no. 1 (2002): 121–38.

46 S. Grundy, "Is Large-Scale Educational Reform Possible?," *Journal of Educational Change* 3 (2002): 55–62; C.P. Henry, "Educating for Human Rights," *Human Rights Quarterly* 13 (1991): 420–23; Katz, Earl, and Olson, "The Paradox of Classroom Assessment"; Rudduck and Flutter, "Pupil Participation and Pupil Perspective."

47 Howe, "The Frontier of Children's Rights Education," *Our Schools/Our Selves* (2005, in press).
48 Howe and Covell, *Empowering Children.*
49 K. Covell, J. O'Leary, and R.B. Howe, "Introducing a New Grade 8 Curriculum in Children's Rights," *Alberta Journal of Educational Research,* 48, no. 4 (2002): 302–13.
50 Howe and Covell, *Empowering Children.*
51 V.C. McLoyd, "Socioeconomic Disadvantage and Child Development," *American Psychologist* 53, no. 2 (1998): 185–204.
52 W.J.G. Evers, A. Brouwers, and W. Tomic, "Burnout and Self-Efficacy: A Study on Teachers' Beliefs When Implementing an Innovative Educational System in the Netherlands," *British Journal of Educational Psychology* 72 (2002): 227–43; O. Lebedev, A. Maiorov, and V. Zolotukhina, "The Rights of Children," *Russian Education and Society* 44, no. 8 (2002): 6–34; Majhanovich, "Conflicting Visions, Competing Expectations."
53 Hancock and Mansfield, "The Literacy Hour"; Katz, Earl, and Olson, "The Paradox of Classroom Assessment."

Bibliography

Alderson, P. 1999. "Human Rights and Democracy in Schools—Do They Mean More Than 'Picking Up Litter and Not Killing Whales?'" *International Journal of Children's Rights* 7: 85–205.

Bickmore, K. 1999. "Teaching Conflict and Conflict Resolution in the School: (Extra-)Curricular Considerations." In A. Raviv, L. Oppenheimer, and D. Bar-Tal, eds., *How Children Understand War and Peace.* San Francisco: Jossey-Bass Publishers.

Cairney, R. 1999. "Confronted." *See Magazine,* June 24. http://www.see magazine.cm/Issues.

Canadian Association for Health and Physical Education, Recreation, and Dance. 2005. http://www.cahperd.ca.

Commonwealth Secretariat. 2000. Communique: 14th Conference of Commonwealth Education Ministers, Halifax, 26–30 November. London: Commonwealth Secretariat, Information and Public Affairs Division.

Conference of Commonwealth Education Ministers. 2000. "Education for Our Common Future: The Halifax Statement on Education in the Commonwealth." London: Commonwealth Secretariat.

Council of Ministers of Education of Canada. 2005. "CME Update June 2005." http://www.cmec.ca.

Covell, K. 2005. *Violence against Children in North America.* Report to the UN Global Study on Violence. Toronto: UNICEF Canada.

Covell, K., and R.B. Howe. 1999. "The Impact of Children's Rights Education: A Canadian Study." *International Journal of Children's Rights* 7: 171–83.

———. 2001. "Moral Education through the 3 Rs: Rights, Respect, and Responsibility." *Journal of Moral Education* 30, no. 1: 31–42.

Covell, K., J. O'Leary, and R.B. Howe. 2002. "Introducing a New Grade 8 Curriculum in Children's Rights." *Alberta Journal of Educational Research* 48, no. 4: 302–13.

Decoene, J., and R. De Cock. 1996. "The Children's Rights Project in the Primary School 'De vrijdagmarkt' in Bruges." In E. Verhellen, ed., *Monitoring Children's Rights*. The Hague: Martinus Nijhoff.

Dewey, J. 1933. *How We Think*. Buffalo: Prometheus Books.

Evers, W.J.G., A. Brouwers, and W. Tomic. 2002. "Burnout and Self-efficacy: A Study on Teachers' Beliefs When Implementing an Innovative Educational System in the Netherlands." *British Journal of Educational Psychology* 72: 227–43.

Grover, S. 2005. Grover Children's Rights and Peace Education Publishers. http://www.groverbooks.net.

Grundy, S. 2002. "Is Large-Scale Educational Reform Possible?" *Journal of Educational Change* 3: 55–62.

Hall (Litigation guardian of) v. Powers (2002). O. J. No. 1803. File No. 02-CV-227705CM3.

Hamm, M., and D. Adams. 2002. "Collaborative Inquiry: Working toward Shared Goals." *Kappa Delta Pi Record* (2002): 115–18.

Hancock, R., and M. Mansfield. 2002. "The Literacy Hour: A Case for Listening to Children." *Curriculum Journal* 13, no. 2: 183–200.

Heath, N.L., H. Petrakos, C.A. Finn, A. Karagiannakis, D. McLean-Heywood, and C. Rousseau. 2004. "Inclusion on the Final Frontier: A Model for Including Children with Emotional and Behavior Disorders in Canada." *International Journal of Inclusive Education* 8, no. 3: 241–60.

Henry, C.P. 1991. "Educating for Human Rights." *Human Rights Quarterly* 13: 420–23.

Hodgkin, R., and P. Newell. 1998. *Implementation Handbook for the Convention on the Rights of the Child*. New York: UNICEF.

Howe, R.B. 2005. "The Frontier of Children's Rights Education." *Our Schools/Our Selves*. In press.

Howe, R.B., and K. Covell. 1998. "Teaching Children's Rights: Considerations and Strategies." *Education and Law Journal* 9, no. 1: 97–113.

———. 2005. *Empowering Children: Children's Rights Education as a Pathway to Citizenship*. Toronto: University of Toronto Press.

Hughes, A., and H. Filer. 2003. *The Rights of the Child: Impact of Teaching in Year 6 Class*. Andover, UK: Knights Enham Junior School.

Joyal, R., J.F. Noel, and C.C. Feliciati, eds. 2005. *Making Children's Rights Work: National and International Perspectives*. Cowansville, QC: Editions Yvonne Blais.

Katz, S., L. Earl, and D. Olson. 2001. "The Paradox of Classroom Assessment: A Challenge for the 21st Century." *McGill Journal of Education* 36, no. 1: 13–26.

Lanotte, J.V., and G. Goedertier. 1996. "Monitoring Human Rights: Formal and Procedural Aspects." In E. Verhellen, ed., *Monitoring Children's Rights*. The Hague: Martinus Nijhoff.

Lebedev, O., A. Maiorov, and V. Zolotukhina. 2002. "The Rights of Children." *Russian Education and Society* 44, no. 8: 6–34.

Lowe, L. 2004. "What's the Fucking Problem?" *The Coast.* http://www.thecoast .ca/BAS04/fucking.html.

Majhanovich, S. 2002. "Conflicting Visions, Competing Expectations: Control and De-skilling of Education." *McGill Journal of Education* 7, no. 2: 159–76.

McLoyd, V.C. 1998. "Socioeconomic Disadvantage and Child Development." *American Psychologist* 53, no. 2: 185–204.

Murray, E. 1999. *Exploring Children's Emerging Conceptions of Their Participation Rights and Responsibilities.* Unpublished dissertation, University of Victoria.

———. 2002. Impact of Children's Rights Education on Primary-Level Children. Unpublished paper, Mount Royal College, Calgary.

Priestly, M. 2002. "Global Discourses and the National Reconstruction: The Impact of Globalization on Curriculum Policy." *Curriculum Journal* 13, no. 1: 121–38.

R. v. M. (M.R.), [1998] 3 S.C.R. 393.

Rodgers, C.R. 2002. "Voices Inside Schools: Seeing Student Learning: Teacher Change and the Role of Reflection." *Harvard Educational Review* 72, no. 2: 230–53.

Rudduck, J., and J. Flutter. 2000. "Pupil Participation and Pupil Perspective: Carving a New Order of Experience." *Cambridge Journal of Education* 30, no. 1: 75–90.

Seaton, A. 2002. "Reforming the Hidden Curriculum: The Key Abilities Model and Four Curricular Forms." *Curriculum Perspectives* 22, no. 1: 9–15.

Sitch, G., and S. McCoubrey. 2001. "Stay in Your Seat: The Impact of Judicial Subordination of Students' Rights on Effective Rights Education." *Education and Law Journal* 11: 173–202.

Slavin, R. 1995. Cooperative Learning: Theory, Research, and Practice. Boston: Allyn & Bacon.

Wall, D., M. Moll, and G. Froese-Germaine. 2000. *Contemporary Approaches to Citizenship Education.* Ottawa: Canadian Teachers Federation.

Aboriginal Children's Rights
Is Canada Keeping Its Promise?

Marlyn Bennett

A young girl will continue to be sexually abused because substance abuse has taken hold of her family ...

An Aboriginal foster child will not be returned to his or her family of origin because a social worker does not know enough about the importance of children to the overall well being of the family and community to which the child belongs ...

An infant boy will continue to be neglected because the only social worker has too many cases, enough for 10 workers ...

A young boy with special needs dies in an institutional hospital setting because neither the federal or provincial governments can settle on which government will pay for his medical and/or foster home care needs ...

A depressed adolescent develops a drug problem and ends up in jail because there is no place for him to go for help and no one to help him stay in school ...

An urban Aboriginal family living in poverty will move multiple times because substandard and affordable housing eludes them, compelling them to move multiple times within a year ...

A federal government will try to cut funding to Aboriginal child welfare agencies and may succeed in continuing to discriminate if no one stands up to speak out ...

And a culture will die slowly and invisibly if we fail to protect and ensure the rights of our children ...

Marlyn Bennett, First Nations Child and Family Caring Society of Canada

Introduction

The protection of children and youth from abuse and neglect has long been a principle of Canadian public policy and law. Unfortunately, conditions for Canada's Aboriginal children continue to be extremely deplorable. The United Nations Development Program consistently has ranked Canada as one of the best countries in the world in which to live based on the criteria of life expectancy, adult literacy, school enrolment, and economic prosperity. Given Canada's high standard of living and relatively low level of internal conflict, few would immediately refer to Canadian citizens as typical examples of victims of forced displacement, discrimination, or extreme poverty. However, Canada's history of colonization and displacement of its Aboriginal populations tells a story of centuries of domination, discrimination, and assimilation.

This chapter examines the rights of Aboriginal children and discusses whether or not Canada has lived up to its responsibilities of ensuring equitable access to and support for the rights of Aboriginal children. It assesses the extent to which Canada's compliance with the United Nations Convention on the Rights of the Child (CRC) and Canada's Indian Act has been effective in protecting the rights of Aboriginal children specifically. I also address the collective resistance of the Aboriginal people in the face of continued domination by the Canadian government. It is written from the perspective of Aboriginal children's welfare, given that awareness of and solutions for addressing these problems have been placed squarely on the shoulders of those who work within Aboriginal child welfare agencies, often without adequate resources and attendant funding in which to address these demanding issues.[1]

Historical Context

The current generation of First Nations children and youth are experiencing the multigenerational effects of a colonial system that was based on government policies designed to destroy Aboriginal cultures, traditions, and ceremonies. The residential school system targeted Aboriginal children and forced them to reject their own languages and heritage and even their own families. Parents forgot how to parent in a responsible traditional manner, and this has continued over several generations. The misguided efforts of mainstream child welfare systems in particular, which took up where the residential school systems left off, have contributed to the further fragmentation and breakdown of families and overall to the negative legacies that are endemic in many communities both on and off reserve.[2] The policies developed and implemented by early Canadian governments have produced intergenerational and cumulative stress and what some have called post-traumatic stress disorder or "historical trauma," which has numerous symptoms affecting the psychological, social, economic, intellectual, political, physical, and spiritual realms of Aboriginal peoples.[3] The symptoms resulting from historical trauma are many. Psychological responses to trauma manifest themselves as unresolved grief experienced across generations; such responses include high rates of alcoholism and substance abuse, depression, suicide, self-destructive behaviour, suicidal thoughts and acts, anxiety, low self-esteem, anger, and difficulty recognizing and expressing emotions.[4] Social manifestations include poverty, crime, low educational attainment, high rates of homicide and accidental death, child abuse, and domestic abuse and violence. On the physical plane, historical trauma has manifested itself in elevated mortality rates and high rates of illness (e.g., diabetes) experienced by the Aboriginal population. Spiritually, historical trauma is referred to as wounding of the soul.[5]

The early mass violation of human rights led to the widespread disruption of cultures, families, and communities, and this has contributed to the political, cultural, spiritual, and economic decline of indigenous nations in Canada. The present social and economic conditions, low educational achievement, high incarceration rates, and the disproportionate numbers of children in care draw attention to the realities of this devastation today. Compared to other Canadian children and youth, Aboriginal children are more likely to be born into poverty, miss out on early childhood education, and to suffer health problems, maltreatment, incarceration, drug use, depression, and sexual exploitation (among other maladies). These conditions, coupled with cumulative emotional and psychological wounding over the lifespan, emanating from massive group trauma experiences, have increased Aboriginal children's susceptibility to abuse and neglect and, subsequently, their movement into out-of-home placement in the Canadian child welfare system.

Key Issues for Aboriginal Children and Families

Awareness of these historical effects spearheaded the development and establishment of Aboriginal child and family service agencies to respond to the needs of Aboriginal children and their families and also to stem the rise of abuse and neglect within families and communities. There are more than 120 First Nations child welfare agencies across the country, the vast majority of which receive their statutory authority to deliver child welfare programs through provincial/territorial child welfare statutes. This has posed a significant challenge for Aboriginal agencies, which must try to adapt services that reflect the holistic, interdependent, and communal rights framework of the cultural communities they serve with the individual-rights-based child welfare statutes imposed by the Canadian state.[6] The concept of child removal—or "apprehension," as it is known in many provinces/territories—is a foreign concept to Aboriginal communities, which traditionally had adopted a communal parenting system that allowed for the seamless transfer of dominant parental authority from one community member to another in times of stress. The impact of applying Western concepts of child removal to Aboriginal communities has been substantial. The Western system of child care developed child removal in order to respond to isolated incidents of child maltreatment. It was never intended to be the principal community development intervention in communities that had been devastated by colonization. In the absence of focused, Aboriginal-driven community development, child removals will continue to be a symptomatic response to colonization, one that fails to redress the etiological factors that have contributed to the maltreatment of children, and future generations of children will continue to grow up away from home.[7]

Provincial data collection systems vary, but the best estimates are that at present, more than 25,000 Aboriginal children are in the child welfare system—three times the highest enrolment figures in residential schools in the 1940s.[8] In terms of First Nations children on-reserve, it is tragic that the numbers of children entering into care are rising. Data from the Department of Indian and Northern Affairs (DIAND) confirm that between 1995 and 2001, the number of Status Indian children entering into care rose an astonishing 71.5 percent nationally.[9] Especially egregious are the high numbers of Aboriginal children with disabilities who are in care.

Aboriginal children are represented in statistics of children with disabilities and in statistics of children with disabilities who are in care.[10] In Manitoba, for example, the rate of disability for the general population is 14.2 percent; the disability rate for Aboriginal children is 39.1 percent. And an overwhelming majority (78 percent) of children in care who have a disability are of Aboriginal descent. It is noteworthy that three-quarters of the Aboriginal children remanded to state care are permanent wards; fewer than half of non-Aboriginal children with disabilities are permanent wards.

The overrepresentation of Aboriginal children in permanent care has been attributed to past discrimination. The weakening of cultural identity has led to a variety of self-destructive tendencies, including substance abuse and violent behaviour. The result is disability rates among Aboriginal children that are twice as high as for non-Aboriginal children. For example, parental substance abuse leads to a number of developmental disorders among children, most notably those associated with fetal alcohol spectrum disorder (FASD). The services required to meet their special needs rarely are available in the community, so many families turn to child welfare services for the help they need.[11]

The impact of historical policies and the need for Aboriginal solutions are seen also in the high suicide rates among Aboriginal youth. Health Canada identifies youth suicide as an urgent issue for First Nations youth and reports rates to be five to seven times higher than for non-Aboriginal youth. Researchers[12] suggest that the rates are even higher than this—up to twenty times higher than for non-Aboriginal youth—and that the rate of suicide among Canada's Aboriginal youth is the highest known suicide rate of any culturally identifiable group in the world. A comparison of Aboriginal communities with varying rates of youth suicide points to individual and cultural continuity as a protective factor. Where Aboriginal communities have been successful in preserving their heritage culture and in controlling their own destinies, the rates of youth suicide are relatively low. Too often, however, jurisdictional issues interfere with Aboriginal control of programming and resources.[13]

The disregard for Aboriginal culture and the need to shift decision-making authority to First Nations is apparent in the case of K'aila.[14] K'aila Will Paulette was declared to be a child in need of protection by the Alberta (and subsequently Saskatchewan) Department of Social Services because his parents did not want him to undergo a liver transplant—a procedure whose merit had not been agreed upon by qualified medical practitioners. As Jocelyn Downie explains, the case highlights the inappropriateness of applying a non–First Nations standard of care and a non–First Nations child welfare system.[15]

One especially poignant example of the difficulties arising from jurisdictional issues is the tragic case of Jordan, an Aboriginal infant born with complex medical needs. Jordan's period of hospitalization was prolonged by a jurisdictional dispute between the federal and provincial governments over who would pay for which aspects of his care. The dispute lasted more than two years. Jordan's community attempted to resolve the dispute first through mediation and then through legal action. The dispute eventually was settled, but not before Jordan died. His legacy has been the "child first" principle known as Jordan's principle. This principle has been established to ensure that jurisdictional disputes do not result in delays of health and health care services to Aboriginal children.[16]

The UN Convention on the Rights of the Child

On November 20, 1989, the UN General Assembly promised certain things to children by formally adopting the Convention on the Rights of the Child (CRC).[17] This was a significant achievement in that it acknowledged and recognized children's rights around the world. The Convention was the first globally applicable human rights convention to integrate explicitly two broad classifications of rights: civil and political, and economic, social, and cultural.[18] In the Canadian context, the Convention embodied many of the already recognized legal and social principles of Canada's commitment to social justice.[19]

An international leader in children's rights, Canada was among the first countries to ratify the CRC in December 1991.[20] The CRC views children as valuable citizens and as rights holders entitled to the best of what society can offer to support their development in ways that respect their distinct cultures, spirituality, and knowledge. It is also the first international instrument to specifically include protections for indigenous children. Essentially, the CRC provides a framework for all governments to improve, promote, and protect the basic human rights of all children. It calls for ongoing action and progress in the realization of children's rights and it is based on four principles: (1) non-discrimination (article 2), which means that states commit themselves to respect and ensure the rights of all children in their jurisdiction without discrimination of any kind; (2) the best interests of the child (article 3), which means that the interests of the child are recognized as paramount and that budgetary allocations should give priority to children and to the safekeeping of their rights; (3) respect for children's views and for their right to participate in all aspects of democratic society (articles 12 to 15), which asserts that children are not passive recipients, but active contributors to the decisions that affect their lives; and (4) the children's right to survival and development (article 6), which claims he right for children to realize their fullest potential through a range of strategies, from meeting their health, nutrition, and education needs to supporting their personal and social development.[21]

These key themes underpin all other provisions of the Convention and provide a strong framework for the adoption of a child-friendly focus in all of the obligations imposed on the state. The CRC's remaining articles cover a range of issues, including the right to privacy, the right to education, the right to identity, and the explicit right to practise culture, religion, and language freely and without discrimination.

Every five years, State Parties report to the Committee on the Rights of the Child on their progress on implementing its articles. After considering the State Parties' reports, and non-governmental organization (NGO) submissions, the Committee offers concluding observations that indicate areas of accomplishment and improvement.

In recognition of the last year of the International Decade of Indigenous Peoples, the First Nations Child and Family Caring Society of Canada (Caring Society) investigated the lived experiences of First Nations children across a number of dimensions that included poverty, urbanization, substance misuse, education, youth suicide, accidental injury, child welfare, sexual exploitation, and youth justice. The authors recognized that there was no standardized way to determine when the rights contained in the Convention were being upheld, so for their purposes they identified possible rights violations based on the following three situations: (1) where First Nations children and young people face disproportionate risk relating to one or more articles of the CRC; (2) where there is an identified risk to First Nations children and young people relating to one or more articles of the CRC—particularly when the risk is severe and persistent; and (3) where there is little evidence that the State Party has considered how to ensure that the right is being realized for First Nations children and young people.[22]

The findings indicate that First Nations children continue to experience unacceptable and disproportionate levels of risk across all the identified dimensions and that policies developed by the government to redress these risks remain largely unimplemented. As indicated in the Caring Society's report *Keeping the Promise*, the vast majority of cases involve First Nations children facing significant and disproportionate risk. Even though it is a wealthy nation with an international reputation for challenging oppressors of the underclasses, Canada clearly falls short in its treatment of Aboriginal children. As Martha Friendly notes in chapter 3, despite care and education programs such as Aboriginal Head Start, Aboriginal children remain significantly underserved in early learning and child care. Cheryl Van Daalen-Smith, in chapter 4, discusses the disproportionate difficulties faced by Aboriginal children in access to health care, as well as the higher risk for health problems that characterize children in Aboriginal communities. Denov and Moore (chapters 7 and 8) describe the overrepresentation of Aboriginal children in the youth justice system. Examples summarized in this chapter concern child poverty and child welfare.[23]

Aboriginal peoples continue to live far below the standard of living of the general Canadian population. Whether they are living on or off reserve, Aboriginal children's living conditions fall far short of those promised in the CRC. Most Aboriginal children living off reserve live in poverty, with their family conditions deteriorating as their basic needs for food, clothing, and shelter remain unmet. Urban Aboriginal children are twice as likely as their non-Aboriginal peers to live in poverty; to live in young single-parent households; to live in inadequate housing; and to be hungry. The lives of on-reserve families also are characterized by poverty. Aboriginal children living on reserve have little access to services of the type available to non-Aboriginal children across the country (and again, jurisdictional disputes are obstacles). This is especially the case for Aboriginal children with disabilities. Food security is a pervasive problem: national data indicate that Aboriginal people are four times more likely than non-Aboriginals to report experiencing hunger. Aboriginals are over-represented in homelessness, inadequate housing, and overcrowding. Unsafe and inadequate water systems are a continuing problem. In essence, poverty is a problem that pervades all aspects of life for Aboriginal children, and one that retards their healthy development. Poverty reduction also is important to reduce the high numbers of children being taken into care because of parental neglect.

Child welfare policies and practices for Aboriginal children have been and remain inconsistent with the CRC as well as discriminatory. Many people are aware of the "'60s scoop," a time during which children were removed en masse from reserves by non-Aboriginal social workers. Many of these children were placed in non-Aboriginal homes. Not nearly enough has changed since then. Aboriginal children continue to be over-represented among children in the child welfare system. Estimates are that Aboriginal children comprise 30 to 40 percent of all children in care in Canada. Even more bleak are DIAND data showing a staggering 71.5 percent increase in the number of Status Indian children on reserve being placed in child welfare between 1995 and 2001.[24] Inequitable funding and lack of family supports for children at risk have been identified as factors underlying this increase in the removal of children.[25] More funding for "least disruptive measures" would do much to reduce the numbers of children in care.[26] Analyses also indicate that discriminatory treatment toward Aboriginal children is evident at every stage of social workers' decision making.[27] For example, cases are more likely to be kept open for ongoing services, and children are more likely to be removed—again, often to non-Aboriginal homes. Importantly, analyses have also shown that poverty is a root cause of the removal of children. Clearly, present-day practices in child welfare are infringing on the right of children not to be discriminated against (article 2), as well as their right to use their own language and enjoy their own culture (article 30).

The Erosion of Children's Rights through the Indian Act

Aboriginal children represent a precious resource by means of which Aboriginal communities and cultures can be sustained into the future. One of the key ways in which the rights of Aboriginal children are being diminished without interference is found in the discriminatory provisions of the Indian Act, which continues to define who is and who is not a "Status Indian" and therefore entitled to specific rights that arise from the historical relationship between Aboriginal peoples and Canadian governments. This act creates artificial divisions between Aboriginal peoples in an effort to restrict the number of Aboriginal peoples for whom Canada will exercise certain obligations; furthermore, it effectively diminishes the rights of future generations of Aboriginal children. The purpose of the Indian Act is to protect the rights of all Aboriginal peoples in Canada; however, many aspects of it are being constantly challenged as oppressive and paternalistic by various lobby groups advocating for the protection of the rights of Aboriginal people.[28] The federal government itself has acknowledged that the legislation provides an inadequate framework for its contemporary relationship with Aboriginal communities.[29] Lack of recognition under the Indian Act has had devastating consequences for some Aboriginal children, especially for families impacted by Bill C-31.

Bill C-31 is a deceitful piece of legislation that was drawn up in 1985 to redress the discrimination perpetrated against First Nations women who had lost their Indian status when they married non-Indian men; at the same time, it bestowed Indian status on non-Aboriginal women who had married Indian men. Children subsequently born to Indian women who lost their status were also not recognized as having Indian status. Bill C-31 changed everything, by creating thirteen rules as to who could regain and/or retain their Indian status. Aboriginal women who had lost their Indian status were reinstated under different sections—6(1)(a), 6(1)(b), 6(1)(c), 6(1)(d), 6(1)(e)(i), 6(e)(ii), or 6(2). Under these new provisions, the federal government imposed a "second-generation cut-off rule" when it came to reinstating Indian status.[30] Given this cut-off rule, over time, there may eventually be no Status Indians to uphold Canada's promises with respect to the treaty rights of Aboriginal people generally, or to the rights of Aboriginal children under the CRC. This is a government-imposed definition of identity and one that does not honour and respect Aboriginal peoples' ways of recognizing offspring as members of their respective nations. The Indian Act provisions dealing with Indian status are of deep concern, as they are slowly eroding the rights of Aboriginal people to decide for themselves who is entitled to an Aboriginal identity. The cut-off rule imposed by the government under the Indian Act has broken down the rights of Aboriginal children as set out in article 8 of the CRC, which states that "State parties undertake to respect the right of a child to preserve his or her identity, including nationality, name and family relations as recognized by law without unlawful interference." Unfortunately the erosion of identity for Aboriginal children is sanctioned by a provision in the Canadian Human Rights Act (CHRA) that disallows complaints of discrimination under the Indian Act.

. Section 67 of the Canadian Human Rights Act restricts the ability of people living or working in communities operating under the Indian Act to file complaints of discrimination if the discrimination they are complaining about is related to the Indian Act. Section 67 is the only provision in Canadian human rights law that restricts access of a particular group of persons (people living or working in First Nations communities) to the human rights process. As a result of Section 67, some actions carried out by the Government of Canada, or a First Nations government, can be exempt from human rights scrutiny. Such is the case with the second-generation cut-off rules developed as a result of Bill C-31. That bill's provisions have led to revisions of the Indian Act that in essence prevent future Aboriginal children from enjoying the intergenerational rights that had been extended to their ancestors. This is a major concern for future generations of Aboriginal children, who will not be entitled to claim Indian status because of the government's second-generation cut-off rules. In a way this discriminatory provision under the CHRA lets the federal government off the hook when it comes to meeting its fiduciary responsibilities to First Nations peoples. Aboriginal peoples will have to fight to ensure that Canada lives up to its responsibilities, in order to protect the special identity and status that are the right of Aboriginal children (even to the ones that are not here yet). Unfortunately, the longer that Section 67 of the CHRA remains in effect, the bigger the problem. Future generations of children will not be entitled to claim Indian status because the second-generation cut-off rules set out by the federal government have overridden the right of Aboriginal people to decide for themselves who is an Aboriginal.

A review of this issue by the Canada Human Rights Commission[31] notes that Section 67 has had a pernicious impact on the access that First Nations people have to human rights redress processes. Incomplete information and misconceptions regarding this section have led to a widespread belief that *all* actions carried out by First Nations or DIAND are exempt from human rights scrutiny. As a result, many First Nations people who *could* file a complaint of alleged discrimination end up not doing so. The other irony is that self-governing First Nations operating outside the Indian Act *are* subject to the CHRA; given this, there is no acceptable reason for differences in treatment among First Nation communities. Exempting the Indian Act from the CHRA was meant to be a temporary measure only, yet twenty years after Bill C-31, it is still part of the law.[32] However, it is increasingly coming under attack by the various advocacy and joint First Nation and government committees that have been assigned to review the section's constitutionality under the Canadian Charter of Rights and Freedoms and its applicability under international human rights instruments and mechanisms.[33] Section 67 is putting the lie to Canada's role as a human rights leader in the world and is diminishing Canada's credibility internationally.[34]

Other children, like the children of the Innu nation in Labrador—who are clearly recognized as Aboriginal people according to the Constitution Act—are also not recognized under the Indian Act. This lack of recognition has meant that the rights of Innu people and their children are not being protected, as noted by Denov and Campbell.[35] The result: this group, like some other Inuit groups in the North, is not receiving the same range of funding or level and quality of services as are provided to other Aboriginal peoples and children registered under the Indian Act and living on reserve lands. This argument also extends to the rights of Metis peoples and their children and to countless other children (i.e., urban and off-reserve, including non-Status) who are recognized as Aboriginal but who do not have status under the Indian Act and/or live on reserve. In summary, innumerable constitutionally recognized Aboriginal children are not receiving the same access to a range of culturally appropriate services and programming as First Nations children on reserve.[36] The need to repeal Section 67 of the CHRA is an interesting matter of rights and probably requires further analysis from a child welfare perspective regarding its implications for Aboriginal children and the child welfare agencies (as representative government bodies) responsible for ensuring that the rights set out under the CRC for the children in their care are adhered to.

The Debilitating Effects of Poverty on the Rights of Aboriginal Children

On the fifteenth anniversary of the Canadian Parliament's vow to end child poverty, Campaign 2000's report card on child poverty in Canada for 2004 stated that 1,065,000 children (nearly one in six of Canada's children) remained in poverty.[37] Child and family poverty is worsening, with more than one million children in poverty. The same report indicated that child poverty was up for the first time in six years, higher than it had been in

1989. This meant that approximately one-third of all children in Canada had been exposed to poverty for at least one year since 1996. Statistics about the gap between Aboriginal and non-Aboriginal social conditions indicate that the life chances of Aboriginal people as a whole lag far behind those of the general Canadian population. "The Human Development Index (HDI) published by the United Nations Development Programme is a widely quoted measure of well-being. It quantifies the standards of education, income and life expectancy (as a surrogate for health status) prevailing in nation states and ranks them on a composite HDI. Canada has regularly ranked number one in recent years. An analysis done by the Research and Analysis Directorate of Indian and Northern Affairs Canada (INAC) using 1996 census and INAC departmental data indicated that registered Indian people living on-reserve would rank 62nd and registered Indians off-reserve would rank 47th on the HDI."[38] The social and economic conditions experienced by many on-reserve First Nations people are similar to those experienced by families in developing countries. Pervasive poverty, substandard housing conditions, widespread alcohol and solvent abuse involving adults and children, and high suicide rates among youth are the resultant stark realities.

A UN report on a decade of child poverty in Canada found that "among Aboriginal children, whether living on or off reserve, almost one in two lives in poverty. Aboriginal people are 4 times more likely to report ever experiencing hunger than the non-Aboriginal population." This UN report also noted that "among all Aboriginal households (owners and renters), an estimated one-third have 'core needs,' that is, their housing does not meet today's standards for adequacy, suitability and affordability ... Most of the nations that have been more successful than Canada at keeping low levels of child poverty are willing to counterbalance the effects of unemployment and low paid work with substantial investments in family policies."[39]

Many children in First Nations communities do not have access to essential public services or to the services offered by the non-profit sector that most people in Canada take for granted.[40]

The child welfare literature discloses that most children in care appear to come from poor Aboriginal or minority families.[41] Caregivers who are on welfare, who experience major life events, who are urban, low-income, single mothers, or who are Aboriginal or minority parents, are investigated more often by child welfare authorities for child abuse and neglect simply because they are more visible to those placing reports to the child protection authorities.[42] Poverty and the involvement of child welfare authorities often co-occur in families receiving social assistance.[43] Derr and Taylor[44] examined the links between childhood and adult abuse among long-term welfare recipients. They conducted in-depth interviews with more than 280 women on public assistance. High rates of childhood abuse and exposure to adult abuse (violence) were reported among this sample. Two-thirds indicated that they had been physically, sexually, and/or emotionally abused during childhood, and 81 percent lived in physically violent relations as adults. Derr and Taylor's study indicates that there is a strong relationship between childhood and adult abuse among individuals on long-term financial assistance and that more attention needs to be paid to family violence factors in this group.[45] Berger's research has corroborated this finding. Children in low-income families are more likely to be at risk of maltreatment, not, however, because of mandatory reports or reporting, investigation, or removal biases within child protective services, but because parents lack the resources with which to create healthy environments necessary for children's development.[46]

The impact of poverty on Aboriginal children and youth is well documented in Canada. "The government's demonstrated commitment to the cause of children's rights suggests that some populations have been less well-served than others. First Nations, Métis and Inuit children and youth are a case in point. Not only do they suffer from significantly higher rates of morbidity and mortality than other Canadian children, but poverty is endemic in many First Nations and Inuit communities, resulting in a sub-standard quality of life and widespread alienation."[47]

The negative impact of poverty on early childhood development has been well documented in thousands of studies throughout the world.[48] Poverty threatens the health and well-being of children and risks excluding children from the chances and opportunities to succeed. Poverty continues to be one of the most important determinants of life chances.[49]

While the impact of poverty on early childhood development is well understood, the impact of poverty and its attendant problems on First Nations families whose children are placed in out-of-home care owing to child maltreatment is only starting to be fully understood here in Canada. According to the 1998 Canadian Incidence Study of Reported Child Abuse and Neglect (CIS-1998),[50] Aboriginal families experience an extremely high rate of hardship: "Aboriginal families were characterized by significantly less stable housing, greater dependence on social assistance, younger parents, more parents having been maltreated as children, higher rates of alcohol and drug abuse, and being investigated more often for neglect or emotional maltreatment. Higher rates of suspected and substantiated cases and child welfare placement were explained by the disproportionate presence of risk factors among Aboriginal families."[51]

The CIS-1998 study suggested that numerous interrelated factors underlie the overrepresentation of Aboriginal children in the child welfare system. These factors reflect the multiple disadvantages experienced by Aboriginal families: "The high rates of poverty, inadequate housing and substance abuse that seem to be leading to this over-representation are problems that extend beyond the child welfare system. While shifting control of child welfare services to Aboriginal communities should help in the development of services that are more appropriately geared to the needs of Aboriginal children and families, research by Shangreaux and Trocmé, Knoke, and Blackstock[52] states that one should not expect to see a significant decrease in admission rates until resources are allocated to address social problems that undermine parents' abilities to care adequately for their children."

Preliminary findings from the Canadian Incidence Study of Reported Child Abuse and Neglect conducted five years later (CIS-2003) generally concur with the findings from the two analyses conducted on the data from the earlier CIS-1998 study.[53] As in the first cycle of CIS, the profiles of Aboriginal families differ dramatically from the profiles of non-Aboriginal families. Aboriginal caregivers are less likely to have full-time work than non-Aboriginal caregivers. Also, Aboriginal cases predominantly involve situations of neglect, with poverty, inadequate housing, and parent substance abuse creating a toxic brew of risk factors and doing much to explain the overrepresentation of Aboriginal children in out-of-home placements.[54]

The Chance to Make a Difference

Cindy Blackstock, executive director of the First Nations Child and Family Caring Society, emphasized in her report to the Standing Senate Committee on Human Rights in 2005 that it is crucial not to be overwhelmed by the magnitude of the problems of Aboriginal children and that change is possible. The federal government has been urged to examine the difficulties facing Aboriginal children as violations of their CRC rights, to acknowledge its ability to act, and to take responsibility for providing equitable funding and resourcing to community-based strategies that will give priority to the healthy development of Aboriginal children. But perhaps the greatest hope for the future is seen in the recent document *Touchstones of Hope for Indigenous Children, Youth and Families*.[55] This document, based on the Caring Society's October 2005 reconciliation conference, could serve as a foundation for community-based action plans to improve the lives of Aboriginal children.[56] It recognizes the past and reaches for a different future. If followed, this document would be CRC consistent. It is a document full of hope. In the words of Chief David General, Six Nations of the Grand River Territory: "I pray that the Creator gives us what we call in our culture, 'the good mind.' The good mind will work us toward the one mind that we need to establish a network that will encircle the world, dealing with this one issue—child welfare ... We have to invest love back in our families, our communities, our nations. We have to get up every day and be hopeful. We cannot live in a painful past. Part of reconciliation means shedding that. We don't have to forget it, but we cannot let it blind us to where we need to go."[57]

Conclusion

In 2003, on reviewing Canada's record in implementing the CRC, the UN Committee on the Rights of the Child expressed deep concern about the lack of progress in implementing the rights of Aboriginal children. The Committee had good reason to be concerned and could have criticized Canada much more forcefully than it did.

Contrary to children's right to health care and economic welfare, Aboriginal children continue to suffer disproportionately from high rates of child poverty and high levels of infant mortality, infant death syndrome, FASD, and youth suicide. Contrary to the principle of non-discrimination, they continue to experience discrimination through the Indian Act and the Canadian Human Rights Act. Contrary to children's right to be protected from harm and to enjoy their own culture, Aboriginal children continue to suffer disproportionately from high levels of child abuse and sexual exploitation and from a child welfare system that fails to adequately protect them through culturally appropriate services. All Aboriginal children should have access to community-based and culturally appropriate services, which would help them grow up safe, healthy, and spiritually strong—free from abuse, neglect, sexual exploitation, and the damaging effects of substance abuse. All should have a bright future, all should be entitled to a place of safety and nurturance, and all should be seen as a source of pride to their family of origin and community. In order to bring this about, it is important that Aboriginal child welfare agencies be given the resources and the funding to ensure that the rights of Aboriginal children under their care and jurisdiction are upheld and respected. Unfortunately, this has yet to be done. The gap between the rights of the child as provided for in the CRC and those provided for by Canada continues to be very wide.

Notes

1 C. Shangreaux, "Staying at Home: Examining the Implications of Least Disruptive Measures in First Nations Child and Family Service Agencies" (Ottawa: First Nations Child and Family Caring Society of Canada, 2004), http://www.fncfcs.com/docs/Staying_at_Home.pdf; First Nations Child and Family Caring Society of Canada, *Wen:De: We Are Coming to the Light of Day* (Ottawa: First Nations Child & Family Caring Society of Canada, 2005).

2 M. Bennett and C. Shangreaux, 2005, "Applying Maslow's Hierarchy Theory to the Research Needs of FNCFS Agencies Participating in Cycle II of the Canadian Incidence Study of Reported Child Abuse and Neglect," *First Peoples Child and Family Review* 2, no. 1: 89–116.

3 R. Struthers and J. Lowe, "Nursing in the Native American Culture and Historical Trauma," *Issues in Mental Health Nursing* 24 (2003): 254–72; M.Y. Brave Heart, "The Historical Trauma Response among Natives and Its Relationship with Substance Abuse: A Lakota Illustration," *Journal of Psychoactive Drugs* 35, no. 1 (2003): 7–13.

4 Brave Heart, "The Historical Trauma Response."

5 Struthers and Lowe, "Nursing in the Native American Culture."

6 M. Bennett and C. Blackstock, "First Nations Child and Family Services and Indigenous Knowledge as a Framework for Research, Policy, and Practice," in N. Freymond and G. Cameron, eds., *Towards Positive Systems of Child and Family Welfare: International Comparisons of Child Protection, Family Services, and Community Caring Systems* (Toronto: University of Toronto Press, 2006).

7 C. Blackstock and M. Bennett, "National Children's Alliance: Policy Paper on Aboriginal Children," http://www.nationalchildrensalliance.com/nca/pubs/2003/Aboriginal_Children-Blackstock_%20Bennett.pdf.

8 Bennett and Blackstock, "First Nations Child and Family Services."

9 B. McKenzie (2002). "Block Funding Child Maintenance in First Nations Child and Family Services: A Policy Review," report prepared for Kahnawake Shakotiia'takenhnhas Community Services, Winnipeg.

10 See D. Fuchs, L. Burnside, S. Marchenski, and A. Mudry, "Children with Disabilities Receiving Services from Child Welfare Agencies in Manitoba" (2005), http://www.cecw-cepb.ca/DocsEng/DisabilitiesManitobaFinal.pdf.

11 A. Wright, D. Hiebert-Murphy, and G. Gosek, 2005, "Supporting Aboriginal Children and Youth with Learning and/or Behavioural Disabilities in the Care of Aboriginal Child Welfare Agencies" (Ottawa: First Nations Child and Family Caring Society of Canada, 2005).

12 M. Chandler, "Suicide and the Persistence of Identity in the Face of Radical Cultural Change," talk presented at the Assembly of First Nations National Policy Forum, April 19, 2005.

13 T. Lavallee, "Federally Funded Manitoba First Nation Children with Complex Medical Needs," *Paediatrics and Child Health* 10, no. 9 (2005): 527–29.

14 *Saskatchewan (Minister of Social Services) v. P. (F.)* (1990), 69 D.L.R. (4th) 134 (Sask. Prov. Ct.).

15 J. Downie, "A Choice for K'aila: Child Protection and First Nations Children," *Health Law Journal* 20 (1994): 99–120.

16 Lavallee, "Federally Funded Manitoba First Nation Children."

17 United Nations General Assembly, Resolution 44/25, November 20, 1989.

18 M. Denov and K. Campbell, "Casualties of Aboriginal Displacement in Canada: Children at Risk among the Innu of Labrador," *Refuge* 20, no. 2 (2002): 21–34.

19 Ibid.

20 Blackstock and Bennett, "National Children's Alliance"; C. Blackstock, S. Clarke, J. Cullen, J. D'Hondt, and J. Formsma, *Keeping the Promise: The Convention on the Rights of the Child and the Lived Experiences of First Nations Children and Youth* (Ottawa: First Nations Child and Family Caring Society of Canada, 2004), http://www.fncfcs.com/docs/KeepingThePromise.pdf.

21 UNICEF (2000), *First Call for children: World Declaration and Plan of Action from the World Summit for Children and Convention on the Rights of the Child* (New York: UNICEF), pp. 46–51.

22 Blackstock, Clarke, Cullen, et al., "Keeping the Promise."

23 Ibid.

24 McKenzie, "Block Funding Child Maintenance."

25 First Nations Child and Family Caring Society of Canada, *Wen:De*.

26 N. Trocmé, D. Knoke, C. Shangreaux, B. Fallon, and B. MacLaurin, "The Experience of First Nations Children Coming into Contact with the Child Welfare System in Canada: The Canadian Incidence Study on Reported Child Abuse and Neglect," in *Wen:De*, 60–86.

27 N. Trocmé, B. MacLaurin, B. Fallon, et al., "Mesnmimk Wasatek Catching a Drop of Light: Understanding the Overrepresentation of First Nations Children in Canada's Child Welfare System: An Analysis of the Canadian Incidence Study of Reported Child Abuse and Neglect" (CIS-2003) (Toronto: Centre of Excellence for Child Welfare, 2005).

28 M.M. Mann, "Indian Registration: Unrecognized and Unstated Paternity," http://www.swc-cfc.gc.ca/pubs/pubspr/066240842X/200506_066240842X_e.pdf.

29 J. Wherrett, *The Indian Act: Proposed Modifications* (Ottawa: Library of Parliament, 1997).

30 C. Simard, "Status of Non-Status? Play the C-31 Guessing Game to Find Out!" *Brandon Sun*, March 21, 2006.

31 Canadian Human Rights Commission, *A Matter of Rights: A Special Report of the Canadian Human Rights Commission on the Repeal of Section 67 of the Canadian Human Rights Act* (Ottawa: CHRC, October 2005).

32 Ibid.

33 Ibid.

34 B. Vongdouangchanh, "Section of Canadian Human Rights Act Excludes Aboriginal," *Hill Times*, October 31, 2005.

35 Denov and Campbell, "Casualties of Aboriginal Displacement in Canada."

36 K.A.H. Graham and E. Peters, *Aboriginal Communities and Urban Sustainability* (Ottawa: Canadian Policy Research Networks Inc., 2002), http://www.urbancentre.utoronto.ca/pdfs/elibrary/CPRNUrbanAboriginal.pdf.

37 Campaign 2000 and C. Hubberstey, *One Million Too Many: Implementing Solutions to Child Poverty in Canada—2004 Report Card on Child Poverty in Canada* (Ottawa: Campaign 2000, 2004).

38 M. Castallano, *Aboriginal Family Trends: Extended Families, Nuclear Families, Families of the Heart* (Ottawa: Vanier Institute of the Family, 2003).

39 UN Special Session on Children, *Campaign 2000*, May 2002.

40 S. Nadjiwan and C. Blackstock, *Caring across the Boundaries: Promoting Access to Voluntary Sector Resources for First Nations Children and Families* (Ottawa: First Nations Child and Family Caring Society of Canada, 2003).

41 A.G. Zetlin, L.A. Weinberg, and C. Kimm, "Are the Educational Needs of Children in Foster Care Being Addressed?" *Children and Schools* 25 (2003): 105–19; Zetlin and Weinberg, "Understanding the Plight of Foster Youth and Improving Their Educational Opportunities," *Child Abuse and Neglect* 28 (2004): 917–23; L. Pelton, "Child Welfare through the Twentieth Century: Policy and Reality," in *For Reasons of Poverty: A Critical Analysis of the Public Child Welfare System in the United States* (New York: Praeger Publishers, 1989), pp. ix–xvii.

42 L.M. Berger, "Income, Family Structure, and Child Maltreatment Risk," *Children and Youth Services Review* 26 (2004): 725–48; M. McDaniel and K.S. Slack, "Major Life Events and the Risk of a Child Maltreatement Investigation," *Children and Youth Services Review* 27 (2005): 171–95.

43 Pelton, "Child Welfare through the Twentieth Century"; L. Pelton and J.S. Milner, "Is Poverty a Key Contributor to Child Maltreatment?" in E. Gambrill and T.J. Stein, eds., *Controversial Issues in Child Welfare* (Boston: Allyn & Bacon, 1994), pp. 16–28.

44 M.K. Derr and M.J. Taylor, "The Link between Childhood and Adult Abuse among Long-Term Welfare Recipients," *Children and Youth Services Review* 26 (2004): 173–84.

45 Derr and Taylor, "The Link between Childhood and Adult Abuse."

46 Berger, "Income, Family Structure, and Child Maltreatment Risk."

47 M. Dion Stout and G.D. Kipling, "Aboriginal Women in Canada: Strategic Research Directions for Policy Development" (Ottawa: Status of Women Canada, 1998).

48 World Bank (1999); World Health Organization (1999); UNICEF (2003); Campaign 2000 (2004). See, for example, various reports from the World Health Organization (ftp.who.int/gb); UNICEF (www.unicef-icdc.org); and Campaign 2000 (www.campaign2000.ca).

49 Campaign 2000, "The Early Childhood Development Initiative: A Vision for Early Childhood Development Services in Ontario, April 9, 2001," developed in consultation with representatives from Campaign 2000, Ontario Coalition for Better Child Care, Ontario Association of Family Resource Programs, Toronto Public Health, Metro Association of Family Resource Programs, and Toronto Coalition for Better Child Care, http://www.campaign2000.ca/ecdsONvision.pdf.

50 N. Trocmé, B. MacLaurin, B. Fallon, et al., *Canadian Incidence Study of Reported Child Abuse and Neglect* (Ottawa: National Clearinghouse on Family Violence and Health Canada, 2001).

51 C. Blackstock, N. Trocmé, and M. Bennett, "Child Maltreatment Investigations among Aboriginal and Non-Aboriginal Families in Canada," *Violence against Women* 10 (2004): 901–16.

52 Shangreaux, *Staying at Home;* N. Trocmé, D. Knoke, and C. Blackstock, "Pathways to the Overrepresentation of Aboriginal Children in Canada's Child Welfare System," *Social Service Review* 78, no. 4 (2004): 577–601.
53 Trocmé, Knoke, Shangreaux, et al., "The Experience of First Nations Children."
54 Ibid.
55 C. Blackstock, T. Cross, J. George, et al., *Touchstones of Hope for Indigenous Children, Youth, and Families* (Ottawa: First Nations Child and Family Caring Society of Canada, 2006).
56 C. Blackstock, I. Brown, and M. Bennett, "Reconciliation: Rebuilding the Canadian Child Welfare System to Better Serve Aboriginal Children and Youth," in I. Brown, F. Chaze, D. Fuchs, J. Lafrance, S. McKay, and S. Thomas Prokop, eds., *Putting a Human Face on Child Welfare: Voices from the Prairies* (Toronto: Prairie Child Welfare Consortium and Centre of Excellence for Child Welfare, in press).
57 Blackstock, Cross, George, et al., *Touchstones of Hope.*
58 CRC/C/15/Add.215.

Bibliography

Bennett, M., and C. Blackstock. 2006. "First Nations Child and Family Services and Indigenous Knowledge as a Framework for Research, Policy, and Practice." In N. Freymond and G. Cameron, eds., *Towards Positive Systems of Child and Family Welfare: International Comparisons of Child Protection, Family Services, and Community Caring Systems.* Toronto: University of Toronto Press.

Bennett, M., and C. Shangreaux. 2005. "Applying Maslow's Hierarchy Theory to the Research Needs of FNCFS Agencies Participating in Cycle II of the Canadian Incidence Study of Reported Child Abuse and Neglect." *First Peoples Child and Family Review* 2, no. 1: 89–116. http://www.fn caringsociety.ca/pubs/vol2num1/Bennett_Shangreaux_pp89.pdf.

Berger, L.M. 2004. "Income, Family Structure, and Child Maltreatment Risk." *Children and Youth Services Review* 26: 725–48.

Blackstock, C., and M. Bennett. 2003. "National Children's Alliance: Policy Paper on Aboriginal Children." http://www.nationalchildrensalliance .com/nca/pubs/2003/Aboriginal_Children-Blackstock_%20Bennett.pdf.

Blackstock, C., I. Brown, and M. Bennett. (in press). "Reconciliation: Rebuilding the Canadian Child Welfare System to Better Serve Aboriginal Children and Youth." In I. Brown, F. Chaze, D. Fuchs, J. Lafrance, S. McKay, and S. Thomas Prokop, eds., *Putting a Human Face on Child Welfare: Voices from the Prairies,* Toronto: Prairie Child Welfare Consortium and Centre of Excellence for Child Welfare.

Blackstock, C., S. Clarke, J. Cullen, J. D'Hondt, and J. Formsma. 2004. "Keeping the Promise: The Convention on the Rights of the Child and the Lived Experiences of First Nations Children and Youth." Ottawa: First Nations Child and Family Caring Society of Canada. http://www.fncfcs.com/ docs/KeepingThePromise.pdf.

Blackstock, C., T. Cross, J. George, I. Brown, and J. Formsma. 2006. *Touchstones of Hope for Indigenous Children, Youth, and Families*. Ottawa: First Nations Child and Family Caring Society of Canada.

Blackstock, C., N. Trocmé, and M. Bennett. 2004. "Child Maltreatment Investigations among Aboriginal and Non-Aboriginal Families in Canada." *Violence Against Women* 10: 901–16.

Brave Heart, M.Y. 2003. "The Historical Trauma Response among Natives and Its Relationship with Substance Abuse: A Lakota Illustration." *Journal of Psychoactive Drugs* 35, no. 1: 7–13.

Campaign 2000. 2001. "The Early Childhood Development Initiative: A Vision for Early Childhood Development Services in Ontario, April 9, 2001." Developed in consultation with representatives from Campaign 2000, Ontario Coalition for Better Child Care, Ontario Association of Family Resource Programs, Toronto Public Health, Metro Association of Family Resource Programs, and Toronto Coalition for Better Child Care. http://www.campaign2000.ca/ecdsONvision.pdf.

Campaign 2000 and C. Hubberstey. 2004. *One Million Too Many: Implementing Solutions to Child Poverty in Canada—2004 Report Card on Child Poverty in Canada*. Ottawa: Campaign 2000.

Canadian Human Rights Commission. 2005. *A Matter of Rights: A Special Report of the Canadian Human Rights Commission on the Repeal of Section 67 of the Canadian Human Rights Act*. Ottawa: CHRC.

Castallano, M. 2003. *Aboriginal Family Trends: Extended Families, Nuclear Families, Families of the Heart*. Ottawa: Vanier Institute of the Family. http://www.vifamily.ca/library/cft/aboriginal.html.

Chandler, M. 2005. "Suicide and the Persistence of Identity in the Face of Radical Cultural Change." Talk presented at the Assembly of First Nations National Policy Forum, April 19.

Denov, M., and K. Campbell. 2002. "Casualties of Aboriginal Displacement in Canada: Children at Risk among the Innu of Labrador." *Refuge* 20, no. 2: 21–34.

Derr, M.K., and M.J. Taylor. 2004. "The Link between Childhood and Adult Abuse among Long-Term Welfare Recipients." *Children and Youth Services Review* 26: 173–84.

Dion Stout, M., and G.D. Kipling. 1998. "Aboriginal Women in Canada: Strategic Research Directions for Policy Development." Ottawa: Status of Women Canada.

Downie, J. 1994. "A Choice for K'aila: Child Protection and First Nations Children," *Health Law Journal* 2: 99–120.

First Nations Child and Family Caring Society of Canada. 2005a. "A Chance to Make a Difference for This Generation of First Nations Children and Young People: The UNCRC and the Lived Experience of First Nations Children in the Child Welfare System in Canada." Submission made to the Standing Senate Committee on Human Rights. Ottawa: First Nations Child and Family Caring Society of Canada.

————. 2005b. "Wen:De: We Are Coming to the Light of Day." Ottawa: First Nations Child and Family Caring Society of Canada.

Fuchs, D., L. Burnside, S. Marchenski, and A. Mudry. 2005. "Children with Disabilities Receiving Services from Child Welfare Agencies in Manitoba." http://www.cecw-cepb.ca/DocsEng/DisabilitiesManitobaFinal.pdf.

Graham, K.A.H., and E. Peters. 2002. *Aboriginal Communities and Urban Sustainability*. Ottawa: Canadian Policy Research Networks. http://www.urbancentre.utoronto.ca/pdfs/elibrary/CPRNUrbanAboriginal.pdf.

Lavallee, T. 2005. "Federally Funded Manitoba First Nation Children with Complex Medical Needs." *Paediatrics and Child Health* 10, no. 9: 527–29. Ottawa: Canadian Paediatric Society.

Mann, M.M. 2005. "Indian Registration: Unrecognized and Unstated Paternity." http://www.swc-cfc.gc.ca/pubs/pubspr/066240842X/200506_066240842X_e.pdf.

McDaniel, M., and K.S. Slack. 2005. "Major Life Events and the Risk of a Child Maltreatment Investigation." *Children and Youth Services Review* 27: 171–95.

McKenzie, B. 2002. "Block Funding Child Maintenance in First Nations Child and Family Services: A Policy Review." Report prepared for Kahnawake Shakotiia'takenhnhas Community Services, Winnipeg.

Nadjiwan, S., and C. Blackstock. 2003. *Caring across the Boundaries: Promoting Access to Voluntary Sector Resources for First Nations Children and Families*. Ottawa: First Nations Child and Family Caring Society of Canada. http://www.fncfcs.com/docs/VSIFinalReport.pdf.

Pelton, L. 1989. "Child Welfare through the Twentieth Century: Policy and Reality." In *For Reasons of Poverty: A Critical Analysis of the Public Child Welfare System in the United States*. New York: Praeger Publishers.

Pelton, L., and J.S. Milner. 1994. "Is Poverty a Key Contributor to Child Maltreatment?" In E. Gambrill and T.J. Stein, eds., *Controversial Issues in Child Welfare*. Boston: Allyn & Bacon.

Shangreaux, C. 2004. *Staying at Home: Examining the Implications of Least Disruptive Measures in First Nations Child and Family Service Agencies*. Ottawa: First Nations Child & Family Caring Society of Canada. http://www.fncfcs.com/docs/Staying_at_Home.pdf.

Simard, C. 2005. "Status of Non-Status? Play the C-31 Guessing Game to Find Out!" *Brandon Sun,* March 21, 2006.

Struthers, R., and J. Lowe. 2003. "Nursing in the Native American Culture and Historical Trauma." *Issues in Mental Health Nursing* 24: 254–72.

Trocmé, N., D. Knoke, and C. Blackstock. 2004. "Pathways to the Overrepresentation of Aboriginal Children in Canada's Child Welfare System." *Social Service Review* 78, no. 4: 577–601.

Trocmé, N., D. Knoke, C. Shangreaux, B. Fallon, and B. MacLaurin. 2005. "The Experience of First Nations Children Coming into Contact with the Child Welfare System in Canada: The Canadian Incidence Study on Reported Child Abuse and Neglect." In *Wen:De. We Are Coming to the*

Light of Day. Ottawa: First Nations Child and Family Caring Society of Canada.

Trocmé, N., B. MacLaurin, B. Fallon, J. Daciuk, D. Billingsley, M. Tournigny, et al. 2001. "Canadian Incidence Study of Reported Child Abuse and Neglect." Ottawa: National Clearinghouse on Family Violence and Health Canada.

Trocmé, N., B. MacLaurin, B. Fallon, D, Knoke, L. Pitman, and M. McCormack. 2005. "Mesnmimk Wasatek Catching a Drop of Light: Understanding the Overrepresentation of First Nations Children in Canada's Child Welfare System: An Analysis of the Canadian Incidence Study of Reported Child Abuse and Neglect" (CIS-2003). Toronto: Centre of Excellence for Child Welfare.

UNICEF. (2000). *First Call for Children: World Declaration and Plan of Action from the World Summit for Children and Convention on the Rights of the Child*. New York: UNICEF.

Vongdouangchanh, B. 2005. "Section of Canadian Human Rights Act Excludes Aboriginal." *Hill Times,* October 31, 2005.

Wherrett, J. 1997. *The Indian Act: Proposed Modifications*. Ottawa: Library of Parliament.

Wright, A., D. Hiebert-Murphy, and G. Gosek. 2005. "Supporting Aboriginal Children and Youth with Learning and/or Behavioural Disabilities in the Care of Aboriginal Child Welfare Agencies." Ottawa: First Nations Child and Family Caring Society of Canada. http://www.fncaringsociety.org/docs/SupportingAboriginalChildren.pdf.

Zetlin, A.G., and L.A. Weinberg. 2004. "Understanding the Plight of Foster Youth and Improving Their Educational Opportunities." *Child Abuse and Neglect* 28: 917–23.

Zetlin, A.G., L.A. Weinberg, and C. Kimm. 2003. "Are the Educational Needs of Children in Foster Care Being Addressed?" *Children and Schools* 25: 105–19.

The Rights of Children in Care
Consistency with the Convention?

Tom Waldock

Introduction

The UN Convention on the Rights of the Child (CRC) provides a conceptual framework of judgment with which to assess Canada's treatment of children, including the treatment of especially vulnerable children. In what follows, Canada's system of alternative care for children is assessed in relation to the Convention. Has Canada made a substantial and notable commitment to children in need of out-of-home care, in line with its obligations under the CRC? Have developments in child welfare—or child protection—legislation, policies, and practices been in accord with the Convention rights of children requiring alternative care? In this chapter it will be shown that while there have been some discernible advances and improvements in the system of care, substantial commitments have been lacking. Solutions have tended to be short-sighted and of the "Band-Aid" variety. Canada needs to make a much more substantial commitment to children in care if it is to live up to its obligations under the CRC. The first part of this chapter deals briefly with the Convention, the second part with developments in Canada's system of care, and the third part with future directions.

The UN Convention

Article 3 of the Convention has obvious significance for child protection and care. It affirms that the best interests of the child shall be a primary

Tom Waldock, Child and Family Studies Program, Nipissing University consideration in decisions relating to protection and care. Accordingly, when the child's family is not in the best interests of the child, as in cases of abuse and neglect, the child is to be provided with alternative care. According to article 20, "States Parties shall in accordance with their national laws ensure alternative care for such a child." Such care includes "foster placement ... or if necessary placement in suitable institutions for the care of children." Article 19 has clear relevance as well. It requires States Parties to take all appropriate measures to protect children from all forms of abuse and neglect while in the care of "parent(s), legal guardians, or any other person who has the care of the child." Article 19 further stipulates that such measures will include the provision of "necessary support for the child and for those who have the care of the child." The Convention repeatedly acknowledges the need for of supportive environments for children, and article 19 is no different. Abused and neglected children are to be protected, but the need to support those charged with the responsibility of taking care of such children is also acknowledged. Article 27 follows this pattern as well. It recognizes "the right of every child to a standard of living adequate for the child's physical, mental, spiritual, moral and social development" as well as the state's obligation to "provide material assistance and support programmes" to parents and others responsible for the child. It is certainly possible that states may fail to live up to these obligations when children are *in* state care, inadequately supporting caregivers as they endeavour to provide for children's needs.

The best interests of children are paramount. Children have a right to be protected, and they have a right to alternative care when it is needed. They also have a right to be nurtured and supported, and the Convention emphasizes the need for environments conducive to positive childhood development. As article 6 makes clear, states are to "ensure to the maximum extent possible the survival and development of the child." With particular reference to child victims of abuse and neglect, article 39 is even more specific in calling on states to "take all appropriate measures to promote physical and psychological recovery and social reintegration" of such children, in "an environment which fosters the health, self-respect and dignity of the child." The Convention acknowledges the rights of vulnerable and marginalized children to be protected, while also insisting on their right to quality care while "in care." This is an important recognition in terms of understanding the framework of judgment being applied to the system of alternative care. In relation to children generally, article 18 is rightly cited as recognition that the Convention requires the provision of quality day care. It is equally the case that the Convention speaks to the provision of supportive environments for marginalized children, in this case children in state care. The applicability of the Convention then, for children in need of alternative care, relates to protection rights but also to the provision of quality systems of care, systems that are sensitive to their particular needs.

The Convention also emphasizes the need for supportive environments for especially vulnerable and marginalized children in the larger community. Article 2 calls on states to respect the rights set forth in the Convention to each child without discrimination. This article provides a challenge to Canada on a number of fronts, but two will be focused on here in relation to children in need of alternative care. As a federal state, with legislative responsibility for child welfare largely vested in the provincial and territorial governments, Canada is hard pressed to ensure equality of services to children within its jurisdiction. This challenge is political in nature, and if Canada is to meet its obligations under the Convention—in this case, avoiding discrimination "of any kind"—a common sense of purpose and direction will be required, as well as collaboration between the federal and provincial levels of government. Of course, the Convention itself, to the extent that it affects the "mindset" of all levels of government and is incorporated into provincial and territorial child protection legislation, practices, and procedures, could go a long way toward providing this common direction.

Another dimension of article 2 applying to the larger community and culture relates to the requirement that states not discriminate on the basis of any aspect of the child's status, and furthermore that the state should "take all appropriate measures to ensure that the child is protected against all forms of discrimination or punishment on the basis of the status ... of the child's parents." The Convention places an obligation on states to empower children in their communities by addressing all forms of discrimination. Part of this responsibility relates to article 42. Canada is required to make "the principles and provisions of the Convention widely known, by appropriate and active means, to adults and children alike." Article 42 speaks to whether or not governments have fostered a "consciousness" of these rights, and of course it would be particularly important for that awareness to exist among both children and the citizenry as a whole. Consciousness raising and implementation are interrelated and are required in terms of promoting and protecting the rights of children.

Finally, article 12, as noted previously throughout this book, provides "the child who is capable of forming his or her own views the right to express those views freely in all matters affecting the child, the views of the child being given due weight in accordance with the age and maturity of the child." In other words, the child has the right to age-appropriate levels of participation. Article 12 further specifies that the state must provide the child with "the opportunity to be heard in any judicial and administrative proceedings affecting the child," either directly or through representation. The child's right to participate in decisions affecting him or her, both in the judicial arena and in administrative proceedings, is significant for the field of child protection. It means that children have the right to be heard in court proceedings affecting them, as well as in the context of child welfare practices and procedures—for example, in such decision-making forums as plans of care and case conferences. The age and maturity of the child is a factor to be considered, and the Convention allows for advocacy on behalf of the child. But in principle, the right to participation is acknowledged.

Canada's Children-in-Care System

To determine whether Canada is meeting its obligations under the Convention, the situation of children in care needs to be assessed. In what follows, our primary focus is the children-in-care system itself—specifically, developments relating to foster care. Other dimensions of "being in care" are relevant as well, and our assessment branches out to the following: to concerns about the dominant paradigm of social work practice in child welfare and how this affects the relationship between children in care and social workers and child welfare agencies; and to a consideration of children in care and in the context of the larger community and culture. Whether it is in their "homes," in their relationships with workers and agencies, or in their communities, children in care are a marginalized population, and if their rights are to be respected, it is clear that these rights need to be acknowledged in legislation and practice and supported by advocacy. The system of advocacy is pertinent as well, and this also is considered. The picture that emerges is positive on some fronts, but overall the system of alternative care needs significant reform if Canada is to meet its obligations under the Convention.

A System in Crisis

Children coming into care generally come from disadvantaged and marginalized populations. This has been the case historically, and it continues today. Children often come from low-income families. Parental receipt of social assistance is a factor associated with placement, as is job loss, inadequate housing and homelessness, and family stress generally. In addition, lack of social supports, problems of parental substance abuse, and mental health issues put children at greater risk of being placed into care.[1] The problems for Aboriginal children in care were detailed by Marlyn Bennett in the previous chapter. Aboriginal and visible-minority children are much more likely to be admitted to care, which raises questions about the effects of race and ethnicity on placement[2] as well as concerns about the increased stresses on these families. For example, in Ontario, approximately 15 percent of children in care are Aboriginal children; the percentages are even higher in Western Canada, where Aboriginal children account for from one-third to more than one-half of all children in care.[3]

There are, of course, many factors associated with the placement of children in care, including the effects of different approaches to child protection and variations in child welfare policies and practices across jurisdictions. The mandates of child protection agencies and organizations have always been contested "territory." Broadly speaking, and for the purpose of conveying the tensions inherent in child protection as well as shifts in legislation, policies, and practices, commentators have identified two general approaches to child welfare in emphasizing the tendency or orientation of the system. The first is a "family-centred," family welfare orientation or model. In general, this approach emphasizes the importance of families to children and favours state intervention and services to support families under stress, with coercive intervention to remove children viewed as a measure of last resort.[4] This approach emphasizes the potential harm to children and families resulting from the removal of children. Neglect and abuse are contextualized, and "patience" in relation to the family tends to follow from sensitivity to the stresses and challenges that affect family life. The second approach is characterized as "child-centred." In this model, the primary concern is the child, and protecting children from abuse and neglect is the central motivation. There is little "patience" for leaving children in harmful situations, and when risk has been identified, the child's interests are viewed as paramount. Within countries, and certainly within Canada, reference often is made to the swinging of the pendulum from one approach to the other.[5] In a country like Canada, legislative responsibility for child welfare rests with the provinces, so assessments have to take into account not only the general approach of the country but also variations among provincial jurisdictions.

A good deal of attention has been paid to general trends in Canadian child protection and to historical developments over time.[6] No attempt will be made here to duplicate those analyses, but some observations are warranted to assess and update the impact of these general trends as they relate to the children-in-care system. From approximately 1980 to the mid-1990s, Canada's system emphasized a family preservation approach. Beginning in the mid-1990s, in legislation and in practice,

Canada generally moved in the direction of a child-centred model of child protection, as cases involving the deaths of children known to child welfare agencies, but not brought into care, contributed to public outrage and put pressure on governments and child welfare authorities to respond.[7] The shift to a child-centred focus was evident in some provinces (especially Ontario and British Columbia) on two particularly noticeable fronts. First, amendments to legislation emphasized that the protection of children from abuse and neglect was to be a paramount objective, not just one objective among others. Second, the grounds for intervention were broadened, on the presumption that existing legislative parameters were hampering a worker's ability to act decisively in cases of abuse and neglect. Partly in reaction to increasing numbers of children coming into care, more recent legislative, policy, and practice reforms—particularly in Alberta, British Columbia, and Ontario—have revolved around the concepts of differential response and kinship care, whereby more flexibility is being sought in terms of an agency's response to children and families requiring intervention. One of the dimensions of this strategy is the more in-depth investigation of whether or not kinship care (placement with extended family or significant others in the child's life) is a possibility, and thus this represents to some degree a return to a family-centred approach. These recent developments will be evaluated after discussing long-standing pressures on systems of care.

Regardless of approaches to child protection, there have always been insufficient and inadequate placement options for children in need of alternative care. As can be appreciated, with provincial jurisdiction for child welfare and variations between provinces in terms of definitions, policies, and practices, as well as the constant fluctuation of numbers, the collection of national data on children in care is possible but challenging, and comparative assessments are difficult. Nevertheless, the Federal and Provincial/Territorial Working Group on Child and Family Services has facilitated cooperation and data collection on children in care, and the Strategic Policy Branch, Social Development Canada (Human Resources Development Canada), tracks children in care across Canada, although provincial ministries and organizations are often the best sources for the most recent statistics. The general trend of increasing numbers of children in care has been apparent across the country, particularly in the latter half of the 1990s. For example, from 1995–96 to 2000–1, Alberta had an increase in children in care of almost 60 percent (from 4,990 to 7,950 children in care). In the same time frame, Ontario's increase was roughly 50 percent (from 9,870 to 14,970), British Columbia's was over 35 percent (from 7,280 to 9,960), Nova Scotia's was almost 25 percent (from 1,640 to 2,020), and Saskatchewan's was approximately 15 percent (from 2,530 to 2,910 children). From 2000–1 to 2004–5, is trend continued in some jurisdictions, but at a slower rate.

In total, there are between 75,000 and 80,000 children in care across Canada. Calculating numbers in relation to Quebec and nationally is complicated by the fact that Quebec has not had a formal "children in care" reporting category. It is clear, however, that Quebec has the largest number of children in care, in excess of 25,000 (2000–1). The trend of increasing numbers is apparent as well, as Quebec saw an increase of almost 40 percent from 1997–98 to 2000–1.[8] What accounts for the increasing numbers of children in care, and the fact that this process has slowed somewhat in the past five years? Some have suggested that lowered thresholds for bringing children into care in the late 1990s were a factor, associated with the child-centred legislative, policy, and practice changes that occurred, notably in British Columbia and Ontario.[9] Others have questioned this, arguing that children were indeed at greater risk during this period, largely because of socio-economic realities and the fact that families, particularly those on social assistance, were under increased stress.[10] Of the many factors suggested, one stands out. There have been increased referrals to child welfare agencies by professionals, perhaps influenced by the duty to report in most jurisdictions, but undoubtedly reflecting as well increased sensitivities to neglect and emotional maltreatment. In addition, the number of substantiated investigations has increased.[11] Neglect is the most frequently investigated category of maltreatment, having been cited as the principal reason for investigations in 40 percent of the cases. When combined with the category of emotional maltreatment (at 19 percent), which includes exposure to domestic violence, a more recognized and reported subcategory of emotional maltreatment, these two categories of maltreatment now account for roughly three-fifths of all investigations.[12] In terms of children coming into care, the slowing nature of the trend over the past five years is perhaps more difficult to explain. The "reaction" of governments and child welfare agencies to the increasing trends, notably in British Columbia and Ontario, is likely a good place to start, given changes in legislation, policy, and practice denoting a shift back toward a family-centred approach.

Aside from increasing numbers, the high level of children's needs places great stress on systems of care and on caregivers themselves. It goes without saying that children coming into care have been victimized by one or more of the following: physical and sexual abuse, neglect, and emotional maltreatment. That children in care have a high level of needs has long been recognized. It also has been noted that most children in care today have specialized needs, and attempts to distinguish categories of care—such as "regular" care or "specialized"/"treatment" care—are somewhat misleading in this regard.[13] While they require safe environments, children in care also need environments conducive to meeting their developmental and recovery needs.

As we have seen, the CRC provides a broad framework of judgment by which to assess child welfare and children-in-care systems. This framework spans the three categories of rights falling under the rubric of the Convention—namely the provision, protection, and participation rights. Protection and provision rights are intimately related. Article 20 requires states to provide for alternative care if it is determined that a child's family is not in his or her best interests, noting that such children are entitled to special protection and assistance. The more difficult test for Canada concerns the quality of that alternative care. Obviously, this precludes negative environments, and protecting children from neglect and abuse (article 19) would apply to children in care as well. Yet it is in the provision of environments conducive to positive childhood development that the Convention's standards become more demanding. Children, including those in care, have the right to a standard of living adequate for their development (article 27). States also are called on to ensure to the maximum extent possible the survival and development of the child (article 6), and in relation to child victims of neglect and abuse, they are to promote the psychological recovery of these children in an environment that fosters their health, self-respect, and dignity (article 39). The children-in-care system must meet the developmental needs of these marginalized children. Moreover, the Convention calls on states to support caregivers in their role (articles 19 and 27).

A good place to start an assessment of Canada's progress is the persistent "crisis" of foster care, which has been the subject of debate and discussion for decades. The story here is one of incremental improvements but certainly nothing amounting to substantial progress of the kind necessary to meet the needs of children in care. The crisis has many dimensions, but generally the focus has been on the inability of systems to deal with the increases of children coming into care. Aside from the issue of quality of care, in many jurisdictions there is a shortage of foster homes, and this calls into question Canada's adherence to the most basic right of children requiring alternative care: that such systems be provided (article 20). The availability of foster care resources is sometimes cyclical in nature, and varies depending on the number of children coming into care in relation to the ability of systems to recruit new homes as others "age out of" or leave the system. Suffice it to say that reported shortages, particularly in urban areas, exist across the country. At times there are very disturbing signs of such shortages, including children being placed in motel rooms[14] under worker supervision or in group care settings. This practice has been more widespread than one might think, given its complete inappropriateness, yet it has occurred in situations where there were no alternatives due to the shortage of homes. Manitoba, Nova Scotia, Ontario, Alberta, and British Columbia are cases in point.[15]

This situation may be far from the "norm," and some jurisdictions have succeeded in recruitment efforts to meet placement needs, but sustaining this over time has been an ongoing challenge. Moreover, it remains worrisome that "success" in meeting placement needs sometimes occurs during family-centred shifts in legislation, policy, and practice, with fewer children coming into care. This is not a positive development, if it entails any discernible tendencies to leave children in risk situations. Inappropriate placements contribute to placement breakdowns and undermine permanency and stability while in care. In one study, the mean number of placements for children in care was four.[16] The experience of some children far exceeds that, with the National Youth in Care Network reporting "horror stories such as moving eleven times in one year."[17] The phenomenon of multiple placements or foster care drift is related not only to limited placement options but also to the support and competencies of caregivers and the quality of the children-in-care system generally.

There are many reasons for the failure to sustain adequate and appropriate placement resources in many jurisdictions. Recruitment and retention challenges have plagued foster care for some time. It is difficult to recruit caregivers from the younger generation to replace caregivers aging out of the system, since more people are now pursuing careers that require a formal education, and the status of caregiving mitigates against viewing it as an option. The prevalence of two-partner working families is a related factor, sometimes associated with the increased labour force participation of women.[18] Aside from such realities, perhaps the most detrimental factor in relation to recruitment and retention concerns the evolution of caregiving itself, and the failure of governments and agencies to adequately recognize the contribution of caregivers to the welfare of children. The system demands more of caregivers. They are asked to provide care to children with increasingly high levels of need, all the while attending meetings, plans of care, and court appearances and liaising with social workers, therapists, psychologists, and sometimes lawyers. Growing expectations have been the pattern, yet recognition for the role has been lacking. Indeed, it often is argued that role confusion characterizes fostering, with a status somewhere between professionals and volunteers.[19] Caregivers are asked to be professionals, yet their actual status is unclear at best. This contributes to frustration, with caregivers feeling that they are not valued members of the "team," and the effort to retain caregivers is hampered as a result. As Kathleen Kufeldt notes, foster parents are "the underrated, overlooked partners in child welfare."[20]

While the evolution toward professionalized foster care has occurred as a result of the growing demands placed on caregivers, there needs to be a clear recognition that such developments are required to meet the needs of children in care and governmental commitments to move forward in a sustained and coordinated fashion. As well-known child psychiatrist Paul Steinhauer pointed out in the early 1990s, it is overly optimistic, if not frankly naive, to assume that "already damaged children ... will obtain the quality of care they need in most traditional foster families."[21] This has been a continuing theme in the literature,[22] and children in care themselves have identified a higher quality of care as a major priority for the future.[23] Some jurisdictions in Canada have developed more professionalized models of care, but often they have not been sustained, nor have they come to characterize their systems of care generally.[24]

The lack of coordination of systems of care has been a problem within provinces, let alone across the country. In Ontario, for example, it was not until the late 1990s that three levels of care were instituted (at least in terms of the government's funding formula), namely Regular care, Specialized care, and Treatment care. Prior to this, agencies across the province had different levels of care. Agencies continue to use their discretion in having different levels of care, and more importantly, some agencies "rank" or label the children in relation to these levels of care, while others relate these rankings to foster homes themselves, more in line with a professional system of care. Across the country, there is wide variation. In Newfoundland and Labrador and Nunavut, for example, there are only Regular or Basic levels of foster homes, with some provision for specialized rates based on the child's behaviours. In Nova Scotia, there are two levels of care provided in Regular and Parent Counsellor foster homes. Saskatchewan identifies four levels—Intern, Practitioner, Specialist, and Therapeutic foster care—but notes that 80 percent of all care is provided at the Practitioner level. There also are substantial discrepancies in the number of foster children allowed in a home at these different levels of care. In Ontario, for example, four foster children in a home is considered "foster care" regardless of the level of care (Regular, Specialized, and Treatment) and anything beyond four children is considered group care. In Saskatchewan, eight children (including natural or adopted children) can be in Practitioner homes, but only one foster child can be in a Therapeutic home. Alberta follows this pattern of one foster child permitted in a home at their highest level of care, deemed Specialized foster care, and allows up to three foster children at other levels.[25] As mentioned earlier, provincial jurisdiction is a factor here, and coordination of efforts will be required if Canada is to meet its obligations under article 2 of the Convention, which requires non-discrimination—in this case, getting different levels of care and treatment depending on their jurisdiction.

Identifying shortcomings in systems of care should not be the rationale for leaving children in situations of risk. At the same time, there should be a level of confidence that the needs of children will be met while they are in care. To date, this does not exist to the extent that it should. The instabilities of care, and the realities of multiple placements, are factors. Increasingly, however, commentators are focusing on the need for foster care policies and practices to meet the developmental needs of children, beyond their needs for safety and permanency. In this regard, developmental outcomes have become the focus to a greater degree, and the question of whether or not foster care contributes to child functioning is being considered. Outcome studies generally identify areas of concern, such as levels of emotional and behavioural development and educational achievement.[26] Other studies identify negative outcomes for youth who "age out" of foster care—outcomes that include homelessness, failure to maintain employment, and early pregnancies[27]—and some studies suggest connections between the experiences of children in care and the likelihood of future delinquency and imprisonment.[28] Conclusions in relation to caregivers or systems of care can be unfair and are difficult to draw because many variables are involved, including the experiences of children before entering care and the impact of these experiences on outcomes. But they do draw attention to the pressing need for systems of care that will contribute to the welfare and recovery of neglected and abused children.

The competency level of caregivers clearly is relevant to meeting the needs of children in care, and some research suggests that caregivers have parenting difficulties.[29] Equally significant is the context in which caregivers attempt to fulfil their roles and the extent to which they are supported and prepared. The CRC requires that caregivers be supported in their roles (articles 19 and 27). In some respects, the supports provided to caregivers have improved over time, but they remain insufficient. Again, there are wide variations across the country, but generally speaking, there have been improvements in terms of supports, such as the provision for relief care. Caregivers generally are able to access monies for the purpose of relief. Given the stressful and demanding nature of foster caregiving, these are welcomed developments, even if more needs to be done. Such factors are related to the "crisis" of foster care and the challenges associated with recruitment and retention. Also related is inadequate remuneration, particularly at the base or regular level of care. Again, there have been moderate improvements, but the fact that daily daycare costs often exceed foster care rates undermines efforts to attract and retain qualified caregivers, especially since the role is so much more demanding.

In terms of the support for caregivers consistent with obligations under articles 19 and 27 of the Convention, no area is more significant than training, since this directly relates to the ability of caregivers to meet the needs of children in care. For the most part, jurisdictions have provided caregivers with "in house" training. They are required to take fostering training prior to undertaking their role, and most jurisdictions provide certificate courses and learning opportunities for caregivers on an ongoing basis. Again, variations exist and challenges remain in relation to obligations under article 2 of the Convention. But in terms of preparation for the role, there have been some positive developments across the country. The widespread interest in the PRIDE (Parenting Resources for Information, Development and Education) model is a case in point. The model has been piloted in many jurisdictions, and adopted in others, such as Newfoundland and Labrador, Ontario, Nova Scotia, and New Brunswick.[30] This model provides a structured framework and involves a multistep process for recruiting, developing, and supporting caregivers. Significantly, it emphasizes a competency-based approach to training that enhances the capacities of caregivers to meet the needs of children in care, with a specific focus on their developmental needs.

As much as the PRIDE model represents an advance in the "in-house" training provided to caregivers, questions still arise as to why formal education and training provided via the usual avenues (colleges and universities) is not a requirement. It is quite revealing that demands for increased levels of professionalism with regard to other caregiver occupations have not been echoed to nearly the same extent in relation to foster care. For example, legitimate demands for quality daycare are common (article 18 of the Convention is sometimes cited in this regard), with "quality" generally being associated with increased competencies and growing professionalism, including the insistence on education and training, minimally at the college level (Early Childhood Education and Child and Youth Worker, for example). Yet in relation to foster care, and a more challenging population of children with a higher level of needs, such demands are rarely heard, and governments and agencies continue to operate as though this education and training is not a requirement. When you add to this the fact that caregivers have a variety of other responsibilities, there is even less justification for such discrepancies. Sadly, part of the answer seems to lie in the fact that children in care are not "everyone's children," but rather "lesser thans" in terms of society's view of their needs, and collective responsibility for their welfare has not been sufficiently acknowledged. Fortunately, obligations under the Convention are clear on this front. If anything, states are required to do more for these children (article 39, for example), because they have been marginalized and victimized.

Complementing training supports (PRIDE) is another positive development relating to children in care, the Looking After Children (LAC) Project, which has the potential to make a real contribution in terms of making the needs of children in care a dominant focus of child welfare. Originally piloted in six provinces (Newfoundland, Nova Scotia, New Brunswick, Prince Edward Island, Quebec, and Ontario), most jurisdictions are now at least engaged in pilot projects, with others (Ontario, for example) moving to expand its use system-wide.[31] The goal of this approach to working with children in care and caregivers is to focus on children's developmental progress over time, measuring and improving outcomes by employing assessment and action records (AARs) in relation to seven developmental dimensions: health; education; identity; social presentation skills; self-care skills; family and social relationships; and emotional and behavioural development.[32] In terms of the major research question identified by the head researchers—"How effectively do child welfare services meet the needs of children in care?"—the initial three-year study generated mixed results; but clearly, the generation of databases and statistics concerning outcomes for children in care has helped identify areas of concern, such as substantially lower levels of educational achievement.[33] The strength of LAC lies in the fact that it is ultimately a proactive, preventative, child-centred approach, one that not only allows for the identification of areas of concern but also seeks to enhance the quality of care provided to children by making their needs the primary focus of child welfare interventions.

In terms of meeting Convention obligations to the developmental needs of children in care, as well as to support caregivers, LAC represents a positive development. LAC has contributed to the recognition of children's needs and is instructive in terms of encouraging increased caregiver competencies in this regard. Ultimately, however, addressing the issues already alluded to in relation to foster care will require more substantial reforms as well as a real commitment to improving systems of care. LAC researchers have expressed the view that it may be a grassroots approach to influencing child welfare policy,[34] and if this is true, perhaps LAC will pressure and encourage governments to meet children's needs by making more substantial commitments to systems of care.

Substantial commitments have been lacking to date, and the response to the "crisis" in foster care has been varied. At times, the value of foster care itself is questioned. Faced with such realities as recruitment and retention difficulties, placement breakdowns, and unflattering outcome studies, some commentators have called for a shift back to institutionalized settings for children in care.[35] Clearly, turning the clock back is not the answer. In most jurisdictions across Canada, the main reaction to the crisis has been to engage in piecemeal efforts and reforms instead of addressing fundamental issues. For example, in all jurisdictions, money is being spent on recruitment efforts, as governments and agencies constantly swim against the tide of the substantial and underlying reasons for the crisis. Even when such efforts achieve minimal success, there is a nagging feeling that they do little to address the quality of care. For example, placing ads in local papers may generate responses, but when minimal requirements exist, and when these requirements are even less than for other caregiver occupations, it is difficult to argue that the best interests of these children is a primary consideration (article 3), let alone make the case that Canada is to the maximum extent possible ensuring the development and recovery of children in care (articles 6 and 39).

In some instances, "responses" to the crisis have involved the use of outside pay resources (OPRs)—that is, privately run foster, group, and institutional care placements. This has been particularly noticeable in urban areas, where it is a challenge to recruit sufficient placement resources to meet the needs of children coming into care. For example, data from the Catholic Children's Aid Society of Toronto (CCAST) confirm the largely unintended trend toward privatized resources. Using October dates (the number of children in care as of October 31 of the respective year) to provide a "snapshot" of the situation over a fifteen-year period, from 1988 to 2003, it was found that the number of children in internal, agency-run foster and group care decreased from 520 to 386 (a decrease of over 25 percent), while the number of children in outside pay resources increased from 220 to 563 (an increase of over 150 percent).[36]

Such trends are not in the best interests of children in care. When a child is admitted to care, the admitting agency takes on responsibility for the child, in some cases becoming the child's legal guardian. A children's service worker is assigned, and this worker becomes responsible and accountable for the child while in care. The agency is collectively responsible for the child, and the worker assumes an individual responsibility. This situation ensures a direct line of accountability and responsibility flowing from the worker/agency to the child. While there will be variations in the numbers and "titles" of workers that make up the agency team, generally speaking the system ensures a strong and clear connection between the agency/workers on the one hand, and both the child and foster home on the other. From the approval stage onward, there is a direct agency connection to the foster home. Caregivers may have an agency resource worker, or they may have worked closely with other members of the team in the past. All of this is no small matter, of course. After all, the foster home is where the child in care lives. Thus, the overall strength and nature of the agency/child relationship encompasses the agency/foster home connection. Responsibility and accountability to the child in care goes beyond legal requirements, and needs to be supported and fostered by the working dynamics of the system.

The employment of outside-pay foster care resources affects this accountability/responsibility relationship. Effectively, a child coming into the care of an agency is placed in an outside-pay foster home with potentially less connection to that agency. Lines of accountability and responsibility can get muted and blurred.[37] The child's worker will continue to have the most direct connection and responsibility to the child, and other members of the team will be aware of the child as well. However, the child's worker, along with other members of the team, may have only a tenuous connection to the foster home. Indeed, foster home resource workers (employed by some agencies) in the agency will perhaps have little relationship to the home in which the child is placed. Moreover, from the recruitment/approval stage onward, caregivers in the outside-pay foster home will have dealt with individuals/owners in their own private agency. This fundamentally alters the overall strength and nature of the agency/child relationship, and the working dynamics of the system become less supportive of agency responsibility and accountability to the child. Such issues, of course, relate to the increased "distance" between those responsible for the child, and the placement resource. This distance may also affect the extent to which workers and agencies are able to oversee outside resources, which raises additional concerns about whether or not the same standards of care can be assured, especially since these are private businesses under pressure to generate profits, often operating in an environment where placement options for agencies are limited.

Differential Response and Kinship Care

An increased emphasis on kinship care across the country represents another strategy or approach to dealing with the crisis in foster care. The continuing adoption of differential response models, along with changes in legislation, policies, and practices, has facilitated the use of kinship care, with Alberta leading the way. Differential response models provide more flexibility to workers and agencies by expanding the range of intervention options, with multiple "streams" of service delivery.[38] If it is determined that a child can safely remain with the current caregivers, agencies are to provide support and engage community resources. If a child cannot remain at home, the possibilities are expanded. Typically, an "out of care" stream includes the possibility of a voluntary placement with kin, or a supervision order with kin, whereby the agency supervises and monitors the situation for a period of time. The "in care" stream also includes the kinship care option—but with the kin caregivers having to meet more criteria—as well as the option of placement in a non-kin agency resource. Differential response strategies have been advocated partly in reaction to dramatic increases in investigations involving neglect and exposure to domestic violence; in particular, reference is made to the need for strategies and interventions that do not further victimize mothers caught in violent relationships.[39] Differential response seeks to distinguish between protection cases, where agencies need to be aggressively "involved," and cases better dealt with by supporting and empowering families and communities.

The emphasis on empowering families and communities is laudable. Certainly, the CRC calls on states to pursue proactive, preventative measures (articles 18 and 19, in particular), as opposed to simply reactive intervention. Broadly speaking, systems with a family-service orientation pursue proactive, preventative policies and take a therapeutic approach to working with children and families. Belgium, Norway, Sweden, Denmark, and the Netherlands approach child protection in this way, and England and Wales certainly have leanings in this direction as well. Other countries, including Canada and the United States, have a legalistic child protection orientation.[40] Clearly, to meet obligations under the Convention, Canada needs to incorporate a proactive, preventative approach in supporting children and families, and child protection agencies themselves would be expected to contribute in this regard. It also should be noted that part of the mandate of child protection, acknowledged in legislation across the country, is to provide supports to children and families. As Paul Thomas points out, the legislation does not make the provision of these supports imperative, nor is it very detailed at times, but it certainly recognizes the need for child protection agencies, or others with the assistance of agencies, to make a contribution in this regard. Some of the services referred to in legislation include improving the family's financial situation and housing situation; improving child care; and providing counselling and drug or alcohol treatment.[41] The success of differential response strategies will hinge partly on following through with commitments to increased investments in families and communities. A substantial commitment to a family service orientation has been lacking in the past, and this has been true regardless of approaches to child protection.

Aside from the need to support families and communities, the success of differential response strategies will hinge on a number of other factors, among them these two: (1) no increases in the tolerance for risk to children, whichever "stream" of service delivery is employed; and (2) careful and cautious assessment of the appropriateness of kinship care placements, with standards of assessment that ensure the protection and nurturing of children. To the extent that differential response, paired with kinship care, represents a family-centred approach to children's welfare, the lessons learned from strategies like family preservation should be kept in mind. At times, these practices have been associated with increased tolerance for risk and with failures to remove children quickly enough in situations of neglect and abuse. There is a distinction with the formalization of kinship care, and that is the potential option of placing children with kin outside their immediate family setting, although even in this regard the maintenance of family connections can be a positive or negative thing, depending on the situation. Placement with kin may be a viable option, but if it is not to compromise the best interests of children—specifically, their need to be protected and nurtured consistent with the CRC (notably articles 6, 19, and 39)—there should be defined and comprehensive standards of assessment in relation to kinship care, and real vigilance should be exercised in evaluating the appropriateness of such placements.

Recent cases and events across Canada suggest the need for caution, in that they draw attention to the fact that just because someone is identified as kin is no reason to assume that standards of assessment should be relaxed. In Ontario, the tragic 2002 death of Jeffrey Baldwin confirms the need for vigilance and comprehensive standards of assessment. In 1998, along with his siblings, Jeffrey had been removed from his parent's care because of protection concerns and placed in kinship care with his grandparents, with foster care payments provided. When he died from septic shock approaching his sixth birthday, he weighed twenty-one pounds, a victim of gross neglect and maltreatment. Later investigations revealed that both the grandparents had previous convictions for child abuse against their children and that this information was in fact in the agency's own records. Yet at the time, there was little scrutiny of kin placements.[42] British Columbia's child protection system is now under intense and continuing scrutiny (including an inquest) with regard to its kinship care practices.[43] The similarly tragic death of nineteen-month-old Sherry Charlie, who was beaten to death by her uncle while in care, provides another example of compromises being made to facilitate kinship care. Again, both Sherry and her brother had been placed without even the most basic assessments, which in this case would have revealed the uncle's violent background and criminal convictions.[44] Both these cases provide clear testimony to the glaring gaps that existed in kinship care policies and procedures; they also reveal that unwarranted compromises are being made regarding standards of assessment in relation to kin placements. Moreover, they reveal a violation of the rights of children under the UN Convention to protection and care.

While a good deal of literature debates the comparative merits of kinship care versus non-kin foster care, there is nothing that supports the presumptive waiving or lowering of standards for kinship care; if anything, it suggests maintaining the same standards of assessment that are applied to non-kin foster homes. Generally, kinship care is defended on the same grounds as family preservation policies: the child is able to live with a known or trusted caregiver (at times the case, but not necessarily); it reduces separation trauma and preserves attachments (assuming positive relationships exist); it reinforces identity in its connection to "family"; and it avoids the loss of the familiar, being less likely to disrupt schooling and community attachments (assuming placement remains relatively local).[45] On the other hand, literature and research also draws attention to concerns. Neoliberal political philosophies and policies associated with government downsizing and fiscal restraint have been identified as motivating factors behind interest in kinship care.[46] Whether or not philosophical explanations are relevant, the kinship care orientation certainly is to some degree a response to the crisis in foster care—a response that is viewed as attractive because it involves reduced costs in relation to the foster care system. Indeed, in Ontario, program cost estimates assumed a 10 percent reduction in children in care owing to placement in "out of care" kinship homes, with a total cost savings of approximately $28 million per year.[47]

Beyond suspicions regarding fiscal motivations, there are many other concerns relevant to the quality of care, including child safety concerns. Intergenerational aspects of child abuse and neglect have been identified, along with the prevalence of poor parenting practices across generations. Challenges exist regarding the ability to control or monitor access between parents and children when this is not in the best interests of children; kin may allow such access when it is not advised, and even if this is not the case, placing kin in a "policing" role increases levels of stress and can negatively affect family dynamics. Studies also have shown that kinship caregivers may already have family stresses associated with such factors as low levels of income (lower than non-kin caregivers), and that they often rely on social assistance and live in conditions of poverty.[48] Many questions arise. How prepared are kinship caregivers for what they are taking on? Do they feel obligated to take the child, even in situations where they aren't able to meet the child's needs? Unless supports to kinship care homes are adequate, additional stresses may drive some families "over the edge," jeopardizing the welfare of all concerned. In addition, given that many of these children are victims of neglect and abuse, and given the Convention's emphasis on providing environments conducive to meeting their developmental and recovery needs (articles 6, 27, and 39), the practice of placing children back in stressful environments should be challenged.

The issue of standards is fundamental to the consideration of kinship care as a placement option, and enough concerns have been raised to warrant vigilance. Criteria such as criminal record checks and prior involvement with child protection agencies are straightforward, although as we have seen, they have not always been incorporated into policies and practices. Improvements have been made, and increasingly standards are being elaborated that address such factors as income, housing, family composition, history and relationships, and parenting attitudes, and there have been increased efforts to address issues of support.[49] In relation to "out of care" placements in particular, it is still common to waive requirements that non-kin foster homes might be required to meet, such as foster parent training,[50] and it is possible to question the modification of such standards, given the needs of most children requiring alternative care as well as Convention requirements to promote the recovery of children (article 39). Differential response, associated with kinship care, may add flexibility in terms of placement options and may decrease pressures on systems to overreact in cases where the needs of children and families can be met with less intrusive and punitive measures. "Out of care" options such as voluntary placement with kin, or placement under supervision orders, may contribute to this flexibility, but success will depend on a family service orientation to practice in which families and children are supported. The issues are complex, the need for judgment unavoidable. But judgments should not err on the side of compromising the rights of children under the CRC to protection and quality care. Given improvements to policy and practice standards, the jury may still be out on differential response and kinship care, but the evidence to date suggests that such compromises have been made, just as they were made in relation to family preservation policies and practices.

Caregivers, Advocacy, and Children's Rights

Under the Convention, children in alternative care are not to be the objects of discrimination. Rather, they are to be secure in their dignity and to experience a supportive environment of care. There are many indications, however, that Canada's system has failed to achieve this.

First of all, the very discourse of child protection is problematic. Children in care are referred to as "clients," "cases," and "placements"—terminology that is now so taken for granted that it is simply employed without any consideration of its appropriateness for children in care. From a child-centred perspective, there is nothing "normal" about being referred to as a "client" or "case." Brian Wharf laments the fact that individuals are referred to and treated as "cases" in child welfare, a practice associated with classification and categorization, intended to meet the needs of bureaucratic structures and technocratic arrangements. As he says: "Simply put, treating people as cases dehumanizes them." In no way does the term "conjure up the image of a unique and valued individual ... who can contribute to the community." Wharf suggests that those who come into contact with child welfare should be seen and treated as citizens with rights and responsibilities.[51] This applies to children in care as well, especially in light of our focus, since the CRC regards children as citizens, too. If anything, such labels can have a more profound effect on children, since they are often internalized at a younger age.

Other terminology in child welfare is even more problematic. Terms and phrases such as "custody," "ward of the state," "intake," "visits," and "records" are associated with institutional settings, such as mental health facilities and prisons. Youth in care have identified stigmatization as an overriding concern, and they single out the negative portrayal of them in case files or "records" that "read like rap sheets with full documentation of negative behaviours and attitudes."[52] In relation to foster care, despite efforts to categorize homes, the practice of labelling the child as a regular, specialized, or treatment child continues. Such practices are very much in line with the dominant paradigm of social work practice in child welfare, which incorporates a pathological view of "clients"—in this case children in care—by individualizing problems rather than situating them in larger social contexts.[53] The child is expected to adapt—in other words, behave normally—in situations and conditions that are far from normal. If the child does not adapt, there is a tendency to see the child *as the problem,* reducing explanations to the individual level of the child's psyche, instead of facilitating positive environments of the sort that are associated with children's developmental needs.

Children also are "in care" in the context of their communities. For example, children in care are sometimes treated as "outsiders" by those in positions of authority, and challenges exist in terms of meeting the needs of children in areas like education. Schools, for example, may be reticent about taking children in care, assuming that these children will pose a variety of "problems."[54] Again, instead of expressing sensitivity toward conditions and experiences and promoting positive, empowering environments, schools "individualize" issues in a way that constructs the child as the "problem." From discipline practices (such as the excessive use of school suspensions)[55] to the ability to access services in relation to their needs, children in care do not experience school "just like everybody else." Their "in care" status does matter. Schools have tremendous potential to empower children. Howe and Covell argue that children's rights education is a major vehicle through which children can internalize their rights and responsibilities, as well as develop a sense of value as dignified persons and citizens.[56] Developing this sense of value and self-worth would have special meaning and significance for children in care, and for other marginalized groups of children, especially since there are other challenges in relation to the community and culture.

The "in care" status of children is conveyed and experienced in a variety of ways, at times subtle but noticeable nevertheless. For example, parents may discourage their own children's contact with children in care. After all, what exactly does it mean when people say that a child comes from a "good family"? And is there much likelihood that children in care will qualify? There are many such examples of forms of social isolation and discrimination against children in care. Consider the reaction in communities when it is discovered that a group home may be opening up. The Convention places an obligation on states to take responsibility for this social and cultural environment, to take all appropriate measures to protect children from all forms of discrimination (article 2) based on their status, and to promote positive environments that will ensure to the maximum extent possible the development of the child (article 6), thus fostering their self-respect and dignity (article 39). While policies and practices that relate to "systems" (such as child protection) can be addressed or reformed, it might be argued that governments play a limited role in relation to ideas or values within the culture. It is worth noting, however, that article 42 of the Convention requires states to foster a consciousness of children's rights among children and citizens generally, and this would empower children in their communities and cultural environments.

In Canada, the CRC has not been directly incorporated into child welfare legislation, which means that it does not have the force of law in Canadian courts. While there is no direct connection to the CRC, most child welfare legislation across Canada accords rights to children, with some provinces (such as Quebec and Ontario) having more explicit codes.[57] Participation rights sometimes figure prominently—for example, the right to participate in plans of care—although youth in care have pointed out that they are sometimes not informed about their rights.[58] Moreover, as with other areas of child protection, there is wide variation in the rights of children in care across the country, and challenges exist in terms of meeting article 2's requirements. The same is true of advocacy services for children in care,[59] including children's lawyers, child advocates, and ombudsmen. Although most provinces have some combination of these advocacy services, structures of oversight are not uniform. In relation to child advocates in particular, their mandates, as well as their levels of independence, differ across jurisdictions. The issue of independent oversight of child protection is always a matter of concern, and it is often contested through the media, especially in the aftermath of children's deaths. Recently, in Ontario, the ombudsman was highly critical of the government and of the fact that the day-to-day decisions of children's aid societies (which are not government agencies) do not come under the scrutiny of an outside, independent investigative agency.[60] In British Columbia, the government has come under heavy criticism for disbanding the children's advocate (an independent officer reporting to the legislature) and children's commission in 2001 and for replacing that officer with a new child and youth officer. Critics have questioned the independence of this position, since it falls under the attorney general's administration.[61]

Participation rights (article 12) and child advocacy are central to empowering children. The need for children in care to have a "voice" certainly relates to the different "ecologies" of care, from children's home environments to their communities and culture. Discrimination and differential treatment both flourish when victims' voices are not heard or when those voices are ineffectual. Canada needs to incorporate Convention rights, including participation rights, more directly into domestic child welfare legislation so that these rights have the force of law in Canadian courts, and intergovernmental coordination and cooperation is required to eliminate variations across provinces, consistent with article 2. In addition, given the need to "amplify" and support the voices of children, there is a need for improvements to the system of advocacy services, and a strong case can be made for the development of independent children's rights commissions.[62] There is no doubt that reforms of this nature would go a long way to empowering and supporting the "voices" of children in care.

While this level of advocacy is important because it would be independent of those providing protection and care to children, it remains true that these are legislative, bureaucratic approaches to advocacy that are somewhat remote from the actual lives of children. To be sure, children sometimes need independent advocacy in their relations with caregivers, agencies, and others. But much less attention has been paid to the need for advocacy that is embedded in the daily lives of children in care. Advocacy has been regarded as part of the role of social workers, but it is sometimes viewed as a declining part of that role,[63] given the pressures on social workers within bureaucratic and hierarchical agency structures. Within child welfare, the pressures of high caseloads and paperwork alone can mean that workers are unable to become very involved in the actual lives of children. There is certainly a need to reinvigorate advocacy in social work practice, but the fact remains that social workers can not be part of the daily lives of children in care and cannot provide the kind of embedded advocacy that children require. Caregivers are in the best position to provide this, since their advocacy can be immediate and informed, built on the experience of sharing lives and struggles and witnessing firsthand a child's interaction with workers, agencies, teachers, schools, and communities. In their lives, children in care need their voices to be amplified by their caregivers. Since their "natural" advocates (parents) often are not able to provide the kind of support that many children take for granted, children in care need caregivers who are close enough to their experience to address their needs effectively and to make sure their rights are acknowledged and defended.

While caregivers are in the best position to provide such advocacy, their ability to advocate cannot be taken for granted, and this role has to be developed and supported. Just as the increased competencies and professionalism of caregivers are required to meet Convention obligations to provide protection and quality care for victims of neglect and abuse, so too are they related to the participatory rights of children in care, ensuring that their voice is supported and empowered. First and foremost, children in care need to have their own voices heard and respected; and to overcome marginalization and exclusion, their right to participate in matters affecting them should be more fully incorporated into policies, practices, and procedures. But because of the extent of their powerlessness in relation to their environments, justice for children in care also will require advocacy support that goes beyond the needs of most children. There will be heightened environmental challenges, since children in care face discrimination in all its forms and their social isolation sometimes reinforces and intensifies the nature of their needs and experiences. In addition, their interactions with both people and systems are complicated and multidimensional. All children need their voices to be heard, in their families, schools, and communities, but for children in care, the challenges will relate to caregivers, educators, social workers, lawyers, therapists, psychologists, and others. To support their voice, they will need independent advocates as well as competent, credible advocacy embedded in their lives—advocacy that is encouraged, developed, and supported by governments and agencies.

Future Directions

The quality of the child-in-care system has a profound impact on the experiences of children in care; it affects their lives both directly and indirectly, in ways that relate to their immediate foster care environments and that branch out through the support and agency of embedded advocacy to their interactions with families, agencies, the community, and the culture. Meeting obligations under the CRC to provide for the protection, provision, and participatory rights of children in care will require more committed efforts to improve the child-in-care system. The path ahead is clear enough. Reforms can be guided by the evolving consciousness of children's rights and by the standards and expectations associated with the articles of the Convention.

There are progressive approaches to foster care. For example, in the 1990s, two Ontario agencies, the Toronto Children's Aid Society and the Toronto Catholic Children's Aid Society, piloted two fostering programs, known respectively as Family Builders and Family Partners. These programs were examples of "inclusive" foster care.[64] Initially, certain caregivers were chosen to work in these programs. Their task was to provide for the needs of children while working with natural families, providing counselling and support services to parents. The provision of parental support contributed to enhanced parenting skills, with some potential for positive, intergenerational effects as well. In addition, such support could facilitate the child's return home, although this was not inevitable or guaranteed, and children were not put at risk while these services were being provided. It also had the additional benefit of drawing on the experience of caregivers, enhancing their role in the system, and providing services to families in non-oppressive and non-threatening ways, while keeping families "connected" to children in care. Articles 9 and 20 of the CRC recognize continuity of care as a priority, if it is in the child's best interests. In some instances, parents could be quite involved, coming to the foster home to discuss the progress of their children, while making their own efforts, with the help and support of caregivers and agencies, to work through whatever issues or challenges had resulted in their children coming into care. The programs incorporated a family service approach to foster care, without compromising the rights of children to a protective and nurturing environment. The intention was for these programs to expand agency-wide until they characterized the system of foster care generally. Despite positive indications that the approach worked for many families, initiatives such as these fizzed out in the late 1990s, with the shrinking mandates of agencies and the emphasis on policing functions and generally reactive approaches to child protection. These programs showed promise as examples of a progressive family-service approach to child-in-care systems. In terms of "future directions" the key will be to draw on similar experiences and other progressive approaches, ultimately making a steady, substantial, and coordinated commitment to improving systems of care across Canada. To date, this has not happened; for the most part, strategies and initiatives have not addressed the quality of systems of care. There have been some positive developments in the areas of training (PRIDE) and putting children's needs first (LAC), but nothing that addresses the fundamental reasons for the crisis in foster care.

Governments and child welfare agencies bear a special responsibility to fulfill their obligations under the progressive standards and ideals of the Convention. They need to participate in and contribute to the larger project of getting the community to "accept youngsters in distress as collectively theirs, full citizens with equal rights."[65]

Notes

1 B. MacLaurin and N. Bala, "Children in Care," in N. Bala, M. Kim Zapf, et al., eds., *Canadian Child Welfare Law: Children, Families, and the State* (Toronto: Thomson, 2004), pp. 114–15; B. MacLaurin, N. Trocmé, and B. Fallon, "Characteristics of Investigated Children and Families Referred for Out-of-Home Placement," in K. Kufeldt and B. McKenzie, eds., *Child Welfare: Connecting Research, Policy, and Practice* (Waterloo: Wilfrid Laurier University Press, 2003), pp. 27–40.
2 MacLaurin and Bala, "Children in Care," p. 114.
3 See Social Development Canada, *Child and Family Services Statistical Report 1998–1999 to 2000–2001* (Ottawa: Government of Canada).
4 L. Fox-Harding, *Perspectives in Child Care Policy*, 2nd ed. (London: Longman Publishers, 1997), p. 73.
5 Bala, "Reforming Ontario's Child and Family Services Act: Is the Pendulum Swinging Back Too Far?" *Canadian Family Law Quarterly* 17: 121–73.
6 K. Covell and R.B. Howe, *The Challenge of Children's Rights for Canada* (Waterloo: Wilfrid Laurier University Press, 2001), pp. 78–91; Howe, "Implementing Children's Rights in a Federal State: The Case of Canada's Child Protection System," *International Journal of Children's Rights* 9: 361–82; Bala, "Reforming Ontario's Child and Family Services Act"; MacLaurin and Bala, "Children in Care."
7 T.J. Gove, *Report of the Gove Inquiry into Child Protection in British Columbia: Volume I, Matthew's Story* (Victoria: B.C. Community and Social Services, 1995); Hatton Report, *Protecting Vulnerable Children* (Toronto: Ministry of Community and Social Services, 1997).
8 Human Resources Development Canada, Social Development Programs Division, Table 421: "Number of Children in Care under Cost-Sharing Arrangements for Child Welfare, by Province and for Canada, as of March 31, 1979 to

1996" (Ottawa: Government of Canada); Social Development Canada, Strategic Policy Branch, Table 437: "Number of Children in Care of Provincial and Territorial Child Welfare Authorities, by Province and for Canada, as of March 31, 1997 to 2003" (Ottawa: Government of Canada); Ontario Association of Children's Aid Societies, *CAS Facts: April 1, 2004–March 31, 2005* (Toronto: OACAS); Children's Services, "Children in Care," Table 3.a: "Children in Care by Legal Authority in March 2001, March 2002, March 2003, March 2004, and March 2005" (Edmonton: Government of Alberta); Ministry of Children and Family Development, Annual Service Plan Reports 2004–05 (Victoria: MCFD).

9   Bala, "Reforming Ontario's Child and Family Services Act."

10   A.W. Leschield, P.C. Whitehead, D. Hurtley, and D. Chiodo, *Protecting Children Is Everybody's Business: Investigating the Increasing Demand for Services at the Children's Aid Society of London and Middlesex* (London and Middlesex: United Way, 2003).

11   N. Trocmé et al., "What Is Driving Increasing Child Welfare Caseloads in Ontario? Analysis of the 1993 and 1998 Ontario Incidence Studies," *Child Welfare* 84, no. 3 (2005): 341–62.

12   N. Trocmé et al., *Canadian Incidence Study of Reported Child Abuse and Neglect, Final Report* (Ottawa: Ministry of Public Works and Government Services Canada, 2001), p. xv.

13   P. Steinhauer, *The Least Detrimental Alternative: A Systematic Guide to Case Planning and Decision Making for Children in Care* (Toronto: University of Toronto Press, 1991), pp. 185–200.

14   One example of the extent of this problem was seen in Winnipeg in November 2006. A number of news media reported that the 127 children in care living in hotel rooms were being evacuated to accommodate football fans coming to the Grey Cup.

15   News Brief: "Ontario: Foster Home Shortage Puts Children in Motel Rooms," *National Post,* September 28, 2002, A11; S. Edmonds, "Spend to Get Foster Kids Out of Hotels, Manitoba MLA Says," *Edmonton Journal,* January 6, 1998, A8; T. Barrett, "Home Shortage Puts Kids in Hotels," *Edmonton Journal,* June 13, 1998, A6; Nova Scotia Legislature, Standing Committee on Community Services, April 15, 2004.

16   K. Kufeldt, M. Simard, and J. Vachon, *Looking After Children in Canada: Final Report* (Ottawa: Human Resources Development Canada, 2000).

17   National Youth in Care Network, *Current Themes Facing Youth in State Care,* Backgrounder Series #1.

18   M. Baker, *Families: Changing Trends in Canada,* 4th ed. (Toronto: McGraw-Hill Ryerson, 2001); N. Mandell and A. Duffy, *Canadian Families: Diversity, Conflict, and Change,* 3rd ed. (Toronto: Thomson, 2005).

19   T. Waldock, "The Professionalization of Foster Care," *Social Worker* 64, no. 3 (1996): 118–27; B. Galaway, "Clarifying the Role of Foster Parents," *Children Today* (1972): 32–33; M. Tinney, "Role Perceptions in Foster Parent Associations in British Columbia," *Child Welfare* 64, no. 1 (1985): 73–79; J. Brown and P. Calder, "Concept Mapping the Needs of Foster Parents," *Child Welfare* 79, no. 6 (2000): 729–46.

20   K. Kufeldt, "Critical Issues in Child Welfare—Section 1: Underrepresented Voices in Child Welfare," in K. Kufeldt and B. McKenzie, eds., *Child Welfare:*

Connecting Research, Policy, and Practice (Waterloo: Wilfrid Laurier University Press, 2003), p. 397.

21 Steinhauer, *The Least Detrimental Alternative*, p. 185.

22 OACAS, *The Future of Foster Care: Towards a Redesign in 89* (Toronto, 1989); Waldock, "The Professionalization of Foster Care"; Steinhauer, *The Least Detrimental Alternative*, p. 187.

23 S. Roxburg, *What Do Young People Think of This?* (National Youth in Care Network, 2004), pp. 1–5.

24 Steinhauer, *The Least Detrimental Alternative*, pp. 283–299; C. Appathurai, G. Lowery, and T. Sullivan, "An Expanded Role for Foster Care?" *Canada's Mental Health* (1986): 6–12.

25 Social Development Canada, *Foster Care Report—September 2000* (Ottawa: Government of Canada).

26 K. Kufeldt et al., "The Looking After Children Project: Educational Outcomes," in Kufeldt and McKenzie, eds., *Child Welfare: Connecting Research, Policy, and Practice* (Waterloo: Wilfrid Laurier University Press, 2003), pp. 177–189; R.J. Flynn and C. Biro, "Comparing Developmental Outcomes for Children in Care with Those for Other Children in Canada," *Children in Society* 12 (1998): 228–33.

27 T. Reilly, "Transition from Care: Status and Outcomes of Youth Who Age out of Foster Care," *Child Welfare* 82, no. 6 (2003): 727–46.

28 S.A. Kapp, "Pathways to Prison: Life Histories of Former Clients of the Child Welfare and Juvenile Justice Systems," *Journal of Sociology and Social Welfare* 27, no. 3 (2000): 63–74.

29 J. Orme and C. Beuhler, "Foster Family Characteristics and Behavioral and Emotional Problems of Foster Children," *Family Relations* 50, no. 1 (2001): 3–15.

30 Social Development Canada, *Foster Care Report*.

31 Kathleen Kufeldt et al., "A Grass Roots Approach to Influencing Child Welfare Policy," *Child and Family Social Work* 10: 305–14; Child Welfare League of Canada, *Looking After Children: Canadian Update* 1, no. 1 (2002): 1–6.

32 Kufeldt, Simard, and Vachon, *Looking After Children in Canada*.

33 Kufeldt et al., "The Looking After Children Project."

34 Kufeldt, "A Grass Roots Approach."

35 Steinhauer, *The Least Detrimental Alternative*, p. 283; R.B. McKenzie, *Rethinking Orphanages for the 21st Century* (Thousand Oaks: Sage Publications, 1999).

36 Catholic Children's Aid Society, "Children in Care by Placement Type," *Monthly and Accumulative Report on Services*, October 1998–2000; *Management Information System Report on Services*, October 2001–3.

37 T. Waldock, "The Central Region Foster Care Project: Initial Observations," *OACAS Journal* 43, no. 1 (1999): 32–36.

38 N. Trocmé, T. Knott, and D. Knoke, *An Overview of Differential Response Models* (Toronto: Centre of Excellence for Child Welfare, 2003).

39 Trocmé et al., "What Is Driving Increasing Child Welfare Caseloads in Ontario?"

40 Covell and Howe, *The Challenge*, p. 84.

41 P. Thomas, "Charter Implications for Proactive Child Welfare Services," in K. Kufeldt and B. McKenzie, eds., *Child Welfare: Connecting Research, Policy, and Practice* (Waterloo: Wilfrid Laurier University Press, 2003), pp. 363–65.

42 N. Pron, "Jeffrey Became 'Invisible,'" *Toronto Star*, January 18, 2006, A20; idem, "Boy, 5, Beaten, Sister Testifies," *Toronto Star*, November 3, 2005, B1.

43 L. Kines and J. Rud, "Campbell Blasted on Child Welfare," *Times Colonist*, March 9, 2005, A3; R. Matas, "James Demands Children's Ministry Shakeup," *Globe and Mail*, February 20, 2006, S1.

44 J. Mahoney, "Child-Killer Was Known Criminal, Agency Reveals," *Globe and Mail*, February 15, 2006, S1; Kines, "What Happened during and after Sherry Charlie's 23 Months of Life," *Times Colonist*, February 5, 2006, D7.

45 M. Connolly, *Kinship Care: A Selected Literature Review* (New Zealand: Department of Child, Youth, and Family, 2003), p. 5.

46 Connolly, *Kinship Care*, p. 4.

47 Provincial Directors of Service, *Draft Conceptual Model*, May 11, 2004.

48 S. Gennaro, R. York, and P. Dunphy, "Vulnerable Infants: Kinship Care and Health," *Pediatric Nursing* 24, no. 2 (1998): 119–24; S. Beeman and L. Boisen, "Child Welfare Professionals' Attitudes toward Kinship Foster Care," *Child Welfare* 78, no. 3 (1999): 315–37; R.L. Hegar and M. Scannapieco, *Kinship Foster Care: Policy, Practice, and Research* (New York: Oxford University Press, 1999); M. Connolly, *Kinship Care: A Selected Literature Review*, pp. 3–31.

49 Hegar and Scannapieco, *Kinship Foster Care*.

50 R. Chipman, S.J. Wells, and M.A. Johnson, "The Meaning of Quality in Kinship Foster Care: Caregiver, Child, and Worker Perspectives," *Families in Society* 83, nos. 5 and 6 (2002): 508–20.

51 B. Wharf, "Cases or Citizens: Viewing Child Welfare through a Different Lens," *Canadian Social Work* 2, no. 2 (2000): 132–36.

52 National Youth in Care Network, *Current Themes Facing Youth in State Care*, Backgrounder Series #3 (2005b).

53 Wharf, "Building a Case for Community Approaches to Child Welfare," in Wharf, ed., *Community Work Approaches to Child Welfare* (Peterborough: Broadview Press, 2002), pp. 181–86.

54 See BBC News, "Cared-for Pupils' Results 'Shock,'" February 24, 2006.

55 M. Kwong, "School Stats 'Discrimination': Parents, Group Says Suspension Rates Prove Kids with Special Needs Are Treated Unfairly," *Toronto Star*, January 18, 2006, A4; V. Macandrew, "Suspending Special Needs Students Is Passing the Buck," *Hamilton Spectator*, January 23, 2006, A16.

56 R.B. Howe and K. Covell, *Empowering Children: Children's Rights Education as a Pathway to Citizenship* (Toronto: University of Toronto Press, 2005).

57 MacLaurin and Bala, "Children in Care," pp. 132–33.

58 S. Roxburg, *What Do Young People Think of This?*

59 Howe, "Implementing Children's Rights in a Federal State," p. 370.

60 R. Brennan, "Province Must Do More to Protect Kids," *Toronto Star*, February 15, 2006, A5.

61 L. Leyne, "Independent Voices Are Finally Heard," *Times Colonist*, September 22, 2005, A10; J. Rud, "Tragic Case Spurs Call for B.C. Child Advocate," *Times Colonist*, October 2, 2005, A1.

62 S. Grover, "Advocating for Children's Rights as an Aspect of Professionalism: The Role of Frontline Workers and Children's Rights Commissions," *Child and Youth Care Forum* 33, no. 6 (2004): 405–23.

63 J. Dalrymple, "Constructions of Child and Youth Advocacy: Emerging Issues in Advocacy Practice," *Children and Society* 19 (2005): 3–15; J. Boylan and P. Ing, "Seen but Not Heard—Young People's Experience of Advocacy," *International Journal of Social Welfare* 14 (2005): 2–12.
64 Kufeldt, "Inclusive Foster Care: Implementation of the Model," in B. McKenzie, ed., *Current Perspectives on Foster Family Care for Children and Youth* (Toronto: Wall and Emerson, 1994), pp. 84–100.
65 Ibid., p. 44.

Bibliography

Appathurai, C., G. Lowery, and T. Sullivan. 1986. "An Expanded Role for Foster Care?" *Canada's Mental Health* 1986: 6–12.
Baker, M. 2001. *Families: Changing Trends in Canada*, 4th ed. Toronto: McGraw-Hill Ryerson.
Bala, N. 1999. "Reforming Ontario's Child and Family Services Act: Is the Pendulum Swinging Back Too Far?" *Canadian Family Law Quarterly* 17: 121–73.
Barrett, T. 1998. "Home Shortage Puts Kids in Hotels," *Edmonton Journal*, June 13, A6.
BBC News. 2006. "Cared-For Pupils' Results "Shock." February 24.
Beeman, S., and L. Boisen. 1999. "Child Welfare Professionals' Attitudes toward Kinship Foster Care." *Child Welfare* 78, no. 3: 315–37.
Boylan, J., and P. Ing. 2005. "Seen but Not Heard—Young People's Experience of Advocacy." *International Journal of Social Welfare* 14: 2–12.
Brennan, R. 2006. "Province Must Do More to Protect Kids." *Toronto Star*, February 15.
Brown, J., and P. Calder. 2000. "Concept Mapping the Needs of Foster Parents." *Child Welfare* 79, no. 6: 729–46.
Catholic Children's Aid Society. 1998–2003. "Children in Care by Placement Type." *Monthly and Accumulative Report on Services*, October 1998–2000 and *Management Information System Report on Services*, October 2001–2003. Toronto: CCAS.
Child Welfare League of Canada. 2002. *Looking After Children: Canadian Update* 1, no. 1: 1–6.
Children's Services. 2005. "Children in Care," Table 3.a: "Children in Care by Legal Authority in March 2001, March 2002, March 2003, March 2004, and March 2005." Edmonton: Government of Alberta.
Chipman, R., S.J. Wells, and M.A. Johnson. 2002. "The Meaning of Quality in Kinship Foster Care: Caregiver, Child, and Worker Perspectives." *Families in Society* 83, nos. 5 and 6: 508–20.
Connolly, M. 2003. *Kinship Care: A Selected Literature Review*. New Zealand: Department of Child, Youth and Family.
Covell, K., and R.B. Howe. 2001. *The Challenge of Children's Rights for Canada*. Waterloo: Wilfrid Laurier University Press.

Dalrymple, J. 2005. "Constructions of Child and Youth Advocacy: Emerging Issues in Advocacy Practice." *Children and Society* 19: 3–15.

Edmonds, S. 1998. "Spend to Get Foster Kids Out of Hotels, Manitoba MLA Says." *Edmonton Journal*, January 6, A8.

Flynn, R.J., and C. Biro. 1998. "Comparing Developmental Outcomes for Children in Care with Those for Other Children in Canada." *Children in Society* 12: 228–33.

Fox-Harding, L. 1997. *Perspectives in Child Care Policy*, 2nd ed. London: Longman Publishers.

Galaway, B. 1972. "Clarifying the Role of Foster Parents." *Children Today* (1972): 32–33.

Gennaro, S., R. York, and P. Dunphy. 1998. "Vulnerable Infants: Kinship Care and Health." *Pediatric Nursing* 24, no. 2: 119–24.

Gove, T.J. 1995. *Report of the Gove Inquiry into Child Protection in British Columbia: Volume I, Matthew's Story*. Victoria: B.C. Community and Social Services.

Grover, S. 2004. "Advocating for Children's Rights as an Aspect of Professionalism: The Role of Frontline Workers and Children's Rights Commissions." *Child and Youth Care Forum* 33, no. 6: 405–23.

Hatton Report. 1997. *Protecting Vulnerable Children*. Toronto: Ministry of Community and Social Services.

Hegar, R.L., and M. Scannapieco. 1999. *Kinship Foster Care: Policy, Practice, and Research*. New York: Oxford University Press.

Howe, R.B. 2001. "Implementing Children's Rights in a Federal State: The Case of Canada's Child Protection System." *International Journal of Children's Rights* 9: 361–82.

Howe, R.B., and K. Covell. 2005. *Empowering Children: Children's Rights Education as a Pathway to Citizenship*. Toronto: University of Toronto Press.

Human Resources Development Canada, Social Development Programs Division. 1996. Table 421: "Number of Children in Care under Cost-Sharing Arrangements for Child Welfare, by Province and for Canada, as of March 31, 1979 to 1996." Ottawa: Government of Canada.

Kapp, S.A. 2000. "Pathways to Prison: Life Histories of Former Clients of the Child Welfare and Juvenile Justice Systems." *Journal of Sociology and Social Welfare* 27, no. 3: 63–74.

Kines, L. 2006. "What Happened during and after Sherry Charlie's 23 Months of Life." *Times Colonist*, February 5.

Kines, L., and J. Rud. 2005. "Campbell Blasted on Child Welfare." *Times Colonist*, March 9.

Kufeldt, K. 1994. "Inclusive Foster Care: Implementation of the Model." In B. McKenzie, ed., *Current Perspectives on Foster Family Care for Children and Youth*. Toronto: Wall and Emerson.

———. 2003. "Critical Issues in Child Welfare—Section 1: Underrepresented Voices in Child Welfare." In K. Kufeldt and B. McKenzie, eds., *Child Welfare: Connecting Research, Policy, and Practice*. Waterloo: Wilfrid Laurier University Press.

Kufeldt, K., M. Simard, and J. Vachon. 2000. *Looking After Children in Canada: Final Report*. Ottawa: Human Resources Development Canada.

Kufeldt, K., et al. 2003. "The Looking After Children Project: Educational Outcomes." In K. Kufeldt and B. McKenzie, eds., *Child Welfare: Connecting Research, Policy, and Practice*. Waterloo: Wilfrid Laurier University Press.

———. 2005. "A Grass Roots Approach to Influencing Child Welfare Policy." *Child and Family Social Work* 10: 305–14.

Kwong, M. 2006. "School Stats 'Discrimination': Parents' Group Says Suspension Rates Prove Kids with Special Needs Are Treated Unfairly." *Toronto Star,* January 18.

Leong, M. 2002. "Child Charity Faces Suit." *Toronto Star,* June 19.

Leschield, A.W., P.C. Whitehead, D. Hurtley, and D. Chiodo. 2003. Protecting Children Is Everybody's Business: Investigating the Increasing Demand for Services at the Children's Aid Society of London and Middlesex. London and Middlesex: United Way.

Leyne, L. 2005. "Independent Voices Are Finally Heard." *Times Colonist,* September 22.

Macandrew, V. 2006. "Suspending Special Needs Students Is Passing the Buck." *Hamilton Spectator*, January 23.

MacLaurin, B., and N. Bala. 2004. "Children in Care." In N. Bala, M. Kim Zapf, et al., eds., *Canadian Child Welfare Law: Children, Families, and the State*, 2nd ed. Toronto: Thomson.

MacLaurin, B., N. Trocmé, and B. Fallon. 2003. "Characteristics of Investigated Children and Families Referred for Out-of-Home Placement." In K. Kufeldt and B. McKenzie, eds., *Child Welfare: Connecting Research, Policy, and Practice*. Waterloo: Wilfrid Laurier University Press.

Mahoney, J. 2006. "Child-Killer Was Known Criminal, Agency Reveals." *Globe and Mail*, February 15.

Mandell, N., and A. Duffy. 2005. *Canadian Families: Diversity, Conflict, and Change*, 3rd ed. Toronto: Thomson.

Matas, R. 2006. "James Demands Children's Ministry Shakeup." *Globe and Mail*, February 20.

McKenzie, R.B. 1999. *Rethinking Orphanages for the 21st Century*. Thousand Oaks: Sage Publications.

Ministry of Children and Family Development. 2005. Annual Service Plan Reports 2004–05. Victoria: MCFD.

National Youth in Care Network. 2005a. *Current Themes Facing Youth in State Care*. Backgrounder Series #1. www.youthincare.ca.

———. 2005b. *Current Themes Facing Youth in State Care*. Backgrounder Series #3. www.youthincare.ca.

Nova Scotia Legislature. 2004. Standing Committee on Community Services, April 15.

"Ontario: Foster Home Shortage Puts Children in Motel Rooms." *National Post,* September 28, 2002, A11.

Ontario Association of Children's Aid Societies. 1989. *The Future of Foster Care: Towards a Redesign in 89*. Toronto: OACAS.

———. 2005. CAS Facts: April 1, 2004–March 31, 2005. Toronto: OACAS.

Orme, J., and C. Beuhler. 2001. "Foster Family Characteristics and Behavioral and Emotional Problems of Foster Children." *Family Relations* 50, no. 1: 3–15.

Pron, N. . 2005. "Boy, 5, Beaten, Sister Testifies." *Toronto Star*, November 3.

———. 2006. "Jeffrey Became 'Invisible.'" *Toronto Star*, January 18.

Provincial Directors of Service. 2004. *Draft Conceptual Model*. Ontario, May 11.

Reilly, T. 2003. "Transition from Care: Status and Outcomes of Youth Who Age out of Foster Care." *Child Welfare* 82, no. 6: 727–46.

Roxburg, S. 2004. *What Do Young People Think of This?* National Youth in Care Network. www.youthincare.ca

Rud, J. 2005. "Tragic Case Spurs Call for B.C. Child Advocate." *Times Colonist*, October 2.

Savoury, G.R., and K. Kufeldt. "Child Welfare: Protecting Children versus Supporting Families." *Social Worker* 65, no. 3: 146–54.

Social Development Canada. 2000. *Foster Care Report—September 2000*. Ottawa: Government of Canada.

———. 2001. *Child and Family Services Statistical Report 1998–1999 to 2000–2001*. Ottawa: Government of Canada.

Social Development Canada, Strategic Policy Branch. 2003. Table 437: "Number of Children in Care of Provincial and Territorial Child Welfare Authorities, by Province and for Canada, as of March 31, 1997 to 2003." Ottawa: Government of Canada.

Steinhauer, P. 1991. *The Least Detrimental Alternative: A Systematic Guide to Case Planning and Decision Making for Children in Care*. Toronto: University of Toronto Press.

Strong-Boag, V. 2002. "Getting to Now: Children in Distress in Canada's Past." In B. Wharf, ed., *Community Work Approaches to Child Welfare*. Peterborough: Broadview Press.

Thomas, P. 2003. "Charter Implications for Proactive Child Welfare Services." In K. Kufeldt and B. McKenzie, eds., *Child Welfare: Connecting Research, Policy, and Practice*. Waterloo: Wilfrid Laurier University Press.

Tinney, M. 1985. "Role Perceptions in Foster Parent Associations in British Columbia." *Child Welfare* 64, no. 1: 73–79.

Trocmé, N., et al. 2001. *Canadian Incidence Study of Reported Child Abuse and Neglect, Final Report*. Ottawa: Ministry of Public Works and Government Services Canada.

Trocmé, N., T. Knott, and D. Knoke. 2003. *An Overview of Differential Response Models*. Toronto: Centre of Excellence for Child Welfare.

Trocmé, N., et al. 2005. "What Is Driving Increasing Child Welfare Caseloads in Ontario? Analysis of the 1993 and 1998 Ontario Incidence Studies." *Child Welfare* 84, no. 3: 341–62.

Waldock, T. 1996. "The Professionalization of Foster Care." *Social Worker* 64, no. 3: 118–27.

———. 1999. "The Central Region Foster Care Project: Initial Observations." *OACAS Journal* 43, no. 1: 32–36.

Wharf, B. 2000. "Cases or Citizens? Viewing Child Welfare through a Different Lens." *Canadian Social Work* 2, no. 2: 132–39.

———. 2002. "Building a Case for Community Approaches to Child Welfare." In B. Wharf, ed., *Community Work Approaches to Child Welfare*. Peterborough: Broadview Press.

Homeless Children and Street-Involved Children in Canada

Sonja Grover

Introduction

This chapter concerns street-involved children, here defined as children who spend all or most of their time living and/or working on the street. Other groups of homeless children are also considered. The chapter addresses the question of the extent to which Canada has met its obligations to this population of marginalized children as set out in the Convention on the Rights of the Child (CRC).[1] That is, it considers the extent to which Canada has provided adequate services to these children and worked toward their social reintegration. Some of these children are homeless, and/or may have no family alive or have been abandoned; others have family and homes. In the latter case, for whatever reason, these children are unable and/or unwilling to live full-time at home and to be under regular adequate protection and supervision by parents, legal guardians, or other responsible adults. In many instances, the family can provide only very substandard housing owing to extreme poverty, or it offers living conditions that threaten the child's health and safety owing to family violence and other such factors. Children with these backgrounds may live in very unstable circumstances, moving between friends' homes, or from shelter to shelter, or visiting the family home very sporadically, or living full-time on the street. Some children live with their families on the street after becoming homeless and displaced through unemployment or other devastating circumstances. Some only work on the street and sleep at home with family at night or visit their families regularly. Clearly, the

Sonja Grover, Faculty of Education, Lakehead University

situations of children lumped together under the colloquial term "street children" are quite varied.

There is a lack of precision in the definition of the term street-involved child. This inconsistency brings into question the reliability of current statistics regarding the numbers of such children globally. The numbers at hand are likely to be underestimates, given the fact that most countries do not include street people in their censuses if these are at all. Since the presence of [street children is one indicator of societal breakdown and often also of government ineptitude, government statistics are likely to downplay the issue to the extent possible] Recent UN data place the number of street children at over 150 million globally—and rising. Berizina points out that that number translates into one in every sixty people on the planet being a child living on the street most or all of the time.[2] The lack of national data regarding the numbers of street-involved children in Canada and the reasons for the paucity of information on this phenomenon are discussed later in this chapter. A snapshot of the numbers of homeless, including street- involved children, in the Greater Vancouver area is presented in that section as a case example since the study was particularly well done. That case example provides some insight into the possible scope of the problem in Canada's major urban areas, though the problem is by no means confined to urban centres.

Statistics globally indicate that the lifespan of street children is considerably reduced. Canadian studies, for example, suggest increased premature mortality for street youth in Canada.[3] From the reports of UNICEF and other international organizations, it is clear that the phenomenon of homeless street children who have little if any contact with family is becoming an increasing problem also in developed nations, and Canada is no exception.

The Committee on the Rights of the Child has expressed concern over the growing phenomenon of homeless street children.[4] The Committee notes that street-involved children are at [particularly high risk of being the victims of violence, sexual exploitation, self-destructive behaviour, HIV/AIDS, and mental disorders] This is so even though street-involved children have the right under the CRC—as does any other group of children—to access protection, education, health, counselling, and other such services.[5] For instance, article 4 of the CRC guarantees the child's economic, social, and cultural rights; article 6 sets out the child's right to life and good development; and article 19 requires the state to protect the child from all mental and physical violence, abuse, and maltreatment generally. In concert with the aforementioned provisions, the street-involved child has the right under the CRC to the highest standard of available health care the state can provide (article 24), as well as the right to education (article 28 and 29). Furthermore, article 20 of the CRC requires the state to offer the child special assistance and protection where the child has been deprived of his or her family either temporarily or permanently. Other articles of the CRC protect children against those factors that may drive them onto the street (e.g., familial abuse) as well as against human rights violations and abuses that may occur or reoccur on the street. Article 32 protects children against hazardous forms of labour such as child prostitution. Article 33 protects them against exposure to illicit drugs and drug cartels, while article 35 protects them against being trafficked for sexual and other purposes. In short, the street-involved child has the right to all supports necessary to achieve psychological recovery and social reintegration. In fact, article 39 of the CRC specifically refers to the right of the neglected, abused, or exploited child to measures that will foster his or her societal reintegration. The same article further stipulates that reintegration efforts must occur while the child is placed in an environment that respects his or her human rights and dignity. In many instances, reintegration of the street-involved child will initially require outreach clinics and services (i.e., services that are brought to the child). In certain cases, recovery of the street child may require something other than family reunification where that measure would not be in the child's best interest or would not be feasible for any number of reasons.[6]

Street-involved children are often regarded as a threat to the social order, given the lack of adult supervision. Often these children are incorrectly perceived as *inherently* prone to criminality, social deviance, and psychopathology. In fact, street-involved children are a diverse group with varying temperaments, personalities, inclinations, talents, and backgrounds. What they have in common is that they must learn to survive spending most or all of their time on the street. However, the character, personality, and aspirations of these children cannot be inferred simply based on their membership in the social group known as "street children." It has been pointed out that when the word "street" is associated with the word "children," aspects of the child's situation are inappropriately merged with the child being discussed[7] (i.e., while the street is a dangerous and brutal place, any particular street child may not share those characteristics).

Clearly, the provisions of the CRC are responsive to the needs and rights of the street-involved child in a broad range of domains. The extent to which Canada is meeting these obligations under the CRC is addressed next.

The Child's Economic Rights under International Human Rights Law

The right to housing and to a decent standard of living is regarded as an economic right. The CRC[8] recognizes the right of the child to the basic necessities of life and to a decent standard of living. For instance, the right to a habitable shelter is implicitly covered under article 27(1). That article sets out the state's obligation to recognize "the right of every child to a standard of living adequate for the child's physical, mental, spiritual, moral and social development."[9] Normally, the child's parents or legal guardians are responsible for providing such a basic necessity as adequate housing. Where they are unable or unwilling to provide it, the obligation shifts to the state. The CRC stipulates in article 27(3)[10] that the state must help parents provide for the child's basic needs, including housing, where such assistance is necessary. However, article 27(3) permits the state to decide what is "within its means" in terms of extending assistance to the parents in providing for their child. Hence, the child is dependent on the state exercising its discretion in such a way as to consider homeless street children a priority. Unfortunately, these groups of highly vulnerable children have so far not been a priority in Canada or in most countries. At the same time, there have been in Canada some important provincial and federal attempts to reduce homelessness and poverty since the early 1990s. Ken Battle details such initiatives against poverty in chapter 2 of this book. However, the gaps in providing for homeless and poor children are still considerable. Covell and Howe note, for instance, that child poverty actually worsened in Canada after this country signed the CRC in 1991. These authors also point out that child poverty in Canada has been worse than in many other industrialized countries such as Sweden, Japan, and Italy.[11] In Canada from the late 1990's to early 2000s, 15 percent of children were living in families whose income was less than half the median disposable income for all people in the country. This compared to a poverty rate in Sweden, Finland, and Norway of less than 5 percent, using the same measure over the identical time period.[12]

The situation for homeless children is exacerbated by the fact that across Canada, shelters designated only for youth, or for families with young children, are rare commodities. Moreover, they are often largely funded by "soft monies" (i.e., unstable funding sources such as private donations), and they are designed as very short-term emergency shelters. These cannot provide the stable, supportive living arrangements that are necessary to facilitate the efforts of youth or families with young children to address such issues as may be contributing to their homelessness. Among these issues are the need to pursue further education or training.

Nor are emergency shelters conducive to the health and well-being of street-involved children or younger children and their families. Underlying this problem is a well-documented[shortage of low-income housing for poor families in Canada.][3]

Children under sixteen who are living with families in very substandard living situations that are hazardous to health and safety can be removed from that situation on a temporary or longer-term basis at the discretion of whichever child welfare agency has legal jurisdiction. This has been the outcome especially for Aboriginal children. As noted by Bennett (chapter 11) and Waldock (chapter 12), Aboriginal children are over-represented among children in care in Canada, and unsafe housing appears to be a factor in a significant proportion of these cases.[14] In practice, many children are not removed unless there are additional circumstances that place the child at risk. The concern is that the agency involved not be viewed as punishing the poor for their poverty by placing the integrity of the family at risk through a child apprehension. Additional factors working against removal are the large numbers of families in this situation and the shortage of alternative placements. In any case, youth sixteen years and over but under eighteen generally are not eligible for such protective services in most provinces. The exceptions are situations where there are voluntary agreements between the child and the child welfare agency or where the youth has been in care prior to his or her sixteenth birthday. The end result is that many children in Canada continue to live in home situations that are hazardous to their development and that increasing numbers are turning to the streets.

Contributing to Canada's homeless problem is the [fact that access to a basic, decent standard of living—which would include adequate housing—is not considered a constitutional right in Canada] This point was made painfully clear by the Supreme Court of Canada in the *Gosselin* case, which concerned a woman on welfare living on a *below*-subsistence level of social assistance in Quebec in the 1980s. In *Gosselin*, the majority of the Court rejected the notion that the Section 7 Charter right to security of the person implies the right to a basic acceptable standard of living or that the state has a positive obligation to provide minimally acceptable living conditions.[15] It is essential that cases be brought to the Supreme Court of Canada that can establish a decent standard of living, including adequate housing, as a constitutional right. Only then is Canada likely to vigorously enforce article 27 of the CRC, which guarantees children a standard of living conducive to their healthy and good development.[16] It may take several seminal and well-crafted cases presented to the Court before progress is made in this area. As Canada does not regard adequate housing and a decent standard of living as a constitutional right, it is perhaps not surprising that Canada does not have an official definition of poverty. Rather, the definition of poverty varies from agency to agency.[17] Next let us consider the barriers to Canada meeting its international human rights obligations with regard to providing acceptable housing and a decent standard of living for every child in the country.

The Homeless as Invisible

While the exact numbers of homeless children in Canada are not known, statistics from major Canadian urban areas suggest that children and youth make up a sizable portion of this country's homeless population.[18] It is especially difficult to count and track street-involved children, as this group tends to be highly mobile. For instance, in one study of street-involved youth, it was found that two-thirds of this group in Vancouver and one-third in Victoria had come from other provinces.[19] It has often been noted that there has been no systematic attempt to count the number of homeless in Canada, including the number of homeless children. The federal government notes in its Initiative on Homelessness reports that no reliable method for counting the number of homeless in Canada has yet been developed. Indeed, the UN Committee on the Rights of the Child has repeatedly criticized Canada for its lack of national, systematic data specifically on vulnerable child groups.[20] Hence, the numbers of homeless children in Canada that are reported are likely to be underestimates. Complicating the matter is the fact that the definition of homelessness may vary from study to study. Whatever the difficulties, there is no justification for the absence of a working definition of homelessness in Canada. Furthermore, any such definition ought to include children who live in substandard housing as well as those on the street who have no viable long-term alternative. National data are required, then, on the numbers of homeless children in Canada, and the data should be broken down to reveal the various subcategories of homeless children (e.g., street-involved children, children living in shelters, children living in substandard housing or in cars or in other unsafe situations). The absence of accurate statistics on the number of homeless in Canada, including children, is not consistent with the federal and provincial governments' stated objective to be accountable to the public for its handling of the major social issue of homelessness. Moreover, the lack of national data on the numbers of homeless street-involved children in Canada reveals an inadequate level of commitment to meeting this group's protection needs and to ensuring their rights entitlements under the CRC and the Canadian Charter.[21]

Since there are no accurate national statistics on the numbers of street-involved children and the homeless in Canada, the most reliable statistics at present are the ones that provide a snapshot at a certain point in time of particular urban areas. The Social Planning Council of Vancouver completed one such study in 2005.[22] The council examined the numbers of persons, including children, who had no place to stay beyond thirty days as well as those who were actually on the street. The study measured homelessness during one twenty-four-hour period on March 15, 2005. That study corroborated the findings in other centres across Canada that the numbers of homeless adults and accompanied and unaccompanied homeless children in Canada are steadily increasing. As in other locales, Aboriginal persons (both children and adults) were found to be overrepresented among the homeless in the region. The numbers and percentages of Aboriginal homeless were highest among the street homeless as opposed to the sheltered homeless. The numbers of homeless in the region had doubled since 2002. The numbers of street homeless (as opposed to persons living in shelters) had grown by 235 percent since the last count in 2002. Forty families with children were enumerated on homeless count day, with most staying in shelters but some on the street. Forty-seven percent of those counted had been homeless for more than one year. As a measure of the desperate situation that faces these individuals, consider that *of those homeless enumerated*, 169 adults and 6 children had been turned away from shelters on count night compared to 111 in 2002, presumably due to lack of space in most instances. Almost 45 percent of the street homeless interviewed reported they were reluctant to stay in shelters owing to safety concerns, the lack of hygiene in the shelters, and other concerns. The numbers of youth under twenty-five comprised 15 percent of the total count during the snapshot period. Homeless youth suffered the highest rates of substance abuse compared to all the other groups of homeless counted, although health problems were very common among the entire population of homeless. The street homeless were found, in addition, to more often report more than one health condition, and they were in worse physical and mental condition generally than the sheltered homeless.

Despite certain major federal government initiatives such as the National Homeless Initiative, in Canada there is still a severe lack of affordable housing for low-income families and children. Until 1950, Canadians spent no more than 20 percent of their income on housing. Today, many low-income people spend more than half of their income on rent;[23] in these circumstances, they simply cannot afford the rest of the basic necessities. For instance, the Canadian Council on Social Development reported in 2000 that more than 40 percent of the food bank users in Canada at that time were under eighteen.[24] Single-female-headed families are strongly overrepresented among the poorest families in Canada, and this is especially so for such women who have children under seven. Furthermore, most preteens who are homeless are part of single-parent female-headed households.[25] There is in Canada inadequate emergency shelter, especially longer-term transitional housing. Transitional housing is essential as it allows people, including youth, to have a more stable shelter situation while they re-establish themselves. Such transitional housing is part of a longer-term solution to homelessness. Clearly, this lack of affordable low-income housing in Canada is contrary to various articles of the CRC that guarantee children a standard of living conducive to their long-term well-being (e.g., article 27).[26] The lack of safe and easily accessible emergency and transitional longer-term shelter services is also contrary to those articles of the CRC which refer to children's protection needs (e.g., article 6).[27] In addition, this lack of adequate service to children, especially those living on the street, is counter to the article 19 guarantee.[28] This latter article requires the state to assist in the social reintegration of children who have been abused and exploited, as so many street-involved children have been (before and/or after arriving on the street) or are destined to be the longer they remain homeless.

The situation is acute enough in Canada that homelessness and poverty among children and youth is a reality of which more fortunate young people are now keenly aware. A study by Health Canada in 2000 involving online consultations with children and youth (conducted in conjunction with the UN Special Session on Children)[29] revealed that only 6 percent of child respondents (ages 5 to 8), 13 percent of preteens (ages 9 to 12), and 7 percent of adolescents (ages 13 to 18) reported that poverty is not a problem or is rarely a problem for some young people in Canada. Most children (82 percent), pre-teens (87 percent), and teens (84 percent) in the study also agreed that it is important for countries globally to meet the basic needs of children and youth. Among the suggestions these young people made for addressing the poverty of young people in Canada: an increase in financial expenditure in this area; additional affordable housing; and an increase in the numbers of shelters and food banks. The latter are not unlike suggestions that have been advanced by experts in the field. Cuts in programs providing social support, new onerous regulations regarding access to "employment insurance," inadequate education and training supports for those who have dropped out of school, and job shortages, as well as the shortage of affordable housing, are but a few of the factors that have helped perpetuate homelessness in Canada. We turn next to a more detailed consideration of the plight of children colloquially referred to as "street children" and more recently in the literature as "street-involved" children.

Street-Involved Children

Street-involved children, especially those on the street separated from parents or legal guardians, are an especially vulnerable group. Flying against its Convention obligations to these children, Canada has launched few, if any, national initiatives directly targeting street youth in Canada.[30] Pare has noted that children living mostly on the street have not been identified under international human rights law as a vulnerable group in and of themselves.[31] Indeed, [street-involved children are not mentioned at all in any international human rights convention] although they have been discussed in documents prepared by the UN and various NGOs.[32] Hence, to date, few legal cases have been brought in defence of these children, and they as a group have generally been unable to assert their human rights effectively. It is important to understand that [a good proportion of children on the street are members of designated groups that do have protection under international human rights law.] These include, for instance, trafficked children (covered under articles 32 and 34 of the CRC)[33] and internally displaced and refugee children (covered under article 22 of the CRC).[34] Many are members of persecuted ethnic, religious, language, and other minority groups and thus fall under the protections afforded by article 2 of the CRC, which guarantees every child equal access to the human rights embodied in the CRC.[35] In order to meet its obligations to street-involved and other homeless children and families as well as to poor families in general, Canada will need to provide much more accessible and high-quality support and outreach service to this population.

In Canada as in the United States, the findings suggest that street-involved children are overrepresented among those who come from homes marked by high levels of abuse and neglect. One study has reported that street youth are five times more likely than domiciled youth to report having been the victims of sexual abuse.[36] Ironically, these are then the most likely children to run away from home, and while on the street they once more become the victims of various forms of violence.[37] One of the key predictors of marginalization of youth and the risk of street life is dropping out of school or being unable to continue in school, especially if this is combined with inadequate family supports. Indeed, youth who have not completed their schooling make up the majority of young people on the street in Canada and internationally.[38] Children who have been in care in the past (e.g., in a foster home, a government group home, or the like) are at increased risk of turning to the street if their time in care has not met their basic emotional needs (in some cases, that care has even included abuse and/or neglect). Unfortunately, children in care in Canada [do not have easy access to provincial child advocacy offices, even where such offices exist.]As noted by Campbell and Rose-Krasnor in chapter 9, not all Canadian provinces/territories have such advocates. Provinces with provincial child advocates include British Columbia, Alberta, Saskatchewan, Manitoba, Ontario, Quebec, and Nova Scotia. In Quebec this advocacy function is performed by a division of the provincial human rights commission dedicated to protecting the rights of children and youth as set out in domestic and international laws such as the CRC. In any event, even when a child in care overcomes the fear of retaliation and contacts the provincial child advocate about some significant problem, the advocate is generally restricted to a mediation role. It is crucial then, if Canada is to comply with the protection provisions of the CRC, that all provinces and territories establish regional child advocates. Furthermore, these advocates must be independent of the government child welfare department; best would be if they reported directly to the legislature regarding their monitoring of the well-being of children in care. This currently is not the case in every Canadian province or territory (e.g., British Columbia recently eliminated the independent aspect of the children's advocacy office).

[An especially vulnerable period with respect to street involvement occurs when the child in care is no longer considered a ward of the government.] In provinces such as Ontario, this moment typically arises just when the child is of legal school-leaving age. In other words, Ontario offers child protective services only to age sixteen, as do certain other provinces (although some provinces, such as Prince Edward Island and Quebec, offer child protective services up to age eighteen). Youth at age sixteen who have been in government care for long periods thus are often left to their own devices with little support when transitioning out of care in provinces that provide <u>protective service only</u> until the age of sixteen. This, even though (using Ontario as an example) the provincial child protection legislation lists the child's best interests as a key consideration. In essence, the province in cases like this appears to be redefining childhood to end at age sixteen for the purpose of child protective services rather than age eighteen. This is contrary to the more general definition of "child" in article 1 of the CRC (although, unfortunately, article 1 of the CRC permits states to have variations in the age of majority in various domestic statutes, thus potentially weakening protection for certain age groups under eighteen in various jurisdictions). Thus, in many provinces vulnerable children sixteen and over may be at high risk for a life on the streets owing to the inaccessibility of child protective services.[To better protect children from homelessness and street involvement, it is essential that protective services be accessible up to the age of at least eighteen.] This would bring

Canada into better compliance with articles 6 and 20 of the CRC, for instance, which deal with the state's obligation to provide protection to children who are separated from family.[39]

Extending compulsory schooling to the end of high school or age eighteen in every Canadian province and territory would also serve as a protective factor against homelessness and street involvement (compulsory schooling to the end of secondary or age eighteen is already in place in New Brunswick, which is the only province in Canada to extend mandatory schooling beyond age sixteen).[40]

Recognition of the child's best interests as a key consideration has led to its taking priority over the notion of "family preservation at all costs," most notably in British Columbia, Ontario, and New Brunswick. Where family support services are not sufficient to ensure the child's well-being and safety, the child is more likely to be removed from the family home than was previously the case. The removal may be temporary or permanent. However, improvements in and commitments to child protection have been quite uneven across Canadian jurisdictions.[41]

A study for the National Homeless Initiative[42] provides some preliminary insights into the relationship between a history of involvement with the child welfare system and the risk of an individual becoming a homeless street youth. The study included qualitative interviews with youth in four big Canadian cities: Vancouver, Winnipeg, Toronto, and Montreal. In each city, ten youth were interviewed from the following groups: youth who had been in care and had been homeless; youth who had been homeless but not in care; and youth who had been in care but had not been homeless. Thus every possible combination of homelessness/lack of homelessness and past care/no past care was addressed in the study. A total of forty youth were interviewed; more than half were under twenty-two. Of these, thirty-six were found to meet all the criteria for the study. Aboriginal youth made up more than half the homeless youth in the sample with a history of having been in care. The data suggested that youth with more positive experiences in care were less likely to become homeless and that such positive experiences may be less frequent for Aboriginal children. More positive experiences in care tended to be associated with placement in foster care (a family-type setting) as opposed to a group home; as well as with having fewer and more stable placements. The findings revealed that it was the age of leaving care rather than any transitional preparation or lack of preparation that was the more powerful predictor as to whether a young person would become a street-involved child. This was the case although transitional preparation was found to be a protective factor. Youth who left care at sixteen or younger were especially vulnerable to homelessness. The younger the age of leaving care, the higher was the risk of becoming homeless and living on the street. A significant supportive relationship with anyone was found to be a protective factor in avoiding a life on the streets. The study also revealed that lack of education and associated low employment skills and not lack of affordable housing were major contributors to these youths' homelessness.

Regarding the issue of homelessness and educational attainment, the Canadian National Youth in Care Network school achievement report indicates that much more needs to be done to provide adequate educational supports for youth in care.[43] These youths too often report that they are not adequately encouraged by social workers or teachers to complete their education. Some also report being stigmatized by school personnel and peers *because* they are in care. The National Youth in Care report makes several suggestions for increasing the chances of better educational achievement among youth in care; these, however, are beyond the scope of this chapter. What is clear is that better educational achievement for youth in care would considerably reduce the risk of homelessness and street life for this vulnerable population once they leave care.

In Canada, charitable NGOs are assuming most of the burden of caring for street-involved children. They do so as best they can, typically with woefully inadequate funds. The federal government's failure to implement adequate recovery programs that are targeted specifically for street-involved children amounts to a violation of its CRC obligations to provide for children's protection. The lack of prevention and recovery programs with regard to child street involvement also infringes the Charter guarantee to ensure the right of children to security of the person.[44] In most Canadian provinces, governments have especially failed children sixteen and over, who are barred from accessing protective services under the provincial child welfare statutes. Yet this age group is at high risk for street involvement when the conditions are right. These older children are being denied protective service even though the government owes them a fiduciary duty.[45] That fiduciary duty is evident in the fact that their status as children and their dependency on the state is recognized in many other ways in other contexts (e.g., under-eighteens have no voting rights, cannot marry without parental consent, and cannot enter into a contract).

Street-Involved Children as Persons with Inherent Human Rights

Street-involved children are deserving of assistance not simply because they are children in need, but also because they are persons and citizens of the larger community, albeit marginalized members.[46] This recognition in Canada of street-involved children as bearers of fundamental human rights is increasing. One example of the trend toward viewing street-involved children as persons with inherent rights, at least to some degree, is reflected in the court rulings dealing with the Alberta Protection of Children Involved in Prostitution Act (PChIP), described by Anne McGillivray in chapter 6.[47] However, these rulings also reveal that street-involved children in Canada have yet to achieve full recognition of their human rights. As we shall discover in examining one of these cases, the child on the street is still largely caught in a legal limbo, viewed neither as entirely a child nor as a full adult. The result has been that for the most part, street-involved children are viewed as being the causal agents in their own misery. Let us turn then to the Alberta cases, which help illustrate these points.

Under the PChIP Act,[48] a "child" is a person under eighteen. In 1999, K.B. and M.J., both seventeen-year-olds, were apprehended pursuant to the act without court order by the Calgary police. These apprehensions were the consequence of the officers' suspicion that the girls were involved in, or at imminent risk of involvement in, child prostitution. The children were transferred to a government-designated safe house for protection and assessment without a court order. There, they were assessed for substance abuse, nutritional status, psychological and physical status, suicide risk, and the like. At the time of writing, children under the act can still be transferred to a safe house for detention and assessment without court order on the grounds of reasonably based concerns among the police or the Director of Child Welfare for the children's safety relating to their involvement or possible involvement in prostitution.[49] Under the new PChIP Act, amended in 2000, these children can be held for up to five days initially, with the possibility of two extensions with court order up to twenty-one days each for a total of forty-seven days. Where there is no court order when the child is initially apprehended, a "show cause" hearing must be held within three days of the child's confinement to establish that there was sufficient cause to believe that the child was involved in, or at imminent risk of being involved in, prostitution (a "child in need of protection" as defined under the act). Where no show cause hearing is held, the child has the right to file a form and challenge his or her detention, thus triggering a hearing on the matter. The child is to be informed of his or her right to representation by counsel at such a hearing and is given information about how to secure such counsel. Thus, there has been some improvement in terms of greater recognition of the right of the child to be heard in such circumstances and to be treated as a person with the legal right to due process, consistent with articles 37 and 40 of the CRC.[50] The process also is consistent with article 12 of the CRC, which requires that the child be heard in any judicial proceeding.[51]

Notwithstanding better recognition of the child's legal rights as a person, it is noteworthy that no "best interests of the child" language appears in the PChIP Act.[52] Rather, the act under the preamble refers to children involved in or at risk of engaging in prostitution as "victims of sexual abuse" and as requiring "protection." The absence of language in the act to the effect that best interests of the child shall be a primary consideration is inconsistent with the requirements under CRC article 3(1).[53] The absence of such language is, however, consistent with the fact that children detained under the protection against child prostitution statute are not automatically assigned child welfare status. The latter may be assigned if the child is detained beyond the maximum initial detention period allowable without such status. Hence, children detained under the PChIP Act do not have access to the provincial child advocate, for instance, since that right is reserved for children in care. It is ironic that one of society's most vulnerable child groups (street-involved children) cannot access free government child advocacy services in Alberta or in most other provinces. The PChIP Act thus does not automatically confer child welfare status on the apprehended street-involved child. This means that under the provincial statute (the PChIP Act), the provincial government considers that it does not have a continuing duty of care to the child once he or she is released from the government-designated safe house. Hence, there is often no post-detention substantive investigation of the child's living situation, nor is there any longer-term monitoring of safety issues affecting the young person. The difficulty is that in Alberta, as in most Canadian provinces, child welfare statutes are not intended to cover the child who is sixteen or older and separated from family. As a result, older street-involved children especially are, for the most part, left to their own devices save for brief government interventions in some instances such as under the PChIP Act. In Alberta, for instance, the older street-involved child is expected to initiate contact with community support programs after leaving the safe house. This again shifts the burden onto the child. Furthermore, among street-involved children, narrow target subgroups such as child prostitutes are the focus of the legislation. The problem to be addressed, however, is that *any* child is on the street in Canada. Outreach services ought to be available and accessible for *every* such child. Clearly, the mandate of the PChIP is too narrow. Furthermore, consider that any child on the street is at potential risk for prostitution or a myriad of other forms of abuse and maltreatment, given the need to survive and the lack of protection. Yet the PChIP targets only those children *already* involved in prostitution or at imminent risk. The act thus targets cases where there is some direct evidence of contact with those elements that have involved or hope to involve the child in prostitution. The PChIP Act is thus largely retrospective in orientation; it calls for intervention only after considerable damage has already been done to the child as a result of the child having been on the street.

The long-term involvement of service agencies with street children and comprehensive free regular outreach services funded by government are vital. In order to provide effective services to these children, it will be necessary to have trained outreach workers who have the skills to deal with the children's fears and mistrust. Services must be provided in a compassionate manner, and the confidentiality of the child must be respected. Furthermore, the services provided must be of high quality and non-discriminatory.[54]

what to do

The cost to society of providing such longer-term quality service to street-involved children will be decidedly less than the consequences of not doing so. It is necessary to understand that street-involved children are often wrongly stereotyped as completely alienated and as generally unwilling to reintegrate into society. In fact, interview studies with these children reveal that the problem is more often one of not having access to the means and the support required for reintegration. In some cases the children have not been treated with respect at shelters or by those attempting half-hearted, short-lived interventions. The children may as a result erroneously conclude that the street is their only viable option. Most such children, however, have the desire to complete school, get a good job, and live a normal life.[55]

Too often, the street-involved child is considered too labour and financially intensive a target population for the government to readily focus upon. The sad fact is that the obvious great need of street-involved children for assistance actually appears to reduce the likelihood of significant government intervention. In the final analysis, not much hope for improvement in their life situation is extended by governments to street-involved children in Canada. It is essential that street-involved children be a Canadian provincial and territorial priority in terms of funding for vulnerable children. This group represents a target population with its own unique needs that must be addressed. This, rather than being subsumed under the category of "poor children," or "children in difficult circumstances," or some other moniker that rarely results in street-involved children receiving the attention and specialized services they require. Meeting the protection and quality-of-life needs of this distinct group of children (covered under the CRC's articles 3, 6, 19, 20, 25, 27, 32–35, and 39), including providing access to good health care and other supports (article 24) and access to education (articles 28 and 29), while respecting their right to participate in decision making (covered under article 12 of the CRC), would allow for compliance with Canada's international obligations under the CRC.[56]

In accord with the CRC, governments must attempt to support families in the raising of their children and effect family reunification for street-involved children where possible (article 18, 19, 25)[57] and where it is in the child's best interest. However, in some instances this will not be possible and the child will have to be supported in other ways. This may need to include supporting the child for independent living with social assistance, and providing social work and psychological support as well as education and job training. These emancipated youth (living independently from parents) will require housing subsidies that guarantee them a safe and habitable living space. In other cases, a child welfare placement may be necessary as referred to in CRC article 20.[58] Access to dedicated child and youth emergency shelters (where the clientele is restricted to those under twenty-one, with special provisions for the protection of children under sixteen) are thus imperative. These will provide the initial shelter and support for many street-involved children. Such emergency shelters for street-involved children must receive stable government funding and provide free access to child-centred social work, health, and psychological services. Transitional longer-term sheltered environments for some older children who are independent from family will also be required to help transition these children from the streets into stable and healthy living situations.

In a real sense, neither home nor street belong to the homeless child in Canada. Street-involved children are not welcome in public spaces, yet they have no decent place of their own to inhabit.[59] They are forced to be constantly on the move within the community and between communities as their integration at even the most marginal level is blocked in a myriad of ways. This strategy only serves to exacerbate the risk of the homeless youth being victimized and of having to rely on illicit activities to survive. The failure to regard street-involved children as members of the larger community with a right to occupy public and semipublic spaces in accordance with normal regulations is a violation of their right under the CRC to be protected from discriminatory treatment (article 2).[60] It also violates the right of children under the CRC to freedom of association (here, the right to mingle with non-street people in a public space) and the right of peaceful assembly (street-involved children often wish to congregate with one another) (article 15).[61] The failure to meet the needs of this group is a function of social exclusion processes that are decidedly undemocratic and that must at last be challenged at every level, from front-line worker to government bureaucrat and in the courts. A critical step toward meeting the needs of all children in Canada would be for Canada to incorporate the CRC into domestic law. This would help ensure equity in the provision of services as well as respect for the fundamental human rights of every child in Canada—including street-involved children, whatever their age.

Notes

1 The United Nations Convention on the Rights of the Child (CRC) was adopted by the UN General Assembly on November 20, 1989. It was signed by Canada on May 28, 1990, and ratified on December 13, 1991, and entered into force on January 12, 1992.

2 E. Berezina, "Street Children" (Youth Advocate Program International), http://www.yapi.org.

3 For a case study on mortality rates among street youth in a large Canadian urban centre, see L. Roy, N. Haley, P. Leclerc, et al., "Canada: Mortality in a Cohort of Street Youth in Montreal," *Journal of the American Medical Association* 292, no. 5 (2004): 569–74.

4 Committee on the Rights of the Child, *Thirty-Third Session: Adolescent Health and Development in the Context of the Convention on the Rights of the Child* (General Comment No. 4, May 19 to June 6, 2003).

5 Ibid. It is evident that the provisions of the CRC are responsive to the needs and rights of street children in a broad range of domains. The question is this: To what extent Canada is meeting its obligations under the CRC?

6 T. Feeney, "In Best or Vested Interest? An Exploration of the Concept and Practice of Family Reunification for Street Children," report prepared for the Consortium for Street Children, 2005. http://www.streetchildren.org.uk.

7 B. Glauser, "Street Children: Deconstructing a Construct," in A. James and A. Prout, eds., *Constructing and Reconstructing Childhood: Contemporary Issues in the Sociological Study of Childhood* (London: Falmer Press, 1990), pp. 138–56; A. Veale, M. Taylor, and C. Linehan, "Psychological Perspectives of 'Abandoned' and 'Abandoning' Street Children," in C. Panter-Brick and M.T. Smith, eds., *Abandoned Children* (Cambridge: Cambridge University Press, 2000), pp. 131–45.

8 CRC, *Thiry-Third Session*.

9 Ibid., article 27.

10 Ibid., article 27.

11 For a detailed discussion of child poverty issues in Canada, see K. Covell and R.B. Howe, *The Challenge of Children's Rights for Canada* (Waterloo: Wilfrid Laurier University Press, 2001).

12 UNICEF, "State of the World's Children" (2005), http://www.unicef.org.

13 Government of Canada, National Homelessness Initiative, "Understanding Homelessness: Reviewing the Numbers" (2003), http://www.homelessness.gc.ca.

14 P. Gough, N. Trocmé, I. Brown, D. Knoke, and C. Blackstock, "Pathways to Overrepresentation of Aboriginal Children in Care" (Centre of Excellence for Child Welfare, 2005), http://www.cecw-cepb.ca.

15 *Gosselin v. Quebec* (Attorney General) 2002 SCC 84. For a discussion of the SCC decision in *Gosselin* see S.C. Grover, "The Equality and Liberty Rights of the Destitute: A Canadian Case Example," *International Journal of Minority and Group Rights* 12, no. 1 (2005): 43–61.

16 CRC, article 27.

17 Canadian Social Development Council, "Canadian Fact Book 2000," http://www.ccsd.ca; S. Leon, "Living on the Edge: Women and Homelessness in Canada," report prepared for the National Anti-Poverty Organization, 2000, http://www.napo-onap.ca.

18 K. Covell, "Canada's Non-Governmental Organizations Report to the United Nations Special Session on Children September 19–21, 2001" (2002), http://www.rightsofchildren.ca.

19 R. Tonkin, "Street Youth Not Just an Urban Issue in B.C.," study for the McCreary Centre Society (2001), http://www.mcs.bc.ca.

20 Government of Canada, "Understanding Homelessness: Reviewing the Numbers," http://www.homelessness.gc.ca. The National Homeless Initiative is a Canadian federal program designed to assist communities in meeting the immediate and longer-term needs of those who are homeless or at high risk of becoming homeless. The CRC's concluding comments on Canada's periodic reports regarding compliance have noted the absence of systematic data collection. See CRC/C/15/Add.215 (34th Session), http://www.unhchr.ch.

21 The Charter of Rights and Freedoms was enacted as Schedule B to the Canada Act 1982 (U.K.) c. 11 and entered into force on April, 17, 1982. http://laws.justice.gc.ca. Note that the CRC and the CRSR have not been incorporated into Canadian domestic law and therefore are not binding on Canadian courts. They are binding on government only as a moral imperative in terms of enforcement, though they are legally binding international agreements.

22 Social Planning and Research Council of B.C., "On Our Streets and In Our Shelters: Results of the 2005 Greater Vancouver Homeless Count" (2005), http://www.gvrd.bc.ca; C. Blackstock, S. Clarke, J. Cullen, et al., *Keeping the Promise: The Convention on the Rights of the Child and the Lived Experience of First Nations Children and Youth* (First Nations Child and Family Caring Society of Canada, 2004).

23 R. Neal, "Voices: Women, Poverty and Homelessness in Canada," report prepared for the National Anti-Poverty Organization (2004), http://www.napo-onap.ca.

24 Canadian Council on Social Development, "Progress Report at a Glance: What Contributes to Child and Youth Well-being?" (2000); idem, "Canadian Fact Book on Poverty 2000." For both, http://www.ccsd.ca.

25 Canadian Feminist Alliance for International Action, "Towards Women's Equality: Canada's Failed Commitment. Women's Poverty and Economic Inequality" (2000), http://www.fafia-afai.org; Covell, "Violence against Children in North America: North American Regional Consultation for the United Nations Secretary-General's Study on Violence against Children" (2005), http://discovery.uccb.ns.ca/children/.

26 CRC, article 27.

27 Ibid., article 6.

28 Ibid., article 19.

29 Health Canada, "Your Voice Matters: Young People Speak Out on Issues Related to the UN Special Session on Children" (2001), http://www.phac-aspc.gc.ca.

30 S.C. Grover, "Why Aren't These Youngsters in School? On Meeting Canada's Charter Obligations to Disadvantaged Adolescents," *International Journal of Children's Rights* 10 (2002): 1–37.

31 M. Pare, "Why Have Street Children Disappeared? The Role of International Human Rights Law in Protecting Vulnerable Groups," *International Journal of Children's Rights* 11 (2003): 1–32.

32 Ibid.

33 CRC, articles 32 and 34.

34 Ibid., article 22.

35 Ibid., article 2.

36 S. Gaetz, "Safe Streets for Whom? Homeless Youth, Social Exclusion, and Criminal Victimization," *Canadian Journal of Criminology and Criminal Justice* 46, no. 4 (2004): 423–56; M. Rotherman-Baus, K.A. Mahler, C. Koopman, and K. Langabeer, "Sexual Abuse History and Associated Multiple Risk Behavior in Adolescent Runaways," *American Journal of Orthopsychiatry* 66 (1996): 390–400; N. Trocmé et al., "Canadian Incidence Study of Reported Child Abuse: Final Report" (2001), http://www.hc-sc.gc.ca. For a discussion of aspects of the Canadian Criminal Code dealing with familial violence (a risk factor for children turning to the street), see Grover, "Negating the Child's Inclusive Right to Security of the Person: A Charter Analysis of the s. 43 Canadian Criminal Code Defense to Corporal Punishment of a Minor," *Murdoch University Electronic Journal of Law* 10, no. 4 (2003), http://www.murdoch.edu.au/elaw/issues/v10n4/grover104.txt. See also idem, "The Impact of Perceived Domestic Public Opinion on Judicial Interpretation: A Commentary on *Canadian Foundation for Children, Youth and the Law v. Canada Attorney General*," *Murdoch University Electronic Journal of Law* 11, no. 1 (2004).

37 Grover, "Why Aren't These Youngsters in School."

38 Ibid.

39 CRC, articles 6 and 20.

40 Grover, "Why Aren't These Youngsters in School?"

41 R.B. Howe, "Implementing Children's Rights in a Federal State: The Case of Canada's Child Protection System," *International Journal of Children's Rights* 9 (2001): 361–82.

42 L. Serge, M. Eberies, M. Goldberg, et al., "Pilot Study: The Child Welfare System and Homelessness among Canadian Youth," prepared for the Government of Canada, National Secretariat on Homelessness, 2002), http://www.cecw-cepb.ca/DocsEng/HomelessnessAndCW.pdf.

43 National Youth in Care Network, "Who Will Teach Me to Learn? Creating Positive School Experiences for Youth in Care" (2001), http://www.youthincare.ca. Note that in certain provinces there has been a recognition of the need to provide longer-term support for youth who have been in care and who are transitioning out of care. Alberta has met this need to some extent for at least a limited number of youth with a history in care. This through a bursary program called "Advancing Futures Bursary Program," which provides financial support for post-secondary education. Information on this initiative is available at http://www.child.gov.ab.ca.

44 Review note 21.

45 "Fiduciary burden" refers to the state's legal and moral responsibility to care for its most vulnerable and dependent members, to act in the best interests of dependent individuals such as children, and to avoid any conflict of interest.
46 Pare, "Why Have Street Children Disappeared?"
47 Protection of Children Involved in Prostitution Act, R.S.A. 2000 (S.A. 1998, Chapter P-19.3), http://www.canlii.org/ab/laws/sta/p-28/20050927/whole.html.
48 Ibid.
49 *Alberta (Director of Child Welfare) v. K.B.* (2000), ABQB 976, http://www.alberta courts.ab.ca.
50 CRC, articles 37 and 40.
51 Ibid., article 12.
52 Protection of Children Involved in Prostitution Act, R.S.A. 2000 (S.A. 1998, Chapter P-19.3).
53 CRC, article 3(1).
54 Pare, "Why Have Street Children Disappeared?"
55 Tonkin, *Street Youth Not Just an Urban Issue;* Pare, "Why Have Street Children Disappeared?"
56 CRC, articles 3, 6, 12, 19, 20, 24, 25, 27, 28, 29, 32–35, and 39.
57 CRC, articles 18, 19, and 25.
58 CRC, article 20.
59 Gaetz, "Safe Streets for Whom?"
60 CRC, article 2.
61 CRC, article 15.

Bibliography

Berezina, E. "Street Children." Youth Advocate Program International. http://www.yapi.org.
Blackstock, C., S. Clarke, J. Cullen, J. D'Handt, and J. Formosa. 2004. *Keeping the Promise: The Convention on the Rights of the Child and the Lived Experience of First Nations Children and Youth.* Ottawa: First Nations Child and Family Caring Society of Canada.
Canadian Council on Social Development. 2000. "Progress Report at a Glance: What Contributes to Child and Youth Well-being?" http://www.ccsd.ca.
———. 2000. "Canadian Fact Book on Poverty 2000." http://www.ccsd.ca.
Canadian Feminist Alliance for International Action. 2000. "Towards Women's Equality: Canada's Failed Commitment. Women's Poverty and Economic Inequality." http://www.fafia-afai.org.
Canadian Social Development Council. 2000. "Canadian Fact Book 2000." http://www.ccsd.ca.
Committee on the Rights of the Child. 2003. Thirty-third Session: Adolescent Health and Development in the Context of the Convention on the Rights of the Child (General Comment No. 4), May 19 to June 6.
Covell, K. 2002. "Canada's Non-Governmental Organizations Report to the United Nations Special Session on Children, September 19–21, 2001," http://www.rightsofchildren.ca.

————. 2005. "Violence against Children in North America." North American regional consultation for the UN Secretary-General's Study on Violence against Children. http://discovery.uccb.ns.ca/children.

Covell, K., and R.B. Howe. 2001. *The Challenge of Children's Rights for Canada*. Waterloo: Wilfrid Laurier University Press.

Feeney, T. 2005. "In Best or Vested Interest? An Exploration of the Concept and Practice of Family Re-unification for Street Children." Report prepared for the Consortium for Street Children. http://www.streetchildren.org.uk.

Gaetz, S. 2004. "Safe Streets for Whom? Homeless Youth, Social Exclusion, and Criminal Victimization." *Canadian Journal of Criminology and Criminal Justice* 46, no. 4: 423–56.

Glauser, B. 1990. "Street Children: Deconstructing a Construct." In A. James and A. Prout, eds., *Constructing and Reconstructing Childhood: Contemporary Issues in the Sociological Study of Childhood*. London: Falmer Press.

Gough, P., N. Trocmé, I. Brown, D. Knoke, and C. Blackstock. 2005. "Pathways to Overrepresentation of Aboriginal Children in Care." Prepared for the Centre of Excellence for Child Welfare. http://www.cecw-cepb.ca.

Government of Canada. n.d. "Understanding Homelessness: Reviewing the Numbers," http://www.homelessness.gc.ca.

Government of Canada, National Homelessness Initiative. 2003. "Understanding Homelessness: Reviewing the Numbers." http://www.homelessness.gc.ca.

Grover, S.C. 2002. "Why Aren't These Youngsters in School? On Meeting Canada's Charter Obligations to Disadvantaged Adolescents." *International Journal of Children's Rights* 10: 1–37.

————. 2003. "Negating the Child's Inclusive Right to Security of the Person: A Charter Analysis of the s. 43 Canadian Criminal Code Defense to Corporal Punishment of a Minor." *Murdoch University Electronic Journal of Law* 10, no. 4 (2003). http://www.murdoch.edu.au/elaw/issues/v10n4/grover104.txt.

————. 2004. "The Impact of Perceived Domestic Public Opinion on Judicial Interpretation: A Commentary on *Canadian Foundation for Children, Youth, and the Law v. Canada Attorney General*." *Murdoch University Electronic Journal of Law* 11, no. 1 (2004).

————. 2005. "The Equality and Liberty Rights of the Destitute: A Canadian Case Example." *International Journal of Minority and Group Rights* 12, no. 1: 43–61.

Health Canada. 2001. "Your Voice Matters: Young People Speak Out on Issues Related to the UN Special Session on Children." http://www.phac-aspc.gc.ca.

Howe, R.B. 2001. "Implementing Children's Rights in a Federal State: The Case of Canada's Child Protection System." *International Journal of Children's Rights* 9: 361–82.

Leon, S. 2000. "Living on the Edge: Women and Homelessness in Canada." Prepared for the National Anti-Poverty Organization. http://www.napo-onap.ca.

National Youth in Care Network. "Who Will Teach Me to Learn? Creating Positive School Experiences for Youth in Care." http://www.youthincare.ca.

Neal, R. 2004. "Voices: Women, Poverty, and Homelessness in Canada. Report prepared for the National Anti-Poverty Organization. http://www.napo-onap.ca.

Pare, M. 2003. "Why Have Street Children Disappeared? The Role of International Human Rights Law in Protecting Vulnerable Groups." *International Journal of Children's Rights* 11: 1–32.

Rotherman-Baus, M., K.A. Mahler, C. Koopman, and K. Langabeer. 1996. "Sexual Abuse History and Associated Multiple Risk Behavior in Adolescent Runaways." *American Journal of Orthopsychiatry* 66: 390–400.

Roy, L., N. Haley, P. Leclerc, B. Sochanski, J. Boudreau, and J. Bovin. 2004. "Canada: Mortality in a Cohort of Street Youth in Montreal." *Journal of the American Medical Association* 292, no. 5: 569–574.

Serge, L., M. Eberies, M. Goldberg, S. Sullivan, and P. Dudding. 2002. "Pilot Study: The Child Welfare System and Homelessness among Canadian Youth." Prepared for the Government of Canada, National Secretariat on Homelessness. http://www.cecw-cepb.ca/DocsEng/HomelessnessAndCW.pdf.

Social Planning and Research Council of B.C. 2005. "On Our Streets and In Our Shelters: Results of the 2005 Greater Vancouver Homeless Count." http://www.gvrd.bc.ca/homelessness/pdfs/HomelessCount2005Final.pdf.

Tonkin, R. 2001. "Street Youth Not Just an Urban Issue in B.C." Study for the McCreary Centre Society. http://www.mcs.bc.ca.

Trocmé, N., B. McLaurin, B. Fallon, et al. 2001. "Canadian Incidence Study of Reported Child Abuse: Final Report." http://www.hc-sc.gc.ca.

UNICEF. 2005. "State of the World's Children." http://www.unicef.org.

Veale, A., M. Taylor, and C. Linehan. 2000. "Psychological Perspectives of 'Abandoned' and 'Abandoning' Street Children." In C. Panter-Brick and M.T. Smith, eds., *Abandoned Children*. Cambridge: Cambridge University Press.

On the Rights of Refugee Children and Child Asylum Seekers

Sonja Grover

Introduction

In the previous chapter, the rights violations of homeless and street-involved children were discussed. This chapter focuses on a second group of especially vulnerable children: refugees and asylum seekers. These are children who have been put at continuing high risk in their home countries and who are attempting to escape those circumstances by seeking asylum in Canada. The chapter considers the extent to which Canada has met its obligations to these refugee children under the CRC and how to remedy any shortfalls. According to Human Rights Watch, refugee children are among the most vulnerable children in the world. Also considered are special populations of victimized children—in particular, those who arrive at a Canadian border point as a result of human trafficking. The latter group of children is in especially dire need of a voice in the international forum and of the protections afforded by the United Nations Convention on the Rights of the Child (CRC). I will examine the extent to which Canada affords these highly vulnerable child groups their rights under the CRC.

Children seeking asylum have suffered the consequences of war or various forms of persecution in their countries of origin. Many of these children continue to suffer human rights abuses in the countries of asylum that have become their temporary or permanent sanctuary. Of the approximately 17 million people worldwide who are seeking asylum as refugees outside their home country, or who are internally displaced, about half are

Sonja Grover, Faculty of Education, Lakehead University

children.[1] Even though more than half the world's refuges are children, their rights and special protection needs as children are often neglected.[2] The number of *unaccompanied* children seeking refugee status has increased steadily in recent years. Growing numbers have come to Canada. It is estimated that by 2002 more than 1,800 unaccompanied minors age seventeen and under had entered Canada, with more than half coming to Ontario.[3] This increase has been due to a number of international factors, including expanded armed conflict, economic dislocation, epidemics, and extreme poverty.

Several articles in the CRC address the issue of state and international obligations to protect child refugees. Article 22 in particular requires states to *ensure* that children seeking refugee status "receive appropriate protection and humanitarian assistance." The same article stipulates that these protections are to apply whether the child seeking asylum is accompanied by parents or others or is unaccompanied. However, article 22 presumes that the determination of who is a child refugee under domestic and international law reflects a just and non-discriminatory process that is respectful of the child's human rights and humanitarian basic needs. This is not always the case in Canada—or in other states. Nor is it always the case that unaccompanied asylum-seeking children receive the same consideration as do accompanied children. Article 22 of the CRC also requires that states make every effort to trace the parents or other family members of the asylum-seeking or refugee child in order to reunify the child with his or her family wherever this is feasible and in the child's best interests.

Typically, the child refugee is attempting to escape from a situation in his or her home country such as civil war or persecution based on gender, ethnicity, sexual orientation, social status, religion, or certain other personal characteristics. Not all countries recognize all of the same grounds for refugee claims. For instance, Canada is among a handful of countries (along with France, the Netherlands, and the United States) that recognizes gender persecution as a basis for a refugee claim.[4] The value of non-discrimination is articulated in article 2 of the CRC. Extreme poverty may be the reason for seeking escape to Canada and often is correlated with high risk to the child's good development or even life. Extreme poverty, however, is not regarded as a basis for a refugee claim under Canadian law—or indeed under international humanitarian law. In contrast, the CRC under article 27 guarantees children a standard of living adequate for their overall good development.

Overview of Some Key Aspects of the Canadian Refugee System Affecting Children

Canadian refugee law has been revised since Canada ratified the CRC in 1991. These revisions, including the ones found in Canada's new Immigration and Refugee Protection Act (2002), are among other things an attempt to make the legislative scheme more consistent with the requirements of the CRC. I now examine the most important of these revisions and consider the extent to which they comply with the CRC.

Family Reunification

An application for refugee status can be made either from within Canada (in the case of those who fear returning to their home country); from within the home country; or from within a third country that can offer only temporary asylum or where the individual is still at considerable risk. Child refugee claimants who are separated from their parents or legal guardians when they arrive at a Canadian cross-border point, however, may or may not present themselves voluntarily to immigration officials or other Canadian authorities. In some cases, as with children who have been trafficked, the child may be discovered by Canadian immigration or other authorities during routine checks or special investigations (e.g., while he or she is stowed away on a cargo ship). Reunification with the child's family, either in Canada or in the home country, is an issue in such cases. When a child who is seeking asylum arrives separated from parents or guardians, it may be impossible for the child to reunite with his or her family or at least to do so expeditiously. These children, if they succeed in obtaining refugee status in Canada, may apply for permanent residency for themselves. One barrier for separated children with regard to obtaining permanent residency in Canada on their own (once they have succeeded with their refugee application) is the high application fees for residency applications filed by separated children.[5] Canadian refugee law does not permit children to include their biological or adoptive parents or other immediate family members in an application for permanent residency and thus bring the primary caretaker(s) to Canada. The reverse is, however, possible. For instance, a refugee parent who achieves permanent resident status in Canada can sponsor his or her children as immigrants to Canada. This is a form of age discrimination, and it is contrary to article 2 of the CRC, which prohibits all forms of discrimination affecting the rights of children.

The Canadian Council of Refugees reports that 50 percent of family members wait more than thirteen months and that one in five wait more than twenty-six months to be re-united.[6] Such delays are inconsistent with article 10 of the CRC, which requires that states deal expeditiously with applications by children or parents to enter a country for the purpose of family reunification.

In some cases the primary caregiver arrives in Canada before the separated child and before obtaining refugee status or permanent residency. If the child later arrives and succeeds in obtaining refugee status and then permanent residency, this will not necessarily assist the parents in their own applications for the same. A denial of refugee status to the parents or child, however, can be reviewed by the minister of Immigration and Citizenship on humanitarian or compassionate grounds. If the parents who initially arrived as refugees are on social assistance (welfare), or are in default to the Canadian government with regard to resettlement monies, the parents are barred from sponsoring their separated child (even if a minor) as a child refugee to Canada. It also sometimes happens that the parents have listed their child on their own application for permanent residence, when the child was displaced and not yet located or was erroneously presumed to be dead or living with another relative in the home country. In these cases it is generally not possible for the parents to later sponsor their child to come to Canada. Furthermore, an unaccompanied child on seeking entry to Canada can be sponsored as a family-class immigrant only by someone who is an immediate biological family member of the child (e.g., a parent or sibling) or who is related through adoption. This child may wait years abroad in circumstances that place him or her at high risk before reunification with the parents or other family members in Canada can take place. Moreover, a person who was the child's primary caregiver in the home country, even if a Canadian citizen or permanent resident, cannot sponsor the child as a family-class immigrant if he or she is unrelated to the child either through adoption or biologically. A guardianship provision that would have permitted sponsorship of an unaccompanied child to Canada as a family-class immigrant by people unrelated to the child has recently been repealed.[7] This provision was a potential avenue for these unaccompanied children who may have lost their biological parents to enter Canada as immigrants, and ultimately to achieve permanent residency. The guardianship provision was repealed even though in many countries adoption is not considered acceptable. In the latter cases, the child is raised by an unrelated guardian when the need arises. In sum, the Canadian refugee system raises many barriers that make it difficult for a separated child to reunite with his or her family in Canada, and chances are high that such reunification will take many years if it occurs at all. These barriers must be eliminated if Canada is to comply with article 22 of the CRC, which calls for facilitation of family reunification wherever feasible.

An accompanied or unaccompanied child who has been trafficked, or who for some other reason has not voluntarily presented himself or herself to Canadian authorities on arrival at a Canadian border point, may still be eligible to apply for refugee status. It is then up to Canadian immigration and refugee authorities processing the claim to determine whether to grant the child refugee status and, ultimately, permanent residency. The process can be quite lengthy. Where feasible, authorities will attempt to reunite the unaccompanied child with his or her family who are still in the country of origin. In the case of a child who has been trafficked, however, this may not be possible. For instance, it may be that the parents or other family members actually participated in trafficking the child. Canada's refugee guidelines regarding cases of unaccompanied minors must be revised to better ensure their well-being while their eligibility for making a refugee claim is considered and then throughout the disposition process. This is to ensure, for example, that a child who is suspected of being trafficked and who has entered or was about to enter Canada is placed in a safe and, wherever possible, familial environment in Canada. When a familial-type placement is not available, another safe, hospitable, non-punitive care environment must be arranged for these children. This would bring Canada into compliance with, for instance, the CRC requirement to provide for the child's mental and physical health (article 25) and to provide whatever special protections are necessary and in the child's best interests (e.g., articles 3, 6, and 20). To effect such a strategy, the federal government will have to enter into formal agreements with the provincial governments regarding the provision of child welfare services to child asylum seekers and child refugees under eighteen.

Resettlement and the Child Refugee

To help refugees who have met the government's requirements and who have initiated the effort to come to Canada with little, if any, assistance, Canada has a resettlement program. Under this program, Canada has an annual number of refugees that it wishes to resettle in Canada. Typically, these people are living in refugee camps abroad, which offer temporary protection as an interim measure until a permanent country of refuge can be found. These people are referred by the UN High Commission on Refugees, by private organizations, or by individuals to various countries for resettlement. These resettlement refugees are sponsored by private individuals or non-governmental organizations, although the Canadian government assists with some resettlement funds. It has been found that 2 to 5 percent of international refugees are unaccompanied children who have been abandoned or orphaned.[8] Some of these children, however, may have family in their home country with whom they need to be reunited, and investigating this takes time. The processing of applications is especially difficult and time consuming if the child lacks proper identity papers or was never registered with the relevant domestic government agency at birth. Others have no remaining family left as a result of civil war or other factors. Once an application for refugee status has been made to Canada, the child claimant's problems are not necessarily over. For instance, an unaccompanied child who achieves refugee status in Canada may be unable to achieve permanent residency, since the residency card must be signed by the child's guardian. The child, however, may have no guardian in Canada recognized by a Canadian court.

To comply with CRC article 22 (i.e., the state must act to facilitate the protection of child refugees), Canada must take steps to ensure the safety and well-being of child asylum seekers. For instance, Canada must more expeditiously reunite unaccompanied children with their families where feasible. There is also an urgent need for Canada to facilitate granting the child asylum seeker refugee status and ultimately permanent residency when the claim is legitimate and/or when the child's well-being cannot be ensured if he or she is removed from Canada. This will mean appointing a legal guardian where necessary, and often this guardian will have to be the provincial child welfare agency.

Best Interests of the Child

Under Canadian refugee law, "child" is defined as a person under eighteen. Hence, the definition is consistent with article 1 of the CRC.[9] Article 3 requires the state to ensure that the children's best interests are "a primary consideration" in any decision making that affects children, including in the area of refugee decision making. Consistent with article 3, Canadian procedures set the best interests of the child as *a* central consideration during refugee determination hearings and appeals and at various other stages.[10] This requirement relating to children's best interests was affirmed in *Baker v. Canada (Minister of Citizenship and Immigration.*[11] In that case, the Supreme Court of Canada ruled that "children's rights, and attention to their interests, are central humanitarian and compassionate values in Canadian society." Thus, the Court found that a reasonable exercise of the immigration officer's discretion in deciding whether to deport a parent for a technical violation of the application process must consider the welfare of the appellant's Canadian-born children. Yet it remains the case that parents can be deported for a mere technical violation of the immigration and refugee regulations where there has been no misrepresentation to the authorities. The outcome in such cases depends on how the immigration officer chooses to weigh the best interests of the child in the particular circumstance.

Notwithstanding certain procedural safeguards, serious weaknesses in the Canadian refugee system persist that may jeopardize the well-being of child refugee claimants in Canada. The principle of best interests of the child is espoused in Canadian refugee law, yet the eligibility criteria for refugee status in Canada are the same for children as for adults. For example, no consideration is given to the child's need for refugee status based on child-specific forms of persecution such as child trafficking. Furthermore, despite certain procedural safeguards in hearings involving child refugee claimants, there is no certainty that the outcome will be in the best interests of the child. Indeed, the 2002 Immigration and Refugee Protection Act of Canada (IRPA)[12] does *not* guarantee that the child refugee's best interests will be met, only that they will be "taken into account." However, the denial of a child's refugee claim is still open to challenge where there is an inconsistency with the Charter of Rights, the CRC, or other international human rights conventions.

References to taking children's best interests into account are made at several points in the IRPA.The IRPA allows for consideration of the child's best interests with regard to the granting of an exemption from certain residency requirements for permanent residency status in Canada. The same act protects their right to a basic education while they are waiting for their applications to be processed and for hearings on their cases to be held. This education entitlement under the IRPA is consistent with the right to education guaranteed under article 28 of the CRC.Unaccompanied children who are independent refugee claimants are, under the IRPA, exempt from exclusion on health grounds, and this is clearly in their best interests. Child refugees often suffer from temporary or longer-term psychological and physical health issues, as a result of the traumatic experiences that most of them have faced in their home country and during their transit to Canada—which often involves a long and dangerous journey. Also, children who have been sponsored by a family member or parent in Canada who has permanent residency or citizenship are exempt from health restrictions when applying for immigration or refugee status. If the child is over sixteen and has a spouse or common-law partner in Canada who is a permanent resident or citizen and who is acting as a sponsor, then the child may also be exempted from health restrictions. These exemptions are consistent with the CRC's articles 2 and 23, which protect children against the derogation of their rights based on disability. Refugee claimants to Canada, including minors, also are eligible for health care,[13] putting Canada in compliance with articles 3, 6, and 24 of the CRC, which set out the child's right to the highest attainable standard of health.

The principle of children's best interests underlies various aspects of the Canadian refugee process. Children are assigned a representative during Refugee Board hearings, and certain safeguards are in place for children who have failed in their refugee application. The Canadian refugee system entitles children to appeal a deportation order to an appeal body within the refugee system. However, the appeal process is not fully consistent with the CRC's article 12 requirement that the child be heard in any administrative or judicial proceeding, since the appeal is restricted to matters of procedural error (such as failure to be assigned a representative at a hearing). Thus, a hearing for contesting a deportation order, for instance, is more like a review than a full-fledged appeal on the facts of the case. This limitation conflicts with Canada's obligation under article 22 of the CRC to ensure that the child's protection needs and circumstances are fully and adequately addressed.

Unaccompanied child refugees who are still in their home country and who are selected for resettlement in Canada, unlike their adult counterparts, are not expected to have the potential to be economically self-sufficient within a relatively short period.[14] Also, the "best interests" factor exempts unmarried children without a legal guardian in Canada or the United States from the safe country agreement with the United States.[15] Adults who pass through the latter country are considered to have come from a safe third country and thus are ineligible to apply for refugee status in Canada at a U.S.–Canada cross-border point. This is not the case, however, for children seeking refuge in Canada. The latter exemptions for child asylum seekers are thus consistent with the best interests principle in article 3 of the CRC.

Barriers in Refugee Law to Meeting the Child's Best Interests

Under Canadian refugee law, the child's best interests are not guaranteed; however, this is not inconsistent with article 3 of the CRC, which stipulates only that best interests of the child be *a* primary consideration in decision making about the child. It does not have to be *the* primary consideration.[16] This was a key point in a 2004 Supreme Court of Canada case involving children's security rights in the context of Canadian criminal law.[17] What is considered to meet the stipulation to "take into account" the child's best interests may, furthermore, not adequately address the child's fundamental rights and needs. The low standard represented by "taking account" of children's best interests often merely amounts to certain procedural niceties (e.g., appointing a designated representative for the child at hearings, who most often is the parent). In the final analysis, it is the state that stipulates what is in the particular asylum-seeking child's best interests. The government guidelines for dealing with child refugees, especially if those children are unaccompanied, aside from some procedural safeguards at hearings and "appeals," are often absent or at best vague.[18] They often offer little if any guidance as to best practice in specific cases. In other respects, the guidelines may do more harm to children than good—for example, when they permit the detention of unaccompanied children owing simply to the child's lack of identity papers. As early as 1996, the Supreme Court of Canada made it clear that in the Canadian legal context, wording in statutes expressing the best-interests-of-the-child principle did not offer the child any certainty regarding legal protections and guarantees.[19] In other words, unless the child's specific entitlements are set out in the statute and/or accompanying regulations, the interpretation of "best interests of the child" is wide open. There is no doubt that some flexibility is required in applying the best-interests-of-the-child principle in specific cases, as the Supreme Court of Canada suggests. Nevertheless, there is also a need for better protection of the child refugee's civil and legal rights under Canadian refugee law and regulations. At present, children suspected of having been trafficked, and other highly vulnerable child asylum seekers, are routinely refused asylum in Canada as Convention refugees, and for less than substantive reasons.[20]

Absence of Child-Specific Forms of Persecution as a Basis for a Refugee Claim

Even though Canadian child refugee law makes reference to the best-interests principle, children do not have any grounds for refugee status in Canada that are unique to them as children.[21] There is no recognition of child-specific forms of persecution such as child abuse, child trafficking, child selling, and hazardous child labor as a ground for claiming refugee status in Canada. Canada does not recognize these child-specific forms of persecution as a basis for refugee claims, though these abuses bear the hallmarks of crimes against humanity. This failure is inconsistent with recognition in the CRC that "there are children living in exceptionally difficult conditions, and that such children need special consideration."[22] Compounding the plight of child refugees is the fact that article 22 of the CRC leaves the standard for protection of the child asylum seeker to the discretion of individual states. This is in deference to individual states' domestic laws. Let us consider now whether the Canadian refugee system is meeting its obligation to accord unaccompanied and accompanied child asylum seekers equity in terms of fair process and outcomes as required by the CRC.

Canadian Definitions of Accompanied versus Unaccompanied Child Asylum Seekers

Most child refugee claimants have a refugee claim filed on their behalf by parents or immediate family as part of a family unit that is seeking refuge together at the same time or that is seeking to be reunited. "Child refugee claimant" here refers to a person under eighteen. A child who arrives at the same time as the parents or the legal guardian, or some time thereafter, is considered an "accompanied" child under Canadian refugee regulations. In addition, a child who arrives with a family member who is not the parent or guardian, but whom the Government of Canada determines to be a family member, is considered accompanied. Finally, a child who arrives alone, but who has a family member in Canada who is acknowledged by Canada as a family member, and who is willing to care for the child, is also considered an accompanied child.[23] Hence, not all children separated from parents or legal guardians are classed as "unaccompanied" children by Canadian immigration and refugee officials.

If there is any doubt that an accompanying adult or the potential caregiver in Canada is in fact a bona fide family member of the child, then the child is considered an "unaccompanied" child. Children who arrive with adults who are suspected of trafficking the child are also considered "unaccompanied" for the purposes of refugee determination.[24] Furthermore, should the child arrive alone at a Canadian entry point and /or not have a potential family member as a caregiver in Canada, the child is likewise considered an unaccompanied child.[25] Children who arrive alone at a Canadian entry point usually, but not always, have been sent by their parents. In those cases it is uncertain whether they have been sent for their own protection or for other, more questionable reasons—for example, to work in the sex trade, or as couriers for drug dealers, or as indentured labourers in illegal sweatshops.[26] That matter will require a thorough investigation by Canadian immigration authorities. The circumstances are sometimes such that the child should be reunited with family in the home country, provided the situation in that country is safe for the child. An example of a situation requiring such family reunification would be if the child, against the family's will or without their knowledge, had been the subject of an illicit transfer abroad. Reuniting the family in this circumstance would be in accord with article 11 of the CRC, which requires states to return children to their home country who are the victims of an illicit transfer.[27]

At present, there is no national policy in Canada regarding the reception and care of unaccompanied minors seeking asylum, other than some guidelines regarding hearing processes. For instance, Ontario, which receives the highest numbers of child asylum seekers, has no arrangement with Child Welfare to place the children when this is necessary during the refugee determination process. Some provinces, including British Columbia and Quebec, do have such arrangements with the provincial child welfare authorities.[28] A national standard is needed in order to bring Canada into compliance with articles 3 and 22 of the CRC regarding the State's obligation to act in the child's best interests and to provide the child asylum seeker or child refugee with effective access to humanitarian assistance and protection.

Screening of Child Refugee Applicants to Canada

All child refugee applicants to Canada, as well as any accompanying adults, are subject to an initial screening, termed "front end processing," that focuses on their eligibility to make a refugee claim. At that initial point the child is not yet assigned representation, as there is no requirement for this under the IRPA.[29] Unlike countries such as the Netherlands, Canada does not automatically assign an independent legal guardian to unaccompanied children seeking asylum.[30] A guardian such as a social worker would be concerned with the child's well-being overall and would be legally responsible for the child's welfare. Provincial child welfare legislation in Canada does *not* exclude non-nationals from receiving child welfare services. However, as mentioned, not all provincial child welfare agencies have entered into agreements with Immigration and Citizenship Canada to provide such services. Furthermore, sometimes it is difficult to assess the actual age of the individual claiming to be under eighteen and therefore eligible for child protective services. In Canada there is no national policy regarding which procedures, medical or otherwise, are to be used to determine age that are respectful of the child's human dignity. Assistance to unaccompanied children via the appointment of a legal guardian through Child Welfare would bring Canada into compliance with article 22 of the CRC. In particular, it would result in compliance with that section of article 22 requiring the state to help children seeking refuge access their protection rights.

The unaccompanied child refugee claimant may have been given a review of his or her case by an immigration officer (a preremoval assessment); however, few of these reviews are successful for child applicants.[31] The only other option then is to apply to the minister for refugee status on humanitarian or compassionate grounds or to the courts. Without effective advocates or counsel, the child is unlikely to have the psychological and other resources to file such written applications for review. Deportation of an unaccompanied minor from Canada is a method of last resort, but such deportations do occur. The child is entitled to representation before a deportation order is enforced. Should all "appeals" fail, the government must then ensure, prior to removing the child, that the child will be met by family or child welfare officials in the home country.[32] Yet, there are no written guidelines in Canada telling officials how to inquire into the safety concerns regarding who will meet and take care of the child who is deported from Canada.[33] This is inconsistent with Canada's obligation under article 6 of the CRC to ensure the child's survival and good development to the extent possible. If the child is under thirteen, he or she is to be accompanied by an escort on the flight to the home country.[34] Children between thirteen and eighteen are to be escorted if the airline will not accept responsibility for their safety, if there are other safety concerns, or if the flight is not direct.[35]

Canada's willingness to deny entry to unaccompanied child asylum seekers in certain cases owing simply to a lack of information on the child (e.g., absence of identity papers, or less than the full story regarding persecution in the homeland) is inconsistent with the best-interests principle of the CRC. Child refugees *must* be given entry to Canada barring any substantive, established, and compelling reason for exclusion (such as the feasibility of family reunification outside Canada in a safe setting). Only then will Canada meet its obligations under the CRC to protect such highly vulnerable children.

Detention of Children during Initial Screening or Processing of the Refugee Claim

A child refugee claimant in Canada can be detained if he or she does not have identity papers or has inadequate identity documents, or is thought to pose a security risk, or has made serious misrepresentations, or for some other reason. Yet it is not unusual for people who are fleeing persecution or who have fled their homeland during a crisis to be without identity papers. Despite this, children who arrive at a Canadian border point without identity papers and who have fled their home country on their own accord or have been trafficked are routinely treated as security risks. This can result in a lengthy stay in detention or even an unjustified deportation. The detention and/or deportation of children who have suffered any form of human rights abuse before their arrival in Canada may be contrary to article 39 of the CRC, which requires the state to promote the physical and psychological recovery of such children. In the case of children who have been trafficked, the deportation is also contrary to the requirements of article 35 of the CRC, which requires the state to take measures to block child trafficking. It also violates article 36, which requires the state to prevent all forms of child exploitation. This is because the child may, as a consequence of the deportation, once again be put at risk of being trafficked in their home country. To comply with articles 3, 35, and 36 Canada must provide trafficked children with refuge when there is no compelling reason to decline to offer asylum (or provide for their asylum in some other country).

Under Canadian refugee law, if there is a suspicion that the child may have been abducted, then the child may be fingerprinted provided that certain authorizations are issued. This may, in some instances, be in the child's best interests in terms of expediting the return of the child to his or her parents where this is a viable option.[36] Fingerprinting and photographing the child for identification purposes can then be part of a strategy that is consistent with the article 22 requirement to facilitate family reunification whenever feasible and justified.

According to Canadian policy, detention is supposed to be a method of last resort; in practice, though, this is not always the case, because placement elsewhere may not be available. Between October 2003 and November 2004, an average of seventeen minors seeking refugee status were in detention each week in Canada, and of these, five were unaccompanied.[37] Provincial child protection authorities are not always willing to accept unaccompanied minors claiming refugee status. These child welfare agencies are often concerned that the child may be a flight risk or create other difficulties for the agency. Also, in provinces such as Ontario, which receives the majority of unaccompanied minors and other refugees, child protective services are available only for children up to age sixteen. In Ontario, special arrangements can be made for children over sixteen who wish to come voluntarily into care. However, it is the child who would normally be expected to initiate the process. This is unlikely to occur with child refugees, especially unaccompanied child refugees, unless they have highly effective representation or counsel acting on their behalf. An unaccompanied child refugee may not speak English and may be so traumatized as to be unable or unwilling to provide the advocate with the information necessary to secure a foster home or other temporary child welfare placement. The potential placement may be reluctant to accept a child refugee, whom they may know little about in terms of exact age, potential risk to self, and similar factors. Neither the federal government nor the provincial ones can compel a children's aid society (or any other provincial child welfare authority) to provide services to unaccompanied minors seeking refugee status (unless there is a formal agreement to this effect). As a result, in most provinces unaccompanied asylum seekers over sixteen are not generally offered services by child welfare authorities. This, even though children over sixteen have a great need for various forms of child welfare support and protection services both during and after the refugee determination process. Compliance with the CRC's best-interests-of-the-child principle and with article 22 regarding the provision of necessary assistance to child asylum seekers and refugees will require Canada to offer child protective services to asylum-seeking children. These services would, in addition, need to be extended also to children over sixteen.[38]

Adherence to the CRC also requires that unaccompanied minors be detained only in very exceptional circumstances that are not inconsistent with international humanitarian law. Detention should not be used as a means to discourage unaccompanied children from seeking refuge in Canada. The use of detention for such purposes is a violation of article 37 of the CRC, which provides protection against arbitrary deprivation of the child's liberty. Arbitrary detention is also a violation of articles 3, 19, and 22, whose purpose is to ensure that children are provided with needed protection, treated with dignity, and shielded from mental and/or physical harms.

The Hearing and "Appeal" Process

If it is determined that the child is eligible to make a refugee claim in Canada, hearings are held by the Immigration and Refugee Board to determine the outcome of that claim. A request for review of a negative decision is available on issues of fair process only, *not* on the merits of the case. In other words, no appeal is available regarding the facts of the case; the review can only address whether the Government of Canada has followed its own laws. As long as proper procedures have been followed by the one-member board, the denial of the refugee claim is likely to be upheld by the review body and by the courts. Furthermore, the child does not have automatic access to the courts. A written application for leave to appeal to the courts must be made, and it is not always granted. In addition, the child is not provided with free, competent legal counsel, and this creates further barriers to accessing the courts. The child's only other option is to ask for consideration by the minister on humanitarian or compassionate grounds. Alternatively, the child can apply for a review on the grounds that return to the home country would place him or her at high risk of serious harm. The absence of an appeal process on the merits has been recognized as a fundamental flaw in the Canadian refugee system.[39] To comply with child refugee rights under article 22 of the CRC, Canada will have to implement an appeal division within the Canadian refugee system.

How the child asylum seeker's claim is handled is influenced in part by whether the child is accompanied. In Canada, the IRPA (under Section 69) requires that the child have a representative designated by the Convention Refugee Determination Division (CRDD) during all hearings.[40] That representative is not counsel. If the child is accompanied, the child's representative is usually the parent or another adult family member. This can raise problems. For example, the parent may be ineligible for refugee status while the child may be eligible, or the parent may misrepresent facts and negatively affect the child's claim. Some have therefore suggested that the child should always have *independent* representation at such hearings.

Canada was the first country to establish special guidelines for the refugee hearing process and other procedural matters where the refugee applicant was an unaccompanied minor.[41] These guidelines were an attempt to bring Canadian refugee practices for child asylum seekers in line with the CRC. Besides appointing a representative for the child at hearings, the guidelines incorporate several additional features. These Canadian guidelines also require that the child be identified as unaccompanied as quickly as possible, that the same officials deal with the case throughout, and that the case be assigned a high priority. The guidelines require that precautions be taken to safeguard the child's emotional well-being and dignity, as the child may be called on to give evidence during the hearing and any subsequent "appeal." Also, consideration in eliciting evidence is to be given to such factors as the child's chronological age and stage of mental development both at the time of the hearing and when the events to which the child is testifying took place. Also to be considered is the time lapse since the events that are the basis for the refugee claim and the child's communicative abilities at the time of the hearing, given the circumstances and history of the child.[42]

It is not always the case that the appointed representative for the child is versed in the hearing procedures or skilled in communicating with the child so as to adequately represent the child's best interests.Where it has become obvious that the child's representative is not acting in his or her best interests, the IRB has unfortunately not always replaced that representative. The representative is responsible for hiring a lawyer, as the child has a right to counsel, but the latter is *not* provided by the government to the child free of charge. Counsel may be paid through legal aid, but those monies generally need to be repaid over time by whoever is assigned that debt. The child who is seeking refugee status is likely to be under emotional strain and may in fact be suffering from post-traumatic stress. The child may also be facing certain cultural barriers that make it even more difficult than it would normally be for the child to share relevant aspects of his or her case with his or her designated representative or counsel. These aspects include information about various forms of persecution of the group to which the child belongs. If the child is to be afforded due process, it is imperative for Canada to ensure that every asylum-seeking child has a designated representative who understands the refugee hearing process, as well as counsel trained to handle child refugee cases. Timely appointment of these individuals acting in the child's best interests will bring Canada into better compliance with article 22 of the CRC, which requires the state to assist the child in securing his or her protection rights.

Some counsel have complained that parents and other representatives for the child designated by the refugee board do not always understand their role and cannot properly consult with counsel on the child's behalf.[43] Also, it is not uncommon that representatives and counsel for unaccompanied children have been appointed only a short time before the refugee hearing. If the representative is the parent, that parent will usually already have tried to act on the child's behalf before being officially designated as the child's representative. For these accompanied children, there are generally fewer problems than for unaccompanied children provided that the parent understands and acts on his or her role as representative. The consequence of delay in appointing representatives and counsel for unaccompanied children is much different. In these cases, counsel has had very little time to study the case or get acquainted with the child and is therefore unable to offer the best representation possible. Often, no one has been acting to protect the unaccompanied child's best interests during case presentation. This is because the designated representative of the child was not appointed before the hearing commenced.[44] The same may occur if the child is with a parent but for some reason the child is making an independent refugee claim to be heard separately from that of the parent. There are also frequent complaints that legal aid funds are insufficient and that some counsel have little incentive to adequately prepare the child's case.[45]

There is considerable anecdotal evidence suggesting that child asylum seekers who are separated from their parents or legal guardians are significantly less likely to obtain refugee status compared to adults. This seems to be for various reasons, such as difficulty accessing adequate counsel and inordinate delays and interruptions in the processing of the case.[46] In most countries, the chances of children's refugee claims succeeding are much less if the child is unaccompanied.[47] There are no accurate statistics available on the numbers of *unaccompanied* minors removed from Canada after failing in their claim for refugee status (or for those that were removed after being deemed to be ineligible to make an application for refugee status).[48] In 1998–99, 1,147 children were removed from Canada; of these, 874 were under fourteen and 273 were between fifteen and eighteen.[49] Furthermore, Save the Children estimates that only 1 to 2 percent of children separated from their primary caregiver(s) succeed in achieving permanent status in the destination country.[50] Thus in many ways the Canadian refugee scheme adversely affects separated, unaccompanied minors who are seeking asylum in Canada. This differential adverse impact of the Canadian refugee system on unaccompanied minors amounts to a violation of the non-discrimination principle of the CRC. Here, the discrimination is based on an aspect of family status (e.g., being separated from the parent) and/or social status (e.g., being a trafficked child).

Special Child Refugee Populations

Problems also exist in Canada's refugee system with regard to special child refugee populations. They may be described as follows.

Child Refugees Who Are the Common-Law Partners, Conjugal Partners, or Married Partners of Adults

The term "child" is defined under Canadian immigration and refugee law as a person under eighteen. However, children sixteen years and over but under eighteen are treated as adults when they are married or have been living common law. If a child is sixteen or over and is married to, or in a common-law relationship with, an adult who has permanent residency, citizenship, or refugee status in Canada, that child is considered admissible to Canada as a spouse or common-law partner. There is no consideration in the immigration and refugee regulations regarding the relationship between gender persecution and child marriage. This, even though child spouses are likely to be female and there is most often a wide age disparity between the child and the adult spouse. Many of these children will have been married by traditional customary practice at age ten (or even younger) with or without additional formal legal proceedings. International organizations such as UNICEF have documented that child marriage poses certain health risks and most often leads to an abrupt end to the girl's schooling.[51] Yet there is no concern about this under Canadian refugee law as long as the child who is married or in a common-law relationship is sixteen or older on arrival at the Canadian border.

The complacency in Canadian refugee law and policy regarding child–adult marriages or common-law relationships is contrary to several articles of the CRC. Arguably, it represents an infringement of Canada's obligation under article 19 to protect the child from sexual abuse or exploitation.[52] Children, especially in cultures that practise early child marriage, are not in a position to give truly free, informed consent to sexual activity with an adult. This is the case given coercive societal forces, the girl's young developmental age, and her lack of life experience and/or cultural conditioning. Many of these children come from destitute or very poor and otherwise disadvantaged families. These families may see the child marriage as an opportunity for the child to have a better life. The family may not always understand that there are significant negative psychological, health, and educational impacts deriving from child marriage. Other parents may have essentially trafficked the child for their own financial benefit under the alleged legitimizing rationale of a child marriage. Given familial pressure for child marriage in some cultures, even older children are unlikely to have given genuinely voluntary, informed consent. Also, children on the street and other children separated from family may be at risk of being lured and/or coerced into adult–child marital or common-law arrangements. For all the above reasons, there is then also a violation of article 24 of the CRC, which requires all states to work toward abolition of customary practices that jeopardize any aspect of the child's health; and of article 13 regarding freedom of expression.[53] Child marriage places the child's physical and psychological health at risk (e.g., there is the health risk associated with premature pregnancy; the psychological risk of a loss of childhood and liberty; the negative consequences of the hard labour, which is often performed both inside and outside the family dwelling by a female child, who is expected to help support a family; the high risk of becoming the victim of spousal battering [more likely where one of the spouses is a vulnerable child]; and the risk of AIDS contracted from an adult sexual partner). Similarly, Canadian refugee policy and law with respect to child marriage violates article 6 of the CRC, which requires States to take all measures to ensure the child's good development and well-being.[54]

Canada's failure to consider child marriage as a basis for an independent refugee claim by a minor also violates article 2 (non-discrimination) of the CRC. Discrimination based on gender occurs in this context in the sense that girls are more often child spouses and thus more adversely affected by Canada's refusal to consider child marriage as grounds for a refugee claim by a minor.

Children Who Were Former Child Soldiers

Articles 38 and 39 of the CRC, together with an accompanying protocol concerning children's involvement in armed conflict, set out the rights of children to the protections afforded by humanitarian law.[55] These include the right of civilians under eighteen to be free from forced duty in the armed forces. Yet at present there at least 300,000 child soldiers globally taking part in innumerable armed conflicts.[56] With regard to former child soldiers, the CRC requires states to provide recovery and reintegration services for these children. The reality is, however, that such services are rarely offered and often inadequately so. Furthermore, many of these children are at high risk of abduction and forced re-recruitment either in their home country or in neighbouring countries. When they do manage to escape forced recruitment and flee in search of asylum, these former child soldiers generally arrive at a Canadian or other border point unaccompanied.

Notwithstanding the protections afforded by the CRC and the relevant accompanying protocol, Canada most often excludes former child soldiers from refugee consideration. This is in direct contravention of international human rights and humanitarian obligations such as those stipulated in article 39 of the CRC. Canada's obligation to ensure that the child is returned to a safe situation most often precludes the return of the former child soldier to his or her native country. This is because such children are often persecuted in their home country and because they face the ongoing risk of forced armed service. Article 38 of the CRC and articles 3 and 4 of the Optional Protocol to the CRC on the involvement of children in armed conflict prohibit the returning of a child to the borders of a state where there is a risk of underage recruitment (or re-recruitment) or participation in armed conflict. Canada's reluctance to accept the refugee claims of minors who at one time were child soldiers places these children at risk of being returned to an unsafe situation in the home country.

Changes are necessary to ensure fairer consideration of the refugee claims of unaccompanied children who at one time were child soldiers. One possibility is to designate minors who were former child soldiers as a persecuted social group under Canadian refugee law. Indeed, such children are often the targets of persecution and discrimination in their home country, even after armed hostilities have ceased. This is because they may have been forced to participate with armed groups vehemently opposed by the local population and/or government. These minors would qualify for Convention refugee status under the proposed changes. The current situation is that such children are often excluded from refugee consideration owing to their inability to provide the needed documentation and evidence concerning forced recruitment and the like. Under the present regulations, they may also be considered security risks though often there is no independent evidence to that effect. If the child has committed a crime against humanity such as participating in a genocidal war, the child may not be allowed to proceed to a refugee determination board hearing.

The courts have recognized that persons, especially children, cannot be held responsible for crimes against humanity or war crimes when they were acting under extreme duress such as pain of death. The International Court of Criminal Justice (ICCJ) under article 26 of its enabling statute does not prosecute children for war crimes (that is, where the crimes were committed while the individual was under eighteen).[57] The presumption of the ICCJ seems to be that children, for a variety of reasons, are especially vulnerable to extreme duress and manipulation by adult armed forces. Hence, they cannot be held criminally responsible for war crimes they may have committed. However, currently in Canada, at the case-screening stage, the government is not required to ensure that the child has representation. Therefore, there may be no one to assist the former child soldier in obtaining counsel who could argue that there are grounds for review of the case. Adequate representation by counsel from the beginning of the child's case, and recognition of former child soldiers as a persecuted group, are both necessary additions to Canadian refugee law and policy if Canada is to act in accordance with the requirements of the CRC.

Stateless Children

Statelessness can result from many different factors, including the failure to have a legal identity owing to the lack of birth registration, displacement through ethnic cleansing by oppressive groups, denial of nationality as the child's father is not a citizen of the country in question (even though the mother is a citizen), and a host of other reasons. Statelessness can leave an individual in legal limbo and serve as a barrier to gaining refugee status and permanent residency. Stateless people may be in dire need of a safe haven since no country will accept them as their own. Yet the stateless person may not fall under any traditional definition of "refugee" under international law.[58] The CRC places a burden on governments to eliminate statelessness. For Canada to meet its obligations under article 7 of the CRC (providing for the right to acquire a nationality), it must ensure that stateless children are not left in legal limbo. Either Canada must grant such a child a national identity and permanent residency, or through negotiation with international partners, the child must be granted a national identity in some other state that meets the child's needs.

Conclusion

There is no doubt that Canada has greatly advanced just treatment of unaccompanied child refugees through the development of a set of general guidelines. These govern certain procedural matters in dealing with such cases at hearings and with regard to removal orders. However, some additional elements need to be incorporated into Canadian refugee law and policy in order to better protect child refugee claimants—in particular, unaccompanied children such as trafficked children. Addition of these elements would bring Canadian refugee policy into better compliance with the CRC. Recognition of specific forms of child persecution as a valid basis for refugee status would bring Canadian law into the compliance with the CRC provision on the state's obligation to provide special protections to children who have been the victims of human rights abuses of various forms (article 39).[59] These forms of child persecution include child marriage, child trafficking, child soldiering, the worst forms of child labor such as bonded labor, sexual slavery, and child prostitution. One implication of recognizing child persecution as a basis for a child's refugee claim would be a ban on sponsoring a child spouse or partner (a spouse or partner under eighteen). At the same time, a provision would be added allowing for the possibility of a child spouse or partner making out a refugee claim independently as a victim of child marriage. The latter provision regarding child marriage would bring Canada into better compliance with articles 3, 6, 19, and 24 concerning the state's obligation to ensure the child's well-being; it would also enforce measures to counteract abuse, neglect, and practices detrimental to the child's education, and promote good psychological and physical health and development.[60]

The provision of independent, free, and expert legal counsel for accompanied and unaccompanied child refugee claimants would allow children to participate effectively in hearings, as required under article 12 of the CRC.[61] Where repayment of legal aid fees would be an absolute barrier to the unaccompanied child retaining counsel, remedies should be provided so that no child is denied legal representation at refugee hearings. In accordance with article 12, in all such hearings it is essential that the administrative panel, tribunal, or court seriously consider the views of the child asylum seeker in any decision making affecting the child.[62] The Refugee Board needs to ensure that the child is afforded such counsel in a timely fashion well before any hearing process begins. Providing this support would bring Canada into compliance with article 22, which requires that states provide such assistance as necessary to permit refugee children to access their protection and other rights under the CRC.[63] For children held in detention while their eligibility to make a claim is being determined or while that claim is being processed, provision of such counsel would also ensure compliance with article 37 of the CRC.[64] Article 37 sets out the right of the child to prompt legal assistance when deprived of his or her liberty for whatever reason. Having such counsel act on behalf of the child would also mean that especially vulnerable groups such as trafficked children and former child soldiers with more complex cases would have a fair chance of filing a refugee claim and succeeding with it. Fair process and full compliance with the child's right to be heard in proceedings as per article 12 of the CRC requires that Canada allow for appeals on the merits of a case and not just on procedural errors that may have been committed. At present, only reviews based on procedural error are possible.

The requirement that all unaccompanied child asylum seekers to Canada be assigned an independent legal guardian would help ensure that the state acted in compliance with article 3 of the CRC, which requires the state to act in the child's best interests.[65] Normally that guardian would be a social worker or some other child welfare professional. The social worker would act to ensure that the child receives the support services he or she requires (e.g., interpretive, educational, health, and legal services). Effective implementation of this provision would require that child welfare services be made available to all children in such need of protective service up to at least age eighteen across all provinces. For unaccompanied children, where there is no established security risk (or other compelling exceptional reason), the child would be placed with a foster family or in a group home or other supportive environment. This would allow for compliance with article 20 of the CRC, which obliges the state to provide special assistance and protection to children temporarily or permanently deprived of their family environment.[66] Hospitable and appropriate child-friendly centres must be made available if the child must be detained in a more secure setting while his or her refugee application is being processed. In child-friendly facilities, the children would be grouped together away from adults in detention and receive appropriate support services suitable to their unique needs.

In some instances—for example, when trafficked by parents—even a child who was accompanied may require placement. In these cases as well, a social worker will be required to act as independent legal guardian for the child. Providing an independent legal guardian when the child is unaccompanied, or when there is a conflict of interest with the adults accompanying the child, would allow for compliance with article 20 of the CRC. That article obligates the state to assist children who are unable to rely on their parents for protection. At present, no independent legal guardian such as a social worker is provided to children under these circumstances to ensure that their rights are protected.

Abolition of the automatic lifetime ban on the possibility of being sponsored under the family class owing to significant misrepresentations made by a particular sponsor would allow Canada to act in the child's best interests. It often would allow for family reunification, given the facts of a particular case. The abolition of the lifetime ban would bring Canada into better compliance also with article 10 of the CRC, which requires states to facilitate family reunification. Furthermore, to facilitate family reunification for child refugees in accordance with article 22 of the CRC, it will be necessary to allow parents or guardians to sponsor a child who was not initially listed on the adult's refugee application. In addition, parents or legal guardians should be permitted to sponsor a non-accompanying child to come to Canada at a later date (a non-accompanying child may include a child who is still with the other parent in the home country at the time the sponsorship application is made). Reinstatement of the guardianship provision to allow the sponsorship of child refugees by a *non-related* private sponsor who acts as the child's legal guardian is also a necessity. This latter step would allow Canada to better meets its obligation to provide for the protection needs of child asylum seekers as guaranteed under articles 6 and 22 of the CRC.

Also, greater compliance with the CRC requirements of article 10 regarding state facilitation of family reunification would result if it were possible to sponsor family members as immigrants at the time they arrived at a Canadian entry port.[67] Currently, the family member who is being sponsored must remain outside Canada while his or her application is being processed. These family members undergo lengthy delays before they are permitted to come to Canada, and this significantly delays family reunification. As well, it would facilitate compliance with article 10 if separated children who arrive first at a border point were permitted to apply for family reunification. Canada would also be brought into greater compliance with the best-interests provision of the CRC if it stopped deporting parents for mere technical violations of immigration and refugee regulations and for infringements genuinely motivated by the need to ensure the safety of the children and integrity of the family.

Canada, at present, is not in full compliance with article 7 of the CRC, which requires the state to respect the child's right to acquire nationality when, through one circumstance or another, the child is or has become stateless. Nearly fifty million children globally were not registered at birth in 2000 and hence they have no legal identity.[68] The fact that these children are not registered makes it extremely difficult to trace family and reunite these children with their parents or guardians. Canadian refugee law and policy must be modified so that the fact that a child does not have adequate identification documents or may be stateless is not considered a sufficient basis in itself for detention or denial of a refugee claim. Such a policy would be consistent with Canada's obligations under article 6 of the CRC, which requires the state to meet the child's protection needs and rights. The registration of children without birth registration is also an international effort to which Canada should contribute. Furthermore, Canada should ratify the UN Convention on the Status of Stateless Persons, which offers certain fundamental protections to stateless people who may not in all instances be classed as refugees.This would help ensure that Canada will grant the stateless child a Canadian nationality or work to have another state assign the child a nationality.

A comprehensive national set of standards in Canada regarding the treatment of child refugee claimants would greatly reduce the risk of discriminatory treatment of unaccompanied child refugees and would be consistent with articles 2 and 22 of the CRC. This would lead to more equitable adjudication of the refugee claims of especially vulnerable groups of unaccompanied child asylum seekers. These standards would include guidelines for the thorough investigation of the safety and adequacy of care the child would receive in the home country from family, relatives, or the government of the home country if removed from Canada. This would ensure that no child can be removed from Canada if there is a continuing risk of trafficking or of any other form of child persecution or other significant harm.

Articles 9(1) and 10 of the CRC guarantee the child's right to family unless it is contrary to the child's best interests. To comply with these articles, Canada must provide increased support to UN agencies with regard to family re-unification. This includes collaboration on measures to prevent children from being separated from families in the first instance, and on the tracing of families of separated children whether the child is or is not still in the home country. Investigations into family history and whereabouts must be thorough and must meet acceptable written domestic guidelines.

As a corollary of national standards, it should be possible to make available interdisciplinary professional expertise in dealing with child refugees, including those who are unaccompanied. These specialist practitioners would be available to the refugee branch to offer advice and guidance on the legal, social work, psychological, health, and educational needs and rights of the child asylum seeker. The latter approach would further enhance Canada's compliance with article 22 of the CRC, which obliges states to provide humanitarian assistance to children at various stages of the asylum-seeking process. Provision of support services to asylum-seeking children is also consistent with article 19, which requires that children who have suffered any sort of significant maltreatment or trauma be provided with such services as are necessary for their social integration and recovery.

The collection of basic systemic data on the treatment of accompanied versus unaccompanied child asylum seekers by Canadian immigration authorities and consultants would assist in developing adequate national standards of care and treatment for all child refugees. This would allow for public accountability and ongoing evaluation of needed improvements in service to these various groups of highly vulnerable children who are seeking asylum in Canada.

Notes

1 Internally displaced persons are those who have been forced to move from their normal geographic place of residence but are still within their home country. Many of these persons may be eligible also for refugee resettlement in Canada, depending on the circumstances relating to their displacement; UN High Commission on Refugees, "The Protection of Refugee and Asylum-seeking Children, the Convention on the Rights of the Child, and the Work of the Committee on the Rights of the Child" (2005), http://www.unhcr.ch.

2 Human Rights Watch, "Promises Broken: An Assessment of Children's Rights on the 10th Anniversary of the Convention on the Rights of the Child (Refugee Children)," http://www.hrw.org.

3 Castan Centre for Human Rights Law, *Detention, Children, and Asylum Seekers: A Comparative Study* (Australia: Castan Centre for Human Rights Law, Monash University), http://www.law.monash.edu.au; M.A. Ali, S. Taraban, and J.A. Gill, "Policy Matters: Unaccompanied/Separated Children Seeking Refugee Status in Ontario: A Review of Documented Policies and Practices," Joint Centre for Excellence for Research on Immigration and Settlement, *Ceris* 13 (2004), http://ceris.metropolis.net.

4 Canadian Council for Refugees, "Refugee Women Fleeing Gender-Based Persecution" (2001), http://www.web.net/~ccr/gendpers.html.

5 Canadian Council for Refugees, "Impacts on Children of the Immigration and Refugee Protection Act" (2004), http://www.web.ca/~ccr/children.pdf.

6 Canadian Council for Refugees, "Annual Status Report on Refuges and Immigrants" (2004), http://www.web.net/~ccr.

7 Canada Gazette, "Regulation Amending the Immigration and Refugee Protection Regulations," *Canada Gazette* 139, no. 2 (2005); Citizenship and Immigration Canada, "Notice: Repeal of Guardianship Provisions," http://www.cic.gc.ca.

8 UN High Commission for Refugees, *Refugee Children: Guidelines for Protection and Care.* Geneva: UNHCR, 1994.

9 Article 1 defines "child" as "every human being below the age of eighteen years." That same CRC article permits individual states to stray from that definition under varying statutes according to domestic definitions of age of majority.

10 Canadian Immigration and Refugee Board, "Guideline 3: Child Refugee Claimants: Procedural and Evidentiary Guidelines," issued by the chairperson on August 26, 1996, http://www.irb-cisr.gr.ca.

11 *Baker v. Canada (Minister of Citizenship and Immigration)* [1999] 2 S.C.R. 817.

12 Immigration and Refugee Protection Act of Canada (IRPA) 2001, c. 27, s. 75; 2002, c. 8, s. 194 (entering into force 28 June, 2002), http://www.cic.gc.ca.

13 Ibid.

14 Canadian Coalition for the Rights of the Child, "UN Convention on the Rights of the Child: How Does Canada Measure Up?" (UN Reporting Category: Special Protection Measures Convention Article 22: Refugee Children, 1999), http://www.rightsofchildren.ca. See also refugee regulations at the CIC website: http://www.cic.gc.ca.

15 CIC Safe Third Country Agreement (exemption for *unmarried* unaccompanied minors at article 4) (2002), http://www.cic.gc.ca/english/policy/safe-third .html.

16 CRC, article 3.

17 *Canadian Foundation for Children, Youth and the Law v. Canada* (Attorney General).

18 The vagueness of the "best interests of the child" principle as currently interpreted in Canada is reflected in the following statement by the CIRB: "Guideline 3: Child refugee claimants: Procedural and Evidentiary Guidelines Issued by the Chairperson August 26, 1996," states that "the phrase best interests of the child is a broad term and the interpretation to be given to it will depend on the circumstances of each case. There are many factors which may affect the best interests of the child ... and this multitude of factors makes a precise definition of 'best interests' principle difficult."

19 *Gordon v. Goertz* [1996] 2 S.C.R.

20 S.C. Grover, "Denying the Right of Trafficked Children to Be Classed as Convention Refugees: The Canadian Case Example," *International Journal of Children's Rights* 14, no. 3 (2006): 235–49; J. Bhabha, "Seeking Asylum Alone: Treatment of Separated and Trafficked Children in Need of Refugee Protection," *International Migration* 42, no. 1 (2004): 141–48.

21 Bhabha, "Seeking Asylum." The grounds of persecution listed under the CRSR include "race." Hence, the term is used here in reference to that convention. Note, however, that the concept of race has been shown to have no scientific credibility and really ought to be substituted by the notions of ethnicity or cultural identity.

22 CRC, preamble.

23 Legal Services of the Immigration and Refugee Board, "Key Point Guide for CRDD Members" (2000), http://www.irb-cisr.gc.ca. See also CIC Refugee Board, "Guideline 3: Child Refugee Claimants."

24 Legal Services of the IRB (2000).

25 Ibid.

26 J. Frecker, P. Duquette, D. Galloway, et al., "Representation for Immigrants and Refugee Claimants" (Department of Justice, 2002), http://canada.justice.gc.ca.

27 CRC, article 11.

28 M.A. Ali, S. Taraban, and J.A. Gill, "Policy Matters: Unaccompanied/Separated Children Seeking Refugee Status in Ontario: A Review of Documented Policies and Practices," Joint Centre for Excellence for Research on Immigration and Settlement, *Ceris* 13. http://ceris.metropolis.net.

29 W. Ayotte and K. Peloffy, *Separated Children in Canada: Immigration Procedures* (2003), http://www.web.net/~ccr.

30 Ali et al., "Policy Matters."

31 Ibid.

32 Ayotte and Peloffy, "Separated Children in Canada."

33 Ali et al., "Policy Matters."

34 Ibid.

35 Ayotte and Peloffy, "Separated Children in Canada."

36 Ibid. See also UNHCR, "The Protection of Refugee and Asylum-Seeking Children," for international guidelines on the identification of unaccompanied children with the objective of family reunification.

37 Canadian Council for Refugees, "Annual Status Report on Refugees and Immigrants."

38 CRC, article 22.

39 Amnesty International, KAIROS, Canadian Ecumenical Justice Initiatives, and Canadian Council for Refugees, "Joint Statement on the Refugee Appeal Division" (World Refugee Day, June 20, 2005), http://www.web.net~ccr/jointst RAD.html.

40 Ayotte, "Separated Children Seeking Asylum in Canada" (prepared for UNHCR, 2001), http://www.web.net~ccr/seprated.pdf. See also Ayotte and Peloffy, "Separated Children in Canada"; Legal Services of the CIRB, "Key Point Guide for CRDD Members."

41 CIRB, "Guideline 3: Child Refugee Claimants."

42 Ibid.

43 Frecker et al., "Representation for Immigrants and Refugee Claimants."

44 Ibid.

45 Ibid.

46 Ibid.

47 Ali et al., "Policy Matters."

48 Ibid.

49 Ayotte, "Separated Children Seeking Asylum in Canada."

50 Bhabha, *Seeking Asylum Alone.*

51 UNICEF, "Early Marriage: A Harmful Traditional Practice," http://www.unicef .org/publications/files/Early_Marriage_12.lo.pdf.

52 CRC, article 19.

53 CRC, articles 13 and 24. Note that the Universal Declaration of Human Rights refers more directly to the right to provide "free and full consent" to marriage for persons who have reached "full age." The CRC does not mention marriage specifically but covers the matter under various articles that are broader in scope. "Full age" in the UDHR is not defined in terms of arbitrary domestic law cut-offs; rather, it implies something more fundamental regarding development and the ability to give free and full consent. The UDHR is available at http://www.un.org/Overview/rights.html.

54 CRC, article 6. See also Grover, "Children as Chattel of the State: Deconstructing the Concept of Sex Trafficking," *International Journal of Human Rights* (in press).

55 CRC and the Optional Protocol on the involvement of children in armed conflict.

56 P.W. Singer, *Children at War* (New York: Pantheon Books, 2005).

57 *Canadian Youth for International Justice* 5, no. 4 (1998), http://collections.ic.gc
.ca.
58 A. Brouwer, "Statelessness in the Canadian Context" (prepared for the
UNHCR, 1993), http://www.unhcr.ch.
59 CRC, article 39.
60 CRC, articles 3, 6, 19, and 24.
61 CRC, article 12.
62 S. Austin, R. O'Neill, and K. Vandergrift, "Separated Children in Canada:
Family Reunification" (2002), https://www1.worldvision.ca.
63 CRC, article 22.
64 CRC, article 37.
65 CRC, article 3.
66 CRC, article 20.
67 CRC, article 10.
68 UNHCR, "The World of Children at a Glance" (2001), http:/www.unhcr.ch/
children/glance.html.

Bibliography

Ali, M.A., S. Taraban, and J.A. Gill. 2004. "Policy Matters: Unaccompanied/Sep-
arated Children Seeking Refugee Status in Ontario: A Review of Docu-
mented Policies and Practices." Joint Centre for Excellence for Research
on Immigration and Settlement. *Ceris* 13. http://ceris.metropolis.net.
Austin, S., E. O'Neill, and K. Vandergrift. 2003. "Separated Children in
Canada: Family Reunification." World Vision Canada. http://www.ibcr.org/
Publications/Trafficking_SC/2003_BP6_Family_Reunification.pdf.
Ayotte, W. 2001. "Separated Children Seeking Asylum in Canada." Report
prepared for the UN High Commission on Refugees. http://www.unhcr.ch.
Ayotte, W., and K. Peloffy. 2003. "Separated Children in Canada: Immigration
Procedures." http://www.web.net/~ccr.
Bhabha, J. 2004. "Seeking Asylum Alone: Treatment of Separated and Traf-
ficked Children in Need of Refugee Protection." *International Migration*
42, no. 1: 141–48.
Brouwer, A. 1993. "Statelessness in the Canadian Context." Report prepared
for the UN High Commission on Refugees. http://www.unhcr.ch.
Canada Gazette. 2005. "Regulation Amending the Immigration and Refugee
Protection Regulations." *Canada Gazette* 139, no. 2.
Canadian Charter of Rights and Freedoms. Enacted as Schedule B to the
Canada Act 1982 (U.K.) c. 11 entering into force on 17 April, 1982.
http://laws.justice.gc.ca.
Canadian Coalition for the Rights of the Child. 1999. "UN Convention on the
Rights of the Child: How Does Canada Measure Up? UN Reporting Cat-
egory: Special Protection Measures Convention Article 22: Refugee Chil-
dren." http://www.rightsofchildren.ca.
Canadian Council for Refugees. 2001. "Refugee Women Fleeing Gender-Based
Persecution." http://www.web.net/~ccr/gendpers.html.

————. 2004a. "Annual Status Report on Refugees and Immigrants." http:// www.web.net/~ccr.

————. 2004b. "Impacts on Children of the Immigration and Refugee Protection Act." http://www.web.ca/~ccr/children.pdf.

Canadian Immigration and Refugee Board. 1996. "Guideline 3: Child Refugee Claimants: Procedural and Evidentiary Guidelines Issued by the Chairperson, August 26, 1996." http://www.irb-cisr.gr.ca.

Canadian Youth for International Justice. 1998. Volume 5, no. 4. http://collections .ic.gc.ca.

Castan Centre for Human Rights Law. Detention, Children and Asylum Seekers: A Comparative Study. Australia: Castan Centre for Human Rights Law, Monash University. http://www.law.monash.edu.au.

Citizenship and Immigration Canada. "Notice: Repeal of Guardianship Provisions." http://www.cic.gc.ca.

Committee on the Rights of the Child. 2005. "Treatment of Unaccompanied and Separated Children outside Their Country of Origin." General Comment 6. http://www.ohchr.org.

Frecker, J., P. Duquette, D. Galloway, F. Gauthier, W. Jackson, and G. James. 2002. "Representation for Immigrants and Refugee Claimants." Report prepared for Department of Justice, Canada. http://canada.justice.gc.ca.

Grover, S.C. 2006. "Denying the Right of Trafficked Children to Be Classed as Convention Refugees: The Canadian Case Example." International Journal of Children's Rights 14, no. 3: 235–49.

————. 2005. "Children as Chattel of the State: Deconstructing the Concept of Sex Trafficking." International Journal of Human Rights (in press).

Human Rights Watch. "Promises Broken: An Assessment of Children's Rights on the 10th Anniversary of the Convention on the Rights of the Child (Refugee Children)." http://www.hrw.org.

Legal Services of the Immigration and Refugee Board. 2000. "Key Point Guide for CRDD Members." http://www.irb-cisr.gc.ca.

Singer, P.W. 2005. Children at War. New York: Pantheon Books.

United Nations High Commission for Refugee Children. 2001. "The World of Children at a Glance." http://www.unhcr.ch/children/glance.html.

UN High Commission for Refugees. Refugee Children: Guidelines for Protection and Care. Geneva: UNHCR, 1994.

————. 2000. "Comments on Canadian Immigration and Citizenship. Draft Discussion Paper. Unaccompanied Minor Refugee Claimants." http:// www.unhcr.ch.

————. 2005. "The Protection of Refugee and Asylum-Seeking Children, the Convention on the Rights of the Child, and the Work of the Committee on the Rights of the Child." http://www.unhcr.ch.

UNICEF. n.d. "Early Marriage: A Harmful Traditional Practice." http://www .unicef.org/publications/files/Early_Marriage_12.lo.pdf.

————. n.d. "Impact of Armed Conflict on Children: Unaccompanied Children." http://www.unicef.org.

Implementing the Rights of Children with Disabilities

Richard Sobsey

Introduction

This chapter reviews the rights of children with disabilities in Canada as specified under the United Nations Convention on the Rights of the Child (CRC). Canada's support of the Convention signals its recognition of the universal rights of all children as well as its support for the specific rights of children with disabilities.

This chapter focuses on actual practices rather than laws or policies, which are addressed only occasionally as they affect practice. There are at least two important reasons for this focus on practice rather than law. Because most of the relevant legislation and policy in Canada is provincial rather than federal, a thorough analysis of the relevant laws and policies would require a province-by-province analysis of dozens of statutes and policies on child welfare, guardianship, health facilities, and a variety of other topics: that is beyond the scope of this chapter. More importantly, actual practice often differs substantially from the formal law and policy. For example, Section 15 of the Canadian Charter of Rights and Freedoms explicitly prohibits discrimination on the basis of mental or physical disability, but it would be naive to assume that no such discrimination exists in Canada.

Estimated numbers of children with disabilities in Canada vary from approximately 250,000 to more than 1,000,000. According to Statistics Canada, roughly 3.5 percent of Canadians under fourteen have

Richard Sobsey, JP Das Developmental Disabilities Centre and the John Dossetor Health Ethics Centre, University of Alberta disabilities.[1] Of these approximately 250,000 Canadian children with disabilities, about 57 percent have mild to moderate disabilities and 43 percent have severe to very severe disabilities. Provincial education ministries, however, identify much larger numbers of children with disabilities. They identify about 10 percent of all school-aged children as having disabilities. This suggests that about 1,000,000 Canadian children have disabilities. The primary difference in these estimates appears to be one of definitions, with schools identifying more children with mild disabilities that affect learning and behaviour. As a result, they identify about 90 percent of children as having mild to moderate disabilities and only 10 percent as having severe disabilities. Whereas the estimates of how many children have mild disabilities vary greatly, the number of children with severe disabilities is similar (about 100,000) in both estimates.

The CRC does not specifically define disability or provide guidelines regarding which children should be considered to have disabilities. It does, nonetheless, describe special rights for children with disabilities in article 23; and as described below, other articles of the Convention are of particular importance to the lives of children with disabilities regardless of the nature or severity of the disability.

Articles 1, 2, and 23: Universal and Special Rights

While article 23 identifies specific rights of children with disabilities, article 1 and article 2 are essential to understanding the nature of those special rights. Article 1 is vital to our understanding of the universal rights of children because it defines them as "every human being below the age of eighteen years unless under the law applicable to the child, majority is attained earlier."[2] This definition is important because it precludes the restriction of "universal" rights through definitions that exclude some children from status as a child. As discussed later in this chapter, societies have sometimes attempted to deny basic human rights to some children with severe disabilities by constructing definitions that exclude them from status as a child or as a person. Article 1 clearly prohibits this approach.

The article 2 prohibition against discrimination provides a passive assurance that children with disabilities cannot be deprived of their universal rights, while article 23 requires an active effort to ensure that children with disabilities can exercise those rights. Because article 23 is designed to ensure that children with disabilities are able to benefit from the same universal rights as all other children, the implementation of that article must be evaluated by examining how well children with disabilities are provided with the universal rights that are recognized and protected by the CRC.

Article 2(1) emphasizes that *all* children have universal rights without discrimination on the basis of personal or family characteristics: "State Parties shall respect and ensure the rights set forth in the present Convention to each child within their jurisdiction without discrimination of any kind, irrespective of the child's or his or her parent's or legal guardian's race, colour, sex, language, religion, political or other opinion, national, ethnic or social origin, property, disability, birth or other status."[3]

Articles 1 and 2 make it clear that all of the universal rights specified in the subsequent articles of the Convention apply to every living human being who has not yet reached the age of majority, without discrimination of any kind, including discrimination based on a disability of the child or the child's parent or guardian. This unambiguous statement in articles 1 and 2 is essential to understanding the special rights of children described in article 23 because it makes it clear that these special article 23 rights are *in addition* to the universal rights of all children, and that special rights cannot be viewed as a substitute for universal rights.

Of course, one might ask why children with disabilities (or why any specific group of children) need special rights if they are provided with all of the other universal rights granted to all children. The authors of the Convention did not include article 23 to give children with disabilities more rights than other children. Article 23 simply recognizes that children with disabilities may require special assistance in order to exercise their universal rights, and it promises children with disabilities the necessary assistance to enable them to meaningfully exercise their universal rights. Without special assistance, universal rights might be meaningless. For example, if all children are given a right to education, but in order to receive education all children are expected to climb the schoolhouse steps, some children with disabilities might be excluded from exercising their right. Article 23 simply promises that extra assistance will be given to ensure that children with disabilities can exercise their rights.

Article 23 also provides a guideline on how this special assistance will be given by stating that special assistance must be provided "in a manner conducive to the child's achieving the fullest possible social integration and individual development, including his or her cultural and spiritual development."[4] This means that any special help given to children with disabilities has to be provided in a manner that maximizes social inclusion and that minimizes intrusion on the child's normal social participation. To return to the previous example, the problem of the inaccessible school could be addressed in one of two ways: children with disabilities could be given the help they need to attend the same school as other children, or a separate accessible school could be constructed for children with disabilities. The article 23 requirement for achieving the "fullest possible social integration," however, mandates the more inclusive approach and prohibits a segregated alternative.

Applying articles 1, 2, and 23, each of the universal rights of children can be considered according to four criteria. First, are children with disabilities given the same opportunities to exercise their rights as are all other children? Second, when children with disabilities are disadvantaged in exercising their universal rights, are special efforts undertaken to compensate for this disadvantage? Third, when special efforts are undertaken to compensate for any disadvantage, are these efforts adequate to ensure equal outcomes for children with disabilities or, if not fully adequate, to substantially narrow the gap between outcomes for children with and without disabilities? And fourth, when special efforts are made to ensure equal outcomes or to narrow the disadvantage experienced by children with disabilities, are they provided in a manner that ensures "the fullest possible social integration and individual development?"

Articles 6 and 24: The Right to Life and Survival and Health Care

Article 6 requires states to recognize "that every child has the inherent right to life"[5]; furthermore, "States Parties shall ensure to the maximum extent possible the survival and development of the child."[6] This is the first article of the Convention that specifies a universal right, and indeed the right to life can be viewed as the most important of all rights, since any child deprived of his or her life is no longer able to exercise any other right.[7] This article requires states to actively protect children from death as well as to refrain from actions that might result in the death of children. Since article 2 prohibits discrimination on the basis of mental or physical disability and article 23 requires that states undertake special efforts to ensure that children with disabilities are not placed at a disadvantage, children with disabilities should be fully protected. In addition, article 24 recognizes the universal "right of the child to the enjoyment of the highest attainable standard of health"[8] and requires states to take action to minimize mortality. Because the right to health care is essential to the right to life, these two articles are considered collectively in this chapter. The general rights of children to health care are discussed in chapter 4 of this book.

Compliance with article 6, then, requires Canada to provide the same protection for the lives of children with disabilities as for all other children, to recognize that some children with disabilities may be at higher levels of risk for loss of life, and to take necessary measures to substantially compensate for this excess risk. Three factors make the assessment of Canada's compliance with this obligation difficult. First, some children have disabilities caused by underlying conditions that substantially increase their risk of dying. While our best efforts may reduce their excess risk and narrow the gap in survival rates between these children and the general population, the gap cannot be eliminated completely with contemporary medical intervention. As a result, it would be an unreasonable standard to judge Canada's compliance with its obligation to make special efforts to protect the lives of children with disabilities by an absolute standard of ensuring a death rate equal to or lower than that of the general population. Therefore, Canada's efforts to narrow this gap must be judged according to qualitative standards, such as *reasonable* and *adequate*. Second, very few data are available on which to base an accurate assessment. There have been few studies about the relative survival rates of children with disabilities and the impact of efforts to improve survival over time. Third, the protection of the right to survival may play out very differently for children with different kinds of disabilities. Most children with specific learning disabilities, for example, have no significantly increased risk of dying, while children with disabilities resulting from some genetic syndromes (e.g., Tay-Sachs disease) rarely live more than four or five years. The right to life and survival, however, is an individual right of each child. Therefore, evaluating the protection of this right requires more than collective data for Canadian children as a group. It requires careful consideration of whether any subgroups or individual children are unprotected.

Finally, the lives of children with disabilities might be protected from different kinds of risk. The increased risk of disability-related medical issues is one kind of risk; but other risks, such as death by homicide, are not inherently related to the child's disability and may require very different kinds of protection.

In this chapter, Canada's efforts to ensure the right to life and survival for children with disabilities is examined in two important areas. First, we must consider the efforts of the health care system to protect children with disabilities from death. Health care is also protected under article 24, which protects the right of every child the child "to the enjoyment of the highest attainable standard of health and to facilities for the treatment of illness and rehabilitation of health"[9] and requires states to ensure that "no child is deprived of his or her right of access to such health care services."[10] Second, we must consider the efforts of the justice system to protect children with disabilities from homicide or potentially fatal abuse and neglect. Children are also protected against abuse and neglect under article 19, which requires states to "take all appropriate legislative, administrative, social and educational measures to protect the child from all forms of physical or mental violence, injury or abuse, neglect or negligent treatment."

The Right to Life-Saving Treatment

The CRC requires Canada and all other nations that are signatories of the Convention to provide health care in a manner that attempts to protect the life of each child with a disability with the same vigour it provides health care for other children, and to take any additional efforts required to overcome or at least reduce any disadvantage experienced by a child with a disability.

One group of Canadian children whose disabilities are often associated with medical conditions that can threaten survival are children with birth defects. One of the few Canadian studies of mortality of children with and without disabilities matched 45,000 children with birth defects with 45,000 children without birth defects in Ontario and followed both cohorts for seventeen years.[11] The death rate in the group with birth defects was thirteen times higher than the death rate among controls. While death rates for both groups of children were highest in the first year of life, the death rate for children with disabilities was about sixteen times the rate for other children during the first year, and death rates remained several times higher among children with birth defects at every age. Children with severe birth defects and children with multiple birth defects were much more likely to die than children who had single, mild birth defects. The huge disparity in death rates makes it clear that Canada has not provided equal right-to-life and survival outcomes for children with disabilities; that said, Canada has unquestionably increased the survival rates for some children with birth defects and other disabilities. For example, the life expectancy has been greatly increased for children with cystic fibrosis,[12] and for those with many kinds of heart defects.[13]

Certainly, some children with birth defects are likely to die even with the best possible care. And even with special efforts made to ensure the survival of children with disabilities, the death rate among children with birth defects is likely to be much higher than among children without birth defects. To better understand the meaning of the relative risk of death for Canadian children with birth defects, we can compare the Canadian findings to similar ones from other countries. The authors of the Canadian study reported that the first-year relative risk of death for children with disabilities in Canada was very similar to the relative risk identified for children with disabilities in similar studies in Norway, which has a lower overall infant mortality rate than Canada, and in the United States, which has a higher overall infant mortality rate than Canada.

This suggests that Canada's efforts to protect the lives and ensure the survival of children with disabilities are similar to the efforts in these two other countries and probably in other developed countries with sophisticated health care systems. In other words, Canada appears to be doing about as well as other developed countries in protecting the rights of children with disabilities under article 6.

Unfortunately, doing about as well as other developed countries probably reflects the common inclination of nations to ignore the right to life and survival for some children with disabilities. Many children with disabilities die in Canada simply because parents and health care professionals decide that their lives are not worth continuing. A study of deaths in an Ontario pediatric intensive care unit indicated that 60 percent of child deaths were the direct result of decisions made not to give life-saving treatment, and that only 40 percent of children died in spite of treatment.[14] Simply put, this implies that more children died because of the decision to end their lives than because of the inability to maintain their lives. One might assume that decisions to let a child die are based on the fact that prolonging life would only permit a brief reprieve, and this was true in about two-thirds of cases. Of the physicians involved in a decision to withhold lifesaving treatment, 68.5 percent indicated that further treatment would probably not have succeeded in saving the child. About three in ten children who were denied treatment, however, probably could have been saved with treatment. The physicians indicated that their reasons for withholding life-saving treatment were unsatisfactory quality of life (19.1 percent of cases) and potential for poor quality of life in the future (12.3 percent). In other words, in approximately 19 percent of all pediatric ICU deaths, parents and physicians decided to let the child die rather than live with a severe disability. This finding from Ontario is very similar to the results of a study conducted in a California hospital by Wall and Partridge, who reported that 20 percent of all deaths occurred because treatment for viable infants with severe disabilities was withdrawn because of decisions that their lives would not be of high enough quality to justify the efforts necessary to keep them alive.[15]

The Canadian study left it unclear whether all of these children actually died as a result of the withholding of life-sustaining treatment or whether some were actively killed as a result of receiving strong sedatives, analgesics, and paralyzing agents, although it presented some evidence of active euthanasia. Decisions to withhold or withdraw life-sustaining treatment were made by consensus among members of the health care team and the parents. After a decision was reached to let the child die, actions were initiated to bring about death within a few hours, and once these actions were taken, the children died within an average of eighty minutes. A consensus approach involving physicians and parents offers very few due process or natural justice protections beyond presumed good intentions, in spite of potential conflicts of interest that exist for parents (e.g., the financial costs and time demands of caring for the child) as well as for members of the health care team (e.g., if there is medical liability for the child's condition, awards are lower for children who do not survive than for children who require lifetime care). There is no common standard for determining potential quality of life or the circumstances under which death is preferable to life. In the Ontario study, an ethicist was part of the discussion in only one out of seventy-two cases, and none of those cases involved a judge or a court proceeding.

While it has been argued often that these decisions are usually ethically and legally defensible and made in the best interests of the child, decisions to withhold life-saving treatment based on presumed quality of life for children with severe disabilities are in clear conflict with the CRC. The Convention clearly mandates survival as a right of every child and requires that special efforts be made to ensure the survival of children with disabilities. It makes no exception based on the severity of disability or perceived quality of life, and article 23 actually requires special efforts to reduce the increased risk of death faced by children with disabilities. Withholding treatment from children with severe disabilities clearly provides less than equal protection for the lives of children with severe disabilities, in stark contrast to the requirement to make extra efforts to preserve their lives.

Many bioethical perspectives are in direct conflict with the notion of a universal right to life and survival. For example, Joseph Fletcher, one of the key architects of modern bioethics, suggested that not all infants, children, or adults should be considered as *human*, and therefore, not all human beings are entitled to rights or moral consideration.[16] Fletcher proposed that a minimum IQ should be required for personhood. The prominent, contemporary utilitarian bioethicist, Peter Singer from Princeton University, presents a similar view of personhood. Singer considers the universal right to life and survival to be an outmoded concept and suggests replacing the traditional "Thou shalt not kill" with his own commandment: "Recognize that the worth of human life varies."[17]

For the most part, the Convention is simply ignored by the field of bioethics. For example, Englehardt[18] specifically discusses the rights of infants and young children in "Ethical Issues in Aiding the Death of Young Children," a chapter in *Bioethics, Justice, & Health Care* (2001); in that book, Englehardt's ethical analysis is reprinted unchanged from its original publication in 1975.[19] From the perspective of bioethics, the CRC was a non-event—nothing of substance has occurred to change our ethical analysis of child euthanasia over the past three decades. Englehardt's analysis does not even consider the possibility that children have a universal right to life and survival. Rather, decisions about who lives and who dies are based on (a) the probable degree of disability and its effect on "expected lifestyle";[20] (2) the cost of treatment; and (3) the degree of burden the child may impose on parents. In his view, the decision rests with parents, "who should not be obliged to take on severe burdens on behalf of their children."[21] He explicitly states that a child cannot be considered a person and has no individual rights. The physician's role is only to provide parents with information. The parents should be the sole decision makers, and society has no right to intervene unless "it is clear that the burden [of caring for the child] is light" and "the chance of the child achieving a good quality of life is high."[22] In other words, he believes that society has no right to intervene to protect or preserve the life of a child with a significant disability, but it can actively intervene to save a child who has no significant disability.

From a human rights perspective, the notion that children have no rights and that parents have the right to end a child's life either because they doubt they will lead happy lives or because they do not wish to be burdened with the care of the child is unacceptable. From the perspective of non-discrimination, however, the fundamental question must be this: If parents have the discretion to end the lives of their children with disabilities, why are they not granted the same rights to end the lives of any other child? For example, parents of twins or triplets might find raising "extra" children burdensome, and the parents' perception that the "extra" child is unwanted might negatively affect the child's quality of life. Yet, there is no recommendation that parents be allowed to dispose of children without disabilities. The Canadian practice of letting children with severe disabilities die is a clear contravention of its obligations under the Convention; yet that practice appears to be similar to those of most other countries, and children's rights and human rights organizations have shown little interest in taking on this issue.

Protection from Filicide

In 2004 the *International Disability Rights Monitor: Regional Report for the Americas* rated twenty-four countries, including Canada, on their protection of the rights of people with disabilities. Each country was rated in five critical areas using a three-level rating system: (1) adequate protection, (2) partial protection, or (3) poor protection. Overall, Canada received top ratings in three of these areas (Accessibility, Health Services and Housing, and Communication), but received second-class ratings in two important areas (Legal Protections, and Education and Employment). Canada's second-class rating in basic legal protections for people with disabilities was better than those in only one other country (Belize), the same as in seven other countries (Jamaica, Chile, Mexico, Paraguay, Guyana, Honduras, and Suriname), and worse than in the fifteen remaining countries (e.g., Bolivia, Brazil, Columbia, Costa Rica, and the United States). Contributing to Canada's second-class rating was a failure of the justice system to protect the lives of people with disabilities: "Homicide and filicide (the murder of a child by a parent) deserve special attentions in Canada. In the last ten years, such crimes against people with disabilities have been increasing, yet there has been a decrease in the rates of homicide among the general population."[23]

Of course, filicide is a significant problem for children with and without disabilities in all countries. It is the most common type of homicide against children and typically represents the majority of all murders of children. Some years, filicides have accounted for as high as 80 percent of all child murders in Canada.

While the overall homicide rate in Canada has dropped since 1990, child homicides have increased. Dalley studied homicides of Canadian children between 1990 and 1997 and found that the percentage of children killed by their parents rose sharply between 1994 and 1997 while the number of children killed by non-parents fell. There has been no systematic study on whether children with disabilities are more likely to be victims of filicide than other children, although there is some indirect reason to suspect that this is so. For example, research suggests that Canadian children with disabilities are two or more times as likely to be victims of child abuse than other Canadian children,[24] and filicide is commonly correlated with child abuse. In addition, research from a variety of countries and cultures suggests that children with disabilities are at particular risk for filicide. For example, De Haan's analysis of 924 cases of potentially fatal child maltreatment in Oregon found that 40 of 42 children (95 percent) who were actually killed had been diagnosed previously with disabilities or related conditions.[25]

Since there is no official source of data on filicides of children with disabilities in Canada, no precise figure can be given for the incidence of these events or their frequency relative to the filicides of other children. Anecdotal accounts from the mass media, however, indicate that filicides of children with disabilities occur regularly in Canada and that the Canadian justice system, instead of responding to provide special protection for children with disabilities, is exhibiting a clear pattern of excusing parents for killing children with disabilities. Among 40 apparent Canadian cases of filicide (38) and attempted filicide (2) of children with disabilities analyzed for this chapter, 7 parents committed suicide, leaving 33 cases to the criminal justice system. Of these, no charges were laid in eight cases and charges were dropped or stayed in two additional cases. The reasons for the lack of charges were sometimes not clear, but in at least a few cases, charges were not laid because of discretionary prosecution. In one of these cases, an inquest determined that the cause of the child's death was homicide while under care and supervision of the mother, yet the mother was not charged owing to a lack of public interest in the prosecution. In another case of apparent attempted filicide, the RCMP investigated and recommended laying charges, but the Crown prosecutor declined to charge the mother.

Regarding the 22 cases in which parents were charged, charges were not dropped, and information on trial outcomes was available, there were 11 acquittals. Almost none of the acquittals, however, was based on a defence that the parent had not killed the child. Virtually all acquittals were based on the conclusion that the parent had killed the child but should not be held criminally responsible owing to stress or depression. Many of the accused presented a secondary informal defence that the child may actually have been better off dead or at least that the filicidal parent believed that the child was better off dead than disabled.

Of those few who were convicted, most were convicted of lesser charges, and most sentences were light. Three received suspended sentences or no jail time, and three more were given a maximum sentence of two years or less. Three received a maximum sentence of more than two but not more than four years. Only two parents received a sentence of more than four years.

These two fathers—the only two parents convicted of murder or attempted murder—received a mandatory life sentence. However, one of these two had killed a second child who did not have a disability and an adult in the same incident, leaving it unclear whether a lighter sentence might have been given if only the child with a disability had been killed.

The only parent sentenced to life with no parole for ten years for killing a disabled child was a Saskatchewan farmer named Robert Latimer.[26] The case was the subject of repeated trials and appeals, but ultimately ended with the Supreme Court of Canada upholding his second-degree murder conviction and minimum allowable sentence.[27] It is highly probable that the main reason for him receiving a much more severe sentence than other parents who killed children with disabilities was his refusal to negotiate a plea agreement for a lesser charge or to defend his actions as wrong but a result of diminished capacity. In the end, the courts rejected his defence, which was based on the assertion that killing his daughter was a moral and legally justifiable act. Based on the distinction between this case and others in which parents who killed disabled children and pleaded various forms of diminished responsibility were acquitted, Canadian courts have been willing to treat the killing of children with disabilities as understandable and excusable, although they have not endorsed the practice as justifiable or heroic. Generally, the Canadian justice system as a whole has been lax in responding to the filicides of children with disabilities but has stopped short of endorsing the practice, as illustrated by the Latimer case. A more systematic study of its response to these cases is needed, but even now it can be said that Canada, instead of offering special protections to ensure the right of survival for children with disabilities, seems to be offering weak protection for the lives of these children. While disability advocacy groups have been vocal about the apparent lack of equal protection of the law, the Canadian public generally appears to support even lighter penalties for killing children with disabilities. For example, one national poll found that 71 percent of Canadians favoured reducing the ten-year sentence in the Latimer case or pardoning him outright, even though the sentence was already the minimum allowed by law.[28]

Summary of Article 6 Rights

Canada's protection of the right of children with disabilities to life and survival is inconsistent. For many children with mild disabilities, particularly those without mental disabilities, access to health care is good and produces significant improvements in survival. For many children with more severe disabilities, especially those with both mental and physical disabilities, both health care and justice systems appear to be failing to provide the most basic protections.

Articles 9, 20, 25: The Right to Family

Article 9 requires states to strive to keep families intact and, when families break down, to provide alternatives that approximate natural families so that institutional care is unnecessary. Since about 1970, institutional care of children with disabilities has been in decline. Nevertheless, various provinces still have some children who live in institutional settings. Some provinces continue to defend their provision of institutional care as giving families choice.

The Convention does not necessarily eliminate this choice, but it does call for efforts to support families. From an economic perspective, institutional care of children is expensive—typically, the costs are well in excess of $100,000 per year per child excluding facility costs, which are excluded because they fall under a different ministry. However, the provinces seem reluctant to grant families the same level of support to keep children in their homes. In other words, provinces are willing to spend more money to take children out of their families than to keep them in their families. This clearly contravenes the Convention. Nevertheless, provincial family support programs do assist many Canadian families of children with disabilities. In doing so, they have allowed some families to keep children with disabilities in the home instead of institutionalizing them, and they have improved the quality of life for many more families.

Alberta, for example, proclaimed a new Family Supports for Children with Disabilities Act[29] in 2004, replacing related provisions of its Child Welfare Act that had been in place since 1972. The new act provides for individual contracts with families to pay for the cost of specialized child care, family counselling, incidental expenses for special services, and other related expenses. All provinces and territories provide some supports to families, but there is considerable variation across Canada in the kinds of assistance given, the ages of children included, the types and severities of disabilities, and other program characteristics.[30] In addition, some provinces provide direct income support to families, and the federal government provides additional income tax exemptions to families of children with disabilities. Various other forms of assistance are available from other governmental and community-based organizations. Overall, Canada has been less than fully successful in supporting families and preventing the institutional care of children with disabilities, but it should also be acknowledged as a leader in providing quality family support programs.

Article 19: Freedom from Abuse and Neglect

Article 19 provides a universal right to all children to protection from abuse and neglect. It requires states to actively engage in child protection. Joan Durrant (chapter 5) and Anne McGillivray (chapter 6) have discussed the violations of article 19 in terms of corporal punishment and childhood sexual abuse. Children with disabilities are at heightened risk of abuse in general. In Canada, as in most other countries, children with disabilities are disproportionately represented among victims of child maltreatment. The degree of their overrepresentation, however, is difficult to state with precision, because of inconsistencies in the criteria used to determine which children have disabilities. A reasonable estimate of the excess risk for Canadian children with intellectual disabilities or developmental delays suggests that they experience abuse and neglect at a rate between 2.9 and 8.6 times the rate experienced by other Canadian children.[31] This level of excess risk appears to be similar to the excess risk of

3.8 to 4.0 times experienced by American children with intellectual disabilities,[32] and is consistent with the opinion presented in a review paper of the Public Health Agency of Canada, National Clearing House on Family Violence: "Research in Canada suggests that the risk estimate of abuse of people with disabilities may be as high as five times greater than the risk for the general population."[33]

The reasons for a strong association between child maltreatment and disability are multiple, complex, and only partially understood,[34] but there is no question that Canada is required both to take action to protect all children from abuse and to take special action to reduce the excess risk experienced by children with disabilities. Although individual provinces have responsibility for child welfare in Canada, the federal government plays a significant role in enforcing criminal law and in supporting research and public education. Children with disabilities are sometimes seen as a small subgroup of children in need of protection; they are not. For example, a study of children in Alberta's child protection system found that 60 percent of all children being served were known to have disabilities.[35]

Unfortunately, children with disabilities often experience barriers in prevention, intervention, and enforcement programs.[36] For example, many personal-safety skill training programs for children assume that participants have entry-level skills—skills that are lacking among many children with disabilities. Or such programs fail to consider functional alternatives for children with disabilities. Telling a child who cannot walk to run away, or telling a child who cannot speak to tell someone, may only increase the child's sense of powerlessness and victimization. Children with disabilities are often more difficult to place in foster care or adoptive homes, and investigation and prosecution may be more complicated and difficult when the alleged victim has limited communication.

It is difficult to assess Canada's performance in responding to the abuse of children with disabilities. Canada was among the first countries to acknowledge this problem and appears to be making some genuine efforts to address it. Unfortunately, most efforts to date seem to be primarily research or demonstration projects, and there is little evidence of actual progress toward reducing the overall incidence of child maltreatment or narrowing the gap between the risk for children with disabilities and the risk for other children. As discussed previously regarding filicide, there is some indication that violence against children with disabilities is more acceptable to Canadians than violence against other children. Considering these factors, Canada should be acknowledged for recognizing the problem and making some efforts to address it. But Canada must do much more to respond to the grim reality of maltreatment that affects the lives of too many Canadian children with disabilities. Moving forward on making a meaningful difference will require not only commitment and resources, but also research to generate the necessary knowledge to guide the effort. Finally, the article 23 requirement for developing inclusive solutions must guide Canada's efforts to protect Canadian children with disabilities from maltreatment. The preferred approach must be to ensure that children with disabilities are considered and included in efforts to protect all Canadian children.

Articles 28 and 29: The Right to Education

Article 28 recognizes the universal right of every child to a free and appropriate education, and article 29 provides criteria for curriculum content. In Canada, education is a provincial responsibility with a limited role for federal involvement. The right of all Canadian children to a basic education has been clearly acknowledged.[37] Although there is no specific right to education in the Canadian Charter of Rights and Freedoms, it is commonly viewed as a welfare right or as an equality right. The rationale for education as a welfare right is based on the premise that an education is so fundamental to a decent life that depriving an individual of his or her education would necessarily result in harm. The equality-right rationale is less controversial. It simply reasons that since provinces provide education and require most children to attend school, they cannot deny education to specific groups or individuals. This equality rationale is specifically supported by Section 15 of the Charter, which requires "equal benefit of the law without discrimination ... based on ... mental or physical disability."[38] The human rights acts of most provinces prohibit discrimination based on disability.[39] In addition, Canada is a party to a number of international agreements, besides the Convention, that recognize a universal right to education. An example is the UN International Covenant on Economic, Social, and Cultural Rights.

Historically, some children in Canada have been denied their right to education, but policy reforms and court decisions have gradually improved access. For example, in 1978 the courts ruled that Alberta could not use a series of *temporary* exclusions (permitted by law) to permanently exclude a child with cerebral palsy from school, and in 1985 the courts determined that British Columbia schools had to provide a program appropriate to the needs of student with disabilities. As a result, as Katherine Covell noted in chapter 10, violations of the rights of children with disabilities to some education now appear to be rare in Canada, and most children with special needs receive special assistance as required by article 23 of the CRC. Canada, however, falls short on the last requirement of article 23—that children with disabilities receive this special assistance in the most inclusive manner possible.

While there has been considerable progress in Canada toward inclusive education for children with disabilities, significant numbers of children with disabilities continue to be denied their right to access to the same classrooms and schools as other children from their own neighbourhoods. Most provinces have a policy promoting inclusive education but generally stop short of mandating it, and most decisions on inclusive education versus segregated alternatives are made by local districts, individual schools, or even individual teachers through "right of refusal" policies. In Alberta, for example, Ministerial Order 4.2.3—Standards for Special Education requires schools to "ensure that educating students with special education needs in inclusive settings in neighbourhood or local schools shall be the first placement option considered by school boards, in consultation with parents, school staff and, when appropriate, the student." Thus, schools are required to consider inclusive education but not necessarily to provide inclusive education.[40]

In 1997 the Supreme Court of Canada ruled in the case of Emily Eaton.[41] Emily was a nine-year-old girl with multiple disabilities who was refused an inclusive education by the Brant County Board of Education in Ontario. Although she had been successfully included in grade one, school authorities sought to segregate her for the rest of her schooling, arguing that she could not be successfully included beyond that grade. Her parents appealed, contending that her right to equal treatment and freedom from discrimination under Section 15 of the Canadian Charter of Rights and Freedoms had been violated. Under Ontario's Education Act, the Ontario Special Education Tribunal heard the case and ruled in favour of the school, based on its conclusion that Emily's educational needs could not be met in a regular classroom. The Ontario Divisional Court agreed with the tribunal. But in 1994, the Ontario Appeals Court determined that the decision denying Emily the right to inclusive education violated her rights. The Supreme Court of Canada, however, reversed the appeal and ruled in favour of the school's right to determine what is best for the child. While the Supreme Court found that inclusion should be the norm and that it generally results in what is best for the child, it left it to the discretion of school authorities to determine what is best in each case.

Not surprisingly, Canadian advocates for people with disabilities and their families were horrified by this decision and were convinced that the Supreme Court got it wrong. A number of legal authorities agreed that Court had erred. For example, UBC law professors Mossoff and Grant argued that the Court erred in its conclusion that discrimination on the basis of disability should not be considered as problematic as discrimination on the basis of race or gender, since Section 15 of the Charter explicitly includes all of these categories. Perhaps the ultimate irony of the *Eaton* case was that by the time the Supreme Court ruled that the Ontario Special Education Tribunal had been correct in ruling that Emily could not be successfully included beyond grade one, she already was in grade six and had, in fact, been successfully included for five additional years. After the Supreme Court decision, Emily continued to be successfully included in a regular classroom in another district with more inclusive policies.

Of course, Canada's obligations under international laws were not considered in *Eaton*, which solely considered Section 15 of the Charter. Whether or not the Supreme Court decision was correct according to the Charter, the decision stands, and it clearly falls short of Canada's responsibilities under article 23 of the CRC.

In conclusion, Canada has a well-developed system of universal education. The vast majority, if not all, children with disabilities can access education, and in most cases some special assistance is provided to children with disabilities. In these respects, children with disabilities have been served well by Canada's schools. However, Canada falls substantially short of the goal of providing these services in the most inclusive manner possible. Many children in Canada continue to be denied access to high-quality inclusive education.

Article 37: Freedom from Cruel Treatment or Punishment

Article 37 recognizes the universal right of children to be protected from cruel, inhuman, or degrading treatment or punishment. One controversial issue in the application of this article to children with disabilities is the use "aversive treatments." Some experts have recommended aversive treatments for children with autism, intellectual disabilities, brain injuries, psychiatric diagnoses, and other disabilities that affect learning or behaviour. These aversive treatments include slapping, arm twisting, ammonia mist spray, cutaneous electric shock, and other painful or noxious stimuli. Advocates claim that these procedures are sometimes effective when non-aversive alternatives fail, that they reduce the risk of abuse by providing an alternative, and that they are used only to address extreme behaviour problems that would produce greater harm if allowed to continue. Critics of these practices argue that the procedures are inherently cruel, often ineffective, model the misuse of power to control others, dehumanize the individual, and promote abuse. In addition, they argue that since these procedures would be considered abuse or torture if applied to people without disabilities, they should be equally unacceptable for use with people with disabilities. The argument that procedures prohibited for use with children without disabilities should be equally prohibited for use with children with disabilities is the critical issue for consideration under the Convention.

The legality of these procedures typically hinges on consent. The right to be free from torture or cruel treatment does not necessarily prohibit a competent adult from giving informed consent and receiving such treatment. Regarding children and adults who are considered incompetent to consent, this raises another issue: Can a substitute decision maker consent to aversive treatment? Currently, in Canada there appears to be no simple answer. Ontario's Substitute Decision Act of 1992, for example, states: "The guardian shall not use electric shock as aversive conditioning and shall not give consent on the person's behalf to the use of electric shock as aversive conditioning."[42] This might seem a clear answer, but it appears in a section of an act that pertains only to individuals over sixteen, does not address aversive treatments other than electric shock, and is followed by the qualification, "unless the consent is given to a treatment in accordance with the Health Care Consent Act, 1996, c. 2, s. 43 (5)." This suggests that substitute consent may be appropriate in some circumstances. Ontario is not alone in its lack of clarity on which aversive treatments are permitted, who can consent to them, and who is qualified to carry them out.

There are no clear standards for behaviour therapists in Canada. While psychologists and teachers are often involved in planning and administering behavioural programs, there is nothing that restricts the use of behavioural programming to these or any other professional groups, and the professional bodies that certify Canadian professionals provide few guidelines for these practices.

The use of aversive procedures with children with disabilities does not appear to be widespread, and the frequency of their use is difficult to estimate. Nevertheless, it does occur and it remains poorly regulated. In order to fulfill the Canada's commitment to the Convention, provinces and professional bodies must address and acknowledge these issues and prohibit or carefully regulate the use of these procedures.

Summary and Conclusion

This chapter has reviewed Canada's performance in a number of areas of children's rights as they are applied to children with disabilities. Overall, Canada ranks fairly highly, relative to other nations, in its degree of compliance with the provisions of the CRC. Canada's performance, however, receives substantially lower grades when judged by the relatively strict standards of the Convention, regardless of comparison with other countries. Canada's apparent non-compliance and utter disregard for article 6 protection of the right to life and survival for children with severe disabilities is particularly troubling. Although Canada needs to do more to ensure that children with disabilities remain in families and are not abandoned to institutions, its strong commitment to family support programs is certainly commendable. There has been progress toward educational inclusion, but there is considerably more work to be done to meet the standards of the Convention. There has been recognition of the special problems that children with disabilities face related to abuse and neglect, but little evidence toward reducing the impact of this problem on the lives of children with disabilities. The lack of clear laws and policies regulating the use of aversive procedures needs attention, and protections need to be put in place so that treatments and punishments that would be unacceptable when applied to children without disabilities cannot be applied to children with disabilities.

Notes

1 Statistics Canada, Housing, Family, and Social Statistics Division, *A Profile of Disability in Canada, 2001 Tables* (Ottawa: StatsCan, 2002). http://www.statcan.ca:80/english/freepub/89-579-XIE/free.htm.

2 UN Convention on the Rights of the Child (CRC), General Assembly Resolution 44/25 of 20 November 1989, Article 1.

3 CRC, article 2, section 1.

4 Ibid., article 23, section 3.

5 Ibid., article 6, section 1.

6 Ibid., article 6, section 2.

7 M. Nowak, *Article 6: The Right to Life, Survival, and Development: A Commentary on the United Nations Convention on the Rights of the Child* (Boston: Martinus Nijhoff, 2005).

8 CRC, article 24, section 1.

9 Ibid., article 24, section 1.

10 Ibid., article 24, section 1.

11 M.M. Agha et al., "Determinants of Survival in Children with Congenital Abnormalities: A Long-Term Population-Based Cohort Study, Birth Defects Research Part A." *Clinical and Molecular Teratology* 76, no. 1 (2006): 46–54.

12 M. Corey and V. Farewell, "Determinants of Mortality from Cystic Fibrosis in Canada, 1970–1989," *American Journal of Epidemiology* 143, no. 10 (1996): 1007–17.

13 K.A. Issekutz et al., "An Epidemiological Analysis of Charge Syndrome: Preliminary Results from a Canadian Study," *American Journal of Medical Genetics* 133, no. 3 (2005): 309–17.

14 D. Garros, R.J. Rosychuk, and P.N. Cox, "Circumstances Surrounding End of Life in a Pediatric Intensive Care Unit," *Pediatrics* 112, no. 5 (2003): e371.

15 S.N. Wall and J.C. Partridge, "Death in the Intensive Care Nursery: Physician Practice of Withdrawing and Withholding Life Support," *Pediatrics* 99, no. 1 (1997): 64–70.

16 J. Fletcher, "Indicators of Humanhood: A Tentative Profile of Man," *Hastings Center Report* 2, no. 11 (1972): 1–4.

17 P. Singer, *Writings on an Ethical Life* (New York: HarperCollins, 2000), p. 212.

18 H.T. Englehardt, Jr., "Ethical Issues in Aiding the Death of Young Children," in W. Teays and L. Purdy, *Bioethics, Justice, and Health Care* (Toronto: Wadsworth, 2001), pp. 394–400.

19 Englehart, "Ethical Issues in Aiding the Death of Young Children," in M. Kohl, *Beneficent Euthanasia* (Amherst, NY: Prometheus Books, 1975), pp. 130–35.

20 Englehardt, "Ethical Issues," in W. Teays and L. Purdy, *Bioethics, Justice, and Health Care* (Toronto: Wadsworth, 2001), p. 397.

21 Ibid., p. 397.

22 Ibid., p. 397.

23 International Disability Rights Monitor, *Regional Report for the Americas* (Winnipeg: Disabled Peoples International and International Disability Network, 2004), http://www.cirnetwork.org/idrm/reports/americas/countries/canada.html.

24 D.C. Reinke, *Child Maltreatment in Canada: A Developmental-Ecological Perspective* (2005). PhD thesis, University of Alberta.

25 B.D. de Haan, *Critical and Fatal Child Maltreatment in Oregon: Escalating Violence or Distinct Behavior?* (Portland: Portland State University, 1998).

26 R. Enns, *A Voice Unheard: The Latimer Case and People with Disabilities* (Halifax: Fernwood Publishing, 1999).

27 *R. v. Latimer,* [2001] 1 S.C.R. 3, 2001 SCC 1.

28 D. Laframboise, "Have Mercy on Robert Latimer," *National Post,* April 26, 2001, A19.

29 Family Supports for Children with Disabilities Act, 2004, S.A. 2004, c. F-5.3.

30 F. Valentine, *Enabling Citizenship: Full Inclusion of Children with Disabilities and Their Parents* (Ottawa: Canadian Policy Research Networks, 2001).

31 I. Brown, *Abuse and Neglect in Children with Intellectual Disability: Results from a National Study* (Toronto: Faculty of Social Work, University of Toronto, 2002); A.F. Schormans and I. Brown, "An Investigation into the Characteristics of the Maltreatment of Children with Developmental Delays and the Alleged Perpetrators of This Maltreatment," *Journal on Developmental Disabilities* 9, no. 1 (2002): 1–20.

32 P.M. Sullivan and J.F. Knutson, "Maltreatment and Disabilities: A Population-Based Epidemiological Study," *Child Abuse and Neglect* 24, no. 10 (2000): 1257–73.

33 C. Frazee, *Abuse of Children with Disabilities* (Ottawa: Public Health Agency of Canada, National Clearinghouse on Family Violence, 2000).

34 R. Sobsey, "Violence," in W.N. Nehring, *Health Promotion for Persons with Intellectual and Developmental Disabilities* (Washington, DC: AAMR, 2005), pp. 205–34.

35 Alberta Family and Social Services and Alberta Association for Community Living, *Children with Disabilities in Care: Summary Report* (Edmonton: AFSS and AACL, 1997).
36 Sobsey, *Violence and Abuse in the Lives of People with Disabilities* (Baltimore: Paul H. Brookes, 1994).
37 D. Poirier et al., *Educational Rights of Exceptional Children in Canada* (Toronto: Carswell, 1988).
38 *Constitution Act*, Canada 1982. Section 15.
39 Poirier et al., *Educational Rights of Exceptional Children in Canada*.
40 Alberta Education, *Ministerial Order 4.2.3—Standards for Special Education* (Alberta, 2004).
41 *Eaton v. Brant County Board of Education* [1997] 1 SCR 241.
42 *Substitute Decisions Act*, 1992, S.O. 1992, c. 30.

Bibliography

Agha, M.M., et al. 2006. "Determinants of Survival in Children with Congenital Abnormalities: A Long-Term Population-Based Cohort Study, Birth Defects Research Part A." *Clinical and Molecular Teratology* 76, no. 1: 46–54.

Alberta Education. 2004. Ministerial Order 4.2.3—Standards for Special Education. Edmonton.

Alberta Family and Social Services and Alberta Association for Community Living. 1997. *Children with Disabilities in Care: Summary Report*. Edmonton: Alberta Family and Social Services and Alberta Association for Community Living.

Brown, I. 2002. *Abuse and Neglect in Children with Intellectual Disability: Results from a National Study*. Toronto: Faculty of Social Work, University of Toronto.

Constitution Act. Canada 1982. S. 15.

Corey, M., and V. Farewell. 1996. "Determinants of Mortality from Cystic Fibrosis in Canada, 1970–1989." *American Journal of Epidemiology* 143, no. 10: 1007–17.

de Haan, B.D. 1998. *Critical and Fatal Child Maltreatment in Oregon: Escalating Violence or Distinct Behavior?* Portland: Portland State University.

Englehardt Jr., H.T. 1975a. "Ethical Issues in Aiding the Death of Young Children." In W. Teays and L. Purdy, eds., *Bioethics, Justice, and Health Care*. Toronto: Wadsworth, pp. 394–400.

———. 1975b. "Ethical Issues in Aiding the Death of Young Children." In M. Kohl, *Beneficent Euthanasia*. Amherst: Prometheus Books, 1975, pp. 130–35.

Enns, R. 1999. *A Voice Unheard: The Latimer Case and People with Disabilities*. Halifax: Fernwood Publishing.

Family Supports for Children with Disabilities Act. 2004. c. F-5.3.

Fletcher, J. "Indicators of Humanhood: A Tentative Profile of Man." 1972. *Hastings Center Report* 2, no. 11: 1–4.

Frazee, C. 2000. *Abuse of Children with Disabilities*. Ottawa: Public Health Agency of Canada, National Clearinghouse on Family Violence.

Garros, D., R.J. Rosychuk, and P.N. Cox. 2003. "Circumstances Surrounding End of Life in a Pediatric Intensive Care Unit." *Pediatrics* 112, no. 5: e371.

International Disability Rights Monitor. 2004. *Regional Report for the Americas*. Winnipeg: Disabled Peoples International and International Disability Network. http://www.cirnetwork.org/idrm/reports/ americas/countries/ canada.html.

Issekutz, K.A., et al. 2005. "An Epidemiological Analysis of Charge Syndrome: Preliminary Results from a Canadian Study." *American Journal of Medical Genetics* 133, no. 3: 309–17.

Laframboise, D. 2001. "Have Mercy on Robert Latimer." *National Post*, April 26, A19.

Nowak, M. 2005. *Article 6: The Right to Life, Survival, and Development: A Commentary on the United Nations Convention on the Rights of the Child*. Boston: Martinus Nijhoff.

Poirier, D., et al. 1988. *Educational Rights of Exceptional Children in Canada*. Toronto: Carswell.

Reinke, D.C. 2005. *Child Maltreatment in Canada: A Developmental-Ecological Perspective*. PhD thesis, University of Alberta.

Schormans, A.F., and I. Brown. 2002. "An Investigation into the Characteristics of the Maltreatment of Children with Developmental Delays and the Alleged Perpetrators of This Maltreatment." *Journal on Developmental Disabilities* 9, no. 1: 1–20.

Singer, P. 2000. *Writings on an Ethical Life*. New York: HarperCollins.

Sobsey, R. 1994. *Violence and Abuse in the Lives of People with Disabilities*. Baltimore: Paul H. Brookes.

———. 2005. "Violence." In W.N. Nehring, *Health Promotion for Persons with Intellectual and Developmental Disabilities*. Washington, DC: AAMR, pp. 205–34.

Statistics Canada, Housing, Family, and Social Statistics Division. 2002. *A Profile of Disability in Canada, 2001 Tables*. Ottawa: StatsCan.

Sullivan, P.M., and J.F. Knutson. 2000. "Maltreatment and Disabilities: A Population-Based Epidemiological Study." *Child Abuse and Neglect* 24, no. 10: 1257–73.

Valentine, F. 2001. *Enabling Citizenship: Full Inclusion of Children with Disabilities and Their Parents*. Ottawa: Canadian Policy Research Networks.

Wall, S.N., and J.C. Partridge. 1997. "Death in the Intensive Care Nursery: Physician Practice of Withdrawing and Withholding Life Support." *Pediatrics* 99, no. 1: 64–70.

Conclusion
Canada's Ambivalence toward Children

16

R. Brian Howe and Katherine Covell

The question for this book was this: At what level is Canada's commitment to the rights of the child, as revealed in its record of implementing the UN Convention on the Rights of the Child? The possibilities included these: (1) symbolic commitment, where words have been used as substitutes for deeds; (2) wavering commitment, where deeds have been sporadic, uneven, and halting; (3) expanding commitment, where deeds have shown a pattern of steady progress; and (4) deep commitment, where there has been sustained, vigorous, and comprehensive implementation of children's rights on all fronts.

As discussed in chapter 1, at first glance there is good reason to be suspicious of Canada's commitment: symbolism would appear to be the most fitting description. One reason for suspicion has been a general failure of Canadian governments to incorporate the Convention into domestic law or into the goals of public policy. Indeed, rarely has reference even been made to the CRC in legislation or in the objectives of child-related public policies. Another reason for doubt has been the failure to establish a national children's commissioner responsible for child advocacy and for promoting the implementation of the Convention on a nationwide basis. Provincial child advocacy offices do exist, but their mandates are limited to particular areas of children's rights in particular provinces. A third reason for doubt has been Canada's failure to establish an effective monitoring and coordinating mechanism, as long urged by the UN Committee on the Rights of the Child. Still absent is a permanent body to track

R. Brian Howe and Katherine Covell, Cape Breton University

developments on a regular basis and to coordinate efforts among Canadian governments in translating the rights of children into realities. Yet despite these shortcomings in processes and procedures, it still may be the case that Canada has made progress in the substance of implementing the rights of children. The task of this book has been to examine substantive developments and to determine whether Canada's level of commitment has risen above the symbolic.

Canada's Level of Commitment

Our chapters indicate that we can rule out symbolic commitment as a characterization of Canada's record. Words have not been used as substitutes for deeds. Action has been taken. In the area of provision rights, measures have been undertaken to reduce child poverty, expand child care, and improve child health. As explained in chapter 2, child benefits have been steadily enlarged and have had a modest impact in countering child poverty. In the area of protection rights, laws have been enacted to protect children—more so than before—from sexual abuse and exploitation, and a new Youth Criminal Justice Act has been established to reduce the use of custody and to give more attention to the rehabilitation and reintegration of youth in conflict with the law. In the area of participation rights, initiatives have been taken at all levels of government to give youth a greater voice in decisions that affect them. These developments cannot be dismissed as insignificant. To characterize them as merely symbolic would be grossly inaccurate.

But at the other extreme, we can easily rule out deep commitment. If deep commitment were the case, Canada's record on reducing child poverty and improving child care would be among the best in developed nations, not among the worst. Not only that, but Canada would have removed the legal defence for corporal punishment and would have ensured the stricter enforcement of laws against sexual abuse and exploitation. Furthermore, Canada would have taken comprehensive measures—not sporadic ones— to ensure that children have a voice in decisions that affect them and to educate children about their human rights. As noted in chapter 10, for a country officially committed to the Convention, it is amazing that the rights of the child can be described as one of Canada's best-kept secrets.

Finally, if deep commitment were the case, Canada's Aboriginal children would not be living in such poverty, nor would they be experiencing such high rates of infant mortality, inadequate health care, and suicide. They also would not be so overrepresented in the child welfare system, and Aboriginal Child and Family Services would not have to deal with so many cases with so few resources and so little funding. Children in alternative care would not be subject to the severe and persistent shortages in foster care and in quality and stable placements. Street-involved children would not be left without services and programs to attend to their basic needs. The claims of refugee children would not be going unrecognized on the basis of child-specific forms of persecution such as child trafficking. Children with disabilities would not be so often denied life-saving treatment, judicial involvement to protect their interests, and inclusive education.

This leaves the choice between wavering and expanding commitment. The overall evidence of the preceding chapters suggests that Canada's level of commitment is—at best—characterized as wavering. If expanding commitment were the case, there would have been clear evidence of growing efforts and steady progress on all or most fronts of children's rights. But this has not been the case. What the record shows instead is an overall pattern of vacillation, sporadic or halting efforts, and spotty and uneven policy and legal developments. The CRC has rarely even been mentioned in legislation and child-related policy, and this reflects the lack of political concern or even awareness of the rights of the child. As noted in chapter 1, recognition of children's rights and incorporation of the Convention into Canadian law is not necessarily enough. For real progress to be made, the courts have to be willing to provide broad interpretations of rights, and governments have to be motivated to put these rights into effect. However, putting aside the issue of the lack of incorporation, it is revealing that the Convention has rarely been referred to in legislation and policy initiatives and—at the same time—that government efforts have been spotty and uneven. This speaks volumes about Canada's wavering commitment to children. Such wavering is evident in developments as summarized below.

In the area of provision rights, for example, although important efforts have been made to decrease child poverty through child benefits, the measures taken have been inadequate. There has been no significant long-term reduction in the rate of child poverty, and the problem of Aboriginal child poverty has remained very serious. Among developed countries, Canada's record on child poverty has been among the worst. Similarly, in the area of early learning and child care, although measures have been taken to increase the number of regulated spaces, access to child care has remained substantially the same as at the time the CRC was ratified. The child care system is still plagued not only by a shortage of spaces but also by a lack of standards and quality assurance. Like child poverty, Canada's system of child care has been ranked as among the worst in developed countries. In regard to child health, progress has been made in the delivery of services, such as through Telehealth and other programs, yet rates of childhood cancers, respiratory illnesses, and obesity have risen. Moreover, accessibility to health care has remained uneven across the country, contrary to the Convention principles of non-discrimination and best interests.

In the area of protection rights, although efforts have been made to better protect children from violence, the practice of corporal punishment continues to be defensible in Canadian law. On the one hand, the practice is no longer allowed in Canadian schools, and the Supreme Court of Canada has circumscribed its use by parents. But on the other, against the recommendations of the UN Committee on the Rights of the Child, and unlike many other state parties to the CRC, the federal government has failed to review the issue and to consider making the practice illegal. In regard to protecting children from sexual abuse and exploitation, progress has been through the enactment of new laws and procedures dealing with child pornography, Internet luring, child prostitution, child sex tourism, and child witnesses. But a major problem continues to be a lack of serious enforcement of the law, reflecting the low priority and low status that children continue to have in Canadian society. In youth justice, considerable progress has been made thanks to the new Youth Criminal Justice Act. In accord with the Convention, the use of custody has been lessened and more focus has been placed on the rehabilitation and reintegration of youth. Especially progressive has been provision for the increased use of restorative justice for less serious offenders. But even here there are inconsistencies with the rights of the child. The principle of the best interests of the child has not been incorporated into the new law, the expanded use of adult sentences for more serious offenders has been a step backward, the separation of young and adult offenders has not been assured, and no assurance has been made for consistency in the use of restorative justice and community programs across the country.

In the area of participation rights, there are even more serious problems. On the one hand, since the ratification of the Convention, there have been a number of promising initiatives. As noted in chapter 9, the federal government has provided considerable funding for research on child participation. At provincial, territorial, and municipal levels, parent education programs have been launched in support of democratic parenting styles, school policies and programs have been changed to allow for the wider input of youth, and government structures have been adjusted to provide broader opportunities for the civic involvement of youth. These initiatives, however, have been sporadic and uneven. For the most part, legislation has not been enacted to ensure youth a voice (it is simply a policy to do so in some jurisdictions), and programs of participation have not been implemented on a comprehensive and systematic basis. Laws typically provide children and youth with a right to make decisions or to consent or withhold consent at a particular age. But they generally do not ensure the child a voice before that arbitrary age. Furthermore, children in Canada remain unaware of their right to participate. Apart from a few scattered programs of children's rights education, Canadian governments have failed to educate children (as well as adults) about the rights of the child, contrary to their dissemination duty under the Convention. Provincial ministers of education and federal officials could have collaborated in support of a strong program of citizenship education in schools that would have included knowledge about the human rights of children. But they failed to do so. They chose to keep children in the dark.

In addition to the general shortcomings in implementing provision, protection, and participation rights, there also has been a major failure to advance the rights of vulnerable or marginalized children. Efforts on behalf of Aboriginal children, children in alternative care, homeless children, and refugee children have been grossly inadequate. Aboriginal children continue to experience disproportionately high levels of child poverty and poor health care and to be greatly overrepresented in an inadequate child welfare system. Children in alternative care continue to face insufficient and inadequate placement options and an inadequacy of resources for meeting their developmental and recovery needs. Street-involved children continue to suffer from problems of poverty, inadequate health care and education, and sexual exploitation. That national data on their situation are lacking reflects the government's lack of concern about their problems. Refugee children continue to face hearings in a system that does not equip them with adequate legal representation and participation rights and that continues to discriminate against unaccompanied and stateless refugee children. Unaccompanied child refugees also face the problem of being at higher risk of detention owing to the lack of available child protection services in many provinces. Finally, children with disabilities continue to face a situation in which their basic right to life and survival is under threat and in which segregated classrooms and schools compromise their right to education and to equality.

In summary, in light of the inadequate and incomplete implementation of the rights of the child in Canada, together with the shortcomings in process as discussed in chapter 1, Canada's commitment to the rights of the child can best be described as wavering. To characterize it merely as symbolic or to describe it as deep or expanding commitment would be to understate or overstate Canada's performance. An obvious question is this: What accounts for Canada's wavering commitment to the rights of children? Is it simply the case that the obstacles to translating the rights of the child into practice—federalism, inadequate resources, lack of public and political pressure—are too great?

Why the Wavering Commitment?

One possible reason for the wavering commitment is Canada's complicated and difficult system of federalism. Without question, the federal system poses problems. Given the fact that many child-related matters are in the provincial (and territorial) jurisdiction, successful implementation requires a high degree of intergovernmental collaboration and cooperation. Difficulties arise because of the complexities and uncertainties of jurisdiction and because different jurisdictions have different priorities and different resources. Alberta, for example, refused to endorse the Convention until 1999, and even then with considerable reluctance. But the problem is not simply one of provincial resistance or apathy or inertia. There is also the legal question as to whether the federal government has the ultimate constitutional authority to compel the provinces to implement an international convention, despite its power to sign and ratify treaties.[1]

However, although federalism is an obstacle, it does not fully account for Canada's wavering commitment. Some matters are entirely or largely in the federal jurisdiction (e.g., youth justice) or provincial jurisdiction (e.g., child protection), and there is no legitimate jurisdictional excuse for inaction. Moreover, in matters where collaboration is required, difficulties do not have to mean inaction. In the area of child benefits, for example, federal and provincial governments have been able to cooperate to steadily enrich the amounts of benefits, as discussed in chapter 2. Furthermore, under the Vienna Convention on the Law of Treaties, to which Canada is bound, lack of federal authority is not a valid excuse for failure.[2] As noted by the UN Committee on the Rights of the Child, the federal government has a legal obligation to ensure that the provinces and territories are aware of their responsibilities and to ensure that the overall implementation of the rights of the child takes place. Federalism cannot be used as a valid legal excuse for shortcomings in Canada's performance. In short, although it must be acknowledged that the federal system presents difficulties in particular areas of children's rights, federalism alone cannot explain Canada's wavering commitment to children. If financial resources were available for children, and if there were sufficient public pressure on behalf of children, the difficulties posed by federalism might well be overcome.

Another possible explanation for wavering commitment is a shortage of financial resources. This, too, cannot be dismissed as a factor. Economic considerations are important, especially in relation to higher-cost items such as child care and the reduction of child poverty. Beginning in the late 1980s and increasing during the 1990s, federal and provincial governments across Canada became concerned—even preoccupied—with deficits and debts. In varying degrees and with considerable public support, these governments pursued policies of deficit reduction, balanced budgets, debt reduction, and cuts or restraints on government spending. In the mid-1990s, federal Finance Minister Paul Martin made deficit reduction a national mission.[3] The Canadian public became convinced of the need for such action, and this allowed federal and provincial governments to proceed. In such an environment, spending on matters related to children became difficult. To the extent that funding was made available for social programs, health care was the priority.

However, like federalism, fiscal restraint in itself does not account for Canada's wavering commitment. First, not all areas of children's rights involve high costs. The extension of participation rights, for example, involves simple adjustments to legislation and policies, not major expenditures. Second, with budgetary surpluses in the late 1990s and early 2000s, the financial situation and capability of the federal government improved substantially. Although a fiscal imbalance remained between the federal government and the provinces, the federal government now had the financial capability to act on its own or to support the provinces and territories in social spending, including on child-related matters. Third, at the World Summit for Children in 1990, Canada had agreed to the principle of "first call for children": the needs of Canadian children were to be given first priority in hard economic times as well as good. That this agreement was not honoured reflects not simply an apparent shortage of financial resources but lack of fear of political embarrassment or public condemnation. It is reasonable to believe that had the Canadian public expressed greater support for children and for the principle of first call, the needs and rights of children would have been a greater government priority.

Another possible reason for Canada's wavering commitment is lack of public and political pressure for action. Together with federalism and financial issues, this would seem an important part of the explanation. Children lack political power and thus depend on pressures from child advocacy organizations and from the public to protect and advance their interests. Child advocacy organizations, however, have limited influence. Within government, provincial child advocacy offices perform very important functions in reviewing the situation of children and youth in care and in addressing grievances and problems. But these offices do not have the mandate to monitor the rights of the child on a comprehensive basis and to press for a fuller implementation of the Convention. Outside of government, child advocacy groups play an important role in raising child-related issues and periodically criticizing governments for inaction. But they are too few in number and inadequately staffed and organized to raise national awareness of the rights of the child and to mount a strong and sustained campaign to implement the CRC.

Child advocacy organizations have not even been able to make politicians and government officials fully aware of the Convention and of Canada's obligations to children under the CRC. For example, in its report on the hearings of the Standing Senate Committee on Human Rights in 2005, the Senate Committee expressed major concern that few politicians or officials had even the most basic knowledge of the CRC.[4] To some extent, stated the Committee, this lack of awareness was due to the absence of a government mechanism or structures for spreading awareness and for reminding government officials on an ongoing basis of their international obligations. It also was due to the secretive approach of the Continuing Committee of Officials on Human Rights, the body responsible for preparing Canada's reports to the UN Committee on the Rights of the Child. In addition, said the Committee, lack of awareness was the result of the failure of the federal government to establish a national children's commissioner, who would have been responsible for, among other things, spreading governmental and public awareness about children's rights. Apart from these points made by the Senate Committee, the general lack of resources among child advocacy organizations, both within and outside of governments, has been a major obstacle to the provision of education on the rights of the child to officials and politicians. Lack of resources has seriously restricted the capacity of child advocacy organizations to pressure governments to make progress in implementing the rights of the child.

This leaves the advance of children's rights dependent on pressure from the Canadian public. However, there is very little pressure. Despite Canada's obligation under article 42 of the Convention to spread awareness of the rights of the child, the Canadian public has remained uninformed. Thus it is not surprising that there is little public pressure. Public opinion can be and often is a significant force in the making of public policy if an issue is salient and if public opinion is solidly on one side of the issue.[5] In such a situation, it is in the political interests of politicians to respond. This could have been the case for the advancement of children's rights in Canada had the Canadian public been educated about the CRC, had it seen value in the principle of children's rights, and had it believed in the importance of implementing the rights of the child in Canada. But given the lack of systematic and comprehensive education on the rights of the child in schools, and given the lack of a strong and effective public information campaign, such has not been the case.

There is another and deeper problem. Although most Canadians remain uninformed and uneducated about the rights of the child as described in the Convention, most do have general views about children and about children's rights, views that are based on misperceptions. These misperceptions have fuelled fears about the loss of parental rights and adult authority and about unwanted state intrusion into the affairs of the family. Many Canadians do believe in the general principle of children's rights, but they also believe that these rights should be restricted or circumscribed and balanced against the rights of parents and adult authorities. This qualified support and ambivalence has been reflected in a number of areas, including political decisions to endorse the Convention and in debate surrounding public policy involving children. First of all, it was reflected in Alberta's conditional support for the Convention. As in the United States, citizens and politicians in Alberta were reluctant to agree to the Convention for fear that children's rights would undermine parental rights. Thus, unlike other provinces that approved the Convention in 1991, Alberta refused to approve it until 1999. When Alberta finally endorsed it, it expressed its support "based on the understanding that the UN Convention does not usurp or override the authority of parents."[6]

Ambivalence or opposition to children's rights also has been expressed during debate about children's rights education in schools. In celebration of the tenth anniversary of the adoption of the Convention, UNICEF Canada and Elections Canada jointly organized an election for schoolchildren. A key purpose of the election was to stimulate thinking about children's rights and to educate young people about the rights of the child as described in the Convention. Students across Canada were to be given the opportunity to discuss and to vote on the relative importance of children's rights in the general areas of education, family, food and shelter, health, safety, name and nationality, and the expression of opinions. The participation of many students was prevented by vociferous opponents, who argued that allowing children to know and to discuss their rights would undermine family and adult authority, involve children in undesirable political activity, and invite an undue degree of state intrusion into the family. As one school trustee in British Columbia stated, the Convention "undermines the integrity of the family and involves children in a political undertaking. There is a gradual erosion of parental authority and this is one more step in that direction."[7]

Nonetheless, three-quarters of a million students in more than 1,900 schools across Canada were informed about their Convention rights and did vote on the rights that they thought were most important. It is noteworthy that contrary to expectations that students would give priority to their own personal freedoms, the results of the election showed that the right held to be most important to children and youth was the right to a family upbringing.

Reservations about children's rights also have been expressed in decisions and in discussions in the areas of physical abuse, sexual exploitation, child care, and child poverty. Canadians generally believe that children should have a fundamental right to be protected from all forms of abuse. However, fears about parental accountability have so far precluded the elimination of Section 43 from the Criminal Code (the section that allows a defence for physical assault of children with limits recently set down by the Supreme Court as detailed in chapter 5). In a 2003 Decima poll, only 30 percent of respondents agreed strongly that parents should not be allowed to use physical punishment. However, 60 percent said they would agree if guidelines were in place to prevent prosecutions for "mild spankings."[8] There is, of course, no definition provided of mild spankings. It may well be that any physical punishment that does not require medical treatment arguably can be mild. The public wants children to have a right to be protected from physical punishment, but only if they, as parents, can continue to exercise their "right" to use physical punishment without fear of prosecution. Ambivalence is seen also in attitudes toward sexual exploitation.

Canada ranks third in the world in the production of child pornography.[9] This may be, at least in part, a consequence of the outcome *R v. Sharpe*, described in chapter 6. In brief, the Supreme Court of Canada in 2001 upheld the constitutionality of the possession of child pornography, exempting from prosecution written or visual works of the imagination held for personal use only, as well as visual recordings created by or depicting the accused that do not show unlawful sexual activity and that are held for personal use only. Although the 2006 Bill C-2 reforms modified these conditions (as explained in chapter 6), it has been argued that the Court has shown more concern with the protection of adults' Charter privacy and freedom rights than for the rights or protection of the child.[10] The consequence, to the present, has been more difficult prosecutions, as well as sentences for convictions of child pornography that are incommensurate with the crime and rarely custodial.[11] Children, it is believed, should have the right to be protected from involvement in child pornography, but within limits that allow protections for the "rights" of adults to consume it.

Children's rights also have been seen as excessive and threatening to women's rights. It has been argued, for example, that it is appropriate for governments to provide for child care only if the explicit primary motivation for that care is the enabling of women's social and economic advancement.[12] According to the argument, when governments such as the Martin Liberal government construct child care as necessary for the healthy development of children, they are marginalizing women and negating the equality gains made by the women's movement. Giving rights to children takes from rights of women.

These examples not only reflect a lack of understanding about the specific nature of children's rights, but also reflect a misunderstanding of the nature of rights. The underlying assumption in each of the above examples appears to be that of rights as a zero sum game: that the provision of rights for children inevitably takes away from rights for adults. Children's rights should be provided for, but not if their exercise allows for parental prosecutions, interference with adult pleasure, or lessened political attention to women. When rights are seen as limited resources, then compromise is necessary and commitment is lacking.

That Canadians want compromise between children's and adults' rights was well demonstrated in a series of consultations held by the Canadian Policy Research Networks.[13] In describing their ideal society, the members of the public who participated in the discussions and polls elected to balance children's rights with family responsibilities and fiscal pressures. There was no desire to give priority to children in social programs or in social spending. Rather, the central theme that emerged was that what was of utmost importance was the empowerment of parents to exercise choice and the provision of supports that would enable parents to assume more responsibility for their children. These data are from 1999. However, the theme is consistent with that of the Conservative Harper government elected in 2006. One major campaign promise of the Harper Conservatives was to provide funding to families to allow their choice in child care arrangements. This was in place of increased expenditures to allow for a more adequate national child care system. Children's rights to child care are believed to be a lower priority than parents' rights to choice.

The tension between children's rights and parental autonomy is seen also in responses to child poverty. The report of the Social Policy Research Unit in Regina, Saskatchewan, on child poverty provides an example here.[14] In their analysis, what is stressed is that interventions to reduce child poverty should target parents. Tax breaks and employment opportunities are the primary initiatives suggested. Programs such as subsidized child care, school meal programs, school uniform programs, and so forth that directly target children are not proposed. Expenditures here may take away from resources available to adults and would certainly limit parental choice.

There also appears to be a belief that children already have too many rights. This is most obvious in perceptions of older children. Adolescents tend to be seen as problems for the adult world. Adolescents are seen as barely rational, unsocialized, and unlawful; there is "a tendency to vilify and pathologize young people."[15] Rights, if provided to such creatures, will be misused. Adults will be taken advantage of. Chaos will reign. Control and punishment are needed to preserve the social order and to prepare youth to take adult responsibilities when they become citizens. Such misperceptions of the nature of youth are maintained through the entertainment media and through the media's focus on high-profile cases of youth crime.

The Canadian public significantly overestimates the incidence and nature of youth crime[16] and has little confidence in the youth justice system.[17] The public, and many politicians, repeatedly call for youth curfews and for harsher responses to youth crime. Youth offending is misattributed to youth having too many rights and too few responsibilities. Discussions about the Youth Criminal Justice Act (YCJA) in 2006 following the death of Teresa McEvoy in Nova Scotia are illustrative.[18] Archie Billard was sixteen years old when, driving a car he had stolen, he hit and killed Ms. McEvoy. This tragic occurrence led to many calls for more and easier incarceration of youth, to hearings on youth justice responses, and to calls to alter the YCJA. During the hearings it was reported that Billard had suffered parental rejection and family instability in early childhood, had been diagnosed with ADHD but had not been provided the necessary medication, had been diagnosed with a learning difficulty but had not been provided the necessary corrective glasses, had suffered emotional abuse by his stepfather, and had been told to leave home by his mother. Despite this litany of rights violations and conditions that are highly predictive of youth criminal offending, the focus of the discussions remained on how to alter the YCJA so that such youth (for whom everything possible had been done, according to one reporter) would not be on the streets and would be held fully responsible for their behaviour.

Sociologist Jordan Titus explains public attitudes toward youth such as Archie Billard in her analysis of current justice responses to children. With the YCJA, there is the wide provision for use of adult sentences for serious youth offenders. Such provision, Titus argues, reflects changes in the conceptions of childhood. Youth, at least those who commit serious crimes, are understood to be mature, antisocial, responsible for their actions, and in need of adult-like punishment. Thus, society deems it acceptable for such children to lose their rights and protections. As she so eloquently puts it, "notions of childhood deprivation become fused with notions of children's depravity."[19] When Canadians ignore, or do not understand the implications of, the typical rearing history of youth in conflict with the law—a history often characterized by rights violations rather than rights excesses—they naturally assume agency and culpability. They then call for harsher penalties.

At the core of views that children have too many rights and are likely to take advantage of those rights is a lack of knowledge about the rights of the child. In a 2005 Ipsos-Reid poll, a majority of the public (61 percent) expressed the conviction that children's rights are already fully realized in Canada. Yet only 46 percent of those surveyed were even aware of the CRC.[20] These data strongly suggest that public perceptions of children's rights are barely connected to the rights set out in the CRC. The result is an ambivalence of attitude that is unlikely to raise the pressure for policies and practices that recognize the rights of the child.

We are a long way from achieving a unitary conception of children as rights-bearing citizens. For Canadians to appreciate the status of children as rights bearers and the status of parents, other adults, and governments as duty bearers, there will need to be a fundamental shift in their attitudes toward children. Such a shift will require not just knowledge of the CRC and its importance to healthy children and healthy societies, but also knowledge of the nature of rights as unlimited and uncompeting resources.

Prospects for Change

A recent development provides some hope that Canada's wavering commitment to the rights of the child can become elevated to deep commitment. In 2004 the Senate of Canada authorized the Standing Senate Committee on Human Rights to examine and report on Canada's international obligations in regard to the rights of children and on Canada's implementation of the CRC. The Senate Committee subsequently held hearings and studied the issue; it completed its interim report in 2005[21] and is scheduled to present its final report in 2007.[22] In its interim report the committee did not back away from pointing out the shortcomings in Canada's performance. It noted several major problems, including the inadequate incorporation of the Convention into Canadian law; the inefficiency of the Continuing Committee of Officials on Human Rights and of the reporting system; the difficulties of federalism and the lack of uniform national standards on children's rights; the lack of governmental and public awareness of the Convention; and the lack of public and parliamentary input into the implementation process. The committee also pointed to substantive problems in Canada's record—to be examined more fully in its final report—with regard to the rights of Aboriginal children, sexually exploited children, refugee and migrant children, children with disabilities, and children caught in the child protection and youth justice systems. The committee urged that Canada take vigorous action to address all of these problems, including a new approach to incorporating the Convention into Canadian law and more vigorous efforts at implementation. It specifically urged that through legislation the federal government declare itself legally bound to implement the Convention, to be held accountable to Parliament and the public for its actions, and to work with the provinces and territories on ensuring incorporation and implementation in provincial and territorial jurisdictions. It also recommended that a national Children's Commissioner be created for the purpose of monitoring and spreading awareness and that a new interdepartmental working group be established for the purpose of facilitating a fuller implementation of the Convention.

The degree to which governments in Canada respond to the Committee's recommendations will be a test of Canada's future commitment to children. The prospects for progress are not good over the short term. Children continue to lack political power, and child advocacy groups continue to lack resources, effective organization, and clout. The system of implementation continues to allow for stalling and inaction. Government officials and the Canadian public continue to be uninformed and uneducated about Canada's obligations under the Convention. Canadians continue to hold ambivalent views about children and their rights.

But over the longer term, the prospects for progress are better. Canada's political culture has been evolving in the direction of greater public support for the value of basic human rights and greater public appreciation for the need to overcome barriers to participation and inclusion. Canadians are becoming what Rhoda Howard-Hassmann has referred to as "compassionate Canadians," aware of the need to give support to historically disadvantaged or marginalized groups including ethnocultural minorities, women, people with disabilities, Aboriginals, and sexual minorities.[23] In this evolving culture, there is good reason to think that child advocates will soon have an easier time in mobilizing public opinion on behalf of children, downsizing the ambivalence and elevating the importance of the rights of children, and pressuring governments into a more vigorous implementation of the rights of the child.

If minorities and women should be treated as citizens with basic rights, and if barriers to their participation in Canadian society should be removed, there is a logic that says children should be treated in the same way. There already has been a certain degree of cultural change in this direction. Most Canadians no longer think of children as the property of their parents. Many believe that children are a vulnerable class of people in need of special protection and care, if not by parents then by the state. However, many have not gone the extra step—as Canada officially has done—to regard children as full citizens and as bearers of rights. Although it will take time, change in the direction of a fully fledged rights-based conception is quite possible provided there is expanded children's rights education in schools and society. Building on the cultural change that already has been going on, and building on programs of children's rights education that already exist, child-friendly educators are a position to develop systematic and comprehensive programs of human rights education in which children learn about their rights and responsibilities and about the importance of implementing the rights of the child across Canada. Children are the voters, child advocates, and government officials of the future. Imbued with children's rights consciousness, they will be in a position to make a difference.

Notes

1 That the federal government apparently cannot enforce the implementation of international treaties is due to the ruling of the Judicial Committee of the Privy Council (Canada's highest court until 1949) in the *Labour Conventions* case (1937). See P. Russell, R. Knopff, and T. Morton, *Federalism and the Charter* (Ottawa: Carleton University Press, 1989), pp. 104–10.

2 R. Andreychuk and L. Pearson, *Who's in Charge Here? Effective Implementation of Canada's International Obligations with Respect to the Rights of Children* (Ottawa: Senate Standing Committee on Human Rights, 2005), pp. 43–44.

3 M. Weinroth, "Rituals of Rhetoric and Nationhood: The Liberal Anti-Deficit Campaign (1994–1998)," *Journal of Canadian Studies* 38 (Spring 2004): 44–79.

4 Andreychuk and Pearson, *Who's in Charge Here?* pp. 69–70.

5 P. Burnstein, "The Impact of Public Opinion on Public Policy: A Review and an Agenda," *Political Research Quarterly* 56 (March 2003): 29–41.

6 A. Pellatt, *United Nations Convention on the Rights of the Child: How Does Alberta's Legislation Measure Up?* (Calgary: Alberta Civil Liberties Research Centre, 1999). www.aclrc.com.

7 R.B. Howe and K. Covell, *Empowering Children: Children's Rights Education as a Pathway to Citizenship* (Toronto: University of Toronto Press, 2005), p. 3.

8 The survey was conducted in late August 2003 through telephone interviews with 2,033 Canadians. The reported margin of error is +2.2% 19 times out of 20. Detailed survey information is found at http://www.toronto.ca/health.

9 ECPAT International, "Commercial Exploitation of Children. Country Profile: Canada," http://www.ECPAT.net.

10 S. Grover, "Oppression of Children Intellectualized as Free Expression under the Canadian Charter: A Reanalysis of the Sharpe Possession of Child Pornography Case," *International Journal of Children's Rights* 9 (2004): 311–31; M. Petrunik, "The Hare and the Tortoise: Dangerous and Sex Offender Policy in the United States and Canada," *Canadian Journal of Criminology and Criminal Justice* (2003): 43–72.

11 C.A.S.E., *Child Exploitation in Canada,* http://www.c-a-s-e.net.

12 A. Dobrowsky and J. Jensen. "Shifting Representations of Citizenship: Canadian Politics of 'Women' and 'Children,'" *Social Politics* 11 (Summer 2004): 154–80.
13 J.H. Michalski, *Values and Preferences for the "Best Policy Mix" for Canadian Children* (Ottawa: Canadian Policy Research Networks, 1999).
14 G. Hunter, *Child Poverty and the Saskatchewan Child Poverty Initiatives* (Regina: Social Policy Research, 2002).
15 P. Aggleton and C. Campbell, "Working with Young People—Towards an Agenda for Sexual Health." *Sexual and Relationship Therapy* 15, no. 3 (2000): 283–96.
16 K. Covell and R.B. Howe, *The Challenge of Children's Rights for Canada* (Waterloo: Wilfrid Laurier University Press, 2001); A. James and C. Jenks, "Public Perceptions of Childhood Criminality," *British Journal of Sociology* 47, no. 2 (1996): 315–31; J.J. Titus, "Juvenile Transfers as Ritual Sacrifice: Legally Constructing the Child Scapegoat," *Youth Violence and Juvenile Justice* 3 (April 2005): 116–32.
17 J.V. Roberts, *Public Confidence in Criminal Justice: A Review of Recent Trends* (Ottawa: Public Safety and Emergency Preparedness Canada, November 2004).
18 Examples are found at the following websites: http://www.nunncommission .ca/home/index.cfm; http://cnews.canoe.ca/CNEWS/LAW2006/01/11/13899229; http://aan.cbc.ca/ns/story/ns-McEvoy20060207.html; http:// www.gov.ns.ca/news/ details/aspid+20050629003.
19 Titus, "Juvenile Transfers as Ritual Sacrifice," p. 119.
20 Ipsos-Reid, *National Children's Day 2005: Canadians Reflect on the State of the Child in Canada* (Toronto: Ipsos Reid, November 2005).
21 Andreychuk and Pearson, *Who's in Charge Here?*
22 The final report was not complete at the time of the writing of this book.
23 R. Howard-Hassmann, *Compassionate Canadians* (Toronto: University of Toronto Press, 2003).

Bibliography

Aggleton, P., and C. Campbell. 2000. "Working with Young People—Towards an Agenda for Sexual Health." *Sexual and Relationship Therapy* 15, no. 3: 283–96.
Andreychuk, R., and L. Pearson. 2005. *Who's in Charge Here? Effective Implementation of Canada's International Obligations with Respect to the Rights of Children.* Ottawa: Senate Standing Committee on Human Rights.
Burnstein, P. "The Impact of Public Opinion on Public Policy: A Review and an Agenda." *Political Research Quarterly* 56 (March 2003): 29–41.
C.A.S.E. n.d. *Child Exploitation in Canada.* http://www.c-a-s-e.net.
Covell, K., and R.B. Howe. 2001. *The Challenge of Children's Rights for Canada.* Waterloo: Wilfrid Laurier University Press.
Dobrowsky, A., and J. Jensen. 2004. "Shifting Representations of Citizenship: Canadian Politics of 'Women' and 'Children.'" *Social Politics* 11, no. 2: 154–80.
ECPAT International. n.d. "Commercial Exploitation of Children. Country Profile: Canada." http://www.ECPAT.net.

Grover, S. 2004. "Oppression of Children Intellectualized as Free Expression under the Canadian Charter: A Reanalysis of the Sharpe Possession of Child Pornography Case." *International Journal of Children's Rights* 9: 311–31.

Howard-Hassmann, R. *Compassionate Canadians*. Toronto: University of Toronto Press, 2003.

Howe, R.B., and K. Covell. 2005. *Empowering Children: Children's Rights Education as a Pathway to Citizenship*. Toronto: University of Toronto Press.

Hunter, G. 2002. *Child Poverty and the Saskatchewan Child Poverty Initiatives*. Regina: Social Policy Research.

Ipsos-Reid. 2005. *National Children's Day 2005: Canadians Reflect on the State of the Child in Canada*. November. Toronto: Ipsos Reid.

James, A., and C. Jenks. 1996. "Public Perceptions of Childhood Criminality." *British Journal of Sociology* 47, no. 2: 315–31.

Michalski, J.H. 1999. *Values and Preferences for the "Best Policy Mix" for Canadian Children*. Ottawa: Canadian Policy Research Networks.

Pellatt, A. *United Nations Convention on the Rights of the Child: How Does Alberta's Legislation Measure Up?* (Calgary: Alberta Civil Liberties Research Centre, 1999). http://www.aclrc.com.

Petrunik, M. 2003. "The Hare and the Tortoise: Dangerous and Sex Offender Policy in the United States and Canada." *Canadian Journal of Criminology and Criminal Justice* 45, no. 1: 43–72.

Roberts, J. 2004. *Public Confidence in Criminal Justice: A Review of Recent Trends*. Ottawa: Public Safety and Emergency Preparedness Canada.

Russell, P., R. Knopff, and T. Morton. 1989. *Federalism and the Charter*. Ottawa: Carleton University Press, pp. 104–10.

Titus, J.J. 2005. "Juvenile Transfers as Ritual Sacrifice: Legally Constructing the Child Scapegoat." *Youth Violence and Juvenile Justice* 3, no. 2: 116–32.

Weinroth, M. "Rituals of Rhetoric and Nationhood: The Liberal Anti-Deficit Campaign (1994–1998)." *Journal of Canadian Studies* 38 (Spring 2004): 44–79.

Appendix
The United Nations Convention on the Rights of the Child

Preamble

The states parties to the present convention,
Considering that, in accordance with the principles proclaimed in the Charter of the United Nations, recognition of the inherent dignity and of the equal and inalienable rights of all members of the human family is the foundation of freedom, justice and peace in the world,

Bearing in mind that the peoples of the United Nations have, in the Charter, reaffirmed their faith in fundamental human rights and in the dignity and worth of the human person, and have determined to promote social progress and better standards of life in larger freedom,

Recognizing that the United Nations has, in the Universal Declaration of Human Rights and in the International Covenants on Human Rights, proclaimed and agreed that everyone is entitled to all the rights and freedoms set forth therein, without distinction of any kind, such as race, colour, sex, language, religion, political or other opinion, national or social origin, property, birth or other status,

Recalling that, in the Universal Declaration of Human Rights, the United Nations has proclaimed that childhood is entitled to special care and assistance,

Convinced that the family, as the fundamental group of society and the natural environment for the growth and wellbeing of all its members and particularly children, should be afforded the necessary protection and assistance so that it can fully assume its responsibilities within the community,

Recognizing that the child, for the full and harmonious development of his or her personality, should grow up in a family environment, in an atmosphere of happiness, love and understanding,

Considering that the child should be fully prepared to live an individual life in society, and brought up in the spirit of the ideals proclaimed in the Charter of the United Nations, and in particular in the spirit of peace, dignity, tolerance, freedom, equality and solidarity,

Bearing in mind that the need to extend particular care to the child has been stated in the Geneva Declaration of the Rights of the Child of 1924 and in the Declaration of the Rights of the Child adopted by the General Assembly on 20 November 1959 and recognized in the Universal Declaration of Human Rights, in the International Covenant on Civil and Political Rights (in particular in articles 23 and 24), in the International Covenant on Economic, Social and Cultural Rights (in particular in article 10) and in the statutes and relevant instruments of specialized agencies and international organizations concerned with the welfare of children,

Bearing in mind that, as indicated in the Declaration of the Rights of the Child, "the child, by reason of his physical and mental immaturity, needs special safeguards and care, including appropriate legal protection, before as well as after birth,"

Recalling the provisions of the Declaration on Social and Legal Principles relating to the Protection and Welfare of Children, with Special Reference to Foster Placement and Adoption Nationally and Internationally; the United Nations Standard Minimum Rules for the Administration of Juvenile Justice (The Beijing Rules); and the Declaration on the Protection of Women and Children in Emergency and Armed Conflict,

Recognizing that, in all countries in the world, there are children living in exceptionally difficult conditions, and that such children need special consideration,

Taking due account of the importance of the traditions and cultural values of each people for the protection and harmonious development of the child,

Recognizing the importance of international cooperation for improving the living conditions of children in every country, in particular in the developing countries,

Have agreed as follows:

Part I

ARTICLE I

For the purposes of the present Convention, a child means every human being below the age of eighteen years unless, under the law applicable to the child, majority is attained earlier.

ARTICLE 2

1. States Parties shall respect and ensure the rights set forth in the present Convention to each child within their jurisdiction without discrimination of any kind, irrespective of the child's or his or her parent's or legal guardian's race, colour, sex, language, religion, political or other opinion, national, ethnic or social origin, property, disability, birth or other status.

2. States Parties shall take all appropriate measures to ensure that the child is protected against all forms of discrimination or punishment on the basis of the status, activities, expressed opinions, or beliefs of the child's parents, legal guardians, or family members.

ARTICLE 3

1. In all actions concerning children, whether undertaken by public or private social welfare institutions, courts of law, administrative authorities or legislative bodies, the best interests of the child shall be a primary consideration.

2. States Parties undertake to ensure the child such protection and care as is necessary for his or her well-being, taking into account the rights and duties of his or her parents, legal guardians, or other individuals legally responsible for him or her, and, to this end, shall take all appropriate legislative and administrative measures.

3. States Parties shall ensure that the institutions, services and facilities responsible for the care or protection of children shall conform with the standards established by competent authorities, particularly in the areas of safety, health, in the number and suitability of their staff, as well as competent supervision.

ARTICLE 4

States Parties shall undertake all appropriate legislative, administrative, and other measures for the implementation of the rights recognized in the present Convention. With regard to economic, social and cultural rights, States Parties shall undertake such measures to the maximum extent of their available resources and, where needed, within the framework of international co-operation.

ARTICLE 5

States Parties shall respect the responsibilities, rights and duties of parents or, where applicable, the members of the extended family or community as provided for by local custom, legal guardians or other persons legally responsible for the child, to provide, in a manner consistent with the evolving capacities of the child, appropriate direction and guidance in the exercise by the child of the rights recognized in the present Convention.

ARTICLE 6

1. States Parties recognize that every child has the inherent right to life.

2. States Parties shall ensure to the maximum extent possible the survival and development of the child.

ARTICLE 7

1. The child shall be registered immediately after birth and shall have the right from birth to a name, the right to acquire a nationality and, as far as possible, the right to know and be cared for by his or her parents.

2. States Parties shall ensure the implementation of these rights in accordance with their national law and their obligations under the relevant international instruments in this field, in particular where the child would otherwise be stateless.

ARTICLE 8

1. States Parties undertake to respect the right of the child to preserve his or her identity, including nationality, name and family relations as recognized by law without unlawful interference.

2. Where a child is illegally deprived of some or all of the elements of his or her identity, States Parties shall provide appropriate assistance and protection, with a view to speedily re-establishing his or her identity.

ARTICLE 9

1. States Parties shall ensure that a child shall not be separated from his or her parents against their will, except when competent authorities subject to judicial review determine, in accordance with applicable law and procedures, that such separation is necessary for the best interests of the child. Such determination may be necessary in a particular case such as one involving abuse or neglect of the child by the parents, or one where the parents are living separately and a decision must be made as to the child's place of residence.

2. In any proceedings pursuant to paragraph 1 of the present article, all interested parties shall be given an opportunity to participate in the proceedings and make their views known.

3. States Parties shall respect the right of the child who is separated from one or both parents to maintain personal relations and direct contact with both parents on a regular basis, except if it is contrary to the child's best interests.

4. Where such separation results from any action initiated by a State Party, such as the detention, imprisonment, exile, deportation or death (including death arising from any cause while the person is in the custody of the State) of one or both parents or of the child, that State Party shall, upon request, provide the parents, the child or, if appropriate, another member of the family with the essential information concerning the whereabouts of the absent member(s) of the family unless the provision of the information would be detrimental to the well-being of the child. States Parties shall further ensure that the submission of such a request shall of itself entail no adverse consequences for the person(s) concerned.

ARTICLE 10

1. In accordance with the obligation of States Parties under article 9, paragraph 1, applications by a child or his or her parents to enter or leave a State Party for the purpose of family reunification shall be dealt with by States Parties in a positive, humane and expeditious manner. States Parties shall further ensure that the submission of such a request shall entail no adverse consequences for the applicants and for the members of their family.

2. A child whose parents reside in different States shall have the right to maintain on a regular basis, save in exceptional circumstances personal relations and direct contacts with both parents. Towards that end and in accordance with the obligation of States Parties under article 9, paragraph 2, States Parties shall respect the right of the child and his or her parents to leave any country, including their own, and to enter their own country. The right to leave any country shall be subject only to such restrictions as are prescribed by law and which are necessary to protect the national security, public order *(ordre public)*, public health or morals or the rights and freedoms of others and are consistent with the other rights recognized in the present Convention.

ARTICLE 11

1. States Parties shall take measures to combat the illicit transfer and non-return of children abroad.

2. To this end, States Parties shall promote the conclusion of bilateral or multilateral agreements or accession to existing agreements.

ARTICLE 12

1. States Parties shall assure to the child who is capable of forming his or her own views the right to express those views freely in all matters affecting the child, the views of the child being given due weight in accordance with the age and maturity of the child.

2. For this purpose, the child shall in particular be provided the opportunity to be heard in any judicial and administrative proceedings affecting the child, either directly, or through a representative or an appropriate body, in a manner consistent with the procedural rules of national law.

ARTICLE 13

1. The child shall have the right to freedom of expression; this right shall include freedom to seek, receive and impart information and ideas of all kinds, regardless of frontiers, either orally, in writing or in print, in the form of art, or through any other media of the child's choice.

2. The exercise of this right may be subject to certain restrictions, but these shall only be such as are provided by law and are necessary:

(a) For respect of the rights or reputations of others; or

(b) For the protection of national security or of public order *(ordre public)*, or of public health or morals.

ARTICLE 14

1. States Parties shall respect the right of the child to freedom of thought, conscience and religion.

2. States Parties shall respect the rights and duties of the parents and, when applicable, legal guardians, to provide direction to the child in the exercise of his or her right in a manner consistent with the evolving capacities of the child.

3. Freedom to manifest one's religion or beliefs may be subject only to such limitations as are prescribed by law and are necessary to protect public safety, order, health or morals, or the fundamental rights and freedoms of others.

ARTICLE 15

1. States Parties recognize the rights of the child to freedom of association and to freedom of peaceful assembly.

2. No restrictions may be placed on the exercise of these rights other than those imposed in conformity with the law and which are necessary in a democratic society in the interests of national security or public safety, public order *(ordre public)*, the protection of public health or morals or the protection of the rights and freedoms of others.

ARTICLE 16

1. No child shall be subjected to arbitrary or unlawful interference with his or her privacy, family, home or correspondence, nor to unlawful attacks on his or her honour and reputation.

2. The child has the right to the protection of the law against such interference or attacks.

ARTICLE 17

States Parties recognize the important function performed by the mass media and shall ensure that the child has access to information and material from a diversity of national and international sources, especially those aimed at the promotion of his or her social, spiritual and moral well-being and physical and mental health. To this end, States Parties shall:

    (a) Encourage the mass media to disseminate information and material of social and cultural benefit to the child and in accordance with the spirit of article 29;

    (b) Encourage international co-operation in the production, exchange and dissemination of such information and material from a diversity of cultural, national and international sources;

    (c) Encourage the production and dissemination of children's books;

    (d) Encourage the mass media to have particular regard to the linguistic needs of the child who belongs to a minority group or who is indigenous;

    (e) Encourage the development of appropriate guidelines for the protection of the child from information and material injurious to his or her well-being, bearing in mind the provisions of articles 13 and 18.

ARTICLE 18

1. States Parties shall use their best efforts to ensure recognition of the principle that both parents have common responsibilities for the upbringing and development of the child. Parents or, as the case may be, legal guardians, have the primary responsibility for the upbringing and development of the child. The best interests of the child will be their basic concern.

2. For the purpose of guaranteeing and promoting the rights set forth in the present Convention, States Parties shall render appropriate assistance to parents and legal guardians in the performance of their child-rearing responsibilities and shall ensure the development of institutions, facilities and services for the care of children.

3. States Parties shall take all appropriate measures to ensure that children of working parents have the right to benefit from child-care services and facilities for which they are eligible.

ARTICLE 19

1. States Parties shall take all appropriate legislative, administrative, social and educational measures to protect the child from all forms of physical or mental violence, injury or abuse, neglect or negligent treatment, maltreatment or exploitation, including sexual abuse, while in the care of parent(s), legal guardians(s) or any other person who has the care of the child.

2. Such protective measures should, as appropriate, include effective procedures for the establishment of social programmes to provide necessary support for the child and for those who have the care of the child, as well as for other forms of prevention and for identification, reporting, referral, investigation, treatment, and follow-up of instances of child maltreatment described heretofore, and, as appropriate, for judicial involvement.

ARTICLE 20

1. A child temporarily or permanently deprived of his or her family environment, or in whose own best interests cannot be allowed to remain in that environment, shall be entitled to special protection and assistance provided by the State.

2. States Parties shall in accordance with their national laws ensure alternative care for such a child.

3. Such care could include, *inter alia,* foster placement, *kafalah* of Islamic law, adoption or if necessary placement in suitable institutions for the care of children. When considering solutions, due regard shall be paid to the desirability of continuity in a child's upbringing and to the child's ethnic, religious, cultural and linguistic background.

ARTICLE 21

States Parties that recognize and/or permit the system of adoption shall ensure that the best interests of the child shall be the paramount consideration and they shall:

(a) Ensure that the adoption of a child is authorized only by competent authorities who determine, in accordance with applicable law and procedures and on the basis of all pertinent and reliable information, that the adoption is permissible in view of the child's status concerning parents, relatives and legal guardians and that, if required, the persons concerned have given their informed consent to the adoption on the basis of such counselling as may be necessary;

(b) Recognize that inter-country adoption may be considered as an alternative means of child's care, if the child cannot be placed in a foster or an adoptive family or cannot in any suitable manner be cared for in the child's country of origin;

(c) Ensure that the child concerned by inter-country adoption enjoys safeguards and standards equivalent to those existing in the case of national adoption;

(d) Take all appropriate measures to ensure that, in inter-country adoption, the placement does not result in improper financial gain for those involved in it;

(e) Promote, where appropriate, the objectives of the present article by concluding bilateral or multilateral arrangements or agreements, and endeavour, within this framework, to ensure that the placement of the child in another country is carried out by competent authorities or organs.

ARTICLE 22

1. States Parties shall take appropriate measures to ensure that a child who is seeking refugee status or who is considered a refugee in accordance with applicable international or domestic law and procedures shall, whether unaccompanied or accompanied by his or her parents or by any other person, receive appropriate protection and humanitarian assistance in the enjoyment of applicable rights set forth in the present Convention and in other international human rights or humanitarian instruments to which the said States are Parties.

2. For this purpose, States Parties shall provide, as they consider appropriate, co-operation in any efforts by the United Nations and other competent intergovernmental organizations or non-governmental organizations co-operating with the United Nations to protect and assist such a child and to trace the parents or other members of the family of any refugee child in order to obtain information necessary for reunification with his or her family. In cases where no parents or other members of the family can be found, the child shall be accorded the same protection as any other child permanently or temporarily deprived of his or her family environment for any reason, as set forth in the present Convention.

ARTICLE 23

1. States Parties recognize that a mentally or physically disabled child should enjoy a full and decent life, in conditions which ensure dignity, promote self-reliance and facilitate the child's active participation in the community.

2. States Parties recognize the right of the disabled child to special care and shall encourage and ensure the extension, subject to available resources, to the eligible child and those responsible for his or her care, of assistance for which application is made and which is appropriate to the child's condition and to the circumstances of the parents or others caring for the child.

3. Recognizing the special needs of a disabled child, assistance extended in accordance with paragraph 2 of the present article shall be provided free of charge, whenever possible, taking into account the financial resources of the parents or others caring for the child, and shall be designed to ensure that the disabled child has effective access to and receives education, training, health care services, rehabilitation services, preparation for employment and recreation opportunities in a manner conducive to the child's achieving the fullest possible social integration and individual development, including his or her cultural and spiritual development.

4. States Parties shall promote, in the spirit of international cooperation, the exchange of appropriate information in the field of preventive health care and of medical, psychological and functional treatment of disabled children, including dissemination of and access to information concerning methods of rehabilitation, education and vocational services, with the aim of enabling States Parties to improve their capabilities and skills and to widen their experience in these areas. In this regard, particular account shall be taken of the needs of developing countries.

ARTICLE 24

1. States Parties recognize the right of the child to the enjoyment of the highest attainable standard of health and to facilities for the treatment of illness and rehabilitation of health. States Parties shall strive to ensure that no child is deprived of his or her right of access to such health care services.

2. States Parties shall pursue full implementation of this right and, in particular, shall take appropriate measures:

  (a) To diminish infant and child mortality;
  (b) To ensure the provision of necessary medical assistance and health care to all children with emphasis on the development of primary health care;
  (c) To combat disease and malnutrition, including within the framework of primary health care, through, *inter alia*, the application of readily available technology and through the provision of adequate nutritious foods and clean drinking water, taking into consideration the dangers and risks of environmental pollution;
  (d) To ensure appropriate pre-natal and post-natal health care for mothers;
  (e) To ensure that all segments of society, in particular parents and children, are informed, have access to education and are supported in the use of basic knowledge of child health and nutrition, the advantages of breast-feeding, hygiene and environmental sanitation and the prevention of accidents.

(*f*) To develop preventive health care, guidance for parents and family planning education and services.

3. States Parties shall take all effective and appropriate measures with a view to abolishing traditional practices prejudicial to the health of children.

4. States Parties undertake to promote and encourage international co-operation with a view to achieving progressively the full realization of the right recognized in the present article. In this regard, particular account shall be taken of the needs of developing countries.

ARTICLE 25
States Parties recognize the right of a child who has been placed by the competent authorities for the purposes of care, protection or treatment of his or her physical or mental health, to a periodic review of the treatment provided to the child and all other circumstances relevant to his or her placement.

ARTICLE 26
1. States Parties shall recognize for every child the right to benefit from social security, including social insurance, and shall take the necessary measures to achieve the full realization of this right in accordance with their national law.

2. The benefits should, where appropriate, be granted, taking into account the resources and the circumstances of the child and persons having responsibility for the maintenance of the child, as well as any other consideration relevant to an application for benefits made by or on behalf of the child.

ARTICLE 27
1. States Parties recognize the right of every child to a standard of living adequate for the child's physical, mental, spiritual, moral and social development.

2. The parent(s) or others responsible for the child have the primary responsibility to secure, within their abilities and financial capacities, the conditions of living necessary for the child's development.

3. States Parties, in accordance with national conditions and within their means, shall take appropriate measures to assist parents and others responsible for the child to implement this right and shall in case of need provide material assistance and support programmes, particularly with regard to nutrition, clothing and housing.

4. States Parties shall take all appropriate measures to secure the recovery of maintenance for the child from the parents or other persons having financial responsibility for the child, both within the State Party and

from abroad. In particular, where the person having financial responsibility for the child lives in a State different from that of the child, States Parties shall promote the accession to international agreements or the conclusion of such agreements, as well as the making of other appropriate arrangements.

ARTICLE 28

1. States Parties recognize the right of the child to education, and with a view to achieving this right progressively and on the basis of equal opportunity, they shall, in particular:

  (a) Make primary education compulsory and available free to all;
  (b) Encourage the development of different forms of secondary education, including general and vocational education, make them available and accessible to every child, and take appropriate measures such as the introduction of free education and offering financial assistance in case of need;
  (c) Make higher education accessible to all on the basis of capacity by every appropriate means;
  (d) Make educational and vocational information and guidance available and accessible to all children;
  (e) Take measures to encourage regular attendance at schools and the reduction of drop-out rates.

2. States Parties shall take all appropriate measures to ensure that school discipline is administered in a manner consistent with the child's human dignity and in conformity with the present Convention.

3. States Parties shall promote and encourage international cooperation in matters relating to education, in particular with a view to contributing to the elimination of ignorance and illiteracy throughout the world and facilitating access to scientific and technical knowledge and modern teaching methods. In this regard, particular account shall be taken of the needs of developing countries.

ARTICLE 29

1. States Parties agree that the education of the child shall be directed to:

  (a) The development of the child's personality, talents and mental and physical abilities to their fullest potential;
  (b) The development of respect for human rights and fundamental freedoms, and for the principles enshrined in the Charter of the United Nations;
  (c) The development of respect for the child's parents, his or her own cultural identity, language and values, for the national values of the country in which the child is living, the country from which he or

she may originate, and for civilizations different from his or her own;

(d) The preparation of the child for responsible life in a free society, in the spirit of understanding, peace, tolerance, equality of sexes, and friendship among all peoples, ethnic, national and religious groups and persons of indigenous origin;

(e) The development of respect for the natural environment.

2. No part of the present article or article 28 shall be construed as to interfere with the liberty of individuals and bodies to establish and direct educational institutions, subject always to the observance of the principles set forth in paragraph I of the present article and to the requirements that the education given in such institutions shall conform to such minimum standards as may be laid down by the State.

ARTICLE 30

In those States in which ethnic, religious or linguistic minorities or persons of indigenous origin exist, a child belonging to such a minority or who is indigenous shall not be denied the right, in community with other members of his or her group, to enjoy his or her own culture, to profess and practise his or her own religion, or to use his or her own language.

ARTICLE 31

1. States Parties recognize the right of the child to rest and leisure, to engage in play and recreational activities appropriate to the age of the child and to participate freely in cultural life and the arts.

2. States Parties shall respect and promote the right of the child to participate fully in cultural and artistic life and shall encourage the provision of appropriate and equal opportunities for cultural, artistic, recreational and leisure activity.

ARTICLE 32

1. States Parties recognize the right of the child to be protected from economic exploitation and from performing any work that is likely to be hazardous or to interfere with the child's education, or to be harmful to the child's health or physical, mental, spiritual, moral or social development.

2. States Parties shall take legislative, administrative, social and educational measures to ensure the implementation of the present article. To this end, and having regard to the relevant provisions of other international instruments, States Parties shall in particular:

(a) Provide for a minimum age or minimum ages for admission to employment;

(b) Provide for appropriate regulation of the hours and conditions of employment;

(c) Provide for appropriate penalties or other sanctions to ensure the effective enforcement of the present article.

ARTICLE 33
States Parties shall take all appropriate measures, including legislative, administrative, social and educational measures, to protect children from the illicit use of narcotic drugs and psychotropic substances as defined in the relevant international treaties, and to prevent the use of children in the illicit production and trafficking of such substances.

ARTICLE 34
States Parties undertake to protect the child from all forms of sexual exploitation and sexual abuse. For these purposes, States Parties shall in particular take all appropriate national, bilateral and multilateral measures to prevent:

(a) The inducement or coercion of a child to engage in any unlawful sexual activity;

(b) The exploitative use of children in prostitution or other unlawful sexual practices;

(c) The explorative use of children in pornographic performances and materials.

ARTICLE 35
States Parties shall take all appropriate national, bilateral and multilateral measures to prevent the abduction of, the sale of or traffic in children for any purpose or in any form.

ARTICLE 36
States Parties shall protect the child against all other forms of exploitation prejudicial to any aspects of the child's welfare.

ARTICLE 37
States Parties shall ensure that:

(a) No child shall be subjected to torture or other cruel, inhuman or degrading treatment or punishment. Neither capital punishment nor life imprisonment without possibility of release shall be imposed for offences committed by persons below eighteen years of age;

(b) No child shall be deprived of his or her liberty unlawfully or arbitrarily. The arrest, detention or imprisonment of a child shall be in conformity with the law and shall be used only as a measure of last resort and for the shortest appropriate period of time;

(c) Every child deprived of liberty shall be treated with humanity and respect for the inherent dignity of the human person, and in a manner which takes into account the needs of persons of his or her age. In particular, every child deprived of liberty shall be separated from adults unless it is considered in the child's best interests not to do so and shall have the right to remain contact with his or her family through correspondence and visits, save in exceptional circumstances;

(d) Every child deprived of his or her liberty shall have the right to prompt access to legal and other appropriate assistance, as well as the right to challenge the legality of the deprivation of his or her liberty before a court or other competent, independent and impartial authority, and to a prompt decision on any such action.

ARTICLE 38

1. States Parties undertake to respect and to ensure respect for rules of international humanitarian law applicable to them in armed conflicts which are relevant to the child.

2. States Parties shall take all feasible measures to ensure that persons who have not attained the age of fifteen years do not take a direct part in hostilities.

3. States Parties shall refrain from recruiting any person who has not attained the age of fifteen years into their armed forces. In recruiting among those persons who have attained the age of fifteen years but who have not attained the age of eighteen years, States Parties shall endeavour to give priority to those who are oldest.

4. In accordance with their obligations under international humanitarian law to protect the civilian population in armed conflicts, States Parties shall take all feasible measures to ensure protection and care of children who are affected by an armed conflict.

ARTICLE 39

States Parties shall take all appropriate measures to promote physical and psychological recovery and social reintegration of a child victim of: any form of neglect, exploitation, or abuse; torture or any other form of cruel, inhuman or degrading treatment or punishment; or armed conflicts. Such recovery and reintegration shall take place in an environment which fosters the health, self-respect and dignity of the child.

ARTICLE 40

1. States Parties recognize the right of every child alleged as, accused of, or recognized as having infringed the penal law to be treated in a manner consistent with the promotion of the child's sense of dignity and worth, which reinforces the child's respect for the human rights and

fundamental freedoms of others and which takes into account the child's age and the desirability of promoting the child's reintegration and the child's assuming a constructive role in society.

2. To this end, and having regard to the relevant provisions of international instruments, States Parties shall, in particular, ensure that:

(a) No child shall be alleged as be accused of, or recognized as having infringed the penal law by reason of, acts or omissions that were not prohibited by national or international law at the time they were committed;

(b) Every child alleged as or accused of having infringed the penal law has at least the following guarantees:

(i) To be presumed innocent until proven guilty according to law;

(ii) To be informed promptly and directly of the charges against him or her, and, if appropriate, through his or her parents or legal guardians, and to have legal or other appropriate assistance in the preparation and presentation of his or her defence;

(iii) To have the matter determined without delay by a competent, independent and impartial authority or judicial body in a fair hearing according to law, in the presence of legal or other appropriate assistance and, unless it is considered not to be in the best interest of the child, in particular, taking into account his or her age or situation, his or her parents or legal guardians;

(iv) Not to be compelled to give testimony or to confess guilt; to examine or have examined adverse witnesses and to obtain the participation and examination of witnesses on his or her behalf under conditions of equality;

(v) If considered to have infringed the penal law, to have this decision and any measures imposed in consequence thereof reviewed by a higher competent, independent and impartial authority or judicial body according to law;

(vi) To have the free assistance of an interpreter if the child cannot understand or speak the language used;

(vii) To have his or her privacy fully respected at all stages of the proceedings.

3. States Parties shall seek to promote the establishment of laws, procedures, authorities and institutions specifically applicable to children alleged as, accused of, or recognized as having infringed the penal law, and, in particular:

(a) The establishment of a minimum age below which children shall he presumed not to have the capacity to infringe the penal law;

(*b*) Whenever appropriate and desirable, measures for dealing with such children without resorting to judicial proceedings, providing that human rights and legal safeguards are fully respected.

4. A variety of dispositions, such as care, guidance and supervision orders; counselling; probation; foster care; education and vocational training programmes and other alternatives to institutional care shall be available to ensure that children are dealt with in a manner appropriate to their well-being and proportionate both to their circumstances and the offence.

ARTICLE 41

Nothing in the present Convention shall affect any provisions which are more conducive to the realization of the rights of the child and which may be contained in:

(*a*) The law of a State Party; or

(*b*) International law in force for that State.

Part II

ARTICLE 42

States Parties undertake to make the principles and provisions of the Convention widely known, by appropriate and active means, to adults and children alike.

ARTICLE 43

1. For the purpose of examining the progress made by States Parties in achieving the realization of the obligations undertaken in the present Convention, there shall be established a Committee on the Rights of the Child, which shall carry out the functions herein-after provided.

2. The Committee shall consist of ten experts of high moral standing and recognized competence in the field covered by this Convention. The members of the Committee shall be elected by States Parties from among their nationals and shall serve in their personal capacity, consideration being given to equitable geographical distribution, as well as to the principal legal systems.

3. The members of the Committee shall be elected by secret ballot from a list of persons nominated by States Parties. Each State Party may nominate one person from among its own nationals.

4. The initial election to the Committee shall be held no later than six months after the date of the entry into force of the present Convention and thereafter every second year. At least four months before the date of each election, the Secretary-General of the United Nations shall address a letter to States Parties inviting them to submit their nominations within

two months. The Secretary-General shall subsequently prepare a list in alphabetical order of all persons thus nominated, indicating States Parties which have nominated them, and shall submit it to the States Parties to the present Convention.

5. The elections shall be held at meetings of States Parties convened by the Secretary-General at United Nations Headquarters. At those meetings, for which two thirds of States Parties shall constitute a quorum, the persons elected to the Committee shall be those who obtain the largest number of votes and an absolute majority of the votes of the representatives of States Parties present and voting.

6. The members of the Committee shall be elected for a term of four years. They shall be eligible for re-election if renominated. The term of five of the members elected at the first election shall expire at the end of two years; immediately after the first election, the names of these five members shall be chosen by lot by the Chairman of the meeting.

7. If a member of the Committee dies or resigns or declares that for any other cause he or she can no longer perform the duties of the Committee, the State Party which nominated the member shall appoint another expert from among its nationals to serve for the remainder of the term, subject to the approval of the Committee.

8. The Committee shall establish its own rules of procedure.

9. The Committee shall elect its officers for a period of two years.

10. The meetings of the Committee shall normally be held at United Nations Headquarters or at any other convenient place as determined by the Committee. The Committee shall normally meet annually. The duration of the meetings of the Committee shall be determined, and reviewed, if necessary, by a meeting of the States Parties to the present Convention, subject to the approval of the General Assembly.

11. The Secretary-General of the United Nations shall provide the necessary staff and facilities for the effective performance of the functions of the Committee under the present Convention.

12. With the approval of the General Assembly, the members of the Committee established under the present Convention shall receive emoluments from United Nations resources on such terms and conditions as the Assembly may decide.

ARTICLE 44

1. States Parties undertake to submit to the Committee, through the Secretary-General of the United Nations, reports on the measures they have adopted which give effect to the rights recognized herein and on the progress made on the enjoyment of those rights:

(a) Within two years of the entry into force of the Convention for the State Party concerned;

(b) Thereafter every five years.

2. Reports made under the present article shall indicate factors and difficulties, if any, affecting the degree of fulfilment of the obligations under the present Convention. Reports shall also contain sufficient information to provide the Committee with a comprehensive understanding of the implementation of the Convention in the country concerned.

3. A State Party which has submitted a comprehensive initial report to the Committee need not, in its subsequent reports submitted in accordance with paragraph I (b) of the present article, repeat basic information previously provided.

4. The Committee may request from States Parties further information relevant to the implementation of the Convention.

5. The Committee shall submit to the General Assembly, through the Economic and Social Council, every two years, reports on its activities.

6. States Parties shall make their reports widely available to the public in their own countries.

ARTICLE 45

In order to foster the effective implementation of the Convention and to encourage international cooperation in the field covered by the Convention:

(a) The specialized agencies, the United Nations Children's Fund, and other United Nations organs shall be entitled to be represented at the consideration of the implementation of such provisions of the present Convention as fill within the scope of their mandate. The Committee may invite the specialized agencies, the United Nations Children's Fund and other competent bodies as it may consider appropriate to provide expert advice on the implementation of the Convention in areas falling within the scope of their respective mandates. The Committee may invite the specialized agencies, the United Nations Children's Fund, and other United Nations organs to submit reports on the implementation of the Convention in areas falling within the scope of their activities;

(b) The Committee shall transmit, as it may consider appropriate, to the specialized agencies, the United Nations Children's Fund and other competent bodies, any reports from States Parties that contain a request, or indicate a need, for technical advice or assistance, along with the Committee's observations and suggestions, if any, on these requests or indications;

(c) The Committee may recommend to the General Assembly to request the Secretary- General to undertake on its behalf studies on specific issues relating to the rights of the child;

(d) The Committee may make suggestions and general recommendations based on information received pursuant to articles 44 and 45 of the present Convention. Such suggestions and general recommendations shall be transmitted to any State Party concerned and reported to the General Assembly, together with comments, if any, from States Parties.

Part III

ARTICLE 46

The present Covention shall be open for signature by all States.

ARTICLE 47

The present Convention is subject to ratification. Instruments of ratification shall be deposited with the Secretary-General of the United Nations.

ARTICLE 48

The present Convention shall remain open for accession by any State. The instruments of accession shall be deposited with the Secretary General of the United Nations.

ARTICLE 49

1. The present Convention shall enter into force on the thirtieth day following the date of deposit with the Secretary-General of the United Nations of the twentieth instrument of ratification or accession.

2. For each State ratifying or acceding to the Convention after the deposit of the twentieth instrument of ratification or accession, the Convention shall enter into force on the thirtieth day after the deposit by such State of its instrument of ratification or accession.

ARTICLE 50

1. A State Party may propose an amendment and file it with the Secretary-General of the United Nations. The Secretary-General shall thereupon communicate the proposed amendment to States Parties, with a request that they indicate whether they favour a conference of States Parties for the purpose of considering and voting upon the proposals. In the event that, within four months from the date of such communication, at least one third of the States Parties favour such a conference, the Secretary-General shall convene the conference under the auspices of the United Nations. Any amendment adopted by a majority of States Parties

present and voting at the conference shall be submitted to the General Assembly for approval.

2. An amendment adopted in accordance with paragraph I of the present article shall enter into force when it has been approved by the General Assembly of the United Nations and accepted by a two-thirds majority of States Parties.

3. When an amendment enters into force, it shall be binding on those States Parties which have accepted it, other States Parties still being bound by the provisions of the present Convention and any earlier amendments which they have accepted.

ARTICLE 51

1. The Secretary-General of the United Nations shall receive and circulate to all States the text of reservations made by States at the time of ratification or accession.

2. A reservation incompatible with the object and purpose of the present Convention shall not be permitted.

3. Reservations may be withdrawn at any time by notification to that effect addressed to the Secretary-General of the United Nations, who shall then inform all States. Such notification shall take effect on the date on which it is received by the Secretary-General.

ARTICLE 52

A State Party may denounce the present Convention by written notification to the Secretary-General of the United Nations. Denunciation becomes effective one year after the date of receipt of the notification by the Secretary-General.

ARTICLE 53

The Secretary-General of the United Nations is designated as the depositary of the present Convention.

ARTICLE 54

The original of the present Convention, of which the Arabic, Chinese, English, French, Russian, and Spanish texts are equally authentic, shall be deposited with the Secretary-General of the United Nations.

In witness thereof the undersigned plenipotentiaries, being duly authorized thereto by their respective Governments, have signed the present Convention.

Copies of the Convention may be obtained from:
Communications Branch
Department of Canadian Heritage
Hull, Quebec K1A 0M5

Copie française aussi disponible

telephone: (819) 997–0797

The United Nations Convention on the Rights of the Child
© Minister of Supply and Services Canada 1991
Cat. No. S2–210/1991E
ISBN 0–662–18588–9

Index

Books in the Studies in Childhood and Family in Canada Series
Published by Wilfrid Laurier University Press

*Making Do: Women, Family, and Home in Montreal during the Great
Depression* by Denyse Baillargeon, translated by Yvonne Klein • 1999 /
xii + 232 pp. / ISBN: 0-88920-326-1 / ISBN-13: 978-0-88920-326-6

*Children in English-Canadian Society: Framing the Twentieth-Century
Consensus* by Neil Sutherland with a new foreword by Cynthia Comacchio •
2000 / xxiv + 336 pp. / illus. / ISBN: 0-88920-351-2 / ISBN-13: 978-0-88920-351-8

Love Strong as Death: Lucy Peel's Canadian Journal, 1833–1836 edited
by J.I. Little • 2001 / x + 229 pp. / illus. / ISBN: 0-88920-389-X /
ISBN-13: 978-0-88920-389-1

The Challenge of Children's Rights for Canada by Katherine Covell and
R. Brian Howe • 2001 / x + 244 pp. / ISBN: 0-88920-380-6 /
ISBN-13: 978-0-88920-380-8

*NFB Kids: Portrayals of Children by the National Film Board of Canada,
1939–1989* by Brian J. Low • 2002 / 288 pp. / illus. / ISBN: 0-88920-386-5 /
ISBN-13: 978-0-88920-386-0

*Something to Cry About: An Argument against Corporal Punishment of
Children in Canada* by Susan M. Turner • 2002 / xix + 317 pp. /
ISBN: 0-88920-382-2 / ISBN-13: 978-0-88920-382-2

Freedom to Play: We Made Our Own Fun edited by Norah L. Lewis • 2002 /
xiv + 210 pp. / ISBN: 0-88920-406-3 / ISBN-13: 978-0-88920-406-5

*The Dominion of Youth: Adolescence and the Making of Modern Canada,
1920–1950* by Cynthia Comacchio • 2006 / x + 302 pp. / illus. /
ISBN: 0-88920-488-8 / ISBN-13: 978-0-88920-488-1

*Evangelical Balance Sheet: Character, Family, and Business in Mid-Victorian
Nova Scotia* by B. Anne Wood • 2006 / xxx + 198 pp. / illus. / ISBN: 0-88920-500-0 /
ISBN-13: 978-0-88920-500-0

A Question of Commitment: Children's Rights in Canada edited by R. Brian
Howe and Katherine Covell • 2007 / xiv + 442 pp. / ISBN: 978-1-55458-003-3